T3-BOH-480

# STUDIES IN HOMOSEXUALITY

A GARLAND SERIES

Edited with
Introductions by

Wayne R. Dynes
Hunter College, City University of New York

and Stephen Donaldson

# Contents of Series

VOLUME XII

# Homosexuality and Religion and Philosophy

Edited with Introductions by
Wayne R. Dynes
Hunter College, City University of New York
and Stephen Donaldson

Garland Publishing, Inc.
New York & London 1992

**Library of Congress Cataloging-in-Publication Data**

Homosexuality and religion and philosophy / edited by Wayne R. Dynes and Stephen Donaldson.
p. cm. — (Studies in homosexuality ; v. 12)
A collection of articles from 20th century scholarly journals.
Includes bibliographical references.
ISBN 0-8153-0767-5
1. Homosexuality—Religious aspects. 2. Philosophy—History. I. Dynes, Wayne R. II. Donaldson, Stephen. III. Title: Homosexuality and religion and philosophy. IV. Series.
BL65.H64H64 1992
291.1'7835766—dc20 92-14514
CIP

Printed on acid-free, 250-year-life paper
Manufactured in the United States of America

# General Introduction

Over the past quarter century powerful currents of research and writing on homosexuality, lesbianism, and bisexuality have rippled through widening channels, finding outlets in scores of journals affiliated with more than a dozen disciplines. While this increase in the volume of publications signals a welcome lessening of the taboo on the subject and a growing sense of its importance, this profusion makes it difficult for even specialists to monitor the progress of scholarship in its many domains. Much of the key material in this area has appeared in hard-to-locate and often unlikely appearing academic periodicals, which have escaped even diligent indexers and bibliographers. Moreover, not a few of these journals appeared in very limited issues and cannot be found today even in the larger research libraries.

To make more accessible to the reader the classic, the pioneering, and the most recent outstanding articles of scholarly work in a wide variety of disciplines, this series gathers a selection of such articles, reprinting them in thirteen volumes organized by discipline. Sifting through thousands of journal articles, the editors have chosen for republication works of scholarly distinction without attempting to impose any uniform ideological perspective on a field still characterized by lively controversies. Dates of original publication of the selections included in these volumes span the twentieth century, from Erich Bethe's landmark 1907 article on Dorian pederasty in *Rheinisches Museum* to current articles embodying the latest techniques of archival research and conceptual analysis. In some cases, it has been impossible to obtain permission to reprint material we felt worth inclusion; Haworth Press, for example, declined to permit republication of any articles from the *Journal of Homosexuality*. Fortunately, that periodical is widely available so that its absence does not detract from our goal of furnishing important but hard-to-find research.

The earlier situation in which work on homosexuality typically found its home in the social sciences and in medicine has significantly broadened, with important work in history, the humanities, and the arts. Attention has also shifted from the isolated individual to the interaction of the gay/lesbian/bi person with his/her peers. Increased attention has also been devoted to cultural representations in novels and poetry, films and popular music.

Each individual volume brings together the best article-length scholarship on homosexuality from that discipline and will save the specialist a great deal of time and effort. Each volume is self-contained; at the same time, the entire series is designed so that the reader seeking a broad understanding of the phenomena of homosexualities and their cultural, literary, and historical manifestations can make profitable use of the volumes representing other disciplines.

The introduction to each volume examines the history of the discipline(s) represented and its approaches to the study of homosexuality, critiques the development of research in the field, notes milestones in the evolution of thought and research, raises methodological issues, discusses conceptual questions, and suggests directions for future investigation and developments in the field. These introductions allow the reader from outside the discipline to survey and appreciate the issues raised. At the same time specialists will find a constructive critique of the state of their discipline as well as an appreciation of its contributions to the overall development of gay, lesbian, and bisexual scholarship. Appended to each introduction is a survey bibliography of important book-length works in that field.

# Introduction

Throughout most of human history, religion and philosophy, both concerned with ultimate questions, have traveled hand in hand; in Asian civilizations, they have never parted company. In the West philosophy originated as a tradition of speculative thought critical of religion among the pederastic Ionian Greeks of the sixth century B.C., but became a captive of Christian doctrine after Constantine in the fourth century, lingering there until it reemerged as a distinct category in the wake of the Renaissance.

Philosophy has tended to favor abstract questions of logic, epistemology, and ontology, though religious writers have also explored all these areas, often in a less than systematic fashion. As a rule, such discussions have little immediate relevance to sexuality, but homosexuality figures in the biographies of many notable philosophers. The nature of love has merited continuing discussion, initially against a pederastic background, and often marked by gender comparison and reflections on what today is often termed "homosociality." Ethics, the most practical branch of philosophy, and one with a strongly articulated parallel tradition under religious auspices, does however address questions relating directly to sexual life and social stigma. For an overview, see Laurence J. Rosán's article, included herein.

## *The Ancient Philosophers*

Resonating throughout the classical age, the skeptical stance of the Ionians prefigured the conflict between science (which traces its roots to them) and religion—a conflict which broke out again with the Enlightenment and which carries over into the contemporary antagonism between fundamentalist religious leaders, who continue to rely on "revealed" authority and ancient texts, and spokespeople for the gay and lesbian movement, who appeal to contemporary secular values.

The Athenian tradition of pederasty, which emphasized the intellectual training of the young beloved by his older lover, set the stage for the flowering of classical philosophy in the person of Socrates (469–399 B.C.). Archelaus, the philosopher of physics and ethics who was his lover and teacher in the pederastic mold, "considered that right and wrong were not by nature but by convention," a position which not only influenced Socrates, and through him the entire subsequent philosophical tradition, but which has echoed down through the centuries in the continuing polemics between proponents of homosexuality and of Christianity.

Socrates' pupil Plato celebrated pederastic love and its usefulness in preparing for contemplation of the Good in his mid-life dialogues such as the *Symposium* (see Donald Levy's article, included herein), but in his old age turned against his earlier views, bitterly denouncing pederasty in the *Laws* as "contrary to nature" and calling for its complete suppression. While this argument found little favor in classical Greece, Christians adopted it (Romans 1:26–27), so that it survived as a basic theme of homophobic rationalization to the present day.

Plato's pupil Aristotle (384–322), tutor of Alexander the Great, had several male lovers, and was the first to distinguish between innate and acquired homosexuality. His study of animals led him to comment on homosexuality among birds. Like Plato, Aristotle was also concerned with the nature of friendship, which to him could only occur between free males.

The Athenian philosophers yielded to the Epicureans, who valued hedonism, and the Stoics, who emphasized natural law and restraint. Neoplatonism, which opposed all sex, dominated philosophy towards the end of the classical age; the homoerotic Marsilio Ficino (1433–1499) revived it and popularized the concept of "platonic love," which he took from Plato's *Symposium* while stripping it of its physical expression.

## *Modern Philosophers*

One of the leaders of the seventeenth-century revival of philosophy, Benedict Spinoza, established the primacy of reason over scriptural authority. Voltaire in the following century attacked the persecution of sodomites as a survival of medieval tyranny. At the end of his life Arthur Schopenhauer (1788–1860), who drew more inspiration from Buddhism than from Christianity, wrote on "pederasty" from a philosophical perspective, deducing from cross-cultural and transhistorical data that homosexuality could not be unnatural (thereby disagreeing with Immanuel Kant). He went on to conclude that homosexuality as such (though the term was as yet unknown) is not reprehensible.

In England Jeremy Bentham (1748–1832) applied his philosophy of utilitarianism to the question of sodomy laws, arguing at length that they should be abolished, though he did not dare publish his writings on the matter.

George Santayana (1863–1952) was an exclusive (though perhaps largely nonpracticing) homosexual, a preference that influenced the decision of this American philosopher to leave his country for the more tolerant climes of France and Italy.

The homosexuality of Ludwig Wittgenstein (1889–1951), iconoclastic logical-positivist and perhaps the most influential philosopher of the twentieth century, is now well established, though many heterosexual Wittgenstein interpreters have shown a reluctance to explore the issue. See the article by William Warren Bartley III, included herein.

## *Ethics*

Little work has been done applying the methodology of philosophical ethics to questions facing those involved in homosexual conduct in the present day. There are numerous ethical issues connected with the "coming out" process, or in living with a concealed sexuality. Most recently, the question of "outing"—the forced revelation of homosexuality—has engendered a lively debate, but not one conducted along the lines of philosophical inquiry.

Sexual objectification raises other issues which seem to fall more easily within the traditional scope of philosophy's generalistic approach.

Gay organizations, publications, and spokespeople have generally neglected to address interpersonal ethical issues, taking a relativistic and individualistic approach when they do so which may still be rooted in antipathy to the type of coercive moralizing which in the past has often had homosexuals as its target. See Thomas Merritt's article, included herein. Regrettably, this approach leaves the question of the construction of a positive ethic up in the air.

A new issue has been the ethical status of homophobia, and more particularly of discrimination against those who practice homosexuality. In some circles, the current of opinion appears to have leapt willy-nilly in the course of a score of years from the view that homosexuality is immoral and to be condemned out of hand to the view that homophobia is immoral and to be condemned out of hand, without in either case subjecting the view in question to rigorous philosophical analysis or comparative ethical examination.

The AIDS epidemic has brought a host of new and still largely inchoate ethical issues with it. Some of them relate to sexual behavior, others (paralleling the "coming out" question) to disclosure. The testing and approval process for experimental drugs and vaccines raises difficult questions of medical ethics. The consensus that discrimination against HIV-positive persons is immoral, which has been written into federal American law, contrasts sharply with the controversy over homophobic discrimination, and with the widespread actual practice of stigmatizing and ostracizing HIV-positives. The question of providing prophylactics—or, as in prisons and jails, prohibiting them altogether despite widespread anal sex—has raised numerous ethical issues.

## *Religion*

Sexuality has been a major concern of religion from earliest times, perhaps because both endeavors tap into the deepest emotional and psychological currents of the human species, perhaps because both activities transcend the limitations of the solitary self and may easily become competitors in the ecology of human energy. Often religion has allied itself with sex, as in the case of sacred temple prostitution or phallic worship; at other times it has worked hard to suppress all sexual energy, as with Christian and Buddhist monastic celibacy, but it has seldom remained silent on sexual questions.

Organizationally, religion has often favored single-gendered and often residentially grouped professional organizations of unmarried and unprocreative clerics. These professions have often attracted those who would otherwise feel obliged by social custom to marry, but were not sufficiently attracted to the opposite sex to wish to do so. They also provided environmental conditions favoring situational homosexuality. Thus homosexuality commonly preoccupies the internal organization of religious groups, even to the point of obsession. Sometimes, by emphasizing a prohibition of premarital or extramarital heterosexuality and heterosociality, religions have unwittingly encouraged homosexuality by the unmarried. Some traditions, such as Hinduism, have favored an androgynous mythology for divinity which has religiously undermined strict gender roles. In shamanism the crossing of gender roles itself provides evidence of advanced spiritual status. Thus there is much more to the general question of religion and homosexuality than the overwhelming homophobia which appears on first examination of the Judeo-Christian tradition.

## *Methodological Problems*

Ancient religious texts and traditions present many hermeneutic problems. Translations into modern Western languages have tended to obscure sexual aspects, reflecting not only a lack of scholarship on the part of translators, but suppression of the literary record in the original language, prejudice by the translators, and in the past century the superimposition of modern concepts (such as "the homosexual" as a type of person) on ancient cultures which knew nothing of them. As a result, for example, the proper translation of all the Biblical passages referring to homosexual behavior has become exceedingly controversial, with conservatives clinging to previous renderings while gay advocates often seem to seek to interpret them out of existence; in the context of this dialogue of the deaf scholarly reconstruction finds little support in the middle. The original and sometimes only Western translations of the texts of other religious traditions were often produced by Christian missionaries, who imposed their own concepts on the translation rather than explore the viewpoints of the culture which produced the text.

Scriptural editing usually preceded translation, and has been responsible for other problems. Often the dating of passages has been controversial, with evidence for the late interpolation of texts (such as the Holiness Code of Leviticus or the pederastic practices of the Greek gods) into earlier material being controversial among fundamentalists, and other problems are raised by clues—not obvious to all believers—to the excision of material (for example, by the early Christian conclaves which determined the biblical canon, or even by the gospel compilers who preceded them).

Usually the context for scriptural utterances is lacking in the text itself and must be sought elsewhere, a process which may be foreign to fundamentalists and controversial even where accepted as a necessary hermeneutic tool. Thus one must see the ancient Hebrew pronouncements on *kedeshim* in the context of religious competition with Canaanite and Mesopotamian traditions which featured these sacred prostitutes, and the Pauline texts in light of the pederastic institutions, mystery cults, and other currents prominent in the Roman empire at the time they were written. But the record of such contexts has often not survived obliteration by the followers of the scripture in question.

Another problem arises in connection with the emphasis or weight given to the texts at different periods of time. Byzantine church fathers (the patristic writers) and late medieval Inquisitors may have found certain texts grave enough to warrant torture and death as their consequences, but early medieval writers and some modernists found in the same texts only peccadillos and minor vices. Looking at the prohibitions of the Buddhist monastic legal code and the widespread unconcern with them today, can we properly deduce that Buddhists took them as lightly two millennia ago? Or examine the Islamic tradition, which is generally taken to penalize homosexuality with death, but at the same time attaches so many evidentiary conditions as to make the penalty a dead letter in practice: what is the actual attitude of the text?

Where there is religion, there is hypocrisy, and the student of religious history can hardly fail to take this linkage into account when he contrasts normative behavior codes with abundant evidence for their transgression by the very clerics who promulgate them, a pattern which has proven remarkably durable from ancient days to the most recent scandals of televangelism.

Another general issue involving the role of homosexuality in the history of religions has been the sublimation of homoerotic emotion, a subject of considerable speculation since Freud's day, but for which evidentiary standards are notably lacking. That many religious professionals have had very strong homoerotic feelings is clear enough, that many if not most have not acted them out sexually seems reasonable enough, and that these feelings have had profound influences on their spiritual work and practice is also obvious to many, but the nature of the connections between these observations remains problematic.

## *Non-Judeo-Christian Religions*

For distributional reasons, the selections in this volume are limited to the Judeo-Christian religious tradition. For other traditions of classical antiquity, see the volume on the ancient world; for shamanism, the volume on anthropology; for Islam, Hinduism and Buddhism, the volume on Asian studies. For comparative purposes, however, a brief survey of these religions follows:

Shamanism, probably the oldest of these traditions, often appears along with gender-crossing behavior in preliterate cultures where the dominant form of homosexuality is gender-differentiated. (This model features one adult who is considered not-male for life and takes a passive sexual role with "normal" insertive adult males, in the male version; among females it involves an aggressive not-female pairing with a typical woman). The shaman is the religious professional of the tribe, the one who mediates between the community and the spirit world. The shaman's cross-gender behavior reflects the influence of the spirits on him, being a sign of his special status, in this system. In those cultures featuring this type of shamanism, the shaman usually cross-dresses, renounces male status, and is married to a typical male of the community. Female shamanism is also known and in some tribes is more common than the male version. Shamanism is a lifelong occupation; shamans sometimes work together but are seldom grouped residentially. The phenomenon of the cross-gendered shaman (often termed "berdache") in the preliterate cultures of Siberia and among the native American tribes has been the focus of extensive study, but it also pops up in Polynesia, parts of Africa, among non-Christian groups in Brazil and Haiti, and elsewhere. Its prevalence has declined under pressure from Christianity. See Edward Carpenter's article, included herein.

Sacred prostitution was common in temples of ancient Babylonia, Assyria, and Canaan, and known to ancient India, with both females and effeminized male slaves servicing male worshippers of deities such as Ishtar and Bel-marduk—perhaps connected with traditions of phallic worship.

Regarding ancient Egypt and Greece, there are no records of a cultic or religious-ritual role for homosexuality, but the mythologies of both religious traditions include a number of instances of homosexual acts on the part of deities. The Egyptian mythology prominently features divine anal rape. There is some evidence that the numerous episodes in Greek mythology of pederastic initiatives on the part of the gods (especially Zeus, Apollo, and Poseidon) stem from the introduction of institutionalized pederasty to Greek culture in the seventh century B.C. rather than forming part of the original Homeric ethos.

Roman mythology pretty much coopted the Greek model, but homosexuality may have played an important role in the secret initiation rites of the "mystery" religions which were very popular in the empire during the last few pagan centuries before Constantine.

Islam doctrinally treats male homosexual acts as a type of adultery, theoretically condemning them with the death penalty, but actually imposing such strenuous evidentiary requirements (sworn eyewitness accounts by four adult Muslims of good character, and whippings for accusers who fail to produce these four) that private conduct is protected. In practice, Islam is concerned with public propriety rather than private behavior and has long displayed great tolerance for pederasty, many of its greatest poets having written of their fondness for boys. "Homosexuality" to the Muslim means the acceptance of a passive, feminine role by an adult male, which is severely condemned. The seclusion of women in Muslim lands has favored pederasty as a sexual outlet for the as-yet-unmarried male. Islamic clerics, especially Sufis, have also developed a reputation for pederastic interests. Crossing ethnic boundaries, the Islamic pederastic tradition flourishes among Turks, Berbers, Persians, Afghans, Muslim Indians and Filipinos, and Indonesians in addition to the Arabs; this points to a religious connection. The Ayatollah Khomeini launched a vigorous persecution, including numerous executions, of "homosexuals" in Iran in the early 1980s, but this campaign appears to have targeted sexually passive adults and political opponents rather than practitioners of traditional pederasty, who held high office in the Khomeini government.

Hindu mythology offers numerous instances of androgyny on the part of the deities, one of Shiva's major forms being Ardhanārīshvara, the right side male, the left female. Vishnu, normally male, assuming a female body becomes pregnant by Shiva, giving birth to Ayappa, who is the focus of a large and growing cult in South India. Hindu *sannyāsin* ("renunciates," the swamis, monks and "holy men") are heterosexually celibate, but temple priests may be married, and laymen are invariable so. Homosexuality appears rarely in the voluminous Hindu scriptures, though one of the best-known incidents has Agni, the god of fire, swallowing Shiva's sperm after the latter god ejaculates following coitus interruptus with his female consort/aspect, Pārvati. There is no consistent Hindu homophobic tradition, though British Victorian taboos and associated homophobia have taken root since the colonial era. Some of the ancient sacred law codes do mention homosexuality, the Code of Manu (first to third century) prescribing minor purification rituals for upper-class males only, but fines and severe punishments for lesbianism. Manu appears to be the only known law code providing heavier punishment for lesbian than for male homosexual activities. In practice, India disregarded Manu's writ, and today Indian law proscribes male but not female homosexuality, following colonial-era British law, though convictions are rare.

Two Hindu sects, the Hijras and the Sakhibhavas, display sacred gender reversal and engage in homosexual prostitution, which takes the gender-differentiated form with "normal" male customers. The Hijras worship the Mother Goddess and seek to identify with her by becoming as feminine as possible, often severing the penis to do so. This sect welcomes many teenage homosexuals who are cast out of their families and have no other niche in a communal-oriented culture.

Buddhism contains no trace of homophobia, but prohibits all insertive (only) sexual activity on the part of monks. For novices (usually teenagers), the orthodox disciplinary code provides mild penalties for homosexual acts and expulsion for heterosexual ones. A pederastic tradition long flourished among the Tibetan and Japanese monks; the northern (Mahayana) Buddhist tradition of Tibet, China, Korea and Japan does not take the disciplinary code as seriously as the southern (Theravada) one of Thailand, Sri Lanka, Burma, and Cambodia. Even the Theravadin monks, however, seem to frequently tolerate homosexual violations of the discipline, though not heterosexual ones. Homosexuality on the part of Buddhist laypersons is not discouraged.

Neither Chinese Taoism nor Japanese Shinto include restrictions on homosexuality. Taoism favors the way of passivity, while Shinto's highest deity is a female, Amateratsu.

The general absence of lesbianism from the descriptions above reflects the lack of concern with female homosexuality characterizing all these traditions of the "higher" religions as distinct from tribal belief systems and practices, which often accord an important place to the priestess or female shaman, who may be either celibate or gender-variant.

## *Judaism*

Many scholars who have examined the relevant texts now believe that homophobic motifs entered Judaism during and after the Babylonian captivity, following a more tolerant era. However this may be, homosexual sacred cult prostitutes (*kedeshim*) were part of the religious life of Judah from about 1200 to 587 B.C.; they appear to have been foreigners and were active in the first temple, but Old Testament writers saw them as religious competitors and criticized them as such.

The well-known story of Sodom has given rise to retroactive interpretations as a harsh divine judgment on homosexuality ("sodomy" as a term originated in late medieval Latin), but scholars find that the crimes involved in the Sodom story are (attempted) rape of males and inhospitality. (Though widely propagated, the notion that the episode concerns inhospitality exclusively does not seem plausible.)

David and Jonathan (beginning of the first millennium B.C.) have reputations in gay circles as homosexual role-model lovers, but a close examination of the biblical narrative indicates that Prince Jonathan was the passionate one and perhaps effeminate, while David was macho and opportunistic; it appears that David was what we would call "straight trade" to Jonathan's passivity, a relationship that would fit better with the gender-differentiated model of homosexuality prevalent in the Middle East at the time than the androphilia (reciprocal relationships between adults) of the current industrial West.

It appears to have been while under Persian rule that Judaism adopted the prohibition against homosexual acts (male only) located in the Holiness Code of Leviticus. This prohibition seems to derive from the Zoroastrianism dominant at the court of Darius I (d. 486 B.C.), its language taken from passages in Avestan writings, and may have been intended to restrict patronage of the sacred prostitutes of the older religions against which both Zoroastrians and Jews struggled.

During the Hellenistic period, diaspora Judaism came into conflict with the widespread practice of pederasty, causing a reinterpretation of the Sodom legend so as to make it a condemnation of pederasty; this was the state of affairs when Christianity arrived on the scene. Later Jewish literature held both active and passive partners to be culpable, in marked contrast to the general practice in the Roman empire of drawing sharp distinctions between the two roles.

Medieval Hebrew literature, imitating Arabic modes, developed an impressive body of pederastic poetry, utilizing imagery from both the Hebrew scriptures and Arabic literature; see Norman Roth's article, included herein.

As a rule Jewish clergy were married and procreative, leaving no hidden traditions of homoerotic clerical brotherhoods. Nevertheless, the German homosexual rights movement was founded by a Jew, Magnus Hirschfeld, in 1897, and it was Kurt Hiller, also Jewish, who in 1921 conceived of the notion that "homosexuals" were members of a minority group deserving of protection, a position which became the dominant ideology of the movement, with numerous consequences. Israel repealed its British-derived sodomy law in 1988 and passed gay rights legislation in 1992. The Reform wing of modern Judaism has witnessed and sometimes encouraged the growth of gay synagogues, and has most recently declared its willingness to accept gay rabbis. See Rav Soloff's article, included herein.

## *Early Christianity*

Jesus made no surviving pronouncements on homosexuality. His bachelorhood was extraordinary for his culture. The late Morton Smith reconstructed a gospel text which may suggest that Jesus engaged in homosexual acts with initiates; see his article herein. The episode of the Roman centurion who pleaded with Jesus on behalf of his boy-slave may indicate Jesus' tolerance of pederasty; see Donald H. Mader's article, included herein. The matter of the disciple "whom Jesus loved" remains shrouded in mystery. Also of interest is Matthew 5:22, where Jesus may have prohibited verbal aspersions on someone's masculinity; see Warren Johansson's article, included herein.

Paul of Tarsus, traditionally the author of much of the New Testament, adopted the sexual attitudes of Hellenistic Judaism but introduced the concept of homosexuality as "unnatural," taken from Plato's *Laws* and unknown to the Old Testament (Romans 1:26–27). Although the contrary is widely assumed, it is unlikely that Paul meant to include lesbianism, which had been ignored to this date, in his condemnation. See the articles by David F. Wright and Bernadette Brooten, included herein.

The post-Pauline church was antisexual, taking its cue from Paul's negative attitude towards marriage, making asceticism an ongoing theme of Christian tradition. The monastic tradition began about the third century, bringing with it an obsession with suppressing homoeroticism in religious communities. John Chrysostom (347–407) intensified Christian homophobia in the Eastern church, leading to capital punishment for homosexuality. His Western counterpart, Augustine (354–430), denounced sexual pleasure in general, grudgingly allowing it only for procreation.

## *Medieval and Reformation Christendom*

The Augustinian view prevailed in the West until the thirteenth century, when Thomas Aquinas emphasized homosexuality as a sin against nature (along with masturbation and heterosexual acts other than vaginal coitus) and hence worse than other sexual sins. Medieval Christianity was relatively mild in its actual treatment of homosexuality until Peter Damian (1007–1072), whose intensified homophobia became increasingly influential. Clerical celibacy became mandatory in the Roman church about the same time. Clerics saw "sodomy" as a type of heresy (hence "buggery"), treated it as worse than incest, and made it punishable by death.

Sodomy was subject to the Christian Inquisition after 1451, leading to numerous burnings at the stake in what became, after Hitler's Holocaust, the second worst persecution of homosexuality in history. The use of torture decreased after 1630, and inquisitional prosecutions became uncommon in the eighteenth century.

Meanwhile the Christian monastery and nunnery saw a good deal of homoerotic friendship and no small amount of homosexual conduct. See Judith C. Brown's article, included. The Renaissance papacy was also notable for homosexuality.

The Protestant Reformation changed little as far as homosexuality was concerned, though reformers abolished clerical celibacy and closed monasteries and nunneries. Reformers and counter-reformers alike accused their enemies of sodomy and heresy interchangeably and sometimes confounded sodomy and witchcraft; Protestants executed sodomites with a zeal sometimes surpassing that of the Inquisitors. Laws were carried over from the sacred to the secular realm in the newly Protestant countries virtually intact, and the Protestants resisted the Code Napoleon reforms which in the early nineteenth century decriminalized sodomy in most Catholic countries. Only the Quakers under William Penn in the colony of Pennsylvania reformed the law in 1682.

The Anglican Church was less austere than most Protestants, harboring large numbers of gay clergymen (especially in the High Church wing; see David Hilliard's article, included). Under the leadership of Canon Derrick Sherwin Bailey in the 1950s, Anglicans eventually championed the cause of British law reform; see Jonathan S. Carey's article, included.

## *Contemporary Christianity*

Under Pope John Paul II the Roman Catholic Church has remained a bastion of resistance to liberalization, reaffirming the doctrines of Aquinas as eternally valid and fighting gay civil rights laws and sodomy repeal with all of its political strength; see G. Coleman's article, included herein. The Eastern Orthodox churches have also maintained their medieval traditions virtually unchallenged.

The fundamentalist wing of American Protestantism has vociferously promoted traditional Christian homophobia, with such leaders as Jerry Falwell and Anita Bryant launching highly visible campaigns to oppose gay rights and even characterizing AIDS as God's judgment on the wicked sodomites.

In other Protestant churches, a wracking debate between those urging changes and the defenders of traditional positions broke out in the 1960s and continues unabated. One milestone came in December, 1964, when Ted McIlvenna, a Protestant clergyman, founded the Council on Religion and the Homosexual in order to bring San Francisco clergy and gay leaders together; the "CRH" soon became involved with police oppression issues and led to similar groups in other cities. Substantial gains have been made, with a few denominations such as the United Church of Canada accepting openly homosexual or lesbian ministers; for most the position has been "we welcome the gay sinner but condemn the sin," a compromise with which reformers cannot in the long run remain comfortable. Denominations with a more educated, upper-income membership seem to have been most willing to overlook or reinterpret their scriptural traditions. See the articles included herein by Georg Strecker and Edward Batchelor, Jr.

Given the large numbers of self-identified homosexuals raised as Christians and the continuing homophobia of the denominations, it was probably inevitable that the growth of the gay movement should foster the foundation of gay churches. The first such, though rather closeted, was Charles Webster Leadbeater's Anglican-derived Liberal Catholic Church, founded in Sydney, Australia, in 1916. It remained for Troy D. Perry to establish an openly homophile congregation, the Metropolitan Community Church, in Los Angeles in 1968; this diverse Protestant group has since grown to over 300 congregations and missions on five continents, and has provided a haven for gay and lesbian fundamentalists and evangelicals driven out of their original churches by those groups' vehement homophobia. See the article by Paul F. Bauer, included herein.

Another response has been the formation of gay and lesbian caucuses within the denominations, sometimes under official sponsorship. At other times the church authorities have banned them from the premises, as with the Mormons' Affinity group or the Catholics' Dignity, founded in 1969 in San Diego and at its zenith the largest such caucus, with seven thousand members. The Quakers even hosted a bisexual caucus in the mid-1970s.

Lesbians often seem to be more involved in the feminist challenge to established Christian practices and thinking than in confrontations with Christian homophobia, which has usually ignored or only sideswiped them. See articles by Mary E. Hunt and Carter Heyward, included herein.

Not all those raised as Christians have been content to remain identified with a tradition they consider their historic oppressor. Many homosexuals have gravitated towards non-Western traditions such as Buddhism and Hinduism, and others have left the realm of organized religion altogether. Still others have flocked to the New Age movement, whose oracular pronouncements have generally been encouraging, or to the Radical Faerie movement, which has looked to pagan European antecedents and to the shamanistic tradition of the American Indian for inspiration in developing a uniquely homoerotic sense of spirituality.

## *The Outlook for Christianity*

Three trends appear likely to continue into the early twenty-first century. The fundamentalist reaction shows no signs of weakening and may indeed gain strength from the abandonment of the homophobic ramparts by other Christian (and secular) defenders of the old order. Those individuals whose strong antipathy to homosexuality derives from psychological roots may find in fundamentalism a reassuring source of comfort and stability in a world of changing values. Whether the Roman Catholic Church will continue its de facto alliance with the fundamentalists is not so predictable, given the mortality of popes and the pressures from more liberal elements of the Roman ecclesia, combined with the ever more urgent problem of staffing a growing church with unmarried clergy. The Orthodox churches are likely to continue their resistance, but with little impact on society in general.

More liberal Protestant groups will continue to be pulled—kicking and screaming—toward an acceptance of homosexuality, though struggles over ordination will continue and a new wave of confrontations over homosexual marriage may prove traumatic.

Finally, some gay-identified persons raised as Christians will continue to find their native religion alien, the struggle to reconcile their own sense of self-worth with the historical hostility of Christianity simply not worth the effort, while the globalization of world culture increases their exposure to the wide array of spiritual traditions outside the Christian fold.

**Bibliography**

Atkinson, D. J. *Homosexuals in Christian Fellowship.* Grand Rapids, Mich.: Eerdmans, 1979.

Bailey, Derrick Sherwin. *Homosexuality and the Western Christian Tradition.* London: Longmans, Green, 1955.

Balka, Christie, and Andy Rose, eds. *Twice Blessed: On Being Lesbian, Gay and Jewish.* Boston: Beacon Press, 1989.

Bartley, William W., III. *Wittgenstein.* 2nd ed. LaSalle, Ill.: Open Court, 1985.

Batchelor, Edward, Jr., ed. *Homosexuality and Ethics*. New York: Pilgrim Press, 1980.

Boswell, John. *Christianity, Social Tolerance and Homosexuality*. Chicago: University of Chicago Press, 1980.

Brundage, James A. *Law, Sex, and Christian Society in Medieval Europe*. Chicago: Chicago University Press, 1987.

Clark, J. Michael. *A Place to Start: Toward an Unapologetic Gay Liberation Theology*. Dallas: Monument Press, 1989.

Coleman, Peter. *Christian Attitudes to Homosexuality*. London: SPCK, 1980.

Curb, Rosemary, and Nancy Manahan, eds. *Lesbian Nuns: Breaking the Silence*. Tallahassee, Fla.: Naiad Press, 1985.

Edwards, George R. *Gay/Lesbian Liberation: A Biblical Perspective*. New York: Pilgrim Press, 1984.

Fortunato, John. *Embracing the Exile: Healing Journeys of Gay Christians*. New York: Seabury Press, 1982.

Foucault, Michel. *The Foucault Reader*. ed. by Paul Rabinow, New York: Pantheon, 1984.

Fraisse, Jean-Claude. *Philia: la notion d'amitié dans la philosophie antique*. Paris: J. Vrin, 1974.

Grammick, Jeannine, ed. *Homosexuality and the Catholic Church*. Chicago: Thomas Moore Press, 1983.

Grammick, Jeannine, and Pat Furey, ed. *The Vatican and Homosexuality: Reactions to the "Letter to the Bishops of the Catholic Church on the Pastoral Care of Homosexual Persons"*. New York: Crossroad, 1988.

Hartmann, Oswald Oskar. *Das Problem der Homosexualität in Lichte der Schopenhauer'schen Philosophie*. Leipzig: Max Spohr, 1897.

Heyward, Carter. *Touching Our Strength: The Erotic as Power and the Love of God*. New York: Harper & Row, 1989.

Holtz, Raymond C., ed. *Listen to the Stories: Gay and Lesbian Catholics Talk about Their Lives and the Church*. New York: Garland Publishing, 1991.

Horner, Tom. *Homosexuality and the Judaeo-Christian Tradition: An Annotated Bibliography*. Metuchen, N.J.: Scarecrow Press, 1981. *Idem, Jonathan Loved David: Homosexuality in Biblical Times*. Philadelphia: Westminster, 1978.

Koertge, Noretta, ed. *Philosophy and Homosexuality*. New York: Harrington Park Press, 1985.

Macourt, Malcolm, ed. *Towards a Theology of Gay Liberation*. London: SCM, 1977.

McNeill, John J. *The Church and the Homosexual*. Kansas City: Sheed, Andrews and McMeel, 1976.

Malloy, Edward A. *Homosexuality and the Christian Way of Life*. Washington: University Press of America, 1981.

Melton, J. Gordon, ed. *Homosexuality: Official Statements from Religious Bodies and Ecumenical Organizations*. Detroit: Gale, 1991.

Nugent, Robert. *A Challenge to Love: Gay and Lesbian Catholics in the Church*. New York: Crossroad, 1983.

Pittenger, Norman. *Time for Consent*. 3rd ed. London: SCM, 1976.

Price, A. W. *Love and Friendship in Plato and Aristotle*. New York: Oxford University Press, 1989.

Scanzoni, Letha, and Virginia Ramey Mollenkott. *Is the Homosexual My Neighbor? Another Christian View*. San Francisco: Harper and Row, 1978.

Schmitt, Arno, and Jehoeda Sofer, eds. *Sexuality and Eroticism Among Males in Moslem Societies*. New York: Harrington Park Press, 1992.

Scroggs, Robin. *The New Testament and Homosexuality*. Philadelphia: Fortress Press, 1983.

Smith, Morton. *Clement of Alexandria and a Secret Gospel of Mark*. Cambridge, Mass.: Harvard University Press, 1973.

Swicegood, Tom. *Our God Too*. New York: Pyramid, 1974.

Thompson, Mark, ed. *Gay Spirit: Myth and Meaning*. New York: St. Martin's Press, 1987.

Walker, Mitch. *Visionary Love: A Spirit Book of Gay Mythology and Transmutational Faerie*. San Francisco: Treeroot Press, 1980.

# Contents

# Homosexuality and Religion and Philosophy

# Wittgenstein And Homosexuality[1]

BY W. W. BARTLEY, III

> A man can bare himself before others only out of a particular kind of love. A love which acknowledges, as it were, that we are all wicked children . . .
>
> Hate between men comes from our cutting ourselves off from each other. Because we don't want anyone else to look inside us, since it's not a pretty sight in there.
>
> — Ludwig Wittgenstein[2]

> If you think I'm an old spinster — think again!
>
> — Ludwig Wittgenstein[3]

*I. A Polemical Reply to My Critics.*

Homosexuality is unlikely to be treated with any equanimity until sexuality itself is so treated. There seems little likelihood, despite the developments of the past century, that that shall soon occur. The original reception of my book *Wittgenstein*[4], on its publication in 1973 and 1974 in New York and London, illustrates this as well as anything.

1 This essay is a revised version of the "Afterword 1982" to the German and Spanish translations of my *Wittgenstein* (Munich: Matthes & Seitz; 1983, and Madrid: Ediciones Catedra; 1982).

2 Ludwig Wittgenstein: *Culture and Value* (Chicago: University of Chicago Press; 1980), p. 46e.

3 Quoted in Norman Malcolm: *Ludwig Wittgenstein: A Memoir* (London: Oxford University Press; 1958), p. 45.

4 New York: J. B. Lippincott, Inc.; 1973: London: Quartet Books Ltd.; 1974.

In my book I had mentioned Wittgenstein's homosexuality only very briefly — on about four or five pages. The information given there was, as I stated, based on confidential reports from some of his friends. Even before the book was published, however, as page proofs were circulating, these reports were vehemently challenged and denied by other of his friends. Since that time, Wittgenstein's homosexuality has been corroborated by his own written statements in his coded diaries. And there is thus no longer any ground for controversy about the fact of his active homosexuality. Yet it continues to be denied, and the controversy continues.[5]

Having treated the matter so briefly in the book itself, I am in two minds about entering into a more extended discussion of it. *Wittgenstein* was my first venture into biography. Since publishing it I have become a bit more thick-skinned: I have published another biography,[6] and am now writing a third.[7] Yet my skin still stings from being called a liar in the *Times Literary Supplement* and elsewhere, from being known as "the man who wrote the dirty book on Wittgenstein," and from being denounced as "an able money-spinner" who "pees on the graves of men whom honest and upright people admire and respect."[8]

There are two more serious reasons for my ambivalence. First, I really do not want to attach undue importance to Wittgenstein's homosexuality. And I find — and here my own experience matches Wittgenstein's — that many people do not "think well" or at all forthrightly when dealing with such issues. And yet, as Wittgenstein himself cautions, it is really difficult "to think, or *try* to think, really honestly about your life and other people's lives. And the trouble is that thinking about these things is not *thrilling*, but often downright nasty. And when it's nasty then it's *most* important."[9]

Lest I make things appear altogether too grim, I should report that part of the reception given my book was refreshing. I had not blamed Wittgenstein for his sexual activities; and many readers seemed to absorb this information in the same understanding spirit in which they had taken similar revelations about Lytton Strachey, E. M. Forster, John Maynard Keynes, Virginia Woolf, Vita Sackville-West, D. H.

5 See the review of Rush Rhees, ed.: *Ludwig Wittgenstein: Personal Recollections* (Totowa: Rowman & Littlefield; 1981) which Desmond Lee published in *The Times Literary Supplement,* January 15, 1982, p. 46.

6 *Werner Erhard: Transformation of a Man* (New York: Clarkson N. Potter, Inc.; 1978).

7 A biography of Sir Karl Popper.

8 The latter quotation is from Wittgenstein's nephew, John J. Stonborough, in *The Human World,* February 1974, p. 78.

9 Quoted in Malcolm, op. cit., p. 39.

Lawrence, and other eminent British thinkers who are commonly associated, directly or indirectly, with Wittgenstein through Cambridge and the Bloomsbury Group, and who also happened to be homosexual.[10] Reflecting this mood, the reviews of the book were tolerably good: *The British Journal for the Philosophy of Science* described it as "extraordinarily concise," "enthrallingly written," "profound," and "more interesting and provocative than anything else written about Wittgenstein."[11] And C. P. Snow, writing in *The Financial Times,* described my treatment of Wittgenstein's homosexuality as "temperate and unusually detached . . . written with neutrality."[12]

But this was only a small part of the story. Several of Wittgenstein's literary executors and relatives threatened legal action to suppress the publication of my book, and also called on my British publishers to attempt to persuade them to stop publication.[13] Controversy raged in the columns of *The Times Literary Supplement,* and in several other publications. Professor G. E. M. Anscombe, of Cambridge University, one of Wittgenstein's literary executors, published two letters suggesting that I could not have known and ought not to have claimed the things I did.[14] Wittgenstein's close friend M. O'C. Drury, after explaining that, since he is a psychiatrist, it is "in the nature of my work to be alert to problems of homosexuality whether latent or active," wrote that "Bartley is in error when he supposes that Wittgenstein was at any time 'tormented by homosexual behaviour' . . . sensuality in any form was

10 Among the many books dealing with these matters, see Michael Holroyd: *Lytton Strachey,* 2 volumes (London: Heinemann; 1967); P. N. Furbank: *E. M. Forster: A Life* (New York: Harcourt Brace Jovanovich; 1978); E. M. Forster: *Maurice* (New York: W. W. Norton & Co.; 1971); Nigel Nicholson: *Portrait of a Marriage* (New York: Atheneum; 1973). See also the *Letters* and the *Diary* of Virginia Woolf.

11 I. C. Jarvie: Review in *British Journal for the Philosophy of Science* 25, 2, June 1974, pp. 195-8. See also *The Economist,* April 6, 1974, p. 107; *Review of Metaphysics,* 27 March 1974, pp. 601-2; *Times Literary Supplement,* August 17, 1973, pp. 953-4; *Los Angeles Times,* July 30, 1973; *The Christian Century,* December 19, 1973, p. 1255; *Philosophy and Phenomenological Research,* 1974, pp. 289-90; *Cross Currents,* Spring 1975, p. 84; et al.

12 C. P. Snow: "Bounds of Possibility," *The Financial Times,* London, 11 April 1974, p. 32.

13 See my letters to *The Times Literary Supplement,* January 11, 1974 and February 8, 1974; and G. E. M. Anscombe's letter of January 18, 1974.

14 *The Times Literary Supplement,* letters as follows: G. E. M. Anscombe: November 16, 1973 and January 4, 1974; W. W. Bartley, January 11, 1974, and February 8, 1974; F. A. von Hayek: February 8, 1974; M. O'C. Drury and Irina Strickland: February 22, 1974; Peter Johnson: December 14, 1973; Brian McGuinness: January 18, 1974; Rudolf Koder: February 8, 1974; William Miller: January 18, 1974.

entirely foreign to his ascetic personality''.[15] Another of Wittgenstein's literary executors, Rush Rhees, of the University of London, used words and phrases like "novellette," and "at the level of gossip columns" to describe my book.[16] A letter campaign was set up: those whom I had mentioned in my acknowledgements were contacted, asked to disassociate themselves from me, and to withdraw permission to use their names. One of those contacted, an eminent British literary critic, wrote to me: "My respect for you and your work are such that I will write in complete frankness. I wonder whether you have a clear notion of the ugliness which followed on the publication of your book here . . . The general line here is that you are to be drummed out of the trade and that no academic invitation of any kind will be extended to you from the United Kingdom henceforth . . ."

The ugliness has continued over the years. Thus in the Wittgenstein Documentation Center in Kirchberg am Wechsel, Austria, the site of the annual international Wittgenstein congress, two display cases were for some years devoted to arguing that Wittgenstein was *not* a homosexual, and that my account was "verfälschend."[17]

15 *Times Literary Supplement,* February 22, 1974. See also Drury's essays: "Some Notes on Conversations with Wittgenstein," and "Conversations with Wittgenstein," in Rush Rhees, ed.: *Ludwig Wittgenstein: Personal Recollections* (Totowa, New Jersey: Rowman & Littlefield; 1981), p. 135, where Drury's point goes uncorrected. For a very different view of Wittgenstein's lack of "sensuality" and "ascetic personality", see Professor Georg Kreisel's report that Wittgenstein often broached the subject of sex in conversations, but Kreisel turned these aside because "it was certainly painful to me, as appropriate to the time, to hear an old man talk of things that were intended only for us young chaps." See Georg Kreisel: "Zu Wittgensteins Gesprächen und Vorlesungen über die Grundlagen der Mathematik," in *Wittgenstein und Sein Einfluss auf die Gegenwärtige Philosophie: Akten des 2. Internationalen Wittgenstein Symposiums* (Vienna: Hölder-Pichler-Tempsky; 1978), pp. 79-81, esp. p. 81, note 7.

16 Rush Rhees: "Wittgenstein," *The Human World,* February 1974, pp. 66-78. Numerous writers — without examining the matter — blindly followed Rhees. See for example Rudolf Haller's review in *Conceptus* 11, 1977, pp. 422-24.

17 I am happy to report that Dr. Adolf Hübner, the director of this Center, has undergone an interesting transformation in this regard, and has now recanted (though privately). In his "Bartley Refuted" (Schriftenreihe der Oesterreichischen Ludwig-Wittgenstein Gesellschaft, 1978), Hübner denied that Wittgenstein was homosexual and called his friends and acquantances in witness against me. By the time he published his book *Wittgenstein* (with Kurt Wuchterl; Hamburg: Rowohlt Taschenbuch; May 1979), Hübner had modified his opinions, and although still denouncing my book wrote of Wittgenstein's "homoerotic tendencies" (p. 67). By September 9, 1979, Hübner wrote to me to say that he would not again write an article "in defense of" Wittgenstein's personality "against reproaches such as yours." Hübner added that he was rather sure that his literary executors know that Wittgenstein suffered from homosexual tendencies. Hübner goes on to say that his article was written in a period in which his admiration for Wittgenstein was "still boundless." But there was no reproach in my own book; and *my* admiration for Wittgenstein was in no way affected by my discoveries about his sexuality.

This entire attack on my book, and on my own *bona fides,* has been based on bluff, on projection, and on plain naivety.

First, as to bluff. The documents confirming Wittgenstein's homosexuality — his own coded diaries — have been in the possession of the Wittgenstein literary estate all along. During the height of their attack, the Wittgenstein literary executors had coded notebooks, in Wittgenstein's own hand — written in a very simple cipher and long since decoded and transcribed — corroborating my statements about his homosexuality. There is also an allusion to his homosexuality in a letter from Wittgenstein to his sister Mining written as early as his days as an engineering student at the University of Manchester (1908-11).

Only two of the coded notebooks appear to have been preserved. It is known that several of his notebooks were destroyed, by Wittgenstein's own order, in 1950, and these appear to include the notebooks for the period 1918-28, the period with which my own book was chiefly concerned.[18] At any rate, they are missing. Of the two books that are preserved, the first dates from the period of the First World War, ending prior to 1918. In it Wittgenstein explicitly discusses his homosexual wishes and longings, recurrences of "sensuality", and the way in which he is tormented by them.[19] But there is as yet no unequivocal evidence of homosexual *activity*, and thus one cannot judge with certainty whether Wittgenstein's relationship with his friend David

18 See my letter, "Wittgenstein and Homosexuality," *Times Literary Supplement,* February 8, 1980, p. 145. I am, incidentally, not the only person to have discussed Wittgenstein's homosexuality. Independent discussion appears in A. L. Rowse: *Homosexuals in History* (New York: Macmillan; 1977), pp. 328-50; and George Steiner: *After Babel* (Oxford: Oxford University Press; 1975), p. 40. See also George Steiner: "The Language Animal," in *Encounter,* 1969, reprinted in his *Extraterritorial* (London: Penguin; 1972), pp. 66-109; and Steiner's "Rare Bird," *The New Yorker,* November 30, 1981, pp. 196-204, esp. p. 202. See also Paul Levy: *Moore: G. E. Moore and the Cambridge Apostles* (London: Weidenfeld & Nicolson; 1979), p. 270. That other persons judged Wittgenstein to be homosexual as early as 1915, we now know from G. E. Moore's diary. In his biography of Moore, Paul Levy reports: "7 August 1915, when Moore was visiting the Wedgwoods and was asked by their great friend Richard Curle (who edited Julia Wedgwood's letters and was also a friend of Joseph Conrad), to talk about his quarrel with Wittgenstein. It was then that Curle and Iris Wedgwood bluntly asked Moore 'about [Wittgenstein's] being normal (about women)' which I don't like!" See Levy: *Moore: G. E. Moore and the Cambridge Apostles* (London: Weidenfeld & Nicolson; 1979), p. 274.

19 B. F. McGuinness, who is writing the official biography of Wittgenstein (which has been announced several times since the early 1970s but has never been published), refers to this very indirectly in his "Wittgenstein's 'Intellectual Nursery-Training'," in *Wittgenstein, the Vienna Circle and Critical Rationalism, Proceedings of the 3rd International Wittgenstein Symposium* (Vienna: Hölder-Pichler-Tempsky; 1979), p. 39.

Pinsent — which is often supposed to have been a homosexual one — involved active sexual relations.

The second notebook dates from a later period, following 1928, and reveals both that Wittgenstein was involved in homosexual activities and that this brought him great distress of mind. In these pages Wittgenstein finds it abhorrent that he should have such desires, yet also comments that he cannot blame himself for having them, and that it is not bad to have them. This notebook also reveals that active homosexual practice was involved in Wittgenstein's relationship with his friend Francis Skinner.[20]

So much for bluff. And so much for Drury's "alertness" to homosexuality.

Then there is projection. I am using the word "projection" in the psychological sense, in which internal subjective states lead to radical misperceptions of the external world. To illustrate how unreliable people often become in the presence of information about homosexuality, I have selected two descriptions of my book by authors who are friendly to it. Any reader of its first chapter will be able to confirm that I do not claim or imply that Wittgenstein's sexual partners were prostitutes or that he despised them. What I *do* say is:

> By walking for ten minutes to the east . . . he could quickly reach the parkland meadows of the Prater, where rough young men were ready to cater to him sexually. Once he had discovered this place, Wittgenstein found to his horror that he could scarcely keep away from it . . . Wittgenstein found he much preferred the sort of rough blunt homosexual youth that he could find strolling in the paths and alleys of the Prater to those ostensibly more refined young men who frequented the Sirk Ecke in the Kärtnerstrasse and the neighboring bars at the edge of the inner city.[21]

20 This testimony by Wittgenstein himself is contrary to that of Fania Pascal, in her discussion of the relationship between Skinner and Wittgenstein in "Wittgenstein: A Personal Memoir," *Encounter,* August 1973, pp. 23-29. Pascal's version is however not corrected in the version reprinted in Rush Rhees, ed.: *Ludwig Wittgenstein: Personal Recollections,* op. cit. If Pascal does not *correct* her remarks, at least she *mentions* Skinner. Although Wittgenstein and Skinner were, in Pascal's words, "inseparable," Malcolm completely omits mentioning Skinner in his *Memoir.* This omission — as serious as Roy Harrod's omission of the question of homosexuality from his biography of John Maynard Keynes — seriously flaws the portrait that Malcolm draws of Wittgenstein.

21 Bartley: *Wittgenstein,* op. cit., American edition, p. 47.

Out of this statement, W. D. Hudson conjures up — for his book *Wittgenstein and Religious Belief* — the following report:

> Bartley's book openly states that Wittgenstein's perpetual bad conscience arose, in part at least, from the fact that he regularly consorted with the most repellent kind of male prostitute in London and Vienna.[22]

And Ben-Ami Scharfstein, in his book *The Philosophers,* writes of Wittgenstein, referring to my book:

> His whole situation would be more intelligible, as would his frequent attacks on his own decency, if he suffered, as has been claimed, from his attachment to rough homosexual men whom he despised.[23]

It is as if the matter is made less threatening by introducing, in the imagination, something which was, to the best of my knowledge, never there: the *repellent, despised prostitute.*

Finally, a word about the quite extraordinary naivety that attended the reception of my book. I will mention only two of the many preposterous arguments that have been published purporting to establish that I could not possibly have obtained the evidence I had for the details of Wittgenstein's homosexuality. First, it is alleged that anyone who could have known about Wittgenstein's sexual activities shortly after the First World War would be either dead or too old to remember. Yet when I obtained my information in the early and mid nineteen-sixties, my informants were of course in their early and mid sixties. Is it seriously suggested that men in their sixties cannot remember the sexual escapades of their youth — particularly when so distinctive a personality as Wittgenstein is involved?

Secondly, it is often argued that Wittgenstein could not have been homosexual since anyone so well known and so distinctive in voice and dress, and so rich, would — had he been homosexual and done the sorts of things I described — have been recognized and blackmailed.[24] This is a very odd argument. Of course Wittgenstein was recognized:

22 W. D. Hudson: *Wittgenstein and Religious Belief* (London: Macmillan; 1975), p. 102.

23 Ben-Ami Scharfstein; *The Philosophers: Their Lives and the Nature of Their Thought* (New York: Oxford University Press; 1980), p. 334.

24 Thus Rush Rhees and John Stonborough in *The Human World,* op. cit., pp. 67 and 80.

otherwise I could not have obtained my original information. Again, although homosexual practice was illegal in Austria prior to and following the first world war (indeed until 1970), and although there was sporadic enforcement of the law, there was little active, serious or sustained persecution or legal prosecution of homosexuals prior to the Hitler period. Thus Count Harry Kessler reports in his diaries the following story about Count Leopold Berchtold, the Imperial Austrian foreign minister:

> On 31 July 1914, when the whole world was waiting for the Serb reply to the Austrian ultimatum, he (Kuh) saw Berchtold in the fun-fair part of the Vienna Prater standing by a merry-go-round notorious as a meeting-place for male prostitutes. An extremely pretty youth, in white trousers and white pullover, winked broadly every time the merry-go-round carried him past a very smartly dressed man whose eyes never left him. When the merry-go-round halted, the youth stepped down and went up to the gentleman, who greeted him and took him along. The gentleman was Berchtold. At the moment that the two were leaving, newspaper sellers rushed on the scene with shouts of 'Serb Answer to the Ultimatum! War with Serbia! Austrian Invasion to Serbia!' — The start of the World War which Berchtold had precipitated.[25]

Berchtold was obviously a far better candidate for blackmail than was Wittgenstein. Yet blackmail is far rarer than is homosexuality. And this is the same Prater where Wittgenstein's nephew John Stonborough suggests that homosexual importuning is hardly to be found.[26]

25 Graf Harry Kessler: *In the Twenties: The Diaries of Harry Kessler* (New York: Holt, Rinehart & Winston; 1971), p. 457. Berchtold seems to have spent quite a bit of time on public view that summer. See Max Graf's vignette in his *Legend of a Music City* (New York, 1945), pp. 69-70: "I can still see the distinguished Count Berchtold on a summer's day in 1914, standing in the doorway of a Ringstrasse Hotel. He had just signed the declaration of war on Serbia. Now he stood here, slender, laughing ironically, a gold-tipped cigarette in his well-manicured fingers, watching the crowds and conversing with the passersby." For comparable information about homosexual assignations, see the Victorian novel *Teleny, or the Reverse of the Medal* (London: Leonard Smithers; 1893), or Brian Reade: *Sexual Heretics* (New York: Coward-McCann, Inc.; 1970), pp. 228-245. Another example of a prominent homosexual during this period is that of Rantzau, Germany's chief delegate to the Versailles conference.

26 *The Human World,* op. cit., esp. pp. 79-82.

## *II. The Question of the Relevance of His Homosexuality to Wittgenstein's Philosophy.*

"It is sometimes said that a man's philosophy is a matter of temperament, and there is something in this".

— Ludwig Wittgenstein[27]

Although Wittgenstein's homosexuality is, it seems obvious to me, of central importance in understanding the man and his influence, I made no attempt in my book to explain his *thought* in terms of it. This too has been criticized. Thus George Steiner, who gave my book a generous welcome, nonetheless suggested that I have evaded the "crux of the matter," and that Wittgenstein's sexual life and theory of language are closely related.[28]

This is a question that I wish to confront in this section.

* * *

I have a good friend named Ben-Ami Scharfstein, who is professor of philosophy in the University of Tel-Aviv, and the author of some splendid books on art and aesthetics, on Chinese and comparative studies, on mysticism, and on the lives of the philosophers. Most philosophers, Scharfstein contends, hide behind façades: their ideas are indeed constructions intended to make those façades the more difficult to penetrate.[29] And sometimes their ideas are the façades themselves.

Such a claim is of course difficult to evaluate fairly. For we are, all of us, so adept at turning a profit out of whatever comes our way, that it is often hard to tell whether we have brought about something to our advantage or whether we have simply *turned* it to our advantage. Doubtless anyone clever enough to invent a philosophy would be clever enough to find a way to hide behind it — if he wanted to hide. Such is the very stuff and prerequisite of any ability to manipulate ideas to corrupt or to confuse understanding.

However this may be, Scharfstein's view would hardly have been advanced were there not at least some philosophers to whom it seemed,

27 *Culture and Value,* op. cit., p. 20.

28 Steiner's notices of my book appeared in *The New Yorker,* July 23, 1973, p. 77, and in *The Listener* (with Anthony Quinton), March 28, 1974, pp. 399-401.

29 See Scharfstein's *The Philosophers,* op. cit., for an account of his views. Steiner seems to argue in a similar vein in *After Babel,* op. cit., pp. 32-3, when he writes that "languages conceal and internalize more, perhaps, than they convey outwardly. Social classes, racial ghettoes speak at rather than to each other."

at least on the surface, to apply. Wittgenstein might appear to be a good example, and I can see how Steiner also could take him to be so. Certainly in his early theory of language Wittgenstein does insist that everything of real importance is unsayable; and he also says that the interior of a person is impenetrable by language. From Scharfstein's perspective, this would be a façade,a façade all too conveniently deflecting the gaze of the curious inquirer (and perhaps Wittgenstein's own attention as well) away from Wittgenstein. As if in confirmation of this, it has been recorded that Wittgenstein "would above all abhor anybody enquiring into his personal life."[30] Wittgenstein himself wrote: "Don't play with what lies deep in another person."[31] And although he himself seriously entertained the idea of becoming a psychiatrist, he advised his disciple M. O'C. Drury — who did become a psychiatrist — that "he [Wittgenstein] would not want to undergo what was known as a training analysis. He did not think it right to reveal all one's thoughts to a stranger."[32] (One cannot know whether Drury is reporting Wittgenstein accurately here either. But if he is, a psychiatrist would likely accuse Wittgenstein of irresponsibility. He would say that anyone who presumes to treat others without having undergone something like a training analysis himself does indeed *play* with his patients' depths.)

In any case, Wittgenstein's friends and literary executors have taken care to carry out his apparent wishes where possible. One of them has written: "If by pressing a button it could have been secured that people would not concern themselves with his personal life, I should have pressed that button."[33] Another executor, when publishing a selection

30 Fania Pascal: "Wittgenstein: A Personal Memoir," op. cit.

31 *Culture and Value,* op. cit., p. 23.

32 See Drury's "Conversations with Wittgenstein" in op. cit., p. 151.

33 G. E. M. Anscombe, quoted by Paul Engelmann in *Letters from Ludwig Wittgenstein, with a Memoir* (Oxford: Basil Blackwell; 1967), p. xiv. In 1953 the Wittgenstein literary estate refused to permit F. A. von Hayek, Wittgenstein's second cousin once removed, the distinguished Nobel-prize winning economist and biographer of John Stuart Mill, to publish some letters of Wittgenstein until they themselves had first published them. As a result, and to our common loss, Hayek abandoned his own biography of Wittgenstein. Later, Anscombe denied that this occurred. See her letter to the *Times Literary Supplement,* January 18, 1974, and F. A. von Hayek's letter in the same journal, February 8, 1974. See also Hayek's "Remembering My Cousin, Ludwig Wittgenstein," *Encounter,* August 1977, pp. 20-22. The hostility of Wittgenstein's executors to biographical and historical investigation has been effective; they have been able to deflect numerous researchers — with the result that every portrait drawn of Wittgenstein is false; not to mention that it is thereby almost impossible to tell the story of — or to direct critical attention to — the formation of his school and the creation of its influence.

from Wittgenstein's notes, "excluded from the collection notes of a purely 'personal' sort — i.e., notes in which Wittgenstein is commenting on the external circumstances of his life, his state of mind and relations with other people . . ."[34] The "love that dare not speak its name," that which is "among Christians not to be named," needed to be shielded from view.

Scharfstein's thesis — that a man's philosophical product is a *disguised* expression of his inner state — is a sophisticated variant of *epistemological expressionism,*[35] the popular idea that a man's work, whether of art or of philosophy, is an expression of his inner state, of his emotions, of his personality.[36] Thus the philosopher and psychologist John Oulton Wisdom has argued that Bishop Berkeley's philosophical idealism is an expression of his internal state as discoverable by psycho-analysis. Berkeley's idealism, his denial of the existence of matter, is, Wisdom argues, linked to and an expression of the same unconscious anality which caused him, physically, to suffer from colitis![37] Elsewhere, Wisdom has argued that Hegel's philosophy is an expression of his isolation, loneliness and depression.[38]

But can Wittgenstein's thought be understood in this way? And if so, what does it express? And what precisely is its connection, if any, with his homosexuality?

Before raising such questions, we need to ask whether *anyone's* thought is appropriately so interpreted. This is a question worth raising, for expressionism is widespread, shifting attention from the quality of the product to the character of the producer, and thereby also encouraging the romantic preoccupation with personality that is so

34 See G. H. von Wright, in his Preface to Ludwig Wittgenstein: *Culture and Value,* op. cit.

35 The term "epistemological expressionism" comes from K. R. Popper: *Objective Knowledge* (Oxford: Oxford University Press; 1972), pp. 146-47. My discussion here is based on my essay: "Ein schwieriger Mensch: Eine Porträtskizze von Sir Karl Popper," in Eckhard Nordhofen, ed.: *Physiognomien: Philosophen des 20. Jahrhunderts in Portraits* (Königstein: Athenäum; 1980), pp. 43-69.

36 On expressionism see E. H. Gombrich: *The Sense of Order* (New York: Phaidon; 1979), pp. 42-4; and *Meditations on a Hobby Horse* (New York: Phaidon; 1963), pp. 56-69 and 78-85. My discussion is much inspired by Gombrich's work. See also K. R. Popper: *Unended Quest* (London: Fontana; 1976), sections 13 and 14.

37 J. O. Wisdom: *The Unconscious Origin of Berkeley's Philosophy* (London: 1953).

38 J. O. Wisdom: "What Was Hegel's Main Problem?," Royal Institute of Philosophy Lecture, London, February 2, 1962. See also Wisdom's *Philosophy and Its Place in Our Culture* (New York: Gordon & Breach; 1975). For a somewhat similar approach see Morris Lazerowitz: *The Language of Philosophy: Freud and Wittgenstein* (Dordrecht: D. Reidel; 1977).

prevalent in, if not an expression of, our culture. It is also an approach — often in the past called physiognomy — sanctioned by age. In the eighteenth century it is found in J. J. Winckelmann, who found the impassive marble fronts of classical statues an expression of the "noble simplicity and quiet grandeur" of the Greek soul; and also in Johann Casper Lavater's *Physiognomische Fragmente* (1775-78), which sought to decipher characters from portrait silhouettes. The approach was later ridiculed by Georg Christoph Lichtenberg who, in his delicious parody of Lavater, showed that those who followed Lavater lost the capacity to discriminate between Goethe's pigtail and Goethe's *Faust*. An even earlier example is G. B. Della Porta, in *De humana Physiognomia* (1586), who sought to develop a science of physiognomics by comparisons between human types and particular animals. Thus a man with an aquiline nose would be noble of spirit, and one with a sheepish face would be sheepish.

Such expressionism might seem palatable to Wittgenstein himself, in that he once wrote, in a physiognomical mood, that "The human body is the best picture of the human soul."[39] More important, such expressionism is often found intertwined with contemporary studies of language; and language is the focus of all Wittgenstein's work. Thus George Steiner asks: "In what measure are sexual perversions analogues of incorrect speech?", whether there are affinities between pathological erotic compulsions and the obsessive search for a private language, and "Might there be elements of homosexuality in the modern theory of language (particularly in the early Wittgenstein), in the concept of communication as an arbitrary mirroring?"[40] Steiner writes that:

> Eros and language mesh at every point. Intercourse and discourse, copula and copulation . . . Sex is a profoundly semantic act . . . To speak and to make love is to enact a distinctive twofold universality: both forms of communication are universals of the human sexuality and speech developed in close-knit reciprocity. Together they generate the history of self-consciousness . . . The seminal and the semantic functions . . . together they construe the grammar of being. . . . If coition can be schematized as dialogue, masturbation seems to be correlative with the pulse of monologue . . . The multiple, intricate relations between speech defects and infirmitives in the nervous and glandular mechanisms

39 *Philosophical Investigations*, p. 178.

40 George Steiner: *After Babel*, op. cit., pp. 39-40. See also his *Extraterritorial*, op. cit., esp. pp. 66-109.

which control sexual and excretory functions have long been known . . . Ejaculation is at once a physiological and linguistic concept. Impotence and speech-blocks, premature emission and stuttering, involuntary ejaculation and the word-river of dreams are phenomena whose interrelations seem to lead back to the central knot of our humanity. Semen, excreta, and words are communicative products. They are transmissions from the self inside the skin to reality outside . . . The grounds of differentiation (between the speech of men and women) are, of course, largely economic and social. . . . But certain linguistic differences do point towards a physiological basis or, to be exact, towards the intermediary zone between the biological and the social . . . Are there biologically determined apprehensions of sense data which precede and generate linguistically programmed conceptualizations?''[41]

This is a delight to read. But is what it says true? For that matter, what exactly *does* it say?

It is easy to mock such approaches: to produce, say, examples of realists who suffer from colitis and happily extraverted Hegelians. Or to recall Winston Churchill's description of a political opponent as ''a sheep in sheep's clothing.'' It is also easy to remark that Steiner's brilliant discourse insinuates an expressionism which he is too sophisticated to state outright — insinuates by the use of provocative questions which are posed and then abandoned, as if the answers to them were obvious. It might even be important to remark that, although Steiner's discussion suggests the contrary, Wittgenstein's early work does *not* contain any ''concept of communication as an arbitrary mirroring,'' and that Wittgenstein, far from obsessively searching for a private language, firmly maintained that such a language was impossible.

In the following, however, I do not wish to make fun of physiognomy or expressionism, and certainly not of Steiner's provocative and brilliantly suggestive studies of language and translation. Rather, I wish to begin to identify some of the basic *scientific* objections to expressionism and to all attempts to reduce human speech and its content to the circumstances, physiological, psycho-sexual, and otherwise, of the individuals who use and create that speech.

41 Steiner, op. cit., pp. 38-39 and 43.

We may begin by placing human expression in a somewhat wider context.

For this purpose I draw on Karl Bühler's famous work, *Sprachtheorie,* concerning the theory of human language.[42] Bühler, who was from 1922 to 1938 Professor of Philosophy and Psychology in the University of Vienna, and whose possible influence on Wittgenstein's later philosophy is discussed in my book, analyzed the communicative function of a language into three components: 1) the *expressive function,* where the communication serves to express the internal states of the speaker; 2) the *signalling* or stimulative or release function, where the communication serves to stimulate or to release certain reactions in the hearer; 3) the *descriptive function,* which is present to the extent that the communication aims to describe some state of affairs. At this third level, the regulative idea of truth emerges, assessing descriptions according to whether they fit the facts. These first three functions are separable in so far as each is accompanied by its preceding one but need not be accompanied by its succeeding one. That is, one may express without signalling; one may express and signal without describing. But one cannot signal without expressing, or describe without both expressing and signalling. Another function has been added to Bühler's set by my teacher Sir Karl Popper (who was Bühler's student in Vienna), and on whose work I shall also draw in the several paragraphs that follow: namely, 4) the *argumentative function.* In terms of this, descriptive statements are appraised with regard to the regulative standards of truth, content, and truthlikeness; and arguments are appraised with regard to their validity. The same hierarchical ordering applies here: one cannot argue without describing, signaling, expressing.[43] The first two functions apply, of course, to animal languages. But the second two functions may be characteristically human — although some of those who research into the life and languages of animals hope for discoveries which will modify some accepted views about the limits of animal communication.[44]

42 Karl Bühler: *Sprachtheorie: Die Darstellungsfunktion der Sprache* (Leipzig, 1934; 2nd edition Stuttgart: Gustav Fischer Verlag; 1965).

43 K. R. Popper: *Conjectures and Refutations* (London: Routledge and Kegan Paul; 1962), pp. 134 and 295; *Objective Knowledge* (London: Oxford University Press; 1972), pp. 41, 120, 160, 235; *The Self and Its Brain* (New York: Springer; 1977), pp. 57-8. See my discussion in my book *Morality and Religion* (London: Macmillan & Co.; 1971), Chapter 2.

44 Frisch's bees are a possible example.

As an aid in the understanding of his ideas, Bühler developed this diagram:

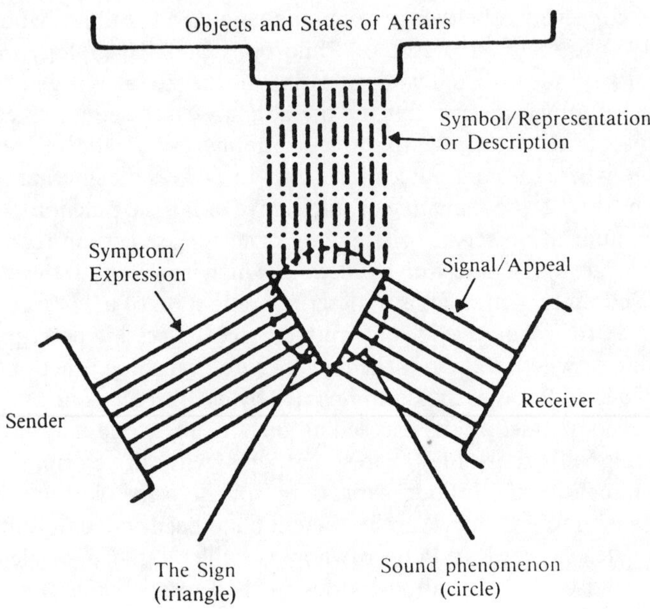


The triangle in the middle denotes the linguistic sign, whatever its character. This sign may be used by the sender or speaker to express himself; it may be received by the receiver or listener as a signal or appeal which may or may not have been intended by the speaker. And the same sign again may be used — by sender, receiver, or both — to symbolize some objective state of affairs independent of the receiver and sender.

The analysis may obviously be applied to contemporary art, music, and poetry — and to a variety of theories about them. Extend the sign beyond language to a work of art. Such a work may express certain subjective states of mind (conscious or unconscious) or intentions on the part of the artist; those who receive or respond to the work of art may or may not decode it (consciously or unconsciously) as it was intended by its sender. And the work of art may or may not be representational.

Let us not pursue this but, instead, with Bühler's account in mind, return to our question: can a philosopher's theories be reduced to the expressive level? Philosopher's ideas are of course self-expressive; in a trivial sense, anything that one does is self-expressive. (And this observation should make us, right from the start, somewhat sceptical of the explanatory power of expressionism: if expression characterizes *everything* that one does, it can have little hope of explaining the particular features of some specific things that one does — such as art or philosophy.) But the question is whether such ideas can (as is maintained in expressionist accounts of philosophy — and of art) be *reduced* to the expressive level, whether they are, ultimately, *only* expression.

The answer to this question is emphatically negative — for a variety of reasons, logical, physical, biological. I shall cite three such reasons or arguments — two very short ones, and another rather longer one.

The first argument is that expressionism is quite contrary to everything we know from biology and from evolutionary theory. It removes the biological *function* from our descriptive statements, and thus leaves the important role that description plays in human life go quite unexplained; unchecked self-expression (i.e., self-expression unchecked by description) in the dangerous environments in which human beings have evolved and continue to live would be biologically lethal.

The second argument is that it is in any case *impossible* to reduce the descriptive and argumentative levels of language to the expressive and signal levels: *no causal physical theory of the descriptive and argumentative functions of language is possible.* Popper shows that the name relationship — which is the simplest case of a descriptive use of words — cannot be causally realized.[45] That is, any purely causal model of naming is intrinsically defective, in that no causal chain alone can represent or realize the relation between a thing and its name. Rather, *interpretation* (which itself cannot be causally realized) *must be added,*

45 Popper has shown this in "Language and the Body-Mind Problem," in *Conjectures and Refutations,* op. cit., pp. 293-98. See also his *The Open Universe: An Argument for Indeterminism,* Vol. II of his *Postscript to the Logic of Scientific Discovery,* ed. W. W. Bartley, III (Totowa: Rowman & Littlefield; 1982), especially sections 20-24, and the three Addenda: "Indeterminism is Not Enough: An Afterword," "Scientific Reduction and the Essential Incompleteness of All Science," and "Further Remarks on Reduction, 1981." See my discussion in "The Philosophy of Karl Popper: Part II: Consciousness and Physics: Quantum Mechanics, Probability, Indeterminism, The Body-Mind Problem," in *Philosophia 7,* July 1978, pp. 675-716; and my "On the Criticizability of Logic," in *Philosophy of the Social Sciences 10,* 1980, pp. 67-77.

in order to pick out or select — and to name — some part of the total physical situation. It follows from this that, to the extent to which a philosopher's theories contain representational descriptive statements, intended to be true or false, and arguments intended to be valid or invalid, those theories cannot be reduced to the expressive level. This argument was originally constructed to refute physicalism and behaviorism, not expressionistic theories of art and philosophy; yet it applies to the latter just as much as to the former.

The argument is strong and general; and *it suffices* to refute the related family of philosophies (materialism, mechanism, determinism, expressionism, etc.) that attempt to reduce the human self, language, and theory to the conditions under which they arise, whether economic, psycho-sexual, physiological, genetic, or otherwise.

But I promised another argument. One which is not only easier to understand but which is also, I believe, particularly revealing, relates to the logical and informative content of theories. When we affirm a theory, we also propose its logical implications (otherwise we should not have to retract it when these come to grief), all those statements that follow from it — as well as those further implications which result from combining this theory with other theories which we also propose or assume. But this means that the informative content of any theory includes an *infinity* of *unforeseeable* nontrivial statements; it also makes clear that the content of an idea is far from identical with some particular person's thoughts about it. For there are infinitely many situations, themselves infinitely varied, to which the theory may be applicable. Yet many of these situations have not only not even been imagined at the time the theory is proposed; they are also, literally, *unimaginable* at that time, in terms of the information then available. For example, part of the informative content of Newton's theory is that Einstein's theory is incompatible with it; yet this could not possibly have been imagined at the time Newton proposed his theory; nor could the test situations or applications that eventually decided against Newton's theory have been imagined then — since such possibilities of observation and testing of *Newton's* theory become *conceivable* only after the invention of *Einstein's* theory.[46]

This startling result means that, literally, "we never know what we are talking about."[47] Even the inventor of a theory cannot possibly

46 There is the related problem that the growth of knowledge is unpredictable in principle. See Popper: *Poverty of Historicism* (Boston: Beacon Press; 1957), Preface; and Popper: *The Open Universe,* op. cit., Chapter 3.

47 See Popper: *Unended Quest,* op. cit., section 7.

fully have understood it — as many historical examples attest. Thus Erwin Schrödinger did not understand the "Schrödinger equations" before Born gave his interpretation of them; and the content and application of these equations is, indeed, still a matter of controversy. Since it is logically impossible, consciously or unconsciously, to anticipate such matters on the basis of what we know about the inventor or discoverer of a theory, it is absurd to think of them in terms of "self expression."

Developing this result, we can see that expressionist accounts must fail in three fundamental ways. First, they suppose that there is a fixed core to the individual, of which his work and thought is an expression. Second, they neglect the objectively unfathomable depths of the product. And third, as a consequence, they are unable to capture the nature of the relationship between a man and his work (any more than they capture the "name relationship"). In sum, expressionism misunderstands the nature of the individual self; the nature of intellectual work and creativity; and the nature of the relationship between the two. The result is altogether too passive and one-directional.

We have already discussed the second point — the objectively unfathomable content of intellectual products or ideas — on which the entire argument hangs. To take the first and third points in turn: the human self, while no doubt in part resulting from inborn dispositions, is also at least in part held together by theories: these help to provide its unity, its individuality, and its continuity; and it is rich, unfathomable, and growing to the extent to which these theories enjoy these characteristics.[48] Once one has acquired descriptive language, one becomes not only a subject but also an object for oneself: an object about which one can reflect, which one may criticize and change. Self-transcendence is a familiar and all-important characteristic of human life, and is attained in large part through the reflective criticism and examination of the theories that hold the self together; the destruction of some of those theories; and the creation of new theories in their place. Hence, for the reasons already mentioned, we can never fully know ourselves any more than we can know what we are talking about in other areas. For both poles are anchored in descriptive language.

The relationship between this unfathomable self and the unfathomable theories which it has somehow produced can then hardly be one of expression of the one by the other! Such an account fails

48 See Popper: *The Self and Its Brain,* op, cit., Chapter P4, esp. section 42; and *Objective Knowledge,* op. cit., pp. 146-50.

to take account either of the nature of language and of theory, or of the constantly changing flamelike quality of the individual, as expressed in his *active* cybernetic relationship with his cultural world, including his own cultural products, and the creative, unpredictable character that is intrinsic to that relationship. This relationship is one of give and take between the individual and his work; it depends upon "feedback" amplified by conscious self-criticism. Such feedback is, as is evident from evolutionary theory, part of any growth process; so it is hardly surprising to find it here.[49]

When one produces an idea — whether about oneself, about the nature of the world, about human society, or language, or whatever — this idea, being formed in descriptive language, takes on an objective life of its own — and particularly so when it is written down and published, and thus made available to others. It has unexplored and sometimes also *unwanted* potential transcending what could possibly have been intended, or expressed, in the moment of its utterance. As one's understanding of such an idea unfolds, it may literally alter the econiche in which one dwells by introducing into it new potentialities and problems. The cultural world, which contains one's self-conceptions and one's theories about the external world, is thus an objective natural exosomatic product, comparable in certain respects to a spider's web. This web of ideas is autonomous in the sense that it generates its own problems and that its content is largely independent of our wishes, existing independently of being realized in the subjective consciousness of any individual.[50] As Nietzsche found: "I discovered and ventured diverse answers; I distinguished between ages, peoples, degrees of rank among individuals; I departmentalized my problem; out of my answers there grew new questions, inquiries, conjectures, probabilities — until at length I had a country of my own, a soil of my own, an entire discrete, thriving, flourishing world, like a secret garden the existence of which no one suspected."[51]

In this context, the unexpected ramifications of one's own ideas about the world, about society, about the individual, about one's own aims and preferences, may — as one pursues them, as one works with them, as one adopts them as problems — have a radical impact on one's self-conception, and also on one's instinctive life. Far from expressing one's

49 See my "Biology and Evolutionary Epistemology" in *Philosophia* 6, 1976, pp. 463-94, esp. pp. 496-77.

50 For a different sort of example, take the table of logarithms or the problem whether there are highest twin prime numbers.

51 Friedrich Nietzsche: *On the Genealogy of Morals,* Preface, section 3.

old self and self-conceptions, they may be radically at odds with them. They may *work against* one's self expression.[52]

Some persons of course exploit this potential rather little. Yet in his interaction with and contribution to this cultural world — and with the descriptive and argumentative levels of language — a person has at least the opportunity to form himself, to transcend his origins, the conditions of his birth, his genes, his instincts, his self expression. In this interaction, one's self is constantly being transcended, together with its expressions of itself.

In the case of an individual such as a scientist or philosopher who is distinguished by his interactions with the world of intellect, one might even be tempted to say that he expresses his ideas, rather than that his ideas express him. Some persons have taken this sort of thinking to an extreme: I am thinking, for instance, of physical therapists in the United States, in the school of Ida Rolf for example, who contend that one's whole body, even the curvature of the spine and the fascia of one's muscles, express one's thoughts. But this too will not do: although the impact of the world of ideas on any person — even on the most original — exceeds the impact which any individual can make on it, the whole model of expression is too passive.

Many other arguments against such attempts at reduction could be added here, serious scientific arguments which are generally ignored in the loose popular talk — literary, historical, and philosophical — about "influences" from the psyche and such like. Such influences of course exist, but it would, for the reasons indicated, be quite impossible for them to work in the direct ways in which they are commonly alleged to work.

Once reminded of these facts about language, thought, and culture, it is hard to take seriously the project of reducing a philosophy to its inventor's personal circumstances, to his personal psychopathology, or to think of it simply in terms of expression. One must set aside such biography, which "explains everything and therefore explains nothing," as empty and unscientific. Such is not biography motivated by the search for deeper understanding; it is biography by recipe.

To understand a philosophy one must study its content and the constellation of objective problems that stand behind its creation; and one must not be distracted *unduly* by the personal circumstances of the philosopher. To do otherwise, to follow an expressionistic program,

52 For a good example, see J. D. Unwin's amusing introduction to his *Sex and Culture* (London: Oxford University Press, 1934).

is for the intellectual historian or biographer to risk turning himself into a kind of graphologist: grasping for insight in deviations from copybook drill; dubiously expressing (or disguising!) his own individuality in his projection-laden interpretations of the scribblings of others. The personal circumstances of the philosopher may *sometimes* play an important role in the network of problems and theories within which he is working and *sometimes they may play no role at all.*

Sometimes they don't; *and sometimes they do.* In arguing against facile forms of expressionism, I do not want to suggest that sexuality *never* decisively shapes the content of the work of a philosopher or scientist. For there are no doubt some cases where this apparently has happened. Walter Kaufmann has contended that this is true of C. G. Jung: that some of the positive content of Jung's psychology, and particularly the argument of his *Answer to Job,* can be understood best in terms of his failure to resolve his own Oedipal conflicts.[52a]

### *III. Some Attempts To Link The Homosexuality And The Thought*

After this review — which ought to form a prolegomenon to any psychologically oriented intellectual history or biography — it is high time to return to the specific case of Wittgenstein.

I know of one interesting detailed attempt to explain the content of Wittgenstein's thought in terms of his homosexuality. It is due to Professor A. W. Levi, of Washington University.[53]

Inspired by Nietzsche's remark that "systems of morals are only a sign language of the emotions", Levi recalls the deep consciousness of personal guilt that runs through Wittgenstein's letters to Engelmann "like a trail of blood." The words Wittgenstein uses to refer to himself, over and over again, are Unanständigkeit, Schlechtigkeit, Schweinerei, Niedrigkeit, Gemeinheit — indecency, badness, filthiness, baseness, vileness. The state in which he finds himself, Wittgenstein writes, "is the state of *not being able to get over a particular fact,*" the only remedy

52a Walter Kaufmann: *Discovering the Mind:* Vol. III: *Freud versus Adler and Jung* (New York: McGraw-Hill Book Co.; 1980), esp. Part IV.

53 A. W. Levi: "The Biographical Sources of Wittgenstein's Ethics," *Telos,* 38, Winter 1978-9, pp. 63-76. See also A. W. Levi: "Wittgenstein as Dialectician," *The Journal of Philosophy,* 61, 4, February 13, 1964, pp. 127-139. See Thomas Rudebush and William M. Berg: "On Wittgenstein and Ethics: a Reply to Levi," *Telos,* 40, Summer 1979, pp. 150-160; Steven S. Schwarzschild: "Wittgenstein as Alienated Jew," *Telos,* 40, Summer 1979, pp. 160-165; and A. W. Levi: "Wittgenstein Once More: A Response to Criticism," *Telos,* 40, Summer 1979, pp. 165-173.

for which, so Wittgenstein suggests, is suicide. Wittgenstein had the conviction, as he sometimes said, that he was "doomed."[54]

Levi's argument is straightforward: Wittgenstein's account of ethics is a kind of reaction formation, aimed at assuaging this heavy burden of guilt.[55] Just as in his daily life he sought out milieux in which he would be protected from his homosexual urges, so "his moral philosophy was unconsciously constructed to protect himself against the moral condemnation which those inclinations might be expected to call out". His theory of ethics is, Levi says, "the subtle strategy of a proud but guilty homosexual who has with great perspicuity and care placed himself beyond the condemnation of rational speech — that is to say — beyond the moral judgement of his fellow men." To do this, Wittgenstein simply created an account of language which rendered moral condemnation meaningless because it went beyond a statement of the factual.

Wittgenstein does this by sharply excluding from ethics anything of a factual character, or anything that may be reduced to factual statements. For example, judgements of value as a means to an end, or as meeting a standard, have nothing to do with ethics since, according to Wittgenstein, they can be translated into factual statements. For the same reason, statements of "tastes or inclinations," Wittgenstein stresses and repeats, are not matters of ethics.[56] Likewise, although "preferences" can be stated in meaningful language, "the fact of being preferred has equally little claim to be something valuable in itself."[57]

In short, personal tastes, inclinations, and preferences — and hence, presumably, sexual tastes and preferences — are not matters of ethics. The "particular fact", the particular state of affairs, of being homosexual — or of being heterosexual, or of acting as preferred by the majority of society, or of acting otherwise — has no coercive moral

54 G. H. von Wright, in Malcolm, *Memoir,* op. cit., p. 20.

55 What very little Wittgenstein wrote about ethics includes the last three pages of the *Tractatus,* his "Lecture on Ethics," (1929-30), and brief remarks in his notebooks and correspondence, in his conversations with Waismann and Schlick, and in the collection of remarks published as *Culture and Value.* (See "Lecture on Ethics," *The Philosophical Review,* January 1965, pp. 3-12.) For Wittgenstein's conversations with Schlick and Waismann, see *Ludwig Wittgenstein and the Vienna Circle* (Oxford: Blackwell; 1979), translated from *Ludwig Wittgenstein und der Wiener Kreis* (Oxford: Blackwell; 1967); these are conversations recorded by Friedrich Waismann. See also *Culture and Value* (Chicago: University of Chicago Press; 1980). Levi takes all except *Culture and Value* (which was not published when he first wrote) into account, and concentrates his attention on the "Lecture on Ethics."

56 "Lecture on Ethics," op. cit., p. 7.

57 *Ludwig Wittgenstein and the Vienna Circle,* op. cit., p. 11.

power, and it is not necessary, Wittgenstein states quite explicitly, to feel guilty about matters of taste or inclination.

So far Levi's interpretation might seem to hold. Such a view of ethics could indeed give at least intellectual relief to a guilty homosexual — or, for that matter, to a heterosexual who was deviant in some way and was inclined to feel guilty about that.

Yet I do not think that Levi's interpretation works. For there is another dimension to Wittgenstein's thought which, it seems to me, Levi's explanation does not capture at all — although he is of course well aware of it, and tried hard to fit it in.

True ethical judgements — what Wittgenstein calls judgements of "absolute value" — transcend the factual, and are *supernatural.* "What is good," he wrote in 1929, "is also divine. Queer as it sounds, that sums up my ethics. Only something supernatural can express the supernatural."[58] As he puts it, the absolute good, *if* it were a describable state of affairs (and it is not), would be one which "everybody, *independent of his tastes and inclinations,* would necessarily bring about or feel guilty for not bringing about."[59] However, no such state of affairs exists: "No state of affairs has, in itself, what I would like to call the coercive power of an absolute judge."[60]

Here we find Wittgenstein himself talking about the supernatural and absolute value. People are not at all deterred from talking about the supernatural, and about the absolute value which is its prerogative, by accounts such as Wittgenstein's which contend that such talk is meaningless. *And Wittgenstein knows this very well.* Moreover, he himself is not deterred. Quite the contrary, as he writes: "My whole tendency, and I believe the tendency of all men who ever tried to write or talk about Ethics or Religion was to run against the boundaries of language."[61] Such an attempt is hopeless; no knowledge can ever come from it. "But it is a document of a tendency in the human mind which I personally cannot help respecting deeply and I would not for my life ridicule it."[62]

What sorts of things do such people thereby want to express? Wittgenstein offers three concrete personal examples: 1) wonder at the existence of the world; 2) the experience of feeling absolutely safe; and 3) the experience of guilt, particularly that God disapproves of one's

58 *Culture and Value,* op. cit., p. 3e.
59 "Lecture on Ethics," op. cit., p. 7.
60 Ibid.
61 "Lecture on Ethics," pp. 11-12.
62 Ibid., p. 12.

conduct. To put these experiences into language, Wittgenstein says, *points to something,* yet leads to nonsense. Nonsensicality is at their very heart: for when we use such expressions *we intend to go beyond the factual* and beyond significant language, and to point to the absolute, the supernatural.

Now a number of serious problems arise here. If people are not deterred from talking about the supernatural by Wittgenstein's theory of the limits of language, they are not likely to be deterred from making moral judgements in matters of taste or inclination either. And thus Wittgenstein's theory of language and ethics — *if devised to protect himself from such judgements* — would be a failure.

Levi tries to circumvent this problem, and to draw Wittgenstein's discussion of the supernatural and the absolute within his interpretation by arguing that Wittgenstein's three experiences place one "in the very center of the moral nightmare of Wittgenstein's moral universe." Thus he says that Wittgenstein's wonder at the existence of the world is really a moral horror at the brute givenness of his "moral deformity." And his concern for absolute safety stems from his fear of the wild homosexual desires raging within him, as well as from the very real threat of physical danger to which he exposed himself in the pursuit of those desires. The third experience, that of guilt, is "obviously" a consequence of his life situation.

But Wittgenstein's discussion simply does not bear Levi's interpretation. Nor would Levi's interpretation work even if it did.

First, there is no evidence that Wittgenstein means moral horror where he speaks of wonder: Wittgenstein chose his words, including his metaphors and his expressions of emotion, carefully. Moreover, the pregnant yet bewildering question why there is anything at all, although formulated in a variety of ways, is familiar in German-language philosophy and goes back at least to Schelling. Karl Jaspers concerned himself with such a question in the 'twenties, and eventually published a book on Schelling (1955) whose central section is devoted to it. The question also arises in Heidegger, in Tillich, and in numerous other writers (including Sartre). I do not know whether Wittgenstein knew the work of Schelling, Jaspers, Sartre, or Tillich; but he did know something of Heidegger, and referred to him briefly in his discussions with Schlick and Waismann.[63] Nowhere in these discussions is there

63 *Ludwig Wittgenstein and the Vienna Circle,* p. 68. See, however, Henry LeRoy Finch's argument in his *Wittgenstein — the Later Philosophy* (New York: Humanities Press; 1977), p. 263, where it is denied that Wittgenstein and Heidegger have the same experience or question in mind.

any discussion of or reference to moral horror; and although Wittgenstein adds something new to the discussion — namely, an argument concerning its nonsensicality — he nowhere suggests that he intended anything so radically different from these other writers.

Second, there is no reason to suppose that Wittgenstein had the dangers, either subjective or objective, of homosexuality in mind when he referred to the feeling of absolute safety. Such an idea of safety is of first importance in Christianity in connection with salvation and the immortality of the soul, with no specific reference to homosexuality; and it also appears, in a different context, in Buddhism, in the striving for liberation from the circumstances of the world. There is no reason to suppose that, when Wittgenstein mentioned this experience, he had in mind other than what he said he had in mind: *religious* experience.

Moreover, there is some further, rather specific, evidence that goes contrary to Levi's interpretation, quite apart from the "Lecture on Ethics". Around 1910 Wittgenstein attended, and was deeply affected by, a performance of the Austrian playwright Ludwig Anzengruber's play, "Die Kreuzelschreiber". At the beginning of the third act, one of the characters states: "Whether you are lying six feet deep in the earth beneath the grass or whether you have to face this many more thousand times again — nothing can happen to you — you belong to all of it and all of it belongs to you. Nothing can happen to you. And this was so wonderful that I hollered to all the others around me: Nothing can happen to you . . . Now be joyful, joyful — Nothing can happen to you."[64] Wittgenstein was struck by this thought, and later described it to Malcolm as a turning point in his attitude towards religion.

The most important objection is that Wittgenstein's third experience simply refutes, rather than supports, Levi's interpretation. For the third experience appeals explicitly to *divine* disapproval. And divine disapproval is precisely what Wittgenstein's account of language would not *remove* — even though it made discussion of it meaningless, and even if it *had* succeeded (as we have seen is doubtful) in removing human disapproval.

For if Wittgenstein conjured up a theory of language and an account of ethics from his unconscious need to deflect human condemnation of his actions, surely his unconscious was ingenious enough to conjure up a philosophy or theology to deflect divine judgement as well!

64 Ludwig Anzengruber: *Gesammelte Werke* (Stuttgart, 1898), Vol 7, p. 279. See Norman Malcolm's account in his *Memoir*, op. cit., p. 70.

Without this second step, his view is hardly the "protective device of incontestable power" that Levi claims it to be.

Levi acknowledges that his argument is problematic, but does not seem aware how problematic it is. We have 1) the fact of Wittgenstein's guilt; 2) his theory of language and account of ethics; 3) the "factually meaningless" yet nonetheless powerful images of God as a terrible judge; 4) the powerful human desire, which Wittgenstein shares and respects, to point to such transcendence. (Levi even suggests that Wittgenstein might have held something like a "cupalogical argument" to argue from the fact of his moral corruption to the need for a Last Judgement and a divine judge.) We are apparently asked to believe that Wittgenstein's ethics functions to *assuage* his guilt, whereas his implicit theology and his account of a human tendency to "run up against the limits of language" — which would also, on such an account, have to be part of a reaction formation — work to *aggravate and increase* it. All this is — as a form of psychopathology — within the realm of possibility. But there is no reason to believe it, as it does not form an economical whole. A deeper account of Wittgenstein's psychopathology, uniting these two disparate strains, would be needed before such hypotheses would, individually, have anything to recommend them.

In any case, there is a straightforward alternative explanation that makes much more sense. Wittgenstein's account of ethics was more or less dictated by his theory of language; it was indeed *an unintended consequence of it,* in the sense explained in the previous section. And the theory of language, in turn, was dictated by the network of thinking that he shared with Russell and the logical positivists. Similar views of ethics were adopted (although without the residual theology) by other philosophers, such as Carnap, who were quite heterosexual. Wittgenstein may well have noticed the limited effect his account of ethics could have in freeing him from the condemnation of his fellow men; and this may account, say, for his explicit mentioning of tastes and preferences in this connection. If this occurred, it could have been of only very limited significance for him. For his guilt continued, and was associated, throughout his life, with images of divine punishment that were not effectively removed by his philosophy.

Levi's attempt to link Wittgenstein's homosexuality to his philosophy focuses on his early work, as represented by the *Tractatus,* and on the "Lecture on Ethics". I could imagine a similar argument being made on the basis of Wittgenstein's later philosophy wherein Wittgenstein suggests that understanding is rooted in and does not occur without shared practice and a common or shared form of life. Thus members or participants in one practice have no basis for criticizing or for judging good and bad those who engage in other practices. If we consider homosexuality as a "form of life", then such a philosophy also effectively insulates it from the moral criticism of others, although now the protective umbrella is constructed rather differently.

Possibly this aspect of his later philosophy, had he noticed it, would have appealed to Wittgenstein. But once again it is hard to accept the suggestion that he was *motivated* to construct his position by such a consideration. There are two reasons why. First, he was forced into such a relativistic position by what I have elsewhere called the "Wittgensteinian problematic", by the objective intellectual problem situation in which he found himself.[65] Many other persons who were neither homosexual nor in any serious moral difficulty also found themselves forced by this intellectual problem situation to accept similar relativistic stances.

More important — and this is a fact about Wittgenstein which Levi's entire discussion neglects — all the biographical evidence suggests that Wittgenstein was never much motivated by or afraid of the opinions of other persons. He repeatedly behaved in disregard of ordinary social convention, and appears to have been singularly self-willed and independent. As he expressed the matter in his notebooks: *"Lass Dich nicht von dem Beispiel Anderer führen, sondern von der Natur!"*[66] That is, "Don't let yourself be led by the example of others, but by nature!"

## *IV. Wittgenstein As Psychopomp.*

"Much of his life will remain forever
unknown to his closest friends."
— Fania Pascal

I have rebutted or cast doubt on various attempts to link Wittgenstein's homosexuality and his thought. Now I must attempt to explain the important connection which I do see between the

65 See my "A Popperian Harvest," In Paul Levinson, ed.: *In Pursuit of Truth* (New York: Humanities Press; London: Hutchinson & Co. Ltd.; 1982); and my "On the Differences between Popperian and Wittgensteinian Approaches," in *Proceedings of the 10th International Conference on the Unity of the Sciences* (New York, 1982).
66 *Culture and Value,* op. cit., p. 41e; see also p. 1e.

homosexuality and the man and his influence — a connection which some might not expect.

The connection that I see relates to the fact that Wittgenstein, although not a thinker of great originality, exerted, and continues to exert, immense influence. If one wanted his ideas, one could go to any number of other, clearer, writers. Those who have been influenced by him, particularly those who were close to him (two of his executors and several of his closest students are converts to Roman Catholicism; several other of his closest students are Anglicans), have responded to him as if to a *psychopomp,* to an *anima mundi,* a spiritual guide of almost supernatural character, to a shaman, priest and medicine man, to a hermetic figure or *spiritus mercurialis* — a spirit concealed or imprisoned in matter. *Wittgenstein fascinates.*[67]

J. N. Findlay expresses this mood when he writes of Wittgenstein:[68] "at the age of 40 he looked like a youth of 20, with a godlike beauty, always an important feature at Cambridge, . . . awesome in its unearthly purity . . . The God received him . . . in an ascetic room, beautiful in its almost total emptiness, where a wooden bowl of fruit on a table made the one note of colour . . . The God was all he had been described as being: he looked like Apollo who had bounded into life out of his own statue, or perhaps like the Norse God Baldur, blue-eyed and fairhaired, with a beauty that had nothing sensual about it, but simply breathed the four Greek cardinal virtues, to which was added a very exquisite kindness and graciousness that bathed one like remote, slightly wintry sunshine . . . what Wittgenstein himself was thinking was of little importance, only much superior to the confusions and half-lights in which most philosophers of his acquaintance lived, despite their very great excellence as *men* . . . There was . . . an extraordinary atmosphere that surrounded him, something philosophically saintly that was also very distant and impersonal: he was the *philosophe Soleil.* One had walked in his sunlight but one had not at all been singled out by the Sun . . . the tea one drank with him tasted like nectar."

For our purposes, three things are important in connection with such responses to Wittgenstein. First, such a response seems to work on the

67 Thus note the ancient, metaphorical meaning of *fascinem* as *membrum virile.* Incidentally, it is not only close disciples of Wittgenstein who respond to him in this way: all sorts of persons claim to be followers of Wittgenstein and to do the "sort" of things that he was doing — though they rarely can state what he *was* doing.

68 J. N. Findlay, "My Encounters with Wittgenstein," pp. 171-4.

instinctual level; it is archaic, and what C. G. Jung calls archetypal, independent of individual training. Second, in the Pythagorean tradition, and in the alchemical and hermetic writings which probe this response, such a shamanic figure is seen as a *sufferer,* "the sufferer who takes away suffering," "the wounded wounder who is the agent of healing." Third, in these same ancient traditions and writings — and elsewhere, as in Plato's myth of lost androgynous unity — such a figure is frequently *hermaphroditic.* Thus for the Neopythagoreans, hermaphroditism is an attribute of deity; so Hermes Trismegistus is said to incorporate the masculine-spiritual with the feminine corporeal, and Hermes Psychopompos is the *filius hermaphroditus.* One could also mention the divine bisexuality often attributed to Brahma and Siva, to Adam, to Baal and Mithras, to Dionysus and Apollo. Thus what are seen as the two great powers of nature, the masculine and the feminine, are combined in one being.[69]

For a human figure, such as Wittgenstein, to have such traits and powers projected on him by his admirers, it is necessary that the homosexuality be there; that it be known or sensed subconsciously by his followers; but that it not be admitted consciously. *Indefiniteness is essential*: the taboo and the temptation must be there together; both must be exploited. Thus what Drury and Pascal both sensed and recorded — Wittgenstein's *noli me tangere* and foreignness to sensuality

69 There is an immense literature here. See for examples, Francis A. Yates: *Giordano Bruno and the Hermetic Tradition* (London: Routledge & Kegan Paul; 1964); Heinrich Zimmer: *The King and the Corpse* (New York: Pantheon; 1948), esp. the discussion of Merlin, pp. 181-201, and Part II, on the Kalika Purana; David Stacton: *Kaliyuga* (London: Faber & Faber; 1965); H. G. Baynes: *Mythology of the Soul* (London: Methuen & Co. Ltd.; 1949), pp. 186, 227, 240; C. G. Jung: *The Psychology of the Unconscious* (New York: Dodd, Mead & Co.; 1937), pp. 33-4, 229; C. G. Jung: *Symbols of Transformation* (Princeton: Princeton University Press; 1956), pp. 125-6, 160n, 221-2; C. G. Jung: *Mysterium Coniunctionis* (Princeton: Princeton University Press; 1963), *passim;* C. G. Jung: *Psychology and Alchemy* (London; Routledge & Kegan Paul; 1953), *passim:* C. G. Jung and C. Kerényi: *Essays on a Science of Mythology* (New York: Pantheon; 1949), pp. 74, 90, 93, 107, 128, 130, 132, 138, 148, 204; Edward Carpenter: *Intermediate Types among Primitive Folk* (New York: Arno Press 1975), p. 71. One should also, in this connection, study the libertine tradition in early Christianity, the understanding of which has been greatly aided by the discovery of the "secret gospel" of Mark. See Morton Smith: *The Secret Gospel* (New York: Harper & Row; 1973), esp. pp. 17 and 115-138; *Clement of Alexandria and a Secret Gospel of Mark* (Cambridge: Harvard University Press; 1973), pp. 254-263, pp. 167-188, esp. p. 185, and p. 217-229. See also his *Jesus the Magician* (New York: Harper & Row; 1978).

(and his intense *suffering* from this) — must be there: so far they told the truth. As did Julian Bell, when he rhymed, in 1930:[70]

I pity Ludwig while I disagree,
The cause of his opinions all can see
In that ascetic life, intent to shun
The common pleasures known to everyone.

But equally required, in order for the mystique to hold, is the subconscious awareness that that is not the whole story.

This indefiniteness must also be present in the message of such a figure, particularly in that aspect of it which relates most closely to issues of morality. So it is not surprising that Wittgenstein's doctrine of ethics is so hard to state: that there is so much *weighty* controversy about what he said — or meant — in saying that what is said in these matters is meaningless . . . and yet of immense importance. As Wittgenstein wrote to Ficker: "My work consists of two parts: the one presented here plus all that I have *not* written. And it is precisely this second part that is the important one."[71] This of course concerned ethics.

Where everything is obscure — the personality, the sexuality, the content of the thought — anything may be projected.[72] And thus, *from his friends and disciples,* Wittgenstein rejected all overtures: interpretations of his thinking were rejected emphatically and even

70 From Julian Bell: "An Epistle on the Subject of the Ethical and Aesthetic Beliefs of Herr Ludwig Wittgenstein (Doctor of Philosophy) to Richard Braithwaite Esq. MA (Fellow of King's College)," a long poem in Drydenesque couplets. Originally printed in *The Venture,* February 1930: quoted from T. E. B. Howarth: *Cambridge Between Two Wars* (London: Collins; 1978), pp. 71-2. See also Peter Stansky and William Abrahams: *Journey to the Frontier: Julian Bell and John Cornford: Their lives and the 1930's* (London: Constable, 1966), pp. 60-1.

71 Ludwig Wittgenstein: *Briefe an Ludwig von Ficker* (Salzburg: Otto Müller Verlag; 1969), pp. 35-5.

72 I do not believe that the *construction* of Wittgenstein is at all restricted to his later disciples in Britain. A similar process seems to have been at work in Vienna with the members of the Vienna Circle. Thus Heinrich Neider writes of "Wittgenstein . . . the halfmythical 'patron saint' of the Vienna Circle . . . I remember that even two years later, during an animated discussion at the philosophers' congress in Prague, a German participant said: 'Herr Wittgenstein, should he be a real person or rather, as I believe, a synthetic figure invented by the Vienna Circle as a mouthpiece to their theses . . . '" See Marie Neurath and Robert S. Cohen: *Otto Neurath: Empiricism and Sociology* (Dordrecht: D. Reidel; 1973), p. 47. In his biography of G. E. Moore, op. cit., p. 9, Paul Levy suggests that Wittgenstein's followers may provide a comparatively rare instance of the "cult of personality" operating within philosophy. See also J. N. Findlay, who writes of Wittgenstein's "magic of personality" and "personal enchantment" in his "My Encounters with Wittgenstein," op. cit.

cruelly. And similarly, "noli me tangere" ruled out in advance most overture-interpretations of his sexuality.

Nothing more is needed to explain the response to the first edition of my book.[73] Thus — as discussed in the first section above — the bluff and coverup, the projection, the naivety. And the pain, affront, and shock. For when this preserve of unnamable privacy was breached, when the details of Wittgenstein's sexuality were reported — however "neutrally" — the mystery was gone. Then it was "just sex."

I wonder then whether eagerness to prevent such aspects of Wittgenstein's life from being explored does not stem from some source such as this? With unconscious prudence and savvy,[74] the "unnamability" of this area is kept safe in order to preserve the power and appeal, the magic, of the man.[75]

73 There is of course more to the explanation than this. Thus any great thinker or artist tends to be romanticized by his followers. Every several years, with remarkable regularity, some outraged doctor or other writes an article denying that Beethoven or Schubert suffered from venereal disease. (See Heuwell Tircuit: "Knocking the 'Great Immortals' Back to Earth," *Review,* August 9, 1981, p. 17. See also Maynard Solomon: *Beethoven* (New York: Schirmer Books; 1977), p. 262; and John Reed: *Schubert's Final Years*). It seems that a heroic effort is made to overcome one's basic distrust of intellectual and artistic effort by making it into a "higher" calling in which the artist must take an elevated role, not prone to the temptations of ordinary mortals. The reverse of the coin here is the tendency to see all artists as libertines.

74 I say "unconscious" prudence; and so it no doubt would have to be. It could not have worked better to the advantage of Wittgenstein's posthumous reputation had it been conscious and deliberate. For by preserving silence about these things, one could avoid affronting the extensive repressed homosexuality and homophobia of American professional academics, and at once titilate and influence them. Hence Wittgenstein's extraordinary influence throughout the arts subjects of American academia. This is not surprising: American children have for years been schooled on the Minnesota Multiphasic Personality Inventory Test, which assigns one a high "femininity quotient" if one prefers going to the museum or reading a book to playing football or selling brushes door to door. In the circumstances it is hardly surprising that many American professors in the arts live with the not quite irradicable fear that they may be not simply homosexual but downright *queer*.

75 I am grateful to a number of persons who have kindly read drafts of this essay and made helpful comments and criticisms, and who are in no way responsible for the opinions and errors that remain. These include Professors Joseph Agassi, I. C. Jarvie, Peter Munz, Steven S. Schwarzschild, and George Steiner.

# Appendix

by Edward Batchelor, Jr.

The following are excerpts from church statements on homosexuality.

AMERICAN BAPTIST CHURCHES

We, as Christians, recognize that radical changes are taking place in sex concepts and practices. We are committed to seeking God's guidance in our efforts to understand faithfully and deal honestly with these changes and related issues. We recognize that there are many traditional problems of family and personal life for which the church's ministries have not been adequate, but we are committed to be used by God to strengthen and broaden these ministries. In this spirit we call upon our churches to engage in worship, study, fellowship and action to provide for meaningful ministries to all persons as members of the 'Family of God' including those who are homosexuals.

THE AMERICAN LUTHERAN CHURCH, Standing Committee for the Office of Research and Analysis, 1977.

The church need not be caught up in the conflicting theories as to how widespread homosexuality is, the factors which cause or foster homosexuality, and whether it is an illness, an arrested state of sexual development, a form of deviant behavior, or a sexual expression of human nature. These are matters for the various scientific disciplines to debate and resolve. The church, however, is concerned that some human beings created in God's image are involved in homosexual behavior, that many people are hurting because of their own homosexuality or that of a loved one, and that the Scriptures speak to the entire issue.

We believe that taken as a whole the message of Scripture clearly is that:

a. Homosexual behavior is sin, a form of idolatry, a breaking of the natural order that unites members of the human community;
b. Homosexual behavior is contrary to the new life in Christ, a denial of the responsible freedom and service into which we are called through baptism;
c. God offers the homosexual person, as every other person, a vision of the wholeness He intends, the assurance of His grace, and His healing and restoration for the hurting and broken.

Nevertheless, we recognize the cries of our homosexual brothers and sisters for justice in the arena of civil affairs. We cannot endorse their call for legalizing homosexual marriage. Nor can we endorse their conviction that homosexual behavior is simply another form of acceptable expression of natural erotic or libidinous drives. We can, however, endorse their position that their sexual orientation in and of itself should not be a cause for denying them their civil liberties.

CHRISTIAN CHURCH (DISCIPLES OF CHRIST), General Assembly. Study Document, 1977.

. . . The standards of membership in the Christian Church (Disciples of Christ) have always rested on confession of faith in Jesus Christ and baptism. Its standards have been "inclusive" rather than "exclusive." In support of these it has appealed to the relationships of Jesus which were inclusive, often, in fact, deliberately directed to those whom society had demeaned and cast aside. It has never acknowledged barriers to fellowship on the basis of dogma or life style. By these principles, rooted in biblical faith, it is difficult to point to any basis upon which homosexual persons might be excluded from membership.

Acknowledging . . . the wide differences of opinion, there does seem to be a minimal consensus to which the church can strive: homosexuals are persons whom God created, loves and redeems and seeks to set within the fellowship of faith communities to be ministered to and to minister. The church can affirm that God's grace does not exclude persons of differing life styles or sexual preferences, nor does the church which is enlightened by the Holy Spirit. Homosexuals may be included in the fellowship and membership of the community of faith where they are to love and be loved and where their gifts of ministry are to be welcomed.

FRIENDS, Philadelphia Yearly Meeting of Friends, 1973.

We should be aware that there is a great diversity in the relationships that people develop with one another. Although we neither approve nor disapprove of homosexuality, the same standards under the law which we apply to heterosexual activities should also be applied to homosexual activities. As persons who engage in homosexual activities suffer serious discrimination in employment, housing and the right to worship, we believe that civil rights laws should protect them. In particular we advocate the revision of all legislation imposing disabilities and penalties upon homosexual activities.

GREEK ORTHODOX CHURCH, Biennial Clergy–Laity Congress, 1976.

The Orthodox Church condemns unreservedly all expressions of personal sexual experience which prove contrary to the definite and unalterable function ascribed to sex by God's ordinance and expressed in man's experience as a law of nature.

Thus the function of the sexual organs of a man and a woman and their biochemical generating forces in glands and glandular secretions are ordained by nature to serve one particular purpose, the procreation of the human kind.

Therefore, any and all uses of the human sex organs for purposes other than those ordained by creation, runs contrary to the nature of things as decreed by God. . . .

The Orthodox Church believes that homosexuality should be treated by society as an immoral and dangerous perversion and by religion as a sinful failure. In both cases, correction is called for. Homosexuals should be accorded the confidential medical and psychiatric facilities by which they can be helped to restore themselves to a self-respecting sexual identity that belongs to them by God's ordinance.

LUTHERAN CHURCH IN AMERICA, Biennial Convention, 1970.

Human sexuality is a gift of God for the expression of love and the generation of life. As with every good gift, it is subject to abuses which cause suffering and debasement. In the expression of man's sexuality, it is the integrity of his relationships which determines the meaning of his actions. Man does not merely have sexual relations; he demonstrates his true humanity in personal relationships, the most intimate of which are sexual.

Scientific research has not been able to provide conclusive evidence regarding the causes of homosexuality. Nevertheless, homosexuality is viewed biblically as a departure from the heterosexual structure of God's creation. Persons who engage in homosexual behavior are sinners only as are all other persons—alienated from God and neighbor. However, they are often the special and undeserving victims of prejudice and discrimination in law, law enforcement, cultural mores, and congregational life. In relation to this area of concern, the sexual behavior of freely consenting adults in private is not an appropriate subject for legislation or police action. It is essential to see such persons as entitled to understanding justice in church and community.

MORAVIAN CHURCH, Synod, 1974

WHEREAS: the Christian Church has the responsibility of reexamining its own traditional sexual stance in the light of more recent interpretation and scientific evidence for the benefit of both youth and adults, and

WHEREAS: the homosexual has too often felt excluded from and persecuted by society, there be it

RESOLVED: (29) that the Moravian Church reaffirms its open welcome to all people by specifically recognizing that the homosexual is also under God's care, and be it further

RESOLVED: (30) that Moravian congregations will extend an invitation to all persons to join us in a common search for wholeness before God and persons, and be it further

RESOLVED: (31) that as Christians, recognizing our common sinfulness and the miracle of God's grace, accepting God's pardon, and together striving to help free each other from bonds of fear, despair, and meaninglessness, fitting us for lives of commitment, responsibility, witness, service, and celebration in God's Kingdom, we will share in this venture as children of God and brothers and sisters in Christ toward wholeness.

THE PRESBYTERIAN CHURCH IN THE UNITED STATES, 117th General Assembly, 1977.

That the 117th General Assembly expresses love and pastoral concern for homosexual persons in our society and the need for the Church to stand for just treatment of homosexual persons in our society in regard to their civil liberties, equal rights, and protection under the law from social and economic discrimination which is due all citizens.

Although we confess our need for more light and pray for spiritual guidance for the Church on this matter, we now believe that homosexuality falls short of God's plan for sexual relationships and urge the Church to seek the best way for witnessing to God's moral standards and for ministering to homosexual persons concerning the love of God in Jesus Christ.

PROTESTANT EPISCOPAL CHURCH IN THE U.S.A., General Convention, 1976.

Resolved, that it is the sense of this General Convention that homosexual persons are children of God, who have a full and equal claim with all other persons upon the love, acceptance, and pastoral concern and care of the Church.

Resolved, this General Council expresses its conviction that homosexual persons are entitled to equal protection of the law with all other citizens, and calls upon our society to see such protection is provided in actuality.

ROMAN CATHOLIC, Vatican Congregation for the Doctrine of the Faith, 1977.

At the present time there are those who, basing themselves on observations in the psychological order, have begun to judge indulgently, and even to excuse completely, homosexual relations between certain people. This they do in opposition to the constant teaching of the magisterium and to the moral sense of the Christian people.

A distinction is drawn, and it seems with some reason, between homosexuals whose tendency comes from a false education, from a lack of normal sexual development, from habit, from bad example or from other causes, and is transitory or at least not incurable; and homosexuals who are definitely such because of some kind of innate instinct or a pathological constitution judged to be incurable.

In regard to this second category of subjects, some people conclude that their tendency is so natural that it justifies in their case homosexual relations within a sincere communion of life and love analogous to marriage insofar as such homosexuals feel incapable of enduring a solitary life.

In the pastoral field, these homosexuals must certainly be treated with understanding and sustained in the hope of overcoming their personal difficulties and their inability to fit into society.

Their culpability will be judged with prudence. But no pastoral method can be employed which would give moral justification to these acts on the grounds that they would be consonant with the condition of such people. For according to the objective moral order homosexual relations are acts which lack an essential and indispensable finality.

THE ROMAN CATHOLIC CHURCH—Great Britain, Statement issued by the Archbishop of Westminster, 1957.

The civil law takes cognizance primarily of public acts. Private acts as such are outside its scope.

However, there are certain private acts which have public consequences in so far as they affect the common good. These acts may rightly be subject to civil law.

It may be, however, that the civil law cannot effectively control such acts without doing more harm to the common good than the acts themselves would be. In that case it may be necessary in the interests of the common good to tolerate without approving such acts.

It has, for example, invariably been found that adultery or fornication (which, however private, have clear public consequences) cannot effectively be controlled by civil law without provoking great evils.

Applying these principles to the question of homosexual acts between consenting males:

1. As regards the moral law, Catholic moral teaching is:
   a. Homosexual acts are grievously sinful.
   b. That in view of the public consequences of these acts, *e.g.*, the harm which would result to the common good if homosexual conduct became widespread or an accepted mode of conduct in the public mind, the civil law does not exceed its legitimate scope if it attempts to control them by making them crimes.

2. However, two questions of fact arise:
   a. If the law takes cognizance of private acts of homosexuality and makes them crimes, do worse evils follow for the common good?
   b. Since homosexual acts between consenting males are now crimes in law, would a change in the law harm the common good by seeming to condone homosexual conduct?

Ecclesiastical authority could rightly give a decision on this question of fact as well as on the question of moral law, if the answers to questions of fact were overwhelmingly clear. As, however, various answers are possible in the opinion of prudent men, Catholics are free to make up their own minds on these two questions of fact.

SOUTHERN BAPTIST CONVENTION, Resolution on Homosexuality, 1976.

Whereas, homosexuality has become an open lifestyle for increasing numbers of persons, and

Whereas, attention has focused on the religious and moral dimensions of homosexuality, and

Whereas, it is the task of the Christian community to bring all moral questions and issues into the light of biblical truth;

Now therefore, be it resolved that the members of the Southern Baptist Convention . . . affirm our commitment to the biblical truth regarding the practice of homosexuality and sin.

Be it further resolved, that this Convention, while acknowledging the autonomy of the local church to ordain ministers, urges churches and agencies not to afford the practice of homosexuality any degree of approval through ordination, employment, or other designations of normal lifestyle.

Be it further resolved, that we affirm our Christian concern all persons be saved from the penalty and power of sin through our Lord Jesus Christ, whatever their present individual lifestyle.

UNITARIAN UNIVERSALIST ASSOCIATION OF CHURCHES IN NORTH AMERICA, General Assembly, 1970.

Discrimination Against Homosexuals and Bisexuals: Recognizing that

1. A significant minority in this country are either homosexual or bisexual in their feelings and/or behavior;
2. Homosexuality has been the target of severe discrimination by society and in particular by the police and other arms of government;
3. A growing number of authorities on the subject now see homosexuality as an inevitable sociological phenomenon and not as a mental illness;

4. There are Unitarian Universalists, clergy and laity, who are homosexuals and bisexuals;

THEREFORE BE IT RESOLVED: That the 1970 General Assembly of the Unitarian Universalist Association: 1) Urges all people immediately to bring an end to all discrimination against homosexuals, homosexuality, bisexuals, and bisexuality, with specific immediate attention to the following issues:
Private consensual behavior between persons over the age of consent shall be the business only of those persons and not subject to legal regulations. Urges all churches and fellowships, in keeping with our changing social patterns, to initiate meaningful programs of sex education aimed at providing a more open and healthier understanding of sexuality in all parts of the United States and Canada, and with the particular aim to end all discrimination against homosexuals and bisexuals.

UNITED CHURCH OF CHRIST, The Tenth General Synod, 1975.

Therefore, without considering in this document the rightness or wrongness of same-gender relationships, but recognizing that a person's affectional or sexual preference is not legitimate grounds on which to deny her or his civil liberties, the Tenth General Synod of the United Church of Christ proclaims the Christian conviction that all persons are entitled to full civil liberties and equal protection under the law.

Further, the Tenth General Synod declares its support for the enactment of legislation that would guarantee the liberties of all persons without discrimination related to affectional or sexual preference.

THE UNITED METHODIST CHURCH, The Quadrennial Conference, 1976.

Homosexuals no less than heterosexuals are persons of sacred worth, who need the ministry and guidance of the church in their struggles for human fulfillment, as well as the spiritual and emotional care of a fellowship which enables reconciling relationships with God, with others and with self. Further we insist that all persons are entitled to have their human and civil rights ensured, though we do not condone the practice of homosexuality and consider this practice incompatible with Christian teaching.

UNITED PRESBYTERIAN CHURCH IN THE U.S.A., 188th General Assembly, 1976.

The 188th General Assembly calls to the attention of our Church that, according to our most recent statement, we "reaffirm our adherence to the moral law of God . . . that . . . the practice of homosexuality is sin . . . Also we affirm that any self-righteous attitude of others who would condemn persons who have so sinned is also sin." The 188th General Assembly declares again its commitment to this statement. Therefore, on broad Scriptural and confessional grounds, it appears that it would at the present time be injudicious, if not improper, for a Presbytery to ordain to the professional ministry of the Gospel a person who is an avowed practicing homosexual.

THE LUTHERAN CHURCH—MISSOURI SYNOD, Convention, 1973.

Whereas, God's Word clearly identifies homophile behavior as immoral, and condemned it (Lev. 18:22; 20:13 and Rom. 1:24–27); and

Whereas, The Law and the Gospel of Jesus Christ are to be proclaimed and applied to all conditions of mankind; therefore be it Resolved, That the Synod recognize homophile behavior as intrinsically sinful; and be it further

Resolved, That the Synod urge that the Law and Gospel of the Scriptures be applied to homophiles as appropriate with a view toward ministering the forgiveness of our Lord Jesus Christ to any and all sinners who are penitent.

UNION OF AMERICAN HEBREW CONGREGATIONS, General Assembly, 1977.

Whereas the UAHC has consistently supported the civil rights and civil liberties of all persons, and

Whereas the Constitution guarantees civil rights to all individuals,

Be it therefore resolved that homosexual persons are entitled to equal protection under the law. We oppose discrimination against homosexuals in areas of opportunity, including employment and housing. We call upon our society to see that such protection is provided in actuality.

Be it further resolved that we affirm our belief that private sexual acts between consenting adults are not the proper province of government and law enforcement agencies.

## Statements by Professional Organizations

AMERICAN BAR ASSOCIATION, House of Deputies, 1973.

RESOLVED that the legislatures of the several states are urged to repeal all laws which classify as criminal conduct any form of non-commercial *sex conduct between consenting adults in private*, saving only those portions which protect minors or public decorum.

AMERICAN MEDICAL ASSOCIATION, Action of the Trustees, 1973.

Passed a resolution urging the endorsement of the Model Penal Code of the American Law Institute, which recommends to legislators that private sexual behavior between consenting adults should be removed from the list of crimes and thereby legalized.

AMERICAN PSYCHIATRIC ASSOCIATION, Board of Trustees, 1973.

Unanimously voted for a resolution urging "the repeal of all legislation making criminal offenses of sexual acts performed by consenting adults in private," and another resolution urged sexual practices (including homosexuality) between consenting adults in private should be removed from the list of crimes. In another resolution, the Board of Trustees voted to remove homosexuality, *per se*, from its official list of mental disorders.

The Trustees also approved the following resolution:

Whereas Homosexuality *per se* implies no impairment in judgment, stability, reliability, or general social or vocational capabilities, therefore, be it resolved that the American Psychiatric Association deplores all public and private discrimination against homosexuals in such areas as employment, housing, public accommodation, and licensing, and declares that no burden of proof of such judgment, capacity, or reliability shall be placed upon homosexuals greater than that imposed on any other persons. Further, the American Psychiatric Association supports and urges the enactment of civil rights legislation at the local, state, and federal level that would offer homosexual persons the same protections now guaranteed to others on the basis of race, creed, color, etc. Further, the American Psychiatric Association supports and urges the repeal of all discriminatory legislation singling out homosexual acts by consenting adults.

AMERICAN PSYCHOLOGICAL ASSOCIATION, Board of Directors, 1975.

The American Psychological Association supports the action taken on 15 December 1973 by the American Psychiatric Association removing homosexuality from the Association's official list of mental disorders. The American Psychological Association therefore adopts the following resolution:

Homosexuality *per se* implies no impairment in judgment, stability, reliability, or general social or vocational responsibilities;

Further, the American Psychological Association urges all mental health professionals to take the lead in removing the stigma of mental illness that has long been associated with homosexual orientations.

# The Homosexual Subculture at Worship: A Participant Observation Study

Paul F. Bauer, Th.D.
*Cecil Community College, Maryland*

*ABSTRACT:* The author worked for ten months as Director of Christian Education at a church serving the homophile community of a large metropolitan area. Using the method of participant observation, he concluded that the group is attempting to solve two problems centering on their sexual orientation and their religious needs. Past social conditioning has told the group that they cannot be both *Christian* and *homosexual.* The group resolves this cognitive dissonance by emphasizing the message that God loves all men, including homosexuals. This religious message is, contrary to expectations, expressed in theologically conservative language.

For ten months I worked as Director of Christian Education at the Metropolitan Community Church (MCC), which serves primarily the Denver, Colorado, homophile community. During that time I employed the methodology of participant observation to record my observations of the gay community at worship. Ten months' time gave me the opportunity to record a large number of observations. Two of these will be dealt with here: the interaction of the religious and social needs in the gay community and that community's theologically conservative stance. It is my contention that these two observations are interrelated.

## The Methodology of Participant Observation

I shared in the life activities of the group by participating in face-to-face relationships. Initially there were difficulties, until rapport and trust could be established between the group and me. Special difficulties were encountered because of my situation. I, a heterosexual,

Dr. Bauer is Associate Professor of Education and Psychology at Cecil Community College, North East, Maryland 21901.

was working in a church that serves primarily the homophile community. This made for some difficulties at the outset. At first, I was both the observer and the observed, and the group tested me. The group was changed simply because I was present. This was especially true in social situations. Most of the effect of my presence involved their hesitation to discuss personal lives and to use language of the gay world. Gradually, as my presence became anticipated, accepted, and even trusted, these difficulties disappeared.

Although I shared the social and religious experiences of the group, however, I was not "of them" in total involvement because of their sexual orientation. Distance was always maintained. The paradoxical role of the participant observer requires both detachment and personal involvement, as I learned in the process of observation. I established, through my behavior, a detachment that did not hinder interaction with the group but did allow me to maintain my own boundaries as a married heterosexual in the midst of a totally gay community.

As a participant observer, I was exposed to the group's concepts and weltanschauung increasingly as I learned to "hear" their language. Being allowed to "hear" the language of the gay world I saw as a privilege, and as my involvement in the group developed, I found it easy to accept. This was possible, I believe, because, from the very beginning, my role as participant observer was understood by the group.

Aware of the need of the participant observer to "bracket" his bias, that is, to suspend as much as possible any preconceived notions about the group before entering into observation, I endeavored to make my biases explicit.[1] The two main areas of bias were *sexual* and *religious.* Concerning sexual bias, I could acknowledge the right of homosexuals to lead the sexual life they desire. My bias was not against homosexuality as such but involved the choice of sexual roles within that orientation. For example, I was aware of a personal bias against the "swish," i.e., the extremely feminine homosexual male. Part of this bias is related to my own concept of masculinity, which is part of my early socialization. Religiously I had a bias against the fundamentalistic orientation of MCC theology. Again my early socialization—some unfortunate intellectual and personal experiences as a youth attending a fundamental church in a small Indiana town—carries some theological implications.

Intellectually, I assumed, even before first entering the MCC's activities, that I would find the MCC fulfilling the definition of a social movement. I had the preconceived notion that within the MCC I would find a significantly large number of people, gathering collectively, to solve the "problem" of their homosexuality: a common problem both religiously and socially. In addition I expected to find a sense of alienation and oppression among the members of the group, because of their sexual orientation.

The MCC in Denver, Colorado, is an attempt of gays to deal with a situation they define as oppression by the heterosexual society. The appeal of the MCC, as a religious community, is to the susceptibilities of the gay community.[2] That is to say, the message of the MCC appeals to the susceptibilities of the homophile community, created by their need for a meaning in life that will remove the instability of the anxiety brought about by living and working in a predominantly heterosexual world in which they are "labeled" as deviant. They also express a fear about whether they can be *Christians* and *homosexuals* at the same time. My task as a participant observer was to isolate the psychological bond that ties the appeal of the MCC to the susceptibilities of the homophile community. After more than 100 hours of observation, I concluded that the appeal of the MCC is that it offers a "solution" to the religious *and* social problems of being gay. "Society may reject us gays, but God does not" is a commonly expressed sentiment. One professional leader of the church was fond of saying, "Jesus Christ is a good friend of mine." MCC's appeal to the susceptibilities of the gay community is best summed up in a frequently heard statement, expressing their search for self-acceptance: "I may be gay, but I'm not queer." The word "queer" has negative connotations for the group, based on its usage by the heterosexual society. This is especially true for the homosexual who wants to believe that "gay is good." The belief that "gay is good" is basic to the world view of the gay movement. The movement's ideology provides a theological legitimation for this belief. The belief appears to contribute to the cohesiveness of the gay community.

## Historical Antecedent: "The Lavender Riot"

Participants in social movements attach significance to the date marking the origin of their existence. Historical antecedents give groups a sense of history and accent their reasons for existing. Minority groups often use the date of physical abuse by a majority group as their point of origin. This is true of the gay movement.

In 1969 New York City Police raided the Stonewall, a gay bar in the Village. Suffering from police brutality and feeling that their oppression had lasted long enough, angry gays took to the Village streets. The result—three days of riots. This first "lavender riot"[3] marks the beginning of an organized gay movement in America. As the Reverend Troy Perry,[4] the MCC founder, puts it, that is the day "we celebrate in Gay Pride; pride in ourselves."

On October 6, 1968, just prior to the riots, the Reverend Mr. Perry, a theological conservative, organized the MCC in Los Angeles. Perceived by its founder as an "out-stretched arm" into the gay community, the MCC has grown from the "mother church" in Los Angeles to more than eighty churches and missions throughout America, England, and Australia.

In June of 1971, the MCC-Denver was founded under the leadership of the Reverend Ronald Carnes. He arrived in Denver with a list of sixteen people who had contacted the Los Angeles congregation about the possibility of starting a church in Denver.[5] Those sixteen have grown to a congregation of 150 official members within a church community of 500. They have moved into shared facilities with a Unitarian church in the inner city of Denver. It is my contention that the MCC has grown so rapidly because it is a workable solution to the two major problems facing the homophile community: religious "respectability" and social acceptance.

## The Search for Human Acceptance

The members of the MCC-Denver face two problems: first, their relationship to God and their quest for religious understanding; and second, complicating the first problem, the member's sexual orientation, being homosexual in a predominantly heterosexual world. For the MCC members both problems are resolved by a search for human acceptance.

For them the two problems are dealt with by one solution: acceptance by God. In the Los Angeles "mother church" (prior to its firebombing on the night of January 25, 1973) hung a large banner saying: "We are not afraid any more." And they are *not* afraid any more. since their interpretation of Scripture and God's message tells them that through the MCC movement God is available to them.

In discussing the history of the MCC movement, Perry begins by saying that the original group of twelve individuals met "just because of our sexual orientation. We believed that God could do a thing like love us! It's true—God moves in strange ways."[6]

Homosexuals have made the assumption, as a part of their view of reality, that Jesus can solve their two problems: social and religious. More concretely, the MCC members see Jesus as available in the MCC worship services and as the best approach to these problems. Many members have either been asked to leave heterosexual churches after publicly admitting their homosexuality or they have sat quietly in the pews hiding their "own being" until they could no longer deny to themselves and to their God that they were homosexual. Gittings described the hostility that is felt toward the heterosexual churches for denying homosexuals the right to worship:

> We feel that we should expect from our churches all of the forms of spiritual, emotional, personal, and social support which they supply as a matter of course to heterosexuals, and that these should be supplied to us in a spirit of acceptance of us as homosexuals, not in a spirit of missionary zeal to convert us to heterosexuality.[7]

*The Religious Message of the MCC*

In this context, a large portion of Denver's gay world has turned to the religious message of the MCC. Growing support is seen in the tremendous increase in both membership and attendance since its founding in June 1971. Apparently many gays in the Greater Denver area find the MCC solution to the combined problems of homosexuality and religious quest to be the best way to seek human acceptance. In the sermons of both Perry and Carnes the constant theme is that "God loves all men . . . God loves us." Jesus is seen as the liberating force in world history, the force that makes it possible for gays to declare that "gay is good" and "Jesus loves me" within the same context. For them the work and love of Jesus Christ in dealing with all types of people is the foundation for their own repentance and acceptance. Through accepting Jesus Christ, each MCC member's efforts to solve his problems become part of a solution to a community problem.

Their belief is that Jesus will listen to the requests of the gay community, just as He listens to those of all mankind. There is strong peer-group need to interpret events in the world as evidence of Jesus' love for them. One member of the MCC often told me that, when someone in the church has a problem, "nothing is more powerful than a church-full of fairies praying." An example of this "power" occurred when a prominent lay leader of the MCC was on vacation in southern California. About a week after he departed from Denver for Los Angeles, the Las Vegas Police found luggage with R.'s name and address in the trunk of a car driven by a man suspected of murder in Los Angeles. Word reached the Denver church that R. had disappeared and that his luggage had been found in the possession of a suspected murderer. A "church-full of fairies" was gathered and an around-the-clock prayer session started. Several days later it was learned that R.'s luggage had been stolen by the suspected murderer and that R. was safe with friends in San Francisco. For the MCC members, Jesus had answered their prayers and safely returned R. to Denver. Their explanation is simple: "God does listen to prayers, even from us gays." Such an attitude leads to a feeling of acceptance from God.

Another example of their perception of God's love for them is the case of C., who is congenitally deaf in one ear. At the second annual conference of the Fellowship in Los Angeles, September 1-4, 1972, C. regained partial hearing during a group prayer session. From previous base lines, the gain in decibels has been verified at the University of Colorado Medical School. To the gays, this provides further evidence that God listens to their prayers.

In addition to a feeling of acceptance by God, there is a strong community support system at work. This community acceptance contributes to the willingness of MCC members to pool their private problems. Individually, many gays are unable to cope with the problem of their homosexuality. Eventually this problem reaches a subjective intolerability of great intensity. As MCC members gain the impression that fellow worshipers share their own perceptions and feelings, a common basis for communication, concerning both sexual and religious problems, is provided. This interrelationship of problems is revealed in the frequent religious messages communicated in the language of the gay community. One evening at Vespers, one of the professional staff said to the gathering, "Jesus Christ was a chicken-queen." The point being made was that Christ loved small children.[8] There is a combination of religious themes and gay language used in the MCC. This combination speaks to the need to address two problems: sexual and religious.

By providing a belief system centering on the affirmation that a better world is concretely available, the MCC offers plausible solutions to an individual's problems. Members feel that something can be done and they want to be a part of that something. The MCC has more than thirty-five percent of its membership involved in church committee work. The average per capita offering at Sunday services is more than four dollars (and this is from a congregation that is predominantly nonprofessional). Recently a Sunday service produced $600 from a gathering of 100 people.

The degree of involvement of MCC members depends upon the orientation of the individual. Some individuals simply come to MCC as a "good place to cruise." For these individuals (cruisers) the worship service is a prelude to the social hour that follows in the church basement. The two events, the worship service and the social hour, are psychologically separated by physical location. The physical change of location allows the two situations to be sharply defined. During the service, individuals do not engage in any social behavior with sexual overtones. But leaving the chapel and walking down stairs to the large social room changes the psychological orientation. Hand-holding, embracing, and cheek-kissing are then permissible.

Those who view MCC as a sexual hunting ground can usually be differentiated from those with a sincere religious interest by the degree of involvement in the church. Seldom are cruisers official members of the church; they are marginal individuals who attend on occasion. Official members take prominent leadership roles in the church. In the terminology used by Fichter, the membership of the MCC is defined by personal criteria.[9] These criteria are intention to be counted as a church member, religious observance, and social participation. Fichter's institutional criteria of baptism, place of residence, and racial (or national) origin are discounted by the sexual orientation of this community. Thus official MCC members exhibit a willingness to be counted on the church rolls, participate actively in the MCC worship activities, and also take part in the MCC non-church-related social activities. The cruiser's behavior does not match this. The cruiser does not fulfill the minimal religious-spiritual requirements necessary to be considered a member.

It should be added that marginal individuals (cruisers) are not frowned upon by the official members. In fact, in most cases, they are welcomed. The attitude is that "They are here, as opposed to a gay bar, and are listening to the word of God." More than one individual who originally came to MCC to look for sexual contacts has been converted and become a full-fledged member. And, as with most new converts to an organization, they work in the church with a zeal often embarrassing to long-term members. One recent convert, P., worked in the church office doing typing, filing, answering the phone, etc., to the point of physical exhaustion. His doctor finally limited him to three days a week at the church office for fear of further physical harm. For the past year P. has held a seat on the major governing body of the church.[10]

Those who do move from cruiser into the convert or membership stage are helped in their decision by the church's authority as a guide in spiritual and social belief systems.[11] Within the gay community the most strongly defended beliefs are those that relate to social problems and to religious problems. Among the authoritative sources is the movement's founder. In a recorded sermon, Troy Perry states that there is a great deal of "phoniness in the straight world. We gays have no hypocrites; we have become a family."[12]

Authority for the belief system comes both from the folklore of gay life concerning heterosexuals and from the Bible. In a Christian Education class, I once asked for biblical references on homosexuality. Immediately I was surrounded by members quoting from memory passages in both the Old and New Testaments. They know their Bible! Because so often biblical passages are used in argument against homosexuality, biblical knowledge provides a strong defense against these arguments. Of particular importance within the belief system, based on the Bible, is a homosexual interpretation of the story of David and Jonathan (1 Sam. 18-20). In addition, some members claim that Jesus "had to be gay because he fits one psychological model of antecedents to homosexuality, i.e., he lacked a father figure, traveled with twelve other men, and never married."

Most of the biblical arguments in the member's belief system center on passages discrediting *other* activities: women wearing pearls and gold (1 Tim. 2:9-10), serving milk with dinner (Heb. 5:13), and women wearing hats in church (1 Cor. 11:5-6, 13). This line of argument is not directed at establishing a biblical position on homosexuality. It is directed rather to biblical passages that today's world considers meaningless. The suggestion here is that the passages cited by "straights" against homosexuality are of the same kind and should, therefore, be discounted. However, some selective perception is at work. Passages on pearls, gold, hats, and milk are discounted, but the story of David and Jonathan is emphasized. Their selective perception of biblical passages speaks to their need for self-protection from traditional Christian arguments against homosexuality. In the MCC community it appears in both their religious and sexual belief systems. The need is to protect the individual from additional anxiety. Turning to the community and to the church provides a source of acceptance and reassurance.

### *"Gay Is Good"*

The gay community has a store of folklore that centers on its superiority to the heterosexual world. That folklore provides data to "prove" that "gay is good." Once "gay is good" is accepted into a belief system, a sense of pride develops and has the effect of affirming the belief system. Gay pride is stressed to help overcome the oppression that many gays experience. On the record "One God," recorded at the MCC-Los Angeles, Troy Perry leads his congregation in the singing of "We Shall Overcome"—a song usually associated with the civil rights movement in the South. On "gay pride," as an authority Perry says that "up until a few years ago no one would think that you could be gay and proud of it." But now gays can be glad that "God in His goodness" created gay people. Realizing this legitimizes the belief that "Gay is good." God's love is the basis for self-pride.

However, it must be added that this pride is often a paranoiac reaction against heterosexuals. Conspiracy beliefs are prevalent among groups regarded as deviant from societal norms. The weltanschauung of gays was difficult for me to comprehend until I understood the conspiracy premise as providing a unifying idea for gays. Recently the Denver Police arrested more than 100 gays in a weekend raid of gay bars and steam baths. The gays viewed this "purge" as further evidence that "gay is good." "Why else should we gays be persecuted unless we are a threat to the straights?"

Consequently, to the MCC member who perceives a conspiracy by straights to persecute him, ideology has an important appeal. This ideology, a conservative theology, has an implicit or latent function not related to its explicit religious referent (God). In reality, the ideology is a belief system used to create a more satisfying reality by removing anxiety about being homosexual. Significantly, increased attendance at Sunday worship, Thursday night Vespers, and Christian Education classes occurred during the "purge." MCC members turned to God for the answer because to them it had become evident that their fellow man would not help.

An interesting point here is that in the face of perceived danger from the heterosexual community, some gays in the MCC turn to a religious solution—the *immediate* return of Jesus Christ—that they adopt to avoid facing the hopelessness of the secular situation. As one professional staff member often said to me, "I wish Jesus would come and make everything right." The turning to a religious solution, which from the viewpoint of an "outsider" has a low probability of occurrence, is part of their past societal conditioning, which tells them that their sexual situation is "insoluble." Thus, not expecting a secular solution today, they turn to a spiritual solution. Their search for meaning in the face of danger is an attempt to find a more satisfying reality. This tends to make gays more susceptible to the theologically conservative message of the MCC.

### "Jesus Loves Me This I Know for My Peer Group Tells Me So"

The most puzzling observation for me was the theologically conservative stance of the church. I was aware of recent movements by several liberal churches to open their doors to the gay community, and, accordingly, I expected the MCC to be theologically liberal. Why did the gay community ignore this new openness and insist on establishing a conservative church organization independent of the heterosexual churches?

Jones claimed that the homosexual identity has been imposed on homosexuals so long that it has become incorporated into their self-image.[13] The homosexual is viewed only in terms of his homosexuality. For the homosexual himself, this sexual identity assumes a disproportionately dominant place in his weltanschauung. So, ironically, the liberal heterosexual churches, eager to amend their past attitudes, have recently opened discussion with the gay community and, in the process, have actually contributed to even greater emphasis upon sexual identity. The liberal churches, in making specific policy statements on homosexuality, identify the individual as first a homosexual and second a possible Christian. However, the homosexual wants to be recognized as Christian first, gay second. Homosexuals in the MCC believe that the attitudes of heterosexual churches have been at odds with the very essence of Christianity: that *all* human beings are children of God.

In addition to a well-intentioned, but misdirected, emphasis by the liberal churches on homosexuality, there is a sociological dimension at work in the conservativeness of the MCC. Fundamentalism is a product of a marginal culture. It is most often dominant in areas or among people isolated by geographic or social distance from the changing modes of thought. The gay community is a vicinally isolated community, set apart by its sexual orientation from the predominantly heterosexual society. One plausible hypothesis, therefore, is that the gay religious community is fundamentalist because it wishes to go back to the purer standards of bygone days, the days "when Jesus loved everyone." While liberals are concerned with changing the social order, the fundamentalist orientation accents an individual's belief system. The MCC has constructed a theologically conservative belief system around their interpretation of Jesus' teachings of love: He loves all people, regardless of sexual orientation.

In liberal churches there is little or no demand made upon the believer; more stress is placed on the corporate body of the church. Thus, gays view the liberal church as an "extension of the closet," allowing the homosexual to remain homosexual without facing the religious and social questions inherent in his sexuality. He can hide his homosexuality amidst the corporate body of the liberal church, which never forces him to deal with its implications for his Christianity. Facing his homosexuality by coming to the realization that according to Jesus' teachings gay can be good requires more than mere membership in a corporate church body. It requires a personal conversion experience.

It is the theologically conservative church that provides avenues for personal conversion. Here the accent is on the individual believer as a human being, as a homosexual. For the MCC member the conversion experiences takes the form: Jesus loves *all* men; He loves even gay people; ergo gay is good. The MCC's theological position, that Jesus loves all men, supported by peer group consensus, allows the homosexual to become a Christian and maintain pride in his homosexual life style. The liberal church, not aware of or stressing the homosexual *dasein*, makes admission into their form of Christianity too "easy" for the homosexual.

The personal religious background of Troy Perry is another major factor in the MCC's conservative stance. In *The Lord Is My Shepherd and He Knows I'm Gay*, Perry talks about his Pentacostal background.[14] Perry himself underwent a dramatic personal conversion, from which he emerged as a Christian and a homosexual. The personal message of Perry's conversion experience has carried over to the MCC by-laws: All men are justified to God through faith. For the homosexual whose sexual existence is justified through faith in God, gay is good.

In general the hostility felt toward heterosexual churches, liberal or not—the result of unfortunate past experiences—makes gays suspicious of recent attempts to begin dialogue. Even if dialogue were established, liberal churches, predominantly heterosexual, cannot provide a common basis for communication. Not having the same need for self-protection, their members operate from a different system of selective perception and hence cannot be a source of acceptance and reassurance to gays.

## Some Conclusions: "No, Honey, We're a Church Group!"

The MCC is a plausible, even necessary, social-religious movement supported by members who are attempting to solve personal problems of sexuality and religion. Observation of the MCC was complicated by the fact that two problems are combined: the need for solution to a sexual problem and the need to relate to God. It was impossible in our observations to determine when the MCC speaks directly to the problems of homosexuality and when it speaks directly to religious problems. We would assume that the two are so closely interwoven that no differentiation could be made. We can say that the MCC community sanctions the interpretation of Jesus' teachings that tells them that their existence is justified through faith in God. Certainly, psychologically, if not always behavioristically, the two needs are being met by the solution of the love of Jesus as interpreted theologically by the MCC.

The members of MCC appear to have been placed, by their sexual orientation, in a position of cognitive dissonance. They enjoy their sexual life and find it impossible to give up, but, at the same time, for most of their lives they have been taught that God cannot "love a faggot." The anxiety from their sexual orientation has its roots in society and in their past religious experience prior to the MCC. To resolve the conflict they add new cognitive elements. These new cognitive elements originate from the group's interpretation of the teachings of Jesus: His love for all men. In part, this interpretation has been done for them in the persons of Troy Perry and Ron Carnes and in the MCC movement. Their anxiety is lessened by their new belief system, which gives them a view of reality necessary for the maintenance of their psychological security: God loves all men; gay is good.

Recently along with 100 MCC members my wife and I attended an international circus on tour in Denver. During the intermission, ten members were posing for a photograph with one of the circus clowns. A woman, passing the group, commented loudly enough to be overheard, "It's a bunch of fairies." One MCC member quickly replied, "No, honey, we're a church group!"

And a church group they are and must be.

## Reference Notes

1. As a further check on my bias and potential "contamination" of my observations, my wife accompanied me on approximately one half of all my visits to the MCC and to homophile social activities.
2. See Hans Toch, *The Social Psychology of Social Movements* (Indianapolis: Bobbs-Merrill, 1965), pp. 12-17, for discussion of the susceptibilities of social movements.
3. The term used by the homophile community.
4. All complete names used are of individuals who have publicly stated their homosexuality. Initials are used to disguise others.
5. The MCC has quite a missionary zeal. Carnes was given a one-way tourist class plane ticket from Los Angeles to Denver, the list of sixteen names, and the blessing of Troy Perry. From that beginning he was to build a church community.
6. Troy Perry, "Editor's Comments," *In Unity*, June/July 1972, no pagination.
7. Barbara B. Gittings, "The Homosexual and the Church," in *The Same Sex: An Appraisal of Homosexuality*, ed. Ralph W. Weltge (Philadelphia: Pilgrim Press, 1969), p. 149.
8. In gay argot a chicken-queen prefers young children for sexual activity.
9. Joseph H. Fichter, *Southern Parish* (Chicago: University of Chicago Press, 1951), pp. 17-32.

10. However, it should be pointed out that P. recently acquired a friend through a gay pen club. Now he has ceased working in the church office and is preparing his home for his friend's arrival. Perhaps the degree of involvement in the church is not always an adequate differentiation of those who are there for cruising and those there for genuine religious reasons.
11. Authority is here used as anything that serves as a source of beliefs.
12. Troy Perry, "One God," Custom Fidelity Records, Hollywood, California, 1972.
13. H. Kimball Jones, "Homosexuality: A Provisional Christian Stance," in *Is Gay Good? Ethics, Theology, and Homosexuality*, ed. W. Dwight Oberholtzer (Philadelphia: Westminster Press, 1971), p. 150.
14. Troy Perry, *The Lord Is My Shepherd and He Knows I'm Gay: The Autobiography of the Rev. Troy D. Perry* (Los Angeles: Nash Publishing, 1972).

Four

# Paul's Views on the Nature of Women and Female Homoeroticism*

*Bernadette J. Brooten*

Paul's condemnation of sexual love relations between women in Romans 1:26 is central to his understanding of female sexuality, nature, and the relationship between women and men. Because of the role of Christianity in the Western world, the New Testament's ethical advice, its images of women and of men, and its attitudes toward sexuality have helped to shape Western concepts of the family and of the proper place of women in society, as well as legislation on marriage and sexuality.

Paul's Letter to the Romans, written in the formative stage of Christianity, came, in the course of time, to be normative for Christian theology. It is one of the most widely read and preached-upon books of the New Testament. In the present church debate on ordination and sexual orientation, Paul's teaching on sexual love relations between women and between men (Rom. 1:26–27) plays an important role. In contemporary public policy debates, fundamentalist groups opposing the right of lesbians and gay men to be protected from discrimination in employment, housing, or custody of their children often quote the Letter to the Romans as an authority.

Sexuality has to do with power. An important insight of the

* This article was written within the context of the "Frau und Christentum" project of the Institut für ökumenische Forschung, University of Tübingen, West Germany. I would like to thank the Stiftung Volkswagenwerk, which is funding this project, as well as the following members of the project team for providing critical comments, typing the manuscript, and doing bibliographical work: Inge Baumann, Christina Bucher, Jutta Flatters, and Linda Maloney. I am currently preparing a book-length study on the topic of the present essay in which I plan to include more extensive documentation and critical discussion.

women's movement has been that, as women, we cannot determine the direction of our lives as long as others control our bodies. Feminists have discovered that sexuality is not simply a matter of romantic love, nor is it a changeless, purely biological phenomenon; rather, sexuality is determined by societal structures. By looking at ethical teachings on female sexuality, as well as by studying the ways in which women experience sexuality, we can learn about hierarchy, about superordination and subordination in a given society. Thus, to understand female sexuality is not simply to understand just one other area of women's lives. It is to understand an area of female existence in which power is acutely expressed.

It is essential to distinguish between what men have taught about women's sexuality and how women have experienced sexuality. What Paul taught is not to be identified with what early Christian women thought or how they lived. Paul's thinking has contributed, nevertheless, in a significant way to the Christian construction of female sexuality, and is therefore intertwined with Christian women's lives. The purpose of this study is to understand Paul within his cultural context. This can help us to examine critically our own thinking about female sexuality and nature, and our appropriation of Paul's thought within our own cultural context.

A central message of Paul's Letter to the Romans is that all who believe in Christ are justified. In Romans 1:18 to 3:20, Paul sets the background for this message by describing how all human beings are in need of justification, how without Christ they live under the power of sin and stand condemned. Everyone has had the opportunity to know God through God's created works, and therefore human beings are without excuse for having turned from God to idols. The result is serious, according to Romans 1:24–27 (RSV).

> **24** Therefore God gave them up in the lusts of their hearts to impurity, to the dishonoring of their bodies among themselves, **25** because they exchanged the truth about God for a lie and worshiped and served the creature rather than the Creator, who is blessed forever! Amen. **26** For this reason God gave them up to dishonorable passions. Their women exchanged natural relations for unnatural, **27** and the men likewise gave up natural relations with women and were consumed with passion for one another, men committing shameless acts with men and receiving in their own persons the due penalty for their error.

Thus, Paul sees sexual relations between women and between men to be a result of idolatry; they signify estrangement between human beings and God.

The focus of this essay is Romans 1:26, in which Paul speaks of the unnatural relations of their women. While the condemnation of male homosexual acts in verse 27 is related to that in verse 26, the issue is not parallel and cannot be subsumed under sexual love relations between women. It is my thesis that Paul's condemnation of female homoeroticism is closely connected with his view that there should be gender differentiation in appearance because of the man's being the head of woman (see 1 Cor. 11:2–16). Paul could well share with other contemporary authors who commented on female homoeroticism and proper female sexual roles the view that sexual relations between women implied that women were trying to be like men, that is, to transcend the passive, subordinate role accorded to them by nature. Indeed, I interpret Paul's words "exchanged natural relations for unnatural" to mean that the women exchanged the passive, subordinate sexual role for an active, autonomous one. If I am correct, it should be clear that Paul's condemnation of sexual love relations between women is of fundamental significance for his understanding of female sexuality.

## Female Homoeroticism in the Greco-Roman World

Paul's theological thinking about women was culturally conditioned by his environment. To understand his views, we must determine where Romans 1:26 fits into the ancient spectrum of views on female homoeroticism. Understanding the historical context is necessary so we do not interpret Paul anachronistically, but rather locate his thinking within the contemporary discussion about female sexuality of his own time.

### *Jewish Authors*

The Hebrew Bible does not prohibit sexual relations between women, although it does forbid male homosexual intercourse: "If a man lies with a male as with a woman, both of them have committed an abomination; they shall be put to death, their blood is upon them" (RSV, Lev. 20:13, cf. Lev. 18:22). Postbiblical Jewish literature does take up the issue of sexual intercourse between women. *The Sentences of Pseudo-Phocylides,* a Greek poem probably written by a Jewish author of the Diaspora, contains a section on proper sexual behavior, marriage, and family life.[1] Following upon a prohibition of male homosexual behavior is a similar prohibition to women: "And let not women imitate the sexual role [literally, "marriage bed"] of men" (line 192). The author describes male homosexuality as a transgression of nature (line 190) that is not found in the animal world (line 191). The reader is warned not to let a son have long, braided or knotted hair, as long hair is for voluptuous women (lines 210–212). Further, beautiful boys are to be protected from homosexual advances and virgins kept locked up until their wedding day (lines 213–216). The sexual ethics presented in the poem are thus based on strict gender differentiation in dress and sexual role. Girls are to be kept fit for marriage and, once married, are not to stray outside the boundaries of marriage. A woman having sexual relations with another woman is viewed as imitating a man.[2]

*Sifra,* a rabbinical commentary on Leviticus composed of sayings from the tannaitic period (before ca. 220 C.E.), also discussed the issue:

> Or: "You shall not do as they do in the land of Egypt . . . and you shall not do as they do in the land of Canaan" (Lev. 18:3). One could [interpret it as meaning] that they may not build buildings or plant plants like them. Therefore scripture teaches, "You shall not walk in their statutes" (Lev. 18:3). . . . And what did they do? A man married a man and a woman a woman, and a man married a woman and her daughter, and a woman was married to two men.[3]

Thus we see that, in light of the lack of a biblical verse prohibiting sexual relations between women, another verse in Leviticus is taken as referring to such relations. This is not a specific negative commandment. Rather, the Egyptians and the Canaanites are described as practicing male homosexual and lesbian marriage, and the Israelites are forbidden to follow statutes that allow such things.

In the Jerusalem Talmud, the compilation and editing of which was completed around the fifth century C.E., there is reference to women having intercourse with each other, literally to "swinging back and forth" with each other.[4] The text records a difference of opinion between two rabbinical schools of the first century on whether such intercourse made women unfit for the priesthood, that is, unfit to marry into the priesthood and to eat the priestly offerings. The background is that a priest may not marry a woman who has committed harlotry (Lev. 21:7), and the high priest must marry a virgin (Lev. 21:13). The question is whether sexual relations between women counts as intercourse, thereby making marriage to a priest forbidden. According to the text, the School of Shammai says that it does count, and the School of Hillel does not count sexual relations between women as making a woman unfit for marriage into the priesthood. Later Jewish sources also occasionally discuss the issue.[5]

In sum, the earliest Jewish sources (known to me) on sexual relations between women are from the Roman period. The emergent awareness of the issue may indicate increased openness on the part of women and possibly a greater frequency of sexual expression within female friendships, for anxiety about a phenomenon usually shows that it in fact exists. Paul's inclusion of women fits in well with the Jewish concern developing at precisely his time.

### *Non-Jewish Authors*

The earliest clear reference to female homoeroticism in Greek literature[6] seems to be that in Plato's *Symposium.*[7] Aristophanes, in discoursing on the origins of humanity, speaks of *hetairistriai,* women who are attracted to women, as having their origin in primeval beings consisting of two women joined together. This parallels the original creatures who were two men joined together and those who consisted of one woman and one man. Aristophanes imagines that each human being seeks a partner of the gender to which she or he was originally attached. In Plato's last work, the *Laws,*[8] he speaks of sexual relations between men and between women as "contrary to nature" (*para physin*), and adds that "the first who dared to do this acted through lack of self-control with respect to pleasure." [9] Thus, the passage in the *Symposium* presupposes that same-sex love is as natural and normal as heterosexual love, while that in the *Laws* does not. The reason for the discrepancy is unclear.

In the third century B.C.E., Asclepiades composed an epigram on two Samian women, Bitto and Nannion, who did not want to live in accordance with the laws of Aphrodite; instead, deserting sexual activities of which she would approve, they turned to other, "not beautiful" ones. Asclepiades calls upon Aphrodite to hate these women, who are fleeing intercourse within her realm. An ancient commentator added as an explanatory note that he was accusing them of being *tribades,* which is the most common Greek term for women who engage in same-sex love.[10]

In the Latin literature of the early Empire, there are a number of references to a woman's expressing her love for another woman sexually, and all of them are derogatory. Seneca the Elder (ca. 55 B.C.E. to 40 C.E.) composed one of his fictitious legal controversies around the case of a man who caught two *tribades* in bed, his wife and another woman, and killed them both. One declaimer describes the husband's first reaction: "But I looked first at the man, to see whether he was natural or sewed-on." Another declaimer notes that one would not tolerate the killing of a male adulterer under these circumstances, but adds that if he "had found a pseudo-adulterer. . . ." The reader is left with the shock of the monstrosity, having been led to see that the husband's act was justified.[11]

Ovid's (43 B.C.E. to 18 C.E.) *Metamorphoses* contains the tale of two girls, Iphis and Ianthe, who loved each other and were engaged to marry.[12] Because of her husband's wish to have a boy, Iphis's mother had raised her as a boy and concealed it from her husband. Iphis now bemoans her predicament, saying that the love she possesses is "unheard of," and even "monstrous." If the gods wished to destroy her, she bewails, they should have given her a "natural woe," one "according to custom." Among animals, females do not love females, she says, and, in her despair, she wishes she were no longer female. Iphis knows that she should accept herself as a woman and seek what is in accordance with divine law and love as a woman ought to love. And yet she loves Ianthe, though knowing that "nature does not will it, nature more powerful than all." [13] It is against the background of the tragedy of freakish circumstances—against divine will, against nature, against custom, unheard of—that the reader is relieved when Isis intervenes and changes Iphis into a boy, making the marriage possible.[14]

The poet Phaedrus (died mid 1st c. C.E.) composed a fable in which he describes the origin of *tribades* and passive homosexual men (*molles mares*) as an error on the part of Prometheus. For Prometheus, on returning intoxicated and sleepy from a dinner party, mistakenly placed female sexual organs on male bodies and male members on women. "Therefore lust now enjoys perverted pleasure." [15]

Martial (ca. 40 to 103/104 C.E.) dedicated two epigrams to Philaenis, "tribad of the very tribads." [16] He depicts Philaenis as sexually aggressive toward both boys and girls, the latter of whom she, "quite fierce with the erection of a husband," batters eleven in a day. She spends much time on athletics: handball, heavy jumping weights, wrestling. She engages in the pleasure of being whipped by a greasy teacher.[17] Before dining she vomits seven portions of unmixed wine. After consuming sixteen meat dishes, she returns to the wine. "When, after all of these things, her mind turns back to sex, she does not engage in fellatio, which she thinks is not manly enough." Instead she "devours girls' middles." Martial can only scorn the logic of this last act, for how could she consider cunnilingus manly? He also says of Philaenis "you rightly call the woman with whom you copulate a girlfriend."

In a third epigram,[18] Martial addresses one Bassa, a woman whom he had first thought to be as chaste as the famed Lucretia, for he had never seen Bassa coupling with men and had heard no scandals about her. On the contrary, she was always surrounded by women. But now he realizes that she was a *fututor* (m., "fucker").[19] Her "monstrous lust imitates a man." That without a man there should be adultery is worthy of the Theban riddle.

In interpreting Martial one must be cautious. The vulgar and violent language and imagery we encounter here are not peculiar to these three epigrams, but are typical of Martial's style. Of particular note is his precise imagery. A *tribas* is a woman who is trying to be like a man. Philaenis is unlimited in her sexual prowess, trying to win as many boys and girls as she can by her aggressive pursuits. The reference to what seems to be sadomasochistic pleasure at the hand of the trainer is designed to evoke special horror in the reader. Could it be that the voluntary submission to violence symbolizes Philaenis's control even over violence toward herself? It appears here that a man's violence toward a woman is a cultural outrage only when she allows such violence. By virtue of such autonomy, Philaenis has ceased to be a woman, as culturally defined, and has become a man. To Martial, it can then appear only ridiculous that she show interest in female genitalia. For how could anyone of sound mind consider cunnilingus (because it can be pleasurable to women?) virile? Thus, for all her carryings-on, Philaenis is not a real man after all. Martial generates a creative tension in the poems by exaggerating women's attempts to be virile and then exposing these attempts as ridiculous. But they are not simply laughable. Such behavior is dangerous, and therefore deserves the term *monstrous.*

Judith P. Hallett, in a very insightful paper entitled "Autonomy as Anomaly: Roman, and postclassical Greek, reactions to female homoerotic expression," [20] suggests that Martial consciously portrays Philaenis as physically masculine, as physically capable of penile penetration (for example, of the boys).[21] She further notes that in the epigrams on Philaenis and elsewhere, Roman authors depict female homoeroticism as Greek and therefore distanced from their own reality. This occurs through such devices as the use of Greek[22] or Greek loanwords, of which there are a number in Martial's epigrams on Philaenis. The word *tribas* itself is a Greek loanword and must have evoked a nuance of foreignness. Hallett's hypothesis is this:

> To some extent, therefore, this male preoccupation with physical masculinity, and particularly penis possession, as a necessary component of female sexual autonomy and homoeroticism, and this characterization of female sexual autonomy as distanced and non-Roman, seem to reflect an effort to describe such female behavior in symbolic language, as an imaginary super-deviation from the limits of prescribed female sexuality explicable to Roman males only in male terms.[23]

Hallett argues that whereas Roman men passed beyond the passive sexual stage during which they could be penetrated by another male when they reached their early twenties, Roman women were to remain in the passive role throughout their adult lives. The easiest way to understand women's rejection of the passive sexual role was to imagine that they, like the men, had passed on to the next stage, which implied penetrating behavior.

Juvenal's (ca. 67 C.E. to ?) *Sixth Satire* contains a reference to women who set down their litters at the ancient altar of Chastity in Rome: "and in turn they ride horseback, and what is more they throb with the moon as a witness." [24] Elsewhere Juvenal has a woman, Laronia, contrast women with homosexual men, saying that among women "such an abominable specimen of conduct" will not be found.[25]

Authors writing in Greek in the Roman period were also nearly always quite negative in their depictions of female homoeroticism.

The philosopher and biographer Plutarch (ca. 45 to ca. 120 C.E.) is an important exception. He describes boy-love in the Sparta of the legendary founder of the Spartan constitution, Lycurgus, in rather favorable terms as promoting the education of the youth. By way of side comment, Plutarch adds, "though this love was so approved among them that also the noble and good women loved the virgins; there was no jealous love in it." [26] There is no mention that such love might be perverse or abominable. Nevertheless, we should not assume that Plutarch's admiration of ancient Spartan customs meant that he would have accepted love relations between women, or female sexual autonomy, in his own day.[27]

The references to female homoeroticism in Greek authors of the second century C.E. and beyond represent a continuation of the motifs outlined thus far. The novelist Iamblichus (after 100 to ?) characterizes the love of Berenice, the daughter of the king of Egypt, for Mesopotamia, with whom she slept, as "wild and lawless amours." [28] In his *Dialogues of the Courtesans,* the second-century author Lucian devotes the fifth dialogue to an experience that Leaena has had with her fellow courtesans Megilla and Demonassa. Megilla, a wealthy woman from Lesbos, has succeeded in seducing Leaena, in spite of Leaena's shame at the strange activity. It turns out that Megilla sees her true self as Megillus and Demonassa as her wife. She wears a wig to conceal her short hair and says that although she does not have a male organ, she does have some sort of substitute. Leaena refuses to describe the exact nature of the sexual encounter, since it is too "shameful." [29] Also cast in the dialogue form is the *Amores* by Pseudo-Lucian (probably early 4th cent.) in which one of the discussants speaks of "tribadic licentiousness," and describes female homoeroticism as women behaving like men.[30]

In his treatise on dream interpretation, the second-century author Artemidorus mentions dreams in which one woman sexually possesses another.[31] The second-century treatises *On Chronic Diseases* and *On Acute Diseases* by Soranus are only available to us in the Latin translation by the African medical writer Caelius Aurelianus (5th cent.). Here we read of the disease of the *tribades,* so called because of their interest in both kinds of love, although they prefer women, whom they pursue with a jealousy that is almost masculine.[32]

A number of ancient astrologers mention sexual relations between women, which they see as a disorder caused by the stars and the planets. Ptolemy (2d cent.) writes of *tribades* who are "lustful of sexual intercourse contrary to nature," who "perform the deeds of men," and who sometimes even designate their partners as "lawful wives." Elsewhere he speaks of *tribades* as "castrated (men)." [33] Vettius Valens (mid 2d cent.) speaks of *tribades* who are "licentious, servile, perpetrators of filth." [34] Manetho (probably 4th cent.) refers to *tribades* as ones who "perform deeds after the manner of men." [35]

In sum, most of the writers discussed do not seem to find a place for female homoeroticism within the realm of the lawful and natural, although the Aristophanes of Plato's *Symposium* and Plutarch in describing the Sparta of Lycurgus do represent another view. Among the other authors there is a strong tendency to depict *tribades* as like men, or trying to be like men (Seneca the Elder, Martial, Phaedrus, Lucian, Pseudo-Lucian, Caelius Aurelianus in his translation of Soranus, Ptolemy, Manetho, Firmicus Maternus, and possibly Artemidorus). The real issue may be that of women overstepping the bounds of the female, passive role assigned to them in Greco-Roman culture. The underlying issue would then be female sexual autonomy. If this is indeed the real issue, it would explain why Martial, for example, associates assertive sexual behavior toward males with the *tribas* Philaenis.[36] Lucian and Ptolemy speak of the women calling their partners wives.[37] The authors in question describe female homoeroticism as against the laws of Aphrodite and not beautiful (Asclepiades), monstrous (Ovid, Martial), unnatural (Plato, Ovid, Ptolemy, by implication Seneca the Elder), shameful (Lucian), and lawless (Iamblichus). According to Caelius Aurelianus's translation of Soranus, homoeroticism was a disease of the mind, to be treated by controlling the mind; in Phaedrus's view it was the result of a divine error; and in the astrologers' view, it was caused by the stars and the planets.

### *Other Sources*

Two Greek vase paintings that document erotic attraction between women should be mentioned here, even though they are from an earlier period. A plate dating to circa 620 B.C.E. from the Greek island Thera depicts two women, of approximately equal height, in a typical courting position; that is, one is placing her hand below the chin of the other.[38] An Attic red-figure vase (ca. 500 B.C.E.) shows one woman caressing the clitoris of another.[39] We cannot exclude the possibility that the second vase was used for male titillation; the vase was a *kylix,* a drinking vessel for wine. But this could hardly be the case with the first, since both women are fully clothed; in the second they are nude. Neither vase depicts the women as in any way masculine or pseudomasculine, and they differ from the Greek vases showing male couples, nearly all of which consist of a bearded adult and a beardless youth.[40]

Also relevant is the image of the poet Sappho in the Roman period. The earliest Sappho biography (P.Oxy. 1800, fr. 1, 2d to 3d cent.) notes, "She has been accused by some of immorality and of being a lover of women." Horace, in commenting on her verse technique, calls her "masculine Sappho," but this may not be a reference to her sexuality.[41] Both Plutarch[42] and Maximus of Tyre[43] compared her with Socrates, who was known for his preference for men. Ovid writes that she loved girls and takes up the legend that she fell in love with a man, Phaon, who did not love her in return, a story that is possibly a reaction to the image of Sappho as one who loved women.[44] On the Christian side, the second-century writer Tatian describes Sappho as a *hetaira* and as a "love-crazy harlot of a woman, who sang her own licentiousness." [45] The context is a list of disparaging remarks concerning fourteen Greek women writers, the works of nearly all of whom are lost to us. According to the *Suda,* a medieval lexicon that contains many earlier traditions, Sappho was accused by some of "shameful love" for women.[46] Thus, beginning in the Roman period there is an increasing preoccupation with Sappho's love for women, usually combined with disapproval of that love. This fits in well with the broader development noted thus far for the Roman period: an increased attention to and vehement rejection of sexual relations between women.

## Paul's Condemnation of Female Homoeroticism

In Romans 1:18–32, Paul describes a series of tragic *exchanges.*[47] Human beings, though they had the opportunity to recognize God through God's created works, exchanged the truth about God for a lie and worshiped images resembling those same created works. As a result of this fundamental disorder and confusion in human beings' relation to God and to God's creation, other exchanges occurred: God handed them over to impurity, to the dishonoring of their bodies (verse 24); God handed them over to dishonorable passions (verse 26); God handed them over to an unapproved intellect and unfitting conduct (verse 28). The disorder and confusion that are idolatry are repeated in the disorder and confusion of same-sex love (verses 26–27)[48] and of other forms of unfitting behavior (verses 29–32).

We have seen that the motif of the *tribas* becoming, being, or trying to be like a man recurs throughout the discussion of *tribades* in the literature of the Greco-Roman world. *Tribades* are women who cross the boundary of their femaleness as it is culturally defined. They are an anomaly, for they fit neither the proper category of female nor that of male. The structure and terminology of Romans 1:18–32 and of 1 Corinthians 11:2–16 show that Paul was deeply concerned that what he saw to be the order of creation be maintained with respect to sex roles and gender polarity. Like other ancient authors who discuss *tribades,* Paul saw female homoeroticism as an improper crossing of boundaries, a blurring of the categories of male and female.

### *Impurity in Romans 1:24*

The insights of anthropology can help us understand the complex concept of impurity. Mary Douglas argues that one must study purity laws in a systematic way.[49] With respect to ancient Israel, she writes:

> The purity laws of the Bible . . . set up the great inclusive categories in which the whole universe is hierarchised and structured. Access to their meaning comes by mapping the same basic set of rules from one context on to another.[50]

There is a symmetry among the classifications for animals, peoples, sacrificial victims, priests, and women. According to Douglas,

> the underlying principle of cleanness in animals [in Leviticus 11 and Deuteronomy 14] is that they shall conform fully to their class. Those species are unclean which are imperfect members of their class, or whose class itself confounds the general scheme of the world.[51]

These considerations are of help in interpreting the concept of impurity in Romans 1:24.

The exchange of natural relations for those contrary to nature in verses 26–27 is a concretization of the "impurity, to the dishonoring of their bodies," described in verse 24.[52] Thus, same-sex love constitutes impurity and a dishonoring of one's body. The categories of classification, namely, "male" and "female," are now no longer clear. Sexual intercourse with a member of the opposite sex implies clarity of sex roles; with a member of one's own, confusion. The biological male could become like a female, as culturally defined, and the biological female—could she become like a male? A class is created that "confounds the general scheme of the world." This crossing of gender-role boundaries is one clear point of contingency between female and male same-sex love. Paul's contemporary, the Jewish philosopher Philo of Alexandria, writes of male homosexuality:

> In former days the very mention of it was a great disgrace, but now it is a matter of boasting not only to the active but to the passive partners, who habituate themselves to endure the disease of effemination, let both body and soul run to waste, and leave no ember of their male sex-nature to smoulder. Mark how conspicuously they braid and adorn the hair of their heads, and how they scrub and paint their faces with cosmetics and pigments and the like, and smother themselves with fragrant unguents. For of all such embellishments, used by all who deck themselves out to wear a comely appearance, fragrance is the most seductive. In fact the transformation of the male nature to the female is practised by them as an art and does not raise a blush. These persons are rightly judged worthy of death by those who obey the law, which ordains that the man-woman who debases the sterling coin of nature should perish unavenged, suffered not to live for a day or even an hour, as a disgrace to himself, his house, his native land, and the whole human race. And the lover of such may be assured that he is subject to the same penalty. He pursues an unnatural pleasure and does his best to render cities desolate and uninhabited by destroying the means of procreation. Furthermore he sees no harm in becoming a tutor and instructor in the grievous vices of unmanliness and effeminacy. . . .[53]

Philo's presupposition that sexual intercourse implies an active and a passive partner (normally a man and a woman), his view that passive male homosexuals become like women, in fact are afflicted with the disease of effeminacy, and his abhorrence of cross-dressing are not untypical of ancient condemnations of male homosexuality.[54] Both Paul and Philo disapprove of male homosexuality; both use the term *para physin,* "unnatural" or "contrary to nature";[55] both reject men wearing hair styles also worn by women (see 1 Cor. 11:2–16); and both imagine physical recompense for male homosexual behavior. Further, as Diaspora Jews, both lived with the conflict between the open male homosexuality around them and the Levitical prohibition thereof.

Underlying Philo's words is disgust, and even horror, at the ambiguous, anomalous being created by male homosexuality. This fits in well with the understanding of the impure as that which does not conform fully to its class.

For Paul, the opposite of impurity is righteousness (Rom. 6:19) or holiness (1 Thess. 4:7; 1 Cor. 7:14). According to Mary Douglas, "Holiness requires that individuals shall conform to the class to which they belong. And holiness requires that different classes of things shall not be confused." [56] In 1 Thessalonians 4:3–8 it is holiness that separates Christians from "the gentiles who do not know God." Holiness implies abstention from forbidden sexual intercourse, that each man should "take a wife [literally, "vessel"] for himself in holiness and honor" (RSV, 1 Thess. 4:4;).[57] Here holiness defines Christians as separate from the outside world, and is manifest by maintaining the proper boundaries within the realm of sexuality.

In Romans 1:24–27, dishonor and shame are closely related to impurity. Bruce Malina, in applying anthropological categories to New Testament studies, writes:

> From a symbolic point of view, honor stands for a person's rightful place in society, his social standing. This honor place is marked off by boundaries consisting of power, sexual status, and position on the social ladder. From a structuralist functionalist point of view, honor is the value of a person in his or her own eyes plus the value of that person in the eyes of his or her social group.[58]

The "dishonoring their bodies among themselves" (verse 24) and the "dishonorable passions" (verse 26) would then mean that those engaged in same-sex love no longer occupy their rightful place in society. Malina contends that honor is not the same for women and men.[59] In the passage at hand, the men have relinquished the honor due their sex. "Their women"—note the subordinating, relativizing word *their*—have not maintained the shame due their sex,[60] and have departed from their proper sexual role. Thus, having crossed the boundaries delineating their respective social positions, their positions in the order of creation, they live in impurity and dishonor. In contrast, a Christian man who respects these boundaries will take for himself a wife in "holiness and honor" (1 Thess. 4:4–8).

It is not an accident that same-sex love is underscored in Romans 1:24–27 as a repetition of the pattern of exchange found in idolatry. Idolaters, that is, followers of all the Greco-Roman religions except Judaism, exist totally outside the realm of holiness. It is therefore clear that a complete confusion of categories, or impurity, should exist among them. The confusion of maleness and femaleness stands for fundamental "symbolic confusion." [61] That Paul saw sexual purity to be more basic than, for example, the cleanness and uncleanness of foods is evident in his statement that the terms *clean* and *unclean* do not apply to foods (Rom. 14:20–21; cf. 1 Cor. 8, 10; Gal. 2:11–14) while he continued to apply the classification system of impurity and holiness to sexuality (cf. 1 Cor. 5:1–13, 7:14; 1 Thess. 4:3–8).

### *Romans 1:26 and 1 Corinthians 11:2–16*

In 1 Corinthians 11:2–16 Paul is addressing himself to a concrete conflict in a community founded by himself, one that he knows well, whereas Romans 1:26–27 is meant for a community not founded by him and is in the context of a discourse on universal human sinfulness. In spite of the differing contexts, 1 Corinthians 11:2–16 helps us to see why Paul describes same-sex love as "impurity" and as the "dishonoring of their bodies among themselves." He sees a blurring of the distinction between the sexes as contrary to nature and against the hierarchy: God, Christ, man, woman. 1 Corinthians 11:2–16 (RSV) reads:[62]

> **2** I commend you because you remember me in everything and maintain the traditions even as I have delivered them to you. **3** But I want you to understand that the head of every man is Christ, the head of a woman is her husband, and the head of Christ is God. **4** Any man who prays or prophesies with his head covered dishonors his head, **5** but any woman who prays or prophesies with her head unveiled dishonors her head—it is the same as if her head were

> shaven. **6** For if a woman will not veil herself, then she should cut
> off her hair; but if it is disgraceful for a woman to be shorn or
> shaven, let her wear a veil. **7** For a man ought not to cover his head,
> since he is the image and glory of God; but woman is the glory of
> man. **8** (For man was not made from woman, but woman from
> man. **9** Neither was man created for woman, but woman for man.)
> **10** That is why a woman ought to have a veil on her head, because
> of the angels. **11** (Nevertheless, in the Lord woman is not inde-
> pendent of man nor man of woman; **12** for as woman was made
> from man, so man is now born of woman. And all things are from
> God.) **13** Judge for yourselves; is it proper for a woman to pray
> to God with her head uncovered? **14** Does not nature itself teach
> you that for a man to wear long hair is degrading to him, **15** but
> if a woman has long hair, it is her pride? For her hair is given to
> her for a covering. **16** If any one is disposed to be contentious, we
> recognize no other practice, nor do the churches of God.

In this passage Paul requires strict gender differentiation with respect to hair style and headdress. Women and men should not look the same. For Paul, this is a theological issue. The reasons for gender polarization in dress are that the man is the head of the woman, just as the head of the man is Christ and the head of Christ is God; that woman is the glory of man, while the man is the image and glory of God; and that woman was created from man and for him. There is a difference between woman and man, a difference that implies woman is to be oriented to her head, to man, in whom she has her origin. (Paul's concessive remarks in verses 11 and 12 do not alter this basic structure.) The boundaries between femaleness and maleness are not to be blurred by women cutting their hair short or men wearing it long. Nor is long hair on women sufficient to mark the difference; women require a veil as a visible sign of their place in the order of creation.

As in Romans 1:26–27, Paul appeals to nature: Nature teaches that for a man to wear long hair is a "dishonor" (*atimia* [RSV] "degrading") to him (while for a woman it is "shameful," *aischron,* to wear short hair, and an unveiled woman "dishonors," *kataischynei,* her head). Thus, nature is the basis for strict gender differentiation in dress. For a man to defy nature means a loss of honor; that is, he no longer occupies his rightful place in society.

This discussion of headdress and hair style is quite reminiscent of the ancient discussions of same-sex love. For the man, the fear is that by looking like a woman a man loses his masculinity and can sink to the level of a woman. Short hair on a woman is one of the signs of her becoming like, or trying to become like, a man. One thinks of the Megilla/Megillus of Lucian,[63] who pulls off her wig to reveal short hair and announces herself to be Demonassa's husband. A woman cannot sink to the level of a man. She can only make ridiculous, yet nevertheless threatening, attempts to rise to that level.

Several exegetes have recognized that same-sex love could be an issue in 1 Corinthians 11:2–16. Early church discussions on same-sex love often included reference to the passage.[64] In the nineteenth century, Johannes Weiss wrote that the woman who shaved her head was trying to look like a man for lascivious reasons, that the "lesbian vice" of perverse women was at stake here.[65] The most recent scholar to see such a connection is Jerome Murphy-O'Connor, who detects in the Corinthian behavior a response to Galatians 3:28:

> If there was no longer any male or female, the Corinthians felt free to blur the distinction between the sexes.... The consistent infantilism of the Corinthians rubbed him on the raw, and the hair-dos raised the disquieting question of homosexuality within the community.[66]

### *Paul and Female Nonsubordination*

Paul is not simply opposed to nonsubordination of the female. By recommending celibacy to women (1 Cor. 7:8–9, 25–35, 39–40) he actually promotes women as anomalies, as not directly subordinate to a husband. Further, by quoting the baptismal formula, "There is neither Jew nor Greek, there is neither slave nor free, there is neither male nor female; for you are all one in Christ Jesus" (RSV, Gal. 3:28), he is opening the way for a blurring of gender roles that could alter social structures. That the slogan was powerful is evident, for he quotes a different version of the formula, one without the "male and female" portion, in 1 Corinthians 12:13, probably because he recognizes that the Corinthians had indeed understood the implications of the phrase "not male and female." Paul acknowledges the work of women in the gospel (Rom. 16:1–16; Phil. 4:2–3), as well as women's right to prophesy in the liturgical assembly (1 Cor. 11:5). If the admonition to women to be silent in the churches and subordinate is by Paul (1 Cor. 14:33b–36) and not a later interpolator, it would be a further example of the already documented tension in his thinking. Thus, any ambiguity about gender roles in the Christian community resulted at least partly from Paul himself. But when pressed, as in the case of gender differentiation in appearance in Corinth, he calls for strict differentiation and bases it on a hierarchical ordering of the sexes, at the same time omitting the "not male and female" phrase that apparently endangered established gender roles. Perhaps it was precisely Paul's promotion of celibacy, itself a potential threat to patriarchal marriage, that caused him to be so adamant about gender polarization, implying female subordination, in dress and in sexual intercourse. Against the belief of the end being near and Christ being the head of both man and woman, Paul could allow a woman to devote herself solely to Christ, thereby circumventing a male head in the form of a spouse. What he could not accept was women experiencing their power through the erotic in a way that challenged the hierarchical ladder: God, Christ, man, woman.[67]

## Conclusions and Implications

This brief survey of sources has demonstrated that little tolerance for sexual love relationships between women can be found among male Greco-Roman writers. This is different from the recorded attitudes toward male homosexuality, which are quite mixed. The sources reviewed should teach us that it is methodologically questionable to subsume love relations between women under male homosexuality, as the following examples show. John Boswell, from whom I have learned much in spite of our differing interpretations, summarizes his findings on Roman society:

> . . . intolerance on this issue was rare to the point of insignificance in its great urban centers. Gay people were in a strict sense a minority, but neither they nor their contemporaries regarded their inclinations as harmful, bizarre, immoral or threatening, and they were fully integrated into Roman life at every level.[68]

Robin Scroggs, upon completion of a survey of ancient sources on male homosexuality, writes:

> *Thus what the New Testament was against was the image of homosexuality as pederasty and primarily here its more sordid and dehumanizing dimensions* [such as lack of mutuality]. One would regret it if somebody in the New Testament had not opposed such dehumanization.[69]

Scroggs specifically notes that he is speaking here only of male homosexuality. His discussion of women occurs in a four-and-one-half-page appendix entitled "Female Homosexuality in the Greco-Roman World."[70]

Boswell and Scroggs, drawing upon the same sources, come to radically different conclusions. Boswell claims that his thesis applies to women; Scroggs does not. What is clear is that the conclusions of neither apply to women. The Roman authors surveyed *did* regard sexual relations between women as harmful, bizarre, immoral, and threatening. And one would be hard pressed to say that the authors discussed disapproved of women giving sexual expression to their affection for one another because it was dehumanizing by being, for example, nonmutual. On the contrary, hierarchy seemed normal to the authors discussed; what was abnormal was women not submitting to it. There is no good reason for Scroggs not to have asked why the sources on women do not support his thesis on men.

It should be noted that what I have been discussing is not lesbian history, that is, the history of women who found their primary identification in other women and who may or may not have expressed that sexually.[71] Rather, I have been treating sources that attest to male attitudes toward, and male fantasies about, lesbians, and the men writing are heavily genitally oriented. These male attitudes are important for women's history insofar as they shaped the culture in which women lived. The extent of that determination remains to be established. The conclusions for women's history can only be tentative and general. The increasing preoccupation with sexual relations between women in the Roman period could indicate that lesbians were living more openly and were perceived as a greater threat. Two ways of dealing with the lesbian threat are utter silence and vehement rejection, whereby a sudden shift in method is not unusual. The sources surveyed seem to represent such a shift from silence to open rejection, although marginalization and containment through the technique of silencc continued throughout the period discussed.

One must be clear about the significance of these sources for Paul, and not assume that Paul personally knew or read any of the sources discussed. Indeed, some were written after the Letter to the Romans. The sources are relevant because their broad variety documents attitudes that were most likely known to him and his readers. In light of widespread disapproval of female homoeroticism, Paul's condemnation is not surprising, nor is his use of the expression *para physin,* "unnatural" or "contrary to nature." The motif of a woman becoming or trying to become like a man was most probably known to him, as well as men's association of female homoerotic activity with sexual aggressiveness and licentiousness, which may be a way of describing—in caricature—female sexual autonomy. Further, it may not be an accident that Paul takes up this question in his Letter to the Romans. In the decades surrounding that letter, several authors who had been trained or lived in Rome (Seneca the Elder, Ovid, Martial, Phaedrus) expressed themselves on the matter, as did Juvenal (Rome) and Soranus (Rome and Alexandria, according to the fifth-century translation) in the early second century. This geographical clustering results partly from the high level of literary productivity in Rome in this period, but may also indicate a special concern with this issue in the city of Rome.

According to the sources, Paul and his culture understood maleness and femaleness hierarchically. The structures of Paul's culture were based on a hierarchical definition of maleness and femaleness, a definition that found an acute expression in the rejection of physically intimate love relations between women and in the accompanying requirement of gender polarity in physical appearance. It is this definition that is behind Paul's condemnation of female homoeroticism. Therefore this issue cannot be dismissed as a marginal question affecting only a small number of women. Anyone concerned about the human costs of a definition of women and men based on enforced polarity and hierarchy must take on the issue of the Christian rejection of lesbian existence, as well as that of male homosexuality, for which Paul is a primary source.

The churches and theology have the task of thinking through the implications of the fact that Romans 1:26 cannot be extricated from its immediate context or from Pauline thinking about women and men. In Paul's eyes a woman who physically expressed love for another woman was repeating the pattern of idolatry, that is, of estrangement from God. It is inconsistent to call for equality between the sexes and yet to require that women either orient themselves toward men or remain celibate. Consistency would also require that if one declares Romans 1:26 (and 27) not to be normative for theology, one cannot adopt the rest of Pauline theology and theological anthropology. Therefore, a careful analysis and fundamental rethinking of Paul's theology is required. Since Paul's thought has deeply affected Western society, this is a task for everyone, not just for Christians.

## *Notes*

1. Lines 175–227. P. W. Van der Horst, trans., *The Sentences of Pseudo-Phocylides,* Studia in Veteris Testamenti Pseudepigrapha 4 (Leiden: Brill, 1978), pp. 225–257. Van der Horst dates the work to between ca. 30 B.C.E. and 40 C.E., and suggests Alexandria as the place of origin (Van der Horst, *Sentences,* pp. 81–83).

2. Were line 192 not in its present context, it could also refer to a woman imitating a man sexually in another way, such as by taking the sexually active role in heterosexual intercourse. Disapproval of lesbians and disapproval of nonpassive heterosexual women are not unrelated to each other, as will be seen below.

Another Greek-language Jewish source deserving mention is Psalms of Solomon 2:14–15, which speaks of the daughters of Jerusalem having defiled themselves with a "confusion of mingling." This could refer to incest or to intercourse with animals or with other women.

3. A. H. Weiss, ed., *Sifra* (Vienna: Schlossberg, 1862), on Lev. 18:3 (Aḥarei Mot, Parasha 9). Translation my own.

4. *Y. Gittin* 49c. 70–71.

5. Babylonian Talmud: *Shabbat* 65a–b; *Yebamot* 76a (see the medieval commentator Rashi on both passages); Maimonides, *Mishneh Torah, 'Issurei Bi'ah* (Forbidden Intercourse) 21:8; *'Even Ha'Ezer* 20.2.

6. The fragment of Parmenides quoted in Caelius Aurelianus, *Chronic Diseases* 9.134–135 (5th cent. C.E.), does seem to refer to both women and men, and could thus be considered a yet earlier mention. See the edition and translation by I. E. Drabkin (Chicago: University of Chicago Press, 1950), pp. 902–903.

7. 191E.

8. 636B–C.

9. John Boswell points out the possible ambiguity of the phrase *para physin,* but does not address himself to the expressions "daring or shameless act" or "lack of self-control." See his *Christianity, Social Tolerance, and Homosexuality: Gay People in Western Europe from the Beginning of the Christian Era to the Fourteenth Century* (Chicago: University of Chicago Press, 1980), pp. 13–14, n. 22.

10. Hugo Stadtmueller, ed., *Anthologia Graeca* 5.206 (Leipzig: Teubner, 1894), vol. 1, pp. 168–169; see schol.[B].

11. *Controversiae* 1.2.23.

12. *Metamorphoses* 9.666–797.

13. *Metamorphoses* 9.726–763.

14. The story of Caenis/Caeneus, a woman with no interest in sexual intercourse with men who was changed into a man, should also be mentioned here. Ovid is one of the main sources for the tale: *Metamorphoses* 12.171–535.

15. Phaedrus, *Liber Fabularum* 4.16. Phaedrus probably composed the fables of book 4 when he was an old man. See Peter L. Schmidt, *Der Kleine Pauly,* s.v. "Phaedrus." Note that actual physical organs are involved. Does the author consider them necessary for the female to play the active role in sexual intercourse?

16. *Epigrammata* 7.67, 70. A woman named Philaenis was known in the Greek-speaking world as the author of a book on sexual positions, although some considered the attribution of the work to her to be malicious. See Pauly-Wissowa, *Real-Encyclopädie der classischen Altertumswissenschaft* 19, 2 (1938), p. 2122. Martial may have had this association in mind.

17. Cf. Juvenal, *Saturae* 6.423.

18. Martial, *Epigrammata* 1.90.

19. The verb *futuo* used in line 2 of 7.70, which I have translated as "copulate," is from the same root. Both refer to men's copulating with women.

20. Unpublished paper presented at the Fifth Berkshire Conference on the History of Women, Vassar College, New York, June 1981.

21. Peter Howell also sees Martial as envisaging physical penetration in 1.90 (Bassa) and 7.67 (Philaenis). He notes that some women are said to have a clitoris large enough to "be able to copulate, or even sodomise," but sees it as more likely that the use of an artificial phallus is meant. See Howell, *A Commentary on Book One of the Epigrams of Martial* (London: Athlone Press, 1980), p. 298. Phaedrus's depiction of *tribades* possessing actual male organs would also support Hal-

lett's interpretation, especially since Martial knew and used the work of Phaedrus. See Schmidt, *Der Kleine Pauly*, s.v. "Phaedrus."

22. See Seneca, *Controversiae* 1.2.23.

23. Hallett, "Autonomy," p. 15.

24. Juvenal, *Saturae* 6.306–313. E. Courtney gives references to metaphors for horse riding applied to sexual activity (*A Commentary on the Satires of Juvenal* [London: Athlone Press, 1980], p. 298). Ludwig Friedländer describes the issue here as "tribadic fornication" (*D. Iunii Iuvenalis Saturarum Libri V. Mit erklärenden Anmerkungen*, 2 vols. [Leipzig: S. Hirzel, 1895], vol. 1, p. 319).

25. Juvenal, *Saturae* 2.43–48. Laronia does not necessarily represent Juvenal's view, and it seems nearly certain that he is referring to sexual activity among the women mentioned at 6.306–313.

26. Plutarch, *Vitae, Lycurgus* 18.9.

27. For Plutarch's views on female marital duties, see especially his treatise *Conjugal Precepts* (*Moralia* 138A–146A). On this work see Kathleen O'Brien Wicker, "First-Century Marriage Ethics: A Comparative Study of the Household Codes and Plutarch's Conjugal Precepts," in James W. Flanagan and Anita Weisbrod Robinson, eds., *No Famine in the Land: Studies in Honor of John L. McKenzie* (Claremont, Calif.: Institute for Antiquity and Christianity, 1975), pp. 141–153. It is female subordination, rather than female autonomy, that Plutarch advises in this treatise.

28. This fragment of Iamblichus, *Babyloniaca*, was preserved in the *Bibliotheca* of the tenth-century patriarch Photius. See René Henry, ed. and trans., *Photius: Bibliothèque*, 8 vols. (Paris: "Les Belles Lettres," 1959–77), vol. 2, pp. 44–46. See also the critical edition of the fragments of Iamblichus by Elmar Habrich (Leipzig: Teubner, 1960), pp. 58–65, and the discussion in Boswell, *Christianity, Social Tolerance, and Homosexuality*, p. 84, Boswell's translation of *ekthesmos* as "inordinate" rather than "lawless" or "contre nature" (Henry) is not supported by the evidence; see the references for *ekthesmos* in the standard Greek lexica: Liddell-Scott-Jones, Lampe, and Preisigke.

29. See also Alciphron (2d cent.), *Letters of Courtesans* 14, which contains an account of an all-female party with erotic overtones.

30. *Amores* 28.

31. *Oneirocritica* 1.80.

32. *Tardarum passionum* 4.9.132–133.

33. *Tetrabiblos* 3.14; 4.5.

34. *Anthologiarum Libri* 2.36.

35. *Apotelesmatica* 4.24. See also the fourth-century Latin writer Firmicus Maternus, who, in his systematic work on astrology, repeats the motif of women becoming like men (*Matheseos Libri VIII* 7.25.1).

36. See also Caelius Aurelianus, *Tardarum passionum* 4.9.132 ("women who are called *tribades* because they perform both kinds of love").

37. A third second-century author who speaks of women is the Christian Clement of Alexandria: "Men passively play the role of women, and women behave like men in that women, contrary to nature, are given in marriage and marry" (*Paedagogus* 3.3.21).

38. K(enneth) J. Dover, *Greek Homosexuality* (Cambridge, Mass.: Harvard University Press, 1978), CE34, discussion on p. 173; G. M. A. Richter, *Korai: Archaic Greek Maidens* (London: Phaidon, 1968), pl. VIII-C.

39. Dover, *Greek Homosexuality*, R207, discussion on p. 173; John Boardman, Eugenio La Rocca, and Antonia Mulas, *Eros in Griechenland* (Munich: List, 1976), pp. 111–112; J. D. Beazley, *Paralipomena: Additions to* Attic Black-Figure Vase-Painters *and* Attic Red-Figure Vase-Painters *2d ed.* (Oxford: Clarendon, 1971), p. 333.

40. Whether the use of dildos is relevant here is not certain. See Dover, *Greek Homosexuality*, pp. 102–103, 132–133; Sarah B. Pomeroy, *Goddesses, Whores, Wives, and Slaves: Women in Classical Antiquity* (New York: Schocken, 1975), pl. 12; Robin Scroggs, *The New Testament and Homosexuality: Contextual Background for Contemporary Debate* (Philadelphia: Fortress, 1983), pp. 141, 143.

41. *Epistulae* 1.19.28. See also Horace's reference to Folia of Ariminum, to whom he attributes "masculine libido," in *Epodon* 5.41–46.

42. *Moralia* 406A.

43. 18.7.

44. *Tristia* 2.365–366; *Heroides* [XV]; cf. also Ovid, *Metamorphoses* 9.666–797.

45. *Oratio ad Graecos* 33.

46. Ada Adler, ed., *Suidae Lexicon*, 1 vol. in 5 parts (Leipzig: Teubner, 1928–38; repr. Stuttgart: Teubner, 1967–71), vol. 1.4, pp. 322–323.

47. On Romans 1:18–32 as a whole, see the commentaries on Romans by C. E. B. Cranfield, Ulrich Wilckens, Heinrich Schlier, Ernst Käsemann, Otto Michel, C. K. Barrett, Hans Lietzmann, M. J. Lagrange, and William Sanday and Arthur Headlam, which contain references to further literature. For a survey of views on the structure of the pericope, which is an especially disputed point, see Wiard Popkes, "Zum Aufbau und Charakter von Römer 1.18–32," *New Testament Studies* 28 (1982): 490–501. On Romans 1:26–27 see also Boswell, *Christian-*

*ity, Social Tolerance, and Homosexuality*, pp. 107–117; Peter Coleman, *Christian Attitudes to Homosexuality* (London: SPCK, 1980), pp. 88–93; Else Kähler, "Exegese zweier neutestamentlicher Stellen (*Römer 1, 18–32; 1. Korinther 6,9–11*)," in Theodor Bovet, ed., *Probleme der Homophilie in medizinischer, theologischer und juristischer Sicht* (Bern: Paul Haupt; Tübingen: Katzmann, 1965), pp. 12–43.

48. My primary reason for interpreting verse 26 as referring to same-sex love, and not to another form of sexual behavior that Paul would call unnatural, is the word *likewise* of verse 27, which clearly refers to male homosexuality. If it were to refer to women taking the active role in heterosexual intercourse, the interpretation that follows would still hold. There does not seem to me to be sufficient basis for taking it to refer to anal or oral intercourse.

49. See esp. *Implicit Meanings: Essays in Anthropology* (London: Routledge and Kegan Paul, 1975); *Natural Symbols: Explorations in Cosmology* (New York: Random House, 1970); *Purity and Danger: An analysis of concepts of pollution and taboo* (London: Routledge and Kegan Paul, 1966). See also Sheldon R. Isenberg and Dennis E. Owen, "Bodies, Natural and Contrived: The Work of Mary Douglas," *Religious Studies Review* 3 (1977): 1–17; Jacob Neusner, *The Idea of Purity in Ancient Judaism: The Haskell Lectures, 1972–1973.* With a Critique and a Commentary by Mary Douglas, Studies in Judaism in Late Antiquity 1 (Leiden: Brill, 1973).

50. In Neusner, *The Idea of Purity*, p. 139.

51. *Purity and Danger*, p. 55.

52. For this interpretation see Ulrich Wilckens, *Der Brief an die Römer*, EKK 6,1–3 (Zurich: Benziger; Neukirchen-Vluyn: Neukirchener, 1978–82), vol. 1, p. 109, and others.

53. *De specialibus legibus* 3.37–39, trans. F. H. Colson, *Philo*, Loeb Classical Library (Cambridge, Mass.: Harvard, 1937), vol. 7, pp. 499, 501; cf. Wilckens, *Der Brief*, vol. 1, p. 325; *De Abrahamo* 133–139; *De vita contemplativa* 59–63.

54. For sources on male homosexuality in antiquity, see esp. Robin Scroggs, *The New Testament and Homosexuality;* Boswell, *Christianity, Social Tolerance, and Homosexuality*, pp. 61–87; Dover, *Greek Homosexuality*. On male cross-dressing, see esp. H. Herter, "Effeminatus," *Reallexikon für Antike und Christentum* 4 (1959): 620–650.

55. See Helmut Koester, "*Physis*," in Gerhard Kittel and Gerhard Friedrich, eds., *Theological Dictionary of the New Testament*, vol. 9 (1974), pp. 251–277, esp. pp. 262, 264–265, 267–269, 271–275.

56. *Purity and Danger*, p. 53.

57. See Wayne A. Meeks, *The First Urban Christians: The Social World of the Apostle Paul* (New Haven: Yale University Press, 1983), pp. 100–101, 228.

58. *The New Testament World: Insights from Cultural Anthropology* (Atlanta: John Knox, 1981), p. 47.

59. Ibid., pp. 42–48.

60. In commenting on Romans 1:26, John Chrysostom writes that it is "more disgraceful that the women should seek this type of intercourse, since they ought to have a greater sense of shame than men" (*PG* 60.417).

61. Ruth Tiffany Barnhouse's book bears the apt title *Homosexuality: A Symbolic Confusion* (New York: Seabury, 1979).

62. It is not possible to discuss here the complex exegetical issues of 1 Corinthians 11:2–16 (such as the meaning of *kephalē* or the reasons for believing that the passage has something to do with veiling). For a different interpretation, see Elisabeth Schüssler Fiorenza, *In Memory of Her: A Feminist Theological Reconstruction of Christian Origins* (New York: Crossroads, 1983), pp. 46, 226–230, 239–240; see also the literature cited there.

63. Note that Lucian is a second-century author and therefore later than Paul. See also Lucian, *Fugitivi* 27.

64. For several of these references, see Bernadette J. Brooten, "Patristic Interpretations of Romans 1:26," in Elizabeth A. Livingstone, ed., *Proceedings of the Ninth International Conference on Patristic Studies* (forthcoming).

65. *Der erste Korintherbrief*, 9th ed. (1910; repr. Göttingen: Vandenhoeck and Ruprecht, 1977), p. 272.

66. "Sex and Logic in 1 Corinthians 11:2–16," *Catholic Biblical Quarterly* 42 (1980): 490. See also Richard Kroeger and Catherine Clark Kroeger, "St. Paul's Treatment of Misogyny, Gynephobia, and Sex Segregation in First Corinthians 11:2–6 [*sic*]," in Paul J. Achtemeier, ed., *Society of Biblical Literature 1979 Seminar Papers*, vol. 2 (Missoula: Scholars Press, 1979), pp. 213–221; John P. Meier, "On the Veiling of Hermeneutics (1 Cor. 11:2–16)," *Catholic Biblical Quarterly* 40 (1978): 219, n. 15; Robin Scroggs, "Paul and the Eschatological Woman," *Journal of the American Academy of Religion* 40 (1972): 297; C. K. Barrett, *The First Epistle to the Corinthians*, Black's New Testament Commentary (London: Black, 1968), p. 257.

67. See Audre Lorde, *Uses of the Erotic: The Erotic as Power* (New York: Out and Out Books, 1978).

68. *Christianity, Social Tolerance, and Homosexuality*, p. 87. It is

important to underscore the great value of Boswell's book; he includes sources that do not support his thesis, which is one of the marks of good scholarship.

69. *The New Testament and Homosexuality*, p. 126.

70. Ibid., pp. 140–144.

71. On the definition of the term *lesbian,* see Adrienne Rich, "Compulsory Heterosexuality and Lesbian Existence," *Signs* 5 (1980): 631–660; see also the responses by Martha E. Thompson in *Signs* 6 (1981): 790–794, and by Ann Ferguson, Jacquelyn N. Zita, and Kathryn Pyne Addelson in *Signs* 7 (1981): 159–199.

On women's history in antiquity as distinct from male attitudes toward women, see Bernadette J. Brooten, "Early Christian Women and Their Cultural Context: Issues of Method in Historical Reconstruction," in Adela Yarbro Collins, ed., *Feminist Perspectives on Biblical Scholarship* (Chico, Calif.: Scholars Press, 1985).

# Lesbian Sexuality in Renaissance Italy: The Case of Sister Benedetta Carlini

Judith C. Brown

The archival discovery of an ecclesiastical investigation containing what is probably the earliest detailed account of a sexual relationship between two nuns is a tale of serendipity. Several years ago, when I was revising a book manuscript on the economic and social history of Renaissance Pescia,[1] I looked through the inventory of a collection entitled *Miscellanea Medicea* at the Archivio di Stato of Florence. One entry in the inventory immediately caught my eye. It read: "The case of a nun from Pescia who claimed to be the object of miraculous events but who upon further investigation turned out to be a woman of ill repute."[2] I thought the case would probably involve the sexual affairs of a nun with some of the local priests. There are hundreds of such documented examples. Renaissance convents were notorious for their loose moral standards and their sexual license, which is not surprising since they were largely warehouses for middle- and upper-class women sent there by parents who were unwilling or unable to raise a dowry large enough to find a suitable husband.[3]

What I found instead was much more interesting. The document, consisting of roughly one hundred unnumbered pages, included a de-

1. Judith C. Brown, *In the Shadow of Florence: Provincial Society in Renaissance Pescia* (New York: Oxford University Press, 1982).

2. Florence, Archivio di Stato, *Miscellanea Medicea*, 376, ins. 28. The translation of this material is mine.

3. Brown, pp. 42–43. The moral problems of Renaissance convents and other religious institutions are outlined in Arnaldo D'Addario, *Aspetti della controriforma a Firenze* (Rome: Pubblicazioni degli Archivi di Stato, 1972), pp. 107–14.

[*Signs: Journal of Women in Culture and Society* 1984, vol. 9, no. 4]

tailed account of the sexual relationship between two nuns. What I originally thought might be a footnote in a larger history has now developed into a separate book on a woman whose sexual, emotional, and intellectual experiences shed new light on the life of women in early modern times.[4]

The ecclesiastical investigation into the case of Benedetta Carlini, Abbess of the Convent of the Mother of God, dates from the years 1619–23. The records of the inquiry tell of the tragic life of a woman whose parents brought her to the convent in 1599, at age nine, to fulfill a vow they made at her birth. Since information about her early years is scant, her social background, relationship to her family, and adjustment to convent life can be reconstructed only with slow and painstaking care. Benedetta belonged to a relatively well-to-do family in a small mountain town near Pescia. She appears to have had a close relationship with her father. She was literate and obviously very intelligent and persuasive—so much so that she became an abbess before she reached the age of thirty and was able to convince many both inside and outside her convent that she was the recipient of special divine favors. She asserted, among other things, that Christ and several male angels spoke through her and that she had received the stigmata. These extraordinary mystical claims brought her to the attention of the authorities, who launched an investigation. The details of her sexual life that were brought to light during the inquiry make the document unique for this period.

Among the hundreds if not thousands of cases of homosexuality tried by lay and ecclesiastical authorities in medieval and early modern Europe, there are almost none involving sexual relations between women.[5] The Venetian archives, for instance, which are replete with prosecutions against clergy and laymen for sodomy as well as for sexual relations with nuns, have not turned up a single case of sexual relations between women.[6] Thus far records from Spain have also yielded little. One ambiguous reference by the sixteenth-century jurist Antonio Gomez discusses two nuns who were burned for using "material instruments." Another report on prison conditions states that some female inmates are tough and manly and make artificial male genitalia. In France, four cases are mentioned by various sixteenth-century writers, but two of these ended in acquittal for insufficient evidence and the other two are simply mentioned in passing by authors who did not dwell on the details.[7] The

4. A more detailed account than that provided here will appear in my forthcoming book (New York: Oxford University Press, in press.)

5. John Boswell points out the absence of women in many legal sources concerned with homosexuality in *Christianity, Social Tolerance, and Homosexuality: Gay People in Western Europe from the Beginning of the Christian Era to the Fourteenth Century* (Chicago: University of Chicago Press, 1980), p. 290.

6. I would like to thank Carlo Ginzburg and Guido Ruggiero, both of whom have had extensive experience with the inquisitorial and criminal records of Venice, for informing me of this. See Guido Ruggiero, "Sexual Criminality in the Early Renaissance: Venice 1338–1358," *Journal of Social History* 8 (Summer 1975): 18–37.

7. Cited in Louis Crompton, "The Myth of Lesbian Impunity: Capital Laws from 1270 to 1791," *Journal of Homosexuality*, no. 1–2 (Fall 1980–Winter 1981): 17–20; also Mary

first record for Germany dates to 1721.[8] And Swiss sources reveal one case in sixteenth-century Geneva in which the rarity of the accusation is underscored both by the authorities' appeal to the well-known jurist Germain Colladon for advice on how to proceed and by the secrecy with which the case was disposed. In the opinion of the authorities, "A crime so horrible and against nature is so detestable and because of the horror of it, it cannot be named."[9]

Crimes that cannot be named, not surprisingly, leave few traces in the historical records. While this enhances the importance of the document that describes Benedetta's sexual relations with another nun, it also raises a number of difficult historical problems, some of which I would briefly like to discuss here.

First, when such records do turn up, they are usually judicial or inquisitorial documents of some sort. This means that they often veil the truth in various ways. What is said and what is recorded will have been filtered through the minds of the authorities, always male, who conduct the proceedings. Moreover, those accused of sexual crimes are likely to say things in ways that minimized or excused their own misconduct. Both of these factors enter into the record of Benedetta's relationship. The information is circumscribed by the questions asked, most of which do not survive and must be surmised from the answers. The responses are also conditioned by what the witnesses believed the male judges wanted to hear and by what they thought would be least damaging to themselves. Hence, for example, the account of Benedetta's sexual acts is related by her lover as if the lover had been an unwilling participant who was forced into the relationship. The historian's task is to disentangle the complex web of motives that influenced the form of the narrative. This can be accomplished by cultivating an awareness of the circumstances that led to the creation of the historical record and by conducting a close and sensitive reading of the documents themselves. As any lawyer knows, it is very difficult for witnesses to sustain a lengthy fiction without falling into contradictions. Sometimes the truth is revealed by an unguarded word spoken in a different context.

A second problem facing the historian involves determining the extent of sexual relations between women. How common were they? Is the paucity of historical evidence related to the ways in which the male world dealt with such relations? Or did women engage less extensively then men in sexual activities with one another? Satisfactory answers are difficult to come by, although a number of reasonable observations can be

---

Elizabeth Perry, *Crime and Society in Early Modern Seville* (Hanover, N.H.: University Press of New England, 1980), p. 84.

8. Brigitte Erikson, "A Lesbian Execution in Germany, 1721: The Trial Records," *Journal of Homosexuality*, no. 1–2 (Fall 1980–Winter 1981), pp. 27–40.

9. E. William Monter, "La Sodomie à l'époque moderne en Suisse romande," *Annales: Economies, Sociétés, Civilisations* 29 (1974): 1023–33. The nineteenth-century court case of two Scottish school mistresses accused of sexual relations reveals a similar concern about not divulging the details of the case for fear of giving ideas to otherwise innocent female minds. See Lillian Faderman, *Scotch Verdict* (New York: William Morrow & Co., 1983).

made. Undoubtedly, sexual relations between women existed in medieval and Renaissance Europe, especially, though not exclusively, within the world of the convent. It was there, where at times close to 10 percent of the adult female population lived, that such relations had the most opportunity to flourish. To imagine that sexual relationships were absent from these all-female communities strains the limits of credulity. But to move from the probable to the realm of evidence, the discussion in several medieval and Renaissance penitentials of penances for women who engaged in "vice against nature" implicitly acknowledges that such relations existed.[10] The paucity of historical evidence regarding these relations must therefore be related in some measure to the ways in which the masculine world perceived the bonds between women.

Although medieval theologians and other learned men were not totally unaware of sexual relations between women, they for the most part ignored them. The world of the Middle Ages and the Renaissance was not prudish. It was a world that was fully cognizant of human sexuality, but it was also phallocentric. The thought that women could bring sexual pleasure to each other without the aid of a man occurred to very few theologians and physicians. For the millennium that followed the decline of Rome, many laws and commentaries that deal with male homosexuality survive; only a handful, however, mention sexual relations between women. So little was written on the subject that the few authors who discussed it were often uninformed about what others had written and therefore disagreed on what this "unnatural" vice was and how it should be punished. Ignorance about sexual relations between women was so pervasive that one Italian cleric in the eighteenth century, Lodovico Maria Sinistrari, decided to write a treatise on "female sodomy." While moralists claimed that sodomy among women existed, none, he lamented, explained how such a thing could occur. After exploring the subject at great length, he concluded that, except in rare instances, it could not.[11]

What women did with each other is precisely the topic that the document appended below illuminated for Benedetta's male superiors. Yet because they lacked an imaginative schema to incorporate the sexual behavior described, they had a rather difficult time assimilating the account. So disturbed was the scribe writing down what had been said that the heretofore neat and legible handwriting of the report totally breaks down in the section covering Benedetta's sexual relations with another nun. The words are illegible, crossed out, and rewritten.

If the scribe had difficulties comprehending what was taking place, he was not the only one. That Benedetta herself could not easily fit her

10. Some of these penitentials and other medieval literature dealing with lesbianism are cited in Derrick S. Bailey, *Homosexuality and the Western Christian Tradition* (London: Longmans, Green & Co., 1955); Boswell; and Crompton.

11. Lodovico Maria Sinistrari, *De sodomia: Tractatus in quo exponitur doctrina nova de sodomia foeminarum a tribadismo distincta* (Paris, 1843), excerpted from his larger work, *De delictis et poenis* (Rome, 1700). This conclusion had to do with Sinistrari's narrow definition of sodomy rather than the belief, more common in the nineteenth century (see Faderman), that women had no sexual desires.

sexual behavior into a mold that was acceptable to her raises the larger issue of labeling and sexual identity. Do the terms "lesbian" and "lesbianism" best describe the person and activities outlined in the investigators' report? Recent studies of sexual identity and sexual preference have stressed the difficulties inherent in definitions. Human sexual behavior, like other aspects of human activity, defies easy or stereotypical categorizations. Women who have had fulfilling sexual and emotional relationships with other women do not necessarily view themselves as lesbian. Conversely, there are those who have never had sexual relationships with other women who consider themselves lesbians nonetheless. The range of sexual experience and self-identification is immensely varied and operates to a large extent within socially defined categories that influence both identity and behavior.[12]

This problem of labeling becomes particularly acute when dealing with sexual behavior and identity in past times. Although considerable legislation and concern about homosexual practices arose prior to the nineteenth century, the concept of the homosexual, as we know it today, did not exist.[13] This was all the more true for the notion of the lesbian.[14] Adrienne Rich has attempted to surmount this difficulty by positing a lesbian continuum in which lesbian identity is tied not so much to a self-conscious identity or even to sexual relations or attractions as to the emotional bonds that emerge between women in the midst of patriarchal society. While such an approach has the merit of emphasizing the complexity of ties among women and the resistance to oppression implicit in so many of their actions, it is also too encompassing and at heart ahistorical. Closer to the mark is Ann Ferguson's argument that, while some women can be described as sexually deviant in that they departed from the norm, the term "lesbian" cannot accurately be applied to women who

12. See, among others, Allan P. Bell, Martin S. Weinberg, and Sue K. Hammersmith, *Sexual Preference: Its Development in Men and Women* (Bloomington: Indiana University Press, 1981); Sherry Ortner and Harriet Whitehead, eds., *Sexual Meanings* (Cambridge: Cambridge University Press, 1981).

13. There has been considerable debate about whether the category of homosexual can be applied to premodern periods. Among the most clearly articulated arguments against employing the category anachronistically are those of Jeffrey Weeks in *Coming Out: Homosexual Politics in Britain from the Nineteenth Century to the Present* (London: Quartet Books, 1977). Opposing this view is John Boswell, "Towards the Long View: Revolutions, Universals and Sexual Categories," *Salmagundi*, no. 58–59 (Fall 1982–Winter 1981), pp. 89–113. There is even disagreement over when the homosexual role emerged within the modern period. While Mary McIntosh argues for the late seventeenth century, Jeffrey Weeks and John Marshall, among others, favor the late nineteenth century. See their respective essays in Kenneth Plummer, ed., *The Making of the Modern Homosexual* (London: Hutchinson Publishing Group, 1981).

14. Even if there is some merit to Boswell's argument that the concept of the homosexual, albeit in altered form, existed prior to the modern age, his claim cannot readily be extended to the concept of the lesbian since women's restricted cultural and social roles precluded the development of the types of communities that he analyzes for males. For a discussion of some of these problems, see Annabel Faraday, "Liberating Lesbian Research," in Plummer, ed., pp. 112–32.

lived before its emergence as a cultural category in the late nineteenth century.[15]

Benedetta Carlini's case illustrates the complexity of these issues. Benedetta engaged in sexual acts that today would be labeled lesbian. Furthermore, she entered into a sexual relationship with another female even though she could have secured male partners without much difficulty. Her apparent preference for a relationship with a woman is not, however, indicative of a clearly articulated choice. When she made love to Bartolomea Crivelli, she imagined herself to be a male angel. Her voice and even her appearance became more like a man's when she assumed the guise of the angel Splendidiello. Since male-female sexual relations were the only ones she seemed to recognize, her male identity allowed her to have sexual and emotional relations that she could not conceive between women. Attaining the object of her sexual desires required a complete reversal of her own gender and sexual roles.[16] But because Benedetta was a nun for whom *all* sexual activities were prohibited, she could not pass for an ordinary male; she required an angelic disguise to preclude the possibility of sin. In this double role, as male and as angel, Benedetta absolved herself from any possible wrongdoing.

Equally important, the ecclesiastical authorities who heard the case also lacked the terms of sexual identification that would be used in a twentieth-century context. Although an extended discussion of medieval and Renaissance notions of female sexuality is not feasible within the narrow confines of an archival note, suffice it to say that on a scale of sinful sexual acts Benedetta's behavior at worst would have been labeled sodomy (that is, engaging in coitus in an unnatural vessel), which was punishable by burning at the stake. Some theologians and lawyers of her time, however, might have viewed her actions merely as pollution brought on by the rubbing together of the pudenda. Still others might have called them mutual masturbation. Both of these sinful acts were of a lesser degree than sodomy. But no matter how grave the sin or the secular crime that her contemporaries thought Benedetta had committed, they would not have applied the term "lesbian" as a discrete category of female sexual identification. This is not to argue that Benedetta's relationship with her lover was not emotionally or sexually fulfilling but simply to say what is after all rather obvious: sexuality and culture are intertwined, and Benedetta's and the authorities' interpretations of her behavior while different from each other are also necessarily different from our own.

15. Adrienne Rich, "Compulsory Heterosexuality and Lesbian Existence," *Signs: Journal of Women in Culture and Society* 5, no. 4 (Summer 1980): 631–60; Ann Ferguson, "Patriarchy, Sexual Identity, and the Sexual Revolution," *Signs* 7, no. 1 (Autumn 1981): 158–66.

16. In this respect, Benedetta's perceptions coincide with Victorian notions of sexual inversion even though the latter originated in quite different conceptions of female gender and sexuality. See George Chauncey, Jr., "From Sexual Inversion to Homosexuality: Medicine and the Changing Conceptualization of Female Deviance," *Salmagundi*, no. 58–59 (Fall 1982–Winter 1983), pp. 114–45.

How the authorities ultimately disposed of the case is a complex story that cannot be recounted here. The immediate task of the investigators was simply to ascertain the facts and if need be to restore order by their very presence. Having accomplished this to their satisfaction after the initial stages of the investigation, they refrained for the moment from taking any other action. For all their measured and deliberate procedures, however, the investigators' horror at what they heard of the relationship between Benedetta and Bartolomea comes through very clearly in the following account. Yet theirs is not the only voice that emerges from the text. Though refracted through the perceptions of other participants—the clerics, who wrote down what they heard or thought they heard, and Bartolomea, who told them what happened or what she thought would implicate her the least—the voice and the longings of Benedetta Carlini can still be heard.

*Department of History*
*Stanford University*

* * *

For two continuous years, two or three times a week, in the evening after disrobing and going to bed and waiting for her companion, who serves her, to disrobe also, she would force her into the bed, and kissing her as if she were a man she would stir herself on top of her so much that both of them corrupted themselves because she held her by force sometimes for one, sometimes for two, sometimes for three hours. And [she did these things] during the most solemn hours, especially in the morning, at dawn. Pretending that she had some need, she would call her, and taking her by force she sinned with her as was said above. Benedetta, in order to have greater pleasure, put her face between the other's breasts and kissed them, and wanted always to be thus on her. And six or eight times, when the other nun did not want to sleep with her in order to avoid sin, Benedetta went to find her in her bed and, climbing on top, sinned with her by force. Also at that time, during the day, pretending to be sick and showing that she had some need, she grabbed her companion's hand by force, and putting it under herself, she would have her put her finger in her genitals, and holding it there she stirred herself so much that she corrupted herself. And she would kiss her and also by force would put her own hand under her companion and her finger into her genitals and corrupted her. And when the latter would flee, she would do the same with her own hands. Many times she locked her companion in the study, and making her sit down in front of her, by force she put her hands under her and corrupted her; she wanted her companion to do the same to her, and while she was doing this she would kiss her. She always appeared to be in a trance while doing this. Her Angel, Splendidiello, did these things, appearing as a boy of eight or nine years of age. This Angel Splendidiello, through the mouth and hands of Benedetta, taught her companion to read and write, making her be near her on her knees and kissing her and putting her hands on her breasts. . . .

This Splendidiello called her his beloved; he asked her to swear to be his beloved always and promised that after Benedetta's death he would always be with her and would make himself visible. He said I want you to promise me not to confess these things that we do together, I assure you that there is no sin in it; and while we did these things he said many times: give yourself to me with all your heart and soul and then let me do as I wish. . . .

The same Angel managed it so that neither Benedetta nor her companion did the usual [spiritual] exercises that the nuns did prior to general confession. He made the sign of the cross all over his companion's body after having committed with her many dishonest acts; [he also said] many words that she couldn't understand and when she asked him why he was doing this, he said that he did this for her own good. Jesus spoke to her companion [through Benedetta] three times, twice before doing these dishonest things. The first time he said he wanted her to be his bride and he was content that she give him her hand, and she did this thinking it was Jesus. The second time it was in the choir at 40 hours, holding her hands together and telling her that he forgave her all her sins. The third time it was after she was disturbed by these affairs and he told her that there was no sin involved whatsoever and that Benedetta while doing these things had no awareness of them. All these things her companion confessed with very great shame.

# D.S. Bailey and "the Name Forbidden among Christians"

JONATHAN SINCLAIR CAREY*

"Without sexuality there can be no full humanity," declared Emil Brunner in *The Divine Imperative*.[1] His statement appeared in the context of discussing Christian marriage, especially in the light of Pauline theology, and with the acknowledgment that neither in marriage nor in sexual experience itself does a person become fully human. Sexuality, it is true, does reveal part of our response to God and our understanding of the order of creation. In 1937, however, when the first English edition of the book appeared, neither Brunner nor members of the pre-war Church of England could have realized the immense turmoil to come, involving the meaning of both humanity and sexuality after the war.[2] The issue of homosexuality, in particular, provided an important forum and focal point.

The 1957 work of the Wolfenden Committee caused substantial attention to be paid to the issues of homosexuality and prostitution.[3] Ten years later, the Sexual Offences Act of 1967 was passed,[4] allowing homosexual acts committed by two consenting members of the same sex, both over the age of twenty-one, in the privacy of their homes. Yet the Wolfenden Committee paved the way for this legal enactment, bringing

---

* *Editor's Note:* Jonathan Sinclair Carey is a moral theologian and philosopher of medicine. He was educated at Boston College, Princeton Seminary, Yale University, the Society of Apothecaries in London, and Oxford University.

1 *The Divine Imperative: A Study in Christian Ethics*, trans. Olive Wyon (London: Lutterworth, 1937), 356. Note that the same year the first English publication appeared of Havelock Ellis, *Sex in Relation to Society* (London: Heinemann, 1937), which was vol. six of the *Studies in the Psychology of Sex*, and which first appeared in English in 1918 (Philadelphia: Davis).

2 For a general history of the English attitude regarding sexuality during the era, see such books as Jeffrey Weeks, *Sex, Politics and Society: The Regulation of Sexuality Since 1800* (London: Longman, 1981), esp. chap. 12; Weeks. *Coming Out: Homosexual Politics in Britain from the 19th Century to the Present* (London: Quartet, 1977); H. Montgomery Hyde, *The Other Love: An Historical and Contemporary Survey of Homosexuality in Britain* (London: Heinemann, 1970).

3 *Report of the [Wolfenden] Committee on Homosexual Offences and Prostitution* (Cmd. 247; HMSO), 1957. See the Sexual Offences Act, 1956, Section 13: "It is an offence for a man to commit an act of gross indecency with another man, whether in public or private, or to be a party to the commission by a man of an act of gross indecency with another man, or to procure the commission by a man of an act of gross indecency with another man."

4 Sexual Offences Act, 1967.

an issue to a head which had not received as much attention since the trials of Oscar Wilde. Although well over two hundred witnesses appeared before the Committee, what became especially noteworthy was the substantial participation of the clergy and members of the medical profession, arguing that change in the law was overdue.

A significant role was played by the Church of England. Not only did Anglicans help to establish the call for reform in the law, but they also produced influential publications that explored the biblical, theological, and moral aspects of homosexuality and homosexual acts, producing sufficent evidence to refute a number of erroneous views about the subject in the Judeo-Christian tradition and in western society.

The Church of England committee that addressed the homosexual questions, as well as provided testimony to the Wolfenden Committee, was the Moral Welfare Council.[5] In 1952, after two well-known gentlemen were arrested for importuning and tried,[6] the members of the Moral Welfare Council voted that the subject of homosexuality and the law was "timely," especially given the fact that the two convicted gentlemen received unusually severe prison sentences under the law.[7] This admitted severity under certain archaic laws, combined with the increasing awareness of homosexual practices in England, suggested that ecclesiastical attention was due.

Under the guidance of the Rev. Dr. Derrick Sherwin Bailey (1910–84), a group of clergy, doctors, and lawyers studied the existing materials on homosexuality. They then produced a privately printed pamphlet titled *The Problem of Homosexuality*.[8] This interim report, written by Bailey, signalled the first twentieth-century extended treatment of homosexuality by an ecclesiastical body. Not only did it examine the current medical, psychological, and sociological literature, but it also sought to address the role of the Church of England in the issue of reforming the law. The Moral Welfare Council recognized the role of the

---

[5] No adequate history of the Moral Welfare Council and its antecedents exists. The modern Council was established in the 1920s to work with prostitutes and the homeless. With the advent of the Second World War, its duties became much more diversified, as its 1947 Constitution indicates, so that it "shall act as a central council of the Church which aims at the co-ordination of thought and action in relation to the place of sex, marriage and the family in the Christian life. Its activities shall fall under the following heads:—1. Educational work; 2. Protective work; 3. Remedial work."

[6] Peter Wildeblood, once diplomatic journalist of the *Daily Mail*, and Lord Montagu were arrested and tried, convicted and imprisoned. See Peter Wildeblood, *A Way of Life* (London: Weidenfeld & Nicolson, 1956); and Peter Coleman, *Christian Attitudes to Homosexuality* (London: SPCK, 1980), esp. 162f.

[7] Coleman, *Christian Attitudes*, provides a fair historical presentation of the situation.

[8] *The Problem of Homosexuality: An Interim Report by a Group of Anglican Clergy and Doctors*, produced for the Church of England Moral Welfare Council by the Church Information Board [for private circulation], 1954.

State in regulating society, but it was clearly the case that the rights of the homosexual were being violated, and this issue needed to be addressed.

This essay will examine the Anglican response to the problem of homosexuality during the 1954–55 period. The formal work of the Moral Welfare Council will be considered in the three major documents it prepared: *The Problem of Homosexuality* (1954), *The Homosexual, the Law, and Society* (1955), and *The Homosexual and Christian Morals* (1955), all of which were written by Bailey, as was the enormously influential *Homosexuality and the Western Christian Tradition* (1955), still reprinted today.[9]

Bailey's writings helped the Church of England to respond to the theological issue of homosexuality, to homosexuals themselves, as well as to the laws of England. This 1954–55 period in the Moral Welfare Council provided important conceptual guidelines for subsequent discussions about homosexuality, not only in the Church of England but throughout Christendom. Examination of Bailey's writings is especially pertinent and timely, given the renewed debates in the Church about homosexuality and homosexual acts, and especially for the current generation more familiar with John Boswell's influential *Christianity, Social Tolerance, and Homosexuality* (1980) than the foundational work of Bailey.

## I

The 1954 publication of *The Problem of Homosexuality* attracted considerable attention. Copies were circulated in churches and theological colleges, and also to members of Parliament. Sections of the pamphlet were quoted in the House of Lords.[10] It has even been suggested that the pamphlet brought about the call for a public inquiry by the British government into homosexuality. Because the pamphlet received so much attention, it is worth close examination.

*The Problem of Homosexuality* is divided into five sections. The first sought to define the "condition" of homosexuality, trying to identify the distinctions among the bisexual, pervert, casual, and habitual adherents to homosexual practices. These distinctions are still seen as falling under the general heading of pervert, that is, to the person who turns from a

[9] The three documents were compiled in *Sexual Offenders and Social Punishment: Being the Evidence Submitted on Behalf of the Church of England Moral Welfare Council to the Departmental Committee on Homosexual Offences and Prostitutions, with Other Materials Relating Thereto* (London: Church Information Office, 1956), subsequently referred to here as *SO*. The book *Homosexuality and the Western Christian Tradition* (London: Longmans, Green, 1955; reprinted Hamden, Conn.: Archon, 1975) is hereinafter referred to as *HWCT*.

[10] See the Introduction to *SO*; also Coleman, *Christian Attitudes*, 163.

natural attraction for those of the opposite sex to a temporary desire for venereal pleasure with a member of the same sex and who transgresses both natural and civil law. But what needs to be considered is the authentic condition of the invert—the homosexual who does not necessarily commit homosexual acts, but a person with a peculiar attraction for those of the same sex. In other words, the homosexual, whether pervert or invert, must be theologically regarded as a sinner, a person who has turned from the natural order of God's creation. This condition, though, may by psychological in orientation, not just as a genital fixation, as would be the case with the pervert, or a total aversion to members of the opposite sex, a fallacy held by many about homosexuals. The pervert recognizes motivations, whether for ephemeral venereal pleasure (and perhaps financial gain); the invert seeks to be recognized for what he or she is—without preconceived moral expectations.

In the second section the pamphlet explored the various theories of inversion. Physically, the invert is seen to be normal. Whether the condition stems from an unhappy childhood or a particular attachment to one parent, the actual cause cannot be determined. It is agreed that most people experience an attraction for someone of the same sex during youth. That some people do not establish heterosexual relationships in the maturing years would be considered a sign of emotional immaturity; even that consideration, however, does not say much about the aetiology of the homosexual condition. In fact, even the homosexual condition cannot readily be perceived outside of the frank admission of the individual or the social consequences of behavior, especially against the law.

These actions give rise to the inevitable moral and religious aspects of a society: the subject of section three. The point is made that the invert should not be blamed for the condition, nor punished; but "we may expect him by the grace of God to resist the temptations to which his condition gives rise, and to come to terms with his 'condition.'"[11] Heterosexual love is unquestionably the norm because "It is connected with God's purpose in creating Man as a male-female duality."[12] This ordinance culminates in the idea of *henōsis*—the one-flesh union, a theme stressed throughout Bailey's writings.[13] The homosexual cannot achieve this type of union, despite the claims of Alfred Kinsey, who wrote of how the homosexual responds to the same psychological sexual stimuli as does the heterosexual. One critical aspect of the *henōsis* is that it can

[11] *SO*, 13.
[12] Ibid.
[13] In particular, see *The Mystery of Love and Marriage. A Study in the Theology of Sexual Relations* (London: SCM, 1952).

lead to procreation and the development of the family unit, an integral part of humanity and God's command to go forth and multiply.

This does not mean, though, that the homosexual is encouraged to marry. This would present no solution because the spouse would never experience the *henōsis*. Homosexual marriages could not be tolerated because of their failure to allow the *henōsis* and therefore the procreating of offspring, and because of the sociological reality that most homosexual unions tend to last no more than four years.

The invert, according to the pamphlet, warrants sympathetic understanding:

> He is confronted with the "tragic" alternative of doing his duty (the will of God) and suffering a sense of sexual deprivation in the doing of it, or of following his sexual inclinations at the expense of his conscience.[14]

In other words, the invert deserves sympathy and acceptance for his or her condition. When homosexual acts are involved, however, then the Church must respond differently:

> It is a matter of Christian experience that faithful acceptance of a difficult way of life in response to a moral demand always finds reinforcement in a powerful movement from God towards man.[15]

The homosexual, according to the pamphlet, has traditionally found avenues for productive service in society through such vocations as art, drama, teaching, welfare services, and the ministry. Turning to man in service is turning to God, as well as to the moral law, for the homosexual.

Homosexual acts, though, are sins against God—in no uncertain terms. Sodomy—and the term is used in a general sense—means an immoral use of the sexual organs, especially when young children are involved.[16] The Moral Welfare Council thought that the sodomite should confront his sin; for it is his guilt that will prove an incipient means of dealing with homosexual acts, at least in one of three ways:

1. He can rationalize the whole sinful situation so that it seems to pertain to only one particular circumstance. This therefore allows the sod-

---

[14] *SO*, 15.

[15] Ibid.

[16] Civil and canon law use the term *sodomy* for a variety of sexual offenses, and not just those between members of the same sex. See Vern Bullough, *Sexual Variance in Society and History* (Chicago: University of Chicago Press, 1976); Michael Goodich, *The Unmentionable Vice: Homosexuality in the Later Medieval Period* (Oxford: ABC-Clio, 1979); "Sodomy in Ecclesiastical Law and Theory," *Journal of Homosexuality* 1 (1976); "Sodomy in Medieval Secular Law," ibid.

omite to continue with a self-deception of regarding only particular acts, never considering them in light of his own humanity.

2. He can continue in doing what he knows is wrong, living with a perpetually uneasy conscience. Inevitably, however, stress will result, resulting in serious (and inevitable) consequences.

3. He can confront his sin and accept it for what it is. From the recognition of weakness comes the desire for cleansing.

The Church, of course, seeks to promote the third possibility. The confession of sin commences the process of reconciliation. After this confession, moral reinstatement and divine liberation result. The invert must refrain from his old habits and ever-present instincts. He must guard against associating with perverts in particular, the "occasions of sin," and he must earnestly desire to rejoin the Christian community. The sacraments will provide

> the divine provision for this emergency, and many an invert who has passed through such a religious revolution has in his own experience come gradually to enter into that of St. Paul; "Nothing is beyond my powers, thanks to the strength God gives me."[17]

The contemporary reader may consider this account of reconcilation as seeming unduly simplistic. In terms of the history of the Christian church, such is not the case. If anything, the Moral Welfare Council of 1954 was attempting to restore some of the power attached to the ancient penitentials. More about their structure will be said later. The immediate point is that the Church offers the invert a place, just as it seeks to offer all Christians a refuge. This does not mean that anyone ultimately escapes the moral demands of a society, whether homosexual or heterosexual, but that in a sacramental context forgiveness is always possible.

After the treatment of morals and religion, the pamphlet concludes with the crucial topic of the law and the male homosexual. Here the Moral Welfare Council demonstrated its understanding of the past laws that defined homosexual acts.[18] On the one hand, the Council objected to the fact that there was inequality in the existing law: males arrested for importuning received severe punishment; females were hardly bothered. Life imprisonment also seemed unusually cruel. On the other hand, the prevailing law encouraged blackmail; the underworld domain of both inverts and perverts flourished because society allowed them no freedom.

---

[17] *SO*, 18.

[18] *SO* contains a fairly detailed compilation of the relevant sections of law pertaining to homosexuality, as well as statistical information on the increase in homosexual offenses in England and Wales, to indicate that reform in the law was necessary.

Arrest, publicity, trial, and ruin of career were vivid realities. In even more drastic occasions, inverts were known to commit suicide from fear of exposure.

These factors only encouraged citizens to view homosexuality with mixed reactions. Frequently only the activities of the pervert were known, the invert misunderstood entirely. As the pamphlet revealed, many inverts lived lonely and deprived lives because of an intense fear of detection: even as inverts, moral judgments were pronounced upon them. No matter what their conduct, their label spoke louder than their actions.

The Council produced an effective pamphlet in *The Problem of Homosexuality*. It caused public attention, both secular and ecclesiastical, to begin to be paid to the issues involving justice in the private realm of sexual conduct. If the English laws were not prosecuting individuals for fornicating or committing adultery—heterosexual offenses against moral laws—then similar policies had to be enforced in the private conduct of the homosexual. It meant a change in the law and an examination of religious, moral, and legislative principles, all of which would be undertaken in the following years.

That the Church of England should produce such a study deserves more attention. Sigmund Freud and Havelock Ellis, for example, had published sexual studies since the beginning of the twentieth century.[19] Further, specialized groups, such as the British Society for the Study of Sex Psychology, began to appear in the early 1920s. But churches were reluctant to become involved in controversial sexual issues, except with such notable exceptions as birth control and the rise in divorces. To produce a study on homosexuality meant acknowledging the unavoidable need for a theological understanding of the "condition."

This 1954 pamphlet might take on a different significance when contrasted with the remark made by Otto Piper in his book *The Christian Interpretation of Sex* (1942) when he frankly admitted that "innate homosexuality faces us with a very difficult and thus far insoluble problem."[20] Piper went no further with the point. The Moral Welfare Council was likewise unable to resolve the difficulties; yet its presentation of the available material concerning inversion, a term borrowed from Ellis, showed a desire to articulate more about homosexuality in a Christian context.

---

[19] Sigmund Freud, *Three Essays on the Theory of Sexuality*, trans. and ed. James Strachey (London: Hogarth, 1974). First printed in German in 1905, Freud's book acknowledged his indebtedness to Ellis's earlier work, especially his *Sexual Inversion*, in the chapter on sexual aberrations.

[20] Otto A. Piper, *The Christian Interpretation of Sex* (New York: Scribner, 1941; London: Nisbet, 1942), p. 143.

Bailey knew that *The Problem of Homosexuality* was no more than a preliminary work.[21] Many of its central themes—inversion, *henōsis*, sexual justice, and moral responsibility—would be repeated, sometimes clarified or reconsidered, in the rest of his publications. The point, though, must be reiterated that the pamphlet, no matter how incipient its presentation and seemingly simplistic its arguments, had a formidable impact on the political and ecclesiastical realms. It also demonstrated that the Church of England felt a responsibility to address this controversial topic, which concerned not just the question of sexuality but the definition of humanity as well.

The pamphlet also introduced Bailey's participation in a field explored by few theologians. Brunner had written nothing, Piper but little,[22] and Barth only a few passing condemnatory remarks in his *Church Dogmatics*, first published in 1951.[23] The subject of homosexuality was avoided in almost the classic stance of "the name forbidden among Christians." Bailey's inductive work combined such diverse elements as sociology, law, and medical opinion in order to approach the subject without dogmatic or scriptural arguments, the past mode of argumentation. In fact, the pamphlet commenced with a statement that additional materials would be forthcoming to treat the biblical, historical, theological, and moral aspects of homosexuality in England. He meant for his study to be as thorough as possible.

The pamphlet, along with other calls for reform from various influential groups, created the requisite pressures on Parliament. On 28 April 1954 a departmental committee was established, formally constituted on 26 August with Sir John Wolfenden as head.[24]

## II

On 30 March 1955 three members of the Council were interviewed by the Wolfenden Committee. Bailey wrote both of the items submitted as formal evidence; they appeared, with several additional articles he wrote, in *Sexual Offenders and Social Punishment*. In the evidence presented, whether written or spoken, Bailey said they were aware of their Christian responsibilities in coming forth to testify, yet they did not see their immediate function as dealing with morality and theological opinion. Instead, their role was to present a look at current justice toward

[21] *SO*, Introduction.

[22] Piper, *Christian Interpretation of Sex*, 143, 190, 210.

[23] Karl Barth, *Church Dogmatics*, trans. G.W. Bromiley, III/4 (Edinburgh: Clark, 1978), 166.

[24] Coleman, *Christian Attitudes*, 166.

the homosexual from the perspective of the Church of England. As Bailey wrote,

> The church's prime responsibility, both to Christians and to the nation as a whole, was to secure as far as possible an intelligent, unbiased, and calm discussion such as might lead eventually to a solution of the whole problem consistent with the well-being of society and the demands of equity.[25]

Because of certain religious assumptions, scientific ignorance, and biased societal impressions about homosexuality, the homosexual in England was confronted with difficulty. As in the earlier publication, so here the point was made that homosexual acts were not the only consideration in defining homosexuality. The nature of the invert *sui generis* needed attention. Yet where the pamphlet had sought to be precise in defining the four classifications of homosexuals (bisexual, pervert, casual, and habitual) and then treating the invert, the formal evidence submitted in *The Homosexual, the Law, and Society* spoke in considerably broader terms, stressing contributory factors such as the effect of an unhappy marriage on the inverted child, a faulty relationship in the family, death, divorce, or prolonged war service.

Bailey believed that homosexual practices themselves were neither more nor less harmful than heterosexual practices. The point was that only fallacious reasoning would convict the invert of a crime, whether by social ostracism or by the even more serious reality of imprisonment. Prosecution was bad enough; persecution of the invert, intolerable. Exposure and social ruin loom in the back of all homosexuals' minds, and thus there is considerable loneliness complicated by the omnipresent threat of blackmail and the truth that suicides occur upon detection.

For these reasons the homosexual must be protected by justice, not penalized. The Council could not accept the inequality in the law where female homosexuals were relatively unpunished while male homosexuals were severely punished with five- or ten-year imprisonments. As the report stated:

> It is the responsibility of society at large to see that those of its members who are handicapped by inversion are assisted to a constructive acceptance of their condition, and are helped to lead useful and creative lives—thus benefitting both themselves and the community, to the service of which their special gifts can often make an important contribution.[26]

---

[25] *SO*, 25.
[26] Ibid., 36.

Reform of the law might secure justice and understanding for the invert, but that will not solve the admitted problem of homosexuality. Only until better marriages and happier family relationships are established in a more settled and secure condition of life will its main causes be eliminated. Expressed in a different way, the invert must always be considered in relation to the family; to consider the invert solely in relation to himself or herself is to say little about their "condition" and the role they might assume in society and in the Church.

The formal report to the Wolfenden Committee did not contain a section later included in the published report and deserving attention here.[27] In this section the Council discussed the moral and religious aspects of homosexual practice. Their recommendation was that the Church of England must demonstrate leadership in the homosexual issue. Theological and pastoral work were needed in addition to the basic concern of reforming the law; the Church should use its influence to protect the invert as well as to educate the public about the nature of the invert. The State must have a means of protecting the private rights of the individual as well as a proper means of disciplining transgressors. In other words, the homosexual must be accepted in the Church; homosexual acts condemned are to be handled effectively in the rites of the Church of England. Unless the Church can offer such love and support for the homosexual, then its attitude will appear to prefer a discussion of theodicy over a concern for individual Christians.

Critics of this stance by the Council accused the Church of being too lenient. Yet the power of the evidence submitted comes from the admitted recognition of the rights of both heterosexual and homosexual. The Church must not be the only party concerned with moral judgments, nor are moral judgments its sole concern. This realm belongs to individuals and, to a certain extent, to the State as well. A pastoral responsibility must be paramount in the Church if the homosexual, whether male or female, practicing or non-practicing sexually, is to be a part of it. Such a pastoral attitude would enable the Church to speak forth, both to its people and to any laws of the land that might seem unfair.

In this regard, the Council made three specific recommendations: (1) that certain sections of various laws providing harsh penalties for importuning be reconsidered or repealed; (2) that any male or female caught in a homosexual act with someone under the age of consent, or in circumstances constituting a public nuisance, or involving assault, be penalized; and (3) that better facilities for such prisoners be made available, where suitable professional care, spiritual as well as psychological, can be offered. A minor note was also attached to the recommenda-

27 Ibid., 63–79.

tion, raising the age of consent from sixteen to seventeen (eventually it would be made twenty-one, ostensibly to protect the State from undue concern over homosexual offenses in the military service).

The attitude displayed in this particular evidence deserves comment. As was noted earlier, *The Homosexual, the Law, and Society* was not written as an explicitly theological essay; on the contrary, the reader must search long and hard to discover any particular theological position presented, except in the section on morals and religion, which was not a part of the formal evidence submitted. In this regard, Bailey has crafted a statement without precedent in the Anglican Church on the topic.

## III

In addition to the evidence mentioned, which was technically presented by the entire Council, Bailey offered what was called "personal evidence": his book *Homosexuality and the Western Christian Tradition*. For the first time, a theologian had assembled the corpus of materials dealing with homosexuality and the Christian church. The intention of the book was to examine the historical and theological factors that contributed to the formation of the traditional western Christian attitude to homosexuality and homosexual practices. Anthropologists and cultural historians, psychologists and social scientists had all discussed the reality of homosexuality in the world, ranging from Bronislaw Malinowski's classic *The Sexual Life of Savages in North-West Melanesia* (1929), to Margaret Mead's *Coming of Age in Samoa* (1929), to the decisive two volumes of A. C. Kinsey on male (1948) and female (1953) sexuality.[28] Now a theologian approached the topic. His scholarship in this regard remained the unsurpassed treatment of the subject until the 1980 publication of Boswell's *Christianity, Social Tolerance, and Homosexuality*.[29]

In some ways, Bailey's work explicitly responded to a quotation by the famous British jurist Sir William Blackstone:

> The crime against nature was one which the voice of nature and of reason, and the express law of God, determine to be capital. Of which we have a signal instance, long before the Jewish dispensation, by the destruction of two cities by fire from heaven; so that this is an universal, not merely a provincial precept.[30]

---

[28] See Graham Heath, *The Illusory Freedom: The Intellectual Origins and Social Consequences of the Sexual "Revolution"* (London: Heinemann Medical, 1978), chap. 1.

[29] John Boswell, *Christianity, Social Tolerance, and Homosexuality: Gay People in Western Europe from the Beginning of the Christian Era to the Fourteenth Century* (Chicago: University of Chicago Press, 1980). Boswell refers to Bailey's book in an extended footnote on p. 4, *et passim*.

[30] *HWCT*, 153.

Bailey was unconvinced that nature, reason, and the express law of God could be effective agents of condemnation against homosexuality. English society had, for too long, promulgated its hostility on such traditional evidence and attitudes; but what, he demanded, was really being said? By turning to Scripture and law, to the original sources themselves, the actual conscious and unconscious aspects of "the tradition" could be pinpointed.

Without question, the Bible—and, in particular, the story of Sodom—shaped much of the traditional attitudes about homosexuality in the Judeo-Christian heritage. Bailey, though, demanded that the relevant text in Gen 19:4-11 be reconsidered. The story itself is well known and shall not be retold here. Instead, let us consider the crucial text: "Bring them out unto us, that we may know them" (Gen 19:5). Countless generations assumed the line meant that the residents of Sodom desired to commit homosexual acts upon Lot's guests. Yet Bailey argues that such an interpretation was without doubt contrary to the author's intention.

In the first place, based on an extended study of the Hebrew verb *yadha*, which can mean sexual contact as well as the social act of cognizance, Bailey argued that the scriptural citations of *yadha* in a coital fashion occur fewer than ten times, and these all indicate heterosexual intercourse. In the second place, several more plausible accounts of the author's intention can be advanced on careful exegesis. The interpretation favored by Bailey involved hospitality: Lot was a *ger*, a foreigner in Sodom, implying certain liabilities; it was therefore possible that the residents were alarmed by the presence of the visitors and sought *to know* their *bona fides*. Whatever the precise case, Bailey concluded that "It is clear that the destruction of Sodom and Gomorrah was an historical event, and that it was due to natural and not supernatural causes."[31]

Even more important than the actual narrative was how "the tradition" in Judaism and Christianity assumed in later periods that homosexuality was the topic in Genesis 19. Certainly Sodom was depicted throughout the Old Testament as a symbol of utter destruction, but nowhere does Scripture identify Sodom's sin explicitly with homosexual practices. After reviewing extensive corroborating texts of the period, from Scripture and historical accounts, Bailey concluded that the narrative was nothing more than a post-Exilic Jewish interpretation devised and exploited by patriotic rigorists for polemical motives.[32] Such a conclusion still did not speak to how the Christian attitude was developed through the succeeding centuries. The fact that there are only six explicit references to homosexuality in the entire Bible (five refer to males, one to

31 *HWCT*, 8.
32 *HWCT*, 60.

females, one to a general condemnation) would not justify the harsh attitude common to many people.

Bailey assumed that the scriptural writers were only addressing homosexual perverts. The Bible did not speak to the psychological state itself, and hence the invert went unrecognized. The consequences were serious. Rabbis were unsympathetic to transgressors; early Christians, equally antagonistic. By assembling classical and biblical source materials, Bailey was able to undermine many of the common assumptions about homosexuality in religion, such as the case that most of the English Bibles mistranslated the terms normally associated with sexual deviance as in 1 Corinthians 6:9f—"effeminate" and "abusers of themselves with men."[33]

He next focused his attention upon the question of the law and homosexuality. Theodosius and Justinian exerted a tremendous influence when they codified the civil practices, not only on western society, but also on the development of ecclesiastical law. To the time of Justinian, the major law concerning homosexuality was the *lex Scantinia.* This law punished homosexual offenses by imposing a heavy fine; and it revealed the extent to which the Romans considered homosexual offenses. Justinian, though, issued the first *novellae* against homosexual acts in 538. Where Theodosius spoke of the "unnaturalness" of the act and imposed a fine, Justinian emphasized that unnatural lusts would be punished by the law—but only if the accused would not repent and confess his sin. The point at hand was that the law recognized the ecclesiastical privilege in dealing with homosexuality. It must also be stressed that Bailey did not believe there was a "veritable crusade" against homosexuality among the Christian emperors because only four edicts appeared in the course of two hundred years.[34] The law in the Christian West might thereby be seen as remarkably ancillary to the structures imposed by the church on this question.

This did not imply that all the church fathers had lenient ideas about homosexuality. Tertullian wrote:

> All other frenzies of the lusts which exceed the laws of nature and are impious towards (human) bodies and the sexes we banish, not only from the threshold but also from all shelter of the Church, for they are not sins as much as monstrosities.[35]

Augustine and Chrysostom supported this general sense, functioning as hostile critics of perverted activities, using Sodom and Gomorrah as the divine example of transgression and its punishment. Thus the church

[33] See Boswell, *Christianity*, 344–52.
[34] *HWCT*, 79.
[35] *HWCT*, 82.

fathers and the councils responded exclusively to the pervert. Of particular importance was the development of the penitentials in this regard. These penitentials, originating primarily in Wales, presented a detailed means of evaluating both homosexual offenses and concomitant penalties. It must be noted that heterosexual and homosexual offenses were treated with equal zeal.

Bailey did not see the medieval church as being overly concerned with homosexuality, although historians and theologians tended to cite from the penitentials for proof of such a concern. According to Bailey's findings, less than a hundred references to homosexuality appear in all of the penitentials. This would hardly be adequate evidence for suggesting that Christians held an especial vendetta against the practicing homosexual. Certainly the homosexual was denounced as one guilty of grave sin; but he (or she) was not singled out any more than the adulterer was by comparison. Reconciliation with God and man could result through the penitentials. The major shortcoming of this approach, according to Bailey, came from its failure to address homosexuality itself, referring instead to specific homosexual acts. This situation will be addressed shortly.

The subject of English law attracted much attention in *Homosexuality and the Western Christian Tradition*. Bailey believed that local attitudes through the centuries would illuminate another facet of modern assumptions about homosexuality in England. He quoted from the thirteenth-century *Fleta*, one of the earliest accounts of law in the country:

> Those who have dealings with Jews or Jewesses, those who commit bestiality, and sodomists, are to be buried alive, after legal proof that they were taken in the act, and public conviction.[36]

By the year 1290, when the document was written, homosexuality was identified as being a distinctly Jewish problem—and hence its being "the name forbidden among Christians"—and unknown in England. What was noteworthy about the *Fleta* was its identification of sexual transgressions with such an item as talking or doing business with a Jew. In 1533, through, a major change occurred. Under Henry VIII "buggery," as the document retitled sodomitical acts, was still punishable by death; yet now the law alone held responsibility for trying and punishing the culprit. The church no longer could either intervene or usurp the role of punisher and forgiver through the penitential system.

Bailey believed that this sixteenth-century development radically altered the perception of homosexuality in England. It meant that for over

[36] *HWCT*, 145.

three hundred years capital punishment was enacted upon the homosexual offender. Not until 1861 did English law remove the death penalty, and not until 1885 did homosexuality come under the control of criminal law. That the criminal stigma had been attached to homosexuals indicated to Bailey that England had no sympathy for the invert. In more direct terms, the law had commanded responsibilities for which it was totally unsuitable for administering. In the twentieth century more information had been uncovered about the various forms of homosexuality, and indeed of homosexual acts. Without question, moralists, pastors, and psychiatrists were needed as spokesmen, not the law. Bailey thought that the Church especially had much to offer in the way of rectifying several of the dangerous attitudes about homosexuality that had been perpetuated in its name. In some ways, the law had fallen victim to these incorrect attitudes, ironically enough, contorting them even more, influencing public opinion, and increasingly forcing the invert to grow in fear.

The biblical, historical, and legal discussion in the book was undergirded by the assumption that the extent of homosexual practices and perversion in a society indicated its general picture. Bailey believed adamantly that the so-called problem of homosexuality was produced by the corruption in society and, equally as important, the abandonment of moral responsibility in the field of heterosexual relationships. His academic interest in this situation led to his writing *The Man-Woman Relation in Christian Thought* four years later.[37] It also influenced his important contribution to the 1958 Lambeth Conference on *The Family in Contemporary Society*.[38] For Bailey, the heterosexual relationship was the standard, homosexuality aberrant. Only in the context of the family can the rightful nature of creation be established; both law and the Church must work for this man-woman balance.

The balance, admittedly, does not result easily. Homosexuality has not only called the family into question; it has also forced the law and Church to reconsider the definitions of humanity. Part of this work entailed understanding better the phenomenon known as inversion. By Bailey's estimate, Scripture spoke only of those who commit homosexual offenses, not of inversion itself. Therefore, to assume that the dictates of both right reason and nature can be determined in how one both identifies and judges the homosexual is difficult, Bailey found, contrary to Blackstone's forthright declaration quoted earlier, because such oft-cited sources as the Sodom and Gomorrah narrative tell us little. As Bailey declared, "The question of sexual inversion takes us from the anomalies in

37 (London: Longman, 1959).

38 *The Family in Contemporary Society: Report of a Group Convened at the Behest of the Archbishop of Canterbury* (London: SPCK, 1958).

the western tradition to its deficiencies as a guide to the handling of modern problems."[39] In other words, inversion itself must be considered morally neutral. The invert, mindful of this condition, can be a valuable member of society and the Church, and this attitude must be inculcated in modern thinking. Unfortunately, the Christian tradition offered little in the way of assistance, if only in offering scriptural citations to identify the invert and his role in the world. The prejudices, based on a misconceived understanding of the homosexual throughout history, has not helped in promoting a positive reason for welcoming the homosexual. As Bailey reiterated in no uncertain terms, "Our tradition gives us no assistance; nor gives us direction for comprehending inversion."[40]

He was acutely aware of this point as he began to respond to homosexuality in the 1950s. His interpretation of homosexuality and the western Christian tradition was expressly placed into the English context—precisely because of the Wolfenden Committee. Recognizing this explicit theological purpose will defend Bailey from Boswell's criticism in which he acknowledges that Bailey's work still stands as the major work on the subject, even if his scholarship has been superseded, especially on the point of his interpretation of *yadha* as hospitality, but that the book suffers from its "negative sanctions."[41]

Bailey placed his scholarship as "personal evidence" with the Wolfenden Committee, aware of the political and theological climate of the time, trying to frame his work in the perspective of law and Church. That Boswell would not recognize these intentional cultural limitations is understandable. Placed in the context of the 1950s, the book supplied information which neither the psychiatrist nor lawyer would know. This information from a theologian could be seen as interpreting the mindset of a nation about homosexuality through the course of many centuries. That it still promotes controversy and critical response indicates its success.

The formal evidence submitted to the Wolfenden Committee in *The Homosexual, the Law, and Society* and *Homosexuality in the Western Christian Tradition* still did not indicate any particular theological or ethical consideration of homosexuality in 1955. The formal report submitted by the Moral Welfare Council argued for reform of the law on the grounds of justice—homosexuals deserved equal protection with heterosexuals. The personal evidence submitted by Bailey placed homosexuality in its biblical and theological perspective in the course of the Judeo-Christian development. But, as has been mentioned, Bailey and the other members of the Council recognized that their responsibility was in a

39 *HWCT*, 75.
40 *HWCT*, 169.
41 Boswell, *Christianity*, 4.

clearly reasoned exposition of how the Church of England regarded a need for a reform in the law.

## IV

In 1955 Bailey wrote another article precisely on the topic "The Homosexual and Christian Morals." It first appeared in a widely circulated volume of essays entitled *They Stand Apart* and was subsequently published by the Church of England with the formal report submitted to the Wolfenden Committee and several essays by Bailey in *Sexual Offenders and Social Punishment.*[42] This article completed the logical progression of articles on the problem of homosexuality, providing the first major theological response to the difficulty, earlier mentioned by Piper, of labelling and responding to invert and pervert homosexuals by the Church.

Bailey first recapitulated the common themes of his work, including his interpretation of Genesis 19 and the distinctions between invert and pervert. He argued that the scriptural failure to understand inversion should be seen as an admitted concern for twentieth-century England because of the Judeo-Christian heritage that permeated so many of its institutions and common attitudes. Yet Bailey was quick to note that the silence of Scripture did not suggest that moral judgments could not be made. How these moral judgments could be made, in fact, became the challenge and duty for the modern Christian.

His approach therefore began with a re-examination of the existing law, rather than a treatment of the natural law or the nature of revelation in Scripture. He suggested that the Act of 1533, instigating the death penalty, was a retrograde step, which subsequent laws did not reverse, and which signalled a serious misreading of Christianity, both in the sixteenth century and up to his own day. In fact, Bailey believed the British law represented a departure from the developed Christian usage and tradition of the Middle Ages. From this admission Bailey then strived to establish the ecclesiastical position in its history and theological significance so that the ethical import might be developed in a contemporary attitude, reconstructed in great parts, toward homosexuality.

Categorically, homosexuality was perceived by the Bible as an abomination, a reversal of what was sexually natural, ordained by God. The immediate problem was that moral judgments were passed on sodomitical transgressions, never on the condition of inversion. In this

42 John Tudor Rees and Harley Verneau Usill, eds., *They Stand Apart: A Critical Survey of the Problem of Homosexuality* (London: Heinemann, 1955).

case, the penitentials in Christian tradition had a definite system for responding to the pervert. Sodomy and fellatio were commonly punished with the same impositions as fornication, incest, infanticide, homicide, and adultery. But there was no explanation in these documents as to how the penitential system functioned, that is, how the transgressions were conceptually conceived; and certainly no attention devoted to the condition of homosexuality itself.

Turning to Thomas Aquinas provided the next step in seeking to develop a theological understanding of inversion and perversion. According to Aquinas, a moral act is one consonant with right reason.[43] Since procreation was the proper end of all venereal acts, signifying that coitus was necessary between man and woman, homosexual acts were *contra naturam*, by definition, and inconsistent with right reason. This right reason, though, would also include the problem arising where venereal pleasures between man and woman resulted in premature ejaculation; thus, the meaning of the sexual act can be unnatural, lustful, and sinful with heterosexuals or homosexuals, depending on the act. Therefore a person can understandably have homosexual regards for another, Aquinas admitted, at least in an especial regard for him or her, as one Christian might have for another in the love of Christ—but not when it leads to the attainment of forbidden pleasures.

Aquinas' "objective attitude," in Bailey's words, strongly influenced Bailey's own approach. In the first place, Bailey attempted to unseat the popular notion of sex as a physical or venereal term, normally referring to pleasure. Instead, he sought to reinstate its original meaning of referring to the relationship between man and woman. Right reason meant that the sexual organs could only be involved in heterosexual contact in the henotic bond of marriage. In terms of objective morality, homosexual acts are contrary to the will of God for human sexuality, as established in Scripture and reason, and therefore sinful.

But, in the second place, how does the objective attitude address the invert? What of the argument that whereas homosexual desires were natural to him or her it must be the will of God? Bailey stood firm: "The normal and divinely ordained human condition is the heterosexual, and homosexuality, strictly speaking, is an aberration."[44] "Aberration," however, did not mean a *moral* opinion, for the subject may not be necessarily responsible or culpable: "Inversion can no more be regarded as God's will for a person than can, for example, deformity or mental deficiency."[45] Undoubtedly the discussion would have to involve a consideration of free will and the homosexual.

[43] *SO*, 73.
[44] *SO*, 75.
[45] Ibid.

As Bailey defined it, the question became one of the relationship between the objective morality of an act and the moral culpability of the agent. Bailey cited a traditional example of stealing. What would be the degree of blame assigned to the burglar, the kleptomaniac, or the person in desperate need? According to Bailey, the invert existed in a precarious situation, caught between a religious tradition and the demands of society. His response to the question of stealing would indicate his approach to sexual attitudes. On the one hand, if he refrained from sexual acts with someone of the same sex, then he would be obeying the established tradition; if he sought to be honest with himself and engage in sexual, venereal pleasures, then he would be violating the order of creation.

Conscience played a large part, to be sure, although it could not always be trusted even if obeyed. It was authoritative but not infallible. Education became important. Knowledge and conscience do not alter the objective fact of sin. They only determine the extent to which a sinful act was morally imputable. So what was the role of morality here? Bailey insisted that two kinds of sin must be distinguished: formal sin—that committed knowingly or in vincible ignorance, and material sin—that committed in invincible ignorance, good faith, and clear conscience.

The law and the Church can express objective morality: the law, through its expression of enacted opinion; the Church, through the proclamation of the gospel. The casuist can interpret aspects of the law and ecclesiastical proclamation, but this interpretation can produce a double standard, as in the case of the existing law where males were penalized more than females. Moral responsibility became important to respond to inequalities, recognizing all the while the various sins that influence decisions and fall short of objective morality.

Bailey acknowledged that the invert possessed moral responsibility. In freedom he must decide what action to take in regard to sexual abstention or practice. The Church must assume the homosexual understands the ramifications of decision. The complication occurs, however, because studies indicated that some inverts did not possess an intuitive conviction that homosexual acts were immoral. This finding implied that the objective was neither innate nor heeded knowledge. This signified the importance of formal and material sin in the theological response.

If a person were to indulge in homosexual practices, knowing they were wrong, then he would have committed a formal sin. In many cases, this distinction will involve the pervert rather than the invert, and the agent of a formal sin may be blamed morally. The invert, though, must be seen as in a state of invincible ignorance and not held morally accountable. This distinction allowed Bailey to reiterate the necessity of the objective morality, the allegiance to heterosexual sex in marriage as the will of God and the condition for the *henōsis*. Awareness of sin brought both invert and pervert into a theological perspective in the eyes of the Church, permitting discipline and sacramental offering.

Just because the invert earned the distinction, as it were, of not being culpable, in a sense, subjective laxity would not be permitted by the Church regarding sexual practice. The invert was called to celibacy and to service in the family of Man. Here Bailey treated the difference between *crime* and *sin*. Crime signified conduct of which the State disapproved, and for which a penalty will be demanded; sin, a free transgression of the law of God by thought, word, deed, or neglect to what is enjoined therein.[46] An inevitable tension existed between the two: a crime did not necessarily imply moral wrongdoing, while sin cannot be punished by the State. Thus the Church can prove an effective agent in calling for moral restitutions or changes in legal practice. The reality of sexual immorality becomes an especially sensitive issue because the law must pass judgment, and hence establish the crimes of the State, while the Church must ever seek to correct the transgressions of the individual and bring about reconciliation in the Church.

The invert would sin in sexual practice while the pervert would not only sin but commit a crime as well. Bailey's point here was to protect the invert. By and large, society had made the invert the scapegoat, in his estimation, the supposedly key factor in why the moral problems in England had swelled and the family itself seemed threatened. Such was not the case. And unless the society was willing to condemn adulterers and fornicaters, as well as homosexuals, then it had to re-evaluate its attitudes and especially its laws.

*The Homosexual and Christian Morals* examined how the Church defined homosexuality and homosexual practices from a theological perspective. Bailey wrote what must be regarded as a significant contribution, although it is far from definitive when viewed from a later era. For example, his treatment of Aquinas considered only one aspect. Current opinion about Aquinas stresses his ambiguous conclusions about homosexuality. In another way, his conclusion about the vincible and invincible factors could have opened up another way in precisely defining how the Church of England could respond, whether in renewing certain penitential practices, or offering a different form of support to the invert who seeks to be honest to the society and the Church. In defense of Bailey, however, his article did open up the subject. He did seek to explore homosexuals as more than "sexual irregularities."[47] He avoided a casuistry, or behaviorist methodology, and kept his discussion on the theo-

[46] *SO*, 82.
[47] *SO*, 78.

retical level, recognizing the sinner as human being, trying to respond with an honest, integrated Christian theology. Far from conclusive and systematic, the article did tackle a difficult subject and concluded his major work on the topic during the important period 1954–55.

## V

Obviously the role of the family in post-war Britain concerned many thinkers. But Bailey's writings provided the most systematic theology of sexuality—and humanity—from 1941 to 1961. His writings on homosexuality have attracted the most attention. His most immediate concern was legal—the reform of the law. As part of his overall theology, his response to the problem of homosexuality led him to consider it using biblical, historical, medical, sociological, and moral aspects. Although opposed to homosexual practices, he deeply believed in the rights of the homosexual invert. This belief enabled him to approach the topics of humanity and sexuality with critical insights. As he wrote in *The Homosexual and Christian Morals:*

> Heterosexuality and homosexuality are not alternative human conditions, nor is the invert (man or woman) a sort of *tertium quid* between male and female; he is an anomaly whose sexual disorientation bears its own tragic witness to the disordering of humanity by sin.[48]

The theologian thereby has a means of response through the recognition of sin and the means of forgiveness. In this case, by seeking to understand the disorientation of the homosexual—whatever its causes and whatever it subsequently implies about God's will or the issue of theodicy--the theologian can learn more about the will of God as it pertains to man and woman.[49]

Although no extended analytical essay has been written on Bailey's writings, his influence on the Church of England, primarily through his work on the Moral Welfare Council, was extensive even if curiously neglected for over two decades. As we have seen, the 1954–55 period was an especially critical one for his influential work at the time.

Ten years afterwards, Helmut Thielicke wrote in his *Theological Ethics* about Bailey (and the psychiatrist Theodore Bovet):

---

[48] *SO*, 76.

[49] In 1953 Bailey published "Sexual Relationship and the Command of God," *Churchman* 67 (1953): 81–89, in which he argued that sex must be seen as part of the creative purpose of God and as revealed in Scripture. This does not mean that man and woman can ever comprehend their sexuality, but in relationship to God its purpose becomes clearer. This is one of the few articles in which Bailey cites Barth.

It is significant that the only two theological or lay-theological authors who have explicitly pursued the problem of homosexuality and orientated themselves in the medical literature without desiring to compromise the normative criteria of theology—thinking of these criteria not as *given* doctrinaire propositions, but rather *seeking* for them—both recognize the exclusive competence of the physician and the pastor and reject that of the criminal judge. This should give us pause.[50]

In 1955, however, Bailey's publications produced much discussion, much of it controversial, because of their attempts to deal theologically and realistically with the difficult problem of homosexuality. Derrick Sherwin Bailey helped the Anglican Church to come of age regarding sexuality and humanity. His name should not be one forgotten among Christians.

[Research for this article was assisted with a grant from the Blair O. Rogers Medical Research Fund.—*J.S.C.*]

---

50 Helmut Thielicke, *Theological Ethics: Sex*, trans. John W. Doberstein (Grand Rapids: Eerdmans, 1979), 274.

# ON THE CONNECTION BETWEEN HOMOSEXUALITY AND DIVINATION AND THE IMPORTANCE OF THE INTERMEDIATE SEXES GENERALLY IN EARLY CIVILIZATIONS.

By EDWARD CARPENTER.

A curious and interesting subject is the connection of the Uranian temperament with prophetic gifts and divination. It is a subject which, as far as I know, has not been seriously considered—though it has been touched upon by Elie Reclus, Westermarck and others. The fact is well known, of course, that in the temples and cults of antiquity and of primitive races it has been a widespread practice to educate and cultivate certain youths in an effeminate manner, and that these youths in general become the priests or medicine-men of the tribe; but this fact has hardly been taken seriously, as indicating any necessary connection between the two functions, or any relation in general between homosexuality and psychic powers. Some such relation or connection, however, I think we must admit as being indicated, and the question is what it may be.

In the account given in the Bible of the reforming zeal of King Josiah (2 Kings XXIII) we are told (v. 4) that "the King commanded Hilkiah the high priest, and the priests of the second order, and the keepers of the door, to bring forth out of the temple of the Lord all the vessels that were made for Baal, and for the grove, and for all the host of heaven; and he burned them without Jerusalem in the fields of Kidron. . . . And he brake down the houses of the Sodomites, that were by the house of the Lord, where the women wove hangings for the grove."

The word here translated "Sodomites" is the Hebrew word Kedeshim, meaning the "consecrated ones" (males), and it occurs again in 1 Kings XIV, 24; XV, 12; and XXII, 46. And the word translated "grove" is Asherah. There is some doubt, I believe, as to the exact function of these *Kedeshim* in the temple ritual, and considerable doubt as to whether the translation of the word given in our Authorized Version is justified.[1] It is clear, however, that these men corresponded in some way to the *Kedeshoth* or sacred women, who were—like the *Devadasis* of the Hindu temples—a kind of courtesan or prostitute dedicated to the god, and strange as it may seem to the modern mind, it is probable that they united some kind of sexual service with prophetic functions. Dr. Frazer, speaking[2] of the sacred slaves or *Kedeshim* in various parts of Syria, concludes that "originally no sharp line of distinction existed between the prophets and the Kedeshim; both were 'men of God,' as the prophets were constantly called; in other words they were inspired mediums, men in whom the god manifested himself from time to time by word and deed, in short, temporary incarnations of the deity. But while the prophets roved freely about the country, the *Kedeshim* appears to have been regularly attached to a sanctuary, and among the duties which they performed at the shrines there were clearly some which revolted the conscience of men imbued with a purer morality."

As to the Asherah, or sometimes plural Asherim, translated "grove," the most accepted opinion is that it was a wooden post or tree stripped of its branches and planted in the ground beside an altar, whether of Jehovah or other gods.[3] Several biblical passages, like Jeremiah II, 27, suggest that it was an emblem of Baal or of the male organ, and others (*e. g.*, Judges II, 13 & III, 7) connect it with Ashtoreth the female partner of Baal; while the weaving of hangings or garments for the "grove" suggests the combination of female with male in one effigy.[4] At any rate we may conclude pretty safely that the thing or things had a strongly sexual signification.

Thus it would seem that in the religious worship of the Canaanites there were male courtesans attached to the temples and inhabit-

[1]See Frazer's *Adonis, Attis and Osiris,* 2nd edition 1907, pp. 14, 64 note, etc.
[2]*Ibid.*, p. 67.
[3]See Frazer's Adonis, pp. 14, note, etc.
[4]See a full consideration of this subject in *Ancient Pagan and Modern Christian Symbolism,* by Thomas Inman. (2nd edition 1874.) p. 120 *et seq.*

ing their precincts, as well as consecrated females, and that the ceremonies connected with these cults were of a markedly sexual character. These ceremonies had probably originated in an ancient worship of sexual acts as being symbolical of, and therefore favorable to, the fertility of Nature and the crops. But though they had penetrated into the Jewish temple they were detested by the more zealous adherents of Jehovah, because—for one reason at any rate—they belonged to the rival cult of the Syrian Baal and Ashtoreth, the *Kedeshim* in fact being "consecrated to the Mother of the Gods, the famous Dea Syria."[1] And they were detestable, too, because they went hand in hand with the cultivation of 'familiar spirits' and 'wizards'—who of course knew nothing of Jehovah! Thus we see (2 Kings XXI) that Manasseh followed the abominations of the heathen, building up the high places and the 'groves' and the altars for Baal. "And he made his son pass through the fire, and observed times, and used enchantments,[2] and dealt with familiar spirits and wizards, and wrought much wickedness. . . . and he set a graven image of the 'grove' in the house of the Lord." But Josiah his gransdon reversed all this, and drove the familiar spirits and the wizards out of the land, together with the *Kedeshim.*

So far with regard to Syria and the Bible, in the matter of the apparent connection of homosexuality with prophecy and priesthood. But Dr. Frazer points out the curious likeness here to customs existing to-day among the Negroes of the Slave Coast of West Africa. In that region, women, called Kosio, are attached to the temples as wives, priestesses and temple prostitutes of the python-god. But besides these "there are male *Kosio* as well as female *Kosio,* that is there are dedicated men as well as dedicated women, priests as well as priestesses, and the ideas and customs in regard to them seem to be similar.[3] "Indeed," he says, "the points of resemblance between the prophets of Israel and of West Africa are close and curious."[4] It must be said, however, that Dr. Frazer

[1]See Westermarck's *Origin and Development of Our Moral Ideas,* Vol. II, p.488.

[2]All this suggests the practice of some early and primitive science, and much resembles the accusations made in the thirteenth century against our Roger Bacon, pioneer of modern science.

[3]*Adonis,* etc., p. 60.

[4]*Ibid.,* p. 66.

does not in either case insist on the inference of homosexuality. On the contrary, he rather endeavours to avoid it, and of course it would be very unreasonable to suppose any *invariable* connection of these "sacred men" with this peculiarity. At the same time the general inference in that direction—particularly in view of later facts brought forward in this paper—is strong and difficult to evade.

To proceed. Among the tribes in the neighborhood of Behring's Straits—the Kamchadales, the Chukchi, the Aleuts, Inoits, Kadiak islanders, and so forth, homosexuality is common, and its relation to shamanship or priesthood most marked and curious. Westermarck, quoting (Moral Ideas Vol. 1, p. 458) from Dr. Bogoraz, says:—"It frequently happens that, under the supernatural influence of one of their shamans, or priests, a Chukchi lad at sixteen years of age will suddenly relinquish his sex and imagine himself to be a woman. He adopts a woman's attire, lets his hair grow, and devotes himself altogether to female occupation. Furthermore, this disclaimer of his sex takes a husband into the *yurt* (hut) and does all the work which is usually incumbent on the wife, in most unnatural and voluntary subjection. . . . These abnormal changes of sex imply the most abject immorality in the community, and appear to be strongly encouraged by the shamans, who interpret such cases as an injunction of their individual deity. "Further," Westermarck says "the change of sex was usually accompanied by future shamanship; indeed nearly all the shamans were former delinquents of their sex." Again he says, "In describing the Koriaks, Krasheninnikoff makes mention of the *Ke'yev,* that is men occupying the position of concubines, and he compares them with the Kamchadale *Koe'kcuc,* as he calls them, that is men transformed into women. Every *Koe'kcuc,* he says, "is regarded as a *magician* and interpreter of dreams. . . . The *Koe'kcuc* wore women's clothes, did women's work, and were in the position of wives or concubines." And (on p. 472) "There is no indication that the North American aborigines attached any opprobrium to men who had intercourse with those members of their own sex who had assumed the dress and habits of women. In Kadiak such a companion was on the contrary regarded as a great acquisition; and the effeminate men, far from being despised, were held in repute by the people, most of them being wizards."

This connection with wizardry and religious divination is particularly insisted upon by Elie Reclus, in his *Primitive Folk* (contemporary Science Series). Speaking of the Inoits (p. 68) he says:—"Has a boy with a pretty face also a graceful demeanor? The mother no longer permits him to associate with companions of his own age, but clothes him and brings him up as a girl. Any stranger would be deceived as to his sex, and when he is about fifteen he is sold for a good round sum to a wealthy personage.[1] 'Choupans,' or youths of this kind are highly prized by the Konyagas. On the other hand, there are to be met with here and there among the Esquimaux or kindred populations, especially in Youkon, *girls* who decline marriage and maternity. Changing their sex, so to speak, they live as boys, adopting masculine manners and customs, they hunt the stag, and in the chase shrink from no danger; in fishing from no fatigue."

Reclus then says that the Choupans commonly dedicate themselves to the priesthood; but all are not qualified for this. "To become an *angakok* it is needful to have a very marked vocation, and furthermore a character and temperament which every one has not. The priests in office do not leave the recruiting of their pupils to chance; they make choice at an early age of boys or girls, not limiting themselves to one sex—a mark of greater intelligence than is exhibited by most other priesthoods." (p. 71.) The pupil has to go through considerable ordeals:—"Disciplined by abstinence and prolonged vigils, by hardship and constraint, he must learn to endure pain stoically and to subdue his bodily desires, to make the body obey unmurmuringly the commands of the spirit. Others may be chatterers; he will be silent, as becomes the prophet and the soothsayer. At an early age the novice courts solitude. He wanders throughout the long nights across silent plains filled with the chilly whiteness of the moon; he listens to the wind moaning over the desolate floes;—and then the aurora borealis, that ardently sought occasion for 'drinking in the light,' the *angakok* must absorb all its brilliancies and splendors. . . . And now the future sorcerer is no longer a child. Many a time he has felt himself in the presence of Sidne, the Esquimaux Demeter, he has divined it by the shiver

[1]See also Bancroft's *Native Races of the Pacific States.*, Vol. I, p. 82.

which ran through his veins, by the tingling of his flesh and the bristling of his hair. . . . He sees stars unknown to the profane; he asks the secrets of destiny from Sirius, Algol, and Altair; he passes through a series of initiations, knowing well that his spirit will not be loosed from the burden of dense matter and crass ignorance, until the moon has looked him in the face, and darted a certain ray into his eyes. At last his own Genius, evoked from the bottomless depths of existence, appears to him, having scaled the immensity of the heavens, and climbed across the abysses of the ocean. White, wan and solemn, the phantom will say to him: 'Behold me, what dost thou desire?' Uniting himself with theDouble from beyond the grave, the soul of the *angakok* flies upon the wings of the wind, and quitting the body at will, sails swift and light through the universe. It is permitted to probe all hidden things, to seek the knowledge of all mysteries, in order that they may be revealed to those who have remained mortal with spirit unrefined." (p. 73.)

Allowing something for poetic and imaginative expression, the above statement of the ordeals and initiations of the *angakok*, and their connection with the previous career of the *Choupan* are well based on the observations of many authorities, as well as on their general agreement with similar facts all over the world. There is also another passage of Reclus (p. 70) on the duties of the *angakok*, which seems to throw considerable light on the already mentioned *kedeshim* and *kedeshoth* of the Syrian cults, also on the *kosio* of the Slave Coast and the early functions of the priesthood in general:— "As soon as the *choupan* has moulted into the *angakok*, the tribe confide to him the girls most suitable in bodily grace and disposition; he has to complete their education—he will perfect them in dancing and other accomplishments, and finally will initiate them into the pleasures of love. If they display intelligence, they will become seers and medicine-women, priestesses and prophetesses. The summer *kachims* (? assemblies), which are closed to the women of the community will open wide before these. It is believed that these girls would be unwholesome company if they had not been purified by commerce with a man of God."

"Among the Illinois Indians," says Westermarck (Vol. II, p. 473), "the effeminate men assist in [*i. e.*] are present at all the juggleries and the solemn dance in honor of the calumet or sacred tobacco-pipe, for which the Indians have such a deference. . . but they are not permitted either to dance or to sing. They are called into the councils of the Indians, and nothing can be decided without their advice; for because of their extraordinary manner of living they are looked upon as *manitous*, or supernatural beings, and persons of consequence." "The Sioux, Sacs, and Fox Indians," he continues, "give once a year, or oftener, a feast to the Berdashe, or I-coo-coo-a, who is a man dressed in women's clothes, as he has been all his life." And Catlin (North American Indians Vol. II, p. 214) says of this Berdashe:—"For extraordinary privileges which he is known to possess, he is driven to the most servile and degrading duties, which he is not allowed to escape; and he being the only one of the tribe submitting to this disgraceful degradation is looked upon as *medicine* and sacred, and a feast is given to him annually; and initiatory to it a dance by those few young men of the tribe who can—as in the illustration—dance forward and publicly make their boast (without the denial of the *Berdashe*) that" [then follow three or four unintelligible lines of some native dialect; and then] "such and such only are allowed to enter the dance and partake of the feast."

In this connection it may not be out of place to quote Joaquin Miller (who spent his early life as a member of an Indian tribe) on the prophetic powers of these people. He says (Life among the Modocs, p. 360) "If there is a race of men that has the gift of prophecy or prescience I think it is the Indian. It may be a keen instinct sharpened by meditation that makes them foretell many things with such precision, but I have seen some things that looked much like the fulfillment of prophecies. They believe in the gift of prophecy thoroughly, and are never without their seers."

The Jesuit father Lafitau, who published in 1724 at Paris an extremely interesting book on the manners and customs of the North American tribes among whom he had been a missionary,[1] after speaking of warlike women and Amazons, says (Vol. 1, p. 53):—"If some women are found possessing virile courage, and glorying in the profession of war, which seems only suitable to men; there

[1]*Moeurs des Sauvages Ameriquains, comparées aux moeurs des premiers temps*, par le P. Lafitau, Paris, 1724.

exist also men so cowardly as to live like women. Among the Illinois, among the Sioux, in Louisiana, in Florida, and in Yucatan, there are found youths who adopt the garb of women and preserve it all their lives, and who think themselves honored in stooping to all their occupations; they never marry; they take part in all ceremonies in which religion seems to be concerned; and this profession of an extraordinary life causes them to pass for beings of a superior order, and above the common run of mankind. Would not these be the same kind of folk as the Asiatic worshippers of Cybele, or those Easterns of whom Julius Firmicus speaks (Lib. de Errore prof. Relig.), who consecrated to the Goddess of Phrygia, or to Venus Urania, certain priests, who dressed as women, who affected an effeminate countenance, who painted their faces, and disguised their true sex under garments borrowed from the sex which they wished to counterfeit."

Certainly this belief in some kind of relation between homosexuality and divination or sorcery (or the priestly office) is very widespread. Westermarck (p. 477) mentions the ancient Scandinavians as regarding passive homosexuals in the light of sorcerers; and refers (p. 484 note) to Thomas Falkner, who in his *Description of Patagonia*, p. 117, says that among thePatagonians "the wizards are of both sexes. The male wizards are obliged (as it were) to leave their sex, and to dress themselves in female apparel, and are not permitted to marry, though the female ones or witches may. They are generally chosen for this office when they are children, and a preference is always shown to those who at that early time of life discover an effeminate disposition. They are clothed very early in female attire, and presented with the drum and rattles belonging to the profession they are to follow."

With regard to the attribution of homosexuality also to female wizards or witches I believe that, rightly or wrongly, this was very common in Europe a few centuries ago. Leo Africanus (1492) in his description of Morocco[1] says, "The third kind of diviners are women-witches, which are affirmed to have familiarity with divels. Changing their voices they fain the divell to speak within them:

[1]Hakluyt Society, 3 vols. Vol. II, p. 458

then they which come to enquire ought with greate feare and trembling (to) aske these vile and abominable witches such questions as they mean to propound, and lastly, offering some fee unto the divell, they depart. But the wiser and honester sort of people call these women *Sahacat,* which in Latin signifieth *Fricatrices,* because they have a damnable custom to commit unlawful venerie among themselves, which I cannot express in any modester terms. If faire women come unto then at any time, these abominable witches will burn in lust towards them, no otherwise than lustie youngsters do towards young maides, and will in the divel's behalf demande for a rewarde, that they may lie with them; and so by this means it often falleth out that thinking thereby to fulfill the divel's command they lie with the witches. Yea some there are which being allured with this abominable vice, will desire the companie of those witches" (and to that end, he explains, deceive their husbands). Whether this is all true or not—and probably it is quite vulgarly exaggerated—it shows the kind of thing that was believed at that time about witches.

No doubt this list of cases connecting homosexuality with sorcery and priesthood might be somewhat indefinitely extended, but we need not attempt to cover the whole ground. In some cases the customs are accompanied by a change of dress, but not by any means always.

Speaking of the Pelew Islanders, Dr. Frazer[1] attributes the adoption by the priests of female attire to the fact that "it often happens that a goddess chooses a man, not a woman, for her minister and inspired mouthpiece. When that is so, the favored man is thenceforth regarded and treated as a woman." And he continues—"This pretended change of sex under the inspiration of a female spirit perhaps explains a custom widely spread among savages, in accordance with which some men dress as women and act as women through life."

This explanation is certainly not very convincing—though it is just possible that in certain cases of men of this kind in early times, the feminine part of their natures may have personified itself, and presented itself to them as a vision of a female spirit or goddess;

[1]*Adonis,* etc., p. 428.

and thus the explanation might be justified. But anyhow it should not be overlooked that the same impulse (for men to dress as women, and women to dress as men) perseveres to-day in quite a large percentage of our modern civilized populations; and whatever its explanations, the impulse is often enormously powerful, and its satisfaction a source of great delight. It must also not be overlooked, in dealing with this complex and difficult subject, that the mere fact of a person delighting to adopt the garb of the opposite sex does not in itself prove that his or her love-tendency is abnormal—*i. e.*, cross-dressing does not *prove* homosexuality. There are not a few cases of men in the present day (and presumably the same in past times) who love to dress as women, and yet are perfectly normal in their sex-relations; and therefore too sweeping generalizations on this subject must be avoided.[1]

On the whole, however, cross-dressing must be taken as a general indication of, and a cognate phenomenon to, homosexuality; and its wide prevalence in early times, especially in connection with the priesthood, must give us much matter for thought. Dr. Frazer in his *Adonis, Attis* and *Osiris*, continuing the passage I have just quoted, says:—"These unsexed creatures often, perhaps generally, profess the arts of sorcery and healing, they communicate with spirits and are regarded sometimes with awe and sometimes with contempt, as beings of a higher or lower order than common folk. Often they are dedicated or trained to their vocation from childhood. Effeminate sorcerers or priests of this sort are found among the Sea Dyaks of Borneo, the Bugis of South Celebes, the Patagonians of South America. . . . In Madagascar we hear of effeminate men who wore female attire and acted as women, thinking thereby to do God service. In the kingdom of Congo there was a sacrificial priest who commonly dressed as a woman and gloried in the title of the grandmother."

And so on. We need not, I think, delay further over the evidence, but proceed to discuss the meaning and explanation of the facts presented.

[1]See, in these connections, Dr. Hirschfeld's remarkable book "*Die Transvestiten*" (Berlin 1910); also *Die Konträre Sexual-empfindung* by Dr. A. Moll, edition 1893, pp. 82-90.

II.

There seem to me to be two possible and not unreasonable theories on the subject. The first is that there really is a connection between the homosexual temperament and divinatory or unusual psychic powers; the second is (that there is no such particular connection, but) that the idea of sorcery or witchcraft naturally and commonly springs up round the ceremonials of an old religion when that religion is being superseded by a new one. This is of course a well-recognized fact. The gods of one religion become the devils of its successor; the poetic rites of one age become the black magic of the next. But in the case of the primitive religions of the earth their ceremonials were—for reasons which we need not now consider—very largely sexual, and even homosexual. Consequently the homosexual rites, which were most foreign to the later religionists and most disturbing to their ideas, associated themselves *most* strongly with the notion of sorcery and occult powers.

For myself I am inclined to accept both explanations, and—leaving out of course the clause in brackets in the second—to combine them. I think there *is* an organic connection between the homosexual temperament and unusual psychic or divinatory powers; but I think also that the causes mentioned in the second explanation have in many cases led to an exaggerated belief in such connection, and have given it a sorcerous or demoniac aspect.

To take the second point first. Just as, according to Darwin, the sharpest rivalry occurs between a species and the closely allied species from which it has sprung, so in any religion there is the fiercest theological hatred against the form which has immediately preceded it. Early Christianity could never say enough against the Pagan cults of the old world (partly for the very reason that it embodied so much of their ceremonial and was in many respects their lineal descendant). They were the work and inspiration of the devil. Their Eucharists and baptismal rites and initiations—so strangely and diabolically similar to the Christian rites—were sheer black magic; their belief in the sacredness of sex mere filthiness. Similarly the early Protestants could never say malignant things enough against the Roman Catholics; or the Secularists in their turn against the Protestants. In all these cases there is an element of fear—fear because the thing supposed to have been left behind lies after all so close, and is always waiting to reassert itself—and this fear invests the hated symbol or person with a halo of devilish potency. Think, for instance, what sinister and magical powers and influence have been commonly ascribed to the Roman Catholic priests in the ordinary Protestant parlors and circles!

It is easy, therefore, to understand that when the Jews established their worship of Jehovah as a great reaction against the primitive nature-cults of Syria—and in that way to become in time the germ of Christianity—the first thing they did was to denounce the priests and satellites of Baal-Peor and Ashtoreth as wizards and sorcerers, and wielders of devilish faculties. These cults were frankly sexual—probably the most intimate meaning of them, as religions, being the glory and sacredness of sex; but the Jews (like the later Christians) blinding themselves to this aspect, were constrained to see in sex only filthiness, and in its religious devotees persons in league with Beelzebub and the powers of darkness. And of course the homosexual elements in these cults, being the most foreign to the new religion, stood out as the *most* sorcerous and the most magical part of them. Westermarck points out (Moral Ideas, II, 489) that the Mediæval Christianity constantly associated homosexuality with heresy—to such a degree in fact that the French word *herite* or *heretique* was sometimes used in both connections; and that *bougre* or *Bulgarian* was commonly used in both, though to begin with it only denoted a sect of religious heretics who came from Bulgaria. And he thinks that the violent reprobation and punishment of homosexuality arose more from its connection in the general mind with heresy than from direct aversion in the matter—more in fact from religious motives than from secular ones.

But connecting with all this, we must not neglect the theory so ably worked out by Prof. Karl Pearson among others—namely that the primitive religions were not only sexual in character but that they were largely founded on an early matriarchal order of society, in which women had the predominant sway—descent being traced through them, and tribal affairs largely managed by them, and in which the chief deities were goddesses, and the priests and prophets mainly females. Exactly how far such an order or society really extended in the past is apparently a doubtful question; but that there are distinct traces of such matriarchal institutions in certain localities and among some peoples seems to be quite established. Karl Pearson, assuming the real prevalence of these institutions in early times points out, reasonably enough, that when Christianity became fairly established matriarchal rites and festivals, lingering on in out-of-the-way places and among the peasantry, would at once be interpreted as being devilish and sorcerous in character, and the women (formerly priestesses) who conducted them and perhaps recited snatches of ancient half-forgotten rituals, would be accounted witches. "We have, therefore," he says,[1] "to look upon the witch as essentially the degraded form of the old priestess, cunning in the knowledge of herbs and medicine, jealous of the rites of the goddess she serves, and preserving in spells and incantations such wisdom as early civilization possessed." This civilization, he explains, included the "observing of times and seasons," the knowledge of weather-lore, the invention of the broom, the distaff, the cauldron, the pitchfork, the domestication of the goat, the pig, the cock and the hen, and so forth—all which things became symbols of the witch in later times, simply because originally they were the inventions of woman and the insignia of her office, and so the religious symbols of the Mother-goddess and her cult.

The connection of all this with homosexual customs is not at once clear; but it has been suggested—though I am not sure that Karl Pearson himself supports this—that the primitive religions of the Matriarchate may have ultimately led to men-priests dressing in female attire. For when the matriarchal days were passing away, and men were beginning to assert their predominance, it still may have happened that the old religious customs lingering on may have induced men to simulate the part of women and to dress as priestesses, or at least have afforded them an excuse for so doing.[2] In this way it seems just possible that the pendulum-swing of society from the matriarchate to the patriarchate may have been accompanied by some degree of crasis and confusion between the functions of the sexes, homosexual customs and tendencies may have come to

[1]*The Chances of Death and other studies,* by Karl Pearson, 2 vols., 1897. Vol. II, p. 13.

[2]See above, pp. 13 and 14.

the fore, and the connection of homosexuality with the priesthood may seem to be accounted for.

This explanation, however, though it certainly has a claim to be mentioned, seems to me too risky and insecure for very much stress to be laid upon it. In the first place the extent and prevalence of the matriarchal order of society is a matter still very much disputed, and to assume that at any early period of human history the same was practically universal would be unjustified. In the second place granting the existence of the matriarchal order and its transmutation into the patriarchal, the connection of this change with the development of homosexual customs is still only a speculation and a theory, supported by little direct evidence. On the other hand, the facts to be explained—namely, the connection of homosexuality with priesthood and divination — seem to be world-wide and universal. Therefore, though we admit that the causes mentioned—namely the attribution of magical qualities to old religious rites, and the introduction of feminine inversions and disguises through the old matriarchal custom—may account in part for the facts, and in particular may in certain localities have given them a devilish or sorcerous complexion, yet I think we must look deeper for the root-explanations of the whole matter, and consider whether there may not be some fundamental causes in human nature itself.

## III.

I have already said that I think there is an original connection of some kind between homosexuality and divination; but in saying this of course I do not mean that everywhere and always the one is connected with the other, or that the relationship between the two is extremely well marked; but I contend that a connection can be traced and that on *a priori* grounds its existence is quite probable.

And first with regard to actual observation of such a connection, the fact of the widespread belief in it which I have already noted as existing among the primitive tribes of the earth; and their founding of all sorts of customs on that belief, must count for something. Certainly the mere existence of a widespread belief among early and superstitious peoples—as for instance that an eclipse is caused by a dragon swallowing the sun—does not prove its truth; but in the case we are considering the matter is well within the range of ordinary observation, and the constant connection between the *choupan* and the *angakok*, the *ke'yev* and the *shaman*, the *berdashe* and the witch-doctor, the ganymede and the temple-priest, and their correspondence all over the world, the *basir* among the Dyaks, the boy-priests in the temples of Peru, the same in Buddhist temples of Ceylon, Burma and China—all these cases seem to point to some underlying fact, of the fitness or adaptation of the invert for priestly or divinatory functions. And though the tendency already alluded to, of a later religion to ascribe devilish potency to earlier cults, must certainly in many instances shed a sinister or sorcerous glamour over the invert, yet this exaggeration need not blind us to the existence of a residual fact behind it; and anyhow to a great many of the cases just mentioned it does not apply at all, since in them the question of one religion superseding another does not enter.

To come to more recent times, the frequency with which accusations of homosexuality have been launched against the religious orders and monks of the Catholic Church, the Knights Templars, and even the ordinary priests and clerics, must give us pause. Nor need we overlook the fact that in Protestant Britain the curate and the parson quite often appear to belong to some 'third sex' which is neither wholly masculine nor wholly feminine!

Granting, then, that the connection in question is to a certain degree indicated by the anthropological facts which we already possess—is there, we may ask, any rational ground for expecting this connection *a priori* and from psychological considerations? I think there is.

In the first place all science now compels us to admit the existence of the homosexual temperament as a fact of human nature, and an important fact; and not only so, but to perceive that it is widely spread among the various races of the earth, and extends back to the earliest times of which we have anything like historical knowledge. We can no longer treat it as a mere local and negligible freak, or put it in the category of a sinful and criminal disposition to be stamped out at all costs. We feel that it must have some real significance. The question is what that may be. The following is a suggestion that may cover part of the ground, though not I think, the whole.

In the primitive societies the men (the quite normal men) are the warriors and hunters. These are their exclusive occupations. The women (the normal women) attend to domestic work and agriculture, and their days are consumed in those labors. But in the evolution of society there are many more functions to be represented than those simple ones just mentioned. And we may almost think that if it had not been for the emergence of intermediate types—the more or less feminine man and similarly the more or less masculine woman—social life might never have advanced beyond these primitive phases. But the non-warlike men and the non-domestic women necessarily sought new outlets for their energies. They sought different occupations from those of the quite ordinary man and woman—as in fact they do to-day; and so they became the initiators of new activities. They became inventors and teachers of arts and crafts, or wizards (as they would be considered) and sorcerers; they became diviners and seers, or revealers of the gods and religion; they became medicine-men and healers, prophets and prophetesses; and so ultimately laid the foundation of the priesthood, and of science, literature and art. Thus—on this view, and as might not unreasonably be expected—it was primarily a variation in the intimate sex-nature of the human being which led to these important differentiations in his social life and external activities.

In various ways we can see the likelihood of this thesis, and the probability of the intermediate man or woman becoming a forward force in human evolution. In the first place, as just mentioned, not wholly belonging to either of the two great progenitive branches of the human race, his nature would not find complete satisfaction in the activities of either branch, and he would necessarily create a new sphere of some kind for himself. Secondly, finding himself *different* from the great majority, sought after by some and despised by others, now an object of contumely and now an object of love and admiration, he would be forced to *think*. His mind turned inwards on himself would be forced to tackle the problem of his own nature, and afterwards the problem of the world and of outer nature. He would become one of the first thinkers, dreamers, discoverers. Thirdly, some of the Intermediates (though certainly not all) combining the emotionality of the feminine with the practicality of the masculine, and many other qualities and powers of both sexes, as well as much of their experience, would undoubtedly be greatly superior in ability to the rest of their tribe, and making forward progress in the world of thought and imagination would become inventors, teachers, musicians, medicine-men and priests; while their early science and art (for such it would be)—prediction of rain, determination of seasons, observation of stars, study of herbs, creation of chants and songs, rude drawings and so forth, would be accounted quite magical and divinatory.

Finally, and in the fourth place, I believe that at this stage an element of what might really be called divination would come in. I believe that the blending of the masculine and feminine temperaments would in some of these cases produce persons whose perceptions would be so subtle and complex and rapid as to come under the head of genius, persons of intuitive mind who would perceive things without knowing how, and follow far concatenations of causes and events without concerning themselves about the *why*—diviners and prophets in a very real sense. And these persons—whether they prophesied downfall and disaster, or whether they urged their people onward to conquest and victory, or whether by acute combinations of observation and experience they caught at the healing properties of herbs or determined the starry influences on the seasons and the crops—in almost all cases would acquire and did acquire a strange reputation for sanctity and divinity—arising partly perhaps out of the homosexual taboo, but also out of their real possession and command of a double-engine psychic power.

The double life and nature certainly, in many cases of inverts observed to-day, seems to give to them an extraordinary humanity and sympathy, together with a remarkable power of dealing with human beings. It may possibly also point to a further degree of evolution than usually attained, and a higher order of consciousness, very imperfectly realized of course, but indicated. This interaction in fact, between the masculine and the feminine, this mutual illumination of logic and intuition, this combination of action and meditation, may not only raise and increase the power of each of these faculties, but it may give the mind a new quality, and a new power of perception corresponding to the blending of subject and object in consciousness. It may possibly lead to the development of that third order of perception which has been called the cosmic consciousness, and which may also be termed divination. "He who knows the masculine," says Lao-tsze, "and at the same time keeps to the feminine, will be the whole world's channel. Eternal virtue will not depart from him, and he will return again to the state of an infant." To the state of an infant!—that is, he will become undifferentiated from Nature, who is his mother, and who will lend him all her faculties.

It is not of course to be supposed that the witch-doctors and diviners of barbarian tribes have in general reached to the high order of development just described, yet it is noticeable, in the slow evolution of society, how often the late and high developments have been indicated in the germ in primitive stages; and it may be so in this case. Very interesting in this connection is the passage already quoted (page 7) from Elie Reclus about the initiations of the Esquimaux *angakok* and the appearance to him of his own Genius or Double from the world beyond, for almost exactly the same thing is supposed to take place in the initiation of the religious *yogi* in India —except that the god in this latter case appears to the pupil in the form of his teacher or *guru*. And how often in the history of the Christian saints has the divinity in the form of Jesus or Mary appeared to the strenous devotee, apparently as the culminating result of his intense effort and aspiration, and of the opening out of a new plane of perception in his mind! It may be that with every great onward push of the growing soul, and every great crisis in which as it were a sheath or a husk falls away from the expanding bud, the new order within, the new revelation, the new form of life, is seen for a moment as a Vision in glorious state of a divine being or God.[1]

## IV.

This leads to another consideration, which ought not to be omitted here, as germane to the subject—namely, the frequency with which, among early peoples, the gods are represented—both in their forms and in their manners and customs—as hermaphrodite

[1]It is probable also that the considerable degree of continence, to which many homosexuals are by nature or external necessity compelled, contributes to this visionary faculty.

or bisexual. For clearly bisexuality links on to homosexuality, and the fact that this characteristic was ascribed to the gods suggests that in the popular mind it must have played a profound and important part in human life. I will therefore, in conclusion, give some instances of this divine bisexuality.

Brahm, in the Hindu mythology, is often represented as two-sexed. Originally he was the sole Being. But, "delighting not to be alone he wished for the existence of another, and at once he became such, as male and female embraced. He caused this his one self to fall in twain."[1] Siva, also, the most popular of the Hindu divinities, is originally bi-sexual. In the interior of the great rockhewn Temple at Elephanta, the career of Siva is carved in successive panels. And on the first he appears as a complete full-length human being conjoining the two sexes in one—the left side of the figure (which represents the female portion) projecting into a huge breast and hip, while the side right is man-like in outline, and in the centre (though now much defaced) the organs of both sexes. In the second panel, however, his evolution or differentiation is complete, and he is portrayed as complete male with his consort Sakti or Parvati standing, as perfect female beside him.[2] There are many such illustrations in Hindu literature and art, representing the gods in their double or bi-sexual role—*e. g.*, as Brahma Ardhanarisa, Siva Ardhanarisa (half male and half female).[3] And these again are interesting in connection with the account of Elohim in the 1st chapter of Genesis, and the supposition that he was such an androgynous deity. For we find (v. 27) that "Elohim created man in his own image, in the image of Elohim created he him, *male and female* created he them." And many commentators have maintained that this not only meant that the first man was hermaphrodite, but that the Creator also was of that nature. In the Midrasch we find that Rabbi Samuel-bar-Nachman said that "Adam, when God had created him, was a man-woman (androgyne);" and the great and learned Mai-

[1]Quoted from the Yajur-Veda. See *Bible Folk-lore:* a study in Comp. Mythology. London 1884, p. 104.

[2]See *Adams Peak to Elephanta,* by E. Carpenter, 1903, p. 308.

[3]See drawings in *Ancient Pagan and Modern Christian Symbolism* by Thomas Inman, London, 1874.

monides supported this, saying that "Adam and Eve were created together, conjoined by their backs, but this double being God divided and taking one half (Eve) gave her to the other half (Adam) for a mate." And the Rabbi Manasseh-ben-Israel, following this up, explained that when "God took one of Adam's ribs to make Eve with," it should rather be rendered "one of his sides"—that is, that he divided the double Adam, and one half was Eve.[1]

In the Brihadaranyaka Upanishad (1 Adhyaya, 4th Brahmana) the evolution of Brahm is thus described[2]—"In the beginning of this [world] was Self alone, in the shape of a person. . . . But he felt no delight. . . He wished for a second. He was so large as man and wife together [*i. e.,* he included male and female]. He then made this his Self to fall in two; and thence arose husband and wife. Therefore, Yagnavalkya said: "We two are thus (each of us) like half a shell [or as some translate, like a split pea]." The singular resemblance of this account to what has been said above about the creation of Adam certainly suggests the idea that Jehovah, like Brahm (and like Baal and other Syrian gods), was conceived of as double-sexed, and that primitive man was also conceived of as like nature. The author (Ralston Skinner) of *The Source of Measures* says (p. 159) "The two words of which Jehovah is composed make up the original idea of male-female of the birth-originator. For the Hebrew letter Jod (or J) was the *membrum virile,* and Hovah was Eve, the mother of all living, or the procreatrix Earth and Nature."[3]

The tradition that mankind was anciently hermaphrodite is world-old. It is referred to in Plato's *Banquet,* where Aristophanes says:—"Anciently the nature of mankind was not the same as now, but different. For at first there were three sexes of human beings not two only, namely male and female, as at present, but a third besides, common to both the others—of which the name remains, though the sex itself has vanished. For the androgynous sex then

[1]These and some other references are taken from the learned and careful study "Ueber die androgynische Idee des Lebens" by Dr. von Römer of Amsterdam, which is to be found in Vol. 5 of the *Jahrbuch für Sexuelle* Zwischenstufen. Leipzig, 1903.

[2]*Sacred Books of the East,* Vol. XV, p. 85.

[3]See H. P. Blavatsky, *Secret Doctrine,* Vol. II, p. 132, quoted in Vol. V, *Jahrbuch für S. L.,* p. 76.

existed, both male and female; but now it only exists as a name of reproach." He then describes how all these three sorts of human beings were originally double, and conjoined (as above) back to back; until Jupiter, jealous of his supremacy, divided them vertically "as people cut apples before they preserve them, or as they cut eggs with hairs"—after which, of course, these divided and imperfect folk ran about over the earth, ever seeking their lost halves, to be joined to them again.

I have mentioned the Syrian Baal as being sometimes represented as double-sexed (apparently in combination with Astarte). In the Septuagint (Hos. II, 8, and Zeph. 1, 4) he is called ἡ Baal (feminine) and Arnobius tells us that his worshippers invoked him thus[1] "Hear us, Baal! whether thou be a god or goddess." Similarly Bel and other Babylonian gods were often represented as androgyne.[2] Mithras among the Persians is spoken of by the Christian controversialist Firmicus as two-sexed, and by Herodotus (Bk. 1, c. 131) as identified with a goddess, while there are innumerable Mithraic monuments on which appear the symbols of two deities, male and female combined.[3] Even Venus or Aphrodite was sometimes worshipped in the double form. "In Cyprus," says Dr. Frazer in his *Adonis, etc.* (p. 432, note), "there was a bearded and masculine image of Venus (probably Astarte) in female attire: according to Philochorus the deity thus represented was the moon, and sacrifices were offered to him or her by men clad as women, and by women clad as men (see Macrobius *Saturn* III, 7. 2)." This bearded female deity is sometimes also spoken of as Aphroditus, or as Venus Mylitta. The worship of this bearded goddess was mainly in Syria and Cyprus. But in Egypt also a representation of a bearded Isis has been found,—with infant Horus in her lap;[4] while again there are a number of representations (from papyri) of the goddess Neith in androgyne form, with a male member (erected). And again, curiously enough, the Norse Freya, or Friga, corresponding to Venus,

[1]Inman's *Ancient Pagan and Modern Christian Symbolism,* Trubner (1874), p. 119.

[2]*Pagan Christs,* 1908, by John M. Robertson (1908), p. 308.

[3]*Ibid.,* p. 307.

[4]See illustration *Jahrbuch für S. Z.,* Vol. V, p. 732.

was similarly figured. Dr. von Römer says:[1]—"Just as the Greeks had their Aphroditos as well as Aphrodite so the Scandinavians had their Friggo as well as their Friga. This divinity, too, was androgyne. Friga, to whom the 6th day of the week was dedicated, was sometimes thought of as hermaphrodite. She was represented as having the members of both sexes, standing by a column with a sword in her right hand, and in her left a bow."

In the Orphic hymns we have:—

"Zeus was the first of all, Zeus last, the lord of the lightning;
Zeus was the head, the middle, from him all things were created;
Zeus was Man, and again Zeus was the Virgin Eternal."

And in another passage, speaking of Adonis:—

"Hear me, who pray to thee, hear me O many-named and best of deities,
Thou, with thy gracious hair . . . . both maiden and youth, Adonis."

Again with regard to the latter, Ptolemaeus Hephaestius (according to Photius) writes:—"They say that the androgyne Adonis fulfilled the part of a man for Aphrodite, but for Apollo the part of a wife."[2]

Dionysus, one of the most remarkable figures in the Greek Mythology, is frequently represented as androgyne. Euripides in his *Bacchae* calls him "feminine-formed" (θηγήροφσς) or thelumorphos, and the Orphic hymns double-sexed (διφής) or diphues; and Aristides in his discourse on Dionysus says:—"Thus the God is both male and female. His form corresponds to his nature, since everywhere in himself he is like a double being; for among young men he is a maiden, and among maidens a young man, and among men a beardless youth overflowing with vitality." In the museum at Naples there is a very fine sculptured head of Dionysos, which though bearded has a very feminine expression, and is remindful of the traditional head of Christ. "In legend and art,'' says Dr. Frazer,[3] "there are clear traces of an effeminate Dionysus, and in some of his rites and processions men wore female attire. Similar things are reported of Bacchus, who was, of course, another form of Dionysus. Even Hercules, that most mas-

[1]See his study already quoted, Jahrbuch, pp. 735-744.
[2]See *Jahrbuch*, as above, pp. 806, 807 and 809.
[3]*Adonis, etc.*, p. 432.

culine figure, was said to have dressed as a woman for three years, during which he was the slave of Omphale, queen of Lydia. "If we suppose," says Dr. Frazer,[1] "that queen Omphale, like queen Semirimis, was nothing but the great Asiatic goddess, or one of her Avatars, it becomes probable that the story of the womanish Hercules of Lydia preserves a reminiscence of a line or college of effeminate priests who, like the eunuch priests of the Syrian goddess, dressed as women in imitation of their goddess, and were supposed to be inspired by her. The probability is increased by the practice of the priests of Heracles at Antimachia in Cos, who, as we have just seen, actually wore female attire when they were engaged in their sacred duties. Similarly at the vernal mysteries of Hercules in Rome the men were draped in the garments of women."

Such instances could be rather indefinitely multiplied. Apollo is generally represented with a feminine—sometimes with an extremely feminine—bust and figure. The great hero Achilles passed his youth among women, and in female disguise. Every one knows the recumbent marble Hermaphrodite in the Louvre. There are also in the same collection two or three elegant bronzes of Aphrodite-like female figures in the standing position—but of masculine sex. What is the explanation of all this?

It is evident that the conception of double sex, or of a sex combining the characters of male and female, haunted the minds of early peoples. Yet we have no reason for supposing that such a combination, in any complete and literal sense, ever existed. Modern physiological investigation has never produced a single case of a human being furnished with the complete organs of both sexes, and capable of fulfilling the functions of both. And the unfortunate malformations which do exist in this direction are too obviously abortive and exceptional to admit of their being generalized or exalted into any kind of norm or ideal. All we can say is that—though in the literal sense no double forms exist—certainly a vast number of intermediate forms of male and female are actually found, which are double in the sense that the complete organs of one sex are conjoined with some or nearly all of the (secondary) characters of the other sex; and that we have every reason to believe that these

[1] *Ibid.*, p. 431.

intermediate types have existed in considerable numbers from the remotest antiquity. That being so, it is possible that the observation or influence of these intermediate types led to a tentative and confused idealization of a double type.

Anyhow the fact remains—that these idealizations of the double type are so numerous. And it is interesting to notice that while they begin in early times with being merely grotesque and symbolical, they end in the later periods by becoming artistic and gracious and approximated to the real and actual. The Indian Siva with his right side masculine and his left side feminine is in no way beautiful or attractive; any more than Brahma with twenty arms and twenty legs. And the same may be said of the bearded Egyptian Isis or the bearded Syrian Aphrodite. These were only rude and inartistic methods of conveying an idea. The later spirit, however, found a better way of expression. It took its cue from the variations of type to be seen every day in the actual world; and instead of representing the Persian Mithra as a two-sexed monster, it made him a young *man*, but of very feminine outline. The same with the Greek Apollo; while on the other hand the female who is verging toward the male type is represented by Artemis or even by the Amazons.

It may be said:—we can understand this representation of intermediate forms from actual life, but we do not see why such mingling of the sexes should be ascribed to the gods, unless it might be from a merely fanciful tendency to personify the two great powers of nature in one being—in which case it is strange that the tendency should have been so universal. To this we may reply that probably the reason or reasons for this tendency must be accounted quite deep-rooted and anything but fanciful. One reason, it seems to me, is the psychological fact that in the deeps of human nature (as represented by Brahm and Siva in the Hindu philosophy, by Zeus in the Orphic Hymns, by Mithra in the Zend-avesta, etc.) the sex-temperament *is* undifferentiated;[1] and it is only in its later and more external and partial manifestations that it branches decidedly into male and female; and that, therefore, in endeavoring through religion to represent the root facts of life, there was always a tendency

[1]Compare the undifferentiated sex-tendencies of boys and girls at puberty and shortly after.

to cultivate and honor hermaphroditism, and to ascribe some degree of this quality to heroes and divinities. The other possible reason is that as a matter of fact the great leaders and heroes *did* often exhibit this blending of masculine and feminine qualities and habits in their actual lives, and that therefore at some later period, when exalted to divinities, this blending of qualities was strongly ascribed to them and was celebrated in the rites and ceremonies of their religion and their temples. The feminine traits in genius (as in a Shelley or a Byron) are well marked in the present day. We have only to go back to the Persian Bâb of the last century[1] or to a St. Francis or even to a Jesus of Nazareth, to find the same traits present in founders and leaders of religious movements in historical times. And it becomes easy to suppose the same again of those early figures—who once probably were men—these Apollos, Buddhas, Dionysus, Osiris, and so forth—to suppose that they too were somewhat bi-sexual in temperament, and that it was really largely owing to that fact that they were endowed with far-reaching powers and became leaders of mankind. In either case—whichever reason is adopted—it corroborates the general thesis and argument of this paper.

[1]Ali Muhammed, who called himself the Bâb (or Gate), was born at Shiraz in 1820. In 1844 he commenced preaching his gospel, which was very like that of Jesus, and which now has an immense following. In 1850 he was shot, at Tabriz, as a malefactor, and his beloved disciple Mirza Muhammed Ali, refusing to leave him, was shot with him.

Theological Studies
48 (1987)

# THE VATICAN STATEMENT ON HOMOSEXUALITY

In the March 1987 issue of *Theological Studies*,[1] Bruce Williams, O.P., of the Pontifical University of St. Thomas, Rome, published a very thorough and critical evaluation of the Letter "On the Pastoral Care of Homosexual Persons" from the Congregation for the Doctrine of the Faith (CDF) under date of October 1, 1986. Williams admits to having "mixed reactions to this new document"[2] but concludes generally that the Letter "amounts to a significant step ... forward"[3] regarding the Church's official stand on homosexuality.

Although Williams makes numerous positive evaluations of the Letter (summarized in his "Conclusion"[4]), two major significant steps are underlined. First, Williams evaluates the theological articulation of the question of homosexuality in the Letter as a "significant advance"[5] over CDF's previous discussion of this question in the "Declaration on Certain Questions concerning Sexual Ethics" (*Persona humana*, Dec. 29, 1975). Specifically, he concludes that *Persona humana* (*PH*) "based its stand essentially on natural-law tradition," whereas the present Letter "moves Scripture to the center of the argument and leaves the natural-law dimension almost entirely implicit."[6]

Second, although Williams admits that some of the references in this Letter might be "most disturbing,"[7] the entirety of the Letter provides "ample reassurance that the demeaning of gay persons is quite contrary to its basic intention."[8] Williams here underlines the Letter's affirmation of homosexual persons as "often generous and giving of themselves" (no. 7, par. 2), as having a "transcendent nature" and "supernatural vocation" (no. 8, par. 2), as invested with an "intrinsic dignity ... [which] must always be respected in word, in action and in law" (no. 10, par. 1), as possessing "the fundamental liberty which characterizes the human person and gives him his dignity" (no. 11, par. 2), and as having a special claim on the Church's pastoral care (nos. 13–17).[9]

The purpose of this article is not so much to enter into debate with Williams as rather to enter into a dialogue with these two "significant

[1] "Homosexuality: The New Vatican Statement," *TS* 48 (1987) 259–77.
[2] Ibid 259.
[3] Ibid.
[4] Ibid 277.
[5] Ibid 260.
[6] Ibid.
[7] Ibid. 263.
[8] Ibid.
[9] Ibid.

steps" in order to advance further the magisterium's teaching on the question of homosexuality and homosexual activity. This article will thus discuss Williams' evaluation of the scriptural exegesis used in the Letter, as well as the Letter's argument that the homosexual orientation itself is "an objective disorder" (no. 3, par. 2).

## SCRIPTURAL EXEGESIS

As stated above, Williams rightly argues that the Letter "moves Scripture to the center of the argument"[10] regarding homosexuality. He argues that the biblical data in this Letter demonstrates that the Church's condemnation of homosexual activity is based not simply on limited scattered texts but "on the solid foundation of a constant biblical testimony" (no. 5, par. 2). He points out that the Letter's use of Scripture in this area is based largely on the vision of creation as found in the book of Genesis (see no. 6, par. 1) and affirms the basic "complementarity of the sexes" and the intrinsic "spousal significance" (no. 6, par. 1) of the human body. He thus concludes that "primary stress is now placed on the relational aspect of this significance"[11] rather than on the traditional natural-law argument regarding the procreative aspect of sexuality. He quotes the Letter specifically: the homosexual relationship "is not a complementary union, able to transmit life; and so it thwarts the call to a life of that form of self-giving which the Gospel says is the essence of Christian living" (no. 7, parr. 1, 2).

The main point here is to stress that heterosexuality remains normative and any other orientation necessarily falls short of the full spectrum of human relationship. This conclusion rests on the Genesis vision of God's sexual design concerning the complementarity of male and female and the responsibility for the transmission of human life.

While Williams treats this basic vision of Genesis correctly, he does not seem to evaluate well specific Old and New Testament references to homosexual activity. He refers, for example, to various "antihomosexual statements"[12] in the Old and New Testaments. On two other occasions he makes reference to particular "antihomosexual" references and texts found in both Testaments.[13]

This point regarding "antihomosexual references" must be carefully evaluated in order to further the Church's understanding of both homosexuality and the morality of homosexual activity. It is of utmost importance to stress the fact that the *concepts* of "homosexual" and "homo-

[10] Ibid. 260.
[11] Ibid. 262.
[12] Ibid. 260.
[13] Ibid. 261.

sexuality" were unknown during the time of the Bible's composition.[14] The concepts of "homosexual" and "homosexuality" presume an understanding of human sexuality that was possible only with the insights and discoveries of contemporary psychological and sociological analysis.

In *The New Testament and Homosexuality*,[15] Robin Scroggs convincingly argues that the modern concept of homosexuality was unknown to the biblical writers and that the particular aspect of homosexuality condemned as sordid and dehumanizing in the New Testament was likely pederasty. In fact, Scroggs argues, if there is any evidence at all of same-age homosexuality in the New Testament, it is between youths (*meirakia*).

In addition, Richard B. Hays argues in "Relations Natural and Unnatural: A Response to John Boswell's Exegesis of Romans I"[16] that in the New Testament St. Paul sustained no concept whatsoever of a person being "constitutionally homosexual." Hays argues that for Paul homosexual activity was understood to be a tragic distortion of the created order and thus it is incorrect to conclude that Paul "means" to condemn homosexual activity because such acts were being done by persons who were "constitutionally heterosexual." In other words, Paul would not have had a notion of someone being "constitutionally homosexual" as opposed to others being "constitutionally heterosexual."

It is important to conclude, then, that Scripture does not recognize or speak about homosexuality as a sexual orientation *as distinct from* specific genital activity. Biblical writers took it for granted that all people were created with a natural attraction to members of the opposite sex and that their genital activity would and should reflect this fact. As Hays demonstrates, Paul understands all human depravity to *follow from* human unrighteousness: i.e., in this regard, to deny God's created order. In light of the Genesis vision, then, any homosexual behavior was likely to be judged as the capricious and malicious rejection of God's designs for humanity.

Williams' references to "particular antihomosexual references" can thus be misleading, since it is vitally important to stress that biblical statements about homosexuality are statements about certain kinds of homosexual *acts*. In all probability, the biblical writers in each instance were speaking of homosexual acts undertaken by persons whom the authors presumed to be heterosexually constituted. Each biblical refer-

[14] For an excellent treatment of this subject, see Vincent J. Genovesi, S.J., *In Pursuit of Love* (Wilmington, Del.: Michael Glazier, 1987) 244–99. I will summarize here a great deal of Genovesi's analysis.

[15] Philadelphia: Fortress, 1983.

[16] *Journal of Religious Ethics*, 14 (1986) 184–215.

ence to homosexual activity, then, must be interpreted against this presumption.

The famous text of Gen 19 is important in this regard. It should not be overlooked that the Scriptures make numerous references to evils associated with Sodom. Jer 23:14, e.g., indicates that Sodom's sins were adultery, persistent lying, and an unwillingness to repent. Ezek 16:49–50 enlarges these evils to include pride, gluttony, arrogance, complacency, and an unwillingness to help the poor and needy. The Wisdom of Solomon (19:13–14) specifies Sodom's evils as folly, insolence, and inhospitality. Other scriptural references to Sodom include Qoh 16:8, Mt 10:14–15, Lk 10:10–12, 2 Pet 2:4–10, and Jude 6–7.

What is clear from a reading of the entirety of these texts is that the people of Sodom were involved in numerous offenses, homogenital activity being one of those offenses. The Genesis text itself makes clear that the men of Sodom were contemplating homosexual gang rape induced by sexual lust. Gen 19 illustrates well a biblical text where careful exegesis is called for, and further demonstrates that this text alone cannot be used as a justification for prohibiting *all* forms of homogenital activity.

Lev 18:22 is another important Old Testament reference. Appearing in the midst of the holiness code, the text clearly commands the Israelites not to "behave as they do in Egypt where you once lived" or "as they do in Canaan where I am taking you" (Lev 18:3). This concern for cultic purity suggests that homosexual activity was condemned in this text in an attempt to demonstrate the need to avoid practices that might be identified with the occurrences of male and female prostitution common in mid-East religious cults. This prohibition can also be seen in Deut 23:18 and 1 Kgs 14:24, 15:12, 22:47. What seems probable in the entirety of these texts is that homosexual activity is prohibited because of its intimate association with idolatry.

As already stated, St. Paul's treatment of homosexual activity in 1 Cor 6:9–10 and 1 Tim 1:9–10 more than likely is aimed at prohibiting a certain form of pederasty that was widespread in the Greco-Roman culture of his time. Paul is thus not necessarily condemning *all* homogenital behavior as such but the specific practice of pederasty as it appeared in Greco-Roman society.

Paul's basic thesis and theology regarding homosexual activity is clearly detailed in Rom 1:18–32. Paul explains that the pagans have refused to honor the true God and this rejection has resulted in dire consequences, e.g. all sorts of "depravity" (Rom 1:29–31).

The point of looking specifically at these texts is to underline the caution that must be raised in such statements as "particular antihomosexual texts/references" which Williams employs in his article. There is no question that texts in both the Old and New Testament condemn various forms of homogenital activity, but each of these texts must be studied in its own context. In addition, the notion of "sexual orientation" is an anachronism when applied to biblical texts.

## THE HOMOSEXUAL CONDITION: AN OBJECTIVE DISORDER

A second main point in Williams' treatment of the Letter is his interpretation of the homosexual condition as being objectively disordered.[17] He carefully analyzes this concept in conjunction with the Letter's correlative statement that persons who engage in such activity "confirm within themselves a disordered inclination which is essentially self-indulgent" (no. 7, par. 2). He explains that the intent of this designation must be interpreted over against the vision of Genesis already explained regarding sexual complementarity and the potential fruitfulness demanded by the nuptial union embodied in the male and the female.[18]

While Williams takes extraordinary steps to interpret this "disorder" in the best light possible, stressing the fact that the Letter also articulates the dignity of homosexual persons and their "often generous" personalities, he unfortunately gives the impression that homosexual individuals *choose*, in some way or other, this sexual orientation. In explaining the context of "self-indulgent," e.g., he writes of "the preference of one's homosexual proclivity over God's creative design. . . ."[19] Toward the end of his article, he offers interesting reasons why the use of a "gay" identity can be quite self-limiting.[20] The problem, however, is that he clearly implies that a person's homosexual orientation is an identity that in some way or other has been chosen. He writes, e.g., that the gay identity is one that "is typically adopted as a defense mechanism."[21]

This assumption regarding "choice" or "preference" leads Williams to conclude that "readjustment" to a heterosexual orientation is possible, even though not "widely assumed."[22] He seems to affirm the quotation from the Washington State Catholic Conference (WSCC) that homosexual persons would be obliged to try to change their orientation if this were at all possible.[23] The statement of the WSCC does indicate that presently there seems to be no apparent way of "altering" a homosexual orientation; but the assumption is that such an alteration might be

[17] Letter, no. 3, par. 3.

[18] Williams, "Homosexuality" 262.

[19] Ibid.

[20] Ibid. 275.

[21] Ibid.

[22] Ibid.

[23] Washington State Catholic Conference, *The Prejudice against Homosexuals and the Ministry of the Church*, Seattle, April 28, 1983.

discovered, thus giving the impression that somehow one "chooses" a sexual identity or orientation.

He furthers this assumption regarding "choice" by indicating that for a homosexual person a "chaste life" might "refer to eventual heterosexual reorientation and marriage."[24]

It is very important, for obvious pastoral reasons, to recall that *Persona humana* teaches that some homosexuals are "innately" constituted as such and thus their "constitution" should not be thought of as "curable" (no. 8, par. 2).

It is vitally important here to advert to the fact that generally the literature on this subject, as well as the testimony of large numbers of homosexual persons, indicates that the homosexual condition itself is *not chosen.*[25] The homosexual orientation appears to be a given, and an individual gradually discovers that he or she sustains this orientation. To the extent that this is true, the condition of homosexuality itself should not be referred to as evil, as the Letter does not do; but neither should the impression be given that one could choose an *orientation* that is heterosexual, even though it might be possible for a homosexual person to *act* heterosexually. In this regard the following "definition" is applicable. A homosexual person sustains

> a predominant, persistent, and exclusive psychosexual attraction toward members of the same sex. A homosexual person is one who feels sexual desire for and a sexual responsiveness to persons of the same sex and who seeks or would like to seek actual sexual fulfillment of this desire by sexual acts with a person of the same sex. A distinction is drawn by a majority of authors on the subject between the homosexual *condition* and the homosexual *act.*[26]

Williams also employs the scholastic axiom "action follows being" (*agere sequitur esse*) to demonstrate that it is not possible to indicate that it is simply "all right" for someone to "be" homosexual.[27] If one

[24] Williams, "Homosexuality" 274.

[25] Masters and Johnson claimed in earlier research that they were able to assist sexually dysfunctionally homosexual persons to become heterosexual. Much of their therapeutic treatment was later disregarded by competent researchers. See William Masters and Virginia Johnson, *Homosexuality in Perspective* (New York: Little and Brown, 1979), and William Masters, "The Masters and Johnson Treatment Program for Dissatisfied Homosexual Men," *American Journal of Psychiatry* 141 (1984) 173–81. In this regard it is important to consult Alan P. Bell and Martin S. Weinberg, *Homosexualities: A Study of Diversity among Men and Women* (New York: Simon and Schuster, 1978).

[26] George A. Kanoti and Anthony R. Kosnik, "Homosexuality: Ethical Aspects," *Encyclopedia of Bioethics* 2 (New York: Free Press, 1978) 671. See also Judd Marmon, ed., *Sexual Inversion* (New York: Basic Books, 1965) 4, and James B. Nelson, *Embodiment* (Minneapolis: Augsburg, 1979) 201.

[27] Williams, "Homosexuality" 265.

came to this conclusion, he argues, " . . . there can be no plausible basis for a rule which tells such a person 'don't do.' "[28]

It is significant here to recall St. Thomas' teaching on homosexual activity (*in coitu masculorum*):

> Now with regard to pleasures of either of these two kinds, there are some which are unnatural, absolutely speaking, but may be called natural from a particular point of view (*sed connaturales secundum quid*). For it sometimes happens that one of the principles which is natural to the species as a whole has broken down in one of its individual members; the result can be that something which runs counter to the nature of the species as a rule, happens to be in harmony with nature for a particular individual (*fieri per accidens naturale huic individuo*), as it becomes natural for a vessel of water which has been heated to give out heat. Thus something which is "against human nature," either as regards reason or as regards physical preservation, may happen to be in harmony with the natural needs of *this* man because in him nature is ailing. He may be ailing physically: either from some particular complaint, as fever-patients find sweet things bitter, and vice versa; or from some dispositional disorder, as some find pleasure in eating earth or coals. He may be ailing psychologically, as some men by habituation come to take pleasure in cannibalism, or in copulation with beasts or with their own sex (*in coitu bestiarum aut masculorum*), or in things not in accord with human nature.[29]

The point here is that, for Thomas, homosexual activity, because of some "tragic distortion," as St. Paul would write, has become "connatural" for some individuals (*connaturales secundum quid*). Certainly, in the biblical as well as the classical, Thomistic traditions heterosexuality is normative. It may happen, however, that some individuals are acting homogenitally. Although clearly the concept of a "homosexual orientation" would be unknown to biblical and classical writers, it seems logical to conclude that these writers would name the homosexual *activity* of these individuals as "distorted," but would not name the persons themselves as such.

It is crucial, therefore, to give further study to the relationship between "be-ing" and "do-ing." Williams seems to think that the Letter's reference to the homosexual condition as objectively disordered rests upon the necessity of insisting that homosexuality *per se* is evil.

What conclusions might be reached? (1) The homosexual orientation and its accompanying life-styles can take many forms which occur cross-culturally, though perhaps not universally. (2) Most people *discover* their sexual orientation as a given, if an ambiguous and confusing given, rather than choose it. (3) Homosexuality is a variation in human sexual orien-

[28] Ibid.

[29] *Sum. theol.* 1–2, 31–39.

tation that occurs consistently, even though with less frequency than heterosexuality.

## CONCLUSION

This article has attempted to demonstrate that Williams appreciates two major significant steps in the recent Letter of CDF: Scripture plays a central role in argumentation regarding homosexuality, and homosexual persons are affirmed for their intrinsic and fundamental dignity and human liberty. In dealing with both of these points, he has raised certain notions that need more nuanced sophistication and a greater amount of research.

While the Genesis vision of God's sexual design concerns the complementarity of the sexes and responsibility for the transmission of human life, biblical texts dealing with homosexual activity cannot be fully appreciated simply by analyzing them over against this norm. Each text must be considered in its own specificity and context, with the realization that biblical writers had no understanding of the modern concept of "homosexual" and "homosexuality." While both the Letter and Williams' treatment of the Letter underline strong positive affirmations of homosexual persons, numerous complications enter into this affirmation when one attempts to understand the Letter's statement that the homosexual condition itself is an objective disorder. In this regard it is essential to remember that a large amount of bibliography on this question, as well as the personal testimonies of homosexual people, testify that one's sexual orientation is a given rather than a condition which one prefers or chooses. The Letter itself does not claim to be "an exhaustive treatment" of the "complex" homosexual question (no. 2, par. 1) and thus implicitly urges further consideration and reflection regarding this extremely complicated question. In Thomistic language, e.g., if a person is *per accidens* homosexual in orientation, what must we morally conclude about this individual's condition itself? That is, if the orientation has become "connatural" for this individual, is it authentically understandable to refer to *this person's* orientation as disordered? The words of *Persona humana* are thus relevant: not every homosexual person is "personally responsible" for this condition.[30]

*St. Joseph's College*
*Mountain View, Calif.*

GERALD D. COLEMAN, S.S.

[30] *PH*, no. 8, par. 4.

# DIGNITY, Inc. : an alternative experience of church

David Davidson

What is the church? Who is the church? Today that question is difficult to answer. A real marvel of contemporary Catholicism has been its ability to maintain within one church differing and sometimes blatantly opposed groups of believers. Throughout the United States pockets of church offer a spectrum of church experiences. Among those pockets are some 116 local chapters of DIGNITY, Inc., a lay organization of lesbian and gay Catholics and their friends, founded in Los Angeles in 1969. To a growing number of American Catholics, Dignity offers an alternative experience of church. Indeed, for most of its members, Dignity offers the only possible experience; without Dignity they would simply forget about being Catholic.

Certainly Dignity is on the fringe of official Roman Catholicism. Some believe that the October 30, 1986, Vatican '*Letter to the Bishops of the Catholic Church on the Pastoral Care of Homosexual Persons*' officially proscribes Dignity. But only consideration of what the Dignity chapters actually are would determine whether or not they provide an authentic Catholic experience of church. So here a priest who has ministered to various Dignity chapters for over ten years offers an inside picture so judgments to be made may be based on the evidence.

### *DIGNITY as a Local Church*

The chapters of Dignity constitute discrete faith communities alongside other such communities within a universal communion. Dignity chapters serve as 'local churches'; or, in the terminology of liberation theology, they are *comunidades de base*. The explicit self-identity of Dignity certainly maintains as much:

> We believe that gay Catholics are members of Christ's mystical body, numbered among the people of God. We have an inherent dignity because God created us, Christ died for us, and the Holy Spirit sanctified us in Baptism, making us His Temple, and the channel through which the love of God might become visible. Because of this, it is our right, our privilege, and our duty to live the sacramental life of the Church, so that we might become more powerful instruments of God's love working among all people.

These local church groups relate to the broader Catholic Church both institutionally and communally, though their status in both cases is ambiguous. As the Statement of Position and Purpose above makes clear, Dignity chapters consider themselves part of the Roman Catholic Church. They celebrate the Roman Catholic rituals and maintain Roman Catholic allegiance. Perhaps only their stance on sexual ethics, expressed in a carefully worded statement, presents a notable contrast:

> We believe that gay and lesbian people can express their sexuality in a manner that is consonant with Christ's teaching. We believe that all sexuality should be exercised in an ethically responsible and unselfish way.

In any case, for better or worse, this position merely mirrors other variant positions common in Catholicism today—on birth control, liturgical practice, women's rights, nuclear disarmament, economic policy, and other issues. More on this below.

The degree of institutional legitimacy that Dignity enjoys varies from chapter to chapter, depending on the opinion of the local diocesan bishop. For all practical purposes in San Diego Dignity has long been banned. In New York and Philadelphia official support is given to Courage, a gay Catholic support group that believes homosexuality is an emotional disability and that advocates celibacy—though it is an open question whether celibacy is more prevalent among Courage than among Dignity members. Since the recent Vatican document, Dignity chapters in Atlanta, Brooklyn, Buffalo, New York and Pensacola have been expelled from church property. Yet in other dioceses Dignity chapters continue to meet as they had. And in Pensacola, as well as in Baltimore, Cleveland, Colorado Springs, Detroit, and Trenton, for example, bishops have presided at Dignity liturgies. In what has now become a notorious case, the 1983 Dignity International Convention celebrated its main liturgy in the Seattle cathedral. In San Antonio the Archbishop appointed a laywoman and a priest as official chaplains to the gay community, and they serve that community primarily through Dignity. The national Dignity office and local chapters have been in communication with many American bishops. The point is this: whether or not Dignity is or can be part of the institutional church is far from clear. The judgment seems to depend on how diocesan bishops view the issues and how they use local Dignity chapters as vehicles for ministry to the gay community.

Dignity's status as part of the Catholic fellowship is equally ambiguous. In fact, few parishes would welcome Dignity chapters into their church buildings. In its early history Dignity/Boston was evicted from a Catholic church and now meets in a Unitarian church. In 1985, Dignity/San Antonio was evicted from two churches within a month, victim of a slanderous campaign waged by a small, anonymous, conservative, and supposedly Catholic group. Despite Dignity members' commitment to the Catholic Church and all efforts to educate other Catholics about homosexuality, Catholic circles, typical of our society at large, generally do not welcome openly gay people, whether as individuals or as organized groups. Gay Catholics represent members of the mystical body that many would rather amputate then embrace. So lesbian and gay Catholics were forced to form separate faith communities.

*Focus of identity*
What distinguishes Dignity chapters from other local churches? Only the insistence that homosexuality is God-given and so is not to be hidden or repressed.

This position appears to be unquestionable. Recent studies show that sexual orientation is irreversibly determined by about the age of three, so no one could be held responsible for his or her homosexuality. Moreover, there is no evidence that parents or siblings or any others play any decisive or culpable role in determining a child's homosexuality. So homosexuality cannot be the result of actual sin in any sense. Then, even if considered in the most pejorative sense possible—even as the recent Vatican document styles it: 'an objective disorder'—homosexuality would merely be like a natural handicap. And faith has always allowed that such a thing, if not willed by God, is certainly allowed by God and so should be accepted as 'God's will'. So one is called to accept and to make positive use of one's homosexuality and thus to achieve salvation for oneself and others. Note that word 'positive'. As will be made clear later in this article, taking this theological standpoint certainly does not mean that one is trying to countenance the sexual hedonism so widespread in our society—the contrary is the case.

*Some* Dignity members countenance homogenital relationships, but even here opinions differ. Some maintain this position within the legitimacy of broad Catholic teaching. Without explicitly questioning the official position on homogenital activity, they appeal to the Catholic Church's other teaching about the ultimate primacy of conscience in all moral decisions. In this they are like the millions of Catholic couples who practice birth control as a practical necessity but without challenging the official teaching on the subject.

Others do challenge the adequacy of the official Catholic position on homogenital activity. Well versed on this issue, they join the discussion within contemporary Catholicism on sexual ethics in general, aligning themselves with the liberal position on contraception and masturbation, other instances of non-procreative genital experience. Consistent with their self-identity as church, these gay Catholics claim new insight under the inspiration of the Holy Spirit. On the basis of their own experience as homosexual Catholics and on the basis of new information produced by the human sciences and historical and biblical research, they call for a re-thinking of official Catholic teaching.

Nevertheless, in no case do they advocate sexual promiscuity. These people are conscientiously grappling with sensitive ethical questions. If on this one issue their conclusions differ from magisterial teaching, they are certainly respectful of Roman Catholicism and committed to its deep tradition of faith, scholarship and community.

*The formation of DIGNITY Chapters*

People join Dignity for a variety of reasons. Of course, not all members are homosexual, but all would be supportive of the gay community.

Homosexual Catholics join Dignity primarily because they refuse to be cut off from the church and its ministry. Spiritual needs surface and demand to be met. Official affiliation with Dignity may take a long time. But when the decision to belong is finally made, it is usually made for spiritual reasons. Other organizations in the gay subculture could meet every other human need. In a secularized world it makes no sense to come to church except for spiritual reasons. This is clearly the case with Dignity.

This decision to belong is a freely chosen one. Lesbian and gay people are facing, and many have overcome, perhaps the most serious taboo in our culture—homosexuality. They are not easily pushed into anything, especially not into church-going. When they come to Dignity, they are already trekking beyond motivation by guilt or social pressure; they are seeking support to continue a spiritual journey.

They come because they seek God's love and reassurance. They want to feel that they are good and worthwhile, people of dignity. They do not come particularly seeking forgiveness or healing. Their motivation is much more basically religious. They have a deep experience of personal insufficiency. They feel there is more to life than they have been allowing. They seek God, salvation, new life.

Besides, they seek a community that will support them precisely in being themselves—religious *and* gay. Other churches would not understand. Other churches would require that they hide their true selves. These people want to stand before God and themselves as they really are. And being so thoroughly Catholic, they realize they cannot do this unless they stand before others, the Christian community, in all honesty. Together they express thankfulness to God. They speak of experiencing a sense of being blessed, of knowing a new-found worth, freedom and joy, of feeling unburdened after—in some cases—years of suffering oppression, hatred and self-denigration.

Of course, the picture is not universally positive. As in all church groups, some come to Dignity seeking merely social or even sexual contacts. These are usually disappointed. They do not become regular attendants. The principal driving power behind every Dignity chapter known to this author is spiritual.

*A community of mature faith*
The seasoned members of Dignity are people who have by God's grace found God for themselves. They are no longer professing what their parents, teachers, priests, relatives or friends told them. What they profess is their own, learned through a long and difficult life's journey. The spirituality in question here fits the criteria of advanced maturity used by contemporary developmental theorists such as Lawrence Kohlberg, James Fowler and Jane Loevinger.

Needless to say, what is being described here is the ideal. Many come to Dignity to be told what to do. Kicking and screaming, they may fight for years to arrive at adult faith. Yet, here is the point: unlike many other church groups and probably atypical of Catholicism in general, the Dignity community encourages that struggle. The deeply personal focus of the comunity requires that people arrive at their own position. No one can give gay or lesbian people ecclesiastical or societal approval to be themselves. With the help of the Dignity community, they must arrive at this stance as their own.

Such adult faith entails a rediscovery of the meaning of the Gospel—*Good* News. Application of the Gospel to the concrete context of gay lives challenges typical interpretations. Gay Catholics must find a deeper meaning in religious formulas. For example, when they pray Psalm 119 and say, 'O Lord, I love your law,' they understand this to mean, 'I love your plan for me; I am glad to be who I am; I submit to your design for me as a gay person.' And they have to deprogram the other meaning, 'I obey what others impose on me as your will.' Or again, 'I am sorry for my sin' means 'I am sorry for betraying myself, for despairing over my homosexuality, for resisting your plan for me.' It does not necessarily mean, 'I am sorry for developing loving relationships in my life' or 'I am sorry for my parents' disappointment over me' or 'I am sorry for being different from others.' In Dignity one's homosexuality becomes the occasion for experiencing God's inscrutable yet loving Providence. The faith that results is that of adults.

*A Conversion Community*
The Dignity chapters form and grow because their members have conversion experiences. These people emerge from the cocoon of childhood's religious upbringing and rise in the freedom of adult faith, knowing that God made them and loves them as they are.

Such conversion touches different categories of people. Some few are Roman Catholics for whom religion was always important but who hid their homosexuality. When they finally begin to deal with it, they need a religiously supportive community, so they come to Dignity. Quite a number of current or former priests, religious, and seminarians fall into this category.

But the majority of Dignity members are Roman Catholics who gave up their religion when they decided to accept their homosexuality. The belief that one must choose between being religious or being gay is all too prevalent. Unable to deny their homosexuality, many reject their religion. Then, when they realize that the dichotomy must be false, they come to Dignity.

Finally, many non-Catholics come to Dignity seeking a profoundly spiritual gay community. The Roman Catholic tradition fosters such community and attracts spiritually sensitive people. Typical of many contemporary church experiences, the Dignity experience has an ecumenical dimension.

This conversion community grows by inviting others to the same conversion: realize that God loves you as you are; you do not have to stop being religious—or even Catholic—just because you are homosexual. So Dignity chapters become involved in a major contemporary Catholic work: evangelization. The message spreads mostly by word of mouth and personal testimony. But brochures, business cards, ads in the gay press, posters in the bars, and interviews with the media also help spread the word. Friends invite their gay friends to come and see what this 'gay church' is like.

The whole process requires much patience. People who approach Dignity come and go. Apart from the sustaining core, selflessly committed to intense ministry, the typical Dignity congregation may be quite fluid. It takes years before many homosexual people shake off their ingrained sense of guilt and unworthiness and begin to experience God's love for them. 'Coming out' is a long and difficult process. Re-entry into church is frightening and difficult. People attend once, they do not return for months: the initial experience is overwhelming. Coming to Dignity is a complex affair. It does not mean simply coming back to church and being a standard legitimate Catholic again. It requires a rethinking of one's personal life and a new understanding of church. It requires some kind of religious conversion.

*A Prophetic Community*

Dignity challenges everyone. One the one hand, as gay it challenges standard Roman Catholics to rethink their attitudes toward their lesbian sisters and gay brothers and to openly welcome them into the church. It also challenges the churches by urging very disturbing ethical issues.

On the other hand, Dignity also challenges the gay subculture to face questions of sexual ethics and other spiritual issues. The gay subculture tends to be adamantly anti-religious. Since the churches have generally abdicated responsibility for the gay community, sexual mores there often embody the worst of today's confused and perverted sexual values. That community does not want to hear from any moralizing religious do-gooders. Moreover, well aware that church groups are a most powerful opponent of their basic civil rights, most gay people harbour an intense distrust and animosity toward religion—and rightly so. Confusing civil rights with sexual ethics, here the Roman Catholic Church is certainly guilty, as the recent Vatican document makes abundantly clear. So Dignity, both gay and Catholic, is an affront to the gay subculture as well as to the church.

Dignity as church is not and cannot be any form of 'established religion'. It is rather a church of the *diaspora,* a church in exile, and in a most radical way. Dignity is ostracized both from the churches, from society at large, and from the gay community. It functions as a prophet, a lone voice crying in the wilderness of misunderstanding and opposition on all fronts. It this case it exhibits a sure sign of true biblical religion.

Yet not all Dignity members or chapters are willing to accept the prophetic call. They are not yet ready to be martyrs. So Dignity also runs the risk of becoming another closet. Providing the spiritual support that gay people need for their personal lives, it can serve as a cosy hideaway from responsibility for the broader ecclesial, civil, and gay communities. Not all Dignity members feel called to heroic sanctity.

*A Welcoming Community*

Being homosexual has a certain levelling effect. Once one has crossed the horrid barrier of that taboo, other societal categories become insignificant. So gay people can generally be proud that their community accepts people regardless of social class, educational background, economic status, and race. Tolerance within the gay community is relatively high. But the gay community also has its own hierarchy of acceptability. Youth rank high, and the elderly low. Good looks at any age are prized. Besides, there are the supposed dregs of gay society: swish, fluff, fems, bulldykes, drag queens, hustlers, transsexuals, addicts. Every society has its outcasts, even a society of outcasts.

As church in this society, Dignity is a welcoming community. Some chapters have an explicit policy of hospitality: we who have experienced rejection can hardly reject others; we who are accepted by God must accept all others. So the chapters struggle to make room for everyone. The high level of tolerance sometimes even inhibits the smooth running of the organization. But hospitality holds a higher priority than efficiency. Gospel values override secular values.

*An Open and Honest Community*

The Dignity communities are generally small, and their purpose is known to everyone. Whoever comes to Dignity meetings exposes himself or herself to association with society's lepers. Then there is nothing more to hide. So Dignity people know each other. They can talk freely about their lives—about their dreams and hardships, their loves and heartaches, their families, work, and friends. And they will be received and supported. This is true not only for those who have come to know each other as intimate friends but also for people who newly join the group. Table conversation after a Dignity liturgy can cover the whole gamut of human experience, and all is accepted and lovingly received. Humour is not lacking.

Here is a basis for real community. People do not have to hide from one another. Is such basis available in standard church communities, proper and 'respectable'? Is it available in formal religious communities, beset with their rules and taboos and traditions? Dignity offers people a place where they can be who they are and grow spiritually by sharing their life's journey with fellow believers. Members of Alcoholics Anonymous say the same about their meetings.

*A Community of Equals*

Because of the community's openness and because of the stigma of homosexuality, no one in the Dignity community can pretend to be above anyone else. When all are convicted, all are equals. Moreover, gay people have seen enough of life to see through most of it. Pretences are hard to sustain in a gay community. So in Dignity people meet and accept each other as equals, as fellow human beings. Whatever other respect one may have in the community must be earned.

The experience of priests presiding at Dignity liturgies offers an important example. Priests tend to call up a presbyteral poise and a liturgical lilt of the voice when they slip into their albs and chasubles. Such show falls flat in the gay community. So priests often report being nervous before the Dignity community. They know they cannot bluff their way with pious words and learned gestures. They feel the community sees through them. So, if they continue to preside at Dignity liturgies, they gradually learn to be themselves. Then they find themselves much more effective ministers, too.

The Dignity gathering tends to be a community of brothers and sisters. There is certainly an appropriate diversity of roles, and there may be sibling rivalry, but no one will pretend to play the parent. It would not work. Even from a structural point of view, Dignity fosters equality among its members. Dignity is lay organized and lay run. Even if the chapter is lucky enough to have a priest around regularly, the leader of the community is its elected president, not the priest. The priest is the spiritual leader, the chaplain. Other than that, he is just one of the members whose voice is respected because of what he says, not because of his priestly role. Here Church is truly a People of God, a community of brothers and sisters working together, each contributing as each is able, all respected for their dignity before God.

This collegial role of the chaplain in the Dignity organization benefits both the chapter and official Catholicism. On the one hand, since Dignity is a lay organization, its activities and policies are free from clerical control. On the other hand, since the official church is not responsible for Dignity, bishops can use the local chapters as effective contact points for needed ministry to the gay community without thereby endorsing everything that Dignity does. The obvious parallel example is chaplaincy to the military establishment.

*The Parish Community*

The ultimate goal of Dignity chapters as separate local church communities is to become obsolete. The goal is to reintroduce alienated lesbian and gay Catholics into the Church and eventually to make them welcome to participate in ordinary parishes with respect and dignity. But that goal is still a long way off. In the meantime, the list of activities of an active Dignity chapter reads like that of an ordinary parish. In addition to providing regular liturgies and celebration of Reconciliation, Dignity leaders find themselves instructing converts, blessing homes, visiting the sick, burying the dead, writing testimonial letters for sacramental sponsors, counselling, holding socials and fundraisers, providing educational programs, organizing charitable works, making contributions to special causes, collaborating with other religious groups, and much more. The point is that even judging on externals Dignity provides a typical experience of church.

Those who insist on the ideal, that there should be no separate communities, that such groups are divisive to the church, need to remember that without such groups gay and lesbian Catholics would be effectively excluded from the church. More gross division, based on prejudice, would reign. Besides, in other cases the church never hesitates to establish special communities, like deaf communities or ethnic parishes, for people who have particular needs or who are not yet integrated into the church and society at large.

*DIGNITY as Church*

Formerly ecclesiology understood church by analysing its essence as the perfect society or as the Mystical Body of Christ. Today theologians prefer to focus on the mission of the church as a Pilgrim People. In *Church: The Continuing Quest* Richard McBrien outlined three functions constitutive of church. To these a fourth may be added.

Church is *koinonia,* a community of believers who support one another in faith and love and so become a model of hope to others. Church is *diakonia,* service to the world in preparation for the coming of God's reign. Church entails *kerygma,* proclamation of the Good News of God's love and acceptance and of our new life in Jesus Christ. And Church is *eucharistia,* thanksgiving and praise to God in the name of all creation.

As obvious centres of Christian *koinonia, diakonia, kerygma,* and *eucharistia,* Dignity chapters qualify as genuine local churches. They offer an otherwise neglected group of Catholics an alternative experience of Christ's on-going saving work in the world. They provide thousands of lesbian and gay people a rich experience of church. Some may still question whether all this sufficient for qualification also as a *Catholic* experience of church. If the answer is No, anyone with extensive pastoral experience might well wonder how any real parish could qualify.

# HETEROSEXIST THEOLOGY: Being Above It All

*Carter Heyward*

### *Heterosexism*

Sexism is the foundation of heterosexism. Heterosexist theology is constructed on the assumption that male domination of female lives is compatible with the will of God. The rightness of compulsory heterosexuality is predicated on the belief in a natural order or process that alone is good—so that any deviation from it is sinful. Basing contemporary moral theory on medieval concepts of natural law necessitates projecting an image or fantasy of "good order" onto human social relations—thereby denying altogether the role of human agency in determining moral good.[1]

While belief in natural law may not strike us as necessarily heterosexist, in a sexist situation like the praxis of the church the assumption of a natural order is infused with corollary presuppositions about gender and sexuality.[2] It is in this social praxis, historical and contemporary, that the image of heterosexual marriage emerges as the prototype for the Right—i.e. the

This essay is from a panel presentation on Lesbian Feminist Issues in Religion (Women and Religion Section) at the American Academy of Religion, Anaheim, Calif., Nov. 25, 1985. It will be expanded into a book, *A Sacred Contempt: Heterosexism and the Liberal God* (New York: Harper and Row, 1989).

[1] For constructive moral epistemologies which build on creative insights from natural law tradition, see Beverly Wildung Harrison, *Making the Connections: Essays in Feminist Social Ethics* (Boston: Beacon, 1985), especially the introduction by Carol S. Robb and pp. 3–21, 115–34, and 235–63; Anthony Battaglia, *Toward a Reformulation of Natural Law* (New York: Seabury, 1981); Daniel C. Maguire, *The Moral Choice* (New York: Doubleday, 1978); Margaret Farley, "New Patterns of Relationship: Beginnings of a Moral Revolution," in *Woman: New Dimensions*, ed. Walter J. Burghardt (New York: Paulist, 1976); and B. Andolsen, C. Gudorf, and M. Pellauer, eds., *Women's Consciousness, Women's Conscience* (Minneapolis: Winston Press), esp. pp. 211 ff.

[2] See Samuel Laeuchli, *Power and Sexuality: The Emergence of Canon Law at the Synod of Elvira* (Philadelphia: Temple University Press, 1972); Anne Llewellyn Barstow, *On Studying Witchcraft as Women's History* (forthcoming); and the classic, infamous, *Malleus Maleficarum* (Hammer of Witches), by monks Sprenger and Kraemer, for the extent to which Christian assumptions about the natural as moral are steeped in misogyny. See also Harrison on the relation between hatred of women and fear of homosexuality, "Misogyny and Homophobia: The Unexplored Connections," in *Making the Connections*, pp. 135–51.

Natural and Moral—Relation not only between male and female, but also between Christ and his church. Compulsory heterosexuality safeguards this divinely willed Right Relation. To coerce heterosexual bonding is simply to affirm what is natural. And what is natural reflects the good order of the cosmos, thereby revealing the divine purpose. The Be-ing of God involves being heterosexual.

In the church, individualistic psychology is often drawn on for support in upholding the sanctity of compulsory heterosexual relations. Thus church bodies often commission psychiatrists to make clinical judgments of the "maturity" of individual candidates for the ordained ministry. More often than not, "maturity" is understood by the ecclesiastical authority (and often by the psychiatrist) as synonymous with heterosexual marriage or, at least, with the candidate's willingness to abstain from any sexual activity outside such marriage. On this basis, church authorities frequently will deny that they are against homosexuality per se, but rather will insist that they are opposed to all sexual activity outside of marriage, heterosexual as well as homosexual. To the rejoinder that *homosexual* marriages are not permitted in the church, the typical response is, "Of course not," as if the very notion were unintelligible to Christian sensibilities of what is both natural and moral.[3]

It should not be surprising that the church would consecrate psychology as its Great High Priest. Psychology, in large part, remains the most highly individualistic of the modern sciences, and liberals have strong investment in the interior life and yearnings of individuals as the locus of sin and grace, problems and transformation.[4] Moreover, what is psychologically "normal" provides the content for the theologian's understanding of the natural and

[3] At least one seminary (The Episcopal Seminary in Alexandria, Virginia) requires all of its students to sign a pledge that they will not engage in sexual activity outside of marriage while they are students at the Seminary. And at least one psychiatrist who screens candidates for ordination in a liberal Episcopal diocese has indicated to those whom he interviews that their sexual behavior is *the* critical factor in his judging their fitness for ordination. While he expresses interest in hearing details of *heterosexual* lives, he makes no secret of his special disdain for gay men and lesbians, who are, in his judgment, "immature" and unfit for ordained ministry.

[4] For attention to interiorized spirituality as a moral problem, see Dorothee Sölle (with Shirley Cloyes), *To Work and to Love: A Theology of Creation* (Philadelphia: Fortress, 1984), as well as other pieces by Sölle. This same theme is explored in the Amanecida Collective's *Revolutionary Forgiveness: Feminist Reflections on Nicaragua* (Maryknoll, N.Y.: Orbis, 1986), as well as throughout the growing corpus of liberation theologies. See, for example, Ernesto Cardenal, *The Gospel in Solentiname*, 4 vols., trans. Donald Walsh (Maryknoll, N.Y.: Orbis, 1976–82); Gustavo Gutierrez, *The Power of the Poor in History*, trans. Robert Barr (Maryknoll, N.Y.: Orbis, 1983), and Phillip Berryman, *The Religious Roots of Rebellion: Christians in Central American Revolution* (Maryknoll, N.Y.: Orbis, 1984). In her essay, "While Love is Unfashionable: An Exploration of Black Spirituality and Sexuality," in *Women's Consciousness, Women's Conscience*, Toinette M. Eugene examines connections between justice, sexuality, and spirituality in Black experience.

moral. What is specifically lacking is a *critical* analysis of the ways in which unjust power relations between men and women shape the lens through which we view the natural/moral order. Liberal proponents of natural law fail to enter into serious engagement with those whose lives are marginalized by its truth-claims.

My thesis in this essay is that liberal Christianity is morally bankrupt in relation to women and all homosexual persons. In fact, the liberal church damages these people because, as a theo-political ideology, liberalism is not only set against collective advocacy as a primary mode of Christian witness; it is also contemptuous of the particular claims of feminists and all openly gay/lesbian people. In what follows I attempt to illustrate why.

Specifically I shall contend that Paul Tillich, as a paradigmatic modern liberal, presents an amoral, individualistic God-Man as constitutive of Being itself. Moreover, the contemporary liberal church, as represented by the praxis of mainline denominations, operates on the same nonrelational and irresponsible assumptions about divine and human life. Most important, the individual's experience of *normative* Christian life is steeped historically in heterosexism.

## *God above God*

Hannah Tillich, Paul's widow, tells of a conversation between "the old woman and the old man":

> "Why do you always remain on the borderline?" asked the old woman. "Why can't you decide between Yin and Yang, between the mountains and the deep blue sea? . . "
>
> "Why should I decide?" retorted the old man nastily. "I don't know where I belong. Besides, indecision allows for freedom."[5]

Paul Tillich went beyond the romantic reductionism of natural law into a more complex theological reasoning which took some account of the ambiguities of human existence. Still, Tillich's theology suffered from problems classic to liberal philosophy. First, he did not have an adequate understanding of the social, relational basis of either human or divine Being. "Being" is constitutive of the inner life of the individual agent. Second, for this reason, Tillich did not see the *theological* significance of the material, embodied, and economic grounds of human being. His specific focus was on the ability of the well-educated Euroamerican male to cope spiritually within the "structures of existence." His concept of God, a logical companion piece to his anthropology, floats free of the contingencies of relationality, physicality, and material need—and, thus, as Alison Jaggar would suggest, from our actual "ground of being."[6]

[5] Hannah Tillich, *From Time to Time* (New York: Stein and Day, 1973), p. 15. I am grateful to Tom F. Driver for reminding me how vividly Hannah Tillich writes of her husband's liberal disposition.

[6] See Paul Tillich, *Systematic Theology*, 3 vols. (Chicago: University of Chicago Press), 2: esp. 155–58.

Tillich recognizes his own "estrangement" as constitutive of his "existence." He notes a problem with the extent to which Christian theologians traditionally have rendered estrangement—or sin—as rooted in "concupiscence," defined narrowly as sexual desire. Of the church's "ambiguous" attitude toward sex, Tillich writes, "The church has never been able to deal adequately with this central ethical and religious problem."[7]

Interestingly, Tillich seems puzzled by this lingering "devaluation of sex" in Christian tradition. He evidently fails to notice a connection in Christian history between the devaluation of sex and the devaluation of women. This failure itself reflects the bias in Tillich's perspective on the meaning of estrangement, creation, existence, and essence. In other words, his world view—grounded in his experience and articulated in his theology—reveals much about the "actualized creation and estranged existence" of a white male German academic failing to acknowledge (or perhaps even to notice) that the limits of his theological epistemology are set not only by his "finitude" as "man" but more particularly by his experience as one white German male.

Writing on behalf of all men (and I leave intact the linguistic ambiguity of Tillich's theology), Tillich subsumes the conditions of human existence under a series of ontological polarities. Every man lives in tension between the angst of his existence and the divine essence from which he has fallen into this alienated situation. Tillich's fundamental image of human life reflects the [his] experience of existing between death/dying and life/living. While Tillich's academic concern is not, basically, a moral one, and while he does not reduce death to evil or life to good, his theology suggests that human existence is synonymous with a moral struggle against Nonbeing and that, in the struggle, justice is actualized as a moral good. Still, this existential process is located in the life of the individual man.[8] As Norene M. Carter has demonstrated, since Tillich fails to present alienation as a social, material condition, his ontology does not address responsibly the moral issues involved in human alienation from other humans, the rest of creation, or the Creator.[9] For human angst originates not in the individual's psychospiritual ontology but rather in the historical structures of alienated social relations which render each person victor or vanquished in a myriad of relational configurations which are beyond her or his individual capacity to alter.

To those who cannot accept the traditional God of theism, Tillich offers

[7] ST, 2:52.

[8] See ST, 1:182–86 on "freedom and destiny"; and 1:255–56 and 2:29ff on "the Fall." Also *The Courage to Be* (New Haven: Yale University Press, 1952) and *Love, Power and Justice* (New York: Oxford University Press, 1954).

[9] Norene M. Carter, a feminist ethicist who lives and works in the Boston area, discusses Marx's and Tillich's different understandings of alienation in an unpublished essay she wrote for Elisabeth Schüssler Fiorenza's and Carter Heyward's class on The Bible and Feminist Hermeneutics, Episcopal Divinity School, spring semester, 1985.

the image of a "God above God" who is eternally beyond the structures of existence.[10] It is from this God above God that we have fallen into alienated existence. And it is with this God that we can reunite in New Being, through participation and transformation by Christ, the Essential God-Man.[11] In refusing to confuse essence with existence, God with man—even in Christ—Tillich misleads us, drawing us away from realizing the part we may play in the drama of salvation.

Tillich does not deny the importance of human "acceptance" of the New Being.[12] He also does not, however, stress the role of human agency in salvation. This is probably because he does not recognize the corporate character of being—either human or divine—and thus, is stuck both epistemologically and soteriologically in his perception that "man" (the individual white male) must be "grasped" by an ontological force (Being, or the Christ) outside himself, before he can participate in the drama of salvation. Ironically, while Tillich is attempting to present a theology that cuts through the individualism of human existence, he fails to grasp the power of human subjectivity when "humanity" is understood as an *essentially corporate reality:*

> The objective reality of the New Being precedes subjective participation in it . . . Regeneration [and conversion], understood in this way, have little in common with the attempt to create emotional reactions in appealing to an individual in his subjectivity.[13]

Tillich draws us beyond the structures of our existence—however dehumanizing, and oppressive—toward an "essence" that should not be confused with our daily human experiences of love and work, pain and struggle, confusion and play. But does it suffice to suggest that our alienation originates in our fall from God, in the spiritual malaise of individual men and women? It may be small comfort to imagine that the solution to our predicament is to bear up courageously on the basis of whatever mental gymnastics enable us to leap high enough or probe deep enough to be grasped by New Being.

Despite his insistence that it is entirely at the initiative of the "divine Spirit" that "man" is "grasped" by the "New Being," the bulk of Tillich's work reflects his efforts to seek, find, and be open to the "essential God-man."[14] Again, the problem is that Tillich did not acknowledge the collective, relational, sensual and embodied ground on which he stood with others, a "ground of being" on which justice-making has more to do with

[10] Tillich discusses "God above God" in *The Courage to Be*.

[11] See ST, 2, esp. part 2.B:118–24.

[12] ST, 2, esp. 2.E:165–79.

[13] ST, 2:177.

[14] ST, 2:178.

one's acceptance of social, relational responsibility than with one's actualization of "as many potentialities as possible without losing oneself in disruption and chaos."[15]

Tillich takes little account of the social, political, historical character of each individual, thus little account of the limits of the individual's spiritual aspirations. Neither Tillich nor other liberal Christians comprehend deeply creative power—at once human and divine—as historically and ontologically embodied among us, transacted between and among ourselves daily as co-creative agents upon whom the Power of Love in history depends. The liberal deity may, in some anthropomorphic sense, "love" us, but it is likely to tax our understandings of what actual loving involves, because a God above God (or an Essential God-Man) remains eternally unaffected by the clamor and clutter of human struggle, including the passions, problems, and confusions of human sexuality.

On the surface, Tillich's theology has nothing to do with sexism, heterosexism, racism, or any other "ism." That is precisely the point of liberal philosophy. God is simply above the fray. This, more than any other, is the grievance of Latin American, Afro-American, Asian American, and feminist liberation theologians against the "objectivity" espoused by liberal theological scholars. This "objectivity" presupposes the subject's ability to manufacture a critical distance between himself and his object of study (such as "God") in order to produce a theology free of bias or ideology.

A more perceptive hermeneutic suggests, however, that Tillich's theology, his portrait of God, has *everything* to do with holding traditional power arrangements in place. For his God above God is finally indifferent to the details of how we live together on the earth. The Prince of Wales and the prisoner on death row, the murdered gay activist Harvey Milk and his murderer Dan White, have the same ontological constitution and live under the same conditions of existence. Their salvation histories involve, essentially, the same angst. A liberal disposition fails to notice its own moral bankruptcy.

Unlike the traditional GodFather, whose anthropomorphic antagonism toward uppity women and wanton sexual behavior is well documented in Christian history, the liberal God of self-consciousness, human potential, and science controls women and homosexual people not because he is hostile to us (God forbid!), but rather because he is neutral in relation to us. Liberal morality is a basically individualistic realm, in which the subject determines right from wrong. In Friedrich Schleiermacher's words,

> In the sinful nature the bad exists only correlatively with the good, and no moment is occupied exclusively by sin. . . . Insofar as the consciousness of our sin is a true element of our being, *and sin*

[15] *Love, Power and Justice*, p. 70.

> *therefore a reality,* it is ordained by God as that which makes redemption necessary. (italics mine)[16]

Not only are good and evil, grace and sin, necessary correlates in the work of redemption in liberal Protestanism, but the reality of sin is predicated upon our noticing it! And we are first and finally moral monads, accountable to the pangs of our own God-*consciousness*, not to a God whose justice may be calling us to account *regardless* of how we feel about it or what we think.

To believe that we can discern our own ethics, choose from many options, and act on the basis of individual "conscience" is, in effect, to admit defeat in the struggle against the structures of our alienation. It is to give *explicit* assent to the immoral proposition that whether one rapes or not, pays taxes or not, drops the bomb or not are decisions that only the responsible individual or individuals can make. It is furthermore to give implicit assent to the dualistic assumption that such matters, in historical fact, are none of God's business. In the realm of God, the opinions of a Jerry Falwell and a John McNeill are of equal consequence—none at all. For the liberal deity has turned over to us the realm of human affairs. What we do, each of us, about racism, sexism, heterosexism or any other human problem is our business.

To their peril, many women as well as male homosexual Christians draw upon the moral neutrality of Christian liberalism in arguing for their right to live and let live.[17] This is finally a self-defeating argument, for the problems of injustice cannot be solved by appeals to "freedom" as a value-free "right."[18] From a moral perspective, freedom is not value-free; it is the power of personal agency in the context of *just* social relations—that is, relations in which the positive value of all persons has been established as a given. Of course, it is indeed logical that, pleading for "neutrality" and "freedom" in matters of morality, liberal Christians should have no reason to believe that God cares whether people are feminists, lesbians, or gay men. It would seem truer to its own ethical heritage if the liberal church were to say to its members who do not conform to traditional gender roles or sexual practices: "God doesn't care whether you are gay or straight, or whether you are a feminist or an adherent to traditional gender roles. God wants you to be true to yourself and faithful in relation to God and God's people." But this is not what most liberal churches have said.

[16] Friedrich Schleiermacher, *The Christian Faith*, ed. H. R. Mackintosh and J. S. Stewart, English trans. of 2nd German ed. (Philadelphia: Fortress, 1976), pp. 332, 335.

[17] This is the position of many gay advocacy groups in religion. Alternatives to this theology are being given voice by such gay/lesbian activists as David Fernbach, *The Spiral Path: A Gay Contribution to Human Survival* (Boston: Alyson, 1981), Mary E. Hunt, *Fierce Tenderness: Toward a Feminist Theology of Friendship* (San Francisco: Harper and Row, 1987), and Cherríe Moraga, *Loving in the War Years* (Boston: South End Press, 1983).

[18] See James Luther Adams, *On Being Human Religiously*, ed. Max L. Stackhouse (Boston: Beacon Press, 1976), esp. pp. 1–88, and Harrison, pp. 81–190, for interpretations of "freedom" and "rights" on the normative basis of justice.

*Sacred Contempt*

In one sense, the implications of theological liberalism for gay men, lesbians and feminists are identical with those for all women, racial/ethnic minority peoples, the poor and others whose oppression should be of more immediate moral concern to church leaders than the spiritual pilgrimages of individuals. There is another sense, however, in which gender and sexual injustice occupy a special place at the hallowed table of Christian fellowship. Sexism and heterosexism receive a particular "blessing" from the liberal philosophical tradition's *trivialization* of the female gender and human sexuality as embodied, material, "lower" phenomena. The "normative dualism" of Christian liberalism has been shaped by sexism and sealed in heterosexism.[19] I need not elaborate here examples from the works of Christian Fathers who have located created, spiritual power in the hypothetically disembodied male mind.[20] Thus, today, while the material concerns of *men* of color and poor *men* can be subsumed *idealistically* into the liberal vision of a nonracist, nonclassist world, women and openly homosexual persons *embody and represent* the specific material phenomena which, in Christian idealism, came early to its full expression in the contributions of Augustine. From the standpoint of Christian idealism, then, to press seriously for women's liberation or for the affirmation of gay and lesbian sexual activity is to fly in the face of the idealistic tradition itself, in which femaleness and sexual activity are, de facto, ungodly and thus singularly undeserving of the justice that constitutes the liberal vision of the divinely ordained world.[21] Thus does liberal Christianity embody its own contradiction between its

[19] See Alison M. Jaggar, *Feminist Politics and Human Nature*, (Totowa, NJ: Rowman & Allanheld, 1983), esp. pp. 27–50 and 173–206.

[20] Important resources for grasping the extent of misogyny—and women's courage and creativity—in Christian tradition include Kari Børreson, *Subordination and Equivalence: The Nature and Role of Women in Augustine and Thomas Aquinas* (Washington, D.C.: University Press of America, 1981); Rosemary R. Ruether and Eleanor McLaughlin, *Women of Spirit: Female Leadership in the Jewish and Christian Traditions* (New York: Simon and Schuster, 1979); Elizabeth A. Clark, *Jerome, Chrysostom, and Friends: Essays and Translations* (New York: Edwin Mellen Press, 1979); Elisabeth Schüssler Fiorenza, *In Memory of Her: A Feminist Reconstruction of Christian Origins* (New York: Crossroad, 1983); Phyllis Trible, *Texts of Terror: Literary-Feminist Readings of Biblical Narratives* (Philadelphia: Fortress, 1984). See Clarissa W. Atkinson, Constance H. Buchanan, and Margaret R. Miles, eds., *Immaculate and Powerful: The Female in Sacred Image and Social Reality* (Boston: Beacon Press, 1985) for similar themes within and beyond Jewish and Christian religions.

[21] It is interesting to me that, in Thomist theology (in which the spiritual is the *super*natural and the "male principle" is in its image), femaleness is cast as "natural." But in modern liberalism's equation of the natural with divine process, the construct of female "nature" (receptive, passive) is set as different from that male "nature" which is normative for a fully human life. Femaleness is, thus, "unnatural" in liberal theology as are sexual

ideal of one, inclusive world and its sacred contempt for femaleness and sexual passion.[22]

While many liberal churches appear to have attended to the problem of sexism, they fail utterly to take heterosexism seriously and thus, in fact, fail to do justice to any women's lives, whether lesbian, heterosexual, bisexual, genitally active, genitally inactive, or celibate. It is important to note that the liberal churches have always displayed some measure of tolerance toward those women and those homosexual people whose *public* presence has been strictly in conformity with patriarchal social relations.[23] Passive, self-deprecating women, and men and women who have kept their homosexual activities "closeted" from public knowledge have been well received on the whole throughout Christian history. I would even conjecture that such women and men have comprised the larger part of the church. Women and homosexual people pose no practical problem to the church unless they *publicly challenge* the church's sexism and heterosexism. This is exactly what is happening today. Many feminists, gay men, and lesbians have begun to "come out" of concealment and put themselves visibly on the ecclesial line as representative of those women and men who, throughout Christian history and the ecumenical church today, have seen that the liberal Christian emperor has no clothes—no sense of the misogynist, erotophobic, and oppressive character of his realm.

Thus, it is true that from the standpoint of advanced patriarchal capitalist social relations, the liberal deity has begun to incorporate, superficially, the "rights" of women and of racial/ethnic minorities and the poor into his divine agenda, as *idealistic* moral claims which need not disrupt the harmony of life as it is meant to be lived in the realm of God. However, the feminist and gay/lesbian demand (not request) that women and homosexual persons be affirmed (not tolerated) poses a challenge not only to the good ordering of liberal social relations, but also a threat to the essence of liberal religion. For

---

acts which run contrary to human (and divine) "nature." Whether "natural" (beneath the super-natural God-man) or "unnatural" (beneath the natural God-man), women are objects rather than subjects of moral agency in Christian history. Liberalism thus has changed nothing with regard to classical Christianity's sacred contempt for women. Homosexual men, of course, have a very different history. As long as they have been "discreet," they have maintained heterosexist benefits of male privilege and domination. *Openly* gay men—not closeted homosexuals—receive scorn and contempt in Christian history.

[22] For help in understanding the politics of this dynamic, see Zillah R. Eisenstein, *The Radical Future of Liberal Feminism* (New York and London: Longman, 1981), Beverly Wildung Harrison, *Our Right to Choose: Toward a New Ethic of Abortion* (Boston: Beacon Press, 1983), and Jaggar, *Feminist Politics and Human Nature*.

[23] John Boswell explores this in *Christianity, Social Tolerance and Homosexuality: Gay People in Western Europe from the Beginning of the Christian Era to the Fourteenth Century* (Chicago: University of Chicago Press, 1980).

the liberal deity is, above all, a noncontroversial gentleman—the antithesis of much that is embodied by feminists and by openly gay and lesbian people who dare to challenge the moral deficit of liberal Christianity. At stake this time, from a feminist liberation perspective, are not the bodies of witches and faggots, but the nature and destiny of God.

*David Hilliard*

# UNENGLISH AND UNMANLY: ANGLO-CATHOLICISM AND HOMOSEXUALITY

DESPITE THE TRADITIONAL TEACHING OF THE CHRISTIAN CHURCH THAT homosexual behaviour is always sinful, there are grounds for believing that Anglo-Catholic religion within the Church of England has offered emotional and aesthetic satisfactions that have been particularly attractive to members of a stigmatised sexual minority. This apparent connection between Anglo-Catholicism and the male homosexual subculture in the English-speaking world has often been remarked upon, but it has never been fully explored. In 1960, for example, in a pioneering study of male homosexuality in Britain, Gordon Westwood stated:

> Some of the contacts maintained that the highest proportion of homosexuals who are regular churchgoers favoured the Anglo-Catholic churches. . . . It was not possible to confirm that suggestion in this survey, but it is not difficult to understand that the services with impressive ceremony and large choirs are more likely to appeal to homosexuals.[1]

More recently, in the United States, several former priests of the Episcopal church have described some of the links between homosexual men and Catholic forms of religion, on the basis of their own knowledge of Anglo-Catholic parishes.[2]

This essay brings together some of the historical evidence of the ways in which a homosexual sensibility has expressed itself within

[1] Gordon Westwood, *A Minority: A Report on the Life of the Male Homosexual in Great Britain* (London: Longmans, 1960), pp. 54-55. See also Andrew Hodges and David Hutter, *With Downcast Gays: Aspects of Homosexual Self-Oppression* (Toronto: Pink Triangle Press, 1977), pp. 16, 37-38; Tom Sutcliffe, "Husbands of Christ," *Spectator* (London), 5 May 1973, p. 553.

[2] Laud Humphreys, *Out of the Closets: The Sociology of Homosexual Liberation* (Englewood Cliffs, New Jersey; Prentice-Hall, 1972), pp. 79-93, 143-145, 151 and *Tearoom Trade: Impersonal Sex in Public Places*, 2d ed. (Chicago: Aldine Publishing Co., 1975), p. 23; Alan Watts, *In my own Way: An Autobiography, 1915-1965* (New York: Vintage Books, 1973), pp. 230-231.

Anglo-Catholicism. Because of the fragmentary and ambiguous nature of much of this evidence only a tentative outline can be suggested.

## I

Until the late nineteenth century homosexuality was socially defined in terms of certain forbidden sexual acts, such as "buggery" or "sodomy."[3] Homosexual behaviour was regarded as a product of male lust, potential in anyone unless it was severely condemned and punished. In England homosexuality had been covered by the criminal law since 1533 when the state took over the responsibility for dealing with the offence from the ecclesiastical courts. The last executions for buggery took place in the 1830s, but it was not until 1861 that the death penalty was abolished. In the 1880s and 1890s – at the same time that the word homosexuality entered the English language, largely through the work of Havelock Ellis – social attitudes towards homosexuality underwent a major change. From being defined in terms of sinful behaviour, homosexuality came to be regarded as a characteristic of a particular type of person. Because homosexuality was seen as a condition, homosexuals were therefore a species, which it became the object of the social sciences to explore and explain. The principal vehicles of this redefinition were legal and medical. Homosexual behaviour became subject to increased legal penalties, notably by the Labouchère Amendment of the Criminal Law Amendment Act of 1885, which extended the law to cover all male homosexual acts.

[3] The following discussion of changing attitudes to homosexuality in late nineteenth century Britain is based upon the work of Jeffrey Weeks, "'Sins and Diseases': Some Notes on Homosexuality in the Nineteenth Century," *History Workshop*, 1 (1976), 211-219; *Coming Out. Homosexual Politics in Britain, from the Nineteenth Century to the Present* (London: Quartet Books, 1977), chaps. 1-3; "Movements of Affirmation: Sexual Meanings and Homosexual Identities," *Radical History Review*, 20 (1979), 164-179. See also Vern L. Bullough, *Sexual Variance in Society and History* (New York: John Wiley and Sons, 1976), pp. 555-557, 565-575; *Homosexuality: A History* (New York: New American Library, 1979), pp. 38-42, 106-112; Peter Coleman, *Christian Attitudes to Homosexuality* (London: Society for Promoting Christian Knowledge [S.P.C.K.], 1980), pp. 137-158; Barbara Fassler, "Theories of Homosexuality as Sources of Bloomsbury's Androgyny," *Signs: Journal of Women in Culture and Society*, 5 (1979), 237-251; Arthur N. Gilbert, "Buggery and the British Navy, 1700-1861," *Journal of Social History*, 10 (1976), 72-98; A. D. Harvey, "Prosecutions for Sodomy in England at the Beginning of the Nineteenth Century," *Historical Journal*, 21 (1978), 939-948; H. Montgomery Hyde, *The Other Love: An Historical and Contemporary Survey of Homosexuality in Britain* (London: Heinemann, 1970), chaps. 4-5; A. L. Rowse, *Homosexuals in History: A Study of Ambivalence in Society, Literature and the Arts* (London: Weidenfeld and Nicolson, 1977), chaps. 9, 12.

whether committed in public or private.[4] This in turn led to a series of sensational scandals, culminating in the three trials of Oscar Wilde in 1895. The harsher legal sanctions were accompanied over a longer period by an important change in the conceptualisation of homosexuality: the emergence of the idea that homosexuality was a disease or sickness which required treatment. The various reasons for this change in definition are beyond the scope of this essay. The result, however, was that the late nineteenth century saw homosexuality acquire new labelling, in the context of a social climate that was more hostile than before.

The tightening of the law and the widespread acceptance by opinion-makers of the "medical model" of homosexuality produced conditions within which men with homosexual feelings began to develop a conscious collective identity. For although a small homosexual subculture had existed in London and a few other cities in the British Isles since the early eighteenth century, the final development of a homosexual underground was essentially a phenomenon of the late nineteenth century.[5] Such a subculture did not rise in a vacuum. It was a direct consequence of growing social hostility that compelled homosexual men to begin to perceive themselves as members of a group with certain distinctive characteristics:

> The homosexual subculture, in which sexual meanings were defined and sharpened, was then predominantly male, revolving around meeting place, clubs, pubs, etc. Indeed perhaps it was less a single subculture than a series of overlapping subcultures, each part supplying a different need. In its most organized aspect there was often an emphasis on transvestism, a self-mocking effeminacy, an argot [slang] and a predominance of "camp."
>
> (Weeks, "Movements of Affirmation," 175).

Although the homosexual subculture embraced men of all ages and occupations, and there are many recorded examples of close friendships across class barriers, upper middle-class values predominated. This was probably because in late Victorian England only middle-class men had sufficient social freedom to develop a homosexual lifestyle. Most of these middle-class homosexuals were married and lived double lives. Outside or on the fringes of the subculture were many men with a homosexual orientation who avoided giving their behaviour a homosexual interpretation. Until the mid-twentieth century, because

[4] F. B. Smith, "Labouchere's Amendment to the Criminal Law Amendment Bill," *Historical Studies*, 17 (1976), 165-175.

[5] The homosexual subculture of eighteenth century London is described by Randolph Trumbach in "London's Sodomites: Homosexual Behaviour and Western Culture in the 18th Century," *Journal of Social History*, 11 (1977), 1-33.

male homosexuality was so often equated in popular thinking with the display of feminine behaviour and personality traits, it was often difficult for men who combined strong homosexual feelings with a strong sense of male gender identity to regard themselves as homosexual.[6]

One facet of the homosexual subculture was Anglo-Catholic religion. For many homosexual men in the late nineteenth and early twentieth centuries, Anglo-Catholicism provided a set of institutions and religious practices through which they could express their sense of difference in an oblique and symbolical way. A large number of religious and social rebels were similarly attracted to Anglo-Catholicism at this time. Some were drawn by the Anglo-Catholic idea of the church as a divinely constituted religious society and by its emphasis on tradition, dogma, and visible beauty in worship. Others, of radical temperament, found in Anglo-Catholicism a religion "freed from the respectability and the puritanism of the churches in which they had grown up."[7]

Starting in the 1830s Oxford Tractarians had sought to revive in the established church the traditions of the "ancient and undivided Church" in doctrine, liturgy, and devotion.[8] Their teachings included the God-given authority and spiritual independence of the church, a high doctrine of the ministry and of the sacraments, and a rejection of religious liberalism and rationalism. Also central to the Oxford Movement was a "sense of awe and mystery in religion," a feeling for poetry and symbolism as vehicles of religious truth.[9] A feature of the early Oxford Movement was the prevalence among its male followers of intense

[6] John Marshall, "Pansies, Perverts and Macho Men: Changing Conceptions of Male Homosexuality," in *The Making of the Modern Homosexual*, ed. Kenneth Plummer (London: Hutchinson, 1980), pp. 133-154.

[7] Hugh McLeod, *Class and Religion in the Late Victorian City* (London: Croom Helm, 1974), p. 249.

[8] For short accounts of the Oxford Movement, see Owen Chadwick, *The Victorian Church*, 2 vols. (London: Adam and Charles Black, 1966, 1970), I, chap. 3; R. W. Church, *The Oxford Movement: Twelve Years, 1833-1845* (1891; rpt. ed., Chicago, Illinois: University of Chicago Press, 1970); David Newsome, "Newman and the Oxford Movement," in *The Victorian Crisis of Faith*, ed. Anthony Symondson (London: S. P. C. K., 1970), pp. 71-89; S. L. Ollard, *A Short History of the Oxford Movement* (1915; rpt. ed., London: Faith Press, 1963). On the ritualist controversy, see James Bentley, *Ritualism and Politics in Victorian Britain: The Attempt to Legislate for Belief* (Oxford: Oxford University Press, 1978); William Fong, "The Ritualist Crisis: Anglo-Catholics and Authority with Special Reference to the English Church Union, 1859-1882," (Ph.D. diss., University of Toronto, 1977). Late nineteenth century Anglo-Catholicism is examined by J. E. B. Munson, "The Oxford Movement by the End of the Nineteenth Century: The Anglo-Catholic Clergy," *Church History*, 44 (1975), 382-395.

[9] *The Mind of the Oxford Movement*, ed. Owen Chadwick (London: Adam and Charles Black, 1960), p. 28.

and demonstrative friendships. These relationships were not regarded by contemporaries as unnatural, for intimate friendships were common enough at the time in the exclusively male communities of public school and university. What was unusual in John Henry Newman's circle was the prominence given to celibacy and the consequent foundation of religious brotherhoods. This has generally been interpreted by historians as an expression of religious idealism and self-sacrifice: "the idea of celibacy, in those whom it affected at Oxford, was in the highest degree a religious and romantic one" (Church, p. 248). Did it also, in many cases, have a homosexual motivation? It seems inherently possible that young men who were secretly troubled by homosexual feelings that they could not publicly acknowledge may have been attracted by the prospect of devoting themselves to a life of celibacy, in the company of like-minded male friends, as a religiously-sanctioned alternative to marriage. Newman himself believed and taught that celibacy was "a high state of life to which the multitude of men cannot aspire."[10]

This homoerotic motivation was strongly hinted at in the 1890s by James Rigg, a Wesleyan historian of the Oxford Movement, who made much of the "characteristically feminine" mind and temperament of Newman and the lack of virility of most of his disciples.[11] The idea was developed and popularised by Geoffrey Faber in his classic *Oxford Apostles* (1933). His portrait of Newman as a sublimated homosexual (though the word itself was not used) has since been a source of embarrassment to those biographers and theologians who seek to present him as a "Saint for Our Time."[12]

Faber's argument was brilliant but open to attack. Meriol Trevor, in her two-volume biography of Newman, undermined some of his illustrations, as when she pointed out, for example, that Wilfred Ward had given no source for the often-quoted statement that Newman

[10] Letter to G. Ryder, 1832, quoted in Meriol Trevor, *Newman*, 2 vols. (London: Macmillan and Co., 1962), I, 159.

[11] James H. Rigg, *Oxford High Anglicanism and its Chief Leaders* (London: Charles H. Kelly, 1895), pp. 13, 31-32, 109-110, 132, 154-156.

[12] Geoffrey Faber, *Oxford Apostles: A Character Study of the Oxford Movement* (London: Faber and Faber, 1933), pp. 32-35, and generally chap. 6. See also David L. Edwards, *Leaders of the Church of England, 1828-1944* (London: Oxford University Press, 1971), pp. 49-50; William Robbins, *The Newman Brothers: An Essay in Comparative Intellectual Biography* (London: Heinemann, 1966), pp. 83-84. For a critical discussion of the historiography of the Oxford Movement and J. H. Newman, see John Kent, "The Study of Modern Ecclesiastical History since 1930," in J. Daniélou, A. H. Couratin, and John Kent, *Historical Theology* (Harmondsworth: Penguin, 1969), pp. 316-328; also Geoffrey Best, "New Bearings on the Oxford Movement," *Historical Journal*, 12 (1969), 707-710.

lay all night on Ambrose St. John's bed after the death of his inseparable friend, and that in view of other known events of that night the incident could hardly have occurred. Of the intensity of their relationship, however, there can be no doubt. On his death in 1890 Newman was buried at his own wish in the same grave as St. John.[13]

The same aura of ambiguous sexuality surrounds other figures in Newman's circle – notably Richard Hurrell Froude, who died young in 1836, and the effusive Frederick William Faber, who followed Newman into the Roman Catholic church in 1845.[14] Geoffrey Faber, for example, argued that Froude's "temperamental bias" can be inferred from the "fervour of his masculine friendships," the "tone and temper" of his private journal, and especially its "unmistakable language of conflict with sexual temptation" (Faber, p. 218). He claimed that Froude's private writings reveal an intense struggle between an "Old Self" and a "New Self," in which his homosexual instincts ("the beast within him") were sublimated into a positive religious ideal: the "idea of virginity" (Faber, p. 222).

As with Newman the available evidence is open to alternative interpretations. The bitter self-accusations of Froude's journal and the language of striving and self-tormenting have been explained by his most recent biographer as a struggle between lofty religious aspirations and the undisciplined self-indulgence of a romantic imagination, disjoined from Christian conduct. According to this interpretation, Froude's attraction to celibacy had its roots not in a lack of interest in women, but in an idealistic desire to fulfil a counsel of perfection, by which celibacy was to be sought for its "intrinsic excellence."[15]

Any interpretation must remain controversial. It is unrealistic to expect documented proof of overt homosexual behaviour, for if sexual activity of any kind occurred between male lovers in private the fact is unlikely to have been recorded. Nor is it possible, on the basis of passionate words uttered by mid-Victorians, to make a clear distinction between male affection and homosexual feeling. Theirs was a generation prepared to accept romantic friendships between men simply as friendships without sexual significance. Only with the emergence in the late nineteenth century of the doctrine of the stiff-

[13] Trevor, II, 526-527.

[14] On F. W. Faber, see Ronald Chapman, *Father Faber* (London: Burns and Oates, 1961), especially pp. 46-51; *Sexual Heretics: Male Homosexuality in English Literature from 1850 to 1900*, ed. Brian Reade (London: Routledge and Kegan Paul, 1970), pp. 4-5, 11, 67-68.

[15] Piers Brendon, *Hurrell Froude and the Oxford Movement* (London: Paul Elek, 1974), pp. 60-66, 72-76.

upper-lip, and the concept of homosexuality as an identifiable condition, did open expressions of love between men become suspect and regarded in a new light as morally undesirable.[16] In addition there is the general question of whether intimate friendships between members of the same sex can legitimately be labelled homosexual when the individuals concerned may not be conscious at the time of an underlying erotic attraction. On the other hand one should also remember the reluctance of many historians (especially historians of religion) to consider the implications of the fact that the men and women they study did have sexual feelings, and that not all of them were attracted to the opposite sex.[17]

When the Oxford and Anglo-Catholic Movements are examined as a whole, the hypothesis of the existence of a continuous current of homoerotic sentiment would appear to offer a plausible explanation of a great deal of otherwise mysterious behaviour and comment. The extent to which these homosexual inclinations were unrecognised, sublimated, consciously disciplined, or expressed in overt sexual acts cannot easily be ascertained. In view of the weight of the traditional Christian condemnation of any sexual relationship outside marriage and (one may assume) the ambivalent attitudes of the individuals concerned towards their own sexuality, it is likely that the majority of homosexual friendships in Anglo-Catholic circles did not find physical expression. But this is not to deny the strength of the emotions that they generated and their subtle influence on religious attitudes and behaviour.

The Oxford Movement provoked vehement hostility in the Church of England. Evangelical and Broad Church critics claimed that it fostered novel ideas and religious practices, such as the separateness of the professional priesthood and the increased use of ceremonial in church services. They deplored this "sacerdotalism" and "ritualism" as essentially un-English and unmanly.[18] Moreover, there

[16] For changing attitudes to male friendships, see J. R. deS. Honey, *Tom Brown's Universe: The Development of the Victorian Public School* (London: Millington, 1977), pp. 167-196; David Newsome, *Godliness and Good Learning: Four Studies on a Victorian Ideal* (London: John Murray, 1961), pp. 83-89; Alison G. Sulloway, *Gerard Manley Hopkins and the Victorian Temper* (London: Routledge and Kegan Paul, 1972), pp. 21-29.

[17] Some of the problems in the historical interpretation of same-sex relationships are discussed in Jonathan Katz, *Gay American History: Lesbians and Gay Men in the U. S. A.* (New York: Thomas Y. Crowell Co., 1976), introduction to section 6.

[18] Geoffrey Best, "Popular Protestantism in Victorian Britain," in *Ideas and Institutions of Victorian Britain: Essays in Honour of George Kitson Clark*, ed. Robert Robson (London: G. Bell, 1967), pp. 124-126.

was a marked difference between the self-assertiveness and noisy emotionalism of popular Protestantism and the ethos of Tractarian piety, with its concern for reverence and reserve in discussing sacred truths, its delight in symbolism and subtle imagery, and its strict observance of the traditional feasts and disciplines of the church. It may be surmised that Charles Kingsley's deep hostility to Newman was based largely on an instinctive feeling (for the two men never actually met) that there was something rather unhealthy about Newman and his circle. In 1851 at the height of the agitation against "Papal aggression" in England (triggered off by Pope Pius IX's restoration of a Roman Catholic hierarchy), Kingsley had written of Roman Catholics and Tractarians:

> In . . . all that school, there is an element of foppery – even in dress and manner; a fastidious, maundering, die-away effeminacy, which is mistaken for purity and refinement; and I confess myself unable to cope with it, so alluring is it to the minds of an effeminate and luxurious aristocracy; neither educated in all that should teach them to distinguish between bad and good taste, healthy and unhealthy philosophy or devotion.[19]

Kingsley himself was an enthusiastic exponent of the duty of Christian "manliness," which he defined as courage, heartiness, physical vitality, and the procreation of children within marriage. The idea of celibacy he abhorred as both contrary to nature and a sin against God. Thus the violence of his attack on Newman in *Macmillan's Magazine* in 1864 cannot be explained solely in terms of the overt grounds of the conflict – the falsehood and cunning of the Roman clergy versus the Protestant virtues of truth and morality. It should also be seen as a conflict of fundamentally opposing personalities – the subtle misogamy of Newman versus the robust uxoriousness of Kingsley – of which neither man would have been fully aware.[20]

The charge of effeminacy – the usual nineteenth-century caricature of male homosexuality – stuck to the successors of the Tractarians. It was frequently used by Protestant controversialists to smear the Anglo-Catholic party as a whole, though the allegations were more usually in the form of innuendo than direct assertion. It may be true that these suspicions were often founded on prejudice; it is equally likely that in many instances they had some basis in fact. After Bishop Samuel Wilberforce of Oxford founded Cuddesdon College in 1854

[19] *Charles Kingsley: His Letters and Memories of his Life,* ed. Frances Kingsley, 2 vols., 10th ed. (London: C. Kegan Paul and Co., 1881), I, 201.

[20] Newsome, *Godliness and Good Learning*, pp. 197-199, 207-211; Robert Bernard Martin, *The Dust of Combat: A Life of Charles Kingsley* (London: Faber and Faber, 1959), pp. 237-253. For Newman's side of the controversy, see Trevor, II, 317-345.

for the training of ordination candidates according to Tractarian principles, it was rumoured among the country clergy of the Oxford diocese that Cuddesdon-trained curates were unmanly, and that their semimonastic life bred effeminacy. Even Wilberforce himself was inclined to agree that the religious formation provided by his college lacked "vigour, virility and self-expressing vitality."[21] Bishop Edward King of Lincoln, a former chaplain and principal of Cuddesdon, was prosecuted in 1889-90 by a Protestant organisation, the Church Association, for the use of "illegal" ritual, and it is probable that a hidden factor in the decision to launch a prosecution was a dislike of King's personal characteristics. As an unmarried High Churchman who had been devoted to his theological students, and the first English diocesan bishop since the Reformation to wear a mitre and the traditional eucharistic vestments, he "embodied all the Tractarian characteristics which Protestants held in special abhorrence."[22]

The revival of pre-Reformation ceremonial in public worship, justified on historic grounds and as an expression of the sacramental principle, was a product of the second generation of the Oxford Movement. During the 1860s ritualism came into the public eye, and the clergy and congregations of ritualist churches were increasingly subjected to hostile scrutiny. Clergymen of "extreme High Church proclivities," sneered *Punch*, "are very fond of dressing like ladies. They are much addicted to wearing vestments diversified with smart and gay colours, and variously trimmed and embroidered."[23] A Protestant visitor to St. Matthias's, Stoke Newington (London), which with its coloured vestments, incense, and lighted candles was regarded as a centre of advanced ceremonial, wrote in the *Rock* that the "style of dress and the close-shaven face, favoured so greatly by English imitators of Rome, do give to most men a rather juvenile, if not womanly appearance." Unlike most churches, "the Ritualistic world attracts crowds of *men*, both young and old."[24] About the same time a journalist from *The Times* attended a Sunday High Mass at the famous ritualist church of St. Alban, Holborn – "one of the ecclesiastical curiosities

[21] Owen Chadwick, *The Founding of Cuddesdon* (Oxford: Oxford University Press, 1954), pp. 92-93. The existence of homosexual interests among young Oxford-educated Anglo-Catholic clergymen in the 1850s is strongly implied in Samuel Butler's autobiographical novel, *Ernest Pontifex, or The Way of All Flesh* (1903), chaps. 51-59.

[22] E. R. Norman, *Anti-Catholicism in Victorian England* (London: George Allen and Unwin, 1968), p. 110.

[23] "Parsons in Petticoats," *Punch*, 48 (10 June 1865), 239.

[24] *Rock*, 9 and 12 June 1868.

of London." In describing its eclectic congregation, he noted that "foremost, perhaps, among the devotees are young men of 19 or 20 years of age, who seem to have the intricacies of ritualism at their fingers' ends."[25] By the end of the century, the jubilee history of St. Alban's proudly related, the number of young men in the congregation had become "more and more conspicuous": "Pious women there were in abundance – was there ever a church where they did not congregate? – but St. Alban's was from the first a Man's church, and a Young Man's church before all."[26]

Some of the young men who clustered around Anglo-Catholic churches – many of them apparently shop assistants and clerks – were regarded by observers as "unwholesome" and "sentimental."[27] For many of those so described it is possible that Anglo-Catholic ritualism provided a way of escape from the problems of sexual tension and forbidden love into a make-believe world of religious pageantry, ancient titles and ranks, exotic symbolism, and endless chatter about copes and candles, the apostolic succession, and the triumphs of the "true faith." Certainly the more austere Anglo-Catholics were disquieted by the air of levity and unreality they witnessed in some of these circles, and they sought to distance themselves from the popular charge of effeminacy. Charles Fuge Lowder, vicar of St. Peter's, London Docks, for example, was described approvingly in his biography as "not a Ritualist at all in the modern sense of the word, after the gushing, effeminate, sentimental manner of young shop-boys, or those who simply ape the ways of Rome."[28]

The allegations persisted. At the end of the nineteenth century the conflict between Protestantism and Anglo-Catholicism within the Church of England was still regularly depicted by Protestant propagandists as a struggle between masculine and feminine styles of religion. They pointed out the apparent appeal of Anglo-Catholic forms of worship to members of the upper classes – "especially women, in the artificial and luxurious atmosphere of our wealthier classes" – which carried the implication that male Anglo-Catholics were effete,

[25] "Ritualism," *The Times*, 27 August 1866, p. 8.

[26] George W. E. Russell, *Saint Alban the Martyr, Holborn: A History of Fifty Years* (London: George Allen and Co., 1913), p. 306. See also [Eleanor A. Towle], *Alexander Heriot Mackonochie: A Memoir by E. A. T.*, ed. Edward Francis Russell (London: Kegan Paul, Trench, Trübner, and Co., 1890), pp. 99-100; Fong, pp. 146-150.

[27] See, for example, *Autobiography and Life of George Tyrrell*, arranged with supplements by M. D. Petrie, 2 vols. (London: Edward Arnold, 1912), I, 150-152.

[28] [Maria Trench], *Charles Lowder: A Biography, by the Author of "The Life of St. Teresa,"* 12th ed. (London: Kegan Paul, Trench and Co., 1887), p. 284.

decadent, and lacking in manly qualities.[29] In 1898 John Kensit, fanatical founder of the Protestant Truth Society, which specialised in disrupting the services of Anglo-Catholic churches, described to a cheering Protestant meeting in London the "idolatry" of a ritualist church at St. Cuthbert's, Pilbeach Gardens' that he had invaded the previous Good Friday. The service had been conducted by a "priest in petticoats." The congregation were "very poor specimens of men. . . . They seemed a peculiar sort of people, very peculiar indeed." To his listeners, the meaning and intent of his remarks were obvious.[30]

In the second half of the nineteenth century as a result of the Oxford Movement there was a revival of religious brotherhoods and sisterhoods in the Church of England.[31] The first two male communities, Newman's at Littlemore and F. W. Faber's at Elton, followed their founders into the Roman Catholic church in 1845. This development confirmed Protestant suspicions that Tractarianism encouraged sexual aberration and impropriety. The Protestant case against Anglican monasticism in any of its forms was not only that it propagated "Romanising practices and doctrines," but that it was also contrary to God's "natural laws." The "suppression or perversion of natural love" by monastic vows led inevitably to "corruption" and "defilement."[32] Popular imagination was fuelled by "revelations" and exaggerated rumours of sexual scandals (in both Roman Catholic and Anglican religious houses) of a kind which works like the *Awful Disclosures of Maria Monk* (1836) had already made familiar.[33]

In the case of communities of priests such as the Society of St. John the Evangelist (1865) or the Community of the Resurrection (1892) these charges were clearly without foundation. They maintained a close connection with the intellectual life of the universities and followed a strictly disciplined way of life. At the same time, how-

[29] *Rock*, 29 April 1898.

[30] The Protestant Alliance, *Verbatim Report of Speeches Delivered at the Great Demonstration, Held in the Queen's Hall, Langham Place. . . May 3rd, 1898* (London: R. J. Haynes, 1898), p. 23. See also Chadwick, *Victorian Church*, II, 355-356; Munson, pp. 385-387.

[31] A. M. Allchin, *The Silent Rebellion: Anglican Religious Communities, 1845-1900* (London: S. C. M. Press, 1958); Peter F. Anson, *The Call of the Cloister: Religious Communities and Kindred Bodies in the Anglican Communion*, revised by A. W. Campbell, 4th ed. (London: S. P. C. K., 1964), and *Building up the Waste Places: The Revival of Monastic Life on Medieval Lines in the Post-Reformation Church of England* (Leighton Buzzard: Faith Press, 1973).

[32] For example: *Norfolk News*, 24 September 1864; Walter Walsh, *The Secret History of the Oxford Movement* (London: Swan Sonnenschein and Co., 1897), chap. 6.

[33] Chadwick, *Victorian Church*, I, 509; Norman, *Anti-Catholicism*, p. 109; Best, pp. 127-132.

ever, the "Anglo-Catholic underworld" was producing a succession of short-lived, often clandestine, brotherhoods and guilds whose members delighted in religious ceremonial and the picturesque neo-Gothic externals of monastic life. Because these brotherhoods enforced no strict criteria for entry, it is likely that they were especially attractive to homosexually inclined young men who felt themselves drawn to the male environment of a monastic community and the dramatic side of religion. Their histories were punctuated with crises and scandals.[34]

One well publicised incident occurred in 1864 at a monastery in Elm Hill, Norwich, where the eccentric and quixotic Father Ignatius (Joseph Leycester Lyne) was trying to restore the Benedictine life within the English church.[35] A love letter written by a Brother Augustine to a young apprentice printer who sang in the priory's choir was sent to the *Norfolk News*, and on 17 September 1864 it was printed in full in an article headed "Ignatius and his Singing Boys." The Protestant citizenry of Norwich was horrified. The newspaper proceeded to publish a stern editorial on the moral evils inherent in monasticism:

> We tell "Ignatius" plainly, and we tell everybody else connected with this establishment who has the slightest power of reflection, that the herding together of men in one building, with the occasional letting in of young girls – some of them morbid, some of them silly and sentimental – and of boys likewise, with soft, sensitive temperaments, cannot fail to produce abominations.
>
> (*Norfolk News*, 24 September 1864).

A year later the Elm Hill community was almost destroyed when Brother Stanislaus led malcontents in an unsuccessful rebellion against Ignatius's authority, then fled the priory with a boy from its associated Guild of St. William. In 1868 the ex-Brother Stanislaus (James Barrett Hughes) reappeared as a popular guest speaker on Protestant

[34] On the minor brotherhoods, see Anson, *Call of the Cloister*, pp. 90-106. In 1869 Bishop Edward Twells, a missionary bishop in southern Africa and founder of a missionary brotherhood called the Society of St. Augustine, was involved in a homosexual scandal and compelled to flee the country in disguise. A senior clergyman observed: "People's faith in the sanctity of high Churchmen will be a good deal shaken, and celibacy and brotherhoods which were the order of the day in that diocese will certainly be at a discount" (Peter Hinchliff, *The Anglican Church in South Africa* [London: Darton, Longman and Todd, 1963], pp. 80, 140-141). Homosexual tensions in two small Anglo-Catholic mens' communities in the 1920s are recalled in Martin Boyd, *Day of my Delight: An Anglo-Australian Memoir* (Melbourne: Lansdowne, 1965), pp. 124-125; Bruno S. James, *Asking for Trouble* (London: Darton, Longman and Todd, 1962), p. 46.

[35] For biographies of Father Ignatius, see Baroness [Beatrice] de Bertouch, *The Life of Father Ignatius, O. S. B.: The Monk of Llanthony* (London: Methuen and Co., 1904); Donald Attwater, *Father Ignatius of Llanthony: A Victorian* (London: Cassell and Co., 1931); Arthur Calder-Marshall, *The Enthusiast: An Enquiry into the Life, Beliefs and Character of the Rev. Joseph Leycester Lyne alias Fr. Ignatius, O. S. B. . . .* (London: Faber and Faber, 1962). See also Anson, *Building up the Waste Places*.

platforms in London and the provinces, where he scandalised the respectable with revelations of the "semi-Popish and improper practices" established by Ignatius and other ritualists. At a meeting in London two youths brought up from Norwich specially for the occasion "made frightful charges, utterly unfit for publication, against a monk" – a reference to Brother Augustine.[36] Then in the following year another youth alleged that he had lived at the monastery in a sexual relationship with Stanislaus, with the encouragement of Ignatius: "it needed no more to set the Protestant world ablaze with joy and expectation" (de Bertouch, p. 430).

Another monastic brotherhood was the Order of St. Augustine, founded in 1867 by a wealthy and eccentric clergyman, George Nugée. In 1872 it established a priory at Walworth in South London, where it maintained a round of extremely elaborate services. Most of those connected with "St. Austin's Priory" were rich men who enjoyed a comfortable life, and there was "very little of a normal religious community about its spirit or observances" (Anson, *Call of the Cloister*, p. 100). Among those who regularly visited St. Austin's and enjoyed its colourful ritual (without believing yet in Christianity) was Walter Pater, aesthete and historian of the Renaissance.[37] His intimate friend was Richard Charles Jackson (Brother à Becket), a lay brother and so-called professor of Church History at the priory. At Pater's request Jackson wrote a poem for his birthday:

> . . . Your darling soul I say is enflamed with love for me;
> Your very eyes do move I cry with sympathy:
> Your darling feet and hands are blessings ruled by love,
> As forth was sent from out the Ark a turtle dove!
> (Wright, II, 22).

A slightly less bizarre foundation was the "Anglican Congregation of the Primitive Observance of the Holy Rule of St. Benedict." This was founded in 1896 by a former medical student, Benjamin (Aelred) Carlyle, who had been fascinated by the monastic life since the age of fifteen, when he had founded a secret religious brotherhood at his public school.[38] His choice of the religious name of Aelred,

[36] *Rock*, 27 March 1868.

[37] Thomas Wright, *The Life of Walter Pater*, 2 vols. (London: Everett and Co., 1907), II, 31-42. In his last years in Oxford, Pater frequently attended St. Barnabas's, an Anglo-Catholic church known for its elaborate ritual. He was the model for "Mr. Rose" in W. H. Mallock's *The New Republic* (1877).

[38] The Anglican Benedictine community on Caldey Island is described by Peter F. Anson in *The Benedictines of Caldey: The Story of the Anglican Benedictines of Caldey and their Submission to the Catholic Church* (London: Burns Oates and Washbourne, 1940); *Abbot Extraordinary: A Memoir of Aelred Carlyle, Monk and Missionary, 1874-1955* (London: Faith Press, 1958); *Building up the Waste Places*, chaps. 12-15.

after a twelfth-century Cistercian abbot of Rievaulx who had written treatises on "spiritual friendships," was a deliberate one, for a biography of St. Aelred by Newman's companion, J. D. Dalgairns, had revealed to him "a monastic world in which natural and spiritual relations could be fused" (Anson, *Building up the Waste Places*, p. 134). Aelred Carlyle was a man of dynamic personality, hypnotic eyes, and extraordinary imagination. In 1906 his community made its permanent home on Caldey Island, off the coast of south Wales (outside Anglican diocesan jurisdiction), where, largely on borrowed money, he built a splendidly furnished monastery in a fanciful style of architecture. The life of this enclosed Benedictine community centred upon an ornate chapel where the thirty or so tonsured and cowled monks sang the monastic offices and celebrated Mass in Latin according to the Roman rite. As there was nothing like it anywhere else in the Church of England the island abbey inevitably became a resort for ecclesiastical sightseers, and many young men were drawn to join the community out of personal affection for Carlyle.

The self-styled Lord Abbot of Caldey introduced practices into the life of his monastery which many outsiders, accustomed to the austere atmosphere of the existing Anglican men's communities, found disconcerting. "Stories Toto Told Me" by "Baron Corvo" (Frederick Rolfe), which had originally appeared in *The Yellow Book*, were often read aloud to the assembled monks at recreation time, and during the summer months they regularly went sea-bathing in the nude. Nor did Carlyle make any secret of his liking for charming young men. Spiritual friendships were "not discouraged," recalled his biographer, himself a former member of the Caldey community:

> . . . and their expression sometimes took a form which would not be found in any normal monastery to-day. . . . Embraces, ceremonial and non-ceremonial, were regarded as symbolical of fraternal charity, so our variant of the Roman rite permitted a real hug and kisses on the cheek between the giver and the recipient of the *Pax Domini* at the conventual Mass. . . .
>
> (Anson, *Abbot Extraordinary*, pp. 125-126).

Not surprisingly for this and other reasons the more conservative Anglo-Catholics regarded the Caldey Benedictines with deep distrust. The bubble burst in March 1913 when Carlyle and twenty-two of his monks – heavily in debt and convinced by the Anglo-Catholic Bishop Charles Gore that their liturgical and devotional usages could be defended only on a papal basis of authority – were received into the Roman Catholic church. The community continued in existence with Carlyle as abbot. Then in 1921 he suddenly resigned his abbacy and went to Canada, accompanied by another monk from Caldey, to work as a Roman Catholic missionary priest in British Columbia. He renewed his monastic vows shortly before his death in England in 1955.

## II

The world of many Anglo-Catholic clergy was overwhelmingly masculine. Some urban parishes were staffed exclusively by unmarried priests, who lived together in clergy houses. A significant minority was committed to celibacy. Among the more extreme Anglo-Catholics, for a priest to "commit matrimony" was considered to be not only a profound betrayal of the Catholic priestly role, but also an act of personal disloyalty to those who remained celibate.[39] The biographies of Anglo-Catholic notables reveal a number of discreetly drawn examples of deep friendships between men, and of priests who were known for their remarkable ability to work with lads and young men. The possibility of moral danger was widely recognised. Vincent Stuckey Coles, librarian and later principal of Pusey House, Oxford, from 1884 to 1909, had realised while still a schoolboy, declared his biographer, that his "beautiful and ennobling love for his friends might co-exist with much that is faulty and ill-regulated, and even with much that is corrupt, and that, like all passionate enthusiasms, it has untold capacities for good but also carries within it possibilities for evil."[40] It is significant that among Coles's circle of Anglo-Catholic friends at Eton and Oxford in the 1860s had been Digby Mackworth Dolben, whose religious poetry, written before his early death in 1867, has been described as "perfect Uranian verse," and Gerard Manley Hopkins, who apparently became strongly attracted to Dolben and channelled his own anguished feelings into a series of sonnets.[41] An Anglo-Catholic tract published in 1922, advocating clerical celibacy, warned priests against friendships with members of *both* sexes. Friendship with a woman might lead to marriage: "A similar caution is necessary with regard to undue intimacy with boys. If the Cross

[39] For example: Colin Stephenson, *Walsingham Way* (London: Darton, Longman and Todd, 1970), pp. 127-128, 225-229; *Merrily on High* (London: Darton, Longman and Todd, 1972), pp. 77-78.

[40] *V. S. S. Coles: Letters, Papers, Addresses, Hymns & Verses with a Memoir*, ed. J. F. Briscoe (London: A. R. Mowbray and Co., 1930), pp. 7-8.

[41] Briscoe, pp. 6-9; Paddy Kitchen, *Gerard Manley Hopkins* (London: Hamish Hamilton, 1978), chap. 4; Reade, pp. 10-12, 72-76; Timothy d'Arch Smith, *Love in Earnest: Some Notes on the Lives and Writings of English 'Uranian' Poets from 1889 to 1930* (London: Routledge and Kegan Paul, 1970), pp. 188-191; Sulloway, pp. 50-55. Hopkins's homosexuality is discussed by Michael Lynch, "Recovering Hopkins, Recovering Ourselves," *The Hopkins Quarterly*, 6 (Fall 1979), pp. 107-117.

weighs heavily upon some of us in these respects let us pray for grace to be generous in bearing it."[42]

Male friendships within the church took many forms. At a later date, in a different context, some of them would undoubtedly have been regarded as homosexual. The case of Henry Scott Holland, High Church theologian and social theorist, is instructive. Having deliberately renounced marriage as a "willing sacrifice," at the age of thirty-five he wrote of his reactions on hearing of a friend's engagement: "The sudden sense that I alone of all my friends am really going to be wifeless, is born in upon me with unwonted energy, and makes me feel strange, and wondering; and I clench my teeth a little, and feel sterner (but not less resolute)."[43] Later in 1903 when Scott Holland was a canon of St. Paul's Cathedral, London, he appointed as his secretary a young Oxford graduate, Laurence Stratford, who became a "real and close friend," entering fully into Scott Holland's many interests. It was "difficult to speak adequately" of his devotion, and when at last he took up a government post Scott Holland found the parting a "bitter grief" (Paget, p. 224).

Priests who worked among undergraduates at Oxford and Cambridge had many opportunities for intimate relationships with the young men in their pastoral care. For example the friendship of Ronald Knox, when chaplain of Trinity College, Oxford, before the first world war, with a handsome and brilliant undergraduate, Guy Lawrence, was the "strongest human affection" of his early manhood.[44] Forbes Robinson, a theological lecturer and college fellow at Cambridge in the 1890s, was remembered for his "extraordinary interest" in his undergraduate acquaintances: "He loved some men with an intensity of feeling impossible to describe. It was almost pain to him. If he loved a man he loved him with a passionate love (no weaker expression will do)."[45] He prayed for those he loved for hours at a time.

Another type of friendship was between priests of similar ages who were engaged in a common enterprise or who worked in the same parish. At St. Clement's, Bournemouth, for example, in the 1870s, there was a deep if outwardly undemonstrative relationship between the vicar, George Douglas Tinling ("artistic, graceful in manner")

[42] C. Newell Long, *Personal Efficiency: The Priest's Rule of Life*, York Books, no. 34 (London: Society of SS. Peter and Paul, 1922), p. 10.

[43] *Henry Scott Holland . . . Canon on St. Paul's, Memoir and Letters*, ed. Stephen Paget (London: John Murray, 1921), p. 166. See also pp. 94-96 – an exposition, in a letter to his brother, of his views on friendship.

[44] Evelyn Waugh, *The Life of the Right Reverend Ronald Knox* . . . (London: Chapman and Hall, 1959), p. 125.

[45] Forbes Robinson, *Letters to his Friends*, ed. Charles [Robinson], 3d ed. (London: Spottiswoode and Co., for private circulation, 1905), p. 50.

and his curate, Robert Gray Scurfield ("an enthusiastic sportsman").[46] These lifelong friends are said to have held everything in common – "their faith, ideals, aims, occupations and possessions." At the Anglo-Catholic outpost of St. Matthew's, Sheffield, the formidable George Campbell Ommanney (vicar from 1882 to 1936) was buried at his request in the same grave as a favourite curate, who had died in the parish many years previously.[47] These and other relationships which have been recorded can only be a small fraction of the whole.

From the mid-1880s, when a new generation of literary men began accepting homosexual sentiment as "part of the whole range of feeling which waited to be explored," some claimed that homosexuality was often linked to the "artistic temperament" (Reade, p. 31). During the 1890s, a crucial decade in the development of a distinctive homosexual identity, there were many links between this homosexual literary culture and Catholic religion, in both its Roman Catholic and Anglo-Catholic forms. There is, for example, the evidence of the literary magazines, *The Artist*, *The Spirit Lamp*, and *The Chameleon*, which, during this period, published many poems, essays, and stories with homosexual themes (Reade, pp. 40-47). Frederick Rolfe, who in 1890 had been expelled from the Scots College in Rome after five months' training for the Roman Catholic priesthood, wrote poems for *The Artist* on St. Sebastian and other subjects. *The Spirit Lamp*, an Oxford undergraduate magazine, was edited from December 1892 to June 1893 by Lord Alfred Douglas, who turned it into "an expensively produced and serious organ of the aestheticism created by Oscar Wilde" – his lover.[48] Several of its contributors subsequently became Anglo-Catholic priests. *The Chameleon*, which was edited by John Francis Bloxam of Exeter College, Oxford, and lasted for only one issue (December 1894), acquired notoriety for an unsigned short story, "The Priest and the Acolyte."[49] Although written by Bloxam this was widely attributed to Wilde and was used by the prosecution

[46] [Malcolm Thorning], *St. Clement's Bournemouth, 1873-1973* (Bournemouth, 1973), p. 9. "George Tinling's ministry was notable for its fearless teaching of Catholic doctrine at a time of great hostility towards the Oxford movement" (p. 10).

[47] *Ommanney of Sheffield: Memoirs of George Campbell Ommanney, Vicar of St. Matthew's Sheffield, 1882-1936*, ed. Francis G. Belton (London: Centenary Press, 1936), pp. 35, 142.

[48] Compton Mackenzie, *My Life and Times: Octave Two, 1891-1900* (London: Chatto and Windus, 1963), p. 202. One of the founders of *The Spirit Lamp* in 1892 was Leighton Sandys Wason (1867-1950), an undergraduate of Christ Church. Later as a priest he was to achieve temporary fame in ecclesiastical circles as an Anglo-Catholic victim of Protestant fanaticism. In 1919 he was deprived of his village parish in Cornwall for doctrinal and liturgical disobedience.

[49] "The Priest and the Acolyte" is reprinted in *Sexual Heretics*, pp. 349-360. See also *The Trials of Oscar Wilde*, ed. H. Montgomery Hyde (London: William Hodge and Co., 1948), pp. 120-122.

at his first trial in 1895. It was an emotional tale – "the first piece of English fiction to echo the firmly-founded French syndrome of the 'naughty' priest" (d'Arch Smith, p. 56) – about the passionate love of a young priest for a fourteen-year-old golden-haired boy. Following discovery by the priest's rector, and the certainty of disgrace, the two lovers take poison in the chalice at a private Mass and die together, embracing on the steps of the altar.

This was Bloxam's last published work. Following his ordination in 1897 he was an assistant priest at various Anglo-Catholic churches in London, including St. Mary's, Graham Street, in the fashionable West End. (It was attended by the Anglo-Catholic lay leader Viscount Halifax and by his son Lord Irwin, subsequently Viceroy of India.) After service as a chaplain in the first world war, during which he was twice decorated for gallantry, he became vicar of the East End parish of St. Saviour, Hoxton. This Anglo-Catholic church was so "Romanised" that its priests used the Latin Missal and followed all Roman devotions.[50] After Bloxam's death in 1928 a former clerical colleague wrote in the *Church Times* of his "pastoral genius," his work for the young, and his "passionate love of beauty": "In regard to his personal character it would be hard to say whether he was more remarkable for his power of winning affection or for his lavishness in bestowing it."[51]

Another minor literary figure of the 1890s who sought to integrate the two worlds of homosexuality and Catholic religion was André Raffalovich. A member of a rich emigré Russo-Jewish family, he was converted to Roman Catholicism in 1896, shortly after the Wilde trials. In the same year he published a study of homosexuality, *Uranisme et Unisexualité*, in which he argued that homosexuality ("inversion") and heterosexuality are two equally legitimate manifestations of human sexuality, rejected the current view that homosexuality was a disease, and advocated a life of chastity, supported by friendship, as the Christian ideal.[52]

Many others associated with the homosexual literary world of the 1890s and early 1900s found a religious home in either the Anglo-Catholicism of the Church of England or the Roman Catholic church. Among those who joined the latter were Frederick Rolfe, Lord Alfred

[50] S. C. Carpenter, *Winnington-Ingram: The Biography of Arthur Foley Winnington-Ingram, Bishop of London, 1901-1939* (London: Hodder and Stoughton, 1949), pp. 170-175; *Crockford's Clerical Directory*, 1898-1928.

[51] *Church Times*, 27 April 1928.

[52] P. W. J. Healy, "Uranisme et Unisexualité: A Late Victorian View of Homosexuality," *New Blackfriars*, 59 (1978), 56-65; Reade, pp. 32-35.

Douglas, Lionel Johnson, and John Gray, the intimate friend of Raffalovich, who eventually became a Roman Catholic parish priest in Edinburgh.[53] The most famous was Oscar Wilde himself, who had become attracted to Roman Catholicism – "a Church which simply enthrals me by its fascination"[54] – while an undergraduate at Oxford in the 1870s, though he was not received into the Roman church until his deathbed in 1900. During Wilde's final trial in 1895 he received aid from a prominent Anglo-Catholic socialist priest, Stewart Headlam – himself something of an aesthete – who put up part of his bail, accompanied him to the courtroom each day, and scandalised most of his own Christian Socialist supporters in the process.[55] Another convert with a prolific literary output was Robert Hugh Benson, youngest son of Archbishop E. W. Benson of Canterbury and a former priest member of the (Anglo-Catholic) Community of the Resurrection. As a young man, he recalled, he had rejected the idea of marriage as "quite inconceivable."[56] Then in 1904, soon after his ordination as a Roman Catholic priest, he formed a passionate friendship with Rolfe. For two years this relationship involved letters "not only weekly, but at times daily, and of an intimate character, exhaustingly charged with emotion."[57] All letters were subsequently destroyed, probably by Benson's brother.

Several of that group of "Uranian" poets of the late nineteenth and early twentieth centuries who wrote on the theme of boy-love were clergymen in the Church of England. Among them were Edwin

[53] See *Two Friends, John Gray & André Raffalovich: Essays Biographical and Critical*, ed. Brocard Sewell (Aylesford: St. Albert's Press, 1963); Brocard Sewell, *Footnote to the Nineties: A Memoir of John Gray and André Raffalovich* (London: Cecil and Amelia Woolf, 1968).

[54] *The Letters of Oscar Wilde*, ed. Rupert Hart-Davis (London: Hart-Davis, 1962), p. 31.

[55] Coleman, pp. 149-150; Peter d'A. Jones, *The Christian Socialist Revival, 1877-1914: Religion, Class, and Social Conscience in Late-Victorian England* (Princeton, New Jersey: Princeton University Press, 1968), pp. 145-149. Shortly before his release from Reading Gaol in 1897, Wilde was visited by another Anglo-Catholic socialist priest, the Honourable and Reverend James Adderley (James Adderley, *In Slums and Society: Reminiscences of Old Friends* [London: T. Fisher Unwin, 1916], pp. 178-179).

[56] Robert Hugh Benson, *Confessions of a Convert* (London: Longmans, Green and Co., 1913), p. 29.

[57] C. C. Martindale, *The Life of Monsignor Robert Hugh Benson*, 2 vols. (London: Longmans, Green and Co., 1916), II, 96. For other accounts of the relationship, see Betty Askwith, *Two Victorian Families* (London: Chatto and Windus, 1971), pp. 212-217; A. J. A. Symons, *The Quest for Corvo: An Experiment in Biography* (London: Cassell and Co., 1934), chap. 14; Donald Weeks, *Corvo* (London: Michael Joseph, 1971), pp. 249-252, 258-259, 262-267, 387-390; David Williams, *Genesis and Exodus: A Portrait of the Benson Family* (London: Hamish Hamilton, 1979), pp. 163-170, 188-189, 219. The romantic friendships of R. H. Benson's brother, Arthur Christopher Benson, are sympathetically described in David Newsome, *On the Edge of Paradise. A. C. Benson: The Diarist* (London: John Murray, 1980).

Emmanuel Bradford, Samuel Elsworth Cottam, George Gabriel Scott Gillett, Edward Cracroft Lefroy, and Edmund St. Gascoigne Mackie.[58] During their ecclesiastical careers Cottam and Gillett were associated with a number of well-known Anglo-Catholic churches in London and elsewhere, though the latter turned his literary talents from writing poetry on Uranian themes at Oxford in the nineties to editing an Anglican missionary periodical and writing devotional and comic verse in the distinctive Anglo-Catholic genre.[59] Cottam was an enthusiastic collector of Uranian poetry and other publications, and (with Bradford) was a member of a secret homosexual society called the Order of Chaeronea, founded in the late 1890s, and whose members were drawn together by ties of friendship, the hope of reforming hostile attitudes, and secret rituals and symbols (Weeks, *Coming Out*, pp. 122-127). A fellow member of the Order of Chaeronea and a writer of Uranian verse was Alphonsus Joseph-Mary Augustus Montague Summers. As an Anglo-Catholic he was ordained a deacon in the Church of England before being received into the Roman Catholic church in 1909. Rejected from training for the Catholic priesthood (though it is probable that he subsequently received priest's orders through a schismatical source), he became a school teacher and antiquarian scholar, an author of voluminous works on Restoration drama, the Gothic novel, witchcraft, and demonology, and an active member of the British Society for the Study of Sex Psychology.[60]

## III

From the early 1900s until the second world war, the public face of the Anglo-Catholic movement was militant and uncompromis-

[58] See d'Arch Smith and Reade. The Uranians' attempts to provide religious justification for their sexual feelings are analysed in Brian Taylor, "Motives for Guilt-Free Pederasty: Some Literary Considerations," *Sociological Review*, n.s. 24 (1976), 104-106. For details of the clergymen's church careers, see *Crockford's Clerical Directory*.

[59] Two of Gillett's early poems are in *Sexual Heretics*, pp. 227-228, 247-248. For his devotional verse, see Gabriel Gillett, *A Garden of Song: With Pictures by Martin Travers and an Introductory Note by Kenneth Ingram* (Westminster: Society of SS. Peter and Paul, 1923). See also John Betjeman's foreword to S. J. Forrest, *What's the Use?* (London: A. R. Mowbray and Co., 1955), pp. 3-5; Waugh, *Ronald Knox*, p. 115.

[60] "Joseph Jerome" [Brocard Sewell], *Montague Summers: A Memoir* (London: Cecil and Amelia Woolf, 1965); d'Arch Smith, pp. 117-123; Weeks, *Coming Out*, pp. 124, 135-136.

ing.[61] Many younger clergy took delight in shocking the respectable "Church of Englandism" of the ecclesiastical establishment, personified by the canny and cautious archbishop of Canterbury, Randall Davidson.[62] A vociferous ginger-group was the Society of SS. Peter and Paul, founded in 1910 on the initiative of Maurice Child, Ronald Knox (son of the staunchly Evangelical bishop of Manchester), who seceded to Rome in 1917, and Samuel Gurney, a director of the Medici Society.[63] The society made fun of the bishops by describing itself as "Publishers to the Church of England" and by advertising and selling such articles as *Ridley* and *Latimer* votive-candle stands and *The Lambeth Frankincense*. It annoyed the authorities even more by advocating in a series of tracts the adoption by Anglican churches of the liturgical practices and popular devotions of the contemporary Roman Catholic church. The ultimate aim was the "resumption of arrested development," as if the Reformation had not happened, for only then, it was claimed, would the Church of England once again become a genuine "church of the people." The Society of SS. Peter and Paul was behind the great series of Anglo-Catholic congresses held between 1920 and 1933 (the latter being the centenary celebration of the Oxford Movement), at which the Anglo-Catholics went onto the attack and expounded the "Catholic position" to huge and enthusiastic audiences, with the object of demonstrating that it represented nothing less than the "true mind" of the Church of England.[64]

Exerting considerable influence at the centre of the Society of SS. Peter and Paul, and later as general secretary of the Anglo-Catholic congress organisation, was Maurice Child – the "mystery man" of the Anglo-Catholic movement – who was regarded by critics as a flippant and pleasure-loving "sybarite" and by admirers as a dedicated priest

[61] On the Anglo-Catholic movement in the twentieth century, see Francis Absalom, "The Anglo-Catholic Priest: Aspects of Role Conflict," in *A Sociological Yearbook of Religion in Britain: 4*, ed. Michael Hill (London: S. C. M. Press, 1971), pp. 46-61; Anselm Hughes, *The Rivers of the Flood: A Personal Account of the Catholic Revival in England in the Twentieth Century* (London: Faith Press, 1961); Roger Lloyd, *The Church of England, 1900-1965* (London: S. C. M. Press, 1966), chap. 6. There are numerous biographies of Anglo-Catholic leaders. By 1901 at least three out of every ten parochial clergy in the Church of England could be regarded as sympathetic to High Church teaching and practices. Only about two per cent of the parochial clergy, however, can definitely be identified as Anglo-Catholic ritualists. For numbers and geographical distribution, see Munson, pp. 387-391.

[62] For example: "Anglicanus," *My People Love to Have it so*, York Books, no. 20 (London: Society of SS. Peter and Paul, 1916).

[63] The Society of SS. Peter and Paul is described in Peter F. Anson, *Fashions in Church Furnishings, 1840-1940*, 2d ed. (London: Studio Vista, 1965), chap. 30; Eric Waldram Kemp, *N. P. Williams* (London: S. P. C. K., 1954), pp. 31-41; Waugh, *Ronald Knox*, pp. 114-118.

[64] *Church Times*, 23 January 1920.

of remarkable ability.[65] Child was of a type that popped up regularly in Anglo-Catholic circles between the wars. A strong believer in clerical celibacy, he was also rich, witty, versatile, a *bon viveur* – nicknamed "the Playboy of the Western Church." In London he lived with a male companion at a succession of fashionable addresses, where he entertained friends from many different walks of life. His glittering parties bore little resemblance to the usual clerical social gatherings. At one of them a young visitor was startled to see the Lady Margaret Professor of Divinity from Oxford in conversation over a cocktail with the film actress Tallulah Bankhead. As a skilled counsellor, an old friend recalled after his death in 1950, his "greatest forte was with young men" (Hood, p. 25).

In examining the homosexual component of early twentieth-century Anglo-Catholicism, it would be quite wrong to imply that more than a minority of Anglo-Catholic clergy or laity were homosexually inclined. Indeed one of the most common criticisms of Anglo-Catholic priests of this period was not that they were "effeminate" (the favourite allegation of nineteenth-century Protestants), but that so many of them behaved like Roman Catholic priests while having wives and children. Nevertheless, in cities such as London, Brighton, and Oxford, and other places in the south of England which had a high concentration of Anglo-Catholic churches, there are indications that a male homosexual subculture was associated with the more flamboyant wing of Anglo-Catholicism. In some London churches visitors noticed an unusually high proportion of young men in the congregation.[66] In the industrial Midlands and the North, on the other hand, where Low Churchmanship was dominant and Anglo-Catholics were on the defensive, the correlation was much less likely.

The published evidence for the connection is sparse. There are a few references in the posthumously published autobiography of Tom Driberg (Lord Bradwell), who was both a prominent Labour member of parliament, a devout Anglo-Catholic, and well-known in upper-class circles as a homosexual.[67] There are some revealing pas-

[65] On Maurice Child, see Sydney Dark, *Not Such a Bad Life* (London: Eyre and Spottiswoode, 1941), pp. 205-206; Frederick Hood, "Maurice Child," *St. Mary's, Pimlico, Quarterly Review*, (Spring 1950), 18-28; James, p. 34; Desmond Morse-Boycott, *They Shine Like Stars* (London: Skeffington and Son, 1947), pp. 260-262; *The Letters of Evelyn Waugh*, ed. Mark Amory (London· Weidenfeld and Nicolson, 1980), p. 544; Obituary in *Church Times*, 3 February 1950.

[66] For example, All Saints, Margaret Street, and St. Mary's, Graham Street (*Church Times*, 13 March 1925, 3 April 1925).

[67] Tom Driberg, *Ruling Passions* (London: Jonathan Cape, 1977), pp. 15-16, 47-48, 73. The idiosyncratic Anglo-Catholicism of his friend, the poet Wystan Auden, is discussed in Charles Osborne, *W. H. Auden: The Life of a Poet* (New York: Harcourt Brace Jovanovich, 1979), pp. 202-204.

sages in fictional works by writers who themselves had a first-hand knowledge of both worlds. In Evelyn Waugh's *Brideshead Revisited* (1945), an Oxford undergraduate, newly arrived in college, is warned by his cousin: "Beware of the Anglo-Catholics – they're all sodomites with unpleasant accents."[68] Compton Mackenzie's *Sinister Street* (1913) and his Anglo-Catholic trilogy, *The Altar Steps* (1922), *The Parson's Progress* (1923), and *The Heavenly Ladder* (1924), include (despite the author's disclaimers) many vivid and accurate descriptions of typical, often identifiable, Anglo-Catholic clergy and parishes of the 1890s and early 1900s.[69] They are subtly permeated with hints of homosexuality. A minor character in *The Parson's Progress* is Father Hugh Dayrell, assistant priest at "St. Cyprian's, South Kensington," an authority on moral theology, who shows unusual interest in the works of Havelock Ellis, Krafft-Ebing, and Freud, privately admits an antipathy to women, and is finally forced to flee the country in order to avoid an unspecified sexual scandal. In *The Altar Steps* the vicar of an Anglo-Catholic slum church in London expresses his dislike of "these churchy young fools who come simpering down in top-hats, with rosaries hanging out of their pockets." The same novel contains an account of life at "Malford Abbey" in the "Order of St. George" (which is recognisable as the Order of St. Paul at Alton). Many years later an historian of Anglican monasticism recalled: "Octogenarians can vouch for the truth of the period atmosphere. Even the gossip between the monks both during and outside times of recreation revive memories of the chit-chat in at least one Anglican monastic community about the turn of the century" (Anson, *Building up the Waste Places*, pp. 154-155). More recently, the autobiography of a former administrator of the Shrine of Our Lady of Walsingham has described with disarming frankness the semiconspiratorial and light-hearted atmosphere of a section of the Anglo-Catholic world of Brighton and Oxford between the wars (Stephenson, *Merrily on High*).

Archibald Kenneth Ingram, an Anglo-Catholic lay theologian, socialist, and prolific writer, attempted in several works to integrate his sexuality with his religious beliefs. In 1920 he contributed two pieces to a short-lived Uranian literary journal, *The Quorum: A*

[68] Evelyn Waugh, *Brideshead Revisited* (Boston: Little, Brown and Co., 1946), chap. 1, p. 26.

[69] Compton Mackenzie, *Sinister Street*, 2 vols. (London: Martin Secker, 1913), I, book 2, chaps. 5-9; *The Altar Steps* (London: Cassell and Co., 1922), chaps. 2, 16, 23-29; *The Parson's Progress* (London: Cassell and Co., 1923), chap. 19. Among more recent novels which portray homosexuality in an Anglo-Catholic setting are Iris Murdoch, *The Bell* (London: Chatto and Windus, 1958); Barbara Pym, *A Glass of Blessings* (London: Jonathan Cape, 1958); A. N. Wilson, *Unguarded Hours* (London: Secker and Warburg, 1978).

*Magazine of Friendship*, in which he advocated male comradeship as the highest relationship and the only way to bridge the gap between social classes (d'Arch Smith, pp. 140-141). In his view of the positive social value of male friendships, Ingram was influenced by the writings of Edward Carpenter, who saw Uranian men and women ("the intermediate sex") as filling an important function as reconcilers and interpreters and as a potential "advance guard" in the evolution of a new society. To the ideas of Carpenter and the other sexual radicals, Ingram added a religious justification derived from his Anglo-Catholic faith: "Pure love, especially so intense a love as the homogenic attachment, is not profane but divine."[70]

*The Symbolic Island* (1924), Ingram's first novel, included among its characters an Anglo-Catholic priest, Father Evrill, who becomes the spokesman for Ingram's personal views on the need for a revitalised Anglo-Catholicism as the remedy for the ills of modern society. At one point Evrill explains his close friendship with young altar boy Gerald Frayne, and talks with enthusiasm of "a new type of youth" which is coming into existence in English society – light-hearted, artistic, nature-loving, "not so exclusively, so aggressively, male," though by no means effeminate.[71] These youths and young men have a "much keener sense of comradeship" than their forefathers and show little romantic interest in women. Wherever they express themselves religiously, the priest observes with satisfaction: " . . . it is always by the Catholic religion. I think the type is naturally religious, because it is mystical. That Catholicism should be the form of its religious expression is, I think, quite inevitable. There could be nothing else" (Ingram, *Symbolic Island*, p. 163).

Ingram also wrote four books which went beyond the frontiers of Christian orthodoxy by advocating a new sexual morality for the "new age." In his first book on the subject, published in 1922, he described homosexuality as "a romantic cult rather than a physical vice" and reluctantly agreed that there could be "no religious countenance for any physical sex-act outside the sacrament of matrimony" (Ingram, *An Outline*, pp. 71-73). He became increasingly radical. By the 1940s he was arguing that the morality or immorality of any sexual behaviour

[70] Edward Carpenter, *The Intermediate Sex: A Study of Some Transitional Types of Men and Women* (London: Swan Sonnenschein and Co., 1908); (Archibald) Kenneth Ingram, *An Outline of Sexual Morality* (London: Jonathan Cape, 1922), chap. 8.

[71] (Archibald) Kenneth Ingram, *The Symbolic Island* (London: Damian Press, 1924), pp. 158-163.

was determined by the presence or absence of love; where love was mutual there was no sin. Conventional religious opinion was outraged.[72]

To the extent that "camp" (in its meaning of "elegantly ostentatious" or "affected display") was a prominent attribute of the homosexual style as it developed in England from the 1890s onwards, it found ample room for expression in the worship and decoration of many Anglo-Catholic churches. Perhaps its most visible manifestation was the attempt, fostered by the Society of SS. Peter and Paul during the 1920s, to refurnish the interiors of English churches in baroque and rococo styles, justified on the ground that this was the living architecture of Catholic Europe. The medieval restorations, so beloved of an earlier generation of High Churchmen, were denigrated as sterile antiquarianism – "British Museum religion." Under the guidance of ecclesiastical decorators such as Martin Travers, the interiors of a number of Gothic Revival churches were transformed into replicas of churches of Counter-Reformation Austria, Italy, and Spain, with gilded altars and reredoses, baroque candlesticks, tabernacles, and shrines, and ornamental cherubs (Anson, *Fashions in Church Furnishings*, pp. 319-327).

The ornamentation and fittings of these churches were luxuriant, often gaudy, and as such they were profoundly shocking to Low Church bishops and Protestant-minded laity. That was part of the attraction. "Anglo-Catholic baroque" was a theatrical, slightly unreal style which reflected the restless gaiety of the 1920s and the postwar urge to reject established social conventions. High Mass in an Anglican church with baroque interior decor, sung to music by Mozart or Schubert, belonged to the age of the Charleston, Theosophy, the Russian Ballet, and the first dramatic successes of Noel Coward. The same people often sampled them all. One can also sense a covert link between exotic church decoration, liturgical extravagance, and the over-ripe elegance of homosexual "camp."

## IV

What were the reasons for this apparent correlation between male homosexuality and Anglo-Catholic religion? Some homosexuals recog-

[72] (Archibald) Kenneth Ingram, *The Modern Attitude to the Sex Problem* (London: George Allen and Unwin, 1930), chap. 5; *Sex-Morality Tomorrow* (London: George Allen and Unwin, 1940), chap. 5; *Christianity and Sexual Morality – A Modernist View* (London: Union of Modern Free Churchmen, 1944).

nised the existence of an aesthetic attraction, for their sense of the numinous was aroused by the elaborate ceremonial and sensuous symbolism of Catholic worship. "The Church! How wonderful!" exclaims Arthur Wilmot, a homosexual poet in Compton Mackenzie's *Sinister Street* (set in the 1890s): "The dim Gothic glooms, the sombre hues of stained glass, the incense-wreathéd acolytes, the muttering priests, the bedizened banners and altars and images. Ah, elusive and particoloured vision that once was mine!" (Mackenzie, *Sinister Street*, I, 284). And in Bloxam's story, "The Priest and the Acolyte," one can recognise the author's own voice in the priest's attempt to explain his "nature": "The whole aesthetic tendency of my soul was intensely attracted by the wonderful mysteries of Christianity, the artistic beauty of our services. . . . My delight is in the aesthetic beauty of the services, the ecstasy of devotion, the passionate fervour that comes with long fasting and meditation" (Reade, pp. 356-357).

Aesthetic attraction, however, is not a sufficient explanation, simply because many homosexual men were not aesthetes, and many aesthetes were not Anglo-Catholics. The ideology and structure of Anglo-Catholicism in the context of English Christianity must also be considered. In the eyes of their Protestant opponents, Anglo-Catholics were no more than "Anglo-Romanists" – an impression which was reinforced by the small but steady stream of Anglo-Catholic clergy and laypeople who seceded to Rome, "the home of truth."[73] But this verdict is misleading, for the intellectual and social ethos of the Anglo-Catholic wing of the Church of England was very different from that of English Roman Catholicism. Almost all its leaders, clerical and lay, shared a common upper-class background of public school and ancient university. Among its intellectuals the dominant theology from the 1880s until the 1930s was a liberal Catholicism which accepted the legitimacy of biblical criticism, used contemporary philosophical and scientific concepts in the study of theology, and asserted the central importance of the Incarnation – the historical Christ as both fully God and fully man – in its dogmatic system.[74]

"The doctrine of the Incarnation revealed the glory of the Church, but it also revealed the glory that is in man, whose nature

[73] For example: Dean Henry Wace of Canterbury, quoted in J. C. Wilcox, *Contending for the Faith: John Kensit, Reformer & Martyr* (London: Protestant Truth Society, n.d.), p. 119. A number of former Anglo-Catholics published accounts of their conversion to Roman Catholicism. Some are included in *The Road to Damascus*, ed. John A. O'Brien, 4 vols. (London: W. H. Allen, 1949-55).

[74] On liberal Catholicism in the Church of England, see Arthur Michael Ramsey, *From Gore to Temple: The Development of Anglican Theology between "Lux Mundi" and the Second World War, 1889-1939* (London: Longmans, 1960); Roy Philip Flindall, "The Development of Anglo-Catholicism from *Lux Mundi* to *Essays Catholic and Critical*" (M. Phil. thesis, University of London, 1972).

has been united with the divine."[75] In the theology of the Incarnation, human nature was fallen but not depraved; natural man could be raised to holiness through the sacraments of the church; Christianity should penetrate and transform the entire social order. A belief that the "Incarnation is fulfilled in the growing together of every human activity" led some Anglo-Catholic priests in the direction of Christian Socialism – the idea of a society based upon the principles of cooperation and brotherhood, as symbolised by the Christian sacraments.[76] It also encouraged a slightly more accommodating attitude towards homosexuality than was commonly found elsewhere in the Christian church. At a time when hostility to homosexuality was intense, and when the few public statements on the subject by church leaders were full of references to "shameful vice," "grievous sin," and "perversion,"[77] it would appear that many Anglo-Catholic priests were inclined to the view that homosexual feelings were not in themselves sinful; they should be disciplined and controlled, and channelled into the service of others. The advice given in a tract entitled *Letter to a Homosexual* (1955) by the vicar of a leading Anglo-Catholic church in London (All Saints, Margaret Street) may be taken as representing a well-established Anglo-Catholic viewpoint, though this was the first time that it had been presented for a popular readership:

> You cannot help being homosexual: nor can you help it if your sexual feelings are very strong. That is a matter of natural endowment. . . . So it is much better to reconcile yourself to the fact that you are homosexual in outlook and make the best of it. I would go further: I say that your homosexual bias is to be used for the glory of God.[78]

The reactions of homosexual men to the moral condemnation of the church varied widely. If many who had been brought up in the Church of England, or in a nonconformist denomination, were alienated from institutional religion, others were drawn to Anglo-Catholicism because of the attitude of its priests and the method they employed to deal with sexual problems and moral dilemmas – auricular

[75] John Gunstone, "Catholics in the Church of England," in *Catholic Anglicans Today*, ed. John Wilkinson (London: Darton, Longman and Todd, 1968), p. 188.

[76] Ramsey, p. 1; Jones, pp. 85-94; E. R. Norman, *Church and Society in England, 1770-1970: A Historical Study* (Oxford: Clarendon Press, 1976), pp. 246-250, 318-323.

[77] For example: Bishop C. M. Chavasse of Rochester and Archbishop Geoffrey Fisher of Canterbury, quoted in D. J. West, *Homosexuality*, 2d rev. ed. (Harmondsworth: Penguin, 1968), p. 94. See also Selwyn Gummer, *The Chavasse Twins* (London: Hodder and Stoughton, 1963), pp. 213-215.

[78] Kenneth N. Ross, *Letter to a Homosexual* (London: S. P. C. K., 1955), p. 5. See also Lindsay Dewar and Cyril E. Hudson, *A Manual of Pastoral Psychology* (London: Philip Allan, 1932), pp. 184-188. For a survey of the views of Anglican theologians on homosexuality, see Coleman, chaps. 9, 10.

confession. Unlike the conventional Anglican parson, Anglo-Catholic clergymen fulfilled a sharply defined priestly role and had been trained in their theological colleges to be discreet and unshockable confessors. "In the right sense of the word, they were professionals: they knew their job through and through," observed a historian of the twentieth-century Church of England (Lloyd, p. 134).[79] On the subject of sex the teaching of their moral theology textbooks was less detailed and less legalistic than the corresponding Roman Catholic authorities, but no less rigorous. Although homosexuality was not specifically mentioned in Francis Belton's widely used *Manual for Confessors* (1916), his advice in other areas of sexual behaviour was uncompromising. Priests were advised to forbid close friendships between young men and women before marriage as dangerous. Even after the modification by the 1930 Lambeth Conference of the Anglican church's traditional opposition to artificial birth control, Belton's view was unchanged: the prevention of conception was never justified.[80] His viewpoint on contraception was not universally accepted by Anglo-Catholic clergy, for a significant minority defended the legitimacy of birth control at a time when it was by no means fashionable to do so.[81] In other areas of morality Anglo-Catholic teaching was substantially identical to the Roman Catholic position. Homosexual acts were judged to be intrinsically sinful, though the degree of moral guilt varied according to the circumstances of each case. For "true homosexuals," declared an influential guide for Anglican confessors, the "only treatment lies in the strengthening of the will to resist temptation."[82] Nevertheless orthodox doctrine was often tempered with pastoral sympathy. Especially before the 1950s, when homosexuality was a taboo subject, many Anglo-Catholic priests were able, under the seal of the confessional,

[79] Anglo-Catholic theological colleges consciously aimed at the formation of disciplined priests — "the presentation of the ministerial ideal and the development of the devotional life." See, for example, "Ely Theological College," *The Treasury* (London), 1 (1903), 353-360.

[80] Francis George Belton, *A Manual for Confessors: Being a Guide to the Administration of the Sacrament of Penance for the Use of Priests of the English Church*, rev. ed. (London: A. R. Mowbray and Co., 1931), pp. 179-186, 204-205.

[81] One of the most prominent of these priests was Father Stephen Langton of St. Mary's, *Graham Street* (now Bourne Street), Pimlico, in *Graham Street Quarterly*, (Autumn 1972), 7. In the 1930s, however, most Anglo-Catholic leaders regarded the practice of artificial birth control as inherently unnatural and immoral. For the evolution of official Anglican thinking on contraception, see Norman, *Church and Society*, pp. 270, 347-348, 412-414.

[82] [Reginald Somerset Ward], *A Guide for Spiritual Directors, by the Author of "The Way"* (London: A. R. Mowbray and Co., 1957), p. 33. See also Kenneth Ross, *Hearing Confessions* (London: S. P. C. K., 1974), pp. 85-86.

to discuss the personal problems associated with it without show of embarrassment or open hostility, and without informing the police.

There was also the inherent attraction of identifiable and continuous groupings of homosexuals. Many homosexual men, unmarried and therefore outside the regular family structure, had a strong need for companionship with others like themselves. Before the liberalisation of the late 1960s, when public meeting places for homosexual men outside London were virtually nonexistent, and when pubs and clubs in London were difficult to find and regularly harassed by the police, Anglo-Catholicism provided a visible network of supportive and protective institutions – not only in England, but also scattered through the Anglican church in the cities of the United States, Canada South Africa, and Australia. Within these Anglo-Catholic congregations, homosexual men, compelled by social hostility to remain invisible and avoid social disgrace, could make contact with each other and establish discreet friendships across class barriers. Looking back at London's homosexual subculture of the 1930s, a recent writer in the weekly *Gay News* recalled that many of his own youthful contemporaries had "attended fashionable churches where contacts were made with rather rich gays. Some were left substantial legacies."[83]

At the heart of the correlation between Anglo-Catholicism and homosexuality was an affinity in outlook between a sexual minority and a minority religious movement within the established church. Both were at variance with entrenched beliefs and both outraged the older generation. In middle- and upper-class circles in the interwar years, an involvement in the homosexual subculture could be a means of demonstrating rebellion, for since the scandals of the 1890s heterosexuality had been "the key test of respectability": "What better way therefore to declare one's contempt for the official mores of society than to take a whirl among homosexuals?"[84]

Similarly, until the second world war, Anglo-Catholics were a consciously defined party within the Church of England – a "Church-within-the-Church" – in perpetual conflict with the dominant norms of the establishment. In many dioceses Anglo-Catholic congregations were ostracised by their bishops and isolated from neighbouring par-

[83] Gifford Skinner, "Cocktails in the Bath," *Gay News*, 135 (26 January 1978), 22. Another account of London's homosexual subculture of the 1920s and 1930s is by J. R. Ackerley, *My Father and Myself* (London: Bodley Head, 1968), chap. 12.

[84] Noel Annan, "'Our Age': Reflections on Three Generations in England," *Daedalus*, 107 (Fall 1978), 91.

ishes because of doctrinal and liturgical disobedience. In return they viewed the "official diocese . . . with indifference, suspicion, or even hostility" (Gunstone, p. 189). With the adoption of Roman Catholic baroque furnishings and ceremonial, they "tended to become a 'people apart' and their churches almost unrecognisable as Anglican" (Stephenson, *Walsingham Way*, p. 88). At the same time, however, many fashionable Anglo-Catholic churches offered all the trappings of outward respectability, as well as the security and stability of ancient rituals and traditions. Despite their marginal position, Anglo-Catholics chose to remain within the established church and liked to regard their religion as "much smarter" than its rival, Roman Catholicism.[85] Anglo-Catholicism was thus both elitist and nonconformist, combining a sense of superiority with a rebellion against existing authority. As such it provided an environment in which homosexual men could express in a socially acceptable way their dissent from heterosexual orthodoxy and from the Protestant values of those who wielded repressive power in church and state.

*Flinders University of South Australia*

[85] See, for example, Rose Macaulay, *Letters to a Friend, 1950-1952*, ed. Constance Babington Smith (London: Collins, 1961), p. 144.

*CELIBACY: THE CASE AGAINST*

# Liberating Lesbian Nuns

By Mary Hunt

Illustrations by Brian Williams

SISTER JOAN is a member of a canonical community. She lives with Sister Barbara, a member of another congregation. They both work as advocates for poor people in the rural South. They are lovers. Neither plans to leave her community. Both hope that no one will find out about their life together.

Sister Marcia is a member of a progressive religious community that supports her work among people with AIDS. Her lover, Sister Anne, is a doctor. Their community is pleased that they live together since rents in their neighborhood are high. They discuss the contradiction between their public vows and their private conduct, but neither is inclined to leave the community. Their close

friends know about their life-style, but so far no one has brought it to the attention of community leaders. Besides, several of the leaders appear to live in coupled relationships themselves. And the community keeps a running tab at the local women's bookstore.

Sister Susan just broke up with her lover, Kate, a married woman with five children. The relationship had come as a shock to both of them. Work at the local school, where Susan is the principal and Kate the president of the PTA, had spilled over into long evenings. Kate's husband traveled constantly; he was glad she had such a good companion in Susan. And Susan lived alone, so her sisters were glad she had some companionship, too. It was a first for both of them. But, in time, though both were deeply in love, neither could handle the intensity. After all, a nun and a married woman are hardly likely to be lovers—or so it seems.

These stories, composites based on real people, illustrate how compulsory celibacy limits the lives of mature women in religious communities—every time a "particular friendship" is broken up, every time a woman is forbidden to develop a sexual relationship as the price of membership, every time women refuse to touch one another for fear of being misunderstood. Such denials are an intolerably high price to pay for maintaining women's canonical communities.

**Compulsory celibacy, commonly assumed to mean abstaining from heterosexual contact, was not a remarkable burden in the past.**

RELIGIOUS COMMUNITIES, variously called convents or religious orders, and their members, known as sisters or nuns, are an essential part of the Roman Catholic Church. In the United States there are about 100,000 sisters, half as many as 20 years ago. At their peak, communities such as the Franciscans, Dominicans, and Sisters of Mercy had scores of women in their training or formation programs all over the country. Now, such groups are lucky to have three or four. The median age for members is about 60, a sure sign that the end of religious communities as we have known them is near.

Women become nuns for a variety of reasons, all of which are subsumed under the term "having a vocation," that is, a calling to live in community with other women under vows of poverty, chastity, and obedience. In recent years poverty has meant economic sharing rather than impoverishment. Obedience has come to mean communal accountability for decisions on work and living arrangements. But the meaning of chastity has not changed much.

Some women joined religious communities because the work or mission of the group attracted them. Others joined for the access to education and upward mobility that the orders provided. And still others, I would judge the majority, joined for seemingly inexplicable reasons.

When pressed, women often acknowledge the influence of a nun who was a beloved teacher, mentor, or role model and who was living a life-style that looked appealing. Usually that life-style stood in stark contrast to one's mother's in that it included no biological children, no husband, and plenty of self-directed activity. But the vows, especially celibacy, were part of the package as well.

It is no wonder that these groups of religious women seem to have a higher percentage of lesbians among them than in the population at large (though until recent years such matters were unspoken). Nor is it any wonder that compulsory celibacy, commonly assumed to mean abstaining from heterosexual contact, was not a remarkable burden in the past.

CLASSIC FEMINIST theory now includes Adrienne Rich's powerful essay "Compulsory Heterosexuality and Lesbian Existence."* Rich argues that the existence of lesbians is obscured by the fact that heterosexuality is the norm in a patriarchal culture. Until this norm is transformed, she argues, the lives of lesbian women will remain hidden, and the variety of lesbian experiences will be lost. Rich suggests that there is a "lesbian continuum," a way of talking about all women's potential and actual ways of loving women. While the lesbian continuum has generated great debate, the basic argument, that compulsory heterosexuality is a constitutive part of patriarchy and that all women fall somewhere on the continuum, is increasingly well accepted.

Rich is correct that compulsory heterosexuality has a negative impact on all women, especially lesbians. An equally compelling case can be made for the negative impact of compulsory celibacy, even in the freely chosen situation of canonical communities. Compulsory celibacy is the antidote to the fear of what will happen to women who are self- and community-identified without dependence on men. It robs women of choice by circumscribing their possibilities. Without compulsory celibacy, differences between women would diminish and choices would increase. In the church, the artificial, male-constructed barrier between so-called lay women and so-called nun women would fall away. Likewise, society as a whole would be forced to abandon celibacy as the calling card for the "good woman" (symbolized by the Virgin Mary who was not only celibate but had a child—a difficult, if not impossible, act for any woman to follow).

Those who have asked why celibacy is "a given" and what religious communities would look like without it have been given nebulous answers. Many who leave communities because of compulsory celibacy think they have outgrown it rather than that it is unreasonable to begin with. If a woman wants to be a part of a religious community she must still accept this discipline. Amen.

Heterosexual women have been raising questions about compulsory celibacy since the mid-1960s when many decided to leave the church because of it. But lesbian women *within* religious communities open the possibility of a viable option to celibacy within the community without making other substantive changes—such as becoming co-ed, or allowing members who are married or have children.

A lesbian nun has the possibility of living in an emotional/sexual relationship with a woman who may or may not be part of the community—an option that is exercised every day. The challenge to the church comes when people start to acknowledge this situation publicly. Then the compulsory nature of celibacy becomes obvious and conflictual.

**A nun and a married woman are hardly likely to be lovers—or so it seems.**

THE PSYCHOLOGICAL effects of compulsory celibacy are difficult to assess. The prohibitions on loving in an integrated way, which compulsory celibacy invokes, make it extremely difficult for friendships to flourish. It is not that all friendships must include sexual expression. Rather, when sexual expression is denied, a friendship cannot move through the natural cycle of increased intimacy which of-

* Adrienne Rich, "Compulsory Heterosexuality and Lesbian Existence," *Signs*, 5, No. 4, (1980), pp. 631-60.

ten includes some consideration or exploration of sexual dynamics.*

Religious communities, for all of their emphasis on community, produce some very lonely people when celibacy is enforced. Conversely, some of the healthiest people in the communities, those most involved in leadership and innovative ministries, have deep friendships that include sexual expression.

At stake with compulsory celibacy is something even more insidious than a prohibition on sex for nuns. It is the loss of choice over love and life-style that translates finally into a loss of autonomy. Like Benedetta Carlini and Bartolomea Crivelli, two nuns who had a spectacular romance during the 17th century, today's nuns have no choice but to accept celibacy if they wish to live in canonically connected communities. This requirement creates a serious conflict because those same communities are women's spaces that have been created to nurture and enhance women's relationships with one another.

**Lesbian women open the possibility of a viable option to celibacy within the community without making other substantive changes.**

An easy solution would be to say that women should not join these communities in the first place. But, in fact, few organized women's groups have succeeded like religious communities in providing economic sharing, meaningful work, and joint strategizing for social change. To lose the accumulated property, the women's traditions, and the sisterhood of centuries to a patriarchal church seems too high a price to pay. Yet, to maintain these benefits at the expense of choice for individual women is dearer still.

* See my forthcoming *Fierce Tenderness: Toward a Feminist Theology of Friendship*, (San Francisco: Harper and Row), 1989, for a fuller treatment of women's friendships.

THEOLOGICALLY, COMPULSORY celibacy for women is on shaky ground, especially when it comes to lesbians. The definition of celibacy, based on the Latin *coelebs*, meaning bachelor, is clearly founded on male experience, especially that of male sexuality. A man can cause pregnancy, thus his sexual capacity has to be controlled. Since inheritance laws would have permitted a priest's offspring to receive the land and goods of the parish, celibacy was prescribed for priests. Gradually a theological rationale was embellished to promote the "tradition." It is important to realize, however, that material considerations preceded this logic.

Sexual expression between women presents no such specter of pregnancy. To the contrary, sex between women does not require contraception nor threaten the need for an abortion. Thus the fundamental reason for celibacy, based on the false norm of male experience, is undercut.

It is also argued that celibacy is a tradition, that canonical communities have always required it. Without detailing the history of celibacy, it is important to reiterate that this tradition, even if true, is again based on male experience. Several contemporary writers have attempted to distinguish between celibacy for priests and chastity for members of religious communities. Some have tried to develop a notion of the "sexual celibate." No contemporary theological writer seems to face the real issue, namely that compulsory celibacy is an ecclesiastical discipline, not a matter of divine revelation. As such it can be changed if those in power would relinquish their hold.

Compulsory celibacy is used to keep a certain decorum, an order that lesbian nuns, by their very existence, defy. It is not their alleged sexual activity that is the main problem. What is at stake is the challenge that they present to the whole church about the importance of well-integrated and freely chosen sexuality.

**I do not pretend to understand totally what motivates a small number of people to choose celibacy unfettered by connection to a canonical religious community.**

Lesbian nuns who define celibacy for themselves in terms that do not preclude sexual activity, or those who simply consider their public vow invalid because of its patriarchal definition, are left with many contradictions. They run the real risk of being forced, usually by other women and sometimes by their own guilt, to leave their religious families. They may be branded unfaithful or lacking in integrity insofar as their private interpretations of the vows are concerned. And worse, they may be prevented from being open to the serendipitous experience of love that comes when one least expects it.

Heterosexual nuns experience the same veiling as it were, but contemporary lesbian/gay movements, coupled with the women's movement, have given lesbian nuns a newfound boldness. Ironically, while doubly oppressed when compared with their heterosexual counterparts, lesbian nuns seem to be challenging structures that, if changed, will improve the lot for heterosexual women as well.

WOMEN IN canonical communities may charge me with insulting or degrading them by pressing the point that celibacy is compulsory—as if they have been robbed of choice. After all, they assent to their vows. I mean to affirm their choice to be with women in religiously focused communities. But there is no intrinsic reason for celibacy to be a part of that commitment unless the control of women is taken for granted. Moreover, if women were to develop communities free from patriarchal expectations, it is not clear that celibacy would figure in at all. My sense is that as women understand compulsory celibacy, it will disappear, even though some will choose to live celibate for reasons of their own.

It takes time to free ourselves and our imaginations from the shackles of patriarchy, but it can be done. The language of mystery has shrouded many discussions of celibacy. I do not pretend to understand totally what motivates a small number of people to choose celibacy unfettered by connection to a canonical religious community, but I do know that whenever such language abounds there is something dubious to explore.

What makes one person love another is equally mysterious. But "celibacy for the kingdom" is not mysterious. It is a rationale used to mask who is king and what power the kings exercise. Celibate love is raised to a higher level in an exercise in body hating, woman controlling, or both. Such is not the stuff of mystery but of oppression. A free choice for celibacy among members of religious communities would be possible *only* if membership were not conditioned by it. Until then, not even members of canonical communities can claim celibacy voluntarily.

Celibacy is not usually a lifelong choice for people outside of canonical communities. Most people have occasional celibate periods, even if they are married. With the serious health threat of AIDS, some people are choosing celibacy as a way to limit their risks. But in general, celibacy is not something to which most people aspire. Above all, it should not be confused with a sexual preference; celibacy is a choice one makes within the context of sexual preference. It is accepted or chosen for a brief period, rarely celebrated, and cheapened when forced.

As sexually active lesbians in canonical religious communities become increasingly vocal about their experiences, we will have new insights for understanding the impact of compulsory celibacy. For now, women who are sexually active in religious life commonly react by leaving. Canonical communities, fear-

> **"Celibacy for the kingdom" is not mysterious. It is a rationale used to mask who is king and what power the kings exercise.**

ing that their relationships with the Vatican may be in jeopardy if such activities become known, often set ultimatums and subtly encourage women to live out their sexual explorations, both homosexual and heterosexual, beyond the limits of the community.

The first step is usually exclaustration, a period of time away from the community. Then an indult of secularization, popularly known as leaving the community, can follow. The language alone is enough to give a clear message. Secular and not canonically connected people are sexually active; religious life and sexual activity are mutually exclusive.

I SUGGEST THREE preliminary steps toward overcoming compulsory celibacy as we recognize and celebrate the legacy of lesbian nuns and thus honor the dignity of all women.

First, I urge that canonical religious communities sever their ties with the Vatican. I realize this is a radical suggestion, but I consider it *sine qua non* for women's autonomy. The control exercised to maintain compulsory celibacy is the same control that prevents women's ordination and that presumes to dictate women's reproductive choices. Until women and women's experience on their own terms are part of the decision making, the canonical connection is simply a noose.

Second, knowing that the severing of the canonical cord may not happen soon, I urge women in religious communities to develop a trusting context in which frank discussion of women's experiences of love and sex can take place. This might necessitate declaring a moratorium, such as a month during which all such discussions would be considered totally off the record. Only when the terror of telling is broken down can we really call each other sister. Then perhaps the poignancy of love well lived, love lost, of love simply waiting to be shared will be part of what moves the hearts and minds of people in power.

Third, I urge that communities begin to talk about and celebrate their own lesbian heritage. It is important to use the word lesbian to break down the taboo. Again, I realize the radical nature of my suggestion, but I make it as a way of underscoring how deeply ingrained the problem is. We must go to the root of the problem, and dare to speak the unspeakable before we can honor the real memories of our sisters, not the whitewashed, glossed-over images of them that we need in order to keep the whole system from collapsing.

Eventually, compulsory celibacy and all of the repressive apparatus that surrounds it will collapse under its own dead weight. Then healthy, loving, freely chosen relationships can flourish for women who choose to bond in communities. It is to these relationships that women bring our communal and religious best, and it will be because of them that society will move more quickly to a new social order. ▼

---

*Mary E. Hunt, PhD., is the co-director of the Women's Alliance for Theology, Ethics and Ritual (WATER) in Silver Spring, Maryland. She teaches, lectures, and writes on religion and feminism, and is an editor of the* Journal of Feminist Studies in Religion.

# WHOSOEVER SHALL SAY TO HIS BROTHER, *RACHA*

(Matthew 5:22)

**by Warren Johansson**

**[Editor's Note:** The study of the usually condemnatory references to homosexual behavior that are found in the varied body of writings known as the Old and New Testament has given rise to much controversy. Generally accepted, however, has been the conclusion that the four Gospels contain no discussion of the subject—that is to say, that the words and actions attributed to Jesus Christ in these biographical texts yield nothing directly pertinent to homosexual behavior. (Efforts to interpret in this light such passages as Matthew 8:5-13; and John 11:13, 5 and 36, 13:23; 19:26; 20:2; 21:7 and 20 —the "beloved disciple" passages— have carried little force of conviction.) Taken by themselves, the Gospels would appear to render at best a Scotch verdict, "not proven," with regard to the views of the founder of Christianity toward same-sex conduct. Any assertions about such attitudes on the part of Jesus himself would have to be inferred from the other opinions attributed to him, situating them in the historical perspective of Jewish tradition, on the one hand, and the intellectual and moral world in which he lived, on the other. In these contexts, with their restrictivist coloration, it would be rash to assume *a priori* that the absence of evidence signifies tolerance or permission. The problem is compounded by the fact that for many years much advanced biblical scholarship has conceded that we can know nothing of the "historical Jesus," but only something of the image that the Primitive Church constructed of his person for missionary and devotional purposes.

Almost two centuries ago, the English philosopher Jeremy Bentham wrote "Jesus has in the field of sexual irregularity preserved an uninterrupted silence." That silence is about to be broken, for in the following article, Warren Johansson explores for the first time in detail the one word which Jesus is reported as having pronounced on our subject: racha. Until the discovery of certain evidence from papyri. this word of Semitic origin was truly a *hapax legomenon,* that is, a unique term in our surviving record. This rarity may account in part for the obscurity in which the expression has hitherto been shrouded. In the latter part of the paper Johansson adduces some collateral evidence from various later historical strata in Europe, which while not crucial to his argument, vividly attest to the word's later manifestations and penumbra of meaning.]

The word *racha,* until recently a hapax legomenon of the New Testament, is one of the little riddles of the Gospel text that have not as yet found a satisfactory explanation. The passage in which it occurs reads in the King James Version:

> But I say unto you, that
> whosoever is angry with his brother [without a cause],
> shall be in danger of the Judgment:
> and whosoever shall say to his brother, Racha,
> shall be in danger of the counsel:
> but whosoever shall say, Thou fool,
> shall be in danger of hell fire.

Modern printings of the KJV have changed the spelling of the word to *Raca* following the edition of 1638, which altered the reading to accord with the *textus receptus* of the Greek Testament and, indeed, all modern editions except those of Lachmann and Tischendorf.[1]

The general meaning of the passage is clear enough: Where the law of Moses forbade only murder, Jesus sets a vastly higher ethical standard for his followers; not merely physical assault and mayhem, but even anger and verbal aggression are condemned and proscribed. It is a standard so high that later editors had to insert the words "without a cause," which have, however, been stricken by modern critical scholarship.

Simple anger at one's fellow man, in this piece of Oriental hyperbole, is a crime for which the offender should be hailed before the court of first instance; the expression of contempt *racha* is an offense that ranks with the capital crimes trial for which is reserved to the Sanhedrin, the highest tribunal of the Jewish nation; and the malicious utterance, Thou fool, is a transgression for which the perpetrator merits eternal damnation. By this picturesque crescendo Jesus drives home his point: The sins contemplated and willed by the heart are as heinous as those contemplated and realized in deed.[2]

I shall not here go into the complex question of the historicity of Jesus or of the authenticity of the Sermon on the Mount, of which this passage forms a part. In general, I agree with Allard Pierson that the Sermon on the Mount is an uterance of Jesus in the same sense that the Book of Proverbs is the work of King Solomon.[3] I should add that the Solomon—not of history, but of Jewish legend—is the prototype of the Jesus of the canonical gospels. His proverbial wisdom, his healing skills, his power over the world of the demonic, his accession to the throne of David his father—all these traits foreshadow the role of Jesus as the Messiah, the anointed king of Israel.[4]

But what does all this have to do with our subject? This paper addresses the problem: What is the meaning of the word *racha*? The text of the Gospel of Matthew includes no explanatory gloss, as is usual with foreign words that would otherwise have been unintelligible to the Greek reader, yet the commentators and lexicographers of late antiquity unanimously understand the word as Semitic: *raka* = Hebrew *rêqā* "empty, emptyheaded, brainless" and thus as parallel to

Greek *mōrós* "fool" in the final clause. Alongside this explanation of the word as deriving from the root *ryq* "to be empty", there is another, recorded by the Byzantine lexicographer Zonaras and repeated in the first dictionary of the Greek Testament by Georg Pasor, which would render the foreign *raka* as *katáptystos* "fit to be spat upon", hence "despicable", as if from the root *rqq* "to spit."[5]

Not a few of the modern commentators have been dissatisfied with this solution, inasmuch as it can scarcely be reconciled with the minority reading *racha* supported by ℵ*DW and the totality of the Latin witnesses. Edgar J. Goodspeed surmised that the epithet was "a bad name, perhaps so vile that Greek literature has nowhere preserved it, except in Matt. 5:22, where the evangelist mentions it only to forbid its use,"[6] But it remained for an expert on Syriac and Palestinian Christian Aramaic, Friedrich Schulthess, to make the relevant suggestion that it could represent Hebrew *rakh* "soft", with the emphatic form *rakhkha* subsequently losing the doubled consonant. As a Hebrew (or Jewish Aramaic) word it would therefore mean "weakling, effeminate." The Arabic cognate *rakīkun* commonly denotes the physically or morally inferior.[7] At the time when Schulthess wrote this explanation, no other instance of the word was known in Greek, albeit the Semitic derivatives of the root *rkk* "to be soft" were well attested.

Then, in 1934, a papyrus was published that had belonged to the archive of Zenon in Philadelphia, in Ptolemaic Egypt. Dated February 6 or 9 of the year 257 before the Christian era, it includes the phrase *hoi perì Antíochon tòn rachân* "those around Antiochus the *rachas*". The editor, C. C. Edgar, remarks in his introduction to the text: "Amyntas, to whom I have ventured to ascribe this letter, was one of the chief lieutenants of Apollonius" to whom the letter was addressed. "Some of his letters have an individual character rather rare among Zenon's correspondents, and are spiced with uncomplimentary epithets, such as *Kallíánax ho kínaidos*".[8] The full reading of the phrase is *Kallíánax ho téktōn ho kínaidos* "Kallianax the carpenter the cinaedus", which shows that the second term is not to be taken in the sense of "professional dancer."[9]

This passage strengthens the hypothesis advanced by Schulthess twelve years earlier, that *racha* is the vocative of a word derived from Hebrew *rakh* "soft", but specifically a vulgar Greek loanword in which the Semitic etymon has been assigned the semantic value of Greek malakós/malthakós "passive-effeminate male homosexual", attested in this sense in the title of the play *Hoi Malthakoí* by Cratinus, the older contemporary of Aristophanes. The word is a product of the initial contact between Jew and Greek in the newly-founded city of Alexandria, and belonged to the most obscene stratum of the slang of Hellenistic Egypt. It shows, incidentally, that even in the third century before the Christian era the Jews and the pagan Greeks were one in their contempt for the passive male partner in the homosexual act. The Latin transcription of the word further establishes that it was a foreign expression and should, therefore, be written *rachâs,* with smooth breathing, while the vocative form in the New Testament should be *rachâ*.[10]

Another point in support of this explanation—and one that has been totally ignored until now—is that in the *Gaunersprache,* the argot of German thieves and beggars, the word *rach* is recorded in the meaning "tender, soft, effeminate, timid, cowardly."[11] Its origin is to be explained by the fact that three-fourths of the distinctive vocabulary of the *Gaunersprache* is taken from Hebrew and Yiddish. Furthermore, the dictionary of Eliezer ben Yehudah offers Hebrew *rakh* as the rendering of German *moll* = Italian *minore,* English *minor* as a term in music.[12] Last of all, the glossary of the *jenische Sprache* compiled by Cajetan Karmayer (1788-1847) contains the word *Rachas* "wine", which can only be explained with reference to the Romany word *mōl, mōl* "wine".[13] Hence the following pairs:

| | |
|---|---|
| Greek *malakós* "effeminate" | Hellenistic Greek *rachâs* "faggot" |
| Medieval Latin *molle* "minor" | Hebrew *rakh* "minor" |
| Romany *mol* "wine" | Jenisch *rachas* "wine" |

This table illustrates how the Hebrew term has again and again been drawn into the semantic orbit of Greek *malakós* = Latin *mollis.*

Yet one more linguistic consideration is that the word *mōré* "thou fool" in the last clause of the verse is rendered by *nābhāl* in the Vetus Hebraea of St. Matthew,[14] and both that word and the abstract *nĕbhālāh* "folly" have a strongly erotic connotation, as does the Greek counterpart *aphrosýnē.*[15] The *nābhāl* is not merely the one who "hath said in his heart: There is no God," he is also the sexual wrongdoer and aggressor, as in Judges XIX 23-24. Thus the entire passage is not merely a Semiticizing pastiche, it also has an undertone of double entendre and irony that made it too subtle for the pagan readers of the second and third centuries—which is why modern commentators have wrongly attempted to decompose the text and reduce it to a shorter, primary form.[16]

Two other words in the passage require an explanation. The first, *énochos* "in danger of" corresponds to Hebrew *ḥayyābh* "obliged for, answerable to, guilty of, subject to," which causes an apparent loss of parallelism in the Greek, since the first two clauses refer to the venue of the trial and the third to the locus of punishment. The second, *tō synedríō* "the counsel" in KJV, must refer to the Sanhedrin, the highest legislative and judicial body of the Jewish nation. As some Jewish apologists in modern times have sought to prove that *tò synédrion* in the Gospels does not mean the Sanhedrin, but only a political council convened by the ruler, it is necessary to go into the origin of the term.

The starting point for the whole semantic development is the Hebrew word *Kĕneset* "assembly," which was the designation of *ha-kĕneset ha-gĕdōlāh,* "the Great Assembly", the supreme legislative body formed in the days of Ezra the Scribe as the constituent assembly of normative Judaism. In time—possibly after the establishment of the Second Commonwealth—this was succeeded by the *bét dīn ha-gādōl,* literally "the Great House of Law." The former term was rendered in Greek by *synédrion,* the latter by *dikastḗrion* "court, tribunal," and Hesychius obligingly glosses the first by the second.[17] However, *synédrion* not merely persisted, but gave rise to Hebrew and Jewish Aramaic *sanhedrīn, sanhedrī,* whence the name Sanhedrin that entered our language in the second half of the sixteenth century, in the wake of the discovery of that tribunal by the Christian Hebraists of the Renaissance.[18] On the other hand, *bét-ha-kĕneset* became the designation for the house in which the Jewish community assembled for prayer, but this was expressed in Greek by *synagōgé,* whence Latin *synagōga* and French/English *synagogue.* What confirms this interpretation is that the Syriac and Hebrew versions of Matthew render *synédrion* and *synagōgé* alike, the former by *knūštā,* the latter by *kĕneset.* The account of the passion of Jesus in Mark and Matthew leaves no doubt as to the import of the narrative: The highest tribunal of Jewry tried Jesus and found him guilty of a capital crime, and the Jewish mob in the streets of Jerusalem ratified the verdict and even demanded that the prefect of Judea, Pontius Pilate, carry out the sentence by crucifixion.

In conclusion, it may even be admitted that Yoël Arbeitman's rather fanciful interpretation of Matthew V:22 has a core of truth.[19] If *rachâs* denotes the passive-effeminate homosexual, then *mōrós* = *nābhāl* could apply to the active one, as in the account of the outrage at Gibeah whose perpetrators are accused of committing an act of "folly" (nebhalah) without precedent in Israel. The parallelism would be just as in I Corinthians VI:9, where as I have demonstrated, the *malakoí* and *arsenokoîtai* are the passive and active culprits respectively.[20] Oesterley's observation that "as to many actual words, knowledge of Greek is insufficient for understanding them" has turned out to be doubly true, and the assertion that "Jesus never so much as mentioned homosexuality" has proved to be absolutely false.[21]

**Notes:**

[1]A good summary of the evidence is to be found in the article by Eberhard Nestle, "Raca," in *A Dictionary of Christ and the Gospels,* ed. James Hastings (New York, 1912), vol. 2, pp. 467-68.

[2]W. O. E. Oesterley, "The Study of the Synoptic Gospels Exemplified by Matthew v. 21, 22", *Expositor,* 6th series, 12:28-32 (1905).

[3]Allard Pierson, *De Bergrede en andere synoptische fragmenten, een historisch-kritisch onderzoek met een inleiding voor enkele leemten in de methode van de kritiek der Evangeliën* (Amsterdam, 1878), pp. 214ff. See also K. H. Boersema, *Allard Pierson. Eene cultuurhistorische studie* (The Hague, 1924), pp. 310-11.

[4]Moncure Daniel Conway, *Solomon and Solomonic Literature* (Chicago, 1899), pp. 176-233; David J. Halperin, "The *Book of Remedies,* the Canonization of the Solomonic Writings, and the Riddle of Pseudo-Eusebius", *Jewish Quarterly Review,* 72: 269-92 (1982), esp. pp. 287-92: Solomon's self-inflicted penance = the incarnation and crucifixion of Jesus.

[5]Georg Pasor, *Etyma nominum propriorum itemque analysis Hebraeorum, Syriacorum, & Latinorum vocabulorum, quae in Novo Testamento uspiam occurrunt,* pp. 79-80, appended to his *Lexicon graecolatinum... in N. Testamentum* (Geneva, 1637). The modern work on the problem is summarized in Robert A. Guelich, "Mt 5[22]: Its Meaning and Integrity," *Zeitschrift für die neutestamentliche Wissenschaft,* 64: 39-52 (1973), esp. pp. 39-40, where he concludes that even the evidence for *racha* makes "this explanation only slightly less than certain." See also the same author's *The Sermon on the Mount: A Foundation for Understanding* (Waco, Texas, 1982), pp. 184-189 and esp. p. 186.

[6]Edgar J. Goodspeed, *Problems of New Testament Translation* (Chicago, 1945), p. 22.

[7]Friedrich Schulthess, "Zur Sprache der Evangelien. Anhang. A. *racha* (*raka*), *mōre,*" *Zeitschrift für die neutestamentliche Wissenschaft,* 21: 241-43 (1922).

[8]C. C. Edgar, "A New Group of Zenon Papri", *Bulletin of the John Rylands Library,* 18: 112-13 (1934).

[9]In a letter from Amyntas to Zenon of 258/257, published as No. 483 in the *Pubblicazioni della Società Italiana per la ricerca dei papiri greci e latini in Egitto.*

[10]Goodspeed had already suggested such a reading on pp. 22-23 of the work cited.

[11]Christian Heinrich Schweser, *Des klugen Beamten tägliches Hand-Lexicon... Nebst einem Anhange eines vollständigen Wörterbuchs von der Jüdisch-teutschen und Rothwelschen oder sogenannten Spitzbuben Sprache, zum Gebrauch derjenigen, so mit Juden handeln, oder über dieselben gerichtliche Verhöre und Inquisitiones halten müssen*... von Germano Philoparcho. Aufs neue vermehret von Christoph Friederich Krackherr (Nuremberg, 1768), p. 508: *Rach, weich;* Friedrich Christian Benedict Avé-Lallemant, *Das Deutsche Gaunerthum in seiner social-politischen, literarischen, und linguistischen Ausbildung zu seinem heutigen Bestande,* vol. 4 (Leipzig, 1862), p. 456 (*rach* in Judeo-German), p. 588: *Rach: zart, weich, weichlich, furchtsam, verzagt;* Günter Puchner, *Kundenschall, das Gekasper der Kirschenpflücker im Winter* (Munich, 1974), p. 262: *rach: zart, weich.* It is noteworthy that the *Gaunersprache* also has the words *reck, reckam, reik* in the meaning "empty, hollow", hence clearly preserving the distinction between the Hebrew etyma. A possible use of *Racha* in the sense *"Pfui, Verräter"* = "Get lost, stoolie" is recorded by Ernst Rabben, *Die Gaunersprache (chochum loschen). Gesammelt und zusammengestellt aus der Praxis--für die Praxis* (Hamm in Westfalen, 1906), p. 109 (with specific reference to Matthew V 22).

[12]Eliezer Ben Iehuda, *Thesaurus totius Hebraitatis et veteris et recentioris,* vol. 13 (Jerusalem, 1951), p. 6587, quoting Moritz Steinschneider, *Die hebraeischen Uebersetzungen des Mittelalters und die Juden als Dolmetscher* (Berlin, 1893), p. 970, n. 159. The word figures in an elementary treatise on music translated from Italian into Hebrew.

[13]Hans Gross, "Das Gaunerglossar der Freistädter Handschrift", *Archiv für Kriminal-Anthropologie und Kriminalistik,* 3: 305 (1900): *Rachas (der): Wein (der);* Franz Nikolaus Finck, *Lehrbuch des Dialekts der deutschen Zigeuner* (Marburg, 1903), p. 74. The *jenische Sprache* is the argot of South German thieves and vagabonds in contact with the Gypsies.

[14]Adolf Herbst, ed. *Des Schemtob ben Schaphrut hebraeische Übersetzung des Evangeliums Matthaei nach den Drucken des S. Münster und J. du Tillet-Mercier neu herausgegeben* (Göttingen, 1879), p. 9.

[15]Wilhelm Gesenius, *Hebräisches und chaldäisches Handwörterbuch über das Alte Testament.* Siebente Auflage, bearbeitet von Franz Eduard Christoph Dietrich (Leipzig, 1868), p. 548; William F. Wyatt, Jr., "Sappho and Aphrodite," *Classical Philology,* 69: 213-14 (1974).

[16]Konrad Köhler, "Zu Mt 5, 22", *Zeitschrift für die neutestamentliche Wissenschaft,* 19: 91-95 (1920). See also Éd. Massaux, "Le Texte du Sermon sur la montagne de Matthieu utilisé par saint Justin", *Ephemerides Theologicae Lovanienses,* 28: 439-40 (1952).

[17]John Selden, *De Synedriis & Praefecturis iuridicis veterum Ebraeorum,* Liber Secundus (London, 1653), pp. 105-09, 674-76; Jacob Levy, "Die Präsidentur im Synhedrium," *Monatsschrift für Geschichte und Wissenschaft des Judentums,* 4: 266-74 (1855)

[18]See the historical dictionaries of English and the other modern languages. The responsibility of the Sanhedrin for the death of Jesus is a problem of pietistic Christian scholarship, not of medieval theology.

[19]Yoël Arbeitman, "Look Ma, What's Become of the Sacred Tongues," *Maledicta,* 4: 80 (1980).

[20]Warren Johansson, *"Ex parte* Themis: The Historical Guilt of the Christian Church," in *Homosexuality, Intolerance and Christianity: A Critical Examination of John Boswell's Work,* published by the Scholarship Committee of the New York Chapter of the Gay Academic Union (New York, 1981), pp. 2-5.

[21]Oesterley, p. 17. Some homophile apologists have assumed that simply because homosexuality is not mentioned in the Gospels, Jesus condoned it or would have regarded it with toleration. Certainly his strictures on divorce and adultery do not imply any relaxation of Jewish moral teaching on those subjects; if such analogies apply, and no one can say conclusively that they do not, his attitude toward homosexual acts and feelings could scarcely have been positive or approving.

# THE DEFINITION OF LOVE IN PLATO'S *SYMPOSIUM*

By Donald Levy

For anyone who wants to think philosophically about love, the only way to begin is to reflect on the problems first raised in Plato's *Symposium.* The dialogue is original in at least two ways—in that it exposes the presuppositions of Greek sexual morality to the sort of critical scrutiny practiced by Socrates, there is simply nothing like it by anyone else before. In addition, the new theory of love and the new ideal of it developed in Diotima's speech appear to be Plato's own equally original advance over Socrates' philosophy.

The dialogue records the brilliant conversation at a dinner party at which Socrates is a guest. Those who speak before Socrates mainly share what Jeffrey Henderson refers to as the typical Greek tendency to glorify the instinct of sex rather than its particular objects (*The Maculate Muse,* [New Haven, 1975], 205). For them, love *(eros)* is a god whose beauty and goodness they compete with one another in praising. Even Pausanias, who takes care to distinguish noble from base love, claims that "it is always honorable to comply with a lover to attain excellence" (185b)—even if the lover turns out to be bad, it does the boy credit to have been so deceived! It is this almost universally held belief in the intrinsic value of sexual love against which Socrates sets himself from the start; love, he says, is neither beautiful nor good (though he does not mean it is ugly or bad, either). Love cannot be beautiful because it is the desire to possess what is beautiful, and one cannot desire that which one already possesses, Socrates argues. That love is nothing good in itself, but is merely a means to the attainment of things that are good in themselves is emphasized again at the very end of Socrates' recital of Diotima's speech when he says "human nature can find no better helper than love" (212b). Even Socrates' own love of testing the opinions of others is not exempt from this new test; just as Socrates had surprised Agathon by claiming love is not beautiful, so Diotima bewilders Socrates with the idea that "the object of love is to procreate and give birth in the presence of beauty" (206e). It is not enough, she seems to say, for a philosopher, a lover of wisdom, merely to assist at the birth of ideas in others, playing the midwife, herself barren (to which Socrates often compared himself), examining the new-born ideas for soundness. Such activities have no intrinsic worth; they are of value only if they lead the philosopher to bring forth theories of his own. The genuine lover of wisdom must himself conceive.

The new account of love introduced in the final part of Diotima's speech is one she is not certain Socrates can understand, she says. This appears to be Plato's way of signalling the radical shift in what follows from the comparatively simple attempt to define love by finding the element common to all types of love (typical of Socrates' method) when no distinctions of value among types of love are made (202d-209e), to Plato's new approach. Now the different types of love are to be ordered hierarchically, one being judged superior to another because its object is inherently better. Further, this hierarchy of love-objects involves another non-Socratic idea—that there is one ultimate object of love to which all the others must be tending in order for them to be objects of love at all. For those who seek to understand love, this absolute beauty, existing apart and alone, is the final goal of all their previous efforts. To achieve the vision of absolute beauty one must first progress from love of physical beauty in an individual to love of all physical beauty; then, love of beauty in the soul leads to awareness of the beauty of activities, institutions, and sciences. Upon surveying all these different kinds of beauty, one will be led to a glimpse of the science whose object is absolute beauty.

This theory of love has appeared defective in at least two ways to Gregory Vlastos, whose "The Individual as Object of Love in Plato" (in *Platonic Studies,* [Princeton, 1973]) is the most important recent discussion of Plato's views. According to Vlastos, the defects in Plato's account of love can be seen by comparing it with the definition of love Vlastos accepts, and which he adopts from Aristotle—"Love is wishing good things for someone for that person's sake." Vlastos's first objection is that since Plato has already defined love as the desire for oneself to possess what is beautiful, his idea of love, however spiritualized it may be, remains essentially egocentric (*ibid,* 30). Secondly, Plato does not see that love fundamentally and primarily has persons as its object; for Plato, the love of persons is placed far below the love of an abstract entity, absolute beauty. "What we are to love in persons is the "image" of the Idea in them" (*ibid.,* 31). In a note Vlastos says "This is all love for a person could be, given the status of persons in Plato's ontology."

> We are to love the persons so far, and only insofar, as they are good and beautiful . . . the individual . . . will never be the object of our love in Plato's theory . . . [which] does not provide for love of whole persons, but only for love of that abstract version of persons which consists of the complex of their best qualities. (*Platonic Studies,* 31)

So, for Plato, our affections for concrete human beings are "lesser loves," as Vlastos paraphrases it (*ibid.,* 32), to be used "as steps" (211c) to the attainment of absolute beauty. Vlastos concludes his criticism by noting the emphatic frequency of this idea (*ibid.,* 32).

Without trying to deal with the entire array of evidence Vlastos presents to support these criticisms, it is enough to point out in reply to the first objection that Vlastos's definition of love, compared to which he finds Plato's defective, seems a definition not of what love is, but of what love ought, perhaps, to be. Fairly clear examples of love abound which do not always conform to our moral ideals of love; the love of children and parents for one another—often negligent, selfish, confused, slow to develop—is one. So it is probably wrong, in defining love, to lay down as a necessary condition of one's loving a person at all that one seeks what is good for the other for the other's sake. At least some of the time when we love, we may be seeking what is good for others for our own sake, not theirs, as Aristotle recognizes (*Nicomachean Ethics,* Book VIII, ch. 1); and we must also consider the possibility that we may not even be seeking what is good for the other at all—"smothering" mothers, murderously jealous husbands are clear examples. (This matter is discussed in some detail in Alice Balint's "Love for the Mother and Mother Love" in Michael Balint's *Primary Love and Psycho-analytic Technique,* [New York, 1965]). If these examples are granted, then Vlastos's definition of love does not state a necessary condition of love. Accepting his definition would make it impossible to distinguish between a person's loving well, and that person being a genuine instance of a lover.

Vlastos's definition seems not to state a sufficient condition of love any more than it states a necessary condition, since there are cases of persons who seek what is good for others for the sake of the others (i.e., because the others need or deserve good) when love for the others is not the motive, and may not even be present. Nurses, firemen, teachers take care of, seek to do what is good for others, even if love for the others is wholly absent. It may be, as Diotima argues, that love motivates us whenever we achieve anything good; the nurse, firemen, teacher might love the science, art, skill to which each is devoted. But granting this point does not at all narrow the distance between Plato's theory and the requirement laid down by Vlastos.

I have restricted myself to arguing here that Vlastos's definition of love is defective;[1] but even if it were accepted, his conclusion that Plato's idea of love is an egocentric one does not directly follow. For his argument to work, Vlastos must show that desiring for oneself to possess what is beautiful never consists in wishing good things for someone for the person's sake; Vlastos must show that the first *cannot* consist in the second. But suppose the beautiful thing one desires for oneself to possess is the good (*Symposium*, 204e). Further, suppose that some of the time the good one desires for oneself to possess is virtue. At least some of the time, desiring to possess virtue for oneself *consists* in wishing good things for someone for that person's sake. It would not be correct to say that wishing good things for someone for that person's sake is merely a *means* to acquiring virtue for oneself; the good one seeks to possess for oneself is—to be the cause of what is good for another person for that person's sake.[2]

[1] Whether Vlastos is right to suppose that his definition is the same as Aristotle's is a complex question. Certainly most scholars have agreed with Vlastos's interpretation of the definition of love in the *Nicomachean Ethics.* An excellent opposing interpretation can be found in W. W. Fortenbaugh's "Aristotle's Analysis of Friendship: Function and Analogy, Resemblance, and Focal Meaning," *Phronesis*, XX, #1, 1975, 51-62.

[2] One obstacle to seeing that there is nothing essentially egocentric about Plato's definition of love probably comes from our imagining an incompatibility between it and Paul's "Love seeketh not its own" (I *Corinthians* 13). If Paul is interpreted to mean "Love consists in seeking only what is good for others, never for oneself" perhaps there is something to fear here. But, as modern translations make clear, what Paul meant to say was "Love does not insist on its own way" (*Revised Standard Version*), "Love is . . . never selfish" (*New English Bible*). To be selfish means to ignore or neglect the needs and wishes of others in pursuit of one's own good. Not being selfish then consists in not ignoring or neglecting others; it need not consist in not pursuing any goods

Vlastos's second objection is actually three tied together—(1) Plato ranks love of persons far below love of other things such as absolute beauty. According to Vlastos, Plato does so because (2) Plato takes love of individuals in themselves to be impossible—only their good qualities can be loved; and partly because (3) Plato understands love of persons to consist in nothing more than love of absolute beauty by way of individual persons. The individual person we love is merely of use as an image of beauty, as a means to it.

It should be noted, in reply to (3), that Diotima does in a sense speak of using particular objects of affection, for example, other persons, to gain knowledge of absolute beauty—but the use to which they are to be put is as examples, instances of beauty, as W. Hamilton's interpretive translation (of 210d and 211c) suggests. If we use a person in this way, it does not follow that that person cannot really be loved by us—any more than our using Thomas Jefferson as an example of a great president implies that we do not really admire him. Of course, to use a person in that way implies that we do really admire or love him, or in Plato's case, that we do regard the person as a genuine instance of beauty.

Besides, when Diotima speaks of using examples of beauty, she is speaking of those who seek to be initiated into love's mysteries, who seek to learn what love really is. For that, a person must understand absolute beauty, and to achieve that, one must use the objects of one's love as examples, images of absolute beauty. In saying these things, Diotima seems to be thinking of a quite distinctive imaginative process—one people might engage in without being obliged to treat the objects of their affections merely as examples of something else. Certainly, a person might engage in such an activity without necessarily believing that all anyone is ever really doing in loving is using the objects of love as examples of something else, or that using the objects of love as examples of something else is all that we ought to do with them. Diotima's recommendation of this imaginative process does imply that if (and when) we wish to understand the mysteries of love we must go about it by thinking of the beautiful objects to which we have formed attachments as examples of absolute beauty, leading us onward. But not everyone is always engaged in seeking this, and when not so engaged it would be absurd to treat others merely as instances of something else. It does not appear correct to attribute to Plato the view that we cannot love individual persons, or that we can love them only instrumentally, or that we ought to love them only instrumentally. Diotima does say "This above all others . . . is the region where a man's life should be spent, in the contemplation of absolute beauty" (211b); that region is not the only region in which we can spend our lives—or even the only region in which we ought to spend our lives; of all the regions in which life should be spent, it is the highest, Diotima says—so there are others.

---

of one's own at all. It would be an error to make it a necessary condition of love that the lover not be seeking what is good for himself. If this point seems trivial or obvious, the reader might consult Anders Nygren's *Agape and Eros* to see the crucial role played in the minds of some scholars by the interpretation of Paul's remark which I have criticized.

If Vlastos's objections do not reveal any basic flaws in Plato's theory, as I have argued, this does not mean there are no problems in it. The real trouble may be, not as Vlastos thought, that Plato ranks the love of persons far below other sorts of love, but rather that love itself, regardless of its object, has no intrinsic value for Plato, and therefore ranks below things that do have it. The value of love is entirely dependent upon the worth of its object, Socrates had emphasized at the beginning of his discussion; love is at best a mighty helper to human nature—but nothing more.

The oddness of this cannot be avoided, though the logic of the argument may seem good; knowledge, virtue, beauty seem to be inherently superior things to the love we have for them. Whereas they are inherently good, our love for them seems to be good only insofar as it helps us to acquire them. As plausible and insightful as this may sound, it is nevertheless natural to protest that life devoid of love would be worthless, and that love itself therefore must have some great inherent worth. Perhaps Pausanias was not so wrong after all to judge the deceived lover as he did.

But it would be a mistake to suppose that the only alternative to Plato's treatment of love as merely instrumental in value is the typical Greek view Socrates reacted against. That view saw value in love—but merely because it was pleasurable in itself and productive of excellence. Is there no intrinsic value to love higher than mere pleasure? One solution to this problem would be to argue that the intrinsic value of love is to be found in its being constitutive of the soul; that is, to claim that love is the fundamental activity (or one of them) all souls are necessarily always engaged in, whatever else they may be doing. Then, the worth of love is established, if the worth of the soul is. Such a claim is clearly not part of Pausanias's commendation of love, nor is it part of any of the praises of love pronounced by the speakers in the *Symposium* before Socrates. Such a view of love as constitutive of soul might seem to be the one Diotima expresses (205a; 205c) when she says

> Now do you suppose that this desire [for what is good] and this love are characteristics common to all men, and that all perpetually desire to be in possession of the good, or what? (205a)

But Socrates' response leaves it unclear whether he accepts the whole of this view: "That is exactly what I mean; they are common to all men." Diotima made two distinct claims, and Socrates assented only to the weaker of the two, it seems, that is, to the claim that all men love, at some time or other, we might add. This view is associated with the idea that every man has a master passion—love of money, or of physical prowess, or of wisdom—which are all expressions of the desire for good and for happiness, according to Diotima (205d). This view requires that (a) all men love at some time or other, and (b) each man loves some one thing more than any other thing. It is consistent with these conditions that much of what men do is not done out of love at all. We must keep separate the stronger thesis that all human activity is motivated by love, as well as the thesis that love is the essential activity of the soul. These three views are not equivalent, and Plato does not accept the last one. This we know from the *Phaedrus*, where the essential activity of soul is said to be eternal motion, self-motion

(245e), of which love is perhaps a resemblance. To be sure, love is "the greatest benefit that heaven can confer on us" (245b)—but it is not constitutive of soul.[3] Indeed, that love is said to be a type of madness conferred on us at all implies that we are able to exist without it.[4]

A complete resolution of Plato's doubts about the role of love in the soul would have to take up and reply to his view of the emotions (and therefore of love as well) as alien to intellect, "the best part of the soul" (*Phaedrus*, 248b). Part of the answer might also draw upon features of his theory of knowledge as essentially recollection. That is, if there were something which, to be known at all, must be loved, it would be difficult to deny that loving it was intrinsically good if knowing it was held to be good in that way. Even if it were granted that knowing it was intrinsically better than loving it, the intrinsic value of loving it would not be undermined. Whether there are any such objects of love and knowledge is a question lying outside the scope of this paper, though it is at least plausible to say that God is such a being, since it is hard to make sense of the claim that someone knows God but does not love God.

Perhaps a different type of case of the following sort illustrates the same point; suppose the only way, the only conceivable way, to gain self-knowledge (or any other kind of knowledge) is through loving others.

[3] Does the claim that love is the greatest benefit that heaven can bestow upon us imply that love must be greater than knowledge or justice, which are inherently good? The implication would succeed only if it were possible for knowledge or justice to be conferred. However, if we take seriously Plato's doctrine that knowledge is recollection, then even heaven cannot confer knowledge upon us—it must be recollected. That justice cannot be conferred either follows from another of Plato's views—that virtue (and hence justice) is a kind of knowledge.

[4] J. M. E. Moravcsik considers, but dismisses, the idea that when the soul reaches the higher stages of the ascent in the *Symposium* "it no longer has passions or aspirations." ("Reason and Eros in the Ascent Passage of the *Symposium*," in Anton, J. P., and Kustas, G. L., eds., *Essays in Ancient Greek Philosophy*, /Albany, 1971/, 285-302 at 294) He is forced to consider this possibility because there is an evident absence of emotion-steps in the higher stages of the ascent, in contrast to the lower ones. He concludes that though "eros is still at work in the soul in the later stages, it no longer functions as a guide, thus not appearing in the sequence of steps described. No change in over-all aspiration is needed in order to lead the soul from the contemplation of the sciences to the comprehension of the Forms. Like Virgil in the "Divine Comedy" eros helps as a guide only until we reach the final stages; there contemplation becomes self-sufficient" (*ibid.*, 294). But it is unclear how eros can still be at work in the soul when contemplation becomes self-sufficient, since Moravcsik noted earlier

> "in general one can say about the causal influence of eros on the mind that eros is what pushes the mind to new investigations" (*ibid.*, 292).

Presumably, when contemplation becomes self-sufficient, eros ceases to be that which "pushes the mind to new investigations." Incidentally, the Virgil analogy seems unsuited to Moravcsik's point, since Virgil vanishes when he ceases to serve as a guide (*Purgatorio*, Canto XXX); he does not continue to accompany Dante in some non-guidance role.

Further, suppose that loving others well is sufficient for self-knowledge. It would then be hard to deny that love was intrinsically valuable, if the knowledge depending on it was assumed to be intrinsically good. These cases suggest that Plato's worry about love's inherent worth rests upon a presupposition hard to justify, namely, that any knowledge or other good reached as a result of love necessarily can be obtained or possessed without love. This presupposition must be false if, as I suggest, love is at least sometimes a necessary condition of recollection.

The subsequent history of philosophizing about love reflects some of these concerns; it is not until Plotinus, I believe, that love is conceived to be constitutive of the soul.[5] (The idea seems wholly absent in Aristotle's psychology; love is purely an ethical problem for him.) Augustine's famous remark, "My love is my weight. To whatever place I go, I am drawn to it by love" (*Confessions,* Book XIII, chapter nine) implies both that love is constitutive of soul (as he takes weight to be constitutive of body), as well as that whatever good, e.g., knowledge, he achieves, it is the result of that love; this essential connection between love and knowledge receives extended examination in *On the Trinity.* Both of these thinkers can be seen as struggling with the same problem inherited from Plato—that of understanding love in such a way that its intrinsic as well as its instrumental value is made clear.

Brooklyn College of CUNY.

[5] "This being, Love, has from everlasting come into existence from the soul's aspiration toward the higher and the good, and he was there always, as long as Soul, too existed." (*Ennead* III. 5.9, translated by A. H. Armstrong, Loeb Classical Library, [Cambridge, Mass., 1967], *Plotinus,* volume III, at 203).

# THE *ENTIMOS PAIS* OF MATTHEW 8:5-13 AND LUKE 7:1-10

Donald Mader

That the gospels are silent about homosexuality has almost become a truism. At least one writer on homosexuality and scripture has even sought to construct arguments for tolerance upon this supposed silence.[1] Certainly there are no direct references to the practices we today term homosexuality anywhere in the teachings of Jesus, as there are in the Pauline letters.[2]

It has been suggested that there may be an indirect reference to homosexuality in Matthew 19:10-12, one of the "hard sayings" of Jesus, regarding eunuchs, on the ground of the popular belief that classed eunuchs with those who practised sodomy.[3] The argument runs that, because of this popular identification, for Jesus to speak highly of eunuchs would at least imply toleration for homosexuals. Two problems severely limit this possibility. The first arises when we note that it was on the ground of physical imperfection that eunuchs were excluded from the covenant community, not their actions; whatever the popular mind may have thought, we are dealing with two different categories, and to reason from the one to the other is not sound. Second, the meaning of Matthew 19:10-12 is sufficiently obscure on its face that it seems unwise to build much upon it. It is probably best taken merely as an admonition to chastity.[4]

Beyond Jesus' silence on the subject, it is also widely accepted that the very subject of homosexuality is unmentioned in the gospels. Since at least the time of Christopher Marlowe, one of whose "damnable opinions" held that Jesus and John were bedfellows, there have been more or less poetical flights based upon the "beloved disciple", and even the young man who "ran away naked", but these cannot withstand serious exegetical examination.[5] However, while none of the standard gospel commentaries which I have been able to examine nor any of the major texts on homosexuality in the Bible have noted the possibility (aside from a brief mention in Horner's *Jonathan Loved David*), the suggestion has been made in foreign sources and in non-exegetical literature in English that the account of the healing of the centurion's servant, in Matthew 8:5-13 and Luke 7:1-10 (with a parallel in John 4:46-53), may contain a reference to homosexuality in its classical form of paederasty.[6] It is the intent of this paper to examine whether or not this suggestion can be exegeticly supported. The issue will center primarily around the understanding of several words, *pais* (boy/servant) and *entimos* (dear, precious, valued), as found in these passages, against the background of other Biblical and secular usage, and the question of whether a person could reasonably be involved in a paederastic relationship and yet have been a "God-fearer" as the centurion is portrayed by Luke.

### The Passages

In both Matthew and Luke the account of Jesus' healing of the centurion's servant at Capernaum is part of a collection of healing stories which directly follow a major section of Jesus' teaching—the Sermon on the Mount in the case of Matthew; the Sermon on the Plain in the case of Luke. Matthew sets it as the second of three healings, Luke as the first of two. Luke has previously used, in his fifth chapter, the healing of the leper with which Matthew preceeds the Capernaum story, and in his fourth chapter the healing of Peter's mother-in-law, with which Matthew follows it; in their place, Luke follows the centurion's story with an account of a resurrection which is peculiar to his gospel.[7]

The setting of the account of the healing of the centurion's boy makes it clear that the gospel writers intended it to be a miracle story, which is to say that they intended its primary focus to be a revelation of the nature and power of Jesus. This equally means that, just as the parable of Lazarus and the rich man is not to be looked to for authoritative teaching about the afterlife, as its primary purpose lies elsewhere, we must here recognize that, even if it is established that it contains a reference to paederasty, we cannot look to this healing story for authoritative moral teaching on homosexuality, carrying the same force as, for instance, Jesus' teachings on marriage in Matthew 5:31-2. At the same time, just as other healing stories, although they are not intended to be authoritative teaching about disease, give us information about Jesus' attitudes toward disease and its causation (or at least the attitudes imputed to Jesus by the early Christian community which framed the stories—an issue which we will examine later), so too, if paederasty is present, this account will necessarily reveal attitudes about it.

Because of the prominence in its structure of the saying of Jesus regarding faith (Matthew 8:10; Luke 7:9), the account certainly does have a secondary focus in teaching about the nature and importance of faith. Indeed, it is a common observation among commentators that structurally the real point of the story comes in these words and not the miracle of healing itself, which comes almost as an afterthought. Perhaps the strong demonstration of faith and trust on the part of the centurion played a role in the placement of the account directly following sections of teaching dealing with faith and life (Matthew 7:24-27 and Luke 6:46-49), to serve, in effect, as a "bridge" between sections.

It is in relation to the strength of the saying of Jesus in the structure of the story that we may briefly examine the source from which this account enters the gospels. The story is almost universally agreed to have been an element in "Q", the hypothetical source of materials used in common by Matthew and Luke but not found in Mark.[8] As such, it would be the only (or perhaps, if Matthew 9:32-3 is admitted to be from "Q", the only major) miracle story to have stood in that source.[9] As "Q" is commonly regarded to have been a collection of the sayings and discourses of Jesus, and not of stories about him, the fact that this account should have been included supports the supposition that Jesus' words to the centurion regarding faith are an important—and were perhaps originally its primary—focus.

Having briefly surveyed the context and source, let us look at the texts themselves, in the Revised Standard translation:

Matthew 8:5-13:
5As he entered Capernaum,
a centurion came forward to
him, beseeching him 6and
saying, "Lord, my servant is
lying paralyzed at home, in
terrible distress." 7And he
said to him, "I will come
and heal him." 8But the centurion answered him,
"Lord, I am not worthy to
have you come under my
roof; but only say the word,
and my servant will be
healed. 9For I am a man
under authority, with soldiers under me, and I say to
one, 'Go', and he goes, and
to another, 'Come', and he
comes, and to my slave, 'Do
this', and he does it." 10-
When Jesus heard him, he
marveled, and said to those
who followed him, "Truly I
say to you, not even in Israel
have I found such faith. 11I
tell you, many will come
from east and west and sit at
table with Abraham, Isaac
and Jacob in the kingdom of
heaven, 12while the sons of
the kingdom will be thrown
into outer darkness; there
men will weep and gnash
their teeth." 13And to the
centurion Jesus said, "Go;
be it done for you as you
have believed." And the
servant was healed at that
very moment.

Luke 7:1-10:
1After he had ended all his
sayings in the hearing of the
people he entered Caper-
naum. 2Now a centurion had
a slave who was dear to him,
who was sick and at the
point of death. 3When he
heard of Jesus, he sent to him
elders of the Jews, asking
him to come and heal his
slave. 4And when they came
to Jesus they besought him
earnestly, saying, "He is
worthy to have you do this
for him, 5for he loves our
nation, and he built us our
synagogue." 6And Jesus
went with them. When he
was not far from the house,
the centurion sent friends to
him, saying to him, "Lord,
do not trouble yourself, for I
am not worthy to have you
come under my roof; 7there-
fore I did not presume to
come to you. But say the
word and my servant will be
healed. 8For I am a man set
under authority, with soldiers under me; and I say to
one, 'Go', and he goes; and
to another, 'Come', and he
comes, and to my slave, 'Do
this', and he does it." 9When
Jesus heard this, he mar-
veled at him, and turned and
said to the multitude that
followed him, "I tell you,
not even in Israel have I
found such faith." 10And
when those who had been
sent returned to the house,
they found the slave well.

A comparison of the two versions shows key points in common as well as key differences. Matthew and Luke agree in placing the incident at Capernaum, in Galilee, a large and prosperous commercial and fishing center with a Roman military presence. While Capernum, unlike Galilee in general, was primarily Jewish, the city was strongly influenced by the Hellenism of the surrounding Gentile majority. It is famed in Biblical archaeology for its well preserved third-century synagogue, noted for the figural decorations not in accord with Jewish law regarding images—perhaps a replacement to the one claimed by Luke to be the centurion's gift. While it would be dangerous to reason from a third century building to first century social conditions, this is at least suggestive of a certain heterodoxy that might have prevailed there.[10] The two versions are also in agreement about the wording of the centurion's message (Matthew 8:8-9 and Luke 7:6b-8) and Jesus' response (Matthew 8:10, Luke 7:9).

On the other hand there are significant differences. The most obvious is the structure of the story, for while both versions agree that the healing took place at a distance because the centurion felt unworthy to have Jesus under his roof, Matthew has the centurion himself approach Jesus, while Luke has a complicated account of two embassies sent by the centurion, the first of Jewish elders and the second of friends. Contained within this is the further identification of the centurion as a "God-fearer", who had donated a synagogue for the local congregation. Matthew includes an Old Testament quotation from Psalm 107:3 in verse 11 as part of a section which Luke reworks as an independent teaching (Luke 13:28-30).

The other significant difference is somewhat muted by the translation, though still traceable in the Revised Standard Version's use of "servant" and "slave". In identifying the relation of the sick individual to the centurion, Matthew (in verses 6, 8 and 13) consistently uses the Greek term *pais*, a word of multiple meanings which include "son", "boy", "child" (of either sex), and "servant" (either an adult or minor), and here rendered by the RSV as "servant". In verses 2, 3 and 10, parallel to Matthew's verses 6 and 13, Luke instead uses the Greek *doulos*, "born slave", rendered by the RSV as "slave". Significantly, each writer uses the opposite term once in his account: Matthew uses *doulos* in verse 9b, seemingly to emphasize the distinction between the *pais* on whose behalf the centurion makes his request and the hypothetical, less important slave being ordered about; Luke, while consistant with verse 9 of Matthew by using *doulos* in the centurion's speech (vs. 8), also breaks his pattern of using *doulos* and agrees with verse 8 of Matthew by using *pais* in verse 7b, perhaps to stress the more personal relationship this servant enjoyed. On his part, in identifying the relationship between the centurion and the sick individual, Luke does introduce the Greek adjective *entimos*, meaning "honored" or "valued" in verse 2 to describe the slave. It is a word which appears in the Gospels only in the writings of Luke.

With these differences between the passages firmly in mind, we may move to the question of precedence. The question is not which of these passages is primary in the sense of one being a reworking of the other, for it is accepted that Matthew and Luke had no contact with one another's work. Rather the question is which of the passages is probably closer to the hypothetical original source, the "Q" document, from which both authors drew. Obviously, no final answer can be given, without an original with which to make comparisons. However, the preponderance of scholarly opinion favors Matthew as better representing the hypothetical source. Most of the arguments involve the structure of the story, noting the artificiality of Luke's narrative, with its complications of having the centurion invite Jesus by the first embassy, then withdraw the invitation by the second. The unsuitability of the first-person message delivered by Luke's second embassy, which fits perfectly in the mouth of the centurion himself in Matthew's version, is also noted. This unsuitability seems to suggest that the message has been preserved by Luke from another source but used in an incongruous setting. Other scholars, however, also extend their claims for precedence to the text of Matthew's version with particular comment on Matthew's use of *pais*.

Among those who have argued, on one ground or another, for Matthew being closer to a hypothetical original are Loisy, Klostermann, Wendland, Dibelius and Bultmann.[11] Plummer clearly states his opinion that in the use of *pais* Matthew preserved the text of his source while Luke has substituted *doulos*.[12] John Chapman refers to Luke as a "borrower", and also suggests Luke changed *pais* to *doulos*; at the same time he judges Luke "longer and more complete" and more "beautiful" for the addition of the intervention of friends.[13] Vincent Taylor plainly states his opinion that "in its Lucan form the story has received later additions", and appears to consider the first embassy one of them.[14] A. R. C. Leaney says that it is "likely that Luke himself invented the detail of the sending of the elders".[15] In the Anchor Bible Jos. Fitzmyer opts for Matthew being truer to the source in both structure and text, except for the addition of the free-standing saying of Jesus now in verse 11. He states that any argument for Matthean "omission is more difficult to explain than Lucan additions", and offers his opinion that Luke has shifted from *pais* in the original source to *doulos*, though he says it is "not clear why".[16] Among current commentators only those of evangelical slant seem to disagree. Geldenhuis, after citing authorities in favor of Matthean primacy, baldly asks "Why?" and actually suggests that both Matthew and Luke are correct and must be combined to make a full story with two embassies *and* a personal visit![17] I. H. Marshall, after making such comments as "Luke's version is more complicated, if not actually improbable" still finds, in the balance, that Luke better represents the source, though "the possibility of Lucan expansion cannot be excluded."[18] But perhaps the strongest statement of all—in favor of Matthew—comes from Montefiore, who declares "Luke makes diverse changes in the story of the centurion", that Luke's version is "weaker and less natural than in Matthew" and that it is "clearly secondary as compared with Matthew".[19]

Before leaving our examination of the texts themselves, we should also take notice of the parallel to these two passages in John 4:46-54. It is one of the few incidents recorded in the synoptic gospels which appears recognizably in John, where it stands as the second of the "signs" performed by the Christ. While it is recognizable, it is by no means identical: the points of similarity include the location, Capernaum; the personal request by the man for the healing of a child (parallel at least to Matthew), answered by a healing at a distance effected by Jesus' word alone; and the faith of the petitioner as a key element of the account. The differences, however, are also considerable: the man is not a centurion, but rather is identified as *basilikos*, or "king's official", though it is the considered opinion of W. F. Howard that this title would suit the position of a Roman centurion in the service of Herod the tetrarch.[20] It is not clear in John whether the man is Jew or Gentile, though the assumption would seem to be that he is Jewish, where it is implicit in Matthew and explicit in Luke that he is non-Jewish; and the relationship of the man and the sick individual is specifically that of father and son, as John uses *huios*, or "son" in verses 46, 47, 50 and 53. However, curiously, in verse 51, John does use *pais* (here obviously by the context, in the sense of "son"), the only appearence of that word in the Johannine writings.[21]

Given these similarities and differences, the relationship of John's version to that of the synoptics has been hotly debated. Among the Fathers, Irenaeus, in his *Against Heresies*, ii 22:3, treats all three accounts as variants of one incident. Though again evangelical commentators argue otherwise, and Plummer denies any parallel, remarking that in view of the differences, to suggest such a relationship would imply a "startling carelessness" with his sources on the part of John, the majority of modern voices can be represented by Howard, Bernard, and Marsh who remarks that "the present story is unmistakably like that of the synoptics" and that the "assumption seems justified" that this is a parallel account.[22] Streeter more cautiously suggests that this is an account of the same incident, though taken from a source that had early diverged from that used by the synoptic writers.[23] R. E. Brown, in the Anchor Bible series, affirms that all three accounts are versions of the same incident, but then stands alone in proposing that it is John who best represents the original source, which he believes used *huios*, which Matthew for some reason altered to *pais*, and which Luke further changed to *doulos*.[24] If, on the other hand, we accept the opinion of the majority of commentators that *pais* stood in the source used by Matthew and Luke, the unusual appearence of *pais* in John would seem to suggest a fairly direct connection.[25]

### The Meaning of *pais*

If it is accepted that *pais* stood in the original source from which Matthew, who retained the word, and Luke, who substituted another, both drew—and it does appear that this is a justified assumption—we may now move to inquire how the word would have been understood by contemporaries first encountering the narrative. As we have already noted, the word has multiple meanings, which often must be understood from the context: it can mean "boy", "child" (of either sex), "son", or "servant" (of any age). The word occurs 23 times in the New Testament, and is used with almost all of these senses. Five additional occurrences are in Matthew: 2:16, of the "male children" of Bethlehem; 12:18, in a quote from the LXX, "servant"; 14:2, of the "servants" of Herod; 17:18, of the "boy" cured of epilepsy; 21:15, of the "children" on Palm Sunday. Seven additional occurrences are in Luke: 1:54 and 1:69, in the Magnificat and Benedictus, respectively, of Israel and David as "servant"; 2:43, of the "boy" Jesus at the Temple; 8:51 and 8:54, of Jarius' daughter, a female "child"; 9:42, of the "boy" cured of epilepsy; 15:26, of a "servant" in the parable of the prodigal son. Five more uses occur in Luke's second volume, Acts: 3:13 and 26, in Peter's sermon, of Jesus, as God's "servant" or "son"; 4:24, of David as God's "servant"; 4:27 and 30, of Jesus as God's "servant" or "son"; and 20:12, of Eutychus, the "boy" who fell from the window. The final one is of course in John. Secular usage reflects the same spread of meanings. The lexicographer Hesychius, writing in late antiquity, defines *pais* as a descendant, particularly a son (*huios*), more mature than a *neos*, and in contrast to a daughter (*parthenos*), and notes it can also be applied to a slave (*doulos*).[26] Liddell and Scott provide instances of use as "son" or "daughter", "boy" or "girl", and "servant" or "slave" of any age or sex.[27]

There is, however, an additional specific usage which one might not necessarily expect to find in the New Testament, but which should have fallen within Liddell and Scott's field of view. Before launching into this discussion, it will be necessary to make a brief digression.

Perhaps the most difficult mental adjustment to make for anyone from a twentieth century western society who seeks an understanding of classical times involves the recognition of the pervasiveness of paederasty within ancient society. (A recognition of the total acceptance of slavery is perhaps a close second.) Intergenerational sexual relationships between males are today regarded by our society as so perverse and uncommon that we are totally unable to comprehend the centrality, and the widespread practise and acceptance, that paederasty enjoyed in the ancient world. Because this condemnation often arises from religious strictures, we are even less willing to consider the possibility that there might be nonjudgemental references to such practises in scripture.

The ubiquity of paederasty, and its centrality to facets of ancient culture and society ranging from literature and the arts through philosophy, education and even into military training, was first treated in such pioneering works as J. A. Symonds' *Problem in Greek Ethics* (the "problem" being precisely the importance of a practise so reviled as paederasty in a culture so revered as that of ancient Greece) and George Ives' *Graeco-Roman View of Youth*.[28] Within the last decade the centrality and pervasiveness of paederasty has been formidably documented for Greek culture and society by K. J. Dover, and for Rome by John Boswell and Royston Lambert.[29] Lambert conveniently sums up the issue:

> Pederasty was not a mere fashion or aberration in ancient Greece. Wherever and for whatever reasons it originated, by classical times it had clearly come to serve certain profound needs existing in society, at least of the leisured or citizen classes. It had matured into an esteemed social institution, fulfilling precise and vital functions, regulated by law and tradition, elaborated into a culture and

> dignified with a philosophy. So important was its function that it flourished, weakened and adulterated perhaps, all over the Hellenic world under Roman rule... tenaciously surviving even the ineffective edicts of the Christian Emperors of the fourth century A.D., which had to be renewed by Justinian two hundred years later.[30]

A further concise summary of the role of paederasty in ancient society, from the perspective of Biblical scholarship, will be found in Robin Scroggs' work on New Testament texts and homosexuality.[31] While we may question his contention that it was paederasty, and not homosexuality as we know it today with more or less equal relationships between similarly aged persons, that is opposed in New Testament texts that explicitly condemn homosexuality, his review of the background material is most valuable, and his conclusions worth noting:

> The practices of pederasty emerged out of the dominant social matrix of the day. In some quarters pederastic relations were extolled, in almost all quarters condoned... it is important to keep in mind that Greco-Roman pederasty was practised by a large number of people in part because it was socially acceptable, while by many other people actually idealized as a normal course in the process of maturation.[32]

Any reader desiring further documentation regarding the importance and pervasiveness of paederasty in classical times may consult these sources in their entirety.

Bearing these facts in mind, we should now note that within the institution of paederasty, *pais* had a rather specific reference to the younger, passive partner in a paederastic relationship, or the desired object of paederastic affections, whether freeborn or slave. In the general overview at the beginning of his study, Dover observes. "In many contexts, and almost invariably in poetry, the passive partner is called *pais*", and Bernard Sergent, in a discussion of terminology in his study of paederastric myths in Greek religion, comments on Strabo's use of the word *pais* in a description of Cretan paederastic customs, "the term was commonly used to refer to an adolescent, the eromenos, and that is the case here."[33] The usage remains remarkably consistent for close to a thousand years from the poems of Theogenis, through the epigrams collected in Book XII of the Greek Anthology, on through work dating to well after the time of the gospels' composition. The epigrams of Strato of Sardis (fl. 30 A.D.) and Meleager of Gadara (fl. 90 B.C.) are of particular interest, as the former was an almost exact contemporary of the date of the gospel events, and the latter, though slightly earlier than the date of the gospels, was a native of Gadara, about twenty miles from Capernaum across the sea of Galilee in the Decapolis, and site of the healing of a demoniac (Matthew 8:28), and thus they provide evidence on usage at the time and place of the gospels. Strabo of Amaseia, the Geographer, the subject of Sergent's comment, whose dates are roughly 63 B.C. to 24 A.D., provides from prose still another example of this contemporary, paederastic understanding of the word.

This is not to suggest that the word *pais* necessarily carried paederastic implications. In most common usage, it carried only the usual meanings. There were words, such as *eromenos*, or *paidika* when used as a masculine singular noun, which did carry such specific implications, and would have left the nature of any relationship for which they were used entirely beyond doubt.[34] It can, however, be said that *pais* is a word that contemporaries could well have expected in descriptions of paederastic relationships, and, morevoer, a word which appearing in the proper context would have clearly conveyed that meaning.

The difficulty in determining the precise meaning of *pais* in any particular situation is clearly seen in the gospel passages here being examined. If we had only Matthew's version, it would be impossible to say whether the *pais* was the centurion's son or servant. If we had Luke alone, we would clearly understand from his use of *doulos* that the *pais* was a servant. Indeed, it is the strength of Luke's use of *doulos* that makes us also read Matthew as a reference to a servant. Yet if we had Matthew's and John's accounts only, and Luke's version did not exist, we surely would read Matthew, with the indefinite *pais*, in light of John's more specific *huios*, and refer to Matthew's account of the healing of the centurion's son! But in the light of what has been said about the paederastic usage of *pais*, another uncertainty must be introduced: if we were to read through first century eyes, accustomed to the institution of paederasty, and knowing its vocabulary, encountering a story like Matthew's, might we not also read it in terms of a man's concern for his younger lover?

**Luke's *entimos doulos***

Before answering that question, we should briefly examine Luke's use of *entimos*. The word occurs five times in the New Testament altogether, two of those appearances being in Luke, who is the only Gospel writer to use the term. It also is used once by Paul, in Philippians 2:29, and twice in I Peter 2:4 and 6. When applied to things, as in the two references in I Peter, the word means "valuable" or "precious"; when to persons, the sense is generally "honorable", as in Paul's injunction to the Philippian church to count Epaphroditus "honorable", and Luke's other use of the word, 14:8, where Jesus instructs his followers not to take seats of importance at a feast lest they have to make way for someone more "honorable" than they. For secular usage, Liddell and Scott confirm these meanings; T. W. Manson notes also that the word was used as an honorific for soldiers with long or distinguished service.[35] Luke's use of the term in 7:2 then must be seen either as somewhat cold-blooded—a "valuable slave"—or as somewhat anomalous—though as a slave not "honorable" in the sense of reputation, at least valued for personal reasons. As the centurion's motives are portrayed as much warmer than merely protecting a valuable piece of property, the latter is undoubtedly the sense in which the word should be understood.[36] Thus, while the term does not usually imply an emotional attachment, at the least we can say that Luke, in introducing it, was recognizing that the centurion's actions displayed a depth of feeling which was over and above that of an ordinary master-slave relationship.[37]

We can now summarize our findings and offer an answer to the question of how a first century reader would have viewed this account. We have seen that the majority of commentators believe that Matthew's version of the story is closer to the hypothetical source from which both Matthew and Luke drew, and that many extend this to the assumption that *pais* stood in that source. We have also seen that *pais*—though it assuredly had other, and more primary, meanings—was a word that first century readers would have expected in references to paederastic relationships and one which, given the context of such a close, though non-parental, relationship between an adult male and a boy such as this account presents, might have implied a paederastic relationship. Though there is nothing which requires such a reading, given the nature of the story, with the concern shown for the boy, and the ubiquity of paederasty in the experience of first-century readers, I believe that we must answer that this account, as reflected in Matthew's version, certainly could have conveyed to its original audience the suggestion of paederasty. But did it?

I would propose not only that it could, but that it did suggest paederasty to an important early reader—Luke. If we need an answer to the question of why Luke changed terms from *pais* to *doulos*, this would appear to be the obvious reason. The author of Matthew, out of respect for his source, or from having a lesser experience with the Gentile world and its institutions, or for theological reasons, let the account stand, while the author of Luke, with a greater experience of the Gentile world and its institutions, and thus a greater sensitivity to the implications of the story, sought to mute them.[38] That Luke understood the relationship to be non-parental is indicated by his choice of another word expressing servitude, but while a *doulos* also could have been used for sexual purposes (and a reading of ancient literature indicates that many were), the term would not have been as provocative as *pais*.[39] Having made the change, Luke felt the need to acknowledge, by the use of *entimos*, that the centurion's actions on behalf of his servant indicated a remarkable emotional connection, the depth of which was comparable to (and for John, explicable in terms of) what a father would do for his child.

**Paederasty and God-fearers**

We are affirming, then, that the account of the healing of the centurion's boy not only might be read as a reference to paederasty, but that it was read that way by Luke, and further, that the changes made to the story by Luke support this interpretation not only in muting what Luke found in the original, but also by still affirming, in a less provocative way, that the relationship was unusual. At this point a new question arises: could a "God-fearer", as Luke portrays his centurion to be, also have engaged in paederasty?

It would be easy to dismiss this issue by arguing that the identification of the centurion as a "God-fearer" is a Lukan creation. Whatever the answer to the question of whether a "God-fearer" could practise paederasty, the primary argument that in the original and Matthean versions this account would be seen to have reference to a pederastic relationship will not be affected, and there is certainly evidence that could be adduced that this detail did originate with Luke. That the detail occurs in the course of the rather artificial structure of the embassy of elders, with all the evidence we have cited that this is secondary, and the fact that the 'pious centurion' is almost a 'type' in Luke-Acts—Cornelius (Acts 10) being another example, and perhaps the source upon which Luke drew to fill out his portrait of this anonymous centurion—all suggest this is from Luke's hand. However, if we wish to argue that Luke's account, though muted in comparison to Matthew's, still allows a paederastic reading, we must deal with the issue. Nor can we ignore the question of whether the centurion of the original story, by his openness to approach Jesus and his concern—perhaps more than just a sensitivity to Jewish culture—about having a rabbi enter his home, might not have shown himself a God-fearer, though the fact was not stated.

The term "God-fearer" (*phoboumenoi ton Theon*) was applied to a large group of Gentiles who responded positively to the theological and ethical teachings of Judaism, but who stopped short of full conversion. They are encountered fairly frequently in Acts; among the more notable are the Ethiopian eunuch, Cornelius, and Titus Justus (Acts 8, 10 and 18, respectively), and many of those that Paul and other apostles found receptive in the course of their preaching journeys probably fell into the group as well. It is obviously hard to categorize so broad a group, which ranged from individuals philosophically inclined toward monotheism through those who embraced some, but not all, Jewish ethical and cultic practices, through those who would strictly follow all these matters but held back from the rite of circumcision.[40].

Quite apart from debates about the original meaning of Old Testament references to homosexuality, it is clear that first century Judaism found homosexuality, and its expression as paederasty, abhorrent. The wealth of rabbinic literature examined by Scroggs documents this for Palestinian Judaism; for Hellenistic Judaism our source material is narrower, as we see it almost entirely through the eyes of Philo Judeus, but his condemnation is no less thoroughgoing.[41] While reliance on a unique source is always risky, and it is by no means clear how well Philo represents the thinking of other Hellenized Jews,[42] we must assume that paederasty would not be an approved practise for a God-fearer. We must also assume that any God-fearer who was so close to the Jewish community as to endow a synagogue would be among those more observant of Jewish customs. Together, these assumptions would argue against the possibility of the centurion, as portrayed by Luke, being involved in paederasty. However, the case cannot be closed entirely. It is also possible that Hellenistic Jewish communities in general, or the one at Capernaum in particular (which, as we noted above, was later rather heterodox in its attitude toward graven images), may have been more accepting of Hellenistic moral practises than was Philo, and that paederasty, particularly if it conformed to the higher Hellenistic ideals for the practise, as the caring evidenced by the centurion's request suggests this did, might have been tolerated in a God-fearer for whom this remained one area of non-conformity.

**Summary and Conclusions**

In summary, the points of the argument are:

1. Respecting the concensus of critical opinion, it is probable that Matthew 8:5-13 and Luke 7:1-10 are both drawn from the same original account; that Matthew's version better represents that original; and that the word *pais* was used in that account, with Matthew preserving the word while Luke substituted *doulos*.
2. The word *pais*, when used in the context of a close non-parental relationship such as that portrayed here—a relationship that John, when using the account, found fitting and explicable as a parent-child relationship—could have conveyed to a first-century audience the implication of paederasty.
3. Not only could this account have been read as referring to a paederastic relationship, but the author of Luke, by substituting *doulos* for *pais* (thus affirming his understanding that the relationship was non-parental while using a less provocative word), and by adding the qualification that the boy was *entimos*, indicates that he understood it that way.
4. While it is presumed be that a deeply observant God-fearer would not practise paederasty, the possibility that this account does refer to paederasty cannot be eliminated for that reason. There were many levels of observance among God-fearers, and the details that imply that the centurion was an observant God-fearer are probably Luke's composition.

I would therefore conclude that we must seriously consider the possibility that this passage in the New Testament does refer to homosexuality, in its classical form of paederasty, though there is no one fact that requires that it be seen in that way.

What are the implications of this? To begin, this passage will not allow us to reach any sweeping conclusions about Jesus' attitudes toward paederasty or homosexuality. As we noted early in this paper, the story does not contain any authoritative moral teaching on the subject. This is merely a detail in a story which had, for its authors, quite a different purpose than the presentation of ethical teaching. For that matter, it is widely recognized today that the Gospels are neither biographical in their intent nor do they portray for us an "historical Jesus"; while they contain historical materials, they are rather the record of what the Church, at the time of their composition, believed about Jesus. Therefore, the most that can be claimed is that a segment of the early church out of which the "Q" document and Matthew arose, was not concerned, and believed that Jesus was not concerned, when confronted by a responsible, loving paederastic relationship, but rather held it subordinate to questions of faith. This is entirely consistent with the rest of the image created by the Gospels. From accounts such as those of Jesus and the woman taken in adultery (John 8:1-11, where the hostile and self-righteous attitudes of the accusers are shown as more troubling to Jesus than the woman's sin) or, from the same chapter in Luke which holds our centurion's story, that of Jesus at the house of Simon the Pharisee (7:36-50, where it is the woman's act of faith that Jesus notes rather than her violation of moral laws), as well as the repeated statements that Jesus extended table-fellowship to sinners (Mark 2:13-17 and its parallels Matthew 9:9-13 and Luke 5:27-32, Luke 15:1-2) and his own observation that he expected prostitutes to enter the kingdom before the conventionally righteous (Matthew 21:31-2), Jesus is shown as more concerned with the state of a person's faith than with their observation of conventional, and particularly sexual, morality. There is nothing unusual, then, in the response Jesus is shown to have toward the centurion, whose request is evidently based on his real love for the boy as well as his strong trust in the saving power of Jesus. Indeed, Jesus is depicted as affirming the relationship here, and fulfilling the centurion's faith, by restoring his boy to him.

The passage has bearing, nonetheless, on the debate in the church over homosexuality. On the one hand, it surely strengthens the general thesis proposed by Boswell that the early church possessed a greater tolerance for homosexuality than was previously suspected—and than it seems to possess today. On the other hand, there has been a tendency, particularly notable in Boswell and Scroggs, to argue that while the early church was tolerant of adult male homosexuality, condemnation was directed to the vicious and unsavoury side of paederasty. Evidently there was little other side. Boswell relates deteriorating attitudes toward homosexuality in the early church to revulsion against the sale and prostitution of unwanted children, incest and child slavery as associated with paederasty, but also reveals his own view when in his index 'Pederasty' refers one to 'Children, sexual abuse of'.[43] Scroggs takes a much longer route, first arguing that because of the partners' difference in age the nature of paederasty is inequality, and because inequality always leads to domination, and domination to dehumanization and abuse, and second, because the relation is inherently impermanent and intended to last for only a few years, "it is clear that most forms of pederasty had at least the *potential* to create concrete relations that would be destructive and dehumanizing to the participants, particularly the youths... Given this potential and its frequent actualization, that early Christians should repudiate all forms of pederasty is not unduly surprising."[44] He concludes, "what the New Testament was against was the image of homosexuality as pederasty and primarily here its more sordid and dehumanizing aspects".[45] One would never suspect, from all this, that the same society also contained nurturing, self-sacrificing relationships such as those cited by Lambert.[46]

The issue is not, however, whether historically there were positive, nurturing relationships—which there surely were—or destructive, dehumanizing ones—which there also surely were—nor even in what proportion they existed. With the discovery of a New Testament passage which suggests an attitude of toleration toward a non-exploitive, caring paederastic relationship, the focus must move back to where it always should have been: that it is not homosexuality, or paederasty, or any other specific sexual relationship that Christian ethics condemns, but dehumanization and exploitation of another person in any relationship, heterosexual or homosexual, intragenerational or intergenerational.

*Editors Note:*
*D. H. Mader was graduated from Union Theological Seminary, New York, and served for fifteen years as a clergyman. He currently lives in Europe as an artist and writer. He prepared the introduction for the new edition of the early gay poetry anthology* Men and Boys *(New York: Coltsfoot Press, 1978), and his book reviews have appeared in* The Cabirion, Pan *and other journals.*

**NOTES**

1. T. Horner, *Jonathan Loved David* (Philadelphia: Westminster, 1978), p. 110-111.
2. Romans 1:26-7, I Corinthians 6:9, Timothy 1:10. A considerable literature exists dealing with exactly what these passages mean, the most important being J. Boswell, *Christianity, Social Tolerance and Homosexuality* (Chicago: U. of Chicago Press, 1980), Appendix I, also pages 106-113; Horner, op. cit., chapters 7 and 8; J. J. McNeill, *The Church and the Homosexual* (2nd ed., New York: Next Year Publications, 1985), pages 50-56; R. Scroggs, *The New Testament and Homosexuality* (Philadelphia: Fortress Press, 1983), chapter 7. It is not within the scope of this article to enter into the debate over Pauline intentions.
3. Horner, op. cit., p. 123; McNeill, op. cit., p. 65, makes a similar argument including Acts 8:26ff. The Old Testament background is Lev. 21:20 and Deut. 23:1, excluding eunuchs from the covenant community; a similar law regarding castrated animals is found in Lev. 22:24. The context of Lev. 21:16-23, however, makes it clear that the objection is to castration as a physical imperfection.
4. F. F Bruce, *Hard Sayings of Jesus* (Downers Grove, Ill.: Intervarsity Press, 1983), pages 63-5.
5. Horner, op. cit., pages 120-21. One of the more remarkable poetical flights is W. Wattles, "John", *Lanterns in Gethsemane* (New York: Dutton, 1918), and no less than the English philosopher Jeremy Bentham was responsible for seeing a homosexual allusion in Mark 14:15; L. Crompton, *Byron and Greek Love* (Berkeley: U. of California, 1985), p. 281.
6. The mention by Horner, op. cit., p. 122, cites previous

ources but devotes less notice to his than to his theories involving Matthew 19:10-12. The foreign sources include J. Martignac, "Le Centurion de Capernaum", *Arcadie*, March, 1975, p. 17ff, which I have not been able to examine; a thoroughly unscholarly notice in E. Gillabert, *Le Colosse aux pieds d'argil* (Paris: Metanonae, 1975), and a poetic enthusiasm by D. Christianopoulos, "The Centurion Cornelius" (trans. K. Friar), *Gay Sunshine Journal*, No. 47, 1982, p. 170; the earliest mention in English is J. P Rossman, *Sexual Experience Between Men and Boys* (Boston: Association Press, 1976), p. 99. It is also mentioned in J. J. McNeill, "God and Gays: A New Team", *Christopher Street*, 1:4, October, 1976, p. 27; it was with the encouragement of Dr. McNeill that this paper was begun.

7. The parallels between this story and another healing story, that of the Syrio-Phonecian woman's daughter (Matthew 15:21-28 and Mark 7:24-30), must be noted. Both accounts involve an appeal to Jesus by an adult Gentile on behalf of a child, followed by a commendation from Jesus about faith, and a healing effected at a distance by Jesus' word alone. There is even, in Matthew's version, a negative embassy (verse 23b)! On this basis, some of the more thorough form-critics have suggested that there is a common origin for these two stories. Two things appear to militate against this, however: the severe difference in Jesus' initial response to the request; and the different sources from which the accounts came (Mark for the Syrio-Phonecian woman, "Q" for the Centurion). While it is not impossible that, at an extremely primitive level in the development of tradition, both reflect a common event, and there are certainly similarities of motif, we will not here assume any connection.

8. For non-professional readers unfamiliar with this designation and how it came to be proposed, the easiest introduction is still probably that of A. M. Perry, "The Growth of the Gospels", *Interpreter's Bible*, Vol. 7, p. 60ff, or D. T. Rowlingson's article "The Synoptic Problem", *Interpreter's Dictionary of the Bible*, Vol. 4, p. 491ff.

9. S. MacLean Gilmour, "Introduction to St. Luke", *Interpreter's Bible*, Vol. 8, p. 13; B. H. Streeter, *The Four Gospels* (London: MacMillian, 1928), p. 233; S. E. Johnson, in his Exegesis to Matthew includes Matthew 9:32-33 as from "Q" as well: *Interpreter's Bible*, Vol. 7, p. 337 and p. 359.

10. D. C. Pellett, "Capernaum", *Interpreter's Dictionary of the Bible*, Vol. 1, pages 532-4; K. W. Clark, "Galilee", ibid., Vol. 2, pages 346-7.

11. Loisy, Wendland and Klostermann are cited as favoring Matthew by N. Geldenhuis, *Commentary on the Gospel of Luke* (London: Marshall, Morgan & Scott, 1950), p. 221; Dibelius' suggestion that the motif of messengers is a Lucan creation and Bultmann's argument that *pais* stood in the original "Q" source are cited in I. H. Marshall, *Gospel of Luke* (Grand Rapids: Eerdmans, 1978), p. 277 and 279.

12. A. Plummer, *International Critical Commentaries: Gospel According to St. Luke* (Edinburgh: T. & T. Clark, 1901), p. 196.

13. J. Chapman, *Matthew, Mark & Luke* (London: Longmans Green, 1937), p. 103.

14. V. Taylor, *Formation of the Gospel Tradition* (London: MacMillan, 1945), p. 76.

15. A. R. C. Leaney, *Commentary on the Gospel According to Luke* (London: A. & C. Black, 1966), p. 141.

16. J. Fitzmyer, *Anchor Bible: Gospel According to Luke (I-IX)* (N.Y.: Doubleday, 1981), pages 451, 468-9.

17. N. Geldenhuis, loc. cit.

18. I. H. Marshall, loc. cit. Marshall does construct a response to the problem in Luke of a first-person statement in the mouth of a messenger, by citing the oriental practise of ambassadors memorizing statements, and Biblical examples thereof, which is credible but not wholly convincing. T. H. Robinson, *Moffett New Testament Commentary–The Gospel of Matthew* (London: Hoder and Stoughton, 1978) must also be numbered among those favouring Lukan primacy.

19. C. G. Montefiore, *Synoptic Gospels* (N.Y.: KTVA Publishers, 1968), Vol. 2, pages 423-4.

20. W. F. Howard, Exegesis of John, *Interpreter's Bible*, Vol. 8, p. 538.

21. J. H. Bernard, *International Critical Commentary: Gospel Ac-*

*cording to John* (Edinburgh, T. & T. Clark, 1928), Vol. 1, p. 166.
22. Plummer, op. cit., p. 197; Howard, op. cit., p. 536; Bernard, loc. cit.; J. Marsh, *The Gospel of St. John* (London: Penguin, 1968), p. 236.
23. Streeter, op. cit., p. 409.
24. R. E. Brown, *Anchor Bible Gospel According to St. John (I-XII)* (New York, Doubleday, 1966), p. 193.
25. C. K. Barrett, *Gospel According to St. John* (London: SPCK, 1978), p. 248, however, presents arguments that *pais* here is an assimilation from the synoptics.
26. Hesychius Alexandrinus, *Lexicon*, ed. M. Schmidt (Jena, 1858-68), Vol. 2, p. 256.
27. H. G. Liddell and R. Scott, *Greek-English Lexicon* (Oxford: Oxford University Press, 1940), p. 1289.
28. J. A. Symonds, *A Problem in Greek Ethics* (London: Privately Printed by Leonard Smithers, 1901, and subsequent reprints); G. Ives, *The Graeco-Roman View of Youth* (London: Cayme Press, 1926). That both works have the polemic purpose of defending homosexuality by appealing to the classical tradition, and therefore are somewhat unwilling to confront the darker side of paederasty in ancient culture, where it intersected with prostitution and slavery, does not negate their value.
29. K. J. Dover, *Greek Homosexuality* (Cambridge, Mass.: Harvard Univ. Press, 1978); Boswell, op. cit., chapter 3; R. Lambert, *Beloved and God: The Story of Hadrian and Antinous* (New York: Viking, 1984), chapter 6.
30. Lambert, op. cit., p. 78.
31. Scroggs, op. cit., chapters 2, 3 and 4.
32. Ibid., p. 27.
33. Dover, op. cit., p. 16; Bernard Sergent, *Homosexuality in Greek Myth* (Boston: Beacon Press, 1986), p. 10. It is not clear whether Sergent's statement is on his own authority, or is based on Dover, whom he cites.
34 Dover, loc. cit. While we lack any commonly used terms that are the equivalent of *eromenos* or *paidika*, the situation with *pais* might be compared with the contemporary use of the word "boy": while in common usage it would refer to a minor male child, when used of or in a gay setting it carries a distinct sexual connotation.
35. Liddell and Scott, op. cit., p. 576; T. W. Manson, *The Sayings of Jesus* (London: SCM Press, 1949), p. 64.
36. I. H. Marshall, op. cit., p. 279, goes to some pains to point out that *entimos* here should be read more with Luke's other usage and Paul, rather than that in I Peter.
37. Manson, loc. cit., concurs, suggesting that Luke used *entimos* to explain concern that would not normally have been shown to a slave.
38. The issue of the authorship of these Gospels, upon which we touch now, is much too complex to be explored here. For non-professional readers unfamiliar with the controversies surrounding it, the most accessible background is probably that in E. P. Blair's article "Luke", section 1 of V. Taylor's "Gospel of Luke", and section 9 of F. C. Grant's "Gospel of Matthew", *Interpreter's Dictionary of the Bible*, Vol. 3, pages 179, 180 and 312, respectively; and S. E. Johnson's "Introduction to the Gospel of Matthew", section VII, S. M. Gilmour's "Introduction to the Gospel of Luke", section F, and G. C. H. MacGregor's "Introduction to the Acts of the Apostles", section IX, in the *Interpreter's Bible*, Vol. 7, p. 242, Vol. 8, p. 9. and Vol. 9, p. 19, respectively. In brief, there is broad consensus, but by no means unanimity, that the Gospel of Luke was likely written by the individual of that name who, according to the Acts, accompanied Paul, and that the Gospel of Matthew was probably written by an unknown Syrian Christian and attributed to the disciple whose name it bears
39. Horner, loc. cit.
40. M. H. Pope, "Proselyte", section 5b, *Interpreter's Dictionary of the Bible*, Vol. 3, p. 929.
41. Scroggs, op. cit., chapters 5 and 6.
42. E. R. Goodenough, "Philo Judeus", *Interpreter's Dictionary of the Bible*, Vol. 3, p. 796.
43. Boswell, op. cit., p. 143-4.
44. Scroggs, op. cit., chapter 3, particularly pages 36-8 and 43. It is clear that, by these criteria, most human relationships have similar potential for dehumanization, and could therefore be condemned. Almost every human relationship—most marriages, all parental and pedagogical relations, and labour/-management relations, among others—involves inequality, and all accordingly contain po-

tential for abuse, physical, emotional, financial and otherwise. So too does paederasty, no more and no less. Similarly, many human relationships are of limited duration, among them parenting and, increasingly, marriage itself—not to mention heterosexual relations not involving marriage. It is questionable if any of these would be criticised for their limited duration alone. Indeed, classical paederasty might have been less damaging than some of these open-ended relationships, as it was clearly understood by both partners that it was of limited duration.

45. Scroggs, op. cit., p. 126. This allows him to conclude that what the New Testament has to say against homosexuality is irrelevant to today's situation, in which homosexuals seek to attain permanent, fully equal and mutually fulfilling relationships.

46. Lambert, op. cit., p. 83.

# HOMOPHILE ETHICS

by
Merritt M. Thompson

Of all the problems which confront homosexuals, perhaps none is more widespread and penetrating in its effect on the welfare and happiness of the group than that of the rightness and wrongness of homosexual acts, that is, their ethical implications. In the current literature of the day one constantly finds references to homosexuality as perversion, one of the crimes of the period, a characteristic of abnormal and perverse people. Preachers have condemned it; judges have scorned those who practiced it; ridicule has been heaped upon it; and in fact it has been listed in company with the worst human aberrations. Thus homosexuals have been subjected to the most intense feelings of guilt or have defied social standards and lived secret lives apart from and coldly separated from their fellow men, if not victimized by their enemies and classified and secluded as criminals in penal institutions. The voices raised against such inhuman treatment have been few and far between with no organized effort to remedy the situation until our own day when for the first time questions are being raised and discussed in groups of intelligent people.

The reasons for the strong feelings against homosexuality are not wholly clear, but there are some historic facts which throw light upon the subject. The ancient Hebrew people were a small group alienated from their ancestral lands over a long period of time and, when circumstances permitted them to return, they found them occupied by strange and hostile nationalities who must be conquered and driven out by warring activities. Consequently potential warriors were at a premium and a high birth rate was desirable. Polygamy became a virtue and anything which hindered the increase of population would be looked down upon. Thus a point of view was established against irregular sex activities which was later extended to all sex activities. The transition from the Hebrew to the Christian culture carried over the antagonistic attitude toward sex. The views of Paul, the organizer of the Christian Church, are well known. His influence went so far that celibacy became a rule for the priesthood of the growing institution, and morality became practically synonymous with abstinence from sex activities. There may have been a psychological basis in part at least for the identification of chastity and holiness. That nature has made the organs of sex those also of excretion is one of the anomalies which are found in the natural world and which offend the rational mind. Sex thus becomes "dirty" merely by association. A possibly more profound reason may lie in the rise of mysticism, an aspect of human culture which has defied all attempts to define it or set limiting boundaries to it, but which has exerted enormous influence and is clearly recognized in the history of religion. The relation of mystical states of mind and sexual ecstacy is indicated in the writings of mystics, such, for example, as those of Santa Theresa and others, as well as in practices wherein, for example, nuns are called "the brides of Christ." Thus sex and religion are placed in the position of rivals for human allegiance and, to our own day, sin is more vividly portrayed in terms of sex by the teachers of "morality" than in any other area. It is thus natural that the denial of man's basic urges must be accompanied by a philosophy of life which exalts suffering and deprivation in this life only to be assuaged in a life beyond the grave. A curious fact of our times is the enormous increase in the membership of the churches at the same time that there is a very lively exercise of skepticism which feels itself justified in examining and criticising the basic beliefs and doctrines bequeathed to us by tradition. Thus the whole subject of sex in general and homosexuality in particular are subject to the search for a truer and more satisfying basis than ever before. Just what do right and wrong, then, mean for the homophile? The present study is an attempt to develop briefly that aspect of a philosophy of life which is termed ethical or moral.

Ethics has to do with the inner aspects of life, mental and spiritual, and conduct. It studies purpose as determined by outer conditions, or outer conditions of individual behavior or institutions as determined by the inner purpose. To study choice and purpose is psychology; to study choice as affected by the rights of others and to judge it as right or wrong by such a standard is ethics. To study an institution may be economics, or sociology, or law, but to study its activities as resulting from the purposes of persons or as affecting the welfare of persons, and to judge its acts as good or bad from that point of view is ethics. The place of value as related to standards will be taken up later.

Following somewhat the Freudian theory of personality, conduct or behavior may take place on three levels. Behavior on the first or lowest level is initiated by various biological, economic, or other non-moral impulses or needs of the organism, non-moral so long as their ends are merely accepted, but becoming moral when their ends are compared, evaluated, and chosen deliberately. This type of behavior is characteristic of animals, children, and persons who act ordinarily without reflection, instinctively and disregarding of consequences either to one's self or to others. The purpose of moral education is to transform this type of behavior to the higher forms, that is, from non-intelligent action to intelligent action.

The second type of behavior is that which is determined by the "folkways" and "mores" of the group to which one belongs, and is approved by it. The standards are accepted by the individual with little or no critical reflection and are handed down from one generation to the next. They may be termed group habits, and are likely to be quite independent of intelligence and flexibility, although they may have had some utility in a previous age. The history of many of the religious sects illustrates this point extensively. A distinguished leader or a set of circumstances may have pointed out a specific need which became embodied in an ethical code, rational at the time, but later a mere formality imposed by group inertia. Many years ago a non-Prussian minority in Germany resented the arrogance and domination of the Prussian military of whom a notable characteristic was the wearing of conspicuous uniforms with large brass buttons. These buttons became the symbol of the hated overlords, and gave rise to a distaste for all buttons. This minority migrated to the United States and settled in western Pennsylvania. Years afterward, when doubtless the origin of the distaste was wholly forgotten, the religious sect representing this minority considered the wearing of buttons "wicked" and do so to this day. The writer has seen these people in eastern Ohio with their buttonless garments cut to long outmoded styles but conforming to the rigid ethical code of the group.

The third type of conduct is that in which the individual thinks and judges for himself, considers whether a purpose is good and right, decides and chooses, and does not accept the standards of his group without reflection. Complete morality is reached only when the individual recognizes the right or chooses the good freely, devotes himself wholeheartedly to its fulfillment, and seeks a progressive social development which involves the sharing of every member of society. A rational method of setting up standards and forming values must be substituted for habitual, passive acceptance. Voluntary and personal choice and interest must be substituted for unconscious identification with group welfare or instinctive and habitual response to group needs. The ultimate purpose is individual development with the demand that all persons shall share in this development. The worth and happiness of the person and of every person are paramount. Thus one passes from the realm of the instinctive and merely expedient to that of the rational.

A concept that has had great vogue in our time with reference to the nature of personality is that of integration, the hanging together, as it were, of the various aspects of the person. Perhaps this quality can best be seen in connection with its opposite. So-called insanity or mental disease can best be understood in terms of the disintegration of the personality. One is shocked by the conversation of the abnormal as it will contain the most glaring inconsistencies and disharmonies. And the so-called normal is not always as consistent as he thinks he is. Someone has said that the greatest invention of the nineteenth century was the ability to hold two ideas at the same time which cancel each other out. One thinks of the "Free World" and the attitude of many of its citizens towards Negroes. Conduct and character are strictly correlative concepts. Continuity, consistency throughout a series of acts is the expression of the enduring unity of attitudes and habits. In fact conduct may be defined as continuity of action. Deeds hang together because they proceed from a single and stable self. Customary morality tends to overlook the connection between character and action. The essence of reflective morals lies in its consciousness of the existence of a persistent self and the part it plays in what is externally done. Motive is the attitude and predisposition of this self toward ends which are embodied in action. Mere foresight moves to action only when it is accompanied by desire for those ends. A set and disposition of character leads to anticipation of certain kinds of consequences and to the neglect of others. There is no such thing as motive and will apart from anticipation of consequences and from effort to bring them to pass.

The discussion of motive leads directly into the larger area of value, the supreme concept of philosophy and the starting point for all consideration of personality. Closely related to it is the concept of freedom. The fundamental task of intelligent living is that of examining the relative worth of varying and opposed values and of bringing about their most valuable combinations. They assume moral significance in so far as they contribute to human living its worth and reason for being. To live as a rational being man must organize his life and thought about the attainment of goals, which express his ideals and ultimately his values. As a matter of fact men do live the greater part of their lives amidst their ideals and experience their highest moments of enthusiasm when they are working and sacrificing more immediate goods for them. The problem of the moral or supreme form of living is that of selecting and organizing ideals. To be free to choose one's goals does not mean to be free from all determining factors in one's nature, but rather to be free to express in action the preference to which these factors give rise. Custom, tradition, emotion, imagination—all these play their part, but reason must ultimately dominate. Freedom is self-determination leading to self-realization which is the equivalent of living rationally or intelligently, the realization of one's potentialities, the expression of one's natural impulses within the limits of one's ideals. The product of conscious effort is willed action, wherein the motive, which represents the attitude of the total conscious being, is held at a particular time and in a particular act of choosing. One is free in an action when it represents the self as a whole and is not the sporadic and momentary expression of some impulse.

As was suggested above, it is in theories of value that all ethics finds its starting point. The theorists of the subject are divided between those who hold that value is inherent in the cosmic order, objective and ultimate, and those who hold that it is an attribute of a deeper reality, a construction of the mind. G. E. Moore, Bertrand Russell, and John Laird hold value as undefinable. Laird claims that nature itself possesses value. This objective interpretation of value is termed the realistic theory of value and was the one held largely by the older religionists who, however, approached objective idealism and located values, and more particularly ethical values in the mind of a personal God. Thus ethical behavior was reduced to a list of prohibitions. One might use the divided page, listing the "wicked" or "sinful" acts on one side and the permissible acts on the other. The great defect of this procedure lay in the fact that the "mind of God" was confused with social and cultural origins, which, as was illustrated above, were likely to be lost in a historical perspective. And the most trivial and inconsequential acts were forbidden, (when the writer was nine years of age, his father gave him one of the worst scoldings of his life because he and a friend took a walk in the woods on a Sunday afternoon) while great, obvious evils such, for example, as graft and special privileges in business and government, adulteration of food and drugs, etc., were never mentioned. Even some of the so-called realists have not held consistently to the completely objective theory of values. For example Russell holds that values are the creations of man, and R. B. Perry defines value in terms of interest, and anything may acquire value when it is desired. That act which secures in the largest degree the interests of all is morally right. S. Alexander finds that truth, goodness, and beauty involve an "appreciating mind" and involve a relationship between mind and its objects. When satisfactions are organized and made coherent within the individual and in the relation of individuals within the social group, they are morally good. If one holds that ethical values are objective and inherent in the universe, it would seem that he has the obligation to discover them and present them to us. Thus far no one has been able to go beyond purely abstract concepts which turn out to be mere classifications or categories, such, for example, as truth, beauty, and goodness, which give very little help in the actual concerns of living, and arbitrary lists of forbidden acts which obviously do not escape their cultural relativity.

To this writer the philosophy known as personalistic or dynamic idealism seems to offer a more acceptable basis for ethics than realism, although it does not deny an objective world, but sees it in a proper perspective which, in its relation to persons, is an inference rather than a primary datum of experience. The world, or reality, in its ultimate structure is a system of conscious beings whose most profound nature may be expressed in the term *persons*. The total universe is a system of selves or persons, who may be regarded either as members of one all-inclusive person who individuates them by the diversity of his purposing, (this view represents that of absolute idealism) or as a society of many selves related by common purpose, (this view represents a pluralistic idealism and is the one held by this writer). The person or self is the process of conscious experience ever moving forward in a time sequence, and having a two-fold character, first, a reaction to the objective world, and, second, a regurgitation of past experience in memory for the purpose of examination, criticism, and the deepening of meaning, in a word, for the development of insight. This process may be called the consciousness of consciousness, an ever more profound understanding of one's own nature and experience. The physical world is within the world of experience which is the entire world of reality. Some have thought that this view denies the existence of an outer or objective world. (*Esse est percipi,* to be is to be perceived, — has often been interpreted in this way.) It does not do so, but it recognizes that, without a perceiving mind, it lacks reality, that is, an object which no one perceives is merely an inference, or abstraction, by a mind. The most hard-boiled research scientist never escapes himself in the process of his work, and it is becoming better recognized that all scientific conclusions are inferences drawn by the minds of persons without whom there would be, as far as human beings are concerned,— just nothing. Values originate in the self and exist only for the self. They are not substantive, things, but attributes of the on-going process which is the consciousness, the person. The inner feel of the person, that by which he knows that he is a person, may be called the intuition of the self, or more immediately, desire. Ordinary living consists of the rhythm of *desire-satisfaction,* repeated endlessly. And the remote goal may be termed self-realization, the fulfilling of the potentialities of the person, his ultimate welfare and happiness, always recognizing that such fulfillment takes place in a social setting of other persons who are entitled to the same privilege. Thus ethical value, the Good, becomes that which contributes to the ever-increasing welfare and happiness of the individual, that which is constructive of personality, and the ethical social Good is that which contributes to the welfare and happiness of all members of the human race. The sacrifices of individuals are sometimes required for the common good, but such sacrifice comes to be a good in its own right. Welfare and happiness are not entirely satisfactory as definitions of the Good, which is easier to see in specific situations than in purely abstract terms. The next part of the discussion will attempts to bring the matter down to earth.

The idealistic interpretation of value and ethics remains on a level of abstract concepts perhaps to too great an extent. It has remained for the pragmatic and instrumentalist philosophies to bring the discussion to the level of everyday experience. For these views value is the supreme category. Like the idealists they find human experience to cover the sum-total of available data. Absolute standards are not discoverable. Values vary from situation to situation and with specific needs. Facts are those aspects of the stimulus-reaction situation which seem to hold a certain consistency and the reactions to them are as near as we can ever come to absolutes. All objects of value receive their value from the functions they perform in the situations where they occur or in situations related to them. Nothing taken in isolation can be said to possess value. In fact nothing exists in such isolation. And the personal idealist says that nothing has reality in isolation from the person. Thus welfare and happiness must be defined in terms of the activities of actual persons in actual situations. For example in most cases living of the person is better when he is well-nourished than when he is starving, when he is healthy than when he is sick, etc., as the anthropologist gives the activities of human beings everywhere. The fact that those activities are so similar gives rise to the error that the goods of life are absolutes. Moral values arise, not alone when the good of the individual is referred to, but also when the situation is social, that is, when the interests of other people are affected by the object of value. Moral standards and attitudes are accepted because they manifest values in the social situations. There are no absolute and permanent standards other than these. There are no eternal ideas of good and evil. Utility then becomes a concept of high place in the discussion. Value is interpreted in terms of control, mastery, use. One thus returns to intelligence or rationality. Some are disappointed that ethics cannot furnish the list referred to earlier, these acts are moral, and these are immoral. Each individual must exercise his intelligence to determine the quality of his own behavior. The moral person is the one who does so and is not moved by blind impulse or enslaved by a narrow and bigoted society. I suppose no one escapes the necessity of expediency when a society will destroy the individual who departs too conspicuously from the norms which it professes with no regard for origin or rationality. Each person, unless he has a yen for martyrdom, is likely to conform to the point at least of survival, but, from that point on, he would seem to have a moral obligation to do what he can to create more rational attitudes and norms in the society where he finds himself.

Thus far the discussion has dealt with ethics in a general way which applies to all the aspects of life, but now it would seem appropriate to look a little more closely at the ethics of the homophile. It seems somewhat presumptuous, however, to suppose that one can add to what René Guyon has written in his *The Ethics of Sexual Acts,* probably the most complete and rational treatment of the subject now extant. While paying him full honor, this writer differs from him in two points. In the first place Guyon objects to a metaphysical interpretation at the basis of ethics. Like John Dewey, who made the same mistake, he assumes that one can build up a theory without presuppositions and then proceeds to state certain principles which are based upon assumptions. John Dewey's followers were somewhat embarrassed, but found it necessary to specify the unconscious assumptions underlying his work. As a matter of fact there is no genuine thinking without some presuppositions. The most thorough research scientist must assume the uniformity of nature, the reliability of sense observation, the worth of his research, and others. Thus we have attempted in this study to find a legitimate starting point for the elaboration of our ideas and that point lies as always in the realm of metaphysics. Our second point of disagreement with Guyon refers to his separation of the acts of living into two spheres, one involving moral decisions and one quite removed from that sphere, such, for example, as eating, and other acts of physiology, psycho-physiology, hygiene, etc., which cannot be either moral or immoral, but rather amoral. Sexual acts come within this amoral sphere and should not be used as criteria of virtue, utility, or value, since they are incommensurable things. This writer cannot see any act of the human being which is outside the realm of the ethical unless one returns to the view of the older religionists with their division of behavior into the "sinful" and the "righteous". When one sees the world as a whole and a consistent whole, he must recognize that there is a right way and a wrong way to reach even the most ordinary and commonplace goals. In baking a cake, if one does not use the right proportion of baking powder to flour, his cake will fail. To claim that such an activity is amoral in contrast to a personal relationship involving honesty or its opposite, seems to this writer to come close to assuming the bifurcation of the world into natural and supernatural, a view here rejected.

Thus we come to our conclusion that sexual acts, the same as any other, are subject to rational examination and are accepted or rejected as to whether they operate constructively toward the building of the Good Life or its opposite. Now it happens in a given society and a given set of circumstances that a particular act so often operates destructively that it becomes expedient to enact its prohibition into law, but even here one has to be careful not to think of such restrictions as absolutes. For example, in our society and that of Europe it is rather well accepted that unethical sexual behavior includes: relations with underage persons, the use of force or violence, public display, and the conscious transmission of venereal disease. And yet that these prohibitions are not absolutes is proved by the fact that there are other societies which think very differently about them. In some countries of the world where minors are not protected by law, preadolescents are sometimes prostitutes and initiate sex behavior on their own account; the writer once lived in a primitive community where the birth of a child in the family was a festive occasion and all members of the family, old and young, were invited home to witness the event. Privacy had little meaning here. There is a certain inertia in man which leads him to wish to avoid rational thinking and find the situations of life expressed in simple terms of black and white, yes and no, but life is just not built that way and successful living requires a price to be paid, and that price is seeking for constructive goals and the use of rational means in attaining them. There is no other way.

---

Note. The author of this study acknowledges indebtedness to the following books: John Dewey and James H. Tufts, *Ethics;* Clifford L. Barrett, *Ethics;* René Guyon, *The Ethics of Sexual Acts.*

# Philosophies Of Homophobia and Homophilia

By Laurence J. Rosán

This chapter is an introduction to the meta-philosophy of homosexuality. That is, 1) it is an introduction only, not a final or exhaustive study, and only a limited number of examples purposely have been given; but it can help stimulate other, more detailed investigations. 2) "Meta-philosophy" (a recent term) or "the philosophy of philosophy" means, in this case, an analysis of all fundamental types of philosophy from the outside as it were, with as much objectivity as possible. Though everyone has a philosophy of his own, this writer included, this chapter will try to avoid its intrusion in spite of some inescapable clues. 3) "Homosexuality" has here its usual general meaning. But it will immediately be necessary to scrutinize this word and to replace it frequently with "homophilia," the *self-accepting* desire for others of the same sex. "Homophobia" is a convenient term for opposition to this. And we will also need a word for those who are neither favorable, nor opposed, to homosexuality, neutrally regarding it as equally valid as heterosexuality, and for this attitude the writer suggests the term "homoïsaia."[1]

Materialism, idealism, and solipsism will be the philosophies presented first, and under the heading of "clear-cut cases" because they are comparatively easy to understand both in themselves and in their consequences for homosexuality. The second section of "complex cases" will contain most of the varieties of dualism where apparently no simple conclusions can be drawn. The chapter will end with a summary, and a prognosis both for dealing with homophobic philosophies and for constructing homophilic ones.

I. Clear-cut cases.

*Materialism* or "naturalism" is one of the simplest philosophies to expound.[2] This is because it is based on what has been called "naive realism" or the belief that all the objects we experience in the external world are truly real — which is the *daily* philosophy of the greatest number of people, even if many of them additionally have a nominal belief in the existence of spiritual beings. Materialism takes this generally accepted "priority of external things" and constructs a rigorously consistent and total philosophy upon it. Traditionally (in the East as well as in the West), this has been accomplished by reducing all things to ultimate material "building blocks," in the Western tradition called "atoms."[3] (The original Greek word meant "uncuttables"; the recent "electrons," "protons," etc. do not represent any shift from this position, although they are the result of "cutting the atom" in the *modern* sense of this word, because they themselves in turn are "uncuttable" building blocks of all things, that is, they also are "atoms" or "atomic particles.") In the rare case of a naturalistic theory of *one* "material substance," the philosophy's vocabulary would initially appear different from what is presented below, but there would be no essential change in its conclusions.

Almost all materialists therefore are "pluralists"; reality consists of a (nearly?) infinite number of nearly infinitesimal particles, either all alike or of a number of types. There is nothing else. There is no God of course, no "guiding intelligence," not even "Mother Nature" or any personification of this sort. And the "scientific laws" that describe the behavior of the atoms are only the patterns that we human beings observe and then codify into a "system of physics"; these laws are not in themselves realities. *Only the atoms are realities.* And since they are material particles, not intelligences, they have no "intentions of doing anything," no goals whatever. Even the ultimate end of the universe — it might be "the thinly dispersed particles of energy, having lost all their organization through entropy, moving extremely slowly at a temperature just above Absolute Zero" — is clearly not the result of any planning by the atoms.

This is important for our understanding of materialism as a homoïsic philosophy. For nothing can be called either "good" or "bad"; everything occurs by the mechanical interaction of atomic particles, and the result is entirely neutral. To be sure, particles combine to form more complex collections, and these collections seem to behave in ways differing from the original atoms themselves; thus "protoplasm," a very complex collection of particles, seems to behave in distinctive ways such as moving, ingesting, excreting, reproducing, etc. And further there are very complex forms of protoplasm, which took eons of time to evolve, called "animals and/or human beings" (i.e., human beings *are* animals), which in turn seem to behave in their own distinctive ways — they appear to move to, or away from, certain things outside them, (knowing these things by "sensation" or the influence of external atoms on the internal ones of their receptive "sense organs"). This movement toward or away from things is named respectively "desire" and "fear"; and whatever is desired is called "good for that animal or human being," whatever is feared is called "bad." But "desire and fear," "good and bad," are value-judgments relative only to those complex arrangements of protoplasm called "animals and/or human beings" which, having evolved into existence over a long period of time, may very well evolve out of existence in some indefinite future; the universe cares nothing about them! The atoms make no value-judgments; no values have any reality. For this philosophy, therefore, only one "ethics" or value-theory is consistently possible; it has been traditionally called "hedonism" or the "pleasure doctrine": If there are no real values, what else can each person seek but whatever he or she desires at the moment? His object or goal at that moment becomes "good" for *him*, and the satisfaction of his desire, the sensation of achieving that object, will bring him a "good sensation" or pleasure. Conversely, avoiding a feared object will save him from a "bad sensation" or pain. So let everyone do exactly as he pleases; *"Fais ce que voudras."*[4]

And what about homosexuality? Well, what about it? What's the question? Homosexuality and heterosexuality, masturbation and zoerasty, sex itself versus chastity — none of these has any difference in value; none of them is either good or bad in itself. It is each person's pleasure that alone determines what he will choose, his disinclination or "pain" that determines what he will avoid. Homosexuality compared to heterosexuality is like a taste for rye bread as compared to white bread: *there is nothing to say about it.* There is no "problem" here, there is no "question" to begin with. Materialism or naturalism's attitude to homosexuality is purely and totally homoïsic.

So far we have been examining traditionally consistent materialism which usually offers no "political doctrine" (or what might be the best society) because all values are relative to the individual only. Just as among animals where what is "good" for the predator will be "bad" for its prey, so also a materialist in a society which values "justice," "honesty," "humanity," etc., will advance his own interests as a predator by pretending to be just, honest, and humane, playing the part like a good actor or "hypocrite" (original Greek meaning), seeking to obtain and remain in power, even dictating the meaning of "justice" itself, which is therefore only the "advantage of the strongest" (Thrasymachus in Plato's *Republic*, Stephanos II, 338). But, understandably, various efforts have been made to "soften" this corollary of naturalistic ethics and to develop some justification for a society in which at least overt violence could be prevented, mutual contracts might be honored, and so on; probably the best-known effort is Thomas Hobbes' *Leviathan* (see below). To consider this "politicized materialism" and its potential attitude to homosexuality, however, we should first ask is it really consistent with the rest of materialism? And this suggests a short analysis of what "consistency" means, and why it is important particularly for us who are gay to examine the consistency of any philosophy.

If a person says, e.g., "*Only* material particles are real; they are the building blocks of the whole universe, and God will punish sexual deviation," we can immediately and confidently exclaim, "This is an inconsistent philosophy!" Now if he should remove the words "only" and "whole," and connect or relate the third clause with the first two, the sentence could change into "Material particles are real; they are the building blocks of the material portion of the universe; but God also exists, Who created and supervises these material particles, and He will punish sexual deviation." This is a satisfactory statement of a certain type of dualism. But whatever the philosophy may be, *it should be made clear from the beginning.* Only then can we know exactly what kind of philosophy confronts us and, if it appears homophobic, only then could we be fore-armed in our defense.

Returning to "politicized materialism" (Hobbes's version): A hedonist seeks his own pleasure, yes, but he realizes that other hedonists have the same desire; he knows that just as he has no scruples about using violence or trickery for his own ends, so these others could use violence or trickery upon him. Therefore, gathering together with them, he and they all make a kind of contract, an agreement not to harm or be harmed, giving up their possible use of violence against others in return for the clear benefit of not suffering it themselves. Because such an agreement must be guaranteed by some external *power* (since these materialists are not likely to "take an oath on the Bible"!), they arm and authorize the "state," specifically the police power of the state, to intervene should anyone break the agreement by an act of violence, and thus prevent this crime to begin with or else punish it to deter future crime.[5] But when will this "agreement not to harm or be harmed" be consistent with the rest of naturalism? When, say, fifteen people gather together, make this agreement and arm the police, then this contract will be valid *for these fifteen people only* (since only they voluntarily contracted, nor can they obligate even their own children) — and valid *only for as long as they have contracted*; (it is implausible that they would bind themselves for the rest of their lives; rather they would probably make such a contract for a limited period of time, say ten years, and subject to voluntary renewal). Now an agreement not to harm or be harmed made by fifteen people for ten years is reasonably consistent with naturalism. But if we allow this idea to drift into the usual concept of a "social contract" where not only are all the people of a society bound for life but they are bound to a so-called "contract" they themselves never personally made, we have moved far beyond consistent materialism where the individual alone is the creator of all values.

For the fifteen who made an agreement for ten years, however, the implications of their contract will be as homoïsic as before. The police power they authorized will be concerned only with the prevention of violence and trickery as agreed on; it will have not the slightest interest in whether a person eats rye bread or white bread, or whether he or she is homosexual or heterosexual. Any state in which the police *do* take such an interest has surely broken away from its original naturalistic foundation, more likely was never based on it to begin with. We can repeat therefore that materialism or naturalism is a philosophy of homoïsaia, totally neutral to homosexuals and heterosexuals.

*Idealism*, although also a simple philosophy in itself, has been much more difficult to explain to the general public than materialism, partly because in America from about the Twenties to the Fifties it was the least prevalent: Transcendentalism had long lost its hold, "Science" and "the Bible" were felt to be the only two alternatives for life, and small idealistic sects like Christian Science were objects of considerable mockery. But in the last decade or so, two seemingly unconnected popular trends, the interest in the power of the mind over the body ("psychosomatic medicine"), and the "beat" and "hip" generations' fascination with Zen, Yoga, and the occult, have now combined to make the explanation of idealism noticeably easier.

Unlike materialism, idealistic philosophy has appeared in various "traditions," reflecting either different psychological emphases and/or national-cultural characteristics. It will be useful to mention these traditions immediately, not only as a basis for later reference to them, but also because they provide an "ostensive definition" of idealism, a "pointing out" just which philosophies are generally accepted in this category. The major traditions are 1) Taoism, the native idealism of China, its earliest writing the *Tao Teh King* by "Lao-tse" (c. 6th Cen. B.C.); and its later descendant Dhyana/Ch'an/Zen Buddhism. 2) "Brahman"-ism, the native idealism of India, found earliest in the (nearly undatable) *Upanishads*, and formalized into both the "pluralistic" Sāṅkhya-Yoga and the monistic (Advaita) Vendanta. 3) The "Platonic tradition" (including predecessors like Parmenides) which as "Neo-Platonism" later absorbed the previously independent "Stoic tradition" and which continued in both Near Eastern (e.g., Sufism) and Western forms to about the Seventeenth Century. 4) The "non-traditional" and individualistic idealists of Western Europe and America from about the Seventeenth Century to the present, including "Cartesians" such as Spinoza, et al., subjective epistemologists like Berkeley, and "Kantians" such as Hegel, et al., whose influence on the American Transcendentalists, strengthened by hypnotism's newly demonstrated power of the mind over the body, resulted in modern "New Thought" (Christian/Religious Science, etc.).[6]

The word "idealism" comes from the Platonic doctrine of "eternal Ideas" ("idea" is the actual Greek word) which precede all material appearances and themselves derive from the highest Idea, "the One" or "the Good." We can explain this philosophy therefore in two ways: On one hand, idealism almost always claims there is only one "Reality" (Tao, Brahman, Absolute Divine Mind, etc.); there is nothing else; even though to the human mind the world seems composed of nearly infinite things. But these are only "appearances," they come and go like dreams, and idealism demonstrates them to be merely expressions of the One Reality by a variety of cosmologies varying from one tradition to another. On the other hand, idealism almost always claims that only *mind* (consciousness, awareness, etc.) is reality and that what seems to be a material world exists only in our own mind, just as dreams seem at the moment to be a world outside us. These two claims converge toward the same intuition: there is only One Reality which is a kind of consciousness or Mind and within Which every other thing (thought) exists, or from Which all other things (thoughts) "emanate" and decline into Appearance.[7]

This One Reality is not alien to human beings. It is the same mind or consciousness that they have, and they are already portions of or emanations from It. When a person knows this unity of himself, or "his self," with the One, he is said to have found his real "Self." But most human beings continue living in the world of appearances, and idealism claims there can be no lasting satisfaction or happiness in the transient and dream-like experiences which constitute this world. True happiness can be found only by knowing one's Self and by communing or uniting with the One Reality. This is a subjective motivation; but there is also a metaphysical one: just as upon finding we are in error we seek to rectify it by discovering the truth, so also universally error tends to move toward truth, not vice versa. The movement from the "error" or unreality of transient appearances to the truth of the real Self is a necessary tendency, and some idealists interpret the efforts of all animals and human beings as simply the subconscious strivings of lesser minds toward the One. The One Reality is the "Good" therefore not only as the highest happiness or bliss but also as the inevitable Goal of all consciousness.[8]

To specify idealism's attitude to homosexuality we must distinguish the movement of the human mind to the One into two seemingly complementary efforts: first there is the *turning away from* the distractions of the world of appearances, and secondly there is the *progress toward* the Goal itself. But there are a limited number of idealistic traditions which have emphasized only the first, the withdrawal from worldly sensations and desires generally called "asceticism," implying that the ascetic achieves a state of consciousness which is already akin to the One Reality. The (Hinayana) Buddhist "Nirvāna/Nibbāna" (desirelessness) and the Stoic "apatheia" (Eng. apathy, or emotionlessness) are examples; (both terms contain a negative prefix in the original languages).[9] But since asceticism recommends as little involvement in worldly affairs, sensual desires, etc. as possible, it is clearly homoïsic; that is, it makes no difference whether we are being urged to give up heterosexual or homosexual attachments. It is as if a vegetarian were asked which he avoided more, beef or pork; he would answer that they are completely equal to him, namely that he avoided both; he might further add that anyone who felt there was a difference between beef and pork was evidently still attracted to one or the other and so not yet completely a vegetarian! Similarly the (e.g.) Buddhist or Stoic devotee would say that anyone distinguishing between heterosexual and homosexual desires was still involved in the distracting appearance of such desires and therefore did not yet understand the meaning of "Nirvāna" or "apatheia."

But what about the majority of idealistic traditions which, in addition to a program of withdrawal from appearances, cultivate positive techniques by which the individual can experience a hint or revelation of, communion or even union with the One Reality? The answer depends on the technique(s) that are advocated, and there are many possibilities, but it seems that they all fall into three categories (and their combinations):

1) The inner-intuitive technique (found, e.g., in Rāja Yoga and Vedanta almost to the exclusion of other methods), where all effort is concentrated within, by closing one's eyes and ears as it were, to attain that highest (or deepest) point of one's self which is the real Self (Yoga's Purusha," Vedanta's "Ātman"), and to grasp this Self intuitively as the only reality, or as the very substance of the One Reality.[10] This technique is a positive and strenuous effort; but because it focusses attention entirely within and totally away from everything else around us, it involves the same "turning away from" worldly affairs and interpersonal relationships, and so the same attitude to homosexuality, as asceticism. That is, insofar as any idealism recommends the inner-intuitive technique of attaining the One as the *only* method, it too will be homoïsic, since any attachment to another person, whether heterosexual or

homosexual, would equally distract from the goal of knowing one's Self or its identity with the One.

2) The aesthetic technique (found, e.g., in Taoism and Zen Buddhism as a primary though not exclusive method), where attention is focussed on all of what appears around us as "Nature" or "the World" in a quietly receptive effort to "feel" Its totality and unity, and our kinship or unity with It, including whatever other personal aesthetic experiences might contribute to this awareness.[11] And 3) the passionate-emotional technique (found, e.g., in Sufism and the "psychedelic mysticism" of the recent "beat/hip" generations), where the whole consciousness is dynamically and aggressively directed toward an ideal or compelling experience, a symbol or even a person, which serves to inspire, enthuse (Gr. "enthousiazein": to be filled with the divine) and instill in the devotee a sense of communing or uniting with it, a foretaste or actual instance of uniting with the One.[12] These two techniques should be considered together because any idealism in which either or both of them enter *even as partial* components will imply a (qualified) homophilia! Let us therefore analyze them carefully: The aesthetic technique claims that any experience enhancing our feeling of kinship or unity with the World is a means of reaching an awareness of our unity with the One. For example, imagine a panoramic landscape (cf. the great Taoist/Zen landscape painters of the Sung and related periods in China and Japan), or any feeling of kinship with Nature, like a "beautiful" (that is, spiritually-aesthetically stimulating) flower, or a "beautiful" *person*. Now this "beautiful person" could be of the same or opposite sex, depending on one's sexual orientation; but whatever this be, only a beautiful person *congenial* to one's orientation can be the appropriately elevating aesthetic object! In an abstract sense this could be called a homoïsic (and heteroïsic) doctrine since "it makes no difference whether a person is straight or gay," he or she has the same potentiality for an aesthetic experience of this kind. But in the concrete, practical sense this philosophy should be considered homophilic (and heterophilic) because it is *a positive spiritual value for a homophile* to have a spiritually elevating *homophilic* aesthetic experience, (and for a heterosexual to have such a heterophilic experience). (To remove any lingering doubt as to the propriety of the "gay life" in idealism, we should repeat that human consciousness is a portion of or emanation from the One Reality; all "sexual-orientations" therefore are already contained in the One, Its "Divine Mind" is "pansexual," i.e. "straight, gay, bi" and so on.) Turning to the passionate-emotional technique, it claims that any object of passionate devotion can offer a revelation of communion or union with the One. This "object," as mentioned, can be an ideal, person, etc., and in the latter

case the person selected must be congenial of course to one's sexual orientation, while "passionate devotion" will become synonymous with words like "erotic-rapture" or "love." Here again this could more abstractly be called a homoïsic and heteroïsic teaching; but insofar as a spiritually-passionate, erotically-rapturous *homophilic love* is hereby *positively recommended to homophiles* as a means of elevating consciousness into the One Reality, this "doctrine of idealistic love" is truly homophilic (i.e., relative to homophiles).

To summarize idealism's two basic attitudes to homosexuality: if the "ethical pattern(s)" are *only* "the turning away from the distractions of appearances" and/or *only* "the inner-intuitive technique of finding the Self or its identity with the One," then the idealism will be purely homoïsic. But if the idealism involves, *even if only partly* and in combination with the other pattern(s), the technique(s) of "aesthetic contemplation that stimulates the feeling of unity with the World" and/or "passionate-emotional devotion as a revelation of communion or union with the One," then it will be an example of (qualified or relative) homophilia.

As in the case of materialism, efforts have been made to "politicize" idealism; but these efforts are even more inconsistent, in spite of some famous names like Plato and Hegel having been involved.[13] The inconsistency of the expression "idealistic government" is revealed by recalling that in this philosophy there is only one human goal: to turn away from appearances and return toward the One Reality. "The State," "society" or any government has no ethical purpose unless it can help its individual members achieve this awareness of the One. But how could any government do this? Only by leaving its people completely alone to discover their own spiritual needs and techniques! By comparison to governments already in existence therefore, idealism's political structure is a non-entity, a *non*-government, i.e., an "anarchy" ("no government" of anyone by anyone else). If, say, fifteen idealists decided to cooperate in matters of food, shelter, etc. so as to have greater freedom for their spiritual pursuits, then this "society" would be in existence for these fifteen people and for as long as any of them continued cooperating. (Nor would they require a "police power" as in Hobbes's example, since there is no need for violence or trickery against others when the goal of life lies only in the Mind.) But any government that might restrict total human liberty is immediately inconsistent with the doctrine that consciousness must be continuously free to move toward the One, so we will not need to discuss a so-called "idealistic government's" implications for homosexuality.

*Solipsism* (Latin "solus" [only] + "ipse" [oneself] is based on one idea: "Only I exist." Its source is the epistemological intuition that "everything I know is what *I* know," or "for *me* there is nothing that I don't know" (since if I could assert "there is something I don't know" to this extent I would already know it). Called the "egocentric predicament," this problem of knowledge is taken seriously by solipsism and results in the metaphysical conclusion "I ≡ reality," that is, "I am all reality and all reality is me."

No other idea *necessarily* follows. Since the solipsist is all of reality, any other statement he or she makes, no matter how strange it may seem to others, is true for him. He could be a materialist, an idealist, a dualist, or any even seemingly inconsistent combination, simply by the fiat of his decision; and as for homosexuality, he could be homophobic, homophilic, homoïsic, or any combination of these he desires! Solipsism's attitude to homosexuality therefore is "unpredictable."

At this point one might ask, "Why bother to mention solipsism?" to which there are at least two answers: First, this philosophy, although infrequently espoused openly, has been a constant potentiality in Eastern and Western thought, the subject of many efforts at refutation by those who sense its "dangers," and yet is almost impregnable to attack.[14] Secondly, though an extremely homophobic form of solipsism can be imagined and some day may appear in writing, the same holds true for an extremely homophilic form of solipsism. So why not get this going immediately?! It's easy; a solipsist asserts or denies reality as he or she wishes. Start with "other homophiles," particularly "other homophiles congenial to me" (you, the solipsist), and claim them as "the only real creations of my mind, while everything else is comparatively unreal, and some things" (homophobes?) "don't exist at all." In this way a totally, passionately homophilic philosophy can be developed suited to your tastes and unfettered by any of the traditional philosophical requirements because based on nothing but the solipsistic principle "only I am reality."[15]

II. Complex cases (dualisms).

Dualism can be defined as maintaining the ultimate independence of two distinct types of reality, one always being the "material" in the common-sense meaning of the word, the other being called, for convenience, the "non-material," but naturally more difficult to describe. We should in fact distinguish at least three kinds of "non-material realities" (making at least three types of dualism): A. "spirit(s)," a kind of personality that can exist apart from a material body; B. "personalities in bodies," which can exist only within a body;

and C. "formal causes," borrowing the term from Aristotelian philosophy to apply to any non-material essence or quality which usually, though not necessarily, exists in close connection with its individual material expression. Placing dualism under "complex cases" may surprise a person who believes, for instance, in God's creation of the world according to Genesis, for we are so accustomed to this type of doctrine that even non-believers fully understand it. But dualism has a great number of varieties with equally various consequences for homosexuality; on this ground alone it must be separated from the comparatively uniform philosophies already discussed. Moreover it poses several difficult technical problems. Some of these — the metaphysical problem of how the non-material and material can influence each other, the epistemological topic of how the human mind gains knowledge of non-material things, and the psychological problem of how the human body can interact with the mind/soul/spirit — are not directly pertinent to homosexuality and will be omitted for reasons of space. But the "ethical problem," namely, *how to determine the goal of life* for a human being within a dualistic world-view, is not only difficult and complex but obviously of crucial importance for clarifying its attitude to homosexuality. Throughout this section therefore we will be *probing and searching* into the difficult question of what are the ethical consequences for homosexuality of this or that dualistic view; the results will be a series of suggested, tentative hypotheses.[16]

A. Belief in some kind of "spirit(s)" has been almost universal. Without implying any theory of derivation, we will start from the "earliest" or simplest cases of spirits and move toward the "later" more complex ones. (The first two types are pre-sexual but are important as a foundation.)[17] 1) Spirits of inanimate objects that are striking (but non-functional for human needs) such as unusually shaped rocks, mountains, etc.: What might be the ethical consequences when a striking rock formation is felt to be inhabited by a spirit? This rock undoubtedly would not be approached like an ordinary rock; rather whoever nears it would feel a special sense of *awe* — the rock itself is in some way *sacred*, in fact its sacredness may be so great that it becomes *taboo* to approach it. 2) Spirits of plants, trees, etc., particularly those used for food: If a plant has its own spirit, the same sense of awe will be felt in its presence. But if a person wants to use this plant for food, tearing off its leaves and fruit, even killing the plant itself, he will experience a conflict between his inner awe of the sacred/taboo spirit of the plant which he is offending by violating, and his clear need to eat. He undoubtedly will feel *guilt*, an unpleasant subjective condition which automatically suggests its removal through an act of *atonement*. His atonement could be a self-punishment unrelated to the plant, but more likely he may wish to appease the angered spirit directly by *propitiation*. (Yet he cannot promise the plant's spirit never to eat this plant or others like it again). So perhaps he will make a (fertilizing?) offering to a still-living plant of the same species; or, knowing the significance of a seed, he may plant it to insure future growth, stimulating the plant's *fertility*, not for his own selfish purpose (the origin of agriculture), but rather in this case as an act of atonement.

3) Spirits of animals, fish, etc., particularly those used for food: This case is similar to the preceding one. Thus a person who, for food, kills an animal he believes has its own spirit, would feel a sense of guilt and need for atoning propitiation; nor could he promise to give up killing these animals in the future. He might therefore make an offering to the animal's spirit, or try to increase that species' fertility. Let's examine the latter case: animals (this would be less true for birds or fish), being structured much like human beings, (and assuming the "facts of reproduction" were already known), would be understood to have "fertility" in their sex organs; "increasing animal fertility" therefore would mean either mating a male and female of the same species, or simply any effort to stimulate their sex organs with this end directly or symbolically in mind. Thus the beginnings of zoerasty! But here this term does not mean the use of animals merely for satisfying one's own urges (which may be a later result), but rather the propitiatory effort to provide the animals with sexual excitement and its associated fertility, motivated by guilt and contrition over the offending of their spirit(s) by their being continuingly killed for food. This is *propitiatory zoerasty*, and it could easily be either heterosexual or homosexual. Thus a contrite, say, male butcher of sheep may try to mate a ewe with a ram as an atoning reparation, or he may propitiatingly stimulate the sex organs of either a ewe *or* a ram, which latter would be a kind of *homosexual zoerasty*. Insofar therefore as the belief in spirits includes only those categories already discussed (inanimate things, plants and/or animals) and not beyond, its attitude to propitiatory zoerasty, it is suggested, will be homoïsic.

4) Spirits of human beings who are currently living (*not* implying continuation after death): The awe and reverence toward these sacred/taboo "human spirits" would be even greater than that for the animals. Yet in almost all societies there has usually been plenty of killing of other human beings, as in warfare, vendetta, cannibalism, etc. The inner conflict between the reverence for the sacred spirit and the clear violation of the taboo by slaying its body often resulted in a very strong, deep-seated guilt in the slayer's heart and a

consequent need for atonement. (Nor in view of the continuing possibility of war, etc. could he promise to abstain from this slaughter.) — But suddenly the analogy with the previous sections disintegrates! For human beings are not felt to be grouped into "species" governed by overall spirits as plants and animals are, but each "living human spirit" is considered autonomous with its own body, and not continuing after death, cannot be propitiated. Is there any other atonement possible? We recall (above, section 2 on plants) that there could be also a "self-punishment" unrelated to the spirit involved. The atonement for killing the body of a "living human spirit" therefore would have to be of this type, a self-punishment or, what is the same thing, a punishment accepted by the guilty party but administered by another person delegated for this purpose. This idea becomes all the more interesting when we reflect that warfare (this would be less true of vendettas, cannibalism, etc.) has been nearly universally waged by males against males, that is, it has been an intra-sexual phenomenon. In the environment of warfare, the reverence for the sacred human spirit, the violation of that spirit by killing its body and the subsequent deep-seated guilt and need for atonement would all have occurred in a psychological ambience that was male intra-sexual (or "homosexual" in the most abstract sense of the word). So if and when the atoning self-punishment was not directly self-inflicted but administered by a delegate, there is the inevitable suggestion here that it would have been courted by a guilty male seeking it to be inflicted at the hands of another male who, temporarily at least, would play the role of the punisher. This would be the foundation for what could easily become a purely voluntary homosexual sado-masochism. And since in this case of warfare the likelihood of a homosexual relationship is very much greater than a heterosexual one, we can suggest that, wherever there is a belief in spirits up to the "living-human" level and not beyond, we can find the possibility of a *sado-masochistic homophilia.*[18]

5) Ancestor spirits: A wholly new attitude seems to develop with the belief in the *continuation* of the "human spirits" after their bodies have died. For reverence to or propitiation of these spirits must now also continue; and although it might seem that any living person could reverence any or all deceased spirits, practically speaking only their direct decendants are specifically required to remember them. They are truly "ancestors" therefore; a so-called "ancestor spirit" who no longer has any descendants us usually a forgotten spirit! Clearly it immediately becomes crucial for each living person to have as many descendants as possible lest, after death, his spirit some day be in the fearful limbo of having no one remember or reverence him. This is a powerful incentive to have many children and so to enter heterosexual marriage. The belief in ancestor spirits therefore is entirely heterosexually

oriented and could very easily regard homosexuality as a waste of reproductive power and an affront to all the possible ancestor spirits whose memory might be blotted out thereby. Although this is our first confrontation with a truly homophobic philosophy, it must be kept in mind from now on. For there is a tendency among the "later" beliefs in spirits to retain characteristics from previous stages, so that all the remaining types of "spirit dualisms" presented below, in spite of their own specific qualities, will continue to be tinged with this apparently fundamental "ancestor-spirit homophobia."

6) Hero(ine) — spirits, i.e., outstanding ancestors: A hero-spirit (according to the belief) was at one time a living person but no longer needs to have descendants because his deeds and charisma are so great that he is reverenced, and his tale is retold by, *all* the people who acknowledge him. Moreover, there are certain isolated examples of homosexual heroes and heroines.[19] But, as mentioned, if this stage of belief is the "latest yet achieved," any possible homophilia stimulated by these would be in conflict with the still overwhelming number of ordinary ancestor spirits and its consequent strong homophobia.

7) Polytheism or "belief in many gods": There is no sharp line between a "great spirit" and a "god"; heroes were already equivalent to "demi-gods," and Euhemerus' theory (c. 300 B.C.) was that all (Greek) gods were only heroes originally. Usually a "god" has a distinct personality of his or her own and may be only casually connected with this or that natural or psychological phenomenon. Furthermore, like heroes, the gods are generally known through stories or "myths" handed down, spoken or written, about them. The number of possible types of gods is therefore very large. For example, a famous world-wide "gestalt" or syndrome is that of the god(s) of agricultural fertility, human fertility, and human immortality; here the story is recurrently told of the god who dies and is reborn, or who alternates between death and life, thus directly symbolizing and guaranteeing in various degrees both agricultural fertility and human immortality (human fertility however somewhat indirectly and more by association with the other two). But this far-flung belief, still very pervasive up to the present, doesn't seem to have any clear implications for homosexuality.[20] And when we turn to the specific gods or symbols of sexuality, such as Dionysus and Priapus in the West, the Lingam and Yoni in India, etc., we find a heterosexual rather than a homosexual interpretation.[21] On the other hand, if we consider the *priests* (witch-doctors, shamans, etc.) of these polytheistic or spirit religions, we discover a converse tendency: here the ordinary worshipper's desire for a human intermediary with the spiritual realm has favored the development of a spirit-oriented personality that is expected to

be "different" -- unworldly, even eccentric, given to visions, dramatic pronouncements and so on — an ideal opportunity for both male and female homosexuals![22]

8) Henotheism and monotheism: A transitional doctrine, "henotheism" is a polytheism where one of the gods becomes supreme, or in the reverse direction, a monotheism where the one god develops many divine helpers, which occurred in certain branches of Christianity and in the movement from Hinayana to Mahāyana Buddhism. Monotheism of course is "the belief in the existence of only one (personal) God." In both cases what was previously perhaps oral mythology tended to be written down into "sacred scriptures," sometimes considered "divine revelation." These scriptures are generally very old (even most of the newer ones, such as the Book of Mormon or Bāha'u'llāh's writings, are firmly grounded upon the older ones), and therefore like their linguistic function of preserving old words and forms they conserve older patterns such as (for our topic) the need to perpetuate the memory of ancestors by having as many children as possible in the face of high infant mortality.

For an example of a sacred scripture we may concentrate on the Hebrew-Christian-Muslim tradition's common foundation, the Old Testament. In this scripture there are at least seven sentences (Lev. 18,22; 20,13; Deut. 23,18; I Kings 14,24; 15,12; 22,47; and II Kings 23,7; Masoretic numbering) which specifically, and negatively, refer to male homosexuality. In addition to the general suggestion already made, that this homophobic attitude was based on reverence for ancestor spirits, a more immediate reason is strongly implied in Lev. 18,27: After verse 22 ("You shall not lie with a male as with a woman, it is an abomination"), verse 27 continues, "For all of these abominations the men of the land did, who were before you, so that the land became defiled." That is, homosexuality had been current among the indigenous Canaanites, into whose land the Hebrews were at that time moving, and from whom they were very concerned to differentiate themselves, lest the native culture threaten the survival of their group by infiltrating their own distinctive customs — an infiltration which occurred in part as the four sentences from Kings reveal. Now the Canaanite culture at a very early period had involved fraternal polyandry, or the plurality of brother-husbands to one wife, which made homophilic relations among these brothers living together conveniently easy and as natural as fraternal affection itself. Secondly, Canaanite religion was of the agricultural/animal/human fertility type, with a conspicuous place for the sex goddess Ashtart, also known as "Kadesh" (holy), and a sex or fertility god Lahmu; sexual/fertility rites therefore were naturally part of this religion. The combination of these two factors produced male as well as female "temple courtesans," the Hebrew word for whom was "kādēsh" (masculine singular), that is, "holy or cloistered male," and it is this word which has been so pejoratively translated as "sodomite(s)" by the King James and other Versions.[23] Thus what for the Canaanites was a natural expression of their fertility cult as influenced by an ancient polyandry, became for the Hebrews an "abomination," based (it is suggested) on two needs felt necessary to their nation's existence: the retention of their traditional culture in a new land, and the remembrance of ancestral spirits, the purity of whose geneaological lineage indeed was of utterly absorbing interest to them (cf. Gen. 25, 31-34, Esau's selling Jacob his primogeniture, as an example).

In very recent years there have arisen new "gay churches and synagogues" whose general ethical program remains within the Hebrew-Christian tradition but which refuse to accept the homophobic pronouncements in the Old Testament (and their reflections in the New Testament). Since almost the whole orthodox law of the Old Testament was thoroughly reinterpreted and re-cast by the Talmud, and transformed if not nullified by Christianity (including two of the "most sacred Ten Commandments" — "graven images" and "seventh-day Sabbath"), it shouldn't be difficult for gay Jews or Christians to demonstrate to heterosexual Jews and Christians how the essential teachings of these religions ought to transcend any homophobia. And there are isolated homophilic scriptural passages such as the stories of David and Johnathan (I Sam. 20,41; II Sam. 1,26) or Ruth and Naomi (Ruth 14-17) or even Jesus and his "beloved disciple" John (John 13,23) which should help mollify or neutralize the rage of the homophobes. But, as all know, these gay churches and synagogues are being met with continuing hostility.

B. "Personalities in bodies" is a phrase meant to suggest the very frequent attitude of "taking people seriously," being concerned about their opinions, that is, dealing with human personalities *as if* separate from their bodies but without actually thinking of them as in any way continuing after death. Unlike the "belief in living human spirits" (above, section 4), this philosophy does not involve spirits or any other non-material reality, and may be considered the metaphysically weakest type of dualism. But it is ethically strong: these human personalities are of utmost importance in the business of daily living; their opinions can "make or break" a person, i.e., can bestow on him "high status" or "low status." We might call this philosophy "status dualism" therefore, since the goal of life is to retain or increase one's status (or "honor") by remaining in everyone's good opinion, and to avoid blame, shame or "stigma" by falling into general contempt, very much like the "other-directed" personality-type proposed and analyzed by David Riesman in *The Lonely Crowd* (New Haven, 1950, pp. 22 on), a kind of person who gains his or her values only from the members of his immediate peer-group because of his intense desire to conform to their expectations, avoid their disapproval, and obtain a sense of their support.

Since this is purely imitative of others, status dualism cannot ordinarily *create* an attitude to homosexuality, but it can very tenaciously *maintain* whatever happens to be current. And because most current social attitudes are homophobic (for whatever reason), status dualism and its "other-directed" devotees constitute the major social problem for nearly all gay people, namely, how to avoid "exposure" by staying "in the closet" and so on.[24] On the other hand, the same sense of "support" that is offered by the peer-group in status dualism can be developed among homophiles too; they can support one another, and this would seem to justify every gay effort toward and every successful instance of mutual contact, yea, even the bushes, baths, and tearooms! For no matter how "primitive" or "oppressive" these environments may seem, any such meeting between gay persons, even just a conversation between an openly gay man and gay woman, provides a measure of support which counteracts the current "made in Straightland" stigma. And extending this, increasing the number of gays involved, parlaying the momentum into clubs, "cruising areas," whole neighborhoods, etc., could actually create a new *homophilic* version of status dualism, with the same "personalities in bodies" and "other-directed" individuals, but now operating within a framework of values that are homophilic (or at least homoïsic). The Alpine County project in California (which failed) and the maintenance of Cherry Grove on Fire Island, New York as a gay resort (which has been successful for more than 25 years), are examples of environments for such a homophilic status dualism. This philosophy therefore, though mostly homophobic in historical fact, is not inherently so, and can become homoïsic or even homophilic with proper planning and effort.

C. As noted, the term "formal cause(s)" has been borrowed from Aristotelian metaphysics; it means a characteristic of a thing that is co-existent with and inseparable from its material substance or "material cause" which in turn individualizes it from all other identical examples; (e.g., the identical "form of a dime" exists in every dime but the actual metal is different in each one). A very similar metaphysics existed in the "Li School" of Neo-Confucianism (Eleventh Cen. A.D. and after), where there was the same dualism between the matter (ch'i) and form (li) of every particular thing; this type of philosophy therefore has appeared at many times and places.[25] But for our purposes we must ask, how is the form of any particular thing known or discovered? And in both Aristotelian and Neo-Confucian "formal-cause dualism" the answer is that first we experience individual things, finding the characteristics or forms many of them have in common, and then we isolate these forms in our mind and speak of them as logically independent from the material substance of which the original things are also made. So the theory of knowledge for formal-cause dualism is actually the same kind of "empiricism," or "sense perception leading to inductive generalization," which is so consistent with the philosophy of *materialism*, but which in dualism immediately runs the danger of being overly pretentious, as if some new kind of knowledge is being gained of a realm of truth which is, however, only an abstraction from our own experience. For example, what is the "form or true nature of a cow?" In materialism we understood that nothing has any constant "nature"; there are cows and cows, and animals transitional between cows and something else — there is no such thing as a "normal cow." But in formal-cause dualism we evidently look at familiar cows and, generalizing from our experience, develop the idea of what is the "true form of a normal cow." Clearly nothing comes out of this kind of philosophy that was not already put into it! Therefore, if a formal-cause dualist lives in a society that regards heterosexuality as proper and "normal," he will of course find the "form or true nature of a human being" to be heterosexual, so that homosexuality becomes "deviation from the form or norm." But if that dualist lived his whole life in Cherry Grove on Fire Island, New York, he would undoubtedly have exactly the converse definition! The conclusion is that formal-cause dualism, for all its subtlety and traditional philosophical importance, is like status dualism: it cannot create any attitude to homosexuality; it can only maintain some attitude already in existence for other reasons.

III. Summary and prognosis.

We have found consistent materialism always to be homoïsic; consistent idealism always to be at least homoïsic when involving only its pattern(s) of "turning away from distractions" and/or "inner-intuitive technique for attaining

Self/Reality," but relatively homophilic when involving any element of its "aesthetic" and/or "passionate-emotional" techniques; while solipsism we found to be unpredictable. In the case of dualism our conclusions are more complex; they can be summarized by suggesting that 1) a true homoïsaia is found only in the "earliest" forms of the belief in spirits, where inanimate, plant and/or animal spirits are revered. 2) One stage beyond, the belief in spirits of living human beings, may have generated a type of homophilic "sado-masochistic" (i.e., dominant/submissive) pattern based on male intra-sexual guilt and atonement. 3) With the belief in ancestor spirits a distinctive form of homophobia becomes developed which permeates all "later" stages of spirit-dualism up to the concluding monotheisms. 4) Rare exceptions may be found among these homophobic types, such as homophilic heroes, gods, or isolated passages in scriptures. 5) Philosophies such as "status" and "formal-cause" dualisms have no inherent significance for homosexuality and merely reflect already existing attitudes. 6) Actual homoïsic/homophilic examples of status dualism and even Hebrew-Christian monotheism can be and have been developed by gay people.

What are the chances of reducing or removing the world-wide homophobia based on the feeling that our ancestors depend on direct descendants for remembrance and thus for their happiness in the afterlife? I suggest that the idea of *reincarnation* (in which after death we do not enter a "single place of afterlife" but rather repeatedly return to one life, or "plane of existence," (after another) would have two helpful, intertwining results. First, it would mean that everyone has innumerable parents and other forebears, a different set for each of our past and future lives, thereby greatly reducing the uniqueness of our "obligation" to our forebears of *this* life. Secondly, reincarnation implies that our deceased ancestors are already busily living other lives, and are no more remembering "us, their former descendants," than we are currently remembering "our former descendants in previous lives"; and if they do not remember us, they will not *need* to be remembered by us. I suggest, therefore, that the more a reincarnation doctrine supplants the belief of a "single afterlife," the less emphasis will be placed on the production of descendants via heterosexual marriage, that is, the less homophobia.

For readers who are religiously Hebrew-Christian-Muslim, I offer a second suggestion: the idea of *subjective revelation*. This means that God has been, is, and will continue to be revealing Himself, even if in small ways, to individuals throughout the ages. Any person reflecting on his or her life and finding the "hand of God" in it would be justified in accepting this intuition as "God's voice speaking to him" or a "revelation." On July 2, 1969, a man calling himself "Om" was lecturing in New York City on how God had revealed to him that the purpose of life was to have as much sexual intercourse as possible, as a divine ritual of communion with God; and when I asked him if this applied to homosexuals also, he said "yes." Similarly any gay person who sincerely feels that his or her life as a homophile is rewarding enough to see the "hand of God" in it may accept this as his "subjective revelation." And if increasingly many gay people have this same intuition, these subjective revelations will accumulate into a historically new "objective revelation." Bāha'u'llāh, Joseph Smith, Mary Baker Eddy, et al., all have comparatively recently proclaimed their own "objective revelations." So the time may be approaching for a new, objective Divine Revelation of homophilia.

The two preceding paragraphs have been "coping with homophobia"; but what are the chances for a truly homophilic philosophy, one that asserts *gay superiority?* To construct a consistent homophilia the following seem to be requisites: 1) The keystone must be the "essence of homosexuality," that is, the idea of "identity or great similarity" as compared to the heterosexual "difference." 2) To insure the significant use of this "essence," the importance of interpersonal relationships, where alone this distinction properly applies, must be demonstrated. 3) Any philosophy which is inherently non-committal (homoïsic/unpredictable/imitative) must be rejected as an unsafe foundation; (thus the suggestion made earlier of a solipsistic homophilia is vulnerable to solipsism's unpredictability which could just as well spawn homophobia). For a safe foundation we have discovered apparently only two philosophies that could be called homophilic: certain types of idealism, and the belief in (but not "beyond") "living human spirits." Here I will select only the former as perhaps less hypothetical and more currently possible. The reader will recall that in idealism the "aesthetic" and "passionate-emotional" techniques both placed a *cosmic* value on interpersonal relationships as one means of elevating consciousness toward the One Reality. The first method stresses a quiet, receptive appreciation of a "spiritually-beautiful person" who could induce an inner reverberation of a "beautifully-spiritual experience"; the second stresses a dynamic, aggressive love or erotic-rapture leading to an intimate communion or union with another person as a foretaste or revelation of the One. In both cases there is need for the *deepest* kind of relationship, the innermost sympathetic or empathic stimulation and/or response. Sympathy ("feeling with") and empathy ("feeling inside", i.e., the almost physical sensation that we experience when someone, e.g., cuts his finger) are based on similarity; the more similar any two people are, mentally/emotionally (sympathy) or physically (empathy), the more easily they can reverberate or commune with each other. This is the "essence of homosexuality" of course, identity or great similarity. We can suggest therefore that homophilic relationships are better able to produce "spiritually elevating aesthetic experiences" and/or "erotically rapturous feelings of communion or union" than heterophilic ones. And in the world-view of idealism this means that homophiles are more predisposed to attaining the One Reality than heterophiles, or what is actually the same thing, that the One Reality manifests Itself more immediately and clearly in the gay consciousness than in the straight one. Whatever the reader's opinions of this kind of idealism may be, it is at least an example of a consistently-constructed doctrine of gay superiority!

## NOTES

1The word "homosexuality" has two disadvantages: first, it combines the Greek prefix "homo-" (the same, as opposed to "hetero-," other, different) with the Latin root "sexus," a faulty construction to begin with; but more importantly, in our language "sexual" hardly connotes mere anatomical gender (the original intention) but rather stimulation of the sex organs or "sex," and as gay people know, this is only one of the many motivations for homosexuality; but the words "homosexual-ity" will remain useful for a vague, generalized reference. "Homoeroticism," which is purely Greek in derivation, also mostly suggests sexuality; though "erōs" meant love in general, in English "erotic" now implies sex. But "homophilia," from the Gr. verb "philein" (to like, kiss, love), has remained in conformity with its original meaning (helped by the root's continued use as, e.g., the suffix "-phile" as in "Anglophile"); so also the concrete noun "homophile" and the adjective "homophilic." In this chapter these words will have a connotation slightly different from "homosexual-ity"; they will connote a *favorable* attitude to one's own homosexuality as in the popular word "gay(ness)." "Homophobia" is actually an abbreviation for "homophilephobia," since strictly speaking it would mean "dislike for those of one's own sex," clearly not the intention; "male homophobes" do not "dislike other males" but rather "dislike those (male or female) who are attracted to their own sex." For the attitude that is truly neutral about homosexuality, Liddell & Scott's *Greek-English Lexicon* (9th ed., Oxford, 1940; p. 836) gives a somewhat rare but valid noun "isaia" (equality) which has the advantage of only 3 syllables like "philia" and "phobia"; [other, longer possibilities are the 4-syllable "isaxia" (equal worth), and the 5-syllable "isomereia" (equal share), "isonomia" (equal rights) and "isotimia" (equal privilege)]. This gives us the abstract noun "homoïsaia" (spelled with the diaeresis to avoid suggesting the prefix "homoi-," similar to); but notice that this *also* is an abbreviation for "homophileïsaia," since it doesn't mean "neutrality to those of one's own sex" but "neutrality to those who are attracted to their own sex." The adjective "homoïsic" is based on the analogy with "homophilic" and "homophobic"; but the concrete noun should also be "homoïsic" since there is nothing here corresponding to "-phile" or "-phobe"; (nor would "homoïse" be acceptable! and there are many cases in Eng. where the Gr. adjective ending "ikos" serves also as a noun, such as "mystic," etc.).

2Because "materialism" has frequently been used derogatorily by this philosophy's opponents, its adherents have sought other terms, such as "naturalism." Wishing to avoid lurking value-judgments, I will use both words interchangeably as needed, and synonymously.

3For a classic presentation of these ideas see Lucretius, *De Rerum Natura*, Book I, lines 216 f. (basic building blocks of matter); 330 (empty space); 420 f. (nothing but matter and space); 482 f. (solid, eternal atoms); II, 83 (motion of atoms); 402 f. (sensation, pleasure and pain); III, 161 (material nature of mind & "soul"); 417 (mortality of soul). Hedonistic doctrines are found in Epicurus, *Letter to Menoeceus* (e.g., *The Philosophy of Epicurus*, tr. Geo. Strodach; Evanston, Ill., 1963); pp. 178-185.

4"Do as you wish," the only rule in Rabelais' Abbey of Thélème (*Gargantua and Pantagruel*, Book I, Ch. 57).

5"I authorize and give up my right of governing myself to this man or to this assembly of men, on the condition that thou give up thy right to him and authorize all his actions in like manner" (*Leviathan*, p. 132 in orig. 1651 ed., rpt. Oxford, 1909).

6I have omitted the Buddhist tradition because, like the Hebrew-Christian-Muslim tradition, it has been an intermixture of both monistic and dualistic elements, though with greater emphasis on the idealistic/monistic than the H-C-M. Both religions have idealists such as Vasubandhu and Angelus Silesius, but they were more influenced by "Brahman"-ism and Neo-Platonism respectively than by their religions.

7The exposition is naturally abbreviated and some of these generalizations may appear untrue now of this, now of that example. Thus 1) "Tao" was first conceived as the "Essence of Nature" more than a "mind"; but Chuang-tse (only 2 cen. after Lao-tse) already stressed the relativity of waking and dreaming (II, p. 197 in Legge's trans., see note below), the primacy of mind, and Tao more as "Essence of Thought." 2) Sānkhya/Yoga is called "pluralistic" since each person's self (Purusha) is numerically separate from every other, but without *any* further qualitative difference and so hardly distinct from Vedanta which reduces "all selves" to "One Self." 3) Spinoza is sometimes not called an idealist because he makes "mind" and *"extension"* co-equal "attributes of God or Substance"; but since this One Reality is prior to both, It could Itself be grasped only by the highest kind of consciousness or Mind.

[8]Cf. the Neoplatonist Proclus: "O Absolutely Transcendent . . . all keen desires or lusts, all painful passions are yearnings only for Thee" ("Hymn to God"); and "Therefore the whole of our life is a struggle toward that Vision" (*Commentary on Plato's Parmenides*); both quotes from L. J. Rosán, *The Philosophy of Proclus: the Final Phase of Ancient Thought* (New York, 1949), p. 204.

[9]"What now is the Noble Truth of the origin of suffering? It is craving . . . What now is the Noble Truth of the extinction of suffering? It is the complete fading away and extinction of this craving . . . wherever in the world there are delightful and pleasurable things, there this craving may vanish" (*Digha Nikaya*, 22, tr. the Bhikkhu Nyanatiloka (1935), found in *A Buddhist Bible*, ed. Dwight Goddard; Dutton: Boston, 1938). And from the Stoic Epictetus, *Discourses*, Book II, Ch. 17 (tr. Geo. Long; Philadelphia, 189_): " 'I desire to be free from passion and perturbation; . . . not only when I am awake, but also when I am asleep . . . filled with wine [or] melancholy.' Man, you are a god."

[10]Patanjali, *Yoga Sutras*, Bk. I, sutra 51; III, 51,56; IV, 33. Also the Vedantist Śankara's "Blessed am I; I have attained the consummation of my life . . . I am that Self-effulgent, Transcendent Ātman . . . I am verily that Brahman, the One without a second . . . I am the Universal, I am the All . . . " (*Vivekachudāmani*, tr. Swami Madhavananda; Mayavati, India, 1952; slokas 488, 507, 514, 516).

[11]This 2nd and the 3rd techniques' significance for homophilia suggests somewhat fuller quotation here and in the next quote. The Taoist Chuang-tse (*The Texts of Taoism*, tr. Jas. Legge; Oxford, 1891; rpt. Dover: N.Y., 1962; Book XIV, pp. 348-351) says: "You were celebrating, O Tī, a performance of music . . . in the open country near the Thung-thing Lake . . . The Perfect Music . . . showed the blended distinctions of the four seasons and the grand harmony of all things; . . . the brilliance of the sun and moon . . . like the music

of a forest produced by no visible form . . . This is what is called the music of Heaven, delighting the mind without the use of words." In *Zen and the Fine Arts* (Kodansha Ltd., 1971), Shin-ichi Hisamatsu derives all Zen arts from the "Formless Self" and demonstrates how they conversely stimulate awareness of this Self (pp. 51-52 esp.). A western example, Geo. Berkeley (*Principles of Human Knowledge*, Par. 148) writes: "We do at all times and in all places perceive manifest tokens of the Divinity — everything we see, hear, feel, or anywise perceive by Sense being a sign or effect of the power of God."

12The Sufi, Jelālu'ddīn Rūmī says, "O lovers, it is time to abandon the world: . . . With each moment a soul is setting off into the Void . . . O Soul, seek the Beloved, O friend, seek the Friend" ("Divani Shamsi Tabriz," tr. R.A. Nicholson; p. 55 in F.H. Davis, *Jelālu'ddīn Rūmī*, Sh. Muhammad Ashraf: Lahore, India, 1907). Shamsi Tabriz is said by Davis to have been Jelāl's homosexual lover (pp. 31-32). Another Sufi, Farīd al-Dīn 'Attār (*Readings from the Mystics of Islām*, ed. & tr. Margaret Smith; Luzac: London, 1950 & 1972; Pars. 88, 97) writes: "A third moth rose up, intoxicated with love, and threw himself violently into the candle's flame . . . As he entered completely into its embrace, his members became glowing red like the flame itself . . . In truth, it is the one who has lost . . . all trace of his own existence who has, at the same time, found knowledge of the Beloved . . . Now I am made one with Thee . . . I am Thou and Thou art I — nay, not I . . . I have become altogether Thou." A psychedelic example: "I took my pill [mescaline] at eleven . . . The Beatific Vision, *Sat Chit Ananda*, Being-Awareness-Bliss — for the first time I understood, not on the verbal level . . . but precisely and completely what those prodigious syllables referred to" (Aldous Huxley, *The Doors of Perception;* N.Y., 1954; pp. 16, 18.

13In the *Republic* (Stephanos II, 368) Plato slips into his doctrine of the "ideal society" ostensibly to illustrate the relationship of each individual's psychic elements to one another by "magnifying" this into the "larger and more visible picture" of a whole society, though in his philosophy "psyches" are real, mere collections of psyches are not (Hegel (*The phenomenology of Mind*, tr. Baillie, 2nd ed.; Allen & Unwin: London, 1931) clearly says "The goal . . . is Absolute Knowledge or Spirit" (last page, 808), while "state-power" (last mentioned on p. 535) "means nothing else than . . . a moment of self-conscious life, i.e., it *is* only by being sublated [transcended]."

14A famous presentation is Max Stirner, *Der Einzige und sein Eigenthum* (Leipzig, 1845; Eng. tr. S. Byington, *The Ego and Its Own*; N.Y., 1907 & 1918); also a recent defense by William Todd, *Analytical Solipsism* (Martinus Nijhoff: the Hague, 1968).

[15]The respective implications of materialism (neutrality), idealism (neutrality/favorability) and solipsism (unpredictability) for homosexuality would seem to be equally applicable to certain more specialized phenomena in the gay life such as transvestitism, pederasty and sado-masochism. Provided that every relationship is purely voluntary, I feel that the three "clear-cut" philosophies would have nothing different to say about these "specialized phenomena." (This will not hold true for the "more complex dualisms" below.)

[16]Why are dualistic ethics generally more obscure than the other philosophies? In the Fall of 1944, Prof. J. H. Randall, Jr. of Columbia U., himself a kind of Aristotelian dualist, in one of his lectures made a distinction between "holoscopic" and "meroscopic" world-views which contains an implied answer: a "holoscopic" (whole-viewing) system, he said, starts with universal principles, deducing all particulars from them (materialism, idealism, and solipsism are examples); a "meroscopic" (part-viewing) philosophy takes up the many questions of life first, then constructs a total outlook from the various answers found. The dualisms are usually meroscopic, and naturally we cannot swiftly discover a goal of life if we must first respond to the variety of questions that our lives apparently offer.

[17]See "Animism" in Hastings, *Encyclopedia of Religion and Ethics* (Edinburgh, 1908-22); the arrangement of categories is different from mine; also, the definition of "animism" in the *Schaff-Herzog Encyc. of Religious Knowledge* (N.Y., 1910-12), Vol. III, p. 194.

[18]To deal with some possibly strong reader resistance at this point, I must mention A) the pansexual (straight/gay/bi) Eulenspiegel Soc. (founded in N.Y.C., 1971), an "S/M Liberation" group whose 4-year program of forums and C.R. sessions has developed the general consensus that i) "S/M" refers to any case of "dominance vs. submission" (the infliction of *pain* implied by the more extreme term "sado-masochism" being only a special instance, and not necessarily involved even in the text's example!); and ii) not only sexual, but emotional and psychic satisfactions justify the seeking of "S/M experience" (the removal of guilt by atonement is a "psychic satisfaction"); and B) "homophilia" here means "a much greater likelihood of homosexual than heterosexual expression," because, occurring at the stage in "spirit-belief" where homophobia has not yet surfaced, this is tantamount to simple acceptance.

[19]Two examples are Ganymede and Penthesilea. The former name

means either "joyful counsel" (medos) or "joyful genitals" (medea), and the story of how Zeus in the form of an eagle abducted him is well-known. See *New Century Classical Handbook* (ed. C.A. Avery; N.Y., 1962) p. 491: " . . . [he] supplanted Hebe in her function as cup-bearer, . . . in Latin the name appears as Catamitus, whence the English term catamite" (i.e., passive partner in anal intercourse). The first clause symbolically suggests the later, more bisexual attitude in Greece. Penthesilea (possibly "gracious [hileos] in mourning [penthesis]" referring to Achilles' being struck by her beauty after killing her) was an Amazon queen, fathered by Ares, god of war; "P. led her 12 princesses into battle . . . slashed about her mightily and the Greeks fled in panic . . . she leaped like a leopard to meet [Achilles]" (*Handbook*, p. 842).

20A) When the transvestite "Galloi," male priests of the Earth Mother Cybele, occasionally castrated themselves in her honor (Hastings, *Encyc.* IV, 377-378) they were indeed ancient analogues of the modern transsexuals; but transsexuality and transvestitism not being limited to homosexuals, this is not "an implication for homosexuality." B) When the "gay churches" maintain "Jesus died for all people, straight and gay," it seems totally consistent with the Christian doctrine that His death guaranteed immortality for all, transcending "moral" distinctions (cf. the thief in Luke 23, 40-43), which is to this extent homoïsic; but the question is whether, once in heaven, these immortal spirits still require remembrance from their descendants on earth.

21"Phallism," Hastings, 'Encyc. The "Dionysian orgies" involved men and women with probably only incidental homosexuality, while Priapus and his phallic symbols (like other cultures' enormous ithyphallic forms) were worshipped mostly by heterosexual women. Similarly the Lingam (penis) and Yoni (vulva) were revered by the opposite sex, and though among the Lingayats (Hastings, VIII, 69 ff.) both men and women wear the lingam amulets and/or caste marks, it is merely a "group identification symbol" of this sect whose purpose was to overcome caste distinctions. In his documentary motion picture "Phantom India" (viewed on T.V., 8/20/74), Louis Mallé suggests that, though surrounded by extreme visual eroticism of temple bas-relief, Hindus are sexually undemonstrative and more concerned with traditional child-bearing marriage.

22"Shamanism," Hastings, *Encyc.* Also the converse long-standing opinion of male and female homosexuals as "wizards," "witches," etc.

23"Canaanites," Hastings, *Encyc.* References to "temple courtesans"

(Revised Standard Version: "cult prostitutes") in the O.T. are associated with the phallic posts called "ashērīm" from the Heb. root " ⁝ sḫ ṛ" meaning either "to be erect" or "to be happy."

24A valuable analysis in Laud Humphreys, *Out of the Closets: the Sociology of Homosexual Liberation* (Prentice-Hall, 1972; Ch. 8: "Confronting Stigma") lists 5 stages of coping; (based on ideas from Irving Goffman, *Stigma: Notes on the Management of Spoiled Identity*; Pr-H, 1963).

25"Formal cause" in Greek: "eidos," "logos." "Li": third tone: character formed from the 96th radical and a phonetic which is also the 166th radical, thus not the same as the famous "li" or "ṛitual." In Fung Yu-lan, *Short History of Chinese Philosophy* (N.Y., 1948), Chu Hsi, major philosopher of the "Li School" of Neo-Confucianism, says "There is no form without matter and no matter without form" (p. 300), and "for the bamboo chair there is the *li* of the bamboo chair" (p. 296), practically identical with Aristotle's "formal cause," though it is true the *li* were also conceived in a realm by themselves (like "Platonic Ideas").

# "MY BELOVED IS LIKE A GAZELLE": IMAGERY OF THE BELOVED BOY IN RELIGIOUS HEBREW POETRY

*by*

NORMAN ROTH

*University of Wisconsin (Madison)*

The critical study and analysis of medieval Hebrew secular poetry is still in its infancy.[1] Very little has been done, for instance, on the motifs and themes which typify this poetry. One of the most significant and interesting genres of medieval Hebrew poetry is love poetry, which may further be divided into the themes of love of women and love of boys ("boys," and not men, for with the exception of some *muwaššaḥāt*,[2] which occasionally express the emotions and words of the female lover towards her male beloved, all the Hebrew poetry of this type is about an adolescent boy, *ṣeḇî*, "gazelle," or *ᶜoḇer*, "fawn").

While earlier scholars such as Brody and Saul-Joseph were already well aware of the motif of the beloved boy in Hebrew poetry and its dependence on Arabic love poetry about boys (in which the term "gazelle" is also used), the notes in which they discussed this were largely ignored; it was left to the late Ḥayyim Schirmann to demonstrate, although with too much caution, the importance of this motif in medieval verse (Schirmann, 1955).

In a recent article (Roth, 1982), I hope I have demonstrated that, in spite of the critics of Schirmann, the beloved boy was indeed a major theme in medieval Hebrew poetry and literature. It was by no means allegorical or a mere imitation of Arabic verse (as the critics suggested),

1. While many seem to know the work of Don Pagis, less well known is the more significant work of such scholars as Judah Ratzaby, Shraga Abramson, Dov Jarden, and Israel Levin. In English, there is still very little worth mention. A survey of sorts is Roth (1981), where other bibliography may be found, including some quite respectable work in Spanish. I am preparing a volume of translations of secular poetry, with detailed analyses.

2. These are Arabic or Hebrew strophic poems, of a more or less standard length, in which the final rhymed couplet is in Spanish (if the poem is in Arabic or Hebrew) or Arabic (if the poem is Hebrew), or sometimes a combination of both.

but reflected a reality which existed in medieval life—a reality that was not only Jewish and not only in Spain.

While there can no longer be any question that the beloved boy was a genuine motif of medieval secular poetry, there is an aspect of it which is of great interest in that it does serve an allegorical purpose: the image of the *ṣeḇî* as a symbol for God or the messiah, and the use of related love imagery in religious poetry or *piyyûṭ*.

It would appear that this use of secular love imagery, and the use of typical themes found in secular love poetry, is a unique feature of Spanish Hebrew religious verse. There seems to be something of a debate among scholars of religious poetry as to the "uniqueness" of the Spanish school of poets. On the one hand, it appears that Spanish *piyyûṭîm* were greatly influenced by Arabic ascetic poetry, with its emphasis on a pessimistic world view, the inevitability of death, and so forth. Also, it has been suggested that Spanish Hebrew religious poetry was strongly influenced by that of Jews in other Muslim lands, chiefly Iraq, and that it was not as innovative as was secular Hebrew poetry in Spain of the same period (Levin, 1977; Fleischer, 1973 [contradicting what he himself wrote in 1970 in his article in *Sēfer Ḥayyim Schirmann*—see Marcus, 1970, p. 286]).

On the other hand, certain scholars have claimed to recognize in Spanish religious poetry considerable innovation and many new ideas, possibly under the influence of Muslim philosophy, yet still quite distinct from Hebrew religious poetry elsewhere (Mirsky, 1965). While this discussion is best left to experts in religious poetry, it may perhaps be suggested that this use of secular love imagery in religious poetry is an innovation of the Spanish poets which does not, as far as I know, have any similar expression elsewhere. Nor, apparently, do we really find anything like this in Arabic religious poetry, at least until the mystical poetry of the Ṣūfīs of the late Middle Ages, such as that of Ibn al-ᶜArabī (Murcia, 1165–1240) and al-Rūmī (Persia, d. 1273). In some of the poetry of the latter, for example, we find the metaphor of God Himself being addressed as the *sāqī*, the cupbearer (often the object of lust and amorous advances at a wine-party).[3]

Spanish mystical poetry also does not provide us with anything equivalent to this motif in Hebrew *piyyûṭ*. The outstanding example of the allegorization of love in religious verse in Spain is, of course, San Juan

3. See Ibn al-ᶜArabī (1911). Rūmī was also translated by Nicholson, but see now al-Rūmī (1983), a conveniently arranged (by topic) anthology of his poetry. There is a desperate need for a good new anthology, with translations, of Arabic mystical verse, as well as new scholarship to replace the outdated views of the last century and the early part of this century.

de la Cruz (sixteenth century), but his *Cantico espiritual* is obviously based on the Song of Songs; and, while it is of significance because of possible Arabic influences, his doctrine of the *Esposa* (the soul) and her beloved *Esposo* (Christ) has nothing of the audacity of Hebrew religious love imagery, and it is, moreover, well-grounded in perfectly orthodox and traditional Christian theology (at least in Spain, going back to the early medieval period).[4] There has been some conjecture about the influence of religious or mystical vocabulary on *secular* poetry, Arabic and Provençal, but I am unaware of anything which would indicate the influence of secular love motifs on Arabic *religious* verse prior to the late Ṣūfī poetry.[5]

Like the Provençal *fin'amors* (which itself was most probably influenced by Arabic poetry), Hebrew poetry knew nothing of so-called "Platonic love." Its love is sensual, purely physical, and frankly erotic.[6] It is the physical beauty of the boy or the woman which attracts the poet, and the desire is for sexual consummation—or, at the very least, passionate kissing—with the object of the aroused lust. While this very lust is used in Ṣūfī poetry to express mystical union and longing for God, the mystical aspect (union and so forth) is entirely lacking in Hebrew religious poetry. Instead, there is a frank borrowing of the traditional imagery of love poetry, including its language, which is used allegorically to refer to God or to Israel or to the messiah.

So far, only one scholar of medieval Hebrew poetry has taken notice of the existence of this motif in religious Hebrew poetry of Spain.[7] That

4. I am aware that in this brief paragraph I have alluded to matters which are of great importance, and even innovative with regard to the poetry of San Juan de la Cruz. The relationship to the Song of Songs, possible Arabic influence, and even the connection with earlier Christian theological treatises and poetry on the nature of Christ as *Esposo*—all of these things seem to have escaped the attention of scholars, and all deserve fuller treatment than can be given here.

5. For Arabic, see von Grünebaum (1940), a suggestive note which was never followed up. For Provençal, see Lazar (1964, p. 84). Apparently some orthodox Muslims objected strongly to the allegorization of love terminology with reference to Allāh; cf. Latham (1964).

6. For the Provençal poetry, see Lazar (1964, p. 61); for Hebrew, Schirmann (1961), an article studiously ignored by his Israeli critics. There may or may not exist a theme of "Platonic love" in Arabic poetry—the so-called ʿUdhrī poetry which is the subject of some debate. Regrettably, there is no article on ʿUdhrī in the *Encyclopedia of Islam*, nor any mention of it in the brief and unsatisfactory article on poetry (*shiʿr*); perhaps this will be remedied in the new edition.

7. Levin (1972). Previously, Judah Ratzaby had observed that in pre-Spanish *piyyûṭîm* for weddings there was no reference to love or beauty, only the ethical characteristics of the bridegroom and bride were praised (Ratzaby [1970]).

article, important as it is, by no means exhausts the discussion of the subject, and in fact it only scratches the surface. In more than a decade since the appearance of that study, nothing further has been said on the subject. The present article will not tread again the ground well covered previously, but it will add new examples, and hopefully new insights, to those already presented.

What was the cause of this allegorization in Hebrew religious poetry in Spain? Why do we not find it in religious verse—contemporary and later—in other lands? It is difficult, perhaps impossible, to answer these questions. The answer does not appear to be, as in the case of the later Ṣūfī poetry, that it was a reflection of mystical longing. Whether or not the observations of certain French writers (Henri Bremond, Jacques Maritain) are correct in noting that there is a similarity between Christian poetry and mysticism, in that both seek a truth in obscurity under the influence of external "illumination," this does not appear to be true of Hebrew poetry of the Middle Ages—certainly not of secular poetry, and only rarely of religious poetry.[8]

It is important to realize that none of the Hebrew poets who composed religious verse of the genre here being discussed specialized exclusively in liturgical or religious verse, for all of them wrote secular poetry as well. Of them all, only Ibn Gabirol approached what might be termed "mysticism" in some of his verse, but not in any of this particular genre.

This, indeed, may be the key. Uniquely in Spain, we find poets who composed both secular and religious verse on a large scale—not to deny, of course, that some individual poets, such as Ḥayya Gaon of Baghdad, composed both; but these were isolated examples. Our poets lived, as has been demonstrated, in a society where this kind of erotic passion was openly expressed and not uncommon. Much of their own verse contains this kind of secular love poetry. It appears that it was natural, when searching (perhaps) for innovation in religious verse, to employ the themes of secular love poetry in an allegorical fashion.

The Bible, of course, already provided a frame of reference. It is rather astonishing, in the quite proper search for sources and similarities to Hebrew poetry in Arabic verse and literature, that the Bible has been somewhat neglected as an obvious source for medieval Hebrew poetry. Some scholars have virtually denied this influence. Yet, of course, the Song of Songs is the immediate source for most of the love imagery and terminology found in Hebrew poetry—however much the themes, or

8. See Hatzfeld (1976, p. 18). In his various works on Hebrew poetry, particularly on Ibn Gabirol, José M. Millás Vallicrosa also has had some observations to make on this.

ideas, may have been borrowed from Arabic verse. Indeed, the "gazelle," as it appears in the Song of Songs as a term for the beloved, may well have influenced Arabic love poetry, where the term is used (for a discussion of the term, see Roth, 1982, p. 28). The Song of Songs was interpreted, for the most part, quite literally by the medieval commentators of Spain (Ibn Ezra, 1874; Ibn ᶜAqnin, 1964—the first and second [rabbinical] interpretations). In spite of the well-known statement of R. ᶜAqîḇā, it was left to the early Christian exegetes, like Origen, to allegorize the book. Surprisingly, little of this kind of allegory is found in *Song of Songs Rabbah*, although there is some (for example on 1:4; 2:16; 8:14), and the *midrashim* dependent on it.

The Song of Songs served as a source for *piyyûṭîm* outside of Spain, of course; for example, those known as "*ʾAhaḇôt*" (prayers expressing the love of God). Examples are especially to be found in the *piyyûṭîm* of Shimᶜôn b. Yiṣḥāq b. Abûn of Mayence (tenth century), such as the "*yôṣēr*" for Passover "*ʾAhûḇeḵā ʾahēḇûḵā mēšārîm*".[9] The Song of Songs, of course, is read in the synagogue on Passover, and there is no surprise in finding these and other *piyyûṭîm* for Passover devoted to this book.

Whereas the Song of Songs undeniably served as a source for the terminology, it was not the source of the genre—of the idea of using secular love themes and motifs to refer to religious subjects. This is what we mean by "audacity." In itself, such audacity is also not new in Spanish Hebrew poetry. The opposite is found, quite frequently in secular Hebrew poetry: the use of religious terms and ideas, sometimes of the most holy nature, applied to a distinctly secular subject. This further lends support to the theory that it is the nature of the "cross-over"—poets quite accustomed to writing secular verse who also wrote religious verse—which produced this unique and innovative element in the religious Hebrew poetry of Spain.

The subject of some of these poems is clearly God Himself, and He is the beloved "gazelle" sought by the lover. In others, God is the lover, as it were, and the people of Israel the "beloved." In some, the "beloved" is the messiah. There is an intimate relationship between the poet and the messiah; exactly the relationship of the lover and his beloved. It is not so much that the yearning—whether for God or for the messiah—*is erotic*, as that it is expressed in terms employed in secular love poetry.

9. Shimᶜôn bᵉr Yiṣḥaq (1938, pp. 27–30); cf. also "*Beraḥ dôdî*," pp. 34–35, and the "*ʾAhaḇah*" there, pp. 53–54.

As I have shown in discussing that secular poetry, the chief purpose which the poet had in mind was to express not the joys of love (as, for instance, in modern romantic verse), but quite the opposite: the *pain* caused by love, the unrequited love, the deceitful boy who abandons his lover for another. It is precisely this imagery which is borrowed and used in this religious poetry.

Lest too much emphasis be placed on the "religious" nature of these poems (they are not, by the way, liturgical; i.e., they were not intended for use in the synagogue, but for private reading), it should be pointed out that the authors are first and foremost poets. They are all the greatest of the medieval Hebrew poets, with a genius for subtlety of style, wit, and sharpness of language. One cannot escape the feeling that these poems are, in a sense, "word games." That is, the reader is clearly not intended to realize the actual meaning of the poem until very nearly the end of it, when it suddenly becomes clear that it is of a religious, not a secular, nature. This will become clear when we turn to the poems themselves.

Dunash Ibn Labrat was the first Hebrew poet known to us in medieval Spain, and he was apparently the originator of many of the motifs which became common in later poetry. It is not surprising that we also find him to be the originator of our theme (not hitherto noticed), in the following *piyyûṭ:*

"What do you seek? they ask me—
  why is my spirit aching?
The fawn has fled from my tent,
  my soul languishes for his return. [Jer 31:24]
Beloved, whom, since he fled like a gazelle,
  my soul longs to see.
Who will give me the glorious land? [Dan 11:16]
  on the wing of an eagle I shall fly;
Perhaps there I shall find my lover
  and stand in the shade of my beloved.
How many nights in the midst of the fire of sickness
  of separation I lie among the flames, [Ps 57:5]
My slumber wandering from me
  and the sleep of my eyes not sweet; [Prov 3:24]
And my soul thirsts, as [in]
  a thirsty land, and also pines
For him—were it not for his mercy,
  the fire of his separation would consume.
On his wandering I wept for him;
  those who see my reveal my secret.

The fawn has made sick my heart—
  how long he has not come!
From the blood of my heart, for want of a pail,
  my eyes draw my tears."

"My dove has wandered, from greatness
  of sorrow, she said: Perhaps; maybe—
And when she heard his mention, flames
  of separation arose in her heart.
How long has she lain on couches
  of grief defiled by drinking?
She said: Why is it that he who seeks me
  is hidden in the chamber of secrets,
And the hand of the enemy, my robber, is elevated,
  and his bow abides in its strength? [cf. Gen 49:24]
Shulamit, why are you grieving
  and desolate in your soul?
Hope for the coming of your beloved;
  you shall not be hurt by your misfortune.
The day approaches when your balm shall come;
  be comforted, be comforted.
Dove, why do you not eat?
  The time of love approaches;
Lo, now my redeemer comes,
  for his banner over me is love." [Cant 2:4]

(Brody-Wiener, 1963, Appendix, pp. 21–22)

In this case, as with some few other examples we shall discuss, the lover is a female and the beloved a male. The poem is in the form of a dialogue between them (although separated by distance)—actually, between Israel and God. There is nothing to indicate that this is not a typical secular love poem, until line 15 and the following lines, when we first realize the real intent. Here, God replies to Israel's complaint, recalling "her" words in saying: "Perhaps; maybe" (in line 5). Shulamit, a woman's name in the Song of Songs, is also symbolically a name for Israel, and so it is used in the poem.

There are numerous poetic devices in the poem which are typical of medieval Hebrew poetry generally. Of particular interest is the use of *ṣeḇî* (line 4a) to refer to the Land of Israel, "glorious land" (Dan 11:16), and as "gazelle" (beloved boy) in line 3a. Habermann, who edited this text, had difficulty in understanding the use of "For him" in line 9, apparently not realizing that it is the object of the verb "pines" in the previous line; thus, there is no need for his suggested correction.

The notion that Israel (*Keneset Yisrāʾēl*) is symbolized by a gazelle, derived, of course, from the Song of Songs in its allegorical meaning, is found also in a religious poem (again, not liturgical) of Samuel Ibn Naghrillah:

"My people, hide until the indignation is past [Isa 26:20]
on the top of Senir dwell like a fawn or gazelle"
(Ibn Naghrillah, 1966, p. 319, No. 209, line 1)

The image is taken directly from Cant 4:8 and 8:14; but *ṣeḇî* and *ʿōp̱er* ("fawn") here may also be taken literally: hide like animals atop the mountain, where you will be safe. This brings us to the first important aspect to be noted in dealing with this poetry, as with all allegory, and that is that there are two levels of interpretation: "level one," the apparent literal meaning, and "level two," the allegorical.

Although Dunash Ibn Labrat was the first poet to use secular love imagery in a religious poem, and this poem was apparently overlooked by Levin in the important study previously cited, it was not Judah Halevy, but Solomon Ibn Gabirol who was the first to make extensive use of this imagery in his religious verse, a fact also overlooked in that article.

Like Dunash, Ibn Gabirol appears to have employed the motif of the gazelle, but from the female point of view. That is, the lover here is a woman, and she pines for her beloved "gazelle"—a young man who is her beloved. Again, this theme is almost entirely lacking in secular love poetry, except for some of the *muwaššaḥāt* which are written from the female's viewpoint. This convention, and also, of course, the image of the female lover in Song of Songs, explains the use of this motif in the following poems. An interesting example of this is:

"The gate which has been closed, arise and open it;
and the gazelle who has fled, send him to me.
From the day you came to rest upon my breast,
there you left your good scent upon me."
'Who is this, the image of your lover, O beautiful bride,
that you say to me, Send and fetch him?'
"It is he, lovely of eye, ruddy and of goodly appearance.
This is my beloved, my companion; arise and anoint him!"
(Ibn Gabirol, 1973, p. 468; Schirmann, 1954, p. 240; a prayer for Simḥat Tôrāh in Separdic prayerbooks)

The *piyyûṭ* is in the form of an imaginary dialogue, which is also a common device in secular poetry. Apparently (level one interpretation), a lover pines for her beloved (the only clue that we have, incidentally, that it is a woman and not a man is the feminine word forms throughout); but actually (level two), it is a dialogue between Israel (lines 1–2, 4) and God (line 3). This realization does not dawn fully upon us until the end of the poem.

Line 3b, and all of line 4, allude to I Sam 16:11–12, the anointing of David. This provides the clue to the poem, for the "gazelle" is the messiah.

Messianic longing is also the subject of the following:

O recliner upon couches of gold in the palace,
  when will you prepare the couch of God for the ruddy one?
Why, delightful gazelle, do you slumber, when the dawn
  ascends like a banner atop Senir and Hermon?
Turn from the wild ones and incline to the graceful hind—
  behold, I am before you as you are before me.
Who comes to my palace will find in my treasures
  wine and pomegranates, myrrh and cinnamon.

(Ibn Gabirol, 1973, p. 457).

Again, this is an address from the female lover to her beloved (level one); from Israel to the messiah (level two). The "ruddy one" again alludes to I Sam 16:12; hence, the messiah, who is directly addressed from line 2 on (line 1 being apparently directed to God). "Wild ones" of line 3 refers to the Muslims (cf. *Gen. Rabbah* 16:12), a term which appears frequently in polemical statements in *piyyûṭ*. "Graceful hind" is, of course, Israel (*Keneset Yisrāʾēl*).

It should be mentioned that "ruddy one," in addition to alluding to David (and thus the messiah), also refers to the complexion of the beloved in Cant 5:10. It is of interest that also in Arabic literature and poetry, "ruddy" is a term for desirable complexion (actually, light-skinned, or "white"), perhaps again under the influence of the Song of Songs.

Senir and Hermon are clichés for the land of Israel generally (although not, technically speaking, located in Israel); but of course the allusion is to Cant 4:8, where rabbinical allegory interpreted these mountains as being symbolic names for the Temple (*Targum, ad loc.*, and Ibn ʿAqnin, 1964, pp. 194–195). In addition, the messiah is referred to as *ʿōp̱er*, "fawn," by Ibn Gabirol also in the *piyyûṭ* "*Shipʿat reḇîḇîm*" line 5: "Hasten and send the fawn before [the time of] prayers departs" (1973, p. 322).

Similar imagery is also employed by Ibn Gabirol in the following:

"Greetings to you, my beloved, white and ruddy;
  greetings to you from a forehead like a pomegranate.

To meet your sister run, go forth and save;
  and prosper like David in Rabbah of the Ammonites."
'What is with you, loveliest one, that you arouse love—
  your voice ringing like a vestment with the sound of a bell?
The time which you desire of love I shall hasten with it,
  and descend to you like the dew of Hermon.'

(1973, p. 324)

Again, this is a dialogue between Israel (lines 1–2) and God (lines 3–4). The "forehead" (*raqqah*; either "temple" or, as Ibn Ezra says, "forehead") like a pomegranate alludes to Cant 4:3. Of interest is Ibn Ezra's comment in the third recension of his commentary, with respect to the allegorical level, in which he says "pomegranate" refers to the priests (Ibn Ezra, 1874, p. 18). This, perhaps, is also what the poet had in mind here. On the other hand, there is the well-known explanation of the rabbis: even the empty ones among you are full of good deeds like a pomegranate is full of seeds (*Berakôt* 57a; cited also by Ibn ᶜAqnin, 1964, pp. 178–179).

Line 2b refers to 2 Sam 12:26–29, but this is perhaps a "level one" interpretation, for the text actually has *Ben Yishāi*, which I have rendered as "David," but which could have a "level two" allusion to the messiah.

Finally, one of the most difficult of Ibn Gabirol's poems to interpret:

At dawn ascend to me, beloved, and go with me;
  for my soul thirsts to see the face of my mother.
For you I spread out couches of gold in my palace,
  I prepare for you a table; I break for you my bread.
A bowl I shall fill for you from the clusters of my vineyard;
  drink with good heart, may my taste be good to you.
Behold, in you I shall rejoice with the joy of [for] a prince of my people:
Son of Your servant Jesse, head of the Bethlemites.

(1973, p. 460; Schirmann, 1954, p. 241)

(Schirmann needlessly changes line 1b to *benê ᶜammî*, "sons of my people," instead of *penê ᵓimmî*, "face of my mother")

Neither Jarden nor Schirmann entirely succeeded in explaining this difficult *piyyûṭ*. The female lover (Israel) calls to her beloved (the messiah) to go with her at dawn to her home, the house of her mother. The allusion, rather obscure to anyone not thoroughly familiar with the book (as Jews of medieval Spain, of course, were), is to Cant 3:4 (and 8:2). "House of my mother" there is interpreted allegorically as Sinai, or as wisdom and the Torah (*Song of Songs Rabbah*; Ibn ᶜAqnin, 1964, pp. 122–123). Thus, it is far more than simply a longing to go to "my land" (Israel), as Jarden explains; rather, it is a metaphysical yearning for the restoration of the covenant relationship of Sinai.

The reference to dawn, and the longing which has kept the lover awake, is understandable also from a comparison with secular love poetry. In Ibn Gabirol's so-called "Golden Poem" (considered worthy to be written in letters of gold), "*Šûr kî yepepiyyāh,*" there appears the line: (5)—"She [arouses] at dawn lovers, for / they are full of tossing to and fro until the dawn."[10] Here, of course, allegorically the dawn is the dawn of redemption from the exile.

The "palace" of line 2 is surely the Temple, and the table and bread refer to the table and shewbread in the Temple, as Jarden correctly noted. The prince, son of Jesse, of line 4 is, of course, David, and hence the messiah.

Moses Ibn Ezra is the next major poet to use this theme. While Ibn Gabirol certainly wrote several secular love poems about the beloved boy (although it is not true, as has been repeatedly stated, that he wrote love poems *only* about boys, or that he never mentioned women), Ibn Ezra composed more such poetry and utilized a wider variety of imagery. It is interesting to note that, while all of the religious poems of Ibn Gabirol which we have discussed express the love relationship between a woman and her beloved, Ibn Ezra employs "real" *ṣeḇî* imagery—i.e., the "lover" as a man, and the "beloved" a boy. An example is the following:

> What is with my beloved that he is angry and haughty
> towards me, when my heart shakes for him like a reed?
> He has forgotten the time of my walking after him in the ruin of the desert
> desirous, and how can I call today and he not answer?
> Even if he slay me, I shall trust in him; though he hide
> his face, and to his goodness [I shall] look and turn.
> The kindness of a master to a slave shall not change—
> for how can lovely gold darken, and how change?
> (Ibn Ezra, 1957, p. 38, No. 38)

In line 2, *ᶜî*, "ruin," is found in the Bible mostly in reference to Jerusalem (Mic 1:6, 3:12; Ps 79:1). The line as a whole refers, of course, to Jer 2:2. Here the "lover" (Israel) chastises his "beloved" (God) that He has forgotten the time of His faithfulness in the desert. However, the theme of the unhappy lover wandering in the desert and coming upon the ruins of the camp of the beloved, fully developed in Arabic poetry, is

10. Ibn Gabirol (1975a, p. 20); Ibn Gabirol (1975b, pp. 359–360); reading *tāᶜîr* with Brody-Schirmann, instead of *yāšûr*, as emended by Jarden, which makes no sense. For the meaning of "dawn" there, cf. Job 3:9 and 41:10.

not uncommon in Hebrew secular poetry. Note that the word *tā'ēḇ* here, meaning "desirous," is generally used not only in the sense of the appetite (cf. *ᶜEruḇin* 41a) but also of lust (e.g., Jer. *Nedarim* 41d). Therefore, the word is *not* used here in its biblical sense, as suggested by the editor (Brody).

The haughtiness of the boy is a standard theme in secular love poetry, as is his deceitfulness and lack of memory of the good times spent with his lover in the past ("and so every boy is deceitful," says one poem). All of this is here subtly woven into the allusion to the biblical imagery of Israel's idealized past with God and the righteousness of its youth, contrasted with the "deceitfulness" of God.

The martyrdom of love, borrowed from Arabic poetry, is another frequent motif. The lover is willing to die for his love, or imagines that the boy slays him (usually with the glances—"arrows"—of his eyes), or that he will slay him. So Ibn Gabirol in a secular poem entreated his beloved boy: "Take my soul and slay [it] / or if not, heal me, please heal!" And Ibn Ezra implores: "If it is in your soul to give life, revive me— / or if your desire is to kill, kill me!" (Roth, 1982, pp. 40, 45). Here (line 3) the poet combines this motif ("Even if he slay me") with the mystical "hiding of the face" of God. This line might also have been influenced by Ibn Gabirol's famous lines in *Keter malḵût* ("Crown of Kingship"):

> And if I do not wait on Thy mercies
> Who will have pity on me but Thee?
> Therefore, though Thou shouldst slay me, yet
> will I trust in Thee.
> For if Thou shouldst pursue my iniquity,
> I will flee from Thee to Thyself.[11]

Line 4 also contains allusions to standard clichés of love poetry: the boy is the master and the lover the slave, and the beautiful face (or body) is compared to gold, or to the moon. The unusual word *ketem* for gold here may allude to Cant 5:11, where the beloved is said to have a head like fine gold (the complexion must be meant, for his locks of hair are said to be black as a raven).

Another of Ibn Ezra's religious poems, reminiscent of his own secular love poetry, is:

> From old as a seal on [his] heart he placed me;
> However, because of my sins he has turned to hate me
> And in the chambers of his heart he has concealed me.
> Therefore, today on every side they smite me.

11. Ibn Gabirol (1923, p. 118, lines 561–564).

From the wine of his mouth and lips he has given me to drink.
[But] today he has satiated me with drinking poisoned waters.
Please speak to him, please restore me
To him; for I am sick with love.

(1957, p. 39, No. 40)

Many of the images here are found typically in secular love poetry, including the reference to the "sins" (whether real or imagined) of the lover which have caused the beloved to turn from him. The lover drinks the saliva from the mouth of his beloved boy, and it is sweeter than wine (For examples, see e.g., Yosef Ibn Ṣaddîq, in Roth, 1982, p. 32). The beloved (God) has previously bestowed his favors on his lover, but now has become bitter towards him.

Love-sickness, of course, is a frequent motif in Arabic and Hebrew poetry. The saying was ascribed, probably erroneously, to Plato: "I do not know what love is, except that I know it to be a divine madness, which cannot be either approved or blamed."[12] Here we find allusion to this motif when the poet says he is sick with love, and only the restoration of his beloved's favors can cure him.

Isaac Ibn Ghiyāth (note the correct spelling of his name, which is Arabic and almost always wrongly given) also used this idea in one of his *piyyûṭîm*:

Almighty, return the love-sick one [to You]—
Who moans constantly on the deceitful statute.

(Schirmann, 1954, II, p. 320, ll. 1–2).

The "deceitful statute" refers to the broken covenant between God and Israel, according to Schirmann's note there.

In one of the most beautiful, and difficult, of Ibn Ezra's religious poems, he employs the image of the garden:

Wind of my joy and the beauty of its delights,
Blow upon my garden that its spices may flow out.
  From the mount of myrrh and the hills of frankincense,
  O north wind, awake; and come, O south;
Perhaps my fawn will go down to the garden
To eat of my fruits and to gather the lily,
And as the days of his youth renew his days.
  Ask and see, masters of words,
  And seek and read hidden secrets—

12. See Nykl (1946, p. 123). In addition to the references in Roth (1982, p. 32), see also the interesting anecdotes in González Palencia (1929, especially p. 91ff.), and Walzer (1939), and also Manzalaoui (1979). For Spanish literature, see the not-altogether-satisfactory book of Bonilla García (1964, especially pp. 127–135).

Perhaps you shall find healing for my illness.
To my beloved carry the greeting of a wife of his youth—
And arouse his compassion to obtain his well-being.
O gazelle, return to me as before,
And restore to me my ornaments.
The lights of my rejoicing make goodly before me,
And raise up my tents and plead my cause
And the son whose steps have stumbled, wound his enemies!
The words of the son of the maidservant are strong against him,
And daily he digs a pit for his feet
And stirs up contention and offers strife.
A branch bearing poison he makes his food,
And a root of bitterness he makes his delicacies.
(Ibn Ezra, 1957, p. 40; Schirmann, 1954, I, pp. 411–412)

The opening couplet and the first two lines of the first stanza allude to Cant 4:16 and 4:14, with its allegorical level of interpretation making it refer to *Keneset Yisrāʾēl* and the restoration of the Temple (see especially Ibn ʿAqnīn, 1964, pp. 188–189 and 230–233). Thus, the fawn (l. 5) and gazelle (l. 12) here means not the messiah, but God. The north and south winds are called upon to symbolize here the ingathering of the exiles of Israel.

Certain textual explanations are necessary. In line 10, *māzôr* (cf. Jer 30:13) is "healing", according to the commentaries (Rashi, there; Ibn Janaḥ and Ibn Balʿam[13]). The "ornaments" (cf. Isa 61:10) and "lights" of lines 14 and 15 allude to the vessels and candelabrum of the Temple, as Schirmann correctly explained, in keeping with the allegorical interpretation of the rabbis of the previous verses from the Song of Songs. In line 17, the "son" must be Israel, i.e., son of the "gazelle"—God. He is contrasted with the son of the maidservant, i.e., Hagar (thus, Ishmael, symbolizing the Muslims), in line 18, who "daily digs a pit" for the feet of Israel.

Thus, the poem closes on a polemical note, concluding with the strong words about the poison and "bitterness" which Ishmael constantly offers to Israel (cf. Deut 29:17). The word *rōtem* (Job 30:4 and elsewhere), which for want of a better idea I have rendered here "bitterness," is of uncertain meaning. David Qimḥi (on 1 Kgs 19:4) translates it as *xiniesta* (*hiniesta*), which means "broom" (a kind of plant), or *jengibre* ("ginger").

13. Ibn Janaḥ (1896), s.v. *z-ô-r* (this is one of the most important Hebrew dictionaries, absolutely essential for understanding medieval texts); Ibn Balʿam, "*Sēp̱er ha-tajnīs*" in Kokovtsov (1970, p. 76).

On the literal, or "level one," level of interpretation, the garden is a frequent motif in Hebrew and Arabic secular poetry. This was particularly important in Muslim (and Jewish) life in Spain, where the garden was literally the center of the house, and the fragrant scent of flowers was a constant accompaniment to lovemaking and to wine parties throughout the city. Many an invitation to come and drink wine, and many a love poem about the beautiful boy, include the scent and delights of the garden.

Among many structural elements of this poem which deserve mention, the perhaps intentional parallelism of lines 5 and 10 should be pointed out: "*Perhaps* my fawn will go down . . . ," "*Perhaps* you shall find healing." This kind of poetic device frequently adds to what was considered the beauty of a secular poem, but is not so frequent in religious poetry.

Isaac Ibn Ghiyāth was a distinguished talmudic scholar and author of important *piyyûṭîm*, including some with philosophical and even rudimentary astronomical themes.[14] There is at least one *pîyyûṭ* from his pen utilizing our theme:

Do you know, my friends—the gazelle fled from my chamber;
When will he return to my dwelling?
My cherub shall tell you,
After he took my heart;
How can I bear my pain?
He did not know, when he carried with him all my joy,
With whom he left my grief!
I am greatly distressed by his wandering;
He has removed from me his glory,
The light of his brightness and splendor.
Where are the days his lips dripped honey on my tongue,
And his neck [rested upon] my throat?
My graciousness how has he forgotten?
My delights how has he rejected?
And companionship, among the sons of Ham
Which he showed me in Amon, showing his wonder to my oppressors,
And [when he] brought out my people?
He split the Sea of Reeds before me,

14. His poetry is scattered in numerous collections, including rare holiday prayer books. Dr. Menahem Schmelzer, librarian of the Jewish Theological Seminary and devoted friend to all scholars, who has recently given us a superb edition of the poetry of Isaac Ibn ʿEzra, may hopefully publish a complete edition of Ibn Ghiyāth's poems, incorporating at least some of the material in his important doctoral dissertation (there, chapters four and five discuss some of the astronomical poetry, and six and seven some of the philosophical-theological poems).

Showing his light to my eyes.
He spoke his love in my ears
And to his room my beloved turned, to the gracefulness of the voice of my bells
And the scent of my spices.
Transgressors of laws and testimonies
Have removed from me companionship
[Which is] esteemed and precious.
Restore to me the joy of your salvation—and if the chief of my pride has gone,
Please remove my transgression.[15]

This remarkable poem is very nearly a true *ṣeḇî* poem; the complaint of a man about his beloved boy who has abandoned him. There is nothing to "give away" the true meaning of the poem, at first glance, until line 15, at which point it suddenly becomes clear that the "gazelle" here is God. Nevertheless, there are hidden clues even earlier in the poem. In line 2, for example, *maᶜôn*, "dwelling," can also mean "refuge," which is used figuratively of God (Ps 71:3, for example). Thus, it could also be understood: when will my Refuge return? The "cherub" is unusual, and while on "level one" it certainly means the "boy," on the "level two" interpretation it is almost like a guardian angel (Habermann explains it simply as angel or messenger). I know of no similar use of this image.

In line 11 we find the standard reference to the saliva of the boy's mouth, like honey in its sweetness; but there is, of course, a second level here also: knowledge (Torah), and particularly esoteric knowledge.[16]

Amon, in line 16, refers to Egypt, and the whole line to the exodus. Line 21 is again an allusion to the Temple. There seems to be no messianic intent to the poem; rather, it speaks of the relationship between Israel and God.

There are other *piyyûṭîm* by Ibn Ghiyāth which utilize the imagery of love within the context of the poem, although the theme of the poem as a whole is not love; for example, the very interesting "*Baᶜalat ʾoḇ veqesem*," which is an imaginary dialogue between Israel and the prophet Daniel. Following Daniel's exhortation not to abandon God, Israel replies, as if directly to God:

15. Edited in Brody-Wiener (1963, pp. 135–136); previously in Dukes (1842, p. 159), and in Mirsky (1957, pp. 154–155).

16. See especially Moses b. Maimon (1963a, I. 32, p. 69); cf. also Moses b. Maimon (1961, p. 66) and (1963b, p. 35).

I have been made drunk with the wine of your love, O my companion,
In restoring your glory to me and rejoicing my soul.
I shall inscribe on my heart a poem of companionship to my beloved.
My beloved comes to his house; I am his and he is mine,
And in my heart his love is sweeter than honey.
(Schirmann, 1954, I, 319, ll. 23–27)

In the previously mentioned study (Levin, 1972), an attempt was made to compare a *piyyûṭ* of Judah Halevy (Schirmann, 1954, I, 467; Halevy, 1978-82, III, 778–779) with one by Ibn Ghiyāth (Schirmann, 1954, p. 324). True, both of these are on the same theme: the suffering of Israel in exile, particularly at the hands of the Muslims (it has nothing to do with the Christian Reconquest of Spain, as suggested by Levin), but neither of them are in any sense love *piyyûṭim*, nor is there any love imagery in them at all! Schirmann quite correctly explained that Halevy's poem was talking about the well-known talmudic adage of receiving all tribulations with love; i.e., as a sign of God's love. This is not at all the same as the theme we have been discussing. The "quarrelers" in line 2 of Halevy's poem are not, as Levin thought, the typical "rebukers" of secular love poetry, but the literal enemies of Israel (Muslims)—again, as Schirmann correctly noted there. Incomprehensible is Levin's statement (p. 118) that Halevy's poem is an actual poem of love, in which the lover speaks to his beloved in the present tense.

Even less is Ibn Ghiyāth's *piyyûṭ* there related in any way to love poetry or love imagery. Thus, all of the nouns which have a connotation of burden and sorrow, which so surprised Levin in a poem ostensibly based on love imagery, are no surprise at all, for the message is simply that Israel has borne with patience the burdens of its suffering in the exile, even when its enemies have sought to lead it astray and have almost forced it to abandon its religion (a clear allusion to the Almohad persecutions).

However, Judah Halevy did compose some important *piyyûṭîm* which reflect this type of secular love imagery, an example of which is the following:

"What shall I give as ransom for the fawn who wandered?
Perhaps he will yet shine upon me from the east."
'Dove, loveliest of maidens, if you pine for me
Put on embroidered garments—only entreat me,
And I shall wear garments of vengeance to avenge me.
Why do you lie in the dust? The flower of your salvation blossoms.
And I shall remember for my children the love of the son of Terah.'

"The beloved whom I have called from the depths
Has hearkened to the song which I have sung to the skies.
How long, for the sin which I did, must I pay double?
If my sins are written in a book, extend
Your mercy, and upon my transgress rub waters of mercy.
Will you not give to the deserted woman a time of favor,
And grazing in faithful pastures to the remnant of the flock?
How long shall I be tested with the delighters in scorn,
Between the people of Edom and ᶜEfer? before you I cry.
From the pit of affliction of my ruins my unshorn hair I pluck bald."

'Be silent! Behold, now I have restored you to good.
The time of your redemption is near—here, I have told you.
You shall be saved in ease—return, for I have remembered you.
Of flowing myrrh and camphor shall I prepare your gift—
Only my faithful festivals let not be a burden.
Rouse yourself, treasure, from your mourning awake.
I have come to the garden of praise—I have gathered your myrrh.
Your light, as in the beginning, has come; arise, shine!
Your beloved, who like a fawn from your breast fled,
Has returned, and the glory of the Lord shines upon you.'

(Halevy, 1978–82, III, pp. 761–763)

This is a dialogue between Israel (ll. 1–2, 8–17) and God (ll. 3–7, 18–27). The opening stanza, "What shall I give as a ransom for the fawn," immediately calls to mind a typical theme of secular love poetry—I shall give my soul (life) as ransom for the boy I love. Typical is the short love poem by Halevy himself, which incorporates much of the imagery discussed in the present article:

I am a ransom for the fawn who arose at night
to the voice of the lyre and sweet love songs;
Who saw in my hand a cup and said:
"Drink from between my lips the blood of grapes!"
And the moon was like a *yôd* inscribed upon
the covering of dawn in golden liquid.[17]

Thus, the typical reader (or "hearer," for those who insist, with absolutely no evidence, that medieval Hebrew poetry was always recited orally) would assume from this stanza that this is a secular love poem with the usual complaint about the boy who has wandered.

In line 2, *yaṣîṣ* has the meaning of "shine" (as in Ps 132:1, not "flourish," as often translated there), and not the meaning it has in Cant 2:9;

17. Judah Halevy (1894–1930, II, 290).

cf. also line 26 at the end of the poem. In line 4, "embroidered" garments, *reqāmôt*; i.e., of different colors, which is in paranomasia with *neqāmôt*, "vengeance," in the following line.

While "dove" is a typical term of affection for a girl (or boy) in love poetry, it also symbolizes *Keneset Yisrāʾēl* (see *Beraḵôt* 53b). While nearly all the Spanish Jewish poets used the dove in some of their poems, Halevy appears to have been fonder of it than most, and he used it constantly—so much so that it may almost be safe to assume that a newly discovered poem unattributed to any other poet, in which the dove appears, may well be his. The "fawn" here, of course, is God—against whom Israel complains of having been abandoned. Israel is referred to as *ʿagûnāh*, "deserted woman," in line 13. This is a strong rebuke indeed. Line 24 is an allusion to Cant 5:1, in spite of the fact that the *midrashim* do not, in fact, refer this verse to God.

Parts of other *piyyûṭîm* by Halevy also contain love imagery (see, e.g., "*Yigʾal ḥalôm*," Halevy, III, 768–771, especially line 9ff., where the *ṣeḇî* is the messiah, and the "beloved" of line 24 is God), and the following lines:

O sleeper under the wings of wandering,
Slumber in the extremities of imprisonment!
I rest and my beauty is far spent,
Silent with a heart gloomy and sad.
My heart is restored to the gazelle;
My spirit is renewed within me.

(*Ibid.*, I, 218, lines 1–3)

Finally, there is no doubt that Wallenstein was correct in his identification of the author of the *piyyûṭ* which he published from a manuscript as being Judah Halevy, and it also reflects our theme:

May the [gazelle] come back—come back to my chamber;
May he again sit on (the) precious throne.
Enough for my court to be a trampling-place—
(A place) where an alien and strange people is let loose.
Is it time for Thee to support my adversaries—
To make them wield a regal sceptre?
(Surely) when I shall call to my God, the rock of my strength,
He will awaken His kindness to help.
Let them know that are far-off; let the inhabitants of the isle (be aware)
That there be no restraint for the grieved
To (re-)build on the [acceptable day] my wall
Of carbuncle and white and black marble.

(Then) to the glory of His name, facing the Temple,
will king and ruler bow.[18]

## SUMMARY AND CONCLUSION

This article has explored a particular theme, unique to the religious poetry of medieval Spain: that of the allegorical use of the *ṣeḇî* or "beloved boy" motif in a religious setting. Some of this poetry expressed the love imagery from the viewpoint of a female beloved, while most of it follows exactly the secular love poetry of the love of a man for a boy. In all cases, what is common to the poetry is an allegorization of the terms and expressions of love, love-sickness, abandonment, and so forth, which are typical and characteristic of secular love poetry. Through a skillful use of these typical images, the reader is subtly "tricked" into thinking he is reading a secular love poem, and only gradually does the true nature of the poem become evident. In this allegorical religious poetry, the "beloved" is either Israel or God or the messiah. The poems are never left to be completely ambiguous, however; at some point within the poem it is made perfectly clear that it *is* allegory and the true subject is revealed in a manner about which there can be no doubt.

Thus, those who have sought to deny the existence of secular love poetry of the *ṣeḇî* type in medieval Hebrew verse, claiming that it is all allegory, were not entirely wrong, in that there are allegorical uses of this imagery and allegorical examples of this type of poetry. However, these are always and exclusively *religious* poems, in which the subject of the poem is made quite clear, while none of the secular love poetry is allegorical. Furthermore, without the existence of a well-established tradition of a secular love poetry of this type, these religious poems would be inconceivable and unintelligible. This is why we find this type of *piyyûṭ* only in Spain, where just such a tradition of secular poetry existed.

The present study has been restricted only to those "classical" Hebrew poets of the Muslim period in Spain. Abraham Ibn Ezra, whose poetry was by no means all written in Spain, has not been included, nor have other minor poets or poets of the later periods. In addition to the type of poem here discussed, where the allegorized beloved is male, there is a considerable amount of religious poetry where the allegory involves the female beloved (*ṣebiyyāh* or *ᶜofrāh*). This has not been discussed here.

In addition to the use of allegory and the deliberate attempt to "fool the eye" (or ear) by holding off the real meaning and subject of the

18. Wallenstein (1960–61). The translation here is his, with a few minor corrections in brackets.

poem, many of these poems are characterized by "audacity," which is itself something typical of medieval secular Hebrew poetry. In this case, the audacity consists in using imagery and words which are typically associated with erotic verse (such things as drinking the saliva from the mouth of the beloved) in a religious setting. If we may say that the religious setting is the intermingling of *ḥôl* (secular) with *qôdesh* (sacred), then the audacity of secular poetry is in the mingling of *qôdesh* with *ḥôl*—the use of traditionally religious terms and ideas in a secular context.

If we are to fully appreciate the literary genius of the great classical Hebrew poets of Spain, we must understand their world. In their eyes, there was absolutely no inconsistency between leading a religious life, loyal to the observance of the commandments and the love of God, and the sensual enjoyment of wine (drunk, as we know, in company with Muslims at wine parties) and the pursuit of passion in the love of both women and boys. If it was audacious to introduce such ideas into religious poetry, it was no less audacious to lead such a life and to write about it in secular verse.

Their intent was only, perhaps, partially to shock—and to dazzle the reader with brilliance and cleverness. Behind it also lay, possibly, a very sincere desire to express a relationship with God in terms of everyday love and passion, which was a very real part of their lives.

## BIBLIOGRAPHY

Bonílla García, Luis. 1964. *El amor y su alcance histórico.* Madrid.

Brody, Ḥayyim and Meir Wiener. 1963. *Mib̲ḥar haššîrāh haʿib̲rît*, abridged ed., with additions, ed. A. M. Habermann. Jerusalem.

Dukes, Leopold. 1842. *Zur Kenntnis die neuhebräischen Religiosepoesie.* Frankfurt a. M.

Fleischer, Ezra. 1973. "*Ḥiddûšê haʾaskôlāh hapayyṭānît hassep̄ārādît.*" *Hassifrût* 4.

González Palencia, Angel. 1929. "El amor platónico en la corte de los califas." *Boletín de la real academia de ciencias, bellas letras y nobles artes de Córdoba* 8:77–99.

Hatzfeld, Helmut. 1976. *Estudios literarios sobre mística española.* Madrid.

Ibn al-ʿArabī. 1911. *Tarjumān al-Ashwāq*, tr. R. A. Nicholson. London.

Ibn ʿAqnin, Joseph. 1964. *Hitgallût hassôdôt vehôfāʿat hammeôrôt.* Ed. and tr. A. S. Halkin. Jerusalem.

Ibn ᶜEzra, Abraham. 1874. *Pêrûš šîr haššîrîm.* Ed. Henry J. Mathews. London.

Ibn ᶜEzra, Moses. 1957. *Šîrê haqqōdeš.* Ed. Simon Bernstein. Tel-Aviv.

Ibn Gabirol, Solomon. 1923. *Selected Religious Poems.* Ed. Israel Davidson, tr. Israel Zangwill. Philadelphia.

______. 1973. *Šîrê haqqōdeš.* Ed. Dov Jarden. Vol. II. Jerusalem.

______. 1975a. *Šîrê haḥôl.* Ed. Ḥayyim Schirmann and H. Brody. Jerusalem.

______. 1975b. *Šîrê haḥôl.* Ed. Dov Jarden. Jerusalem.

Ibn Janaḥ, Abu'l-Wālid (Jonah). 1896. *Sēp̱er haššorāšîm.* Ed. Wilhelm Bacher. Berlin; rpt. Amsterdam, 1969.

Ibn Naghrillah, Samuel. 1966. *Ben Tehillîm.* Ed. Dov Jarden. Jerusalem.

Kokovtsov, Paul. 1970. *Missiprê habbalšānût haᶜiḇrît bîmê habbênayîm.* Jerusalem.

Latham, J. D. 1964. "The Content of the *Laḥn Al-ᶜAwāmm* . . ." Primero congreso de estudios árabes e islamicos. *Actas.* Madrid.

Lazar, Moshé. 1964. *Amour cortois et "fin'amors" dans la littérature du XIIe siècle.* Paris.

Levin, Israel. 1972. "*Biqqaštî et šeʾahaḇāh nafšî.*" *Hassifrût* 3–4:116–149.

______. 1977. "*habberîḥāh min haᶜôlām ʾel haelōhîm.*" *ᶜAl šîrāh vesiprût.* Ed. Zvi Malachi. Tel-Aviv.

Halevy, Judah. 1894–1930. *Dîvan.* Ed. Ḥayyim Brody. Berlin.

______. 1978–82. *Šîrê haqqōdeš.* Ed. Dov Jarden. Jerusalem.

Manzalaoui, M. A. 1979. "Tragic Ends of Lovers: Medieval Islam and the Latin West." *Comparative Criticism, a yearbook.* Ed. E. Shaffer. Cambridge.

Marcus, Joseph. 1970. "*Šîrîm vepiyyûtîm ḥadāšîm.*" *Sēpẹr Ḥayyîm Schirmann.* 214–215. Ed. Shraga Abramson and Aaron Mirsky. Jerusalem.

Mirsky, Aaron. 1957. *Yalqûṭ piyyûṭîm.* Jerusalem.

______. 1965. *Rēšît happiyyûṭ.* Jerusalem.

Moses b. Maimon. 1961. *Haqdāmāh lammišnāh.* Ed. Mordecai Rabinowitz. Jerusalem.

______. 1963a. *The Guide for the Perplexed.* Tr. Shlomo Pines. Chicago.

______. 1963b. *Mišnāh ᶜim pērûš Mošeh ben Maimôn, Zeraᶜîm.* Ed. Joseph Kafiḥ. Jerusalem.

Nykl, A. R. 1946. *Hispano-Arabic Poetry.* Baltimore.

Ratzaby, Judah. "*Ḥôl beqōdeš: môṭîḇê ʾahaḇāh ḥillôniyyîm bappiyyûṭ hassepardî.*" *Hāʾāreṣ* (newspaper). 10/16/70.

Roth, Norman. 1979. "Satire and Debate in Two Famous Medieval Hebrew Poems From Al-Andalus: Love of Boys vs. Girls, the Pen and Other Themes." *Maghreb Review* 4:105–113.

———. 1979–80. "'Sacred' and 'Secular' in the Poetry of Ibn Gabirol." *Hebrew Studies* 20–21:75–79

———. 1981. "The Lyric Tradition in Hebrew Secular Poetry of Medieval Spain." *Hispanic Journal* 2:7–26.

———. 1982. "'Deal Gently with the Young Man': Love of Boys in Medieval Hebrew Poetry of Spain." *Speculum* 57:20–51.

al-Rūmī. 1983. *The Sufi Path of Love: The Spiritual Teachings of Rumi.* Tr. William Chillick. Albany, N.Y.

Schirmann, Ḥayyim (Jefim). 1954. *haššîrāh ha<sup>c</sup>iḇrît.* Jerusalem.

———. 1955. "The Ephebe in Medieval Hebrew Poetry." *Sefarad* 15:55–69 (also translated in Hebrew in Schirmann, *Letôldôt haššîrāh vehaddrâmāh ha<sup>c</sup>iḇrît* [Jerusalem, 1979], I, 97–105).

Schirmann, Ḥayyim (Jefim). 1961. "L'amour spirituelle dans la poésie hébraique du moyen âge." *Les Lettres romanes* 15:315–324.

Shim<sup>c</sup>on b"r Yiṣḥaq. 1938. *Piyyûṭî.* Ed. A. M. Habermann. Berlin.

von Grünebaum, G. E. 1940. "Penetration of Religious Motive in Arabic Love Poetry." *Journal of the American Oriental Society* 60:23–29.

Wallenstein, M. 1960–61. "Hebrew Ms. 6 in the John Rylands Library." *Bulletin of the John Rylands Library* 43:267–271.

Walzer, Richard. 1939. "Aristotle, Galen and Palladius on Love." *Journal of the Royal Asiatic Society* (no volume number):402–422; rpt. in his *Greek Into Arabic* (Oxford, 1962), pp. 48–59.

Wiener, Meir and Ḥayyim Brody. 1963. *Miḇḥar hāššîrah hā<sup>c</sup>iḇrît*, abridged ed., with additions, ed. A. M. Habermann. Jerusalem.

*HTR 75:4 (1982) 449-61*

# CLEMENT OF ALEXANDRIA AND SECRET MARK: THE SCORE AT THE END OF THE FIRST DECADE

Morton Smith
Columbia University

Late Spring of 1982 will see the tenth anniversary of the full publication of Clement's letter and its gospel fragments.[1] Accordingly, this seems an appropriate occasion to review the discussion of them to date. The following review is based on about 150 published items that have come to my attention. No doubt some have been missed, but I trust these are representative.

In brief, when the new material first appeared, there were many reports in newspapers and periodicals. Though some of these were surprisingly accurate and sympathetic, none went much beyond restatement or misstatement of the facts. Then came a swarm of attacks in religious journals, mainly intended to discredit the new gospel material, my theories about it, or both. Besides these, a few relatively objective studies of the material and/or the theories have appeared. These studies have commonly treated only particular aspects of the many problems raised by the new text. As yet, therefore, serious discussion has barely begun, but in a number of areas preliminary positions have been staked out, not only by the objective studies, but also by the attacks. Prejudiced and even malicious papers sometimes cite evidence and raise questions of scholarly importance.

Of the many publications received, I have listed in the bibliography at the end of this article those that seem to me significant for the scholarly discussion. "Significant" is a deliberately vague term; there are several I think worthless but influential. Since almost all are short, and since I shall not want to prove particular points, but only to categorize, I shall cite them merely by the authors' names.

As with any discovery of an ancient text, the first question was that of authenticity. Since the document consists of a letter, allegedly by Clement, quoting fragments said to come from

[1] In M. Smith, *Clement of Alexandria and a Secret Gospel of Mark* (Cambridge, MA: Harvard University, 1973) hereafter: *Clement*; abbreviated in *The Secret Gospel* (New York: Harper & Row, 1973). *The Secret Gospel* has meanwhile gone out of print but will be republished in 1982, in paperback, by The Dawn Horse Press, Clearlake, CA 95422.

a gospel by Mark, four positions are possible: (1) Both elements are bogus. (2) Both are genuine. (3) The letter is genuine, but the gospel fragments are not by Mark. (4) The fragments are genuine, but the letter is not by Clement. Variants of these positions can be conceived — for instance, one gospel fragment might be accepted, the other rejected. However, no such variants have been proposed, so none need be considered. Even the second and fourth of the above positions have had, I believe, no defenders and can likewise be passed over. All critics have agreed in choosing one of the remaining two: Either, as I initially proposed, the letter is actually by Clement of Alexandria, though he was mistaken in attributing the gospel fragments to Mark, or the whole thing is a fake.

Of these two, the latter has rarely been maintained. Those who have read either *Clement* or *The Secret Gospel* will remember that when I sent the text with a first draft of my commentary to fourteen outstanding scholars, all but two, Munck and Völker, thought Clement had written the letter. Besides these, A. D. Nock held to his first impression that it was not by Clement. Had Nock and Munck lived to consider the whole of the evidence, I think they might have changed their minds — or mine. At all events, we should have had serious discussion. Of the scholars listed in the bibliography here following, twenty-five have agreed in attributing the letter to Clement,[2] six have suspended judgment or have not discussed the question,[3] and only four have denied the attribution, namely, Kümmel, Murgia, Musurillo, and and Quesnell. Quesnell's denial was part of an absurd attempt to prove me the author of the text. Unfortunately, nobody else has had so high an opinion of my classical scholarship. Quesnell, having persuaded himself that I *could* have forged the text, had no difficulty in making up evidence that I *did* do so. For that purpose he simply distorted passages in my earlier works. I must thank Father Clifford, then editor of *CBQ*, not only for permitting me to answer Quesnell, but also for sending me, "in the hope that they will be useful," the comments of two of his associate editors, one of whom wrote, "Smith deserves some redress. I took the trouble to check all *HTR* passages where S. claims Quesnell

[2]To wit: Beardslee, Brown (?), Bruce (?), Donfried, Fitzmyer (?), Frend, Fuller, Grant, Hanson, Hobbs, van der Horst (?), Johnson, Kee, Koester, MacRae, Mullins, Parker, Petersen, Pomilio, Richardson, Shepherd, Skehan, Trevor-Roper, Trocmé, Wink. Those whose names are followed by question marks accepted the letter's authenticity only as a working hypothesis.

[3]Achtemeier, Betz, Kolenko, Merkel, Reese, Schmidt.

has misrepresented him, and S. certainly is correct. Q's reading of those passages is so inaccurate as to be irresponsible."[4]

The dissents of Murgia and Musurillo were on a different level. Musurillo wrote a valuable paper on milieux in which an ancient or seventeenth-eighteenth-century forgery *might* have been produced, and on *possible* reasons for producing one; his conjectures are ingenious and learned, but unlikely and unnecessary. By far the simplest explanation of the text is, that it was written where it was found, copied from a manuscript that had lain for a millennium or more in Mar Saba and had never been heard of because it had never been outside the monastery. Murgia, though he fell into a few factual errors, argued brilliantly that the literary form of the new document is one found often in forgeries — a bogus introductory document, commonly a letter, explaining the appearance and vouching for the authenticity of the equally bogus material it presents. This is true, but the same form is often used for presentation of genuine discoveries or material hitherto secret. Forgers use it because it is regularly used. (So too, when they forge wills, they commonly use the standard legal forms, but this does not prove that any will in a standard legal form is a forgery.) In sum, stimulating, but inconclusive. The question has to be settled by the objective evidence, above all the details of literary style. None of these studies contained any substantial argument to show that Clement could *not* have written the letter; they merely suggested reasons for thinking that someone else *might* have written it. By contrast, Kümmel began by crediting Quesnell, and went on to assemble, as evidence against authenticity, an assortment of secondhand trivialities and several substantial objections I had already answered in *Clement*. His reiteration of these, without any attention to the answers or to the linguistic evidence for Clement's authorship, was a disgrace both to the *Theologische Rundschau* and to the objective tradition of German criticism.

In sum, most scholars would attribute the letter to Clement, though a substantial minority are still in doubt. No strong

[4]This part of Quesnell's paper was adapted without acknowledgment by L. Moraldi in an amusing attack on the Italian edition (*Il Vangelo Segreto* [Milan: Mursia, 1977] "Morton Smith col 'vangelo segreto' scandalizzò l'America," *Tuttolibri* 3 (1977) #38 3. In a letter to *Tuttolibri* (#47 4) I pointed out M's source and the falsehoods he had himself contributed (he is an original thinker).

argument against the attribution has been advanced, and those few who have denied it have either ignored or resorted to fantastic conjectures to explain away the strong evidence presented in *Clement* from the letter's content and style, which attest Clement's authorship. Unless that evidence is faced and explained, no denial that Clement is the author should be taken seriously. Meanwhile, the recent "provisional" inclusion of the letter in the Berlin edition of Clement's works adequately indicates its actual status.[5]

If Clement wrote the letter, the gospel fragments quoted in it must be considerably earlier than his time. Writing between 175 and 200, he speaks of Secret Mark as a treasured heirloom of his church. He was not the sort of man to make up such a story. Consequently the latest plausible date for Secret Mark is about 150, while Clement's report that Carpocrates based his teaching on it would push it back to the beginning of the century, prior, at least, to Carpocrates, who flourished about 125. This brings it close to the canonical gospels, commonly dated about 70 to 100. The question of their relationship becomes sensitive, and resistance to the thrust of the evidence increases. Moreover, the thrust is difficult to determine. The evidence here is complicated, dull — much of it tables of verbal statistics and lists of variant readings — and apparently self-contradictory. The third chapter of Clement, which presents it, is hard reading, and the explanation finally proposed is complex — so complex that most critics did not try to present it, and several of those who did, got it wrong.[6]

Essentially I conjectured that an original Aramaic gospel had been twice translated into Greek; John had used one translation, Mark another. (This accounts for their agreement in outline, but difference in wording.) Each left out some elements and added many. Mark was then variously expanded — by Matthew, by Luke, and by the author of Secret Mark, who imitated Mark's style, but added episodes from the old Greek translation, inserting them where they had stood in the original outline. (Hence the Lazarus story has the same location, vis-à-vis the outline, in Secret Mark as in John.) According to Clement, the Carpocratians, too,

[5] *Clemens Alexandrinus* (GCS 4/1; 2d ed.; eds. O. Stählin and U. Treu; Berlin: Akademie-Verlag, 1980) xvii-xviii; cf. viii.

[6] Donfried, Fuller, Johnson, Merkel, Mullins, Shepherd, Wink.

got hold of Secret Mark and expanded ("corrupted") it yet further.[7]

In this theory the two most important points are: (1) that Mark and John are both based on a single, earlier gospel; (2) that Secret Mark added to Mark elements from that earlier gospel, rewritten in Markan style. Of the dozen scholars who commented on the theory, about half seemed inclined to accept these points.[8] Most commentators, however, after declaring the secret gospel later than Mark, went directly to their own theories of its origin. Then thought it a pastiche composed from the canonical gospels;[9] five thought it a product of free invention like the apocryphal gospels of the second century (they ignored the fact that those differ from it conspicuously both in style and in literary form);[10] five thought it used pre-Markan "floating pericopae" or oral traditions[11] — this comes close to the supposition of a pre-Markan gospel, but differs from it by failing to explain the similarities of order and geographical framework between Mark and John. The preponderance of the pastiche theory is due to three factors: (1) It is naively assumed that any occurrence in early Christian literature of an expression found in one of the canonical gospels is to be explained as a borrowing from that gospel. Though everybody pays lip service to the notion of oral tradition, few realize that it constituted a supply of expressions and motifs from which all Christian writers, including the authors of the canonical gospels, independently drew.[12] (2) No attention is paid to the facts that (a) we have these gospel fragments only in an eighteenth-century manuscript, (b) we must

[7]To this bare outline there were several modifications: Canonical Mark seemed to have been cut down from a longer text; Clement's secret gospel shows some signs of censorship; in sum, there seem to have been many minor alterations and we can grasp securely only the main outlines.

[8]So Beardslee, Donfried, Koester, MacRae, Pedersen, and perhaps Trocmé. *Contra*: Brown, Fuller, Johnson, Merkel, Pomilio, Shepherd. Koester's remarks are particularly important both because of his knowledge of the evidence for the extracanonical material, and for his role in developing the "trajectory" concept. His objection to its mechanical misuse (in his response to Fuller) deserves general attention.

[9]Brown, Bruce, Grant, Hanson (tentatively), Hobbs, van der Horst, Mullins, Richardson, Schmidt (with interesting parallels from the Diatessaron), and Skehan.

[10]Fitzmyer, Kümmel, Merkel, Parker, Shepherd.

[11]Fuller, Frend (?), Johnson, Kee Wink. Frend did not make his position fully clear.

[12]For full evidence of this see H. Köster, *Synoptische Überlieferung bei den apostolischen Vätern* (Berlin: Akademie, 1957).

therefore suppose that they have been to some extent corrupted in transmission, and (c) we know that one of the commonest forms of corruption, in the transmission of gospel texts, is contamination by the wording of more popular gospels. (3) The problems posed by the agreement in *order* of Mark, John, and Secret Mark, and the priority in *form* of the resurrection story in Secret Mark to that in John, are neglected in favor of first impressions based on familiar wording.[13] This reverses the proper ranking of the evidence. Verbal similarities can be accounted for in any number of ways; they may result from common Greek usage, from Christian oral tradition, from a common written source, from one evangelist's use of another's gospel, or from later textual corruption — to mention only familiar causes that have always to be considered. But questions of structural similarity between two stories, and a fortiori between two gospels, are fundamental and imply specific answers. Most people, of course, pay most attention to the superficial.

The positions outlined above allow for some overlap. All critics would recognize some borrowings from canonical gospels

[13]To this generalization the outstanding exception is Brown's paper, which tries to prove "that *it is not impossible* [his italics, p. 474] that SGM [the Secret Gospel of Mark] drew upon John." This attempt, and the clarity with which Brown saw the problem, makes his paper one of the most important of those in the bibliography. However, I think it fails. The attempt to discredit the argument from order fails to explain why, if using John, Secret Mark would not have located the visit to Bethany after that to Jericho. (The suggestion that it was located earlier so that its conclusion could be modeled on that of the Nicodemus story is desperate. Why could that conclusion not have been used in a later location?) The attempt to explain the resurrection story as an adaptation of John's Lazarus story is even weaker. Brown astutely concentrated on the *verbal* similarities, but it is the *structural* differences that are here decisive. He cannot explain how the author of Secret Mark, using John, happened to eliminate one of the two sisters (whose contrast is so important in the Johannine story!), to eliminate the Jews, etc. The appeal to "rewriting in Markan style" does not account for these *structural* changes; Brown accordingly avoids them. As for his presuppositions, let me quote the comment I sent him: "*If* one sets out with a determination to explain the origin of SGM from the canonical gospels, and *if* one supposes that somebody who had a vague memory of John wanted (for what reason?) to produce a copy of Mark which would contain versions of the Lazarus and Nicodemus stories, combined and rewritten in Markan style, and *if* one supposes that his memory of John — in spite of being vague (so that he would leave out and distort most of the stories) — was also extraordinarily good (so that he could range all over the gospel and take one element from here, another from there ... ), and *if* one supposes that his notion of Markan style was such that he could fill his story out at will with words and phrases from other gospels, *then* it would be possible to suppose that he had in this way produced the text we have ... ; *but* one would still be unable to explain ... why he just happened to forget all the clearly secondary, distinctively Johannine traits of the Johannine story which was his main source. (This was the point at which you dropped the effort to explain and took flight to Fortna's reconstruction — scarcely a tower of strength.) ... The main question in my mind is why one should make all these obviously unlikely suppositions."

other than Mark; most would probably admit some invention. The great divide, however, lies between the eleven who think that behind Secret Mark lies some pre-Markan tradition (whether oral or written in one form or another), and the fifteen who think the secret material composed entirely from scraps of the canonical gospels and free invention. For the first, Secret Mark can serve as evidence of what was said in pre-Markan Christian communities, and thence, perhaps, of what Jesus did. For the second, it is evidence only of the second-century community that produced it. The latter group probably gained some adherents because I had shown that the gospel fragments represented Jesus as practicing some sort of initiation, and I had argued that this initiation was a baptism supposed to admit the recipient into the kingdom of God and free him from the Mosaic law, this being effected by an illusory ascent to the heavens, of the sort described in the magical papyri, and by union with Jesus, also magical.

Of course nobody accepted the proposed explanation. I was amazed that so many went so far as to concede that Jesus might have had some secret doctrines and initiatory ceremonies,[14] or to recognize, even if unwillingly and with reservations, that magic did have a role in the first-century Church.[15] The most violent abuse (from scholars) came from two circles, one, the *dévots* (e.g., Fitzmyer, "Faust sells his soul!", "venal popularization"; Skehan, "morbid concatenation of fancies"; etc.), the other, the adherents of current exegetic cliques (form criticism, redaction criticism, etc.) who were outraged that I had not given their literature of mutually contradictory conjectures the attention they thought it deserved.[16] These latter, at least, had a legitimate objection — neglect of much contemporary scholarship — that did deserve an answer. Let me answer it here.

[14]Betz, Johnson, Koester, Grant, van der Horst. That none would go further was due, I think, rather to unfamiliarity with the terrain than to religious prejudice. None had given much attention to the evidence for the outsiders' view of Jesus, none was very well acquainted with ancient magical texts, or had then considered their parallels to the gospels, and, most important, all were used to interpreting the relevant NT texts in other ways, so the new interpretations, because they differed from the accepted ones, seemed "wrong." Here the outstanding exception was Trevor-Roper, who read my work as a professional historian, without the preconceptions of a NT scholar. I am proud of his approval.

[15]Bruce, Frend, Betz, Koester, Grant, van der Horst, Richardson, Trevor-Roper, Wink.

[16]So Achtemeier (a conspicuously incompetent review, swarming with gross errors even in his reports of what I had said), Donfried, Fuller, Merkel, Wink.

To show that a text has been altered, one can use three kinds of evidence: from manuscripts (textual differences, erasures, insertions, etc.), from historical reports indicating changes, and from inconsistencies (changes in wording, content, grammatical usage, etc.). This last kind of evidence is occasionally conclusive,[17] but often uncertain. Whether or not an introduction to a story comes from its original teller, whether details that seem to break the narrative are additions or mere asides — such questions often come down to matters of feeling. Consequently much that passes as form criticism and the like is actually autobiography — "How I feel about this text." Hence the welter of contradictions these schools have produced.

Now the mass of factual data that had to be dealt with in evaluating the letter of Clement and Secret Mark was such that my full presentation, *Clement*, is a dreadfully complex book. To have further cluttered its complexity with innumerable discussions of form-critical theories, leading to conclusions in which nothing could be concluded, would have produced a work practically unreadable. All the more so, *The Secret Gospel*, in which I tried to make the results of *Clement* accessible to ordinary readers, had to be clear of such clutter. A good example of what I mean has been furnished by Fuller, the arbitrariness of whose conjectures was pointed out in my reply to him. In another reply, Hobbs produced a completely different account of the secret gospel's origin by his conjecture that it was a pastiche. Yet another conjectural explanation was offered by Grant.

Admittedly conjectures are necessary, but they must be based on substantial evidence and must accord with historical knowledge of ancient society and of the general course and circumstances of the events concerned. The general historical framework must serve as our guide in locating and assessing all early Christian documents, canonical or not. Within this general framework there are smaller frames that should both limit and guide conjectures concerning smaller fields — the public life of Jesus, the missionary career of Paul, and so on. When writing *Clement* I overestimated the professional readers for whom the book was written, supposing they would recognize, when I merely mentioned them, the elements of these frames, and that they would see their relevance to the argument. *The Secret Gospel*, summarizing *Clement*, suffered

[17]For instance, if one can show, in a text, a series of parenthetical comments, all of which, in the same way, contradict or modify the main argument. But even in such cases piety and perverse ingenuity may continue to defend the text's integrity. See the commentaries on Ecclesiastes.

even more from the same misjudgment. Consequently a number of critics complained of the "lack of historical criteria" to justify distinctions between trustworthy and unreliable material. To these complaints I have responded in *Jesus the Magician*[18] which begins with a study of the evidence for the basic events of Jesus' career and the role he played in his society, ascertains these, and proceeds from them to evaluate particular gospel passages. Only by reference to the historical framework can we discover which pieces fit and which do not.

In sum, "the state of the question" would seem to be about as follows: Attribution of the letter to Clement is commonly accepted and no strong argument against it has appeared, but Clement's attribution of the gospel to "Mark" is universally rejected. As to the gospel fragments, the field is split three ways. The weakest position seems to be that of those who declare them an apocryphal gospel of the common second-century sort; this overlooks their conspicuous differences from that type. The most popular opinion declares them a pastiche composed from the canonical gospels. Since such pastiches are reported, the fact that no early one is extant is a less serious objection to this theory than is its failure to explain the apparent priority of the new resurrection story to John's Lazarus story, and its relation to the Markan-Johannine outline. The third opinion is that the new text comes from an expansion of Mark which imitated Markan style, but used earlier material. This escapes the previous objections, but those who hold it are much divided as to what sort of earlier material was used.[19]

[18] San Francisco: Harper & Row, 1978. This has now been republished in paperback by Harper & Row.

[19] This article has dealt only with the works or passages bearing directly on the origin of the letter of Clement or of the gospel material it contains. A number of other studies, however, have mentioned in passing either the letter or the gospel material. Of these, one group deserves mention — those attempting to explain the mysterious young man of Mark 14:51. These began with an "Addendum" by R. Scroggs and K. Groff on pp. 547-48 of their article "Baptism in Mark" (*JBL* 92 [1973] 531-48). They took the young man as an allegorical figure representing both Christ and the initiate in Christian baptism. This interpretation neglects only the main facts: this young man deserted Christ and saved himself. However, the authors concluded on p. 548 that the initiation reported in the secret gospel "is, or is related to, baptism" and therefore proves that "the baptismal interpretation of 14.51-52 is ... 'orthodox' and fairly early"; they thought the secret gospel "probably ... no later than the second century." Their article initiated a series of implausible suggestions by theologians whose candor compelled them to say nothing at all about the new evidence: P. Beernaert, 1974; J. Crossan, 1978; B. Standaert, 1978; J. Gnilka, 1979; H. Fleddermann, 1979. By contrast, F. Neirynck ("La Fuite du Jeune Homme," *EThL* 55 [1979] 43-66 [= *ALBO*, Ser. 5, 39]) was more thorough. He admitted the existence of the secret gospel story,

TERMINAL NOTE

Since the preceding article was completed, I have learned of three more studies (two of them still forthcoming) dealing seriously with the text. A paper by Prof. Thomas Talley of General Theological Seminary, New York, "Le Temps liturgique dans l'Église ancienne" (*La Maison-Dieu* 147 [1981] 29-60), surveys current discussions of the early dates of the major Christian festivals and points out (pp. 51ff.) that the secret gospel and letter of Clement contain the tradition needed to explain the dating of the early Egyptian baptismal liturgy on the sixth day of the sixth week of a lent beginning immediately after Epiphany. In this connection Fr. Talley reports that he asked about the manuscript of the letter of Clement when he was in Jerusalem in January 1980. The Archimandrite Melito told him that he had

---

but dismissed it as based on John 11, saying nothing of the formal evidence that it is earlier than the Johannine version. Then he argued (pp. 51-52) that it is historically insignificant because composed of random reminiscences of the canonical gospels. His evidence was (1) the fact that it contains many parallels to those gospels; (2) the tacit assumption that, in early Christian literature, all parallels to the canonical gospels must derive from them. This assumption being false, his argument was worthless. He then went on to argue (pp. 62 ff.) that since the words *epi gymnou* in 14:51 are omitted by W and λ, while ϑ, φ, and 565 have a variant, *gymnos*, they should be deleted! (One can hardly imagine what he would say of a proposal to delete, on so little evidence, any phrase which was not embarrassing. And what would the text of the gospels look like if all words against which there is this much evidence were deleted?) Having thus got rid of the embarrassment, the more difficult reading, he placidly observed, "Quant à *gymnos* au v. 52, l'emploi du mot au sens de *en chitōni monōi* n'a rien d'extraordinaire" (p. 64). It never occurred to him that this is just what proves that neither the sense nor the omission can be right. The evangelist was not concerned to report matters which were "in no way extraordinary," and the dramatic position of this detail, at the conclusion of Jesus' free ministry and the beginning of his passion, proves it significant. In the Mar Saba letter Clement tells us that the Gospel of Mark served as a collection of texts from which Christian teachers began their explanations. Those explanations had to be, in many points, apologetic; the opponents of Christianity were still telling their versions of the events — so Justin reports (*Dialogue*, 17, 108, 117) and Celsus proves. This event must have needed a good deal of explaining: "Holy man arrested ... naked youth escapes." No further explanation is needed for the omissions by Matthew and Luke, or the partial bowdlerization by some MSS of Mark. Uncritically accepting the bowdlerized version, Neirynck cautiously concluded that the episode was historical, but he did not think of asking what the young man was doing there. How did he just happen to be present after a secret dinner of Jesus and the disciples? How did he just happen to be alone with Jesus after "all" the disciples had fled? Blessed are the pure in heart, for they shall not see difficulties. The most recent study I have seen is that of M. Gourgues, "À propos du symbolisme ... de Marc 16.5," *NTS* 27 (1981) 672-78. Gourgues cites all the articles referred to in this note, and also alludes in two footnotes to the new evidence, but says nothing of its importance for his subject — its indication that Jesus administered some sort of nocturnal ceremony to which recipients came in the costume customary for initiations.

himself brought it from Mar Saba to the Patriarchal Library. Fr. Kallistos, the librarian there, said that it had been received, but it had been taken out of the volume of Ignatius, was being studied, and was not available for inspection. Talley's article is to appear also in German in *Liturgisches Jahrbuch* and in English in *Studia Liturgica*. In another paper, "Alexandria and the Origin of Lent," given at the International Patristic Congress in 1979, and to be published in the papers of that Congress, he argues that the initiatory text of Secret Mark was the source of a baptismal festival "of Lazarus" celebrated annually in the Alexandrian church prior to the time of Athanasius. A paper by Prof. Helmut Koester of Harvard, "History and Development of Mark's Gospel (from Mark to *Secret Mark* and 'Canonical' Mark)," will appear in *A Time for Reappraisal and Fresh Approaches: Colloquy on New Testament Studies*, ed. Bruce Corley (Macon, GA: Mercer University, 1982). In correspondence about the latter article, Prof. Koester made the following statement, which he has given me permission to quote: "If the letter is 'Pseudo-Clement,' — and I don't think it is — it must be ancient and the fragment from *Secret Mark* that it quotes (as well as the reference to the Carpocratians, etc.) must be genuine. The piece of *Secret Mark* fits the Markan trajectory so well that a forgery is inconceivable."

## BIBLIOGRAPHY

P. Achtemeier, review, *JBL* 93 (1974) 625-28.

W. Beardslee, review, *Int* 28 (1974) 234-36.

H. D. Betz, response to Fuller, see Fuller.

R. Brown, "The Relation of 'The Secret Gospel of Mark' to the Fourth Gospel," *CBQ* 36 (1974) 466-85.

F. Bruce, *The 'Secret' Gospel of Mark* (E. Wood Lecture 1974) London: Athlone Press, 1974.

K. Donfried, "New-Found Fragments of an Early Gospel," *Christian Century* 90 (1973) 759-60.

J. Fitzmyer, "How to Exploit a Secret Gospel," *America* 128 (1973) 570-72. See my reply and his, printed by the editors of *America* under the title, "Mark's 'Secret Gospel'?", 129 (1973) 64-65.

W. Frend, "A New Jesus?" *New York Review of Books* 20 (9 Aug 1973) 34-35.

R. Fuller, *Longer Mark: Forgery, Interpolation, or Old Tradition?* (Center for Hermeneutical Studies, Colloquy 18) ed. W. Wuellner; Berkeley: Center for Hermeneutical Studies, 1975. This contains responses by a dozen scholars, of which some are mere notes, but the following deserve notice: H. D. Betz, 17-18; E. Hobbs, 19-25; S. Johnson, 26-28; H. Koester 29-32; A. Kolenkow, 33-34; C. Murgia, 35-40; D. Schmidt, 41-45; M. Shepherd, 46-52; M. Smith, 12-15.

R. Grant, "Morton Smith's Two Books," *ATR* 56 (1974) 58-65.

R. Hanson, Review, *JTS* 25 (1974) 513-21.

E. Hobbs, response to Fuller (see Fuller).

P. van der Horst, "Het 'Geheime Markusevangelie'," *NedThTs* 33 (1979), 27-51.

S. Johnson, "The Mystery of St. Mark," *History Today* 25 (1975) 89-97.

———, response to Fuller (see Fuller).

H. Kee, review, *JAAR* 43 (1975) 326-29.

H. Koester, review, *AHR* 80 (1975) 620-22.

———, response to Fuller (see Fuller).

A. Kolenkow, response to Fuller (see Fuller).

W. Kümmel, "Ein Jahrzent Jesusforschung (1965-1975)," *ThR* n.s. 40 (1975) 298-303.

G. MacRae, "Yet Another Jesus," *Commonweal* 99 (1974) 417-420.

H. Merkel, "Auf den Spuren des Urmarkus?" *ZTK* 71 (1974) 123-44. See my reply, "Merkel on the Longer Text of Mark," *ZTK* 72 (1975) 133-50.

T. Mullins, "Papias and Clement and Mark's Two Gospels," *VC* 30 (1976) 189-92.

C. Murgia, response to Fuller (see Fuller).

H. Musurillo, "Morton Smith's Secret Gospel," *Thought* 48 (1974) 327-31.

P. Parker, "An early Christian cover-up?" *New York Times Book Review* (22 July 1973) 5.

———, "On Professor Morton Smith's Find at Mar Saba," *ATR* 56 (1974) 53-57.

N. Petersen, review, *Southern Humanities Review* 8 (1974) 525-31.

M. Pomilio, "Il frammento di Mar Saba Un Vangelo Segreto?" *Studi Cattolici* 21 (1978) 10-16.

Q. Quesnell, "The Mar Saba Clementine: A Question of Evidence," *CBQ* 37 (1975) 48-67. See my reply, "On the Authenticity of the Mar Saba Letter of Clement," *CBQ* 38 (1976) 196-99, and Quesnell's "A Reply to Morton Smith," ibid., 200-203.

J. Reese, review, *CBQ* 36 (1974) 434-35.

C. Richardson, review, *TS* 35 (1974) 571-77.

D. Schmidt, response to Fuller (see Fuller).

M. Shepherd, response to Fuller (see Fuller).

P. Skehan, review, *CHR* 60 (1974) 451-53.

M. Smith, responses, see Fitzmyer, Fuller, Merkel, Quesnell.

H. Trevor-Roper, "Gospel of Liberty," (London) *Sunday Times* (30 June 1974) 15.

E. Trocmé, "Trois critiques au miroir de l'évangelie selon Marc," *RHPhR* 55 (1975) 289-95.

W. Wink, "Jesus as Magician," *USQR* 30 (1974) 3-14.

See also the papers cited in n. 19 and the papers by Koester and Talley mentioned in the terminal note.

# *Is There a Reform Response to Homosexuality?*

RAV A. SOLOFF

IT IS CLEAR THAT NEW ATTITUDES AND challenges on the question of homosexuality are being felt throughout the Jewish world. No article entitled "homosexuality" appeared in the *Jewish Encyclopedia* of seventy-five years ago, and no article entitled "homosexuality" appeared in the *Universal Jewish Encyclopedia* of forty years ago. However, in the more recent *Encyclopedia Judaica* there is just such an article, a little over one column in length, by Chief Rabbi Immanuel Jacobovitz of London.

Rabbi Jacobovitz's article and two responsa by the eminent Reform *posek*, Rabbi Solomon B. Freehof, leave no room for doubt about their understanding of the negative biblical and talmudic attitudes toward homosexuality.[1] They follow generations of rabbinic interpreters in regarding the biblical injunctions against *mishkav zakhar* as condemning homosexual relations in general, and only homosexual relations, without regard to any historical context. When Rabbi Walter Jacob collected "Jewish Sources on Homosexuality" from rabbinic literature he did not find any texts that question the *halakhic* prohibition against homosexuality cited above.[2] Very recently, however, Rabbi Allen B. Bennett has argued that the biblical authors would not have had an inkling of what homosexuality was (what anyone today would call "homosexuality") and, therefore, would not have wasted their time legislating against it. In support of his contention he cites *Sex Laws and Customs in Judaism*,[3] and *Sexual Variance in Society and History* whose author holds that "among the Hebrews, the denunciations seem to be not so much against homosexuality as such as

1. Immanuel Jacobovitz, *Encyclopedia Judaica*, volume 8, columns 861, 862; Solomon B. Freehof, "Homosexuality," *Current Reform Responsa* (volume III of the series, HUC Press, 1969), pp. 236ff., and "Homosexual Congregations," *Contemporary Reform Responsa* (volume V of the series, HUC Press, 1974), pp. 23ff.

2. Walter Jacob, "Jewish Sources on Homosexuality" (privately circulated, Pittsburgh, Pa., August, 1978), p. 1.

3. Louis Epstein, *Sex Laws and Customs in Judaism* (KTAV, 1967), pp. 135ff.

RAV A. SOLOFF *is the rabbi of Beth Sholom Congregation, Johnstown, Pa. From 1978 to 1983, he served on the Responsa Committee of the CCAR.*

against the idolatry associated with it, or they spring from fears of assimilation."[4]

The biblical texts at the center of this discussion are in the third book of Torah. Traditionally understood, Leviticus 18:22 directly forbids male homosexuality, listing the act as one of the abominations because of which the Land vomited out its (former) inhabitants. Verse 29 specifies that those who do such things shall be cut off from their people. Two chapters later the law is repeated with a slightly different wording. Leviticus 20:13 says "they have committed an abomination, both of them; they shall surely be put to death; blood guilt (for their death) rests upon their own heads." This verse, however, is in a section with other violations which carry the same penalty (verses 9-13), and with other violations that carry other penalties (verse 14, "burnt with fire;" verses 15-16, "surely be put to death;" verses 17-18, "cut off from their people") leading me to think that the penalty for an act of homosexual intercourse is not the same in Leviticus 18:22 as in Leviticus 20:13. That is, *nikhretu*, the term used in 18:22, *is* used again in Chapter 20, but for a different violation (verses 17-18), so I do not believe that *nikhretu* in Leviticus 18:22 is the same punishment as *mot yumatu* in Leviticus 20:13. I shall return to this difference a little later.

There are a few other biblical references to homosexuality. Although Deuteronomy 23:18 forbids ritual male prostitution[5] (I guess it is assumed that both male and female ritual prostitution services males), references to the persistence of such prostitution are found in the Book of Kings (IK 14:24; 15:12; 22:47; and IIK 23:7). There is, however, no instance of express approval or explicit toleration of homosexuality on the part of the Lord or on the part of the Lord's spokesmen and editors. This is true however one translates the stories of the men of Sodom who demanded to "know" Lot's male visitors, and of the men of Benjamin who demanded to "know" a male traveller.

Some writers have undertaken a non-traditional explanation of these biblical texts in their effort to expound a "gay theology." In an interview published in *Ministry, The International Journal of the Seventh-Day Adventist Ministerial Association*, the editor, J.R. Spangler, talks with Colin Cook, who found deliverance from homosexuality through the power of the Gospel, and now directs Quest Learning Center. . . .

> *SPANGLER:* You say you believe the Bible speaks of homosexuality. But the gay theologian takes the same texts you read and finds no reference to homosexuality in them.

4. Vern Bullough, *Sexual Variance in Society and History* (University of Chicago Press, 1976), pp. 82 and 37.

5. "No Israelite woman shall be a cult prostitute, nor shall any Israelite man be a cult prostitute (v. 19). You shall not bring the fee of a whore or the pay of a dog [here used as a perjorative, to describe a male prostitute] into the house of the Lord your God in fulfillment of any vow, for both are abhorrent to the Lord your God." Translation and comment from *The Torah, A Modern Commentary* (UAHC, 1981), p. 1497.

> *COOK:* You have to understand that there is a basic presupposition underlying gay theology — that true homosexuality is unchangeable, natural, "inverted," as Bailey started calling it. So God wouldn't condemn the expression of something that is basic to some people's nature, the gay theologian says. What God does condemn, he explains, is the *abuse* of homosexuality, as in homosexual rape, or the exploitation of it, as in homosexual cultic prostitution.
> *SPANGLER:* So the gay theologian interprets the homosexuality texts on the basis of these presuppositions?
> *COOK:* Yes, Sodom and Gomorrah, for example, were not destroyed for homosexuality, the gay theologian explains, but for pride, gluttony, and inhospitality, as Isaiah, Ezekiel, and Jesus point out. . . . Genesis sets up man's identity. Man was made to be fully himself only when he identifies with one who is the same as he is, and yet opposite from him — that is, another human of the opposite sex (see Gen. 2:10-24). . . . When we take this unified biblical view, the Sodom account makes sense without clubbing it to death. The same goes for the Levitical proscription (Lev. 18:22, 20:13). That is, homosexual activity is sinful not because of its association with pagan rites, but because of its basic disharmony with the internal structure of creation.[6]

There are biblical texts and rabbinic texts which condemn homosexual acts. Some would say: because of their association with idolatry; because of their disharmony with the structure of creation; because of their abuse as in homosexual rape or their exploitation as in cultic prostitution; because they might lead the husband to abandon his wife or avoid procreation.[7] These and other traditional or anti-traditional explanations, however, do not provide the basis for a Reform response to homosexuality. Should the majority at a CCAR Convention decide to adopt one or another interpretation of those verses in Leviticus, it would leave our question unanswered because so many of our colleagues take a position similar to that of Rabbi Judith S. Lewis:

> I, myself, do not make my Jewish decisions on the basis of *halakha* or "tradition." I would, therefore, not address the question of homosexuality from a *halakhic* point of view unless I were also prepared to take an equally traditional stand on family purity, *kashrut* and other such matters. I think the question which really needs to be addressed is, since we know that large numbers of Jewish men and women are and will continue to be homosexuals, practicing or not, how do we respond, legitimately, as a liberal Jewish movement?[8]

The CCAR Committee on Responsa recognizes the right of the parent body to adopt policies and norms negating *halakhic* teachings. Individually, the rabbis support some of these departures from tradition and oppose others. The new roles that women play in Reform Jewish life, accepting rabbinic ordination, for example, are validated by decisions made in this generation and not by older *halakhah*. If the CCAR and the

6. *Ministry*, Vol. 54, No. 9 (September, 1981): 7-8.
7. Walter Jacob, *Op. cit.*, p. 1.
8. Judith S. Lewis, personal letter of February, 1983, quoted with permission.

UAHC decide that eating pig and wearing *shatnez* are no longer disapproved behaviors for a Reform Jew, then the clear prohibitions in Torah and Talmud should no longer be applied by Reform rabbis or Reform congregations, except as matters of individual guidance and choice. In this frame of reference, a different response to homosexuality may some day be accepted by Reform. I can only report that I have not been personally confronted with evidence of any widespread shift of opinion among my colleagues, away from the biblical and talmudic prohibitions.

However, in my view, there is a second aspect of the question that should be considered, regardless of whether one decides that homosexuality is bad, good, indifferent, or that one has not reached any decision. That is, what should we do about it? I refer back to the two terms in Leviticus which may *not*, traditional interpretations to the contrary notwithstanding, may *not* describe one and the same biblical attitude toward the proper penalty for homosexuality: *karet* and *mavet*.

> . . . Originally, divine punishment was independent of and additional to judicial punishment . . . In one instance, the law explicitly states that where the prescribed capital punishment is not carried out, God will Himself set His face "against that man and his kin, and will cut off from among their people both him and all who follow him in going astray after Molech" (Lev. 20:2-5). This juxtaposition of divine and judicial punishments appears conclusively to disprove the view that *karet* ("cutting off") was not a divine punishment of death, but rather a judicial punishment of excommunication. . . . For a good many offenses, the divine *karet* is the only punishment prescribed. It has been suggested that they are such offenses as are committed in private, for which eyewitnesses will not usually be available; such as, for instance, . . . various sexual offenses (Lev. 20:17-18; 18:29. . . .) Others maintain that these offenses are mostly of a religious or sacerdotal character. . . . There are, however, some offenses, punishable by *karet* only, that do not fit into either of these categories. . . . This fact — together with the gravity of some of the sexual offenses so punishable — led some scholars to assume that *karet*, even though a threat of divine punishment, was at the same time an authorization of judicial capital punishment.[9]

Thus, in our case we might say that *nikhretu* means that they will be cut off by God from the good which is destined for their people, whereas *mot yumatu* means that they will be put to death by decree of a human court.

Leviticus *Rabbah* 18:3 states that the flood came upon the world in the days of Noah because of sodomy, and Genesis 9:22 has been interpreted as a possible homosexual act between Ham and Noah, which resulted in a divine curse.[10] From these rabbinic comments, also, one may argue that at least some authorities saw divine punishment as the appropriate penalty for a homosexual act. Indeed, *Mishnah Keritot* 1:1-2 specifies, "if a man has connexion . . . with a male", as one of thirty-six transgressions punishable by *karet*. But not under all circumstances. It is one of the acts concerning which,

9. "Divine Punishment," *Encyclopedia Judaica*, volume 6, column 121.
10. Walter Jacob, *Op. cit.*, p. 1.

> if in these things he transgressed wantonly he is liable to *karet* (and not to another penalty), and if (he did it) in error, (he is liable) to a sin-offering; and if it was in doubt whether he had committed a transgression, he is liable to a Suspensive Guilt-offering. . . .[11]

Here, the penalty is made to depend upon the nature of the perpetrator's intention or state of mind. On the other hand, *Mishnah Sanhedrin* 7:4 reads, "These are they that are to be stoned: he that has connexion with (then we find included in the list) a male," and later in the same *mishnah* the penalties specified in Leviticus 20:15-16 (including stoning for a homosexual act) are repeated.[12]

The relation of law to morality is complex in every society, and their common source in Judaism, as revelation, does not simplify the issue. Accordingly, we are sure to find support texts in some *halakhic* source about homosexuality for either policy: "leave it to heaven, it's a moral question," or "punish severely, the law forbids." And, as a further caution, harsh legal phraseology regarding penalties may at times indicate rabbinic feelings about the immorality of a behavior, rather than rabbinic judgment about a legally enforceable punishment. For example, the Talmud calls many sinners "liable to the death penalty" when "clearly no court would prescribe such punishment" for their sins.[13] Dr. Robert Gordis simplifies this point succinctly by reference to the rabbinic category of *patur aval asur* as a proper response to private homosexual acts between consenting adults.[14]

For completeness' sake a few words about lesbianism. Female homosexuality is more rarely considered in *halakhic* sources, and the absence of any direct, biblical text prescribing condemnation or punishment leads to some leniency. Still, lesbian acts were considered obscene, with some authorities apparently dictating punishment and others declining to do so.[15]

Now, what should we *do* about homosexuality?

We have Dr. Freehof's responsa on "Homosexuality" and on "Homosexual Congregations," concluding that homosexuality *is* sin, but forbidding the exclusion of sinners from the congregation. A draft of "A Statement on Homosexuals in Leadership Positions" from the Responsa Committee reflects some of our agonizing over the question of "what to do about it." The draft quotes a 1977 resolution of the CCAR supporting civil rights and civil liberties for homosexuals, and encouraging "legislation which decriminalizes homosexual acts between consenting adults, and prohibits discrimination against them as persons."[16] After examining

11. Herbert Danby, *The Mishnah* (Oxford University Press, 1933), "Kerithoth," pp. 562ff.
12. Ibid., "Sanhedrin," pp. 391ff.
13. "Law and Morality," *Encyclopedia Judaica*, volume 10, columns 1480-1484.
14. Robert Gordis, *Love and Sex* (Farrar, Straus & Giroux, 1978), p. 157.
15. Walter Jacob, *Op. cit.*, pp. 2-3.
16. *CCAR Yearbook*, Vol. LXXXVII (1977), pp. 50f.

*halakhic* statements, not only about homosexuality, but also about rabbis, cantors and teachers, our draft notes that,

> among Ashkenazim they were sometimes dismissed on rumor alone. . . . The Sephardic community was more lax in this regard (Maimonides, *Responsa* — Friemann, #18), but it would also dismiss instantly if a charge was proven (R. Ḥai, *Shaarei Teshuvah* #50). These standards referred to all kinds of overt improper sexual behavior, as well as other unacceptable acts. I have found only one reference to an accusation of homosexual practices; although this was not proven, the cantor was dismissed as a preventive measure (Elijah Ibn Ḥayim, *Responsa* #41). The community always sought leaders who were above reproach, and continues to do so. . . .
>
> Overt heterosexual behavior or overt homosexual behavior which is considered objectionable by the community, disqualifies the person involved from leadership positions in the Jewish community. We reject this type of individual as a role model within the Jewish community. We cannot recommend such an individual as a role model nor should he/she be placed in a position of leadership or guidance for children of any age.[17]

It is not the homosexual as a person whom we reject for a leadership position, but a person whose behavior is considered objectionable. In *halakhah*, customs accepted in practice become binding, and local custom is binding upon the local community.[18] The congregation has a right to refrain from hiring a rabbi who picks his nose in the pulpit.

At the core of the problem may be a long standing "revulsion," which Gordis describes[19] and about which I think the philosophy expressed by Joseph Margolis is relevant:

> . . . Assume that a relatively homogenous society accepts some doctrine about "appropriate" or "admissible" sexual practices, usually incorporated into moral convictions. Then admit that, subscribing to that doctrine, the habits of mind and the tastes and feelings of the members of that society are sensitized and trained congruently. Deviations from the admitted norms will, then, be noted, and relatively extreme departures will be viewed as perverted — in the strong sense that representative members of the society will be disposed to find such extreme practices and inclinations abhorrent. (Margolis goes on to describe how *society* may adjust to this tension.)
>
> This corollary is obvious: In order to reduce the sense of abhorrence, a society must extend its tolerance from its own normative preference via intermediary practices, toward the perverted; as it does so, it will inevitably alter its conception of "natural" practices. What the limits of its tolerance may be is difficult to say, but without doubt, they will be substantially in accord with the moral and prudential values prevailing in sectors of community life other than the sexual.[20]

17. Letter from Dr. Walter Jacob to Responsa Committee, dated April 2, 1981 with attached draft, "A Statement on Homosexuals in Leadership Positions," p. 3.

18. "Minhag," *Encyclopedia Judaica*, volume 12, columns 5ff.

19. Robert Gordis, *Op. cit.*, p. 150.

20. Joseph Margolis, "The Question of Homosexuality," *Philosophy and Sex*, ed. Robert Baker and Frederick Elliston (Prometheus Books, 1975), pp. 299ff.

What do we accept as the moral and prudential values of our society? How much change are we willing to accept in the name of Reform Judaism? And is there any consensus beyond that slippery shibboleth, "community standards?"

We have no answer as yet concerning the "*gerut* of a gay goy." What should be our approach to a known and active homosexual who desires to convert to Judaism? Here are some of my thoughts on that question. For one thing, Cook makes a point about lumping all homosexuals into any one category: "It is important to distinguish between homosexuals committed to a gay life style and those desperately trying to resolve what they believe to be an emotional and moral problem." I am reminded of the distinction between a wanton act, punishable by the more severe penalty of *karet* (which, however, only God imposes), and an act committed in error, for which the penalty may be lighter, a sin-offering or lashes imposed by a court. Anyway, I always want to consider the specific behavior, and not the nature or condition of the person concerning whom a decision is called for.

Second, the responsibility of a rabbi who takes part in welcoming a *ger* into Judaism is weighty, indeed. We owe it to *Am Yisrael* that we not weaken or betray our people by knowingly introducing saboteurs, enemies or destroyers into our midst. But we presume that the prospective *ger* is innocent unless proved to be otherwise, and truthful, so that his intentions regarding future homosexual acts would probably be taken at face value. Now, is the rabbi faced with a prospective *ger* whom the rabbi suspects of planning future seductions or rapes? If so, gay or heterosexual, that *goy* should be rejected on the basis that "we cannot accept as a convert someone who is a sinner and intends to continue with his sin." But when the rabbi is faced with a prospective convert whom the rabbi expects to be a good and sincere Jew, not a criminal or a destroyer of Judaism, then that rabbi, in my opinion, must decide *ad hoc* whether the sexual orientation and practices of the *ger* are relevant to the conversion. Some rabbis may feel that a "gay" is *per se* "a destroyer," whereas others may feel that this individual would benefit from conversion to Judaism, and would probably prove to be an asset to *Am Yisrael*, and I think that each rabbi must follow his or her conscience.

In summary I offer the following draft for a Reform response to homosexuality:

> The Central Conference of American Rabbis is on record, supporting full civil rights and civil liberties for homosexual persons and encouraging "legislation which decriminalizes homosexual acts between consenting adults, and prohibits discrimination against them as persons." This marks a shift away from the punitive attitude of many traditional Jewish texts.
>
> Generations of rabbis based their teachings on the premise that the Bible mandates an attitude of revulsion and laws of prohibition against homosexuality as such, citing passages in Leviticus 18 as their prooftexts. However,

recent scholarship questions whether the biblical authors were even addressing the issue of homosexuality at all, holding instead that the prohibited homosexual acts were inextricably linked with idolatry in the context of both heterosexual and homosexual cultic prostitution. Thus, the specific prohibition of a homosexual act was only a part of the picture, one "fence" around the prohibition against the idolatrous practice of heterosexual as well as homosexual cultic prostitution.

The proper interpretation of well known statements about homosexuality from later, classic Jewish texts likewise is subject to debate. But just as rabbis who commented thousands or hundreds of years ago spoke out of their times and cultural settings, so too must we consider the lessons of contemporary scholarship in the fields of psychology, social psychology, sociology, ethics and religious thought. Thus, the inescapable implication of the resolution encouraging legislation to prohibit discrimination against homosexuals as persons is that we must not practice any such discrimination.

We do not discriminate against Jewish persons seeking membership in our congregations on the basis of race, sex, sexual orientation, disability or handicap. We do not discriminate against them in employment. We reject the unfounded fear that the healthy sexual development of children or young adults can be jeopardized by the presence of a qualified, well-behaved adult such as a teacher, administrator, cantor or rabbi who is of any specific race, sex, sexual orientation, stage of pregnancy or limited by a disability or handicap.[21] We recognize that there is the rare case of anti-social behavior or improper behavior on the part of a Jewish professional or layman, irrespective of sexual orientation, which would lead to suspension or dismissal from office. When such a case involves aberrant sexual behavior the appropriate response is professional treatment, not ostracism or discrimination.[22]

It has not been my purpose in this article to argue for a preconceived position, though the present state of my own prejudices and beliefs must be obvious. Rather, with the help of colleagues, those quoted above and others, I have tried to survey an area of shifting discussion and decreasing controversy among us. After more than seven years since the CCAR resolution on the civil rights of homosexuals, we may be close to agreement on a more substantive statement.

21. Richard Green, "Patterns of Sexual Identity in Childhood: Relationship to Subsequent Sexual Partner Preference," *Homosexual Behavior*, ed. Judd Marmor (Basic Books, 1980).
22. Drafted by Rabbis Rav Soloff, Judith Lewis and Allen Bennett for *Shaarei Musar*, at the invitation of the CCAR Family Life Committee, January, 1983.

# Homosexualität in biblischer Sicht

Von Georg Strecker

## 1. *Begriffsverständnis*

1.1 Homosexualität[1] ist „gleichgeschlechtliche Zuneigung, die von der Mehrheit der Bevölkerung im Gegensatz zur Heterosexualität als abartig empfunden wird". Diese *Definition*, die von S. Keil vorgetragen wurde[2], ist weiter zu differenzieren. Nachweisbar sind sehr unterschiedliche Äußerungsformen der Homosexualität: eine latent vorhandenen Neigung, die auch bei heterosexuell Veranlagten aus beiden Geschlechtern vorhanden ist und eine normale Ehe nicht unmöglich macht, da sie sich durch den Willen steuern läßt, bis hin zu einem Trieb, der die Persönlichkeitsstruktur tiefgreifend bestimmt und den Verlust der Entscheidungsfreiheit einschließen kann.

Homosexualität ermöglicht eine stimulierende Geistigkeit, wie die Literaturgeschichte beweist. Als hervorragendes Beispiel für eine lesbische Persönlichkeit ist die griechische Lyrikerin Sappho bekannt. Entsprechendes findet sich u.a. in Männerbünden im Verhältnis von Mann zu Mann. Andererseits kann Homosexualität zu einer Gefährdung der menschlichen Gemeinschaft werden, insbesondere durch Schaffung und Ausnutzung von Abhängigkeitsverhältnissen zwischen Älteren und Jüngeren. Wegen der ihnen nachgesagten Cliquenbildung wurden in der Zeit des Dritten Reiches Homosexuelle ver-

---

[1] *Literatur*: *H. D. Betz*, Lukian von Samosata und das Neue Testament, TU 76, Berlin 1961, 199–201. – *Th. Bovet* (Hg.), Probleme der Homophilie in medizinischer, theologischer und juristischer Sicht, Tübingen 1965. – *G. Friedrich*, Sexualität und Ehe. Rückfragen an das Neue Testament, Biblisches Forum 11, Stuttgart 1977, 46–57. – *R. Goeden*, Zur Stellung von Mann und Frau. Ehe und Sexualität im Hinblick auf Bibel und Alte Kirche, theol. Diss. (Masch.), Göttingen 1969, 163–175. – *H. Herter*, Art. Effeminatus, RAC IV, 620–650. – *S. Keil*, Art. Homosexualität I. Medizinisch, soziologisch, ESL [7]1980, 586f. – *W. Kroll*, Art. Kinaidos, PRE XI, 1922, 459–462; ders., Art. Knabenliebe, PRE XI, 897–906; ders., Art. Päderastie, KP IV, 1972, 1583f. – *H. Licht*, Homoerotik in der Griechischen Literatur. Lukianos von Samosata, Abh. aus dem Gebiet der Sexualforschung III/3, Bonn 1921. – *S. Meurer*, Das Problem der Homosexualität in theologischer Sicht, ZEE 18, 1974, 38–48; ders., Art. Homosexualität II. Theologisch-ethisch, ESL [7]1980, 587f. (Lit.). – *W. S. Schlegel*, Die Homosexualität in biologischer und in ethischer Sicht, ZEE 8, 1964, 30–34. – *H. J. Schoeps*, Homosexualität und Bibel, ZEE 6, 1962, 369–374. – *H. Thielicke*, Erwägungen der evangelisch-theologischen Ethik zum Problem der Homosexualität und ihrer strafrechtlichen Relevanz, ZEE 6, 1962, 150–166. – *W. Trillhaas*, Sexualethik, Göttingen [2]1970, 71–79.

[2] Vgl. *S. Keil*, ESL[7] 586.

folgt unter dem Vorwand der sexualethischen „Abartigkeit", primär jedoch aufgrund machtpolitischer Erwägungen, da die homosexuellen Verbindungen weitgehend der Kontrolle durch die Staatspartei entzogen waren. Steht heute die Homosexualität nicht mehr unter dem Verdikt strafrechtlicher Verfolgung, sondern wird sie von der Gesetzgebung – weniger von der Gesellschaft – toleriert, so bleibt andererseits die Gefahr der Gemeinschaftsgefährdung bestehen; daher die Päderastie, die sogenannte „Knabenliebe", insoweit sie die Entwicklung von Jugendlichen beeinträchtigen kann, auch heute noch unter das gesetzliche Verbot fällt[3].

1.2. Was die *Erklärung* der Homosexualität angeht, so spricht die Tatsache einer latenten Neigung, die jedem Menschen mitgegeben ist, gegen eine einseitige Ableitung. Die biologische Auskunft, Homosexualität sei erbmäßig, durch einen Fehler im genetischen Code bedingt, wird heute nur noch zurückhaltend vertreten. Mag das Problem der Vererbbarkeit bzw. der physischen Komponente noch nicht ausdiskutiert sein[4], so sind jedenfalls die sozialen Faktoren wichtig: so der enge Anschluß an einen gleichgeschlechtlichen Erzieher, besonders in einem Alter, in dem der Mensch entsprechenden Einflüssen leicht zugänglich ist. Durch bestimmte Schicksalsschläge, etwa durch den Verlust einer nahestehenden Person, kann die gleichgeschlechtliche Neigung gefördert werden. Einen hohen Einfluß auf die Entwicklung der Homosexualität hat die Kasernierung von Gleichgeschlechtlichen, z.B. im Wehrdienst, insbesondere, wenn diese längere Zeit andauert und mit dem Gefühl der Isolation verbunden ist. Obwohl Homosexualität als weitgehend sekundär erworben angesehen wird, bezeichnen Mediziner die therapeutischen Aussichten als nicht positiv[5]. Von den Homosexuellen wird ihre Veranlagung nicht nur als eine spezifische Andersartigkeit im Verhältnis zur umgebenden Gesellschaft bejaht, sondern nicht selten als existentielle Belastung erlebt.

Die biblischen Belege sind zahlenmäßig gering. Dennoch ist ihre Bedeutung für die christliche Ethik kaum zu überschätzen. Die Interpretation der einzelnen Texte ist freilich sehr unterschiedlich; auf kaum einem anderen Gebiet spielt bei der Auslegung die persönliche Stellung des Exegeten eine so große Rolle.

## 2. *Altes Testament*

Die Geschichte von den zwei Engeln Jahwes, die bei Lot in Sodom einkehren (Gen 19,1–12), hat für die Beurteilung der Homosexualität im Alten Testament eine exemplarische Bedeutung. Die männlichen Einwohner von Sodom umringen das Haus des Lot und verlangen die Herausgabe der bei

---

[3] Dazu unten 5.1.

[4] Hierzu O. *Frhr. von Verschuer*, Die Frage der Erblichkeit der Homophilie, in: *Th. Bovet* (Hg.), Probleme 79–87 (Lit.); *W.S. Schlegel*, ZEE 8, 1964, 33.

[5] Vgl. *S. Keil*: „Homosexualität ist therapeutisch nicht zu beseitigen" (ESL[7] 587).

ihm eingekehrten Männer: „Bringe sie zu uns heraus, daß wir ihnen beiwohnen" (V.5). Das Verb ידע heißt „erkennen" im Sinne von „geschlechtlich verkehren". Es besteht also kein Zweifel, daß hiermit eine gleichgeschlechtliche Vergewaltigung gemeint ist. – Eine ähnliche Erzählung begegnet Ri 19: Hier übernachtet ein Levit aus dem Gebirge Ephraim mit seiner Nebenfrau, die er aus Bethlehem geholt hatte, in der Stadt Gibea, die im Stammesgebiet Benjamin liegt. Auch hier sind es die Einwohner der Stadt, welche die Herausgabe des Gastes verlangen, „um ihm beizuwohnen" (V.22), und sodann mit der Frau „ihren Mutwillen treiben" (V.25), so daß diese zu Tode gequält wird (V.28; 20,5). In beiden Perikopen wird die Bestrafung der Übeltäter berichtet: der Untergang Sodoms bzw. die Bestrafung der Benjaminiten. Beide Male handelt es sich nicht eigentlich um die Bestrafung des homosexuellen Deliktes selbst, vielmehr um die Ahndung der gewalttätigen Verletzung des Gastrechtes. Die späteren biblischen Erwähnungen des Untergangs Sodoms[6] nennen nicht ausdrücklich das Delikt der Homosexualität, sondern allgemein die Gottlosigkeit der Sodomiter[7]. Dennoch besagt dies nicht, daß Gen 19 und Ri 19 Homosexualität als ein geringes Übel erkennen lassen; im Gegenteil, es besteht kein Zweifel, daß hiermit die Ehrlosigkeit und Schändlichkeit des Handelns von gottlosen Menschen gekennzeichnet werden soll.

Dies geht auch aus zwei weiteren alttestamentlichen Belegen hervor.

*Lev. 18,22:*
„Du sollst nicht bei einem Mann liegen, wie man bei einer Frau liegt, das wäre ein Greuel" (תּוֹעֵבָה).
*Lev. 20,13:*
„Wenn einer bei einem Mann liegt, wie man bei einer Frau liegt, so haben beide ein Greuel verübt; sie sollen getötet werden; ihr Blut komme über sie!"

Beide Texte befinden sich im sog. Heiligkeitsgesetz (Lev 17–26), das durch die Forderung bestimmt ist: „Ihr sollt heilig sein, denn ich bin heilig, der Herr, euer Gott" (19,2). Die Heiligkeit des Gottesvolkes verlangt, daß dieses sich in seinem Verhalten von den heidnischen Völkern unterscheiden muß. Gegensätzlich wird auf die „Bräuche der Heiden", die Gott verabscheut, Bezug genommen (20,23).

[6] Z.B. Ez 16,49f. (keine Fürsorge für die Armen, Übermut und Greuel); vgl. auch Jes 1,10; 3,9; Jer 23,14; Weish 10,7f.; Sir 16,8.

[7] Wie übrigens auch im heutigen Sprachgebrauch „Sodomie" nicht mit Homosexualität identisch ist, sondern geschlechtlichen Umgang mit Tieren bezeichnet; vgl. *H. Maisch*, Art. Sodomie, Lexikon der Psychologie III, Freiburg ²1980, 2096f.

[8] Vgl. Lev 18,3.24–30; 20,22f. – Weitere Belege für das AT sind weniger ergiebig; vgl. Dtn 22,5 (Transvestiten = Homosexuelle?; dazu *R. Goeden*, Stellung 166f.), auch Dtn 23,19: „Du sollst keinen Dirnenlohn und kein Hundegeld in das Haus des Herrn, deines Gottes, bringen auf irgendein Gelübde hin; denn alle beide sind dem Herrn, deinem Gott, ein Greuel" (nach *H.J. Schoeps*, ZEE 6, 1962, 371, handelt es sich bei dem Ausdruck „Hundegeld" um Gewinn aus homosexuellen Praktiken). – Die Erzählung von David und Jonathan preist deren Freundschaft (vgl. 2. Sam 1,26), enthält jedoch keine Aussagen über ein homosexuelles Verhältnis.

Der Schluß scheint sich nahe zu legen, daß vor allem die heidnischen Kultrituale mit homosexuellen Handlungen verbunden gewesen seien und daß von hier aus die alttestamentliche Abgrenzung[8] gegen den heidnischen Kult das Verdikt der Homosexualität begründet. So meint S. Meurer, das Verbot richte sich eigentlich gegen die kultische Prostitution der kanaanäischen Religion[9]. Jedoch, gegen die These, kanaanäische kultische Prosititution sei der eigentliche Anlaß des Verbotes von homsexuellem Umgang in Lev 18 und 20, spricht entscheidend, daß das „Heiligkeitsgesetz" wahrscheinlich in exilischer Zeit entstanden ist, also in einer Zeit, als von einer Bedrohung Israels durch kanaanäische Kulte nicht mehr die Rede sein kann. Das Heiligkeitsgesetz ist zudem nicht auf kultische Anweisungen begrenzt, so sehr diese im Vordergrund stehen. In ihm finden sich neben den Anordnungen zu Schlachtopfern (c. 17), Priestertum (c. 21) und allgemeinen Kultvorschriften (cc. 22.24), zu Festen und zum Sabbatjahr (cc. 23.25) nicht selten ethische Weisungen; so das berühmte Gebot der Nächstenliebe (19, 18), das Gebot, die Alten zu ehren (19, 32), das Verbot, Vater oder Mutter zu fluchen (20, 9), schließlich Ehegesetze (z. B. das Verbot, die Schwägerin zu heiraten: 20, 21). Demnach ist auf das Heiligkeitsgesetz und auf entsprechende Weisungen im Alten Testament nicht einfach der Satz von M. Weber anzuwenden, „daß die Reglementierungen der Sexualvorgänge nicht ethischen, sondern *rituellen* Charakter" haben[10], so daß sämtliche sexualethische Weisungen im Zusammenhang mit dem Kult ständen, sondern es gilt auch umgekehrt: Die Befolgung der Kultvorschriften geht in das ethische Bewußtsein ein und kennzeichnet den Stand der „Moral" des israelitischen Volkes; eben deshalb können kultische und ethische Forderungen ohne Unterschied im Korpus des Heiligkeitsgesetzes Aufnahme finden.

## 3. *Religionsgeschichtliches*

3.1. In der kanaanäischen Religion gehört Homosexualität seit dem 14. Jh. v. Chr. zum Kultritual, nämlich zur kultischen Prostitution. Nach Textfunden aus Ugarit standen die Lustknaben auf gleicher Rangebene neben den Priestern[11]. – Umstritten ist die Auslegung des babylonischen Kodex Ham-

---

[9] Vgl. ZEE 18, 1974, 42; sehr stark betont wird dieser Aspekt durch *H. J. Schoeps*: „Die biblischen Strafbestimmungen gegen die Homosexualität gehören ebenso wie die gegen sexuellen Umgang mit einem menstruierenden Weib, Ehebruch und Sodomie (Lev 18) zu den Taharotgesetzen, die die kultischen Reinheitsvorschriften behandeln. Für sie gilt das gleiche wie über die Verbote betr. Kilajim (Mischungen) und das Speiseritual, daß sie gegen Kultbräuche der Umwelt gerichtet sind" (ZEE 6, 1962, 370).

[10] *M. Weber*, Gesammelte Aufsätze zur Religionssoziologie III. Das antike Judentum, Tübingen ²1923, 204.

[11] Ras-Schamra-Fragment 8252. – Vermutlich sind unter der Bezeichnung „Geweihte" (קְדֵשִׁים) in Hiob 36, 14 derartige „Lustknaben" zu verstehen (so *B. Duhm*, Das Buch Hiob, Tübingen 1897, z. St.; *K. Budde*, Das Buch Hiob, HK II/1, Göttingen ²1913, 228); vgl. auch 1. Kön 14, 24;

murabi (um 1700 v.Chr.), in dem „weibliche Männer“ erwähnt werden; sie sind möglicherweise mit Lesbierinnen identisch. Daneben werden „männliche Eunuchen“ genannt, die sich der kultischen Prostitution hingaben[12].

Im griechischen Altertum ist Homosexualität zunächst nicht bezeugt. Sie scheint seit dem Einfall der kriegerischen Dorer in Griechenland verbreitet worden zu sein. Diese regelten die Päderastie auf gesetzlichem Wege, allerdings offenbar nur für die ritterliche Oberschicht. Homosexualität findet sich sodann auch in Athen. Ein bekanntes Beispiel ist das Verhältnis des Sokrates zu Alkibiades, von dem Platon im „Symposium“ berichtet[13]. – Von hier aus wurde die römische Gesellschaft in ihrer Stellung zur Homosexualität beeinflußt. Diese verbreitete sich vor allem im römischen Reich im Zusammenhang mit Fruchtbarkeitskulten. So durch den Kybelekult, der in Kleinasien entstand, sodann für Griechenland bezeugt ist und im Jahre 204 v.Chr. nach Rom gelangte. Sein Fruchtbarkeitsritual weist eine enge Verwandtschaft mit dem Attiskult auf, der ursprünglich aus Syrien stammt. In beiden Kulten wird die Wiederbelebung der Gottheit gefeiert in ausgelassenen Formen, die bis zur Selbstverstümmelung und Entmannung führen und auch homosexuelle Handlungen eingeschlossen haben[14].

3.2. Es ist nun verständlich, daß in der jüdischen – später auch in der christlichen – Literatur Homosexualität als Kennzeichen der heidnischen Unmoral gilt[15]. Jedoch ist nicht zu verkennen, daß die Homosexualität auch in nichtjudischen Kreisen auf Widerstand stieß. Schon der griechische Gesetzgeber Solon versuchte um 590 v.Chr. in Athen die gewerbsmäßige Päderastie einzuschränken[16]. Im römischen Recht stellt seit 226 v.Chr. die Lex Scantinia bestimmte homosexuelle Handlungen unter Strafe; dies vor allem, um den Schutz von Minderjährigen zu gewährleisten. Selbst die Vermietung von Räumen zwecks Ausübung des gleichgeschlechtlichen Verkehrs wurde bestraft[17]. Diese Tendenz der römischen Rechtsprechung hat sich bis in die

---

15,12; 22,47; 2. Kön 23,7; zur Sache: *B. A. Brooks*, Fertility Cult Functionaries in the Old Testament, JBL 60, 1941, 227–253, bes. 234 ff.

[12] Einzelheiten bei *R. Goeden*, Stellung 166.

[13] *Plato*, Symp 217a ff.; vgl. ebd. 178c ff. (Lobpreis der Homosexualität); auch ders., Charm 155d (Anspielung auf das homosexuelle Verhältnis zwischen Sokrates und Charmides); anders Plato in seiner Spätphase: Leg 636c und 863a ff. (dazu unten Anm. 19). – Plutarch von Chäronea (45–125 n.Chr.) vertritt als Lehrer des „mittleren Platonismus“ die Auffassung, „Knabenliebe“ sei die „einzig unverfälschte Liebe“ (Mor 751a: οὕτως εἷς Ἔρως γνήσιος ὁ παιδικός ἐστιν), wendet sich jedoch gegen homosexuellen Verkehr mit Sklaven (aaO. 751b).

[14] Die „Galloi“ (= Angehörige des Kybele-Kultes) werden als Kinäden bezeichnet, denen homosexuelle Praktiken zum Vorwurf gemacht werden: *W. Kroll*, PRE XI 460f. (Belege!); vgl. Ps-Lucian, Asin 36–38 par Apuleius, Metam VIII 26–29; zur Identifizierung von κίναιδοι mit Homosexuellen: *Lucian*, Cynic 17 u.ö.; *H.D. Betz*, 200f.; zur Sache auch *H. Licht*, Homoerotik 32f.

[15] Vgl. Lev 20,23; OracSib III 595; Röm 1,26 ff.

[16] Im Rückgriff auf Solon wendet sich auch der athenische Redner und Politiker Aischines (geb. um 390 v..Chr.) gegen gewerbsmäßig ausgeübte Homosexualität (Tim 39 ff.)

[17] Dig 48,5,8; vgl. *D.S. Bailey*, Art. Homosexualität, RGG³ III, 441–444, bes. 442.

9*

christliche Kaiserzeit durchgehalten. Für die neutestamentlichen Texte ist von besonderer Bedeutung, daß Stoiker, Epikuräer und Kyniker die Homosexualität ablehnten[18]. Hierbei wird die „Naturerfahrung" ins Feld geführt, welche der homosexuellen Neigung widerspricht; denn Tiere sind nicht homosexuell[19].

Das Verbot der Homosexualität steht demnach im Alten Testament nicht isoliert, sondern hat zahlreiche Parallelen in der paganen Gesetzgebung und in der gesellschaftlichen Wirklichkeit der Antike. Welches ihre eigentliche Begründung im Alten Testament und worauf ihre Aufnahme in das Heiligkeitsgesetz zurückzuführen ist, läßt sich letztlich nicht erklären. Offenbar handelt es sich um ein Verbot „positiven Rechts", das als Ausdruck des heiligen Gotteswillens formuliert ist und von dem Volk Israel als gegeben akzeptiert, tradiert und realisiert wird[20]. Es steht in sachlicher Übereinstimmung mit der Hochschätzung von Familie und Ehe im Judentum, wonach geschlechtlicher Umgang auf Erzeugung von Nachkommenschaft ausgerichtet sein soll[21]. Auch die spätere Literatur des Judentums lehnt die Homosexualität eindeutig ab, wie zahlreiche Texte demonstrieren[22]. Das alttestamentliche Verbot von homosexuellen Handlungen wird in der Geschichte des Judentums nicht relativiert. Es läßt sich nicht einfach aus spezifischen zeit- oder religionsgeschichtlichen Situationen erklären, sondern es gehört zu den Weisungen des Alten Testaments, die für das Selbstverständnis des alttestamentlichen und nachalttestamentlichen Judentums konstitutiv sind[23].

## 4. *Neues Testament*

Im neutestamentlichen Schrifttum gibt es einige wenige, jedoch prägnante Texte, welche zur Homosexualität Stellung nehmen; es sind dies Röm 1,26f.; 1.Kor 6,9f. und 1.Tim 1,10.

---

[18] Belege bei *Wettstein* II 24f.; *Bill.* III 69; *W. Kroll*, PRE XI 904.

[19] Schon *Plato*, Leg 636c; 836c (παρὰ φύσιν); vgl. *W. Kroll*, ebd.; *H. D. Betz*, Lukian 200.

[20] In Verbindung mit der Vorstellung vom Landbesitz, der nicht durch unethisches Handeln verunreinigt werden darf (Lev 20,22).

[21] So schon das Gebot Gen 1,28: „Seid fruchtbar und mehret euch!", das im Judentum in hohem Ansehen stand; vgl. auch *H. Ringeling*, Die biblische Begründung der Monogamie, ZEE 10, 1966, 81–102, bes. 85.

[22] Z.B. Arist 152; OracSib III 184ff.; V. 166f. (gegen Rom: „Ehebruch ist bei dir und ruchlose Vermischung mit Knaben und frevelhafte mit Weibern ..."); Weish 14,22ff.; Test Lev 17,11; Philo, SpecLeg III 37–42; slHen 10,4; PsPhokyl 3. – Weitere, auch rabbinische Belege bei *Bill.* III 68ff. (zu Röm 1,26); *H. Lietzmann*, An die Römer, HNT 8, Tübingen [5]1971 (z.St.).

[23] Gegen *H.J. Schoeps*, *ZEE* 6, 1962, 372: „Es ist ein Treppenwitz der Religionsgeschichte, aus einem derartigen Sachverhalt eine zeitlos gültige sexualethische Regel abzuleiten"; vgl. auch *ders.*, Überlegungen zum Problem der Homosexualität, in: Der homosexuelle Nächste, Stundenbuch 31, Hamburg 1963, 74–114, bes. 91f.

*4.1. Röm 1,26–27:*

„Deswegen hat Gott sie dahingegeben in schändliche Leidenschaften; denn ihre Frauen vertauschten den natürlichen Umgang mit dem widernatürlichen; ebenso die Männer; sie verließen den natürlichen Umgang mit der Frau und entbrannten in ihrer Begierde gegenseitig; Männer taten mit Männern Schändliches und erhielten an sich selbst den verdienten Lohn für ihre Verirrung."

Auch wenn zu V.26 umstritten ist, ob Paulus an lesbische Liebe denkt und/oder an unnatürlichen Geschlechtsverkehr zwischen Mann und Frau[24], so ist doch deutlich, daß gleichgeschlechtlicher Umgang abgelehnt wird. Diese paulinische Stellungnahme befindet sich im ersten Hauptabschnitt des Römerbriefes (1,18–3,20), wo im Anschluß an das voraufgestellte Thema (1,17: Offenbarung der Gottesgerechtigkeit) die Notwendigkeit der Offenbarung der Gottesgerechtigkeit gegenüber Heiden und Juden ausgeführt wird. Paulus will nachweisen, daß die in Jesus Christus manifestierte Gottesgerechtigkeit für alle Menschen Grundlage des Heils ist und niemand aus eigener Kraft zu Gott gelangen kann. Im ersten Unterabschnitt handelt er daher von dem „Zorn Gottes über der Heidenwelt" (1,18–32): Die ὀργὴ ϑεοῦ liegt über den Heiden (von 2,1 an wird aufgezeigt werden, daß sie auch den Juden gilt), denn sie haben Gott zwar an seinen Schöpfungswerken erkannt[25], aber hieraus nicht die notwendigen Konsequenzen gezogen; sie gaben Gott nicht die Ehre (1,21). Sie haben Gott zwar erkannt, jedoch nicht anerkannt. Vielmehr vertauschten sie die Ehre Gottes mit der Verehrung von Götzenbildern (V.23). Wo aber anstelle des Schöpfers die Schöpfung zum Gott erhoben wird, da greift sittlicher Verfall um sich. Wo die Beziehung zum Göttlichen als dem Urgrund menschlichen Lebens gestört ist, da ist echte menschliche Gemeinschaft unmöglich gemacht. Der Gedanke, daß Götzendienst und Sittenlosigkeit aufs engste miteinander verbunden sind, findet sich schon in der jüdisch-hellenistischen apologetischen Literatur (z.B. Weish 13,1ff.). Paulus greift ihn auf, indem er rhetorisch wirkungsvoll ein dreimaliges „und er gab sie dahin" (παρέδωκεν) formuliert (V.24.26.28) und hierdurch anzuzeigen versucht, daß die Sittenlosigkeit menschlichen Lebens die schuldhafte Folge des Unglaubens und die Strafe Gottes für solche Schuld ist.

Nach *V.24–25* stellt sich die Heidenwelt als in „Leidenschaften" (ἐπιϑυμίαι) und „Unreinheit" (ἀκαϑαρσία) befangen war. Dies und die „Schändung der Leiber" (V.24) steht im Zusammenhang mit dem Götzendienst, von dem in V.23 und 25 gesprochen wird. Heidnischer polytheistischer Kult und sexuelle Unzucht sind demnach miteinander verknüpft.

*V.26–27* schildern die Homosexualität als einen Spezialfall der heidnischen ἀκαϑαρσία; die „unehrenhaften Leidenschaften" treten in der Homosexuali-

---

[24] Dazu *D.S. Bailey*, Homosexuality and the Western Christian Tradition, London 1955, 40.

[25] Röm 1,21: γνόντες bezeichnet nicht nur eine theoretische Möglichkeit der natürlichen Gotteserkenntnis, sondern Paulus argumentiert bewußt im Stil und im Inhalt der stoischen „theologia naturalis".

tät zutage und beherrschen die Menschen, die sich von Gott abgewendet haben. Homosexuelles Tun ist Ausdruck der Gottesferne des Menschen. Eine spezielle Konfrontation zu kultischen Praktiken besteht nicht; im Gegenteil, der anschließende Lasterkatalog nennt ausschließlich „ethische" Untugenden.

Dieser Katalog findet sich in *V.29–31*. Er steht unter dem Stichwort: Sie tun „das, was sich nicht ziemt" (τὰ μὴ καθήκοντα: V.28). Dies ist ein stoischer Ausdruck; er läßt erkennen, daß die Aufzählung auch im einzelnen mit pagan-hellenistischen Vorstellungen übereinstimmt, wenn auch der unmittelbare Hintergrund der paulinischen Katalogtradition zunächst vorpaulinische christliche Überlieferung und dahinter zurückgehend das hellenistische Judentum ist[26]. Die aufgezählten Verfehlungen demonstrieren exemplarisch das gottlose Wesen der Heidenwelt, die alle nur erdenklichen Laster ausübt. Das Urteil über solche Sittenlosigkeit ist gesprochen: Sie sind des Todes schuldig (V.32). Dies meint den ewigen Tod, wie er im Endgericht verhängt werden wird. Die Verbindung von Katalogüberlieferung mit dieser jüdisch-apokalyptischen Motivation hat Paulus in der christlichen Paränese vorgefunden[27]; sie weist an dieser Stelle auf 1,18 zurück, wonach der Gerichtszorn Gottes schon jetzt sich über der Heidenwelt offenbart.

Wenn Paulus in diesem Zusammenhang einen ethischen Lasterkatalog anfügt, so wird hieraus deutlich, daß er nicht lediglich gegen den heidnischen polytheistischen Kult polemisiert, sondern gegen das Heidentum selbst, das als solches als von Gott getrennt und als sittenlos dargestellt wird. Wie der anschließende Abschnitt zeigt, gilt gleiches für die Juden, obwohl ihnen durch das Gesetz der Wille Gottes offenbart wurde. Sie alle, Juden und Heiden, haben den rechten Weg verfehlt und „ermangeln des Ruhms (δόξα), den sie vor Gott haben sollten" (Röm 3,23). Deshalb bedarf es der Offenbarung einer Gerechtigkeit aufgrund von Glauben, nicht aufgrund von Werken, wie sie durch Jesus Christus manifestiert worden ist (3,24f.)

Dies also ist das theologische Koordinatensystem, in das hinein die Aussagen über die Homosexualität der Heiden eingeordnet sind. Es handelt sich hierbei um eine ethische Verfehlung neben anderen. Eine spezifische Erklärung gibt Paulus nicht. Selbstverständlich gehört die Homosexualität zum Bereich der σάρξ, die durch ἐπιθυμίαι gekennzeichnet ist[28]. Die Sphäre der σάρξ als Raum der Vergänglichkeit (V.23) ist die eine Seite des paulinischen Dualismus, dessen andere Seite durch das göttliche Pneuma bestimmt ist (Gal 5,13ff).

Fragen läßt sich, ob die jüdische und auch stoische Hochschätzung der Ehe, die auf Erzeugung von Nachkommenschaft ausgerichtet ist, auf die Argumentation des Paulus eingewirkt hat. Jedenfalls läßt die Bezeichnung φυσική

---

[26] Weitere Lasterkataloge im paulinischen Schrifttum: Röm 13,13; Gal 5,19–23; 1Kor 5,10f.; 6,9f.; 2.Kor 12,20f.

[27] Vgl. auch Gal 5,21: „Diejenigen, die solches tun, werden das Reich Gottes nicht erben."

[28] Röm 1,24; vgl. zum Zusammenhang σάρξ und ἐπιθυμίαι: 13,14; Gal 5,16.24.

χρῆσις (V.26f.) bzw. der Begriff φύσις (V.26) erkennen, daß Paulus Homosexualität als widernatürlich ansieht und gegenüber dem ethischen Verfall das „Natürliche" als die gottgewollte Grundlage menschlichen Verhaltens ins Feld führt. Der weitere, von Paulus vorausgesetzte Hintergrund können auch die in hellenistischen Kulten geübte kultische Prostitution oder die Idealisierung der gleichgeschlechtlichen Liebe sein. Von argumentativer Bedeutung sind diese möglichen Erklärungen im Kontext jedoch nicht. Entscheidend ist vielmehr, daß Paulus durch das homosexuelle Verhalten, das eo ipso als unsittlich gilt, die Gottesferne und die Schuld der Heidenwelt demonstrieren will. Er sagt: Diejenigen, die solches tun, haben keine Entschuldigung (2,1); sie alle unterstehen dem Gerichtsurteil (2,2). Dies meint aber auch: Sie alle sind angewiesen auf die Gnade Gottes, wie sie in Jesus Christus angeboten wird.

4.2. Ein anderes Beispiel für die Ablehnung der Homosexualität durch Paulus findet sich *1. Kor 6,9–10:*

„Wißt ihr nicht, daß Ungerechte das Reich Gottes nicht erben werden? Irret euch nicht: Weder Hurer (πόρνοι), noch Götzendiener, noch Ehebrecher, noch Lustknaben (μαλακοί), noch Päderasten (ἀρσενοκοῖται), noch Diebe, noch Habgierige, noch Trunksüchtige, noch Verleumder, noch Räuber werden das Reich Gottes erben."

Paulus schließt sich der Katalogüberlieferung an[29], der die apokalyptische Begründung angehört[30]. Die Aussagen dürfen nicht exegetisch strapaziert werden. Die einzelnen Glieder des Katalogs sind mehr zufällig zusammengestellt; sie umgreifen nicht alle denkbaren Untugenden und überschneiden sich gegenseitig. So ist der Begriff πόρνοι schwerlich gegenüber μαλακοί (nur hier im Neuen Testament) und ἀρσενοκοῖται (auch 1.Tim 1,10) abzugrenzen. Die beiden letzten Ausdrücke bezeichnen den passiven bzw. den aktiven Partner beim männlichen Sexualakt[31]. Diese „Laster" werden gleichwertig mit Götzendienst, Diebstahl, Habsucht u.a. genannt; ein Zeichen, daß religiöse und ethische Verfehlungen nicht grundsätzlich getrennt werden, ohne daß das eine aus dem anderen abzuleiten wäre oder jeweils mit dem anderen in einem unmittelbaren Zusammenhang stünde. Da Paulus auf eine Tradition zurückgreift, dürfen die Einzelaussagen nicht in jedem Fall auf die Gemeindesituation bezogen werden. Allerdings redet der Apostel die korinthischen Christen darauf an, daß einige von ihnen sich einstmals solcher Verfehlungen schuldig gemacht haben. Mit Recht läßt sich hieraus die Folgerung ziehen, daß Paulus Homosexualität nicht als unkorrigierbar versteht[32].

---

[29] Auch 1. Kor 5,10f., wo jedoch Aussagen über Homosexualität nicht erscheinen.

[30] S. oben zu Röm 1,32.

[31] Die Terminologie ist in der griechisch-hellenistischen Literatur verbreitet; vgl. *W. Bauer*, Griechisch-deutsches Wörterbuch, Berlin [5]1958, 966 (μαλακός); *H. Conzelmann*, Der erste Brief an die Korinther, KEK 5, Göttingen [2]1981 (z. St.).

[32] Vgl. *Th. Bovet*, Sinnerfülltes Anders-Sein, Tübingen 1959, 87; *E. Kähler*, Exegese zweier neutestamentlicher Stellen, in: *Th. Bovet* (Hg.), Probleme [s.o. Anm. 1], 12–43, bes. 32ff.; *S. Meurer*, ZEE 18, 1974, 43.

Liegt die Homosexualität – wie auch alle anderen Untugenden – für den Christen grundsätzlich in der Vergangenheit, ist sie durch die Taufe überwunden (V. 11), so richtet Paulus dennoch diese Ausführungen an eine Gemeinde, welche Streitfälle untereinander auszufechten hat und deren Glieder gegeneinander vor heidnische Gerichte ziehen (1.Kor 6,1ff.). Der Lasterkatalog hat eine paränetische Funktion. Der Apostel mahnt die Gemeinde, nicht in die frühere heidnische Lebensweise zurückzufallen. Die Gefahr, daß die genannten Verfehlungen in der Gemeinde aufleben, ist nicht grundsätzlich von der Hand zu weisen. Christliche Gemeinde ist nach paulinischem Verständnis kein „corpus perfectum", sondern stets bedroht, von dem rechten Wege abzuweichen. Dies gilt nicht nur für die Gemeinde insgesamt, sondern erst recht von jedem einzelnen Christen. Daher der Apostel mit dem ethischen Imperativ die Forderung erhebt, das einmal zugesprochene Heil nicht aufs Spiel zu setzen, sondern in einem dem Willen Gottes entsprechenden Leben zu realisieren (vgl. Gal 5,25).

4.3. In den deuteropaulinischen Pastoralbriefen findet sich ein weiterer neutestamentlicher Beleg. *1.Tim 1,10* steht im Zusammenhang eines Katalogs, welcher der Polemik gegen Häretiker eingeordnet ist (V.8–10):

„Wir wissen aber, daß das Gesetz gut ist, wenn man es dem Gesetz entsprechend gebraucht, in der Erkenntnis, daß nicht einem Gerechten das Gesetz gegeben ist, sondern dem Gesetzlosen und Ungehorsamen, den Gottlosen und Sündern, den Unheiligen und Unreinen, den Vater- und Muttermördern, den Totschlägern, Hurern, Päderasten, Menschenhändlern, Lügnern, Meineidigen und wenn irgendetwas anderes der gesunden Lehre entgegensteht, entsprechend dem Evangelium von der Herrlichkeit des seligen Gottes, das mir anvertraut worden ist."

Vorausgesetzt ist, daß Häretiker als Gesetzeslehrer auftreten. Ihnen hält der Verfasser des 1.Tim entgegen, daß Gesetz und Evangelium einander ausschließen; denn das Gesetz richtet sich nicht an die Gerechten, sondern gegen die Gesetzlosen. Die anschließende Liste erläutert den Grundsatz, daß Irrlehre und unrechtes Tun zusammengehören (vgl. 1.Tim 6,3–5). Das Gesetz, auf das sich die Gegner berufen, ist in Wahrheit gegen sie gerichtet. In diesem Zusammenhang hat also der Lasterkatalog (V.9–10) eine antihäretische Spitze. Dabei ist nicht anzunehmen, daß jede Angabe einem „Mißstand" bei den Häretikern entspricht, sondern der Katalog hat einen allgemein-ethischen Sinn. So zeigt es die Tatsache, daß er sich an den alttestamentlichen Dekalog anlehnt: Auf die erste Tafel mit der Aufzählung von Übertretungen, die sich gegen Gott richten (-βεβήλοις: „Unreine"), folgt die zweite Tafel, die sich auf das vierte bis achte Gebot bezieht. Die einzelnen Gebote sind durch besonders abschreckende Beispiele illustriert: Vater- und Muttermörder, Totschläger (= viertes und fünftes Gebot), Hurer und Päderasten (= sechstes Gebot), Menschenhändler (= siebtes Gebot)[33], Lügner

---

[33] So oft verstanden; z.B. G. *Holtz*, Die Pastoralbriefe, ThHK 13, Berlin ³1980, 40. – Das Wort 'ανδραποδιστής kann aber auch den Sinn von „Kuppler" haben; denn es bezeichnet einen

und Meineidige (= achtes Gebot). Dem unsittlichen Tun der falschen Lehre wird die „gesunde Lehre" entgegengestellt. Diese manifestiert die Einheit von theologischer Wahrheit und ethischer Haltung (V. 10). Solche antihäretische Frontstellung ist eine Fortführung der paulinischen Gedankenwelt und geht in der – hier erstmals im Neuen Testament bezeugten – Entgegensetzung von Gesetz und Evangelium über diese hinaus. In der Ablehnung der Homosexualität zeigt sich jedoch kein Wandel; im Gegenteil, indem die Häretiker mit dem Laster der Homosexualität in Verbindung gebracht werden, ist die strikte Zurückweisung durch Paulus bekräftigt worden. Es ist denn auch verständlich, daß in der Alten Kirche die neutestamentliche Tradition ungebrochen aufgenommen werden konnte (Polyk 5,3 = 1. Kor 6,9f.) und homosexuelle Handlungen als schwere Sünde betrachtet wurden[34].

## 5. *Hermeneutische Folgerungen*

5.1. Fragen wir, welche Konsequenzen aus dem biblisch-ethischen Befund für unsere gegenwärtige Situation zu ziehen sind, so stehen wir zunächst vor der Aufgabe, uns den rechtlichen Tatbestand zu vergegenwärtigen. In den 50er und 60er Jahren ist das Problem der Homosexualität in theologischen Kreisen heftig debattiert worden, dies in Auseinandersetzung mit einer strafrechtlichen Regelung, wonach (entsprechend § 175 StGB) die Unzucht zwischen Männern mit Gefängnis, in schweren Fällen mit Zuchthaus bestraft wurde. Dagegen war die Unzucht unter Frauen nicht strafbar, obwohl Artikel 3 des Grundgesetzes die Gleichberechtigung von Mann und Frau ausdrücklich feststellt. Zur gleichen Zeit wurde in der Schweiz die Homosexualität nur als gewerbsmäßige oder bei Mißbrauch eines Abhängigkeitsverhältnisses bestraft. Straffrei ist sie dagegen in den Niederlanden und in den romanischen Ländern.

Unter dem Eindruck der Ergebnisse einer weitreichenden Diskussion (wozu besonders der Hirtenbrief der schwedischen Bischöfe aus dem Jahr 1951, der Griffin-Report 1956, der Wolfenden-Report 1957 u.a. zu zählen sind) sind auch in der Bundesrepublik Deutschland die strafrechtlichen Bestimmungen erheblich gelockert worden. Seit 1969 ist die Homosexualität unter Erwachsenen erlaubt; dagegen bleibt sie zwischen männlichen Erwachsenen und Minderjährigen verboten[35]. Im Vergleich mit der Heterosexualität bedeutet

---

Menschen, der einen anderen (wörtlich: durch Aufsetzen seines Fußes) zum Sklaven macht; dann wäre es mit den beiden voraufgehenden Begriffen zusammen zu sehen und würde ebenfalls das sechste Gebot erläutern.

[34] Belege bei *D. S. Bailey*, RGG³ III 443.

[35] Durch die Neufassung vom 23.11.1973 erhielt § 175 StGB den folgenden Wortlaut: „§ 175: Homosexuelle Handlungen. (1) Ein Mann über 18 Jahre, der sexuelle Handlungen an einem Mann unter 18 Jahren vornimmt oder von einem Mann unter 18 Jahren an sich vornehmen läßt, wird mit Freiheitsstrafe bis zu 5 Jahren oder mit Geldstrafe bestraft. (2) Das Gericht kann von einer Bestrafung nach dieser Vorschrift absehen, wenn 1. der Täter zur Zeit der Tat noch nicht 21 Jahre alt war oder 2. bei Berücksichtigung des Verhaltens desjenigen, gegen den sich die

dies freilich eine verschiedenartige Regelung, da heterosexueller Umgang nur zwischen Erwachsenen und Jugendlichen unter 16 Jahren strafrechtlich geahndet wird. Als unbefriedigend mag erscheinen, daß bei Übertretung nicht nur der Erziehungsberechtigte, sondern jedermann Anzeige erstatten kann[36]. Dennoch ist es ein Fortschritt, daß die Homosexualität generell nicht strafbar ist und im allgemeinen die strafrechtliche Verfolgung nur dann eingreift, wenn homosexuelle Handlungen im Zusammenhang mit anderen, die öffentliche Ordnung gefährdenden Delikten auftreten[37].

5.2. Durch die gesetzliche Regelung sind die Fragen, die sich für das Verhalten des einzelnen Christen wie auch der kirchlichen Institution heute stellen, selbstverständlich noch nicht beantwortet. Welchen Beitrag kann die biblische Exegese für die Suche nach einer sachgemäßen Beurteilung des Phänomens der Homosexualität in der Gegenwart leisten? Ausgeschlossen sollte eine fundamentalistische Lösung sein, wie sie allerdings noch in der „Erklärung zu einigen Fragen der Sexualität" von der römisch-katholischen Glaubenskongregation in Rom 1976 vertreten wurde[38]. Hier beruft man sich auf die „objektive sittliche Ordnung", mit der die biblischen Weisungen in Einklang stünden[39], ohne sich einzugestehen, daß schon der biblische Text die „Objektivität" ethischer Weisungen in Frage stellt. Zum Beispiel stand Jesus der mosaischen Tora kritisch gegenüber, indem er ihre Forderungen teils radikalisierte, teils außer Kraft setzte. Auch die frühchristliche Kirche hat

---

Tat richtet, das Unrecht der Tat gering ist." – Die entsprechende Fassung des § 151 im DDR-Strafgesetzbuch (1975) lautet: „Ein Erwachsener, der mit einem Jugendlichen gleichen Geschlechts sexuelle Handlungen vornimmt, wird mit Freiheitsstrafe bis zu 3 Jahren oder mit Verurteilung auf Bewährung bestraft."

[36] So *S. Keil*, ESL[7] 586. – Im juristischen Sinn handelt es sich bei der Homosexualität im beschriebenen Sinn nicht um ein „Antragsdelikt". „Dieser Lösung stand ... einmal das Bedenken entgegen, daß der Strafschutz in all den Fällen nicht effektiv werden könnte, in denen der antragsberechtigte gesetzliche Vertreter vom Sachverhalt nicht ausreichend informiert wird oder in denen er sich um den betroffenen Jugendlichen nicht kümmert und auch bei Kenntnis des Sachverhalts aus Gleichgültigkeit keinen Antrag stellen würde. Gerade in diesen Fällen sind aber die betroffenen Jugendlichen häufig in besonderem Maße gefährdet und des Schutzes bedürftig" (Deutscher Bundestag – 7. Wahlperiode, Drucksache VII/514 S. 7; ich verdanke diesen und den folgenden Nachweis Herrn Kollegen U. Nembach).

[37] Das Schutzalter der Jugendlichen ist – nach einer vorübergehenden Festlegung bei 21 Jahren – auf 18 Jahre festgesetzt worden aufgrund der Überlegung, „daß Männer von 18–21 Jahren im allgemeinen nicht mehr auf Dauer homosexuell geprägt werden könnten" (Deutscher Bundestag – 6. Wahlperiode, Drucksache VI/3521 S. 30). Die „Befürchtung, Männer dieser Altersgruppe könnten bei Einbeziehung in homosexuelle Handlungen dadurch in der psychischen Entwicklung gestört werden, daß die Ausbildung ihrer heterosexuellen Anlagen gehemmt werde und sie selbst in Konflikt mit der Umwelt gerieten" (ebd.), ist selbstverständlich auch auf Jugendliche unter 18 Jahren zu beziehen. Auch aus juristisch-technischen Überlegungen hat man sich für dieses Schutzalter entschieden, obwohl die Mehrheit der Sachverständigen, die vom 23.–25.11.1970 angehört wurden, die Auffassung vertrat, daß „homosexuelle Prägung schon nach dem 16. Lebensjahr im allgemeinen nicht mehr möglich sei" (ebd.).

[38] HerKorr 30, 1976, 82–87.

[39] AaO. 84.

in eigener Verantwortung ethische Weisungen abgeändert oder neu begründet. So ist Jesu absolutes Ehescheidungsverbot im Verlauf der urchristlichen Überlieferung den faktischen Erfordernissen der Gemeindepraxis angepaßt und hierdurch entschärft worden (Mk 10,1ff.11f. par; Mt 5,31f. u.ö.). Mit guten theologischen Gründen hat Paulus das „objektiv" gegebene alttestamentlich-jüdische Zeremonialgesetz für Heidenchristen aufgehoben. In seinen positiven Mahnungen bindet sich der Apostel – wie wir gesehen haben – zu einem großen Teil an vorgegebene jüdische oder hellenistische Überlieferungen, die nach Maßgabe der Gemeindesituation in seinen Briefen Aufnahme fanden. Paulus kann auch auf die συνήθεια als die verbindliche Sitte verweisen, der sich in Übereinstimmung mit der jüdischen und heidnischen Welt die christlichen Gemeinden verpflichtet wissen sollen (1.Kor 8,7; 11,16). Dies besagt: Bei der Ausrichtung seines Amtes, besonders in der paränetischen Unterweisung, nimmt Paulus ein hohes Maß an apostolischer Autorität und Freiheit für sich in Anspruch.

5.3. Die christliche Freiheit bei der Aufnahme und Weitergabe ethischer Mahnungen darf freilich nicht libertinistisch oder aktualistisch interpretiert werden. Wenn der Apostel von der „Widernatürlichkeit des homosexuellen Umgangs spricht (Röm 1,26), so schließt er sich einem Naturbegriff an, der für ihn und seine Zeit die Relevanz eines normativen Kriteriums hat. Steht solche „naturrechtliche" Weisung in Übereinstimmung mit der jüdischen Hochschätzung von Ehe und Familie, so hat Paulus darüber hinaus durch Verwendung von ethischen Allgemeinbegriffen (Röm 1,28: τὰ μὴ καθήκοντα) die grundlegende, nicht auf die gegebene Situation eingeschränkte Verbindlichkeit der ethischen Forderung hervorgehoben. Das Verbot der Homosexualität ist nach neutestamentlichem Verständnis nicht nur eine zeitgebundene Randerscheinung der Ethik, sondern eine unbedingte Forderung, die sich einer verbreiteten frühchristlichen, jüdischen und hellenistischen Überzeugung anschließt. Sie erhebt den Anspruch, dem Kriterium der „Gerechtigkeit" zu entsprechen (1.Tim 1,9; vgl. Röm 14,17; Phil 1,11), und kann auch heute noch das christliche Gewissen schärfen. Dies um so mehr, als Paulus den Zusammenhang dieses Verbotes mit der Gemeindewirklichkeit betont: Die Gestaltung des christlichen Gemeinschaftslebens darf nicht den Enthusiasten überlassen werden (1.Kor 6,1ff.12ff.). Die Warnung vor ethischen Verfehlungen, wie sie in den Lasterkatalogen ausgesprochen wird, gilt nicht individualorientierten, isolierten Verhaltensweisen, sondern sie steht im Rahmen einer durch das Christusgeschehen begründeten Gemeindewirklichkeit, die das Recht des einzelnen Christen zur Selbstverwirklichung begrenzt, wie Paulus dies besonders in Auslegung des Leib-Christi-Gedankens sagt (Röm 12,4ff.; 1.Kor 12,12).

5.4. Welche Folgerungen sind also aus dem biblischen Befund zu ziehen? Da Paulus die Homosexualität als Auswirkung des eschatologischen Strafgerichts versteht, ist in seinem Urteil für den ausgleichenden Gedanken einer

„ἀποκατάστασις πάντων", wonach Gottes ewige Güte die ethischen Verfehlungen als solche nicht zur Kenntnis nimmt, kein Raum. Wird Homosexualität als Ausdruck des Gerichtswaltens Gottes (κρίμα τοῦ θεοῦ: Röm 2,3) erkannt, so ist von hier aus der Ruf zur „Umkehr" begründet (Röm 2,4; 2. Kor 12,21). Dieser muß zu Konsequenzen im zwischenmenschlichen Bereich führen, dessen „Normalität" durch das Ausleben der homosexuellen Neigung gestört oder aufgehoben wird. Jedoch ist nicht die Gerichtsansage, sondern der Zuspruch von göttlicher Gnade und Vergebung die wichtigste Aufgabe eines Verkündigers des neutestamentlichen Evangeliums; denn „wo die Sünde mächtig geworden ist, da ist die Gnade noch viel mächtiger geworden" (Röm 5,20).

Was besagt dies für das gegenseitige Verhältnis von Nichthomosexuellen zu Homosexuellen in der christlichen Gemeinde? Nach dem Gesagten verbietet es sich, die christliche Verantwortung für die Gemeinde wie auch für den einzelnen Mitchristen in einem gesetzlichen Sinn zu realisieren[40]. Da die ethischen Forderungen des Neuen Testaments grundlegend durch die Christusdimension bestimmt sind, d.h. durch die in Jesus Christus erschlossene „Liebe Gottes" (ἀγάπη θεοῦ), müssen die ethischen Entscheidungen diese Agape reflektieren. Sie sind gegenüber der konkreten Situation offen zu halten und können nicht im voraus ein für allemal normiert werden. Andererseits müssen sie das Ganze der Ekklesia im Blick behalten. Die Entscheidung im Einzelfall muß mit der Eigenart des christlichen Bruders bzw. der christlichen Schwester das Recht und das Ansehen der Gemeinde zu vereinbaren suchen. Dies heißt konkret: Ausgeschlossen ist eine moralische Diffamierung von Homosexuellen, gleichgültig, ob es sich um eine erworbene oder um eine ererbte Anlage handelt; ihr ist die seelsorgerliche Diakonie entgegenzustellen, insbesondere dort, wo die Betroffenen unter ihrer Neigung leiden. Andererseits sollte auch eine Idealisierung ausgeschlossen sein, weil diese in Widerspruch zu Einheit und Selbstverständnis der christlichen Gemeinde steht[41]. Die Frage, ob ein Homosexueller eine pädagogische oder pastorale Funktion ausüben dürfe oder nicht[42], kann nicht

---

[40] Daß sich Apostel und Gemeinde für das Heil der Mitchristen verantwortlich wissen, besagt etwa 1. Thess 5,9–11 („darum ermahnt einander und auferbaut einer den anderen") und kann bis zur extremen Konsequenz des Ausschlusses führen (1. Kor 5,4 f.). Daneben wird der einzelne aufgerufen, seinen grundsätzlich berechtigten Anspruch, sich als Christ und Mensch zu verwirklichen, dem Ziel der „Erbauung" der Gemeinde unterzuordnen (1. Kor 14,1–12; Röm 14,19; 15,2).

[41] Zu *H. J. Schoeps*, ZEE 6, 1962, 373 Anm. 22.

[42] Verneint durch *W. Trillhaas*, Sexualethik 76; auch der Theologische Ausschuß der VELKD vertritt in seiner Stellungnahme zum Problem der Homosexualität von Pfarrern vom 12.9.1979 die Auffassung, „daß die offen gelebte und öffentlich vertretene Homosexualität eines Pfarrers der wegweisenden und orientierenden Aufgabe des Pfarramtes als eines Amtes der Kirche widerspricht" (Texte aus der VELKD Nr. 11/1980 S. 16). – Dagegen ist in den USA der Fall einer Ordination einer lebischen Frau aus der „Episcopal Church" belegt; vgl. The New York Times vom 24. 1. 1977, S. 12.

im allgemeinen Sinn entschieden werden. Sie ist im Zusammenhang von Agape und Gerechtigkeit im jeweils konkreten Fall zu stellen und zu beantworten[43].

Professor Dr. Georg Strecker, Wilhelm-Raabe-Straße 6, 3406 Bovenden

## Summary

### *Homosexuality in the Sight of the Bible*

Homosexuality, in OT-Literature strictly forbidden, was widespread in the ancient world. Thus in OT and NT it could be looked upon as a characteristic element of pagan immorality. Though overcome by baptism (1.Cor. 6, 11), it was still a problem within and therefore attacked by NT-communities.

The biblical prohibition of H. must not be repeated legalistically, but has to be reflected anew in view of God's judgement and grace.

The question, whether a homosexual person may have access to a pastoral or pedagogical function or not, should be answered within the context of agape and righteousness.

---

[43] Vgl. hierzu *G. Strecker*, Strukturen einer neutestmentlichen Ethik, ZThK 75, 1978, 117-146, bes. 139ff.

MARK THOMPSON

# THIS GAY TRIBE: A BRIEF HISTORY OF FAIRIES

I'm not willing just to be tolerated. That wounds my love of love and of liberty.

—Jean Cocteau
*The White Paper*

One of the most remarkable offshoots of American gay liberation in recent years has been the emergence of "radical fairies," a nationwide, grass-roots movement of gay men seeking alternatives within their own subculture and society at large. Many fairie-identified men see little distinction between the two, arguing that as the gay middle-class assimilates into the cultural mainstream, deeper inquiries into the predominant structures of state and spirit are being left unanswered. This loosely organized faction of gay men, largely unknown (even within their own community), remains on the outer edges of both worlds.

In most instances, those who are aware of this underground movement discount its questions and values as naïve remnants of the 1960s. These critics invoke clichéd images of incense and vague Oriental philosophies, as if these things too should remain relics from another decade, trivializing history into sentiment and shameless nostalgia. But, in fact, the fairies are exploring the most personal and relevant of questions: What does it mean to be a gay man—alive, today? And rather than borrow answers from the East, they have gone to the very roots of Western spiritual mythology.

Although *fairie* has long been used as a hateful and self-effacing epithet, gay historian Arthur Evans was among the first to insist that the word—as applied to homosexual men—had an actual, living reality based in fact. We think of fairies today as being mythical creatures, stemming mostly from Northern European folklore, primarily Celtic in origin. The Celts, and the many indigenous tribes that preceded them, were nature-worshipping people with a strong matriarchal religious tradition. The many faces of the Great Mother were celebrated on special days throughout the seasons, often with sacred, sexual rites. Male sexuality, the world of the night, and the spirit of animals were embodied by a male deity known, in various guises, as the Horned One—a satyrlike figure referred to by the Celts as Cernunnos, and named Dionysus, Pan, Minotaur and Osiris in other pre-Christian cultures. The ancient tradition of nature worship persisted through Celtic, Roman and early Christian times, although it was increasingly suppressed by the corporate demands of the church. The archetypes of the Great Mother and her horned consort were eventually assimilated into Christian theology as the Virgin and the Devil.

In his ground-breaking work, *Witchcraft and the Gay Counterculture: A Radical View of Western Civilization and Some of the People It Has Tried to Destroy* (Fag Rag Books, 1978), Evans asserts, "Though outlawed, the worshippers of the matriarchal mix persisted underground and were known in folklore as fairies, named after the fateful goddesses whom they worshipped. Later in the medieval period, various remnants of the 'old religion' were to emerge again, only this time they were called heretics and witches. Their greatest 'crime' was that they experienced the highest manifestations of the divine in free practice of sexuality." Aspects of the Great Mother survived as the image of the three Fates, notes Evans, who were mythologized as fairies by the medieval Christian world (*fairy* coming from the Latin word *fata*, meaning fate).

Evans was a member of the Gay Liberation Front in New York City, which formed immediately after the Stonewall riots in 1969, and later helped found the outspoken Gay Activists Alliance, where he developed a form of militant, nonviolent protest that he called "zaps." Evans's world view of gay people as tribal-shamanic figures was central to his activism; later, when he moved to the West Coast in the mid-1970s, he began to publicly expand on this history. During the spring of 1976, Evans conducted a series of well-attended lectures in San Francisco, presenting a bold conceptualization of gay spirituality based on his research about "Faeries." More privately, he had already begun to give form to his ideas through the practice of ritual with a widening circle of other gay men in locations throughout the city. I remember one afternoon during this time at San Francisco State University, where one of the first gay academic conferences in the country was being held, when Evans and a dozen followers charged through the campus wearing robes, skins and scarves, clanging bells and waving boughs of leaves. A buried heritage was being announced that day, one far removed from the imaginations of those witnessing this pagan procession.

The need to create a new inner vision—and one not based on modern Western morality—was a vital issue for many gay people during this time. Drawing new historical conclusions from old myths was one approach, but others felt compelled to separate themselves physically from the dominant heterosexual culture and to seek alternatives for body, as well as soul, in isolated rural areas. A plan for one such refuge in 1970 touched a collective nerve in gay people across the country, even though the idea was later revealed as elaborate fiction. As a means to raise media awareness, a Los Angeles group also called the Gay Liberation Front (GLF) invented a story about gay people "taking over" remote Alpine County in Northern California. The story was interpreted as real, made national headlines and created controversy and outrage. It also gave hope to many that such a plan might be true. Wishful thinking aside, some gay men and lesbians did actually go on to establish small rural communities, such as in Golden, Oregon (1970); Elwha, on the Olympic Peninsula in Washington state (1973); in Wolf Creek, Oregon (1975); and a few years later (in the late 1970s), the Running Water and Short Mountain sanctuaries in North Carolina and Tennessee.

*RFD,* a magazine focusing on gay country living and radical fairie politics, was created at one such community—in a large, windy farmhouse, actually—outside Grinnell, Iowa, in October 1974. According to Stewart Scofield, the magazine's first editor, "The time was right for a publication for rural gay men. The idea or dream existed in the minds and hearts of many—activists, post-hippies, fairies, queers, hermits and just ordinary guys—from all parts of the country who hadn't yet connected with one another. That deisolating connection manifested itself quite magically as *RFD: A Country Journal for Gay Men Everywhere.*"

Word about the new publication quickly spread, and a deluge of mail began to arrive at the Iowa farm. Two thousand copies of the third issue were distributed by the following spring equinox. Subscribers found packets of pansy seeds stapled to the back cover of their copies. "*RFD* was more than the newsprint, the words and pictures, more than those who were intimately involved," Scofield wrote in the magazine nearly a decade after its inception. "It was the lives of hundreds of early supporters who daily sent energy to it, who told their friends about it, who wrote poetry, who read it cover from cover, who waited by their mailboxes, who dreamed with lovers about that piece of land in the future, who gardened vegetables and flowers, who celebrated the solstice and danced by the light of the moon. The readers made love to *RFD,* and *RFD* responded in kind."

Although the magazine had obviously touched a collective need, Scofield also recalled critical mail from readers who "chided us for being hippie idealist pagan gay liberationists and for the lack of material of 'real' relevance to the thousands of 'ordinary' gay men living in the country in more traditional lifestyles." Harsh words were rare, however, as *RFD* was mainly shaped and written by its far-flung network of readers, many who found the journal an ideal forum in which to express their deepest and most personal concerns.

During the early 1970s, while complex gay business and social infrastructures were emerging in major urban areas, it was rural gays who were largely questioning internal needs and values—an exploration no doubt nurtured by their relative isolation, increased self-reliance and contact with raw nature. These gay men, on the fringes of a newly organized community, provided their movement with some of its most astute and visionary analysis. "*RFD* was the last gay liberation paper to begin," observed Scofield, that "advocated a separate gay culture, a we-are-different-from-straights attitude." It was a time when many gay people began to see rural life as a viable option to urban gay ghettos, and he further noted, "It seems to me no accident that not a small amount of energy in the early days of *RFD* came from gay lib 'heavies' who had either fled the urban madness or had returned to the country of their boyhoods."

Carl Wittman was one such man. He and his companion, Allan Troxler, had helped establish *RFD* from the West Coast and were among the cofounders of the Golden, Oregon, collective, in the area where the magazine was centered for a number of years after it moved from Iowa.*

Wittman, as writer and activist, was keenly interested in the potentialities of gay consciousness throughout his life (he died of AIDS in early 1986). His widely read "Gay Manifesto" was one of the most influential documents during the early years of post-Stonewall gay liberation. Written during the summer of 1969 in San Francisco, the manifesto offered a potent gay vision in which open acceptance of sexuality in all of its forms was an integral part. Later, in the mid-1970s, Wittman participated in several gatherings of gay men in the Northwest.

One of the most far-reaching of these gatherings was the Faggots and Class Struggle conference at Wolf Creek in September 1976, where the word *fairie* was asserted in a political context. But it was through work on *RFD* and his previous exposure to the visionary writings of Harry Hay that Wittman had begun to perceive the word as having a spiritual connotation as well.

Hay and his companion John Burnside were living among the Rio Grande Indian people at San Juan Pueblo (the traditional Tewa Indian

*The magazine, much like a movable feast, has been produced by various collectives of gay men around the country. It resides, at the time of this writing, with a collective in the Southeast and still remains a vital and lively reader-generated quarterly. Write: *RFD*, Route 1, Box 127-E, Bakersville, North Carolina 28705.

village of Oke-Oweenge) in rural northern New Mexico during this time. They had left Los Angeles in May 1970, bringing their small kaleidoscope manufacturing business with them. Six months earlier, the couple had helped found the Gay Liberation Front in Southern California with activists Morris Kight and Jim Kepner. Hay and Burnside had also hoped to carry their concerns about gay liberation to the Indian and Chicano pueblos when they moved to the Southwest. But it turned out not to be an idea whose time had come. According to Hay, northern New Mexico in the 1970s was a crossroads of many peoples, both indigenous and immigrant, "who were coming *from* something—a place, an attitude, an idea—rather that purposely going *to* anywhere." Nevertheless, the couple established their home as a spiritual nexus, named the Circle of Loving Companions, which for a number of years was the only openly gay listed address in the entire state. It was a place for "frightened, lonely people to develop as political gay persons, to be healed and reinspired."

During this period, Hay found himself realizing and deepening many of his ideas about gay spirituality. He began to create a multifaceted approach to what he called "the lovely dream of being gay," an inquiry that required a more subtle and cross-cultural analysis than the politics of gay liberation had demanded up to that time. He had first used the word *faerie* to convey the idea of a separate gay consciousness in 1970, during a speech before the Western Regional Homophile Conference. "But, within this community, let the spirit be betrayed, let coercion or opportunism attempt to bind any of us against our will . . . and *presto*, like the faeries of folklore, suddenly we are no longer there. . . . Our faerie characteristic is our homosexual minority's central weakness . . . and paradoxically, also the keystone of our enduring strength."

Hay continued to expand on his concept of a *faerie* identity in public talks and published papers. It was an idea that many older gay men had difficulty accepting at the time but about which a younger generation was beginning to express curiosity.

Wittman met Hay in the summer of 1975. Hay and Burnside were returning to New Mexico from seminars they had been invited to attend in Seattle, when they stopped to visit Wolf Creek. The two men shared their views about a "circle of loving companions" with members of the Oregon collectives, and Hay asserted the need for a community land trust (a permanent rural site) where "faerie consciousness" could be explored to full potential by gay men. Wittman was especially moved by Hay's vision, and in the autumn of that year he wrote in *RFD* that "the notion of foundling, growing up a foreigner in family and culture, and returning to the larger whole—this notion I put on gently, like a new robe, wondering if it becomes me; afraid of vanity, but yearning for dignity, I find myself saying, yes, it fits. Ah, but politically, is it misleading? Where are my hard-won ideas about separatism, confrontation, group consciousness? Are we not members of a lost and dispersed tribe, rather than errant offspring? Isn't it a bit spiritual, ignoring the real needs to unite politically? I decide not. This vision . . . is a mantle to wear over whatever else is me, one which I feel will become my other attributes."

Wittman's debate echoed the feelings of many others—that the political and the spiritual need not be exclusive of one another. In fact, the synthesis of the two was a reality fully expressed in many gay lives during that time. According to Faygele benMiriam, a political activist since the early 1950s, "There was a time when fairies were the most politically directed of gays. We formed a nucleus of people who were trying to change patterns of dress and attitude and ways of treating each other. We were out there saying, 'We are different than others' —and giving that difference expression. Many fairies were looking at the next step."

BenMiriam was a resident of the Elwah community and then relocated to the Wolf Creek area, where he worked on *RFD* for several years. Later, he moved to North Carolina, and continued to work on the magazine, which had also traveled east. BenMiriam remembers gatherings of gay men in the early 1970s where questions about a unique gay identity were expressed. "We didn't call ourselves 'fairies' back then, but we were."

Groups of outrageously dressed gay men would travel between Boston, Ann Arbor, Seattle and San Francisco in cars painted with slogans proclaiming *Gay Power* or *Faggots Against Facism,* recalls benMiriam, who, in the spirit of the times, once went a year and a half without wearing men's clothing, including the time he was working for the federal government. "We were trying to keep some sort of gay spirit alive during a time of great attack and repression. Fairie-identified gay men refuse to be automatically ghettoized. We have long been on our communities' front lines and, in many cases, have formed its political basis."

The investigation of gay consciousness by small groups of gay men around the country; a growing inquiry by Carl Wittman and many others in the pages of *RFD* and elsewhere; the radical reevaluation of a gay heritage by Arthur Evans, whose work had appeared piecemeal in *Fag Rag* and *Out* magazines during the mid-1970s and then in book form; and the synchronistic reclaiming of a *faerie* identity by Harry Hay were all important foundation stones for the alternative movement soon to come.

The need to retreat and explore gay sensibilities in a protected environment remained a compelling issue within the subculture. But it was a minority opinion, a voice counter to the central thrust of a civil rights movement working hard to downplay the concept of difference. In 1979, Hay and Burnside and two other men decided to take the matter into their own hands and announced the first Spiritual Conference for Radical Fairies. Don Kilhefner, formerly of the GLF and one of the founders of the Los Angeles Gay and Lesbian Community Services Center, and Mitch Walker, a San Francisco writer and counselor, had also emphasized in their individual work the importance for gay men collectively to discover a way of being unique to themselves.

The site chosen to begin this exploration was a remote spot in the Arizona desert, and over two hundred gay men arrived that summer from throughout the United States and Canada. The gathering had a profound impact on many who attended, and despite personal and ideological conflicts that would split its founders a few years later, the fairie movement was born. During the next six years, over a hundred gatherings of "radical fairies" were held across the North American continent, from Key West beaches to Washington state forests, lofts in New York City to the mountains of Colorado, and up and down the coast of California, with anywhere from two dozen to three hundred men in attendance. And, at the time of this writing, there are ongoing gatherings being planned throughout the country.

The phenomenon has spread beyond national boundaries, with gatherings reported in Europe and Australia, and a new set of values, one with its own oral and written traditions differing from mainstream gay culture, has developed. (See Michael Rumaker's *My First Satyrnalia*, San Francisco: Grey Fox Press, 1981.) For several thousand gay men, fairie gatherings have provided a unique opportunity to examine and to reclaim a part of the self previously denied, an intense experience to be digested and then used in the context of everyday life. The fairies, as a kind of constantly rejuvenating tribe (there are no leaders; each gathering is locally organized), remain anarchical in spirit. And while their gatherings are frustrating and too unfocused for some, they remain essential for others.

On the surface, it would be possible to view the fairies as part of the growing popular interest in neopaganism and Wicca—the ancient word for *witchcraft*, meaning "to bend." (See Margot Adler's *Drawing Down the Moon*, Boston: Beacon Press, revised edition, 1986.) Or to regard their retreats as an idealistic leftover from the whole-earth, alternative-culture sentiment of the 1960s. Although the fairies have taken signals from both sources, the energy that propels their movement forward seems to come from a deep place within the gay psyche: a wounded and vulnerable place, but a place perhaps not unfamiliar to "fairies" of previous times. In so actively choosing to reinvent themselves, the radical fairies are dipping into a deep well of human myth and spiritual experience.

In saying this, I am reminded of a passage from Mircea Eliade's *The Sacred and the Profane:* "It is the specialists in ecstasy, the familiars of the fantastic universes, who nourish, increase, and elaborate the traditional mythological motifs. . . . In the last analysis, in the archaic societies as everywhere else, culture arises and is renewed through the creative experiences of a few individuals. But since archaic culture gravitates around myths, and these are constantly being studied and given new, more profound interpretations by the specialists in the sacred, it follows that society as a whole is led toward the values and meanings discovered and conveyed by these few individuals. It is in this way that myth helps man to transcend his own limitations and conditions and stimulates him to rise to 'where the greatest are.' "

I remember these lines by Walt Whitman: "In the need of songs, philosophy, and appropriate native grand opera, shipcraft, any craft, he or she is greatest who contributes the greatest original practical example." And, finally, his declaration, "Who need be afraid of the merge."

To outsiders, the fairies often appear politically naïve, however authentic the spirit that motivates their gatherings may be. Yet, for the men who respond to its call, the fairie movement is rooted in the firm belief that the only liberation movement worth having is one that first begins inside. Personal evolution is the true agent for change: Therefore, the personal *must* be linked with the political. Too many gay people have not really confronted their own homophobia, the internalization of society's stigma, that self-hate that pollutes the soul. It is a painful realization to face; and as a result, many have projected their own feelings of negative self-worth onto others.

Still, at its core, the message of gay liberation has been one primarily of love. And—on the surface, at least—the fairies have embodied this message well, taking to heart and expanding on the most radical impulses of the early gay movement. Their first gatherings appeared like a mirage, a *fata morgana,* on an otherwise arid landscape—an original and healing journey into the pathless lands of inner knowing.

## A Recollection: In the Shadow of the Red Rock, The Radical Fairies Convene

A clipping from the *Farmers' Arizonan Gazette*, Wednesday, September 5, 1979:

> *Benson—A series of "strange doings" were reported by local sheriff, Waldo Pruitt, at a site about ten miles west of this small desert*

*community. Pruitt first made his report Monday night, claiming that he had failed to locate a section of desert land after repeated investigation.*

*The land in question was the site of the Desert Sanctuary Foundation, also known as the Sri Ram Ashram. Locals in the area said they knew little about the activities of the sanctuary. Other sources reported yesterday, however, that a Spiritual Conference for Radical Fairies had been scheduled at the sanctuary over the Labor Day weekend. One organizer for the event was quoted as having said, "With luck we'll learn to levitate, as fairies should." No explanation was offered by the source overhearing the remark.*

*Pruitt first became aware of the event through reports about cattle displaying unusual behavior in the vicinity of the sanctuary. Informants also claimed that large groups of men there were engaging in orgiastic rituals.*

*"They said that all the animals in the area started to act real strange," the sheriff explained. "I guess I don't mind what you do as long as you don't do it in public. But when you start in on plants and animals, well, then you've gone too far."*

*Pruitt and three deputies drove out to the site to investigate the disturbances. He claimed that a flashing of colored lights could be seen from miles around. But when the men arrived, "The land out there had just got up and plumb disappeared. All that was left was an old* Gunsmoke *set a few miles down the road." Pruitt said he will continue his investigation of the incident.*

I arrived at the sanctuary in the middle of the desert amid a great veil of dust. The taste of it lay choking in my mouth; fine rivulets of it slid across the hood of the car. Arizona was the final stop on a long journey that had also taken me across Europe, where I had been picking through the shards of gay heritage.

A castrated Dionysus in the Vatican, myths and legends perverted from original meanings, painters and writers censored by convention were among the relics. Only the men observed gathering night after night, usually at the site of the oldest ruins or wooded groves, offered tangible evidence of a culture that still might survive after centuries of patriarchal, heterosexual domination.

I was tired and wanted to go home. But the sensations before me of a garden in bloom, playful laughter and a beautiful man, flower in hair and hands reached out in welcome, quickened a hope that perhaps I needn't look further. As I stepped out of the dust, I stepped out of time, was hurtled out of gravity. The fairies, at last, had reconvened.

Harry Hay had a vision over thirty years ago when he put out a call for gay men to gather together and at last discover "Who are we?" "Where have we come from?" and "What are we here for?" These questions became the spiritual basis for the early Mattachine Society, a foundation stone for our present-day liberation movement.

Hay's vision was dimmed, however, when the group lost contact with its original purpose and its members "became more interested in being respectable than self-respecting. . . . They believed we were just like everyone else."

Hay left the group profoundly disappointed but eventually met his "other," John Burnside. Together they left for New Mexico where, during the past decade, they have been quietly rearticulating the need for a "circle of loving companions."

A century before, Walt Whitman wrote, "I dream'd in a dream I saw a city invincible to the attacks of the whole of the rest of the earth, I dream'd that was the new city of Friends. . . ."

Hay began to sense the need for reasserting this dream. And so, joining together with other men, the call was put out again. Much had changed in thirty years. Whitman's "new city of Friends" had now emerged as inner city ghettos. Like many of the men drawn to the conference, I had become weary of a "culture" defined by exploitive entrepreneurs, distrustful of religious leaders using spirituality in ways that did not move me, doubtful of a community unable to see beyond the pursuit of civil rights alone.

I remember the sting of a baseball driven hard into the palm of my hand as my father worked for hours trying to "make a man of me." I remember talking to trees and of the wonderful pictures left dream'd in a dream. I came to Arizona to accept and to reclaim, to shed the wounds of conformity as the snake drops its skin on the desert sand, to understand that variations in the human species extend past color and form and into modes of perception as well, to learn of the creative potentials still locked within my sexuality.

I came to shake the magic rattle, to roll in the dust, to take apart the pieces and reinvent myself, to be able to say finally, "I remember now what I want to become."

> Come forth, o children,
> under the stars,
> And take your fill of love!
> I am above you and in you.
> My ecstasy is in yours.
> My joy is to see your joy.
> —*Aleister Crowley*,
> Quoted on the First "Call"

The tall man with the laugh in his voice slowly circled in the middle of the group. "Forget the linear associations you used to get here," he said. "Use fairie physics—turn everything inside out. Imagine, for instance, that the tops of the trees are really the roots." And then Mitch Walker sat down.

Gradually, other men stood up and presented their gifts. Actors, writers, teachers, priests, crop tillers and film directors. Gifts of movement and music, laughter and wit were all brought forth. The experience of age freely mixed with the exuberance of youth. Long-felt anxieties were exposed, tears unashamedly shed. Two hundred gay men forming an oasis in the middle of the desert, linking hands without competition and aggression, without the usual props of status and envy.

Hay had stood up the previous evening and unwrapped the gift of his insights. "We must recognize that there is a qualitative difference between hetero social consciousness and gay social consciousness," he said. "And our first responsibility must be to develop this gay consciousness to its deepest and most compassionately encompassing levels.

"Humanity must expand its experience from people thinking objectively—thinking subject-to-object; that is, in terms of opportunism, competitiveness and self-advantage—to thinking subject-to-subject, in terms of equal sharing, loving healing.

"Early on in human evolution, natural selection set into the evolving whirl a small percentage of beings who appeared to counterbalance the tendency of subject–object thinking characteristic of the emerging human conformity. Humanity would be wise to finally give consideration to these deviants in their ranks—gays—and to begin to grant us the peace and growing space we will need to display and further develop, in communicable words and actions, our gift. [It is] the gift of *analogue consciousness* by which we perceive the world through the gay window of subject-to-subject consciousness."

He continued, the night air carrying his words over the men sitting in front of him. "We must transform the experience of people viewing others as objects to be manipulated, mastered and consumed, to subjects like him/herself, to be respected and cherished.

"We must also remember that the social world we inherit, the total hetero male-oriented and -dominated world of tradition and daily environment—the sum total of our history, philosophy, psychology, culture, our very languages—are all totally subject–object in concept, definitions and evolution.

"To all of this we fairies should be essentially alien. The hetero male, incapable of conceiving the possibility of a window on the world other than his own, is equally incapable of perceiving that gay people might not fit in either of his man–woman categories, that we might turn out to be classified as something very else.

"If we, as people, will but grasp this, flesh it out and exercise this affirmatively, we will discover the lovely gay conscious 'not-man' shining underneath our disguises. We must begin gathering in circles to manifest the new dimensions of subject–subject relationships and to validate the contributions our consciousness is capable of developing within the world vision."

Hay's words for some men were comfortable and familiar; for others, new ideas full of turmoil and self-confrontation. Coming out is more than a prescription to a contained lifestyle; it is an ongoing experience of many dimensions. As the first morning progressed, and more and more men stood up to reveal old attitudes and assumptions, the many secure places left behind outside were, indeed, being turned "inside out."

Being integrated into a world conceived by sexist heterosexual males is not the full measure of equality. The men on the grass that morning, assembled from many points thousands of miles apart, knew that they still felt sad and alienated by the paradox of a culture reaping the benefits of civil liberation but still left spiritually impoverished. As gay men, we have been denied access to the watersheds of our culture and systematically suppressed for fulfilling the roles we once naturally assumed. At one time we embodied the creatures of change in myth and folklore: shamans and ritualmakers, conveyors of spirit, carriers of seed, tenders of the sun and moon; a people encoded with the function of empathizing with the elements.

How appropriate to reclaim the distinction of *fairie*; to return to a spot on the continent that had not felt such a gathering in centuries; to honor the full sum of ourselves and the spinning, biological entity once known as Gaia—the Great Mother of us all. As the hours of this first day passed, the cocoons of many former selves could be seen shriveling under the bright midday sun. New creatures, fairies of many different hues, were emerging.

I left the luxuriant grounds of the sanctuary late that afternoon feeling cynicism encroaching upon my exhilaration. I walked several miles, past groups of men making music, making love, making conversation, to a point where the desert plains begin their sweep up into the Rincon Mountains. I took off my clothes and jumped down to the sandy bottom of a dry riverbed. I cradled myself, rocking back and forth, some part of me wanting to disbelieve the events of the day, yet feeling the invisible currents of the water that had once been there, aware of the life under the desert floor coming up through the soles of my feet.

Now I was on the inside, somehow merged with the sand, the scrub trees, even the insect sounds around me. I felt I was seeing, hearing, consciously for the first time in my life. My "objectivity" had become unglued. Each man here was a companion to love and learn from; my ability and my need for trust was being renewed.

The cynicism sprang from my reluctance to accept yet another label, from my previous distrust of men in general. The term *fairie* seemed comforting, yet alien. I knew I often felt *fairylike*, but the word did not fully encompass the complexities of my thoughts and emotions as a *man-creature*. Still, it seemed the natural progression in the long derivation of words used to describe us: *Uranian, invert, homosexual, homophile, gay, queer, faggot* and, now, *fairie*. Each increment gets closer to the way I have always felt inside. *Fairie* is powerful and seems appropriate for these new ways of approaching ourselves and each other. It helps to define a state of inner awareness for me. *Gay* has always dealt with attitudes of lifestyle and politics.

I decided I was comfortable with the word for now, but I knew I could relinquish it as my evolution continued. If anything, fairies are flexible. Perhaps, someday, words will not be necessary.

Walking slowly back, I noticed an almost physical lightness in the air the closer I got. Entering the grounds, I saw the joy in each man's face as he connected with others and then drifted apart without pretense or stance. The day filled with music and dance.

That night, about seventy of us gathered by the edge of the large swimming pool. Murray Edelman, a group facilitator practicing in New York, arranged us in groups of six. Any clothes still remaining were dropped to the carpet of sleeping bags and blankets beneath us. Slowly, we began to explore each other's bodies—arms and feet, faces and backs. No one was too fat or thin, too perfect or old. Edelman had slipped out of view; the strong moonlight revealed a single body of men laying on hands and mouths to hardened cocks and shining bodies. We were calling forth Hermes, bringer of ecstasy; Luna, keeper of the moon.

The next morning another group of men arose early and went out to the desert, also leaving clothes behind. Buckets of water had been brought to a dry riverbed, and soon a great puddle of mud was produced. Cries for "more mud" rang across the cactus fields as each man anointed the other. Twigs and blades of dry grass were woven through hair, hands were linked and a large circle formed. Coming together, the group lifted one man above it, arms above shoulders, silently swaying in the morning sun.

In other areas of the sanctuary, groups of men were learning that loosening our laughter is as important as setting free our sexuality—that fairies can be silly, too. Elsewhere other discussions were in progress. A ritual was also being planned.

We spent the early part of the third evening carefully dressing ourselves and painting our faces and bodies with the brightest designs imaginable. A deep-toned bell rang and we gathered to take a silent walk through the desert. One by one, in a single line, we were led through the unfamiliar terrain.

Our path was lit by an occasional candle; we stumbled as our clothes caught on the hard branches and sharp thorns. Slowly, our resistance to the desert diminished. Our silence was no longer a nervous suppression but rather a contemplative awareness of our surroundings. The environment ceased to be an obstacle; we were learning to move through it, dance with it.

After twenty minutes we approached the site of the ritual, a large cleared area on the outskirts of the sanctuary. A ring of candles had been set in the middle; a band of musicians serenaded our arrival from the half-lit perimeters. We arranged ourselves in a circle. Nearly all of us were there. A great convocation of fairies!

The music dimmed and, quietly at first, came the evocation of familiar friends and guiding spirits. "I evoke Walt Whitman," said one man. "Marilyn Monroe," the next. "The shadow of my former self." "Peter Pan." "Kali, the creator and destroyer." Then a moanful wail, a collective sigh, arose out of the circle up to the starry sky above. We began to chant, letting each note linger deep in our throats.

The circle split itself in two, and facing each other, we greeted the man in front of us. Fond embraces, tender kisses for all as the two rings intertwined and moved forward with the reverberating sounds of "fairie spirit, fairie love."

Music was heard again. A basket was produced, and each man made an offering. A feather from Woolworth's, a stone from the bank of the Ganges river, some hair, a poem. We began to dance with the music, moving closer together, growing more excited. In the dark shadows surrounding the circle, the outline of a large, horned bull was spotted by some of the men. Normally shy, the animal was inexplicably drawn toward the center of the gathering. The hiss of a rocket being set off frightened him away. The fireworks illuminated the night with a splashy glow.

We left the ritual site and regrouped on the comfortable lawn near the sanctuary entrance. After being led in a Balinese folk dance, we passed around pitchers of clear desert water, each man inviting another to drink. The gathering drifted apart. Some men left together, others in groups; some men stayed to talk and laugh; others curled up and went to sleep, to dream. We all felt changed in ways we could scarcely begin to know.

The next morning was a time of good-byes. One man lying on the grass near his sleeping bag looked blankly up at the sky. "I feel that whole barriers inside me have crumbled," he said. Other men were expressing fears about leaving. Each one of us had come singly, but collectively we had built the nourishing, loving energy that enveloped us all now. There had been no plans beyond the first evening; there had been no messianic ego directing us along a prescribed path. Our experience of the weekend had arisen from a collective awareness, from particles released in the unconscious, from the intuitive, from dreams not remembered in the past.

Yet despite the emotional impact of the past three days, this illuminating conference hardly represented an end in itself. The event had provided a glorious experience for coming together in new ways, but few of us felt it to be an exclusive thing, or even that the word itself—*fairie*—should, or could, be taken so seriously. In a very real sense, our dance had included all other like-minded men, wherever they were, who also longed for a spiritually rooted connection. The conference was an important landmark on the path of our personal and collective unfolding, a lovely reminder of places we had all been, a touchstone for places we still hoped to arrive at.

I left wondering how I would keep my newfound awareness alive, wondering what circles I might find on my return to San Francisco.

Sitting in a car, a friend turned and looked out the rear-view mirror. The sanctuary was being erased from sight by the cloud of dust. "Just like *Brigadoon*," he laughed.

I remembered some words by Herman Hesse, who years ago had taken another *Journey to the East*: "Oh, which of us ever thought that the magic circle would break up so soon! That almost all of us—also I, even I—should again be lost in the soundless deserts of mapped-out reality. . . ."

*Vigiliae Christianae* 38 (1984) 125-153, E. J. Brill, Leiden

# HOMOSEXUALS OR PROSTITUTES?

## THE MEANING OF ΑΡΣΕΝΟΚΟΙΤΑΙ (1 COR. 6:9, 1 TIM. 1:10)

BY

DAVID F. WRIGHT

That translators of the New Testament into English have had not a little difficulty with both μαλακοί (1 Cor. 6:9) and ἀρσενοκοῖται (1 Cor. 6:9, 1 Tim. 1:10) is evident enough from a perusal of a selection of modern translations. The point has been made to good effect by the author of a recent substantial study of attitudes to 'Gay People in Western Europe from the Beginnings of the Christian Era to the Fourteenth Century'.[1] Professor John Boswell of Yale University devotes a lengthy appendix to 'Lexicography and Saint Paul' in the course of which he provides the fullest investigation to date of the meaning of ἀρσενοκοῖται.[2] He concludes that it denotes 'male sexual agents, i.e., active male prostitutes, who were common throughout the Hellenistic world in the time of Paul ... "Ἀρσενοκοῖται" is the Greek equivalent of "drauci".' At the time he grants that Paul may not have understood the difference between active and passive male prostitutes. 'It would not be surprising if he considered active prostitution more reprehensible than passive, but it is not necessary to assume that he understood the precise nuance of "ἀρσενοκοῖται" in terms of sexual roles. Since it was unambiguous in its reference to male prostitution (as opposed to male recourse to female prostitution), he may well have intended it generically' (pp. 344-345).

The 'unambiguous reference' of the term to male prostitution Boswell claims to establish on grounds that vary considerably in weight.

### - *The context, particular and general, in Paul*

The juxtaposition of ἀρσενοκοῖται and πόρνοι in 1 Tim. 1:10 'suggests very strongly that prostitution is what is at issue ... Moreover, prostitution was manifestly of greater concern to Saint Paul than any sort of homosexual behaviour: excluding the words in question, there is only a single reference to homosexual acts in the Pauline writings, whereas the word "πόρνος" and its derivatives are mentioned almost thirty times' (p. 341). Whatever inference might be drawn from the collocation of words in 1 Tim. 1:10, this is clearly a grossly inadequate account of the meaning of πόρνος and its cognates in the New Testament and contemporary literature.[3]

- *The linguistic structure and semantic import of* ἀρσενοκοῖται

- *The absence of the term from most Greek literature on homosexuality*

Boswell speaks of 'the vast amount of writing extant on the subject of homoerotic sexuality in Greek in which this term does not occur. It is extremely difficult to believe that if the word actually meant "homosexual" or "sodomite," *no* previous or contemporary author would have used it in a way which clearly indicated this connection' (p. 345). This argument makes two claims, first, that the word was thus neglected, and secondly, that its non-use in literary references to homosexuality warrants the inference Boswell draws from it.

- *Uses of the term in literature roughly contemporary with Paul*

Occurrences of ἀρσενοκοῖται and its cognates in works written 'within two or three centuries' of the Pauline letters 'offer further evidence that the word did not connote homosexuality to Paul or his early readers' (p. 350). Aristides and Eusebius are cited to this purpose, together with less clearcut supporting testimony from Origen and Chrysostom. Boswell accepts that after the fourth century ἀρσενοκοιτία 'was often equated with homosexuality' (p. 107; cf. pp. 352-353).

Each of these last three grounds alleged by Boswell merits extended examination. The last two obviously overlap and must to some extent be taken together. But first attention must be drawn to the evidence of the Septuagint:

Lev. 18:22 — μετὰ ἄρσενος οὐ κοιμηθήσῃ κοίτην γυναικός
Lev. 20:13 — ὃς ἂν κοιμηθῇ μετὰ ἄρσενος κοίτην γυναικός

Boswell quotes these LXX verses elsewhere in his study (p. 100 n. 28) but never considers their possible significance for the meaning of ἀρσενοκοῖται in the New Testament.[4] The reason is no doubt to be found in his claim that these Levitical prohibitions had little or no influence on early Christian attitudes. 'It would simply not have occurred to most early Christians to invoke the authority of the old law to justify the morality of the new: the Levitical regulations had no hold on Christians and are manifestly irrelevant in explaining Christian hostility to gay sexuality' (p. 105).

It is certainly the case that Lev. 18:22 and 20:13 are rarely cited explicitly in Christian literature of the early centuries, although not as rarely as Boswell makes out. He first asserts that 'many [Greek-speaking theologians] considered that [the behaviour condemned in these verses] had been forbidden the Jews as part of their distinctive ethical heritage or because it was associated with idolatry, not as part of the law regarding sexuality and marriage, which was thought to be of wider application' (p. 102). As witnesses he cites only one passage from Eusebius of Caesarea and the *Apostolic Constitutions*, neither of which substantiates his claim. In his *Demonstration of the Gospel* Eusebius relates the Mosaic ban on γυναικῶν τε πρὸς γυναῖκας καὶ ἀρρένων πρὸς ἄρρενας μίξεις, preceding it with Lev. 18:2-4 and following it with Lev. 18:24-25, but he does not imply for a moment that, although distinguishing Israel from its neighbours, the ban was intended solely for Israel. If that had been his meaning, the context shows clearly that the same would have to be said about child-sacrifice![5] Eusebius's meaning is put beyond doubt elsewhere in the same work when he paraphrases Matt. 5:18 as follows:

> ὁ μὲν Μωσῆς μοιχοῖς καὶ ἀκολάστοις διετάττετο τὸ μὴ μοιχεύειν, μηδὲ ἀρσενοκοιτεῖν, μηδὲ τὰς παρὰ φύσιν ἡδονὰς διωκεῖν ..., ἐγὼ δὲ μηδ' ἐμβλέπειν γυναῖκα μετ' ἐπιθυμίας ἀκολάστου τοὺς ἐμοὺς βούλομαι.[6]

It is surely a safe presumption here that ἀρσενοκοιτεῖν refers to the Levitical proscription of male homosexual activity. Further confirmation that Eusebius did regard it as still binding upon the people of God is found in *The Preparation for the Gospel*, in which he contrasts Plato's recommendation of pederasty with the words of Moses ὃς διαρρήδην τούτοις ἐναντία νομοθετεῖ, μεγάλῃ τῇ φωνῇ τὴν κατὰ παιδεραστῶν προσήκουσαν προφερόμενος δίκην, and proceeds to cite both Lev. 20:13 and Lev. 18:22.[7]

In the *Apostolic Constitutions*, which were probably compiled in the late fourth century in Syria or possibly Constantinople, the argument proceeds as follows:

> 'If the difference of the sexes was made by the will of God for the generation of multitudes, then must the conjunction of male and female be also agreeable to his mind. But we do not say so of that abominable mixture which is contrary to nature,

> or of any unlawful practice; for such are enmity to God. For the sin of Sodom is παρὰ φύσιν, as is also that with brute beasts. But adultery and fornication are παράνομον.... [Sodomists] endeavour to make the natural course of things to change for one that is unnatural.'[8]

Then follow the two texts from Leviticus among others. Although a clear distinction is drawn between heterosexual offences and homosexual, as Boswell points out (p. 103 n. 42), its purpose is *not* to suggest that the prohibition of the latter in Leviticus was valid only for Jews. The implication is rather that offences παρὰ φύσιν are more heinous than offences παρὰ νόμον.[9]

Boswell argues that 'Almost no early Christian writers appealed to Leviticus as authority against homosexual acts' (p. 104). He mentions two exceptions—Clement of Alexandria ('an exception to this as to most generalizations', p. 104 n. 47) and the *Apostolic Constitutions*, which only two pages previously he has cited as attesting the restricted reference of the Levitical enactments against homosexual behaviour—'ceremonially unclean rather than instrinsically evil' (p. 102). As we have seen, his second citation of the work is the more accurate. There are at least two other leading exceptions to be adduced. In his refutation of Marcion Tertullian distinguishes between the *institutio* of marriage and the *exorbitatio* of adultery and other sins, and declares that God punishes with death *incestam, sacrilegam atque monstrosam in masculos et in pecudes libidinum insaniam*, with identifiable allusions to Lev. 20:10, 13, 15.[10] Origen's eleventh homily on Leviticus takes 'Be ye holy ...' (Lev. 20:7) as its text. Lev. 20:13 is not among the verses explicitly cited or alluded to, but the general thrust of the homily does not allow an interpretation that such prohibitions are no longer binding on Origen's Christian congregation.[11] But in his *Commentary on Romans*, now extant only in Rufinus's Latin, Origen quoted first 1 Tim. 1:9-10 and then Lev. 18:22 in the course of a discussion sparked off by Rom. 4:15, *Et statuamus ante oculos, si videtur, duos aliquos, verbi gratia, qui cum masculis non concubuerunt concubitu muliebri; unum ex his praecepto legis prohibitum ...*[12]

A broader range of evidence than Boswell collates can therefore be adduced for the continuing validity of the proscription in Lev. 18:22 and 20:13 in the eyes of early Christian writers. Certainly he is unable to cite any evidence of any degree of explicitness declaring that it had been abrogated, like much else in the Levitical legislation. A more differentiating approach was adopted than Boswell allows. As one of his reviewers commented, 'Sexual prohibitions tend to have a longer life than dietary or dress restrictions. Even if they show no distinctive gravity in early legislation, they are notoriously capable of surviving the dissolution of taboo structures like the heavily ritual Holiness Code of Leviticus and reappearing with increased weight in later patterns of moral offense.'[13]

The argument of the preceding paragraphs may not be strictly relevant to the question wheter the LXX of Lev. 18:22 and 20:13 provides a clue to the meaning ἀρσενοκοῖται had for Paul. It has rather been directed to the reason, so it appears, why Boswell did not investigate this possibility. The parallel between the LXX's ἄρσενος οὐ κοιμηθήσῃ κοίτην and even more κοιμηθῇ μετὰ ἄρσενος κοίτην and Paul's ἀρσενοκοῖται is surely inescapable. If, as seems likely, the ἀρσενοκοίτ- group of words is a coinage of Hellenistic Judaism or Hellenistic Jewish Christianity, the probability that the LXX provides the key to their meaning is strengthened.

If the argument of the last paragraphs is valid, it undermines *ab initio* the force of Boswell's linguistic approach to the meaning of ἀρσενοκοῖται. In short he claims that the first half of the compound (ἀρσενο-) denotes not the object but the gender of the second half (-κοῖται). This is patently not the case if the LXX of the verses in Leviticus lies behind ἀρσενοκοῖται, whether in encouraging the formation of the word itself or in informing its meaning.

But before looking more closely at the evidence of linguistic structure, we should note that Boswell stresses the coarseness and active licentiousness of the 'sleeping' denoted by -κοῖται. 'In this and other compounds [it] corresponds to the vulgar English word "fucker," a person who, by insertion, takes the "active" role in intercourse' (p. 342). This is not a point of great moment, but is worth a brief examination. Unfortunately no parallels are adduced in support of Boswell's assertion, and it is uncertain which other compounds he had in mind. Of two standard listings, comprising twentytwo compounds of -κοίτης, most of them of very rare occurrence, there is scarcely a single example to corroborate Boswell's claim.[14] Only four designate those who engage in nonmarital intercourse—κλεψικοίτης (seeking illicit sex), δουλοκοίτης (sleeping with slaves), μητροκοίτης (engaging in incest), and ἀνδροκοίτης (having intercourse with a man). In none of these compounds, except possibly the last, does the second component -κοίτης appear to carry the weight Boswell seeks to assign to it in ἀρσενοκοίτης. To set against these four are many others in which -κοίτης denotes the literal activity of sleeping or lying (e.g., ἡμεροκοίτης, sleeping by day; χαμαικοίτης, sleeping on the ground; ἐνωτοκοίτης, with ears large enough to sleep in; βορβοροκοίτης, the mudcoucher—a kind of frog), as well as ἀκοίτης and παρακοίτης which both mean 'bedfellow' or spouse. Nor does the picture change much if the enquiry is extended to include compounds of -κοῖτος, -κοιτία and -κοιτέω.[15] (Both ἀρσενοκοιτία and ἀρσενοκοιτέω are not infrequently attested). Here one encounters forms which quite patently exclude Boswell's interpretation, e.g., συγκοῖτος and ὁμοκοῖτος (both meaning 'bedfellow, sleeping together with, having intercourse,' like the verb δευτεροκοιτέω), as well as others, e.g., πολυκοῖτος (sleeping with many women or men) and ἀδελφοκοιτία (incest of brother and sister), which may bear a nuance of coarseness but hardly of thrusting activeness.[16].

Boswell's chief linguistic contention is that 'In general ... those compounds in which the form "ἀρρενο-" occurs employ it objectively; those in which "ἀρσενο-" is found use it as an adjective.... In no words coined and generally written with the form "ἀρσενο-" is the prefix demonstrably objective; overlap occurs on a small scale in words containing "ἀρρενο-" ' (pp. 343, 344).[17] Several comments are in order.

It is in the first place surprising that, having established the particular force of -κοίτης in the compound, Boswell did not go on to enquire whether in other compounds of -κοίτης the first half ever denoted who did the 'sleeping'. In all, it seems, of the comparable compounds the first element in fact specifies the object of the 'sleeping' or its scene or sphere—what one might call its indirect object (e.g., χαμαικοίτης, sleeping on the ground; ἀνεμοκοίτης, luller of winds; ἡμεροκοίτης, sleeping by day). Thus we have δουλοκοίτης (sleeping with slaves, *not* slaves sleeping with others), μητροκοίτης (*not* mother who sleeps around), and πολυκοίτης (sleeping with many others). Invariably -κοίτης has, as one might expect, a verbal force on which is dependent the object or adverb specified in the first half of the word.

Secondly, Boswell does not take sufficient account of the fact that both ἀρσενοκοιτ- and ἀρρενοκοιτ- forms are found. He does discuss one late occurrence of the latter, in an inscription at Thessalonica in honour of Basil I of Macedon, the ninth-century Byzantine emperor (A.D. 867-886), who had defeated the Arabs in Asia in 871 and 880:

βάρβαρον οὐ τρομέεις, οὐχ ἄρρενας ἀρρενοκοίτας.[18]

This is addressed to the city of Thessalonica, assuring its citizens that, thanks to Basil, they need no longer fear the barbarians, a race of men who indulge in sex with other men. To Boswell the phrase makes sense only if ἄρρενας is the object of ἀρρενοκοίτας (p. 344 n. 22). Otherwise ἄρρενας would be wholly pleonastic or, if the gender of ἀρρενοκοίτας needed clarification, one would expect an adjective, ἀρρενικούς, rather than a noun. Such an argument ends up positing a most improbable grammatical construction for the phrase, and also prejudices a plausible meaning of it. In characterizing an alien people there is no little difference between tarring the whole of it with its toleration of male homosexuality and alluding to the obviously more limited prevalence of active male prostitution. Boswell comments on only one other occurrence of ἀρρενοκοιτ-, the noun ἀρρενοκοιτία in a homily ascribed to Macarius the Egyptian.[19] He suggests that the writer had conflated the biblical ἀρσενοκοῖται with 'the more common' ἀρρενομιξία (p. 353 n. 51).

It is presumably true that the variation between the two spellings ἀρσενο- and ἀρρενο- in compounds is no more than a transcript of the variation between ἄρσην and ἄρρην and their respective derivatives. On this subject there has been considerable discussion, but, so far as I can discover, no writer has yet suggested the difference is other than one of dialectal diversity.[20] Not once in the considerable literature on the question is it claimed that there might be some semantic significance in the variation. In summary terms, something of a shift took place from -ρσ- to -ρρ-, affecting especially Attic but not mainstream Ionian.[21] Although -ρσ- spellings predominate in the LXX, the papyri of the Ptolemaic period and the New Testament, they are less common in the Roman and Byzantine eras in which the dominant Attic influence is apparent. Nevertheless fluctuation persists between the two forms, reflecting the diverse dialectal heritage of Koine Greek. Both spellings are found in modern Greek. But if no semantic import attaches to the difference between ἄρσην and ἄρρην, *a fortiori* it can scarcely be pertinent in the case of their compounds.

It is, however, Boswell's contention that 'In no words coined and generally written with the form "ἀρσενο-" is the prefix demonstrably objective' (p. 344). In due course I will argue that this is indeed the case with ἀρσενοκοίτης itself, but first the wider evidence needs to be reviewed. Only some twelve compounds of ἄρσενο- are attested: ἀρσενοβάτης (and -βασία), -παις, -φρων, -θηλυς, -κοίτης (and -κοιτέω, -κοιτία), -μίκτης, -γενής, -θυμος, -μορφος, -πληθής, and ἀρσενάκανθον. (Compounds of ἀρρενο- number twenty). Of these only the last five occur solely with ἀρσενο-; the rest are found also with ἀρρενο- as the first half. So the range of parallels against which Boswell's claim is to be tested is not very wide, nor can one be sure how much flexibility 'generally written' allows. Within these narrow limits (and excepting ἀρσενοκοίτης for the time being) Boswell is correct, but draws from the material untenable conclusions. It is in any case surely extremely hazardous to base the alleged difference of semantic significance of the two forms on so restricted a sample.

In so far as a distinction can be drawn between those compounds of the group in which the first element is the object of the second and those in which it supplies the qualifying gender of the second, we must start at the other end, with the second element, as was hinted above with reference to the compounds of -κοίτης. In most if not all of the compounds in which the second half is a verb or has verbal force, the first half denotes its object, irrespective of whether it is ἀρρενο- or ἀρσενο- (e.g., ἀρρενομιξία, ἀρσενομίκτης, ἀρσενοβάτης, ἀρρενοβασία, etc.). When the second part is substantival, the first half denotes its gender, as in all the five solely ἀρσενο- compounds isolated above, but again irrespective of the spelling (e.g., ἀρσενόφρων and ἀρρενόφρων, ἀρρενοφάνης, ἀρρενόπαις and ἀρσενόπαις, ἀρσενόθυμος, ἀρρενωπία). Such a conclusion does not exactly take one by surprise, but it does suggest how ἀρσενοκοίτης should be interpreted.

To ascertain whether the direction in which all the evidence has so far pointed is the right one, we must now survey the occurrences of the term (and ἀρσενοκοιτέω and ἀρσενοκοιτία) in the literature of the patristic era. Since Boswell's account of the use of the term is far from complete and no lexicon provides a full listing, an attempt will be made to give an exhaustive catalogue of its occurrences.

Of little help in clarifying its meaning are its first certain uses in 1 Cor. 6:9 and 1 Tim. 1:10, although this is not to deny that historical investigation of their sources or backgrounds may provide some evidence. To this we shall return. Likewise straightforward quotations of one or other of these verses are in themselves of no value.[22] Some other isolated uses of the term throw no additional light on its meaning.[23] But there are more occurrences than Boswell allows that do disclose the meaning it bore for the writer in question.

Aristides' *Apology* was addressed to the emperor Hadrian and hence composed by A.D. 138 at the latest. Its polemic against the gods of the Greeks concentrates especially on their immoral behaviour. If human beings were to imitate them, they would become μοιχοὺς καὶ ἀρρενομανεῖς ... Πῶς οὖν ἐνδέχεται θεὸν εἶναι μοιχὸν ἢ ἀνδροβάτην ἢ πατροκτόνον;[24] A little later Aristides argues that if the laws are just, the gods are wholly unjust, having done contrary to the laws ἀλληλοκτονίας καὶ φαρμακείας καὶ μοιχείας καὶ κλοπὰς καὶ ἀρσενοκοιτίας.[25] The coupling with μοιχεία on each of these occasions (albeit separated once by κλοπάς) strongly suggests that ἀρρενομανεῖς, ἀνδροβάτην and ἀρσενοκοιτίας all carry the same basic meaning. Boswell endeavours to distinguish between them, however, in the following terms:

a) ἀρρενομανής designates *female* addiction to adultery or fornication.[26] The context gives no support to this. The preceding paragraph deals solely with the doings of Zeus, the one before that of Kronos. Immediately before the sentence containing ἀρρενομανεῖς Zeus's passion for Ganymede is mentioned. 'Hence it happened, Emperor, to mankind to imitate all these things and to become μοιχοὺς καὶ ἀρρενομανεῖς and to engage in other dreadful practices in imitation of their *god.*' The fuller Syriac text likewise refers only to male sexual malpractice and includes a mention of 'sleeping with men'.

b) ἀνδροβάτης denotes a *stuprator*, one guilty of the rape of a free citizen. There may well be a hint of homosexual assault in the Greek word, but the context in Aristides is precisely the same as for ἀρρενομανεῖς, the Syriac uses the same term for both (= 'sleeping with men'), and other uses of ἀνδροβάτης and its cognates do not appear to specify rape as the homosexual abuse in question.[27]

c) ἀρσενοκοιτία still denotes prostitution, but Boswell fails completely in his attempt to show that Zeus could meaningfully be charged with prostitution.

It seems clear that Aristides employed three different words, each with its own nuance, to incriminate male homosexuality as unworthy of gods and men. The parallelism not only suggests the meaning of ἀρσενοκοιτία but also confirms that the ἀρσενο- element is the object.

Perhaps the most revealing occurrence of ἀρσενοκοιτία is not noted by Boswell at all. It comes in Hippolytus's account of the founder of the Naassene Gnostics:[28]

> ὁ δὲ Νάας παρανομίαν ἔσχε· προσῆλθε γὰρ τῇ Εὔᾳ ἐξαπάτησας αὐτὴν καὶ ἐμοίχευσεν αὐτήν, ὅπερ ἐστὶν παράνομον· προσῆλθε δὲ καὶ τῷ 'Αδὰμ καὶ ἔσχεν αὐτὸν ὡς παῖδα, ὅπερ ἐστὶ καὶ αὐτὸ παράνομον· ἔνθεν γέγονε μοιχεία καὶ ἀρσενοκοιτία.

This could scarely be clearer, and cannot sustain Boswell's version of the word-structure and meaning of ἀρσενοκοιτία.

In reviewing citations and echoes of Lev. 18:22 and 20:13 in early Christian literature we have noted Eusebius's assertion that Moses forbade μοιχεύειν and ἀρσενοκοιτεῖν, μηδὲ τὰς παρὰ φύσιν ἡδονὰς διωκεῖν.[29] Boswell contends that the word cannot here refer to homosexual activities because it is distinguished from 'pleasures against nature', and because Eusebius is here presenting a paraphrase of Matt. 5:28 which has in mind the attitude of men towards *women*. He concludes that Eusebius understood ἀρσενοκοιτεῖν to mean male prostitution servicing women (p. 351).[30] Whether it is a sound inference from μηδὲ κ.τ.λ. that what precedes it cannot be 'contrary to nature' is very dubious,[31] nor does it make bad sense of Eusebius's sequence of thought if ἀρσενοκοιτεῖν means male homosexuality. For if one explains this word in heterosexual terms, one is still left with 'the pursuit of pleasures contrary to nature'. If this phrase denotes non-heterosexual acts between human beings, then why should not ἀρσενοκοιτεῖν denote (non-heterosexual) homosexuality? If it denotes something like (heterosexual?) bestiality, it is still hard to see how this could be appropriate in the context if male homosexuality is not. We could paraphrase Eusebius's paraphrase thus: 'Moses forbade adultery and male homosexuality, but I do not allow my disciples even to look lustfully on a woman [let alone a man]'. In any case, the evidence adduced earlier from Eusebius shows him asserting unambiguously that Moses forbade female and male homosexuality (ἀρρένων πρὸς ἄρρενας μίξεις).[32]

The Syriac writer Bardesanes who flourished at the turn of the second and third centuries records different ethnic attitudes to male homosexual intercourse.[33] Eusebius gives an extract in Greek. Beyond the Euphrates a person accused of murder or of theft will not be angered, ὁ δὲ ὡς ἀρσενοκοίτης λοιδορούμενος ἑαυτὸν ἐκδικεῖ μέχρι καὶ φόνου. The Syriac here denotes 'lying with men', using the same vocabulary as in 1 Cor. 6:9, 1 Tim. 1:10.[34] Male prostitution is definitely excluded. We thus have corroboration that ἀρσενοκοιτία for Eusebius specified male homosexuality activity, whether with youths or adults. (We will return to this aspect of the question.)

We must next note some occurrences of the term in question in which it is paralleled to παιδοφθορία, i.e., male homosexuality with teenagers which was of course the dominant form of male homosexuality among the Greeks. The term was a critical way of referring to παιδεραστία and can certainly not be restricted to child-molesting.

Theophilus of Antioch twice lists the trio of vices, μοιχεία, πορνεία and ἀρσενοκοιτία.[35] Nothing in the context casts further light on the meaning of the latter. Origen groups the three together in a free citation of 1 Cor. 6:9 as exemplifying types of flagrant sinfulness—πόρνοι, μοιχοὶ, ἀρσενοκοῖται, μαλακοὶ, εἰδωλολάτραι, φονεῖς. In an extract of another work preserved only in Latin he instances 'fornicators, adulterers and *masculorum concubitores*' as those who have committed *grandia peccata*.[36] The juxtaposition of these three, which embodies a particular selection from the categories of sinfulness catalogued in 1 Cor. 6:9-10, is paralleled in some later writings. A further occurrence of the triple formula is found in the *Church History* of Theodoret of Cyrrhus completed in A.D. 450. He cites at length a letter by Peter, bishop of Alexandria after Athanasius, which describes the desecration of one of the churches in the city by a pagan mob under the prefect Palladius in league with the Arian party. An abandoned scoundrel was set up to preach, and his message advocated ἀντ' ἐγκρατείας πορνείαν, μοιχείαν, ἀρσενοκοιτίαν, κλοπήν.[37]

A homily dubiously ascribed to Cyril of Alexandria indicts those who do not weep for their sins of πορνεία and μοιχεία, μὴ θρηνοῦντες διὰ τὸ πέταυρον τῆς ἀρρενοκοιτίας, καὶ μὴ ὀλολύζοντες διὰ τὴν μαλακίαν.[38] A letter by Nilus, bishop of Ancyra in the first quarter of the fifth century, declares that every kind of uncleanness, such as πορνεία, μοιχεία, ἀσελγεία καὶ ἀρσενοκοιτία and the like, are called 'winter' by Solomon.[39] The traditional association of the three vices is preserved in the *Sacra Parallela*, a large collection of moral and ascetic teaching attached, not all of it with full certainty, to John of Damascus. One of the divisions of the collection is entitled Περὶ πορνείας, καὶ μοιχείας, καὶ ἀρσενοκοιτίας. Lev. 20:13 is among the biblical texts assembled under this heading.[40]

Comparison is obviously invited with a similar grouping of μοιχεία, πορνεία and παιδοφθορία. The *Epistle* of Barnabas gives the threefold instruction οὐ πορνεύσεις, οὐ μοιχεύσεις, οὐ παιδοφθορήσεις.[41] The same triple command, but in a different sequence, is found in the middle of a longer list in the *Didache*, οὐ μοιχεύσεις, οὐ παιδοφθορήσεις, οὐ πορνεύσεις.[42] There is little doubt that both works are using a common pattern of originally Jewish moral instruction set in a 'two ways' framework. Clement of Alexandria ascribes to Moses the three prohibitions exactly as found in Barnabas,[43] and Origen catalogues the same three offences in the same order when he wishes to adduce gross violations of the law.[44] The *Apostolic Constitutions*, at this point almost certainly heir to the 'two ways' pattern of parainetical instruction, arranges the same three prohibitions in the *Didache's* order in its more expansive review of the law of life—οὐ μοιχεύσεις..., οὐ παιδοφθορήσεις..., οὐ πορνεύσεις.[45]

The elevation of the ban on παιδοφθορία and πορνεία to a rank alongside the Decalogue's prohibition of μοιχεία almost certainly took place in Jewish circles exposed to the immoralities of the Greek world.[46] Within the Mosaic corpus, Lev. 18:22 and 20:13 provided all the authority that was needed to justify the ban on pederasty. What seems clear is that Christian writers associated this prohibition which they took over as part of the ethical legacy of Hellenistic Judaism with the ἀρσενοκοιτία forbidden in 1 Cor. 6:9 and 1 Tim. 1:10. Not only do we find the trio of μοιχεία, πορνεία and παιδοφθορία paralleled by that of μοιχεία, πορνεία and ἀρσενοκοιτία, but in Origen both threefold listings occur. While the meaning assigned to παιδοφθορία in early Christian writings remains to be considered, the parallelism clearly excludes Boswell's interpretation of ἀρσενοκοιτία. Christian writers and teachers identified ἀρσενοκοιτία with by far the commonest form of active homosexuality current in the Hellenistic world, that is, the relationship between an adult male and a youth of teenage years.[47]

We have yet to consider the occurrence of ἀρσενοκοιτεῖν in the *Sibylline Oracles*, which may be one of the earliest appearances of the word after the Pauline writings and may indeed derive from a period roughly contemporary with them. In book 2 are found the following three lines:

71 σπέρματα μὴ κλέπτειν· ἐπαράσιμος ὅστις ἕληται
εἰς γένεας γενέων, εἰς σκορπισμὸν βίοτοιο.
μὴ ἀρσενοκοιτεῖν, μὴ συκοφαντεῖν, μήτε φονεύειν.[48]

They belong to a section of the book (2:56-148) which most scholars hold to be derived from the collection of Jewish-Hellenistic gnomic wisdom attached to the pseudonym of Phocylides (lines 5-79). Since, however, this block of material is present in only one branch of the manuscript tradition, it was presumably interpolated into book 2 after the composition of this book, which is normally placed around the middle of the second century A.D.[49] Furthermore, lines 72-73 above are among the twenty or so lines inserted into this material from Ps-Phocylides (in which *Or.Sib.* 2:71 is line 18). The latest editor of Ps-Phocylides' *Sentences* is inclined to assign their origin to Alexandria within the period 30 B.C. - 40 A.D.[50] A wide variety of scholarly hypotheses has been advanced about the poem's character and purpose. Difficulty in placing it with assurance arises largely because so much of it has parallels in both Jewish ethical teaching, especially the Pentateuch and Wisdom literature of the LXX, and Greek gnomological traditions. Van der Horst draws attention to its heavy use (in lines 9-41) of Lev. 19 as a kind of summary of the Torah, suggesting that at the beginning of the Christian era this chapter was held to be a central one in the Pentateuch. Although the line containing μὴ ἀρσενοκοιτεῖν is not part of Ps-Phocylides, this writer's disapprobation of homosexual conduct, often joined with adultery, is unmistakable:

μήτε γαμοκλοπέειν μήτ' ἄρσενα Κύπριν ὀρίνειν...
μὴ παραβῆς εὐνὰς φύσεως ἐς Κύπριν ἄθεσμον,
οὐδ' αὐτοῖς θήρεσσι συνεύαδον ἄρσενες εὐναῖ...
παιδὸς δ'εὐμόρφου φρουρεῖν νεοτήσιον ὥρην.
πολλοὶ γὰρ λυσσῶσι πρὸς ἄρσενα μεῖξιν ἔρωτος.[51]

The sentiment of the interpolated line 73 therefore accords closely with the source of the block into which it has been inserted, and the inspiration of Leviticus may suggest a more localized connection with the part of the block in which it is found, if the language of Lev. 18 and 20 LXX lies behind ἀρσενοκοιτεῖν, as has been argued above. Considerations of this kind have led some scholars to the conclusion that the Sibyllines' text of this material preserves an earlier form of Ps-Phocylides' lines 5-79. The sequence of *Or. Sib.* 2:71-73 has been specifically appealed to in support of this case.[52]

If, however, we adhere to the consensus which regards *Or. Sib.* 2:56-148 as an interpolated interpolation from Ps-Phocylides, it remains true that the insertion of lines 72-73 fits in remarkably well with the spirit and language of Ps-Phocylides no less than of the Sibylline collection—which is elsewhere repeatedly and emphatically hostile to male homosexual activity.[53] Although the restriction of book 2:56-148 to only one family of the manuscripts would naturally lead one to suppose that the additional insertions not derived from Ps-Phocylides were made at the same time as the main interpolation, and therefore later than c. 150 A.D. and by a Christian hand (for it is agreed that books 1-2 of the Sibyllines represent a Christianized revision of a Jewish original), the block may have come to the Christian interpolator with the further insertions, in particular lines 72-73, already present. We have suggested the common influence of Leviticus 19 and environs on the context of lines 72-73 and on line 73 itself. Line 72 is notably Jewish in character.

It has further been argued that lines 3-4 of Ps-Phocylides, which immediately precede the block incorporated into the Sibyllines, inspired some of the additions inserted in this block.[54] Thus γαμοκλοπέειν (line 3 cited above) is echoed in *Or. Sib.* 2:53 (οἱ δ' ἀγαπῶσι γάμον τε, γαμοκλοπίων τ' ἀπέχονται), and μήτ' ἄρσενα Κύπριν ὀρίνειν evoked μὴ ἀρσενοκοιτεῖν in 2:73. This is entirely plausible and prompts a speculative suggestion about the choice, and perhaps even the very formation, of the word ἀρσενοκοιτεῖν. A Christian editor, when transferring a block of material from Ps-Phocylides replete with Levitical associations, transposed the patently, even offensively, secular Greek reference to ἄρσενα Κύπριν (i.e., originally Aphrodite) into a compound term suggested by the proscription of Lev. 18:22, 20:13 LXX. It perhaps remains more likely that this occurrence of ἀρσενοκοιτεῖν is to be ascribed to the interpolator of the material from Ps-Phocylides, working at some date after c. 150 A.D., but the use of ἀρσενοκοιτεῖν strengthens rather than weakens the case for the existence of this section of the poem *already in its expanded form* before it found its way into one branch of the Sibyllines' manuscript tradition. That is to say, the enlargement of the section by some or all of the insertions but including at least lines 72-73 may well have been carried out by a Jewish writer like Ps-Phocylides himself. Whether this expansion belonged to the textual history of the Ps-Phocylidean collection or to the Jewish, pre-Christian history of book 2 of the Sibyllines can only be a matter of further speculation. The suggestiveness of this possibility for the purpose of the present enquiry consists in its identifying a very plausible milieu for the origination of the word ἀρσενοκοιτεῖν, viz., a Hellenistic Jewish setting under marked Levitical inspiration seeking a decently Jewish way of speaking about ἄρσενα Κύπριν.

The appearance of ἀρρενοκοίτης in a work by Rhetorius, an Egyptian astrologer of the sixth century A.D., provides no precise guidance on the meaning of the term. It occurs twice in lists of vices generated by Aphrodite in those born under the signs of the Ram and the Twins.[55] Rhetorius' use of the word merits a mention only because one of his sources, not least in respect of this chapter, was probably Teucer of Babylon in Egypt. Teucer, who wrote around the beginning of the Christian era, exerted a wide influence, but only fragments of his work are extant. They contain nothing similar to the catalogues of vices including ἀρρενοκοίτης.[56]

It remains to take account of some other occurrences of ἀρσενοκοιτ-, especially some that Boswell has noted. One of the collection of homilies that bears the name of Macarius of Egypt declares that the men of Sodom did not repent ἐπὶ τῇ τῶν ἀγγέλων κακῇ βουλῇ ἀρρενοκοιτίαν εἰς αὐτοὺς ἐργάσασθαι θελήσαντες.[57] Boswell accepts this as 'probably the earliest instance of the use of the word in a context other than prostitution... It implies [sic!] a connection between sodomy and ἀρρενοκοιτία' (p. 353 n. 51). However, he blunts the force of this concession by groundless philological speculation and by invoking the uncertain authorship and date of the collection. In reality, the author can now be placed and dated within half a century with a fair degree of assurance.[58] The use of ἀρρενοκοιτία by this writer clearly carries the implication of forcible homosexual activity, almost homosexual rape.

In one of the earliest Greek penitentials, traditionally attributed to John the Faster (Joannes Jejunator) of Constantinople (d. 595), is encountered a use of ἀρσενοκοιτία which in Boswell's view 'would seem to preclude absolutely interpreting this word as referring to homosexual intercourse'.[59] In order to determine appropriate penance the priest must enquire about the penitent's sexual activity. Amongst other things he must ask about ἀρσενοκοιτία, of which there are three kinds, of escalating gravity—passive, active, and both passive and active. At this point ἀρσενοκοιτία is not defined. Boswell suggests it denotes 'anal intercourse', but acknowledges that semantically this is an impossible construction, and leaves it untranslated (p. 364 n. 25). The reader is given no clue to the grounds on which Boswell finds it to mean 'anal intercourse'. He holds, however, that it cannot refer to homosexual activity generically, partly because of the further occurrence shortly to be discussed, and partly because elsewhere the priest is instructed to enquire about other types of homosexual activity, viz., mutual masturbation (if this is what μαλακία means here) and παιδοφθορία. The latter argument in itself is not conclusive in excluding 'homosexuality between (adult) males' as the meaning of ἀρσενοκοιτία. Much rests on a sentence that comes at the end of a paragraph on incest: τὸ μέντοι τῆς ἀρσενοκοιτίας μῦσος πολλοὶ καὶ μετὰ τῶν γυναικῶν αὐτῶν ἐκτελοῦσιν. Boswell again does not translate ἀρσενοκοιτίας, but he clearly implies that 'their wives' are the sexual partners of many in ἀρσενοκοιτία. It certainly cannot be accommodated within Boswell's standard interpretation of male prostitution; husbands can scarcely be said to serve their own wives as male prostitutes.

Improbable though it may seem at first sight, the proper meaning of ἀρσενοκοιτία should probably be maintained here. The preceding paragraph deals solely with the range of possible female partners in male incest; there is no suggestion of mode or position of incestuous intercourse. The writer's formula for incest is περιπεσεῖν εἰς with the accusative of the female relative involved. Having mentioned sister, cousin, mother-in-law and others, he comes to the peak of perversity: φθάνουσι δέ τινες καὶ μέχρι τῶν ἰδίων μητέρων. Ἄλλο πάλιν τὸ εἰς τὴν ἰδίαν σύντεκνον, καὶ ἄλλο τὸ εἰς ἣν ἐδέξατο θυγατέρα.[60] Τὸ μέντοι τῆς ἀρσενοκοιτίας κ.τ.λ. Boswell's translation fails to bring out the difference in grammatical structure between the last sentence and the rest of the paragraph, rendering both περιπεσεῖν εἰς and ἐκτελοῦσιν μετά as 'commit...with'. May there not be a distinction here between εἰς + accusative of the sex object and μετά + genitive of the companion in sexual licence? This is how the end of the paragraph may be paraphrased: 'Incredibly enough, some men even go as far as having incestuous intercourse with their own mothers, or some again inflict it on their own daughters or goddaughters. Indeed, (would you believe it that) many men even engage in homosexual activity in the company of their own wives' i.e. three to a bed, or while the wives likewise indulge each other homosexually? According to this reading of the sentence it does not speak of another relationship of incest (how could it, if husbands and their wives are the sexual partners?), but of another form of sexual deviancy of the same order of gross perversity as incest with one's mother or daughter. The advantage of this interpretation is that one does not have to unearth a special meaning for ἀρσενοκοιτία, as Boswell seeks to do without any real evidence. The sequence is clear enough in the section of the text as given in Boswell's translation: questioning first centres on heterosexual intercourse, then on ἀρσενοκοιτία, next bestiality, then masturbation (? μαλακία), and finally incest. A whole paragraph devoted to 'anal intercourse', with regard for variations of passive and active roles and of frequency, duration and period of life, carries no conviction in this context. Such a notion has something of the air of irrepressible resourcefulness exemplified by Boswell's earlier comment: 'If it could be shown that "ἀρσενο-" were the object rather than the gender of "-κοῖται" it would certainly refer to this sort of gender inversion [i.e., women taking the active role in 'lying with men'] rather than to homosexuality in general' (p. 345 n. 27). This is desperate reasoning.

Boswell contends that ἀρσενοκοιτ- would not have been absent from so much literature about homosexuality if that is what it denoted. This argument calls for a number of comments.

i) It is pointless to appeal to its absence from Herodotus, Plato and Aristotle (p. 345) since it is patent that the word did not come into use until about the first century A.D., nor from Philo unless he should have been expected to originate it.

ii) It is clear from the evidence cited by Boswell in support of his contention (pp. 345-349) that the Greeks had no lack of terms to designate homosexuality. Chrysostom used 'dozens of words and phrases', and Clement of Alexandria employed 'at least thirteen different expressions'.

iii) Some of the writers whose silence Boswell invokes should be excluded from his catalogue of supporting witnesses. For example, he asserts that the *Didache* 'quotes much of the list of sinners in 1 Corinthians 6:9; conspicuous by their absence are the words "μαλακοί" and "ἀρσενοκοῖται" ' (p. 346), whereas by the common consent of scholarship the work betrays no sign of a knowledge of Paul's letters. It may indeed, at least for the chapter in question, have been written earlier than 1 Corinthians. For a different reason Minucius Felix should be ignored. It is clear that he deliberately avoids citing Scripture.[61] The same probably holds for another African apologist cited by Boswell, Arnobius, although his knowledge of the Bible is altogether more uncertain than Minucius's. For a similar reason Ausonius's failure to cite 1 Cor. 6:9 or 1 Tim. 1:10 is scarcely pertinent. The Christian content of his writings is at best so elusive that it has long been debated whether he was a Christian or a pagan.

iv) Boswell underestimates the use of ἀρσενοκοιτ- in Christian writers. 'One would certainly expect to find such a word among other *Christian* writers in Greek, yet one looks for it in vain among all the discussions of homosexual relations' (p. 346). To some extent the argument is circular. By refusing to allow that the term denotes homosexuality, except in the sense of male prostitution with males, he has disqualified it from taking part in such discussions. But he also omits its use by Hippolytus in one of the clearest texts of all, he fails to notice or mention citations of 1 Cor. 6:9 or uses of the term by Irenaeus, Methodius, Theodoret and the *Acts of John*,[62] and he underplays its use by Eusebius and Chrysostom. The latter merits separate treatment. Most of the evidence for Eusebius has already been given,[63] but criticism must be made of Boswell's statement that 'Eusebius quotes Romans 1:26-27 almost verbatim, excoriating homosexual relations in all their manifestations, yet nowhere does he employ the word which supposedly means "homosexual" in Paul's writings' (p. 346). This turns out to refer solely to *Dem. Evang.* 4:10, a passage which at most alludes to Rom. 1:26-27, if that.[64] Indeed, a citation of any New Testament text would have been quite out of place, for Eusebius is summarising the instructions given to Israel through Moses.

v) Chrysostom is Boswell's star witness. The prosecutor deserves to be heard at length before some rejoinder is entered:

> Saint John Chrysostom probably wrote more about the subject of same-sex sexuality than any other pre-Freudian writer except Peter Damian. In dozens of works he discusses or mentions it. Greek was his native language, the patristic Greek of the later Empire, thoroughly imbued with the Koine of the New Testament. His writings abound with New Testament references, and he quotes from all the Pauline epistles with accuracy and facility. Yet among the dozens of words and phrases used by Chrysostom to name, describe, or characterize homosexual relations, neither "ἀρσενοκοῖται" nor any derivative of it occurs in any of these writings. This absence is particularly notable in several instances where the use of the word would seem almost inevitable if it were indeed related to homosexuality: in his commentary on Romans 1:26, for instance where he quotes 1 Corinthians 6:18 in a discussion of Roman homosexual behavior but does not refer to the place in the text only nine verses before where homosexuality is allegedly mentioned by name (see text in app. 2). It is even more striking that in discussing the supposedly homosexual activities of the people of Sodom, he quotes directly from the list of sins in 1 Corinthians 6:9 and 1 Timothy 1:10,[a] yet he does not mention the one word which translators would have us believe refers specifically to homosexuality.
>
> All this is convincing enough, but the final proof lies in the fact that after writing so copiously on the subject of homosexual relations in every exegetical work where the text could possibly suggest a connection—e.g., Genesis 19, Romans 1—and even some which do not—Titus, for instance—Chrysostom does not mention so much as one word about homosexuality when expounding on the very places where "ἀρσενοκοῖται" occurs; in his commentaries on 1 Corinthians 6:9 and 1 Timothy 1:10 there is not a hint about sexual activity between persons of the same sex. In fact on several occasions Chrysostom copied out the list of sins from Corinthians and actually omitted the one word which is claimed to mean homosexual;[b] considering his feelings on the subject, abundantly evidenced in many works, it is virtually inconceivable that he would have done so had he understood the term to refer to what he had elsewhere called "the worst of all sins."
>
> [a]*De perfecta caritate* 8 (PG, 56:290). It is unlikely that it could be coincidence rather than quotation for such unusual words as "πλεονέκται" and "ἅρπαγες" to occur together with "μοιχοί." Note that in his commentary on Titus he quotes the whole list of sins from 1 Cor. 6:9 verbatim in the same paragraph in which he discusses the homosexual excesses of the Sodomites: but he does not use the word "ἀρσενοκοῖται" or any form of it to name these excesses, contenting himself instead with the circumlocution "παισὶν ἐπεμαίνοντο," and establishing no connection be-

tween the ἀρσενοκοῖται and the Sodomites (*In epistolam ad Titum* 3.5 [PG, 62:693]). Cf. homily 43 on Genesis 3 (PG, 54:399-400) and 42 on Matthew 3 (PG, 57:449).
[b]E.g., homilies 16 and 37 (PG, 61:135, 317).

There are several inaccuracies in these paragraphs, which provide a revealing example of Boswell's type of exposition:

a) His statement that 'neither "ἀρσενοκοῖται" nor any derivative of it occurs in any of these writings' is corrected by his own n. 34 on the same page. Not only does Chrysostom cite 1 Cor. 6:9 in full in his fifth homily on Titus,[65] but in his homily on the passage itself he comments that many were critical that Paul placed the drunkard and the curser alongside the μοιχός, ἡταιρηκώς and ὁ ἀρσενοκοῖτος.[66]

b) According to Boswell, in *De perfecta caritate* 7-8 (PG 56, 288-290) Chrysostom discusses the homosexuality of the Sodomites, 'quotes directly from' the list of sins in 1 Cor. 6:9 and 1 Tim. 1:10 but does not use ἀρσενοκοῖται. This last point is true. After stressing that the one offence of the Sodomites was that they παισὶν ἐπεμαίνοντο, *some thirty lines later* he comes to talk further about divine punishment, in this life and the next. He mentions Pharaoh and the Egyptians and the captivity of Israel. Why are some punished here and not others? οἱ μὲν τῶν μοιχῶν τιμωροῦνται, οἱ δὲ τελευτῶσιν ἀτιμώρητοι; πόσοι τυμβωρύχοι διέφυγον; πόσοι λῃσταί; πόσοι πλεονέκται; πόσοι ἅρπαγες; Does the use of μοιχῶν, πλεονέκται and ἅρπαγες constitute direct quotation from 1 Cor. 6:9-10? (None of Chrysostom's language here is found in 1 Tim. 1:10). The whole construction of the passage is quite different from Boswell's summary.[67]

c) It is difficult to see why in his *Homil. on Titus* 5:4 (*PG* 62, 693-694) Chrysostom should quote 1 Cor. 6:9 between a reference to the punishment of the Sodomites solely because they παισὶν ἐπεμαίνοντο and a rebuke to those of his hearers οἱ τοῖς μὲν ἄρρεσιν ὡς θηλείαις μιγνύμενοι if the connexion did not hinge on ἀρσενοκοῖται. He may not say in so many words 'the Sodomites were ἀρσενοκοῖται' but the implication is clear enough and alone makes sense of the citation.

d) 'On several occasions', asserts Boswell, Chrysostom copied out the list of sins from 1 Cor. 6:9-10 but omitted ἀρσενοκοῖται. Only two examples are given in the footnote, one of which is the homily on 1 Cor. 6, on which, as we have seen, Boswell is mistaken. The other occasion offers a partial citation ('Do not be mistaken: neither πόρνοι nor μαλακοί will inherit the kingdom of God') in the context of a discussion about Paul's authority as a teacher. I have come across no other instance that bears out Boswell's contention.

Yet there is no doubt that Chrysostom rarely used ἀρσενοκοιτ-. But is one justified in supposing that his use of it in commenting on Rom. 1:26 'would seem almost inevitable' if it denoted homosexuality?[68] The homily itself gives an uncompromising, unambiguous and extended indictment of the vice. Is it surprising that in his homily on 1 Tim. 1 he makes no allusion to homosexual activity? He does not explain or discuss any of the sins listed in 1 Tim. 1:10, but would it not be foolish to detect in this exercise of homiletic liberty anything whatsoever about Chrysostom's attitude to *any* of its catalogue of sins?[69]

What is the force of this argument from linguistic silence of which Boswell makes so much (and which he has considerably exaggerated)?[70] Romans 1:26-27 provided a much more explicit biblical condemnation, and παιδοφθορία a term which more closely specified the prevalent form of male homosexual activity in the Greco-Roman world.[71] Failure to use a particular word may indicate any number of things, e.g., greater familiarity with other words or phrases, and reluctance to use a word which, in this instance, clearly never became part of everyday speech and retained a certain technical character. Of itself non-use reveals nothing about a word's *meaning*; only use clarifies meaning. And Boswell has signally failed to demonstrate any use of ἀρσενοκοίτης etc. in which it patently does not denote male homosexual activity. The only possibility is the occurrence in John the Faster, where even Boswell has to resort to a wholly unprecedented meaning. This appearance of the term can therefore scarcely be regarded as determinative for its other occurrences, which are sufficiently revealing to put its meaning beyond doubt.

Professor Boswell devotes only very limited attention to the evidence of the early versions for the meaning of ἀρσενοκοῖται.[72] The three most significant versions are the Latin, Syriac and Coptic. For the pre-Vulgate Latin translations of the term a critical presentation of the evidence is available only for 1 Tim. 1:10.[73] The main preference is for *masculorum concubitores*, with *concubitores* alone and *stupratores* (or *puerorum stupratores*) also indicated. Citations of 1 Cor. 6:9 show a similar preference in the early Latin version of Irenaeus' *Adversus Haereses*, in Tertullian, Gregory of Elvira, Ambrosiaster and Pelagius, but Cyprian's two quotations have *masculorum appetitores* (*adpetitores*).[74] The latter clearly reflects an understanding of ἀρσενοκοῖται in which ἀρσενο- is the object of the second half of the word, and the same is implied by *masculorum concubitores*. The latter word seems to be a coinage of early Christian Latin, and the phrase was scarcely used at all in the early centuries outside of a biblical sphere of reference. In its usage there is nothing to support Boswell's assertion that 'to a Latin speaker the phrase would clearly imply acts of prostitution rather than sexual inclination' (p. 348).

For the Old Syriac version of the New Testament other than the Gospels only quotations provide evidence. The Peshitta text of 1 Cor. 6:9, 1 Tim. 1:10 breaks ἀρσενοκοῖται into three words, literally 'those who lie with men'. This appears to be a direct translation of the Greek word. Confirmation that Syriac speakers read the word in this way is provided by the evidence advanced earlier from Bardesanes and Eusebius's Greek version of part of his text, and from the Syriac translation of Aristides' *Apology* which may be dated c. 350 A.D. and therefore antedates the Peshitta.[75]

Like the Syriac, the Coptic versions in both the Sahidic and Bohairic dialects render the Greek word by two Coptic words 'lying (or sleeping) with-males'.[76] There is no ambiguity about the interpretation of ἀρσενοκοῖται in the Coptic Churches of the third and fourth centuries. The result is that none of the three primary versions of the New Testament affords any support for Boswell's thesis.[77]

This enquiry has concentrated on the use of ἀρσενοκοίτης etc., and on its supposed linguistic form. An alternative approach to its meaning in the New Testament would examine the background to the lists of vices in which it appears in 1 Cor. 6:9 and 1 Tim. 1:10. There is no lack of literature on this subject and no point in retracing well-trodden paths.[78] Most previous studies conclude that the kinds of lists encountered in our two verses developed in late Judaism exposed to strong Hellenistic influences, but they have failed to produce a comparable list in which ἀρσενοκοίτης or its equivalent appeared prior to 1 Corinthians.[79] Nevertheless, that Hellenistic Jewish writings unambiguously condemned the homosexuality encountered among the Greek world is not in doubt.[80] At the same time the moral philosophers of the Hellenistic era were increasingly coming to question homosexual indulgence. The presumption is thus created that ἀρσενοκοιτία came into use, under the influence of the LXX of Leviticus, to denote that homoerotic vice which Jewish writers like Philo, Josephus, Paul and Ps-Phocylides regarded as a signal token of pagan Greek depravity. It is not apparent that investigation of the sources of the New Testament's Lasterkataloge serves to establish further than this the meaning of the term. But it is probably significant that the word itself and comparable phrases used by Philo, Josephus and Ps-Phocylides[11] spoke generically of male activity with males rather than specifically categorized male sexual engagement with παῖδες. It is difficult to believe that ἀρσενοκοιτία was intended to indict only the commonest Greek relationship involving an adult and a teenager. The interchangeability demonstrated above between ἀρσενοκοιτία and παιδοφθορία argues that the latter was encompassed within the former. A broader study of early Christian attitudes to homosexuality would confirm this.

## Notes

[1] This is the subtitle of John Boswell's *Christianity, Social Tolerance, and Homosexuality* (Chicago and London 1980). The fruits of the research that lie beyond the book had some influence on the literature on the subject before it was published. A mention in V.P. Furnish's *The Moral Teaching of Paul* (Nashville 1979) 83, indicates that it was earlier scheduled for publication by Professor Boswell's own university's press at New Haven under the title *Ganymede in Exile: Medieval Christianity, Homosexuality and Intolerance*. Boswell's reinterpretations were extensively adopted by J. J. McNeill, *The Church and the Homosexual* (London 1977). See n. 59 below. Furnish's rendering of the two words is worth quoting (p. 70)—'men who assume the female role in sex, men who have sex with them'.

[2] Appendix 1, pp. 335-353 (pp. 341-353 on ἀρσενοκοῖται). The previous year Fred Craddock in 'How Does the New Testament Deal with the Issue of Homosexuality?', *Encounter* 40 (1979) 197-208, had dared to write that the philological approach to the texts 'has by this time yielded all its fruits' (p. 198)!

[3] This scarcely needs documentation, but cf. *TDNT* 6, 579-595; *NIDNTT* 1, 497-501. Elsewhere Boswell recognizes 'some ambiguity about the Greek word "πορνεία" ' (p. 103; cf. p. 341), and that in Koine Greek it often meant simply 'fornication' (p. 344). For the shift in the meaning of πόρνος and πορνεύειν in New Testament and Christian usage, cf. H. D. Jocelyn, 'A Greek Indecency and Its Students: ΛΑΙΚΑΖΕΙΝ', *Proc. of Camb. Philol. Soc.* 206 (1980) 12-66 at p. 29, cf. p. 25.

[4] Despite the fact that E. A. Sophocles' *Greek Lexicon of the Roman and Byzantine Periods (from B.C. 146 to A.D. 1100)* (Memorial edition, New York 1887), p. 253, s.v. ἀρσενοκοίτης made the connection with Lev. 18:22 LXX.

[5] *Dem. Evang.* 4:10:6 (PG 22, 276; GCS 23, 165). Boswell's reference (*Praep. Evang.* 4:16, PG 21, 276) is inaccurate in three particulars (p. 102 n. 37). Such faults are regrettably frequent in his work.

[6] *Dem. Evang.* 1:6:67 (PG 22, 65; GCS 23, 33). Cf. too *Dem. Evang.* 1:6:33 (PG 22, 56; GCS 23, 27-28): ἔπειτα οὐ φονεύειν, οὐ μοιχεύειν, οὐ κλέπτειν, οὐχ ἐπιορκεῖν, οὐχ ἄρρενας ἄρρεσιν ἐπιμαίνεσθαι... οὐδ' ὅσα τοιαῦτα τοῖς τότε πράττειν ἐξῆν, ἀφόβως συνεχώρει.

[7] *Praep. Evang.* 13:20:7 (GCS 43:2, 251-252).

[8] *Ap. Const.* 6:28 (PG 1, 984; ed. F. X. Funk, *Didascalia et Constitutiones Apostolorum*, vol. 1 (Paderborn 1905) 375-377. Boswell's reference (p. 103 n. 42) is incomplete.

*p. Const.* 7:2 (PG 1, 1000; ed. Funk, p. 390) indirectly confirms the continuing .ity of the Levitical ban. The commands that spell out 'the way of life' include '"You ı not corrupt boys (παιδοφθορήσεις)", for this wickedness is contrary to nature, and ɛ from Sodom.'

*Adv. Marc.* 1:29:4 (CCL 1, 473).

*Homil. in Levit.* 11 (SC 287, 142ff.). Origen did not deal with Lev. 18 at all.

*Comment. in Rom.* 4:4 (PG 14, 973). No critical edition of this work exists. According .he eighteenth-century edition of C. Delarue reproduced in Migne, the text is not certain *c. cit.*, n. 78), but *Biblia Patristica*, vol. 3: *Origène* (Paris 1980), p. 82, takes it as a ference to Lev. 18:22.

Jeremy du Q. Adams in *Speculum* 56 (1981) 351.

P. Kretschmer and E. Locker, *Rückläufiges Wörterbuch der griechischen Sprache*, ith suppl. by G. Kisser (Göttingen 1963) 272; C. D. Buck and W. Petersen, *A Reverse ndex of Greek Nouns and Adjectives* (Chicago 1944) 556. These comments on the com- ounds of -κοίτης etc., ignore chronological and geographical variations of usage. They nerely seek to find out whether *prima facie* evidence can be found to support Boswell's :ontention. Boswell's comment (p. 344 and n. 24) about παρακοίτης does not alter this conclusion. The occurrences he records do not clearly support his contention. Cf. Peter Zaas, '1 Corinthians 6:9ff; Was Homosexuality Condoned in the Corinthian Church?', *Society of Biblical Literature 1979 Seminar Papers*, vol. 2, ed. P. J. Achtemeier (*SBL Seminar Papers Series*, 17; Missoula 1979) 205-212, at p. 208: 'Of the two [*malakos* and *a.*], *arsenokoitēs* is the easiest to define, at least by its etymology, "one who lies with a man."' But Zaas is wrong when he goes on to claim that most examples of the word are found in the moral literature of Hellenistic Judaism and from the syncretistic astrological literature (p. 209), and in his attempt to associate it with idolatry.

15 Kretschmer and Locker, pp. 40 (-κοιτία), 495, 711 (-κοῖτος), 591, 715 (-κοιτέω); Buck and Petersen, pp. 163 (-κοιτία), 491 (-κοῖτος). Together they list 26 compounds of -κοῖτος, 12 of -κοιτία, and 18 (Kretschmer and Locker alone) of -κοιτέω.

16 Boswell suggests (p. 343 n. 20) that ἀδελφοκοιτία yields the same meaning whether ἀδελφο- is the object or the subject of -κοιτία. It is attested solely in Theophilus of Antioch, *Ad Autolycum* 1:9, 3:6 (PG 6, 1037 (not 1023, as Boswell), 1129; SC 20, 76, 214). On the first occasion it is charged against Jupiter together with μοιχεία and παιδοφθορία. On the second Epicurus and the Stoics are accused of inculcating it and ἀρρενοβασία. Since a few lines previously Epicurus is credited with counselling men καὶ μητράσι καὶ ἀδελφαῖς συμμίγνυσθαι, the objective force of ἀδελφο- in ἀδελφοκοιτία is clearly implied. This would agree with the semantics of most other compounds with ἀδελφο-. At one point Boswell claims (p. 343 n. 19) that, had Paul used ἀνδροκοῖται instead of ἀρσενοκοῖται, it would not have been ambiguous. This seems to rest on the assumption that whereas ἀνδρο- is clearly a noun stem, ἀρσενο- may be either a noun or an adjective. This is not the case. If composites of ἀρσενο- are of uncertain meaning, the uncertainty is not rooted here. The ἀρσενο-prefix is a noun stem. In any case, there are compounds of ἀνδρο-, such as ἀνδρόβουλος and ἀνδρόφρων, in which it is not the object of the second part but qualifies it like an adjective.

17 Compounds of ἀρσενο- and ἀρρενο- are rarely discussed in the specialist literature. P. Chantraine, *Dictionnaire Etymologique de la Langue Grecque. Histoire des Mots*, vol. 1 (Paris 1968) 116, translates ἀρσενοκοίτης as 'pédéraste', and merely comments that most of the ἀρσενο- composites are of a technical character and often late.

18 *Anthologia Palatina* 9:686 line 5; *Anthologie Grecque*, pt. 1: *Anthologie Palatine*,

vol. 8 (*Livre IX, Epigr. 359-827*), edd. P. Waltz and G. Soury (Paris 1974) 138, which gives the translation 'tu n'as pas à craindre les mâles qui partagent la couche d'autres mâles'. The translation by W. R. Paton in the *Loeb Classical Library* edition, vol. 3 (1917) 380-381, is blunter: 'fear the barbarian or sodomites'. Boswell (p. 342 n. 17) gives the date wrongly as the sixth century.

[19] *Homil.* 4:22 (PG 34, 489; ed. H. Dörries et al., *Die 50 geistlichen Homilien des Makarios*, Patristische Texte und Studien, 4 (Berlin 1964) 42. Since the sin of the Sodomites is here described as attempted ἀρρενοχοιτία, Boswell's interpretation of the word cannot stand on this occasion.
In addition to these two occurrences, the ἀρρενοχοιτ- form also appears in a homily ascribed to Cyril of Alexandria (n. 38 below) and in the astrologer Rhetorius (n. 55 below). A total of four occurrences is not insignificant for a word of such limited currency overall.

[20] The fullest discussion is by Jacob Wackernagel, 'Hellenistica', in *Programm zur akademischen Preisverteilung* (Göttingen 1907) 3-27, reprinted in *Kleine Schriften*, vol. 2 (Göttingen 1953) 1034-1058, at 1043-1056. See also A. Thumb, *Die Griechische Sprache im Zeitalter des Hellenismus. Beiträge zur Geschichte und Beurteilung der KOINH* (1901; r.p., New York 1974) 77-78; Eduard Schwyzer, *Griechische Grammatik*, vol. 1, Handbuch der Altertumswissenschaft II:1:1 (Munich 1939) 284-286; M. Lejeune, *Traité de Phonétique Grecque* (²Paris 1955) 106-109; S. B. Psaltes, *Grammatik der Byzantinischen Chroniken*. Forschungen zur Griechischen und Lateinischen Grammatik, 2 (Göttingen 1913) 90-91; C. D. Buck, *The Greek Dialects* (Chicago 1955) 59; F. Blass, A. Debrunner, R. W. Funk, *A Greek Grammar of the New Testament and Other Early Christian Literature* (Cambridge and Chicago 1961) 19; F. T. Gignac, *A Grammar of the Greek Papyri of the Roman and Byzantine Periods*. Testi e Documenti per lo Studio dell' Antichità, LV, vol. 1 (Milan, n.d.) 142-144, vol.2 (1981) 140-141. Gignac lists further literature.

[21] Boswell, p. 343, speaks misleadingly of 'the general orthographic shift from Attic "ἄρρην" to Hellenistic "ἄρσην" (Old Attic)', having misunderstood a brief statement in R. Browning, *Medieval and Modern Greek* (London 1969) 31.

[22] Polycarp, *Philipp.* 5:3 quotes 1 Cor. 6:9, likewise Clement of Alexandria, *Paidag.* 3:81 (SC 158, 156). On another occasion Clement quotes 1 Cor. 6:9ff.at *Strom.* 3:18:109 (GCS 52, 246) with the introduction ἐπὶ δὲ τῆς παρὰ τὸν κανόνα ἡδονῆς μὴ πλανᾶσθε φησίν... Irenaeus quotes 1 Cor. 6:9 in *Adv. Haer.* 4:27:4 (SC 100², 748ff.) and 5:11:1 (SC 153, 136f.), but his original Greek is not extant (Latin *masculorum concubitores*). Methodius, *De Resurr.* 1:60, 2:4 (GCS 27, 324, 336) twice quotes 1 Cor. 6:9, but without further clarifying the meaning of our term. Origen quotes the text in whole or part on a number of occasions: *Comm. on Matt.* 13:28 (Latin only—*masculorum concubitoribus*), 14:10 (GCS 40, 256, 299); *Fragm. e Catenis in I Cor.* fr. 27 (ed. C. Jenkins, *JTS* 9, 1908, 369); *Ep. ad amicos Alexandriae, apud* Jerome *Apol. con. Rufinum* 2:18 (PL 23, 462—Latin only—*masculorum concubitores*); *Homil. on Jerem.* 20:3 (SC 238, 262ff.); *Dialog. with Heracl.* 10 (SC 67, 76); *Homil. on Levit.* 4:4 (SC 286, 172—Latin only—*masculorum concubitores*). 1 Tim. 1:9-10 is quoted in *Comm. on Rom.* 4:4 (PG 14, 973—Latin only—*masculorum concubitoribus*).

[23] The *Acts of John* 36 includes ὁ ἀρσενοκοίτης among those whom punishment awaits (*Acta Apostolorum Apocrypha*, edd. R. A. Lipsius, M. Bonnet, vol. 2:1 (1898; r.p.

Hildesheim, New York 1972) 169). *Biblia Patristica*, vol. 3 p. 24, indicates that the occurrence of ἀρσενοκοιτεῖν printed among Origen's *Fragmenta e Catenis in Proverbia* on Prov. 7:12 in PG 17, 181, does not belong to those sections of the catena to be ascribed, not without some uncertainty, to Origen. Boswell, p. 350 n. 43, inclines to find in the passage 'an equation of "ἀρσενοκοῖται" with "γυναῖκες ἄτιμοι", i.e., female prostitutes'. At most it implies that they share condemnation with τῆς ἀτίμου γυναικός. The operative sentence reads: Οἱ μὲν ἐν ταῖς πλατείαις ῥεμβόμενοι μοιχείας καὶ πορνείας καὶ κλοπῆς λαμβάνουσι λογίσμους· οἱ δὲ ἔξω τούτων ῥεμβόμενοι, τὰς παρὰ φύσιν ἡδονὰς μετέρχονται, ἀρσενοκοιτεῖν ἐπιζητοῦντες, καὶ ἄλλων τινῶν ἀπαγορευομένων πραγμάτων φαντασίας λαμβανόντων.

[24] *Apol.* 9:8-9, ed. J. R. Harris and J. Armitage Robinson, Texts and Studies I:1 (Cambridge 1891) 105. The sentence containing ἀρρενομανεῖς is relegated to the appar. crit. by E. J. Goodspeed, *Die ältesten Apologeten* (Göttingen 1914) 12, and J. Geffcken, *Zwei griechische Apologeten* (Leipzig and Berlin 1907) 13-14. However the Syriac text (ed. Harris and Robinson, p. (13)) includes two references to 'sleeping with men' (ET *ibid.*, p. 42). The Syriac word is the noun form of the verb used in the Peshitta text of Lev. 18:22, 20:13. For this and other help with Syriac I am greatly indebted to Dr. A. P. Hayman.

[25] *Apol.* 13:7 (again Boswell's reference is wrong, p. 350), ed. Goodspeed, p. 18; ed. Harris and Robinson, p. 109; ed. Geffcken, p. 21. Boswell argues that ἀρσενοκοιτία cannot mean homosexual behaviour because in the Roman Empire of the second century no laws in any city debarred them. But as Geffcken, p. 80, shows, Aristides' argument was already a commonplace in pagan, Jewish and Christian writers.

[26] P. 351 n. 45. Boswell claims here that ἀρρενομανία in classical Greek applies mainly to males but in patristic Greek almost exclusively to females. Again evidence is hard to come by. The lexicons of Sophocles and Lampe list only one occurrence, in a late work (seventh century at the earliest) falsely ascribed to Caesarius the brother of Gregory of Nazianzus (*Dialog.* 139, PG 38, 1044—ἀρρενομανουσῶν γυναικῶν). Liddell-Scott-Jones give only one secular usage, in an epitome of the fourth-century astrological work of Hephaestion of Thebes, in which ἀρρενομανής is the equivalent of ἄνδρασι συνερχόμενος, *Apotelesmatica* 1:1:18 (ed. D. Pingree, vol. 1, *Bibliotheca Teubneriana*, Leipzig, 1973, p. 16) and *Epit.* IV, 1.107 (ed. Pingree, vol. 2, 1974, p. 147). Boswell also implies in the same note that the LXX usage of the term applies it to females, whereas it does not occur in the LXX. (No compound of ἀρρενο- occurs in the LXX, solely the derivative ἀρρενωδῶς, 2 Macc. 10:35; see E. Hatch, H. A. Redpath, *A Concordance to the Septuagint*, vol. 1, Oxford, 1897, p. 160). Boswell later acknowledges that in Chrysostom ἡ κατὰ τῶν ἀρρένων μανία stands for male homosexual passion (p. 360 n. 18). Cognates of μανία are used to similar purpose in Clement of Alexandria, Eusebius and Chrysostom.

[27] See Liddell-Scott-Jones, *s.vv.*; Lampe, *s.vv.* Boswell quotes (with another incorrect reference) Justin, *2 Apol.* 12:5, Διὸς δὲ καὶ ἄλλων θεῶν μιμηταὶ γενόμενοι ἐν τῷ ἀνδροβατεῖν, but nothing in Justin secures his interpretation of 'rape of males by males'. For a similar critique cf. Tatian, *Adv. Graecos* 10—a god who makes Ganymede his cupbearer and τὴν παιδεραστίαν σεμνύνεται.

[28] *Refut. Omn. Haer.* 5:26:22-23 (GCS 26, 130).

[29] See n. 6 above.

[30] Boswell is left with the task of showing where Moses forbade male prostitution serving women. He suggests (in another incomplete reference, p. 351 n. 46) that Eusebius's ἀρσενοκοιτεῖν may be an allusion to Deut. 23:18 LXX, but the word there is πορνεύων, not ἀρσενοκοιτεῖν.

[31] Cf. as a close parallel in *Praep. Evang.* 1:4:6 (GCS 43:1, 16), μηδ' ἄρρενας ἄρρεσιν ἐπιμαίνεσθαι καὶ τὰς παρὰ φύσιν ἡδονὰς μετιέναι.

[32] See n. 5 above.

[33] *The Book of the Laws of Countries* (*Dialogue on Fate*), ed. and tr. H. J. W. Drijvers (*Semitic Texts with Translations*, III; Assen, 1965), pp. 47, 49, 53, 61 ('Our [Christian] brothers who live in Gaul do not marry with men'—unlike their fellow-Gauls, cf. p. 53).

[34] *Praep. Evang.* 6:10:25 (GCS 43:1, 339); parallel Syriac text, ed. Drijvers, p. 46. Male prostitution is obviously excluded. Elswhere Bardesanes uses two other expressions, literally 'marry the men as wives' (Drijvers, pp. 48-49), and 'take males' as partners in marriage (*ibid.*, pp. 52-53, 60-61).

[35] *Ad Autolyc.* 1:2 (SC 20, 60)—Show me yourself, εἰ οὐκ εἶ μοιχός, εἰ οὐκ εἶ πόρνος, εἰ οὐκ εἶ ἀρσενοκοίτης; 1:14 (SC 20, 91)—for those who are full of μοιχείαις καὶ πορνείαις καὶ ἀρσενοκοιτίαις there awaits wrath.

[36] *Comm. on Matt.* 14:10 (GCS 40, 299. The first four here appear in a slightly different sequence in *Fragm. e Catenis in I Cor.* fr. 27, ed. C. Jenkins, *JTS* 9, 1908, p. 369—πόρνος, μοιχός, μαλακός, ἀρσενοκοῖται.) *Ep. ad amicos Alexandriae*, cited n. 22 above. Cf. *Homil. on Jerem.* 20:3 (SC 238, 262 ff.).

[37] Theodoret, *Hist. Eccl.* 4:22:9 (GCS 44(19), 252).

[38] *Homil. Div.* 14 (PG 77, 1087-1088—yet another wrong reference in Boswell, p. 353 n. 51). The homily may be by Cyril's uncle and predecessor as bishop, Theophilus, who died in A.D. 412.

[39] *Ep.* II. 282 (PG 79, 341).

[40] *Sacra Parall.* litt. Π, tit. xi (PG 88, 248).

[41] *Ep. Barn.* 19:4 (SC 172, 198).

[42] *Did.* 2:2 (SC 248, 148).

[43] *Paidag.* 2:10:89 (SC 108, 174). Cf. *Protr.* 10:108:5 (SC 2, 176): 'And what are the laws? "You shall not kill, οὐ μοιχεύσεις, οὐ παιδοφθορήσεις, you shall not steal....".'

[44] *Fragm. e Catenis in Exodum*, on Exod. 12:15 (PG 12, 284): ὁ τῶν ὅλων Θεὸς ὁ χρηματίζων τοὺς νόμους, ὡς ὀλοθρεύει μοιχὸν, ὡς ὀλοθρεύει πόρνον, ὡς ὀλοθρεύει παιδοφθόρον ...

[45] *Ap. Const.* 7:2:10 (ed. Funk, p. 390). See also the discussion above of 6:28:1-2 (Funk, pp. 375-377), where 'the sin of the Sodomites' (here called παιδοφθορία) against nature is contrasted with μοιχεία and πορνεία which are against law. Cf. the Sahidic *Statutes of the Apostles 6* (tr. G. Horner, *The Statutes of the Apostles*, London, 1904, p. 297), which records the three prohibitions in the same sequence.

[46] Cf. J. P. Audet, *La Didachè. Instructions des Apôtres* (Paris 1958) 286-287. The first occurrence of παιδοφθόρος may be that in the *Testament of Levi* 17:11 (*The Testament of the Twelve Patriarchs*: *A Critical Edition of the Greek Text.* Pseudepigr. Vet. Test. Graece, I:2 (Leiden, 1978), ed. M. de Jonge, p. 45), where it occurs in a list of vices between ἀνόμοι, ἀσελγεῖς and κτηνοφθόροι (= bestiality). However in both date and provenance this may not be far distant from the *Didache* (cf. J. Daniélou, *The Theology of Jewish Christianity*, London, 1964, 12-16). The word is not used by Philo or Josephus.

[47] Cf. K. J. Dover, *Greek Homosexuality* (London 1978) esp. pp. 16, 85-87; L. P. Wilkinson, *Classical Attitudes to Modern Issues* (London 1978) 116-117, 121. Relationships were generally entered into between young men and teenagers of 12-18 years. Reciprocal desire of partners of the same age group was almost unknown in Greek homosexuality. The relationship was essentially that of the ruler and the ruled, which helps to explain why παῖς was used of the younger partner even when reaching adult height.

[48] *Or. Sib.* 2:71-73 (GCS 8, 30, ed. Geffcken). Boswell's reference is wrong, p. 350 n. 42.

[49] A. Kurfess in E. Hennecke, W. Schneemelcher, R. McL. Wilson, *New Testament Apocrypha*, vol. 2 (London 1965) 707-708; J. H. Charlesworth, *The Pseudepigrapha and Modern Research* SBL Septuagint and Cognate Studies, 7 (Missoula 1976) 185.

[50] P. W. Van der Horst, *The Sentences of Pseudo-Phocylides*. Studia in Veteris Testamenti Pseudepigrapha, 4 (Leiden 1978) 81-82. P. Derron, who is producing a new edition for the *Collection des Universitaires de France* has recorded his opinion that its provenance is a Jewish-Greek environment in Egypt probably in the first century A.D., 'Inventaire des manuscrits du Pseudo-Phocylide', *Rev. d'hist. des textes* 10 (1980) 237-247 at p. 237.

[51] Lines 3, 190-191, 213-214 (ed. Van der Horst, pp. 110-111,237-239, 250-251, with ample documentation).

[52] E.g., A. Kurfess, 'Das Mahngedicht des sogenannten Phokylides im zweiten Buch der Oracula Sibyllina', *ZNW* 38 (1939), pp. 171-181, at pp. 172-174: 'Das Verständnis von Or. Sib. II 71 ( = Phok. 18) ist also durch V. 73 μὴ ἀρσενοκοιτεῖν vermittelt, während der Vers bei Ps.-Phokylides eigentlich in der Luft hängt und kaum verständlich ist.' But Kurfess bases his case at this point too heavily on a strained reading of σπέρματα μὴ κλέπτειν. This phrase has given rise to varied interpretations and emendations; cf. Van der Horst, pp. 124-125.

[53] *Or. Sibyl.* 3:185-187 (ἄρσην δ' ἄρσενι πλησιάσει στήσουσί τε παῖδας / αἰσχροῖς ἐν τεγέεσσι), 3:596-597 (κοὐδὲ πρὸς ἀρσενικοὺς παῖδας μίγνυνται ἀνάγνως / ὅσσα τε Φοίνικες), 3:764 (μοιχείας πεφύλαξο καὶ ἄρσενος ἄκριτον εὐνήν), 5:166-167 (μοιχεῖαι παρά σοι καὶ παίδων μίξις ἄθεσμος / θηλυγενὴς ἄδικός τε), 5:387f. (GCS 8, 57-58, 79, 87, 112, 123).

[54] A. Dieterich, *Nekyia: Beiträge zur Erklärung der neuentdeckten Petrusapokalypse* (Leipzig, 1893), pp. 182-183.

[55] *Catalogus Codicum Astrologorum Graecorum*, vol. 8, pt. 4. *Codicum Parisinorum*, 4 (Brussels 1922) 196.

[56] *Ibid.*, 115-116. The fragments are given in F. Boll, *Sphaera. Neue Griechische Texte und Untersuchungen zur Geschichte der Sternbilder* (Leipzig 1903) 5ff., 16ff., 31ff. On Rhetorius and his sources see also W. Gundel, *Dekane und Dekansternbilder. Ein Beitrag zur Geschichte der Sternbilder der Kulturvölker*, Studien der Bibliothek Warburg, 19 (Glückstadt and Hamburg 1936) 411-412, 416-417. *Der Kleine Pauly* vol. 5 (Munich 1975), col. 636, places Teucer probably in the first century B.C., but Gundel in Pauly-Wissowa, vol. 5.A, cols. 1132-1134, puts him in the first Christian century.

[57] See n. 19 above.

[58] See W. Jaeger, *Two Rediscovered Works of Ancient Christian Literature: Gregory of Nyssa and Macarius* (Leiden 1954) 208-230. Jaeger established Macarius's indebtedness to Gregory of Nyssa, which further questions the earlier thesis of Macarius's affinities with Messalianism. The homilies are ascribed to one Symeon in part of the tradition. Jaeger concludes that the unknown writer flourished around the mid-fifth century in the Near East, probably in the Syrian region. The edition by Hermann Dörries *et al.*, *op. cit.*, pp. ix-x, has nothing to add on this question. It continues to ascribe the collection to the Messalian Symeon, and takes no account of Jaeger. Heinz Berthold's edition of other works of Macarius (*Makarios/Symeon Reden und Briefe*, vol. 1:1; GCS, 1973, ixff.) places the author in Syrian monastic circles towards the end of the fourth or the beginning of the fifth century, and maintains the Messalian connexion.

59 P. 364 n. 26. Cf. p. 353 n. 51, and pp. 363-365, where Boswell gives an English translation of the section from PG 88, 1893, 1896. McNeill, *op. cit.* (n. 1 above), p. 53, follows Boswell here and describes this use as of the utmost importance for understanding ἀρσενοκοιτία. The sixth-century Byzantine writer, Joannes Malalas, in his *Chronographia* 18:167-168 (PG 97, 644) uses ἀρσενοκοιτεῖν of homosexual relations interchangeably with παιδεραστία and ἀνδροκοίτης, as Boswell recognizes (p. 172 n. 10). Later, however, Boswell assimilates ἀρσενοκοιτεῖν here to παιδεραστία as 'illicit relations with boys' (p. 353 n. 51). Nothing explicit in Malalas indicates that this was the precise nature of the offence.

60 Apparently 'goddaughter'.

61 'Minucius does not even cite the evidence of the Scriptures except once or twice in a very obscure manner... Where he might easily have gone nearer to the words of the Bible, he is content to allude rather obscurely', H. J. Baylis, *Minucius Felix and His Place among the Early Fathers of the Latin Church* (London 1928) 145, 153. It is nowhere near the mark to say (Boswell, p. 349) of either Ausonius or Cyprian or Minucius Felix that they 'discuss homosexual relations in considerable detail and with large vocabularies'.

62 See nn. 22, 23, 37 above.

63 See above nn. 6, 34. The latter occurrence is not mentioned by Boswell.

64 πάντα ἀπαγορεύσας ἀθέμιτον γάμον καὶ πᾶσαν ἀσχήμονα πρᾶξιν, γυναικῶν τε πρὸς γυναῖκας, καὶ ἀρρένων πρὸς ἄρρενας μίξεις... The last phrase is a common way of describing homosexuality, being found in Plutarch, Josephus and other writers.

65 *Homil. on Tit.* 5:4 (PG 62, 693-4).

66 *Homil. on I Cor.* 16:4 (PG 61, 134-135). Boswell discusses this passage later, on p. 351.

67 If Boswell were right, one would then need to ask why, in connection with discussion of the Sodomites' homosexuality, Chrysostom should think of 1 Cor. 6:9 if ἀρσενοκοῖται did not provide the link. Boswell's reference (p. 348 n. 34) to *Homil. on Matth.* 42(41):3 (PG 57, 449) seems mistaken. The passage contains nothing of relevance.

68 Boswell gives a translation (pp. 359-362) of much of Chrysostom's homily.

69 *Homil. on I Tim.* 2:2 (PG 62, 511-512).

70 Although strictly irrelevant to this investigation of the meaning and use of ἀρσενοκοιτ-, it is worth noting, if only to put the record straight, the inadequacy of Boswell's implication (pp. 348-349) that no Latin father cites 1 Cor. 6:9 in connexion with homosexuality. Gregory of Elvira (*Tractatus Origenis* 10:23, 34; CCL 69, 81, 83) and Salvian (*De gubern. Dei* 7:18:82; CSEL 8, 182) both do so. Tertullian (*De pudic.* 16:4; CCL 2, 1312—*masculorum concubitores*) and Cyprian (*Testim.* 3:65; CCL 3, 155; *De Domin. Orat.* 12; CCL 3A, 96-97—*masculorum adpetitores/appetitores*) both cite 1 Cor. 6:9 but in contexts that do not further clarify its meaning. According to Boswell (p. 349) Lactantius (*Div. Inst.* 5:9; CSEL 19, 425) 'quotes at length from the list of sins' in 1 Cor. 6:9 without using any word for homosexual. In fact, of his enumeration of seven types of sinners, only two (*adulteri* and *fraudulenti*) appear in the African Latin New Testament text reconstructed by H. von Soden, *Das Lateinische Neue Testament in Afrika zur Zeit Cyprians.* Texte und Untersuchungen, 33 (Leipzig 1909), 594.

71 It could be pertinently asked, if one were to take a leaf out of Boswell's book, why neither Philo nor Josephus use παιδοφθορία, nor Josephus παιδεραστία, and why (according to his lists, p. 347 nn. 31, 33) Clement did not use the latter and Chrysostom the former.

72 P. 348 with n. 36. He regards *masculorum concubitores* as a somewhat misleading translation of ἀρσενοκοῖται.

73 *Vetus Latina* 25 (*Epistulae ad Thessalonicenses etc.*) fasc. 6, ed. H. J. Frede (Freiburg 1978) 411.

74 See above nn. 22 (Irenaeus) and 69 (Tertullian, Cyprian, Gregory of Elvira). Cf. H. von Soden, *loc. cit.* (n. 69 above); H. J. Vogels, *Das Corpus Paulinum des Ambrosiaster*. Bonner Bibl. Beiträge, 13 (Bonn 1957) 70, 159; Pelagius, *Expos. XIII Epp. Pauli, ad. loc.* (PL Suppl. 1, 1196).

75 See nn. 24, 33, 34 above.

76 *The Coptic Version of the New Testament in the Northern Dialect...Bohairic*, ed. and tr. G. W. Horner, vol. 3 (Oxford 1905) 144-145, 558-559; *The Coptic Version of the New Testament...Sahidic*, ed. Horner, vol. 5 (Oxford 1920) 438-439 (1 Tim. 1:10 only; Horner's reconstruction leaves over 100 verses missing from 1 Cor., including 6:5-10—see vol. 4, pp. v, 204-205); H. F. H. Thompson, *The Coptic Version of the Acts of the Apostles and the Pauline Epistles in the Sahidic Dialect* (Cambridge 1932) 126, 232. See also W. E. Crum, *A Coptic Dictionary* (Oxford 1939) 225.

77 Ephraem's Pauline commentary is extant only in an Armenian version, to which I have access solely in a modern Latin translation, *S. Ephraem Syri Commentarii in Epistolas D. Pauli nunc primum ex Armenio in Latinum Sermonem a Patribus Mekitharistis translati* (Venice 1893). Ephraem conflates the vice catalogue in 1 Cor. 6:9 (p. 58), but cites the word in question at 1 Tim. 1:10 (p. 245—*masculorum concubitoribus* here). Cf. J. Molitor, *Der Paulustext des hl. Ephräm aus seinem Armenisch erhaltenen Paulinenkommentar untersucht und rekonstruiert*. Mon. Bibl. et Eccl. 4; (Rome 1938) 148.

78 Cf. A. Deissmann, *Light from the Ancient East* (London 1910) 319-322; B. S. Easton, 'New Testament Ethical Lists', *JBL* 51 (1932) 1-12; A. Vögtle, *Die Tugend- und Lasterkataloge exegetisch, religions- und formgeschichtlich Untersucht*. NT Abhandlungen 16:4-5 (Münster 1936); S. Wibbing, *Die Tugend- und Lasterkataloge im Neuen Testament und ihre Traditionsgeschichte unter besonderer Berücksichtigung der Qumran-Texte*. Beihefte zur ZNW, 25 (Berlin 1959); P. Zaas, *art. cit.* (n. 14 above); H. Conzelmann, *A Commentary on the First Epistle to the Corinthians*. Hermeneia (Philadelphia 1975) 100-101.

79 The text cited by Wibbing, *op. cit.*, p. 90, containing παιδοφθόροι following πατροφόνοι and μητροφόνοι, is not relevant. It is no earlier than the fourth century A.D., and parallel texts reveal that παιδοφθόροι is a synonym of παιδοκτόνοι, παιδοφόνοι (*Scriptores Physiognomonici Graeci et Latini*, ed. R. Foerster, vol. 1, Leipzig, 1893, 327).

80 Cf. L. M. Epstein, *Sex Laws and Customs in Judaism* (1948; r.p. New York 1967) 134-137; Furnish, *op. cit.* (n. 1 above) 64-67.

81 Cf. Philo, *Opera* vol. 7, *Indices*, ed. J. Leisegang, pt. 1 (Berlin 1926) 119, and K. H. Rengstorf, *A Complete Concordance to Flavius Josephus*, vol. 1 (Leiden 1973) 235, for convenient listings, *s.v.* ἄρρην, of some of their expressions.

*Edinburgh*, New College, Mound Place

# Acknowledgments

Bartley, III, W.W. "Wittgenstein and Homosexuality." *Salmagundi* 58 (1982–83): 166–196. Reprinted with the permission of Skidmore College. Courtesy of the *Salmagundi*.

Batchelor, Jr., Edward. "Appendix." In Edward Batchelor, Jr., ed., *Homosexuality and Ethics* (New York: Pilgrim Press, 1980): 233–243. Reprinted with the permission of The Pilgrim Press. Courtesy of Yale University Cross Campus Library.

Bauer, Paul F. "The Homosexual Subculture at Worship: A Participant Observation Study." *Pastoral Psychology* 25 (1976): 115–127. Reprinted with the permission of Human Sciences Press, Inc. Courtesy of Yale University Divinity Library.

Brooten, Bernadette J. "Paul's Views on the Nature of Women and Female Homoeroticism." In Clarissa W. Atkinson, Constance H. Buchanan and Margaret R. Miles, eds., *Immaculate and Powerful* (Boston: Beacon Press, 1985): 61–87. Reprinted with the permission of Beacon Press. Copyright 1985 by Clarissa W. Atkinson, Constance H. Buchanan and Margaret R. Miles. Courtesy of Yale University Cross Campus Library.

Brown, Judith C. "Lesbian Sexuality in Renaissance Italy: The Case of Sister Benedetta Carlini." *Signs* 9 (1984): 751–758. Reprinted with the permission of The University of Chicago Press, publisher. Copyright 1984 by The University of Chicago. All rights reserved. Courtesy of Yale University Sterling Memorial Library.

Carey, Jonathan Sinclair. "D. S. Bailey and 'The Name Forbidden among Christians.'" *Anglican Theological Review* 70 (1988): 152–173. Reprinted with the permission of the *Anglican Theological Review*, Richard E. Wentz, Editor-in-Chief. Courtesy of *Anglican Theological Review.*

Carpenter, Edward. "On the Connection between Homosexuality and Divination and the Importance of the Intermediate Sexes Generally in Early Civilizations." *American Journal of Religious Psychology and Education* 4 (1911): 219–243. Courtesy of Wayne R. Dynes.

Coleman, Gerald D. "The Vatican Statement on Homosexuality." *Theological Studies* 48 (1987): 727–734. Reprinted with the permission of *Theological Studies*, Georgetown University. Courtesy of the *Theological Studies.*

Helminiak, Daniel A. (pseudonym: David Davidson). "DIGNITY, Inc.: An Alternative Experience of Church." *New Blackfriars* 68 (1987): 192–201. Reprinted with the permission of the author. Courtesy of the *New Blackfriars.*

Heyward, Carter. "Heterosexist Theology: Being Above It All." *Journal of Feminist Studies in Religion* 3 (1987): 29–38. Reprinted with the permission of Scholars Press. Courtesy of Yale University Divinity Library.

Hilliard, David. "UnEnglish and Unmanly: Anglo-Catholicism and Homosexuality." *Victorian Studies* 25 (1982): 181–210. Reprinted by permission of the Indiana University Board of Trustees. Courtesy of the *Victorian Studies.*

Hunt, Mary. "Celibacy: The Case against—Liberating Lesbian Nuns." *Out/Look* (1988): 68–74. Reprinted with the permission of the *Out/Look.* Courtesy of the *Out/Look.*

Johansson, Warren. "Whoever Shall Say to His Brother, *Racha* (Matthew 5:22)." *Cabirion and Gay Books Bulletin* 10 (1984): 2–4. Reprinted with the permission of the Gay Academic Union, Inc. Courtesy of Wayne R. Dynes.

Levy, Donald. "The Definition of Love in Plato's *Symposium.*" *Journal of the History of Ideas* 40 (1979): 285–291. Reprinted with the permission of the *Journal of the History of Ideas.* Courtesy of Yale University Sterling Memorial Library.

Mader, Donald. "The *Entimos Pais* of Matthew 8:5–13 and Luke 7:1–10." *Paidika* 1 (1987): 27–39. Reprinted with the permission of the Stichting Paidika Foundation. Courtesy of Wayne R. Dynes.

Merritt, Thomas M. (pseudonym of Merritt M. Thompson). "Homophile Ethics." *ONE Institute Quarterly of Homophile Studies* 3 (1960): 262–267. Reprinted with the permission of ONE, Inc. Courtesy of the *ONE Institute Quarterly of Homophile Studies*.

Rosán, Laurence J. "Philosophies of Homophobia and Homophilia." In Louie Crew, ed., *The Gay Academic* (Palm Springs, CA: ETC Publications, 1978): 255–281. Reprinted with the permission of ETC Publishers. Courtesy of Yale University Cross Campus Library.

Roth, Norman. "'My Beloved Is Like a Gazelle': Imagery of the Beloved Boy in Religious Hebrew Poetry." *Hebrew Annual Review* 8 (1984): 143–165. Reprinted with the permission of the Ohio State University. Courtesy of Yale University Sterling Memorial Library.

Smith, Morton. "Clement of Alexandria and Secret Mark: The Score at the End of the First Decade." *Harvard Theological Review* 75 (1982): 449–461. Reprinted with the permission of Harvard University. Courtesy of Yale University Sterling Memorial Library.

Soloff, Rav A. "Is There a Reform Response to Homosexuality?" *Judaism* 32 (1983): 417–424. Reprinted with the permission of *Judaism*. Courtesy of Yale University Divinity Library.

Strecker, Von Georg. "Homosexualität in biblischer Sicht." *Kerygma und Dogma* 28 (1982): 127–141. Reprinted with the permission of Vandenhoeck und Ruprecht. Courtesy of Yale University Divinity Library.

Thompson, Mark. "This Gay Tribe: A Brief History of Fairies." In Mark Thompson, ed., *Gay Spirit: Myth and Meaning* (New York: St. Martin's Press, 1987): 260–278. Reprinted with the permission of St. Martin's Press, Inc. Courtesy of Yale University Sterling Memorial Library.

Wright, David F. "Homosexuals or Prostitutes? The Meaning of Arsenokoitai (1 Cor. 6:9, 1 Tim. 1:10)." *Vigiliae Christianae* 38 (1984): 125–153. Reprinted with the permission of E. J. Brill. Courtesy of Yale University Seeley G. Mudd Library.

# Index